THE ARUNDEL HARINGTON MANUSCRIPT OF TUDOR POETRY

VOLUME II

THE ARUNDEL HARINGTON MANUSCRIPT OF TUDOR POETRY

Edited by RUTH HUGHEY

VOLUME II

Notes & Glossary

COLUMBUS, OHIO

THE OHIO STATE UNIVERSITY PRESS

1960

Printed in the United States of America
by Princeton University Press, Princeton, N.J.

CONTENTS

REFERENCE NOTE

In addition to the works cited by abbreviations and short-titles in the first volume, others are so referred to in the Notes in this second volume. See the Reference List in Volume I for full bibliographical description of the works of the following authors or editors:

Joseph Foster
A. K. Foxwell
John Harington
Sir John Harington
Henry Howard, Earl of Surrey
N. E. McClure
Kenneth Muir
F. M. Padelford
Thomas Park
Thomas Percy, Bishop of Dromore
H. E. Rollins
John Venn
J. A. Venn
Sir Thomas Wyatt

Also cited frequently in the Notes are:

Arber, Edward, ed., *A Transcript of the Registers of the Company of Stationers of London 1554-1640 A.D.*, 5 vols. London, Privately Printed, 1875-1894.

Biblia Sacra Vulgatae Editionis Sixti Quinti Pont. Max. Jussu Recognita Atque Edita Romae Ex Typographia Apostolica Vaticana MDXCIII. Editio Nova Auctoritate Summi Pontificis Leonis XII. Excusa. Francofurti A.M., 1826.

C.S.P.D.: *Calendar of State Papers Domestic*, with editions indicated.

Chaucer: *The Student's Chaucer, Being a Complete Edition of His Works*, ed. W. W. Skeat. Oxford, Clarendon Press, no date.

Historical Manuscripts Commission Reports or *Calendars*, with editions indicated.

N.E.D.: *A New English Dictionary on Historical Principles. Founded Mainly on the Materials Collected by the Philological Society*, ed. James A. H. Murray and others, 10 vols. in 12. Oxford, Clarendon Press, 1888-1928.

Petrarch: Francesco Petrarca, *Le Rime Sparse e i Trionfi*, a cura di Ezio Chiòrboli. *Scrittori D'Italia*, 126: *Petrarca, Opere* I. Bari, Gius, Laterza e Figli, 1930.

Puttenham, George, *The Arte of English Poesie*, ed. Gladys D. Willcock and Alice Walker. Cambridge, at the University Press, 1936.

REFERENCE NOTE

In the first citation of books published since 1900, publisher, place, and date of publication are included. Thereafter the date only is given except in cases of fairly lengthy quotations. For works published before 1900, the date only is listed.

When copies of contemporary books used in collation are not designated, it should be understood that they are in the British Museum Library. Variants and quotations from contemporary editions of the works of the two John Haringtons are from copies in the British Museum with the exception of that of the 1634 edition of Sir John's translation of Ariosto's *Orlando Furioso*. For this I have used a copy belonging to the English Department Library of the Ohio State University.

Notes to Poems
Nos. 1-324

Notes to Poems
Nos. 1-324

[1] *I once had money and my ffrend*

Hand: Tudor secretary. In line 4 "Returne . . . wolde" is written in the same hand over the partially erased words, "as Reason wold I showld." In the right margin in modern italic is the penciled note, "Imprimend." It is not Bishop Percy's hand, as are most of the other penciled notes in the volume.

N, fol. 3^{r}, has Nott's penciled note, "J H," above the poem, the most probable inference being that he attributed the verses to John Harington. He frequently so refers to Harington's authorship.

A copy is in (*A*) Bodleian MS. Gough Norfolk 43, fol. 31^{v}, a commonplace book belonging to the Brampton family, following a poem by Thomas Brampton, dated 1594. The first six lines only are in (*B*) Bodleian MS. Rawl. Poet. 172, fol. 12^{r}, written in a late Elizabethan secretary hand.

1 I once] Once I *A*; my] a *AB*; and] I *B*
3 spar'd] spared *AB*; I well] well I *AB*
4 nor] no *A*: not *B*; as Reason] *omitted* *B*
5 ask] asked *AB*; I] me *AB*; stay] cause *A*;
strange] str$^{\bar{u}}$ *B*
Lines 7 and 8 are wanting in B.
7 You . . . have] He that hath *A*
A adds the following lines:
Yf god sende mony once agayne as I haue had before
I will save mony & kepe my frinde & haue them both in store

The idea for the verses is found in Plautus, *Trinummus*, IV, iii, 43-47:

Si quis mutum quid dederit, sit pro proprio perditum
Cum repetas, inimicum amicum beneficio invenis tuo
Si mage exigere cupias, duarum rerum exoritus optio:
Vel illud, quod credideris, perdas vel illum amicum amiseris.

A much longer poem on the same theme is printed in *A Little Book of Songs and Ballads, gathered from Ancient Musick Books, MS. and Printed*, ed. E. F. Rimbault, 1851, pp. 42-43, taken, according to the editor, from a music book which once belonged to King Henry VIII and later to John Heywood, whose autograph it bears. I have not located the manuscript, but I give below the copy from Rimbault:

I had both monie and a frende,
Of neither though no store;

I lent my monie to my frende,
    And tooke his bonde therfore.

I asked my monie of my frende,
    But nawght save words I gott;
I lost my monie to keepe my frende,
    For sewe hym would I not.

But then if monie come,
    And frende againe weare founde,
I woulde lend no monie to my frende
    Upon no kynde of bonde.

But after this, for monie cometh,
    A frende with pawne to paye,
But when the monie should be had,
    My frende used such delay

That neede of monie did me force,
    My frende his pawne to sell,
And so I got my monie, but
    My frende then from me fell.

Sith bonde for monie lent my frende,
    Nor pawne assurance is,
But that my monie or my frende,
    Therbye I ever misse.

If God send monie and a frende,
    As I have had before,
I will keepe my monie and save my frende,
    And playe the foole no more.

Sir John Hawkins in *A General History of the Science and Practice of Music*, iii (1776), 38-39, prints a copy, without giving his source, which differs from that in Rimbault only in one word, i.e., *clene* instead of *then* in line 20.

It is not hard to account for the popularity of the verses. There may not be much poetry in them, but there is a practical philosophy that Tudor England would fully appreciate. The stanza of *AH* may have originated with John Harington, as Nott suggests, an assumption supported by the fact that it immediately precedes two of Harington's poems. It may be supposed, however, that, if it is his, he developed his rhyme from a current saying.

There remains the possibility that the rhyme may have been written by the noted dealer in proverbial sayings, John Heywood, who owned the manuscript containing the longer version.

[2] *Of person Rare, Stronge Lymbes, and manly shapp*

Hand: same as the preceding. The heading is in quite a different secretary hand, that of "dyvers sentences," preceding No. 24. Emendations are written in the hand of the poem, although they appear to have been put in at a different time. In the right margin is the penciled "Imprimend," as in No. 1.

Henry Harington first printed the poem in the *NA*, 1769, p. 87, with the heading, "*Upon the Lord Admiral* SEYMOUR'S *Picture*," and the ascription, "J.H. 1567" (reprinted, eds. 1779 and 1792, iii, 260; ed. 1804, ii, 329). An explanatory note, which follows Seymour's poem "Forgetting God to love a Kynge" (p. 86), reads:

> This unfortunate man is said to have been an excellent master to those Knights and Gentry that had served under him. In the notes to the nineteenth book of the translation of Ariostos Orlando, mention is made of a copy of verses wrote under a picture of this Nobleman, presented to Queen Elizabeth by John Harington, and hung in Somerset-House, which are here added from a copy in his own hand, dated 1567.

This poem then follows. If the heading of the *NA* copy was also in John Harington's hand, it may be assumed that these are the verses that were attached to the portrait of Seymour. The notes to Book XIX of Sir John Harington's translation of the *Orlando Furioso*, printed in large part in the Note to No. 3, do not specify, however, that these are the particular verses, nor does the heading in *AH* so indicate. If the portrait could be located, this question could, of course, be answered at once.

Without exception the emended readings in *AH* accord with the readings in *NA*:

sarue
2 of] By; ⟨rule⟩] serve
3 of] In; and] or
skill
4 ⟨harte⟩] skill
5 on foote] or foote
7 and] a
8 en'mye] and foe
11 and . . . more] that fed more mouthes with
aduaunste
12 ⟨that Clym'de⟩] advanc'd

Sir Thomas Seymour, created Lord High Admiral after the accession of King Edward VI in 1547, was committed to the Tower, January 17, 1549, on charges of high treason, and was beheaded the following March 20 (*Acts of the Privy Council*, ed. J. R. Dasent, ii [1890], 236, 262; *Chronicle of the Grey Friars of London*, ed. J. G. Nichols, Camden Society, liii [1852], 58). John Harington, who had been in his service certainly since early in 1546 (Letters and Papers of 38 Henry VIII, XXI, i, fol. 79[r], no. 114), was carefully examined at Seymour's trial (Cecil Papers 150; for printed accounts, see the *Burghley State Papers*, ed. Samuel Haynes, 1740, pp. 82-85), when it was said that he labored to go with the master to whom he was devoted. He was committed to the Tower the day after Seymour's internment (*Acts of the Privy Council*, ii, 240). For further indication of Harington's devotion to Seymour, see the Note on No. 3.

The experimental five-rhyme sonnet form should be noticed.

[3] *None can deeme righte, whoe ffaithfull freendes do rest*

Hand: same as the preceding. *N*, fol. 3[r], has Nott's note, "J.H.," above this poem.

This is a translation of the first stanza of Book XIX of Ariosto's *Orlando Furioso*, made, Sir John Harington tells us, by his father. In his Notes to that book in his own translation of the *Orlando*, 1591, p. 151, Sir John says:

> *In the first staffe of this Canto, is an excellent morall of the proofe of frends, which my father many years since did translate, almost word for word as I haue set it downe, applying it to his master, the worthie Lord Admirall* Seymor: *and because the verse was my fathers, I count I may without vsurpation claime it, by inheritance. He applied it to that noble peere (very aptly) diuerse wayes: both for his life, and for his death, but specially (which I count worth the noting) for his seruants, who loued him so dearely, that euen in remembrance of his honorable kindnesse, they loued one another exceedingly: and my father I remember, but a weeke before he died, which was in the yeare* 1582. *wrate with his owne hand the names of those were then liuing of the old Admiraltie (so he called them that had bene my Lords men) and there were then xxxiiij of them liuing, of which many were knights and men of more reuenew then himselfe, and some were but meane men, as armorers, artificers, keepers, and farmers; and yet the memorie of his seruice, was such a band among them all of kindnesse, as the best of them disdained not the poorest, and the meaner had recourse to the greatest, for their countenance and ayd in their honest causes, and many of them are euen now liuing, and yet it wants litle of fortie yeares since that noble man was put to death. His pic-*

ture my father gaue after to the Queenes Maiestie that now is, with a pretie verse written on it, and it now hangs in the gallerie at Somerset house.

On the relations of John Harington and Admiral Seymour and for some discussion of the "pretie verse," see the note on the preceding poem.

The stanza as Sir John prints it, p. 146, forms a strict ottava rima, thus:

None cā deem right who faithful friends do rest
While they beare sway & rule in great degree,
For then both fast & fained friends are prest,
Whose faithes seem both of one effect to be:
But then reuoults the faint and fained guest,
When welth vnwindes, and Fortune seems to flee
But he that loues indeed remaineth fast,
And loues and serues when life and all is past.

By way of comment on the instability of pretended friends, Sir John quotes from Ovid (*Tristia*, I, ix, 5-6) in a marginal note by the stanza:

Donec eris foelix multos numerabis amicos:
Tempora si fuerint nubila solus eris

It is very probable that the *AH* version represents the elder John's translation before it was touched up by his son to fit in with the whole *Orlando*. Copies in the two autograph manuscripts of Sir John's *Orlando*, British Museum Add. MS. 18920, fol. 46r, and Bodleian MS. Rawl. Poet. 125, p. 402, agree exactly with the printed copy. A copy in another Harington MS., *P*, fol. 44r, differs somewhat from that in *AH* and appears to represent the middle stage:

beare sway or rule
2 whilste] whilest; doe . . . Raigne]⟨do rule and rain⟩
6 knowen] knowne
7 in . . . linckt] once vertue linked
lif and
8 euen . . . deathe] whan ⟨hope of⟩ all

[4] *Now hope, now feare, now weale, now wofull cace*

Hand: unidentified late Tudor secretary, not the same as that of the crossed-out version, No. 4a.

A copy in *P*, fol. 46v, agrees exactly with the reading of No. 4a, except for spelling differences. Like these two it has no ascription. The British Museum poetry index attributes the sixain to Sir John Harington.

Very probably it is the work of a Harington, as it seems not to occur in other than Harington MSS.; but since it is placed in *AH* with poems by the elder Harington, one may more reasonably suppose that it is his rather than his son's.

No. 4 may be a Harington versification of an observation in Seneca, *Ad Serenum*, I, 3–II, 1, "petita relinquimus, relicta repetimus, alternae inter cupiditatem nostram et paenitentiam vices sunt." The model may have been John Skelton's *Magnyfycence*, *ca.* 1520, lines 2512-18 (ed. Robert L. Ramsay, E.E.T.S., Extra Series, xcviii [1908], 79):

> Nowe well, nowe wo, nowe hy, nowe lawe degre;
> Nowe ryche, nowe pore, nowe hole, nowe in dysease;
> Nowe Pleasure at large, nowe in captyuyte;
> Nowe leue, nowe lothe, nowe please, nowe dysplease;
> Now ebbe, now flowe, nowe increase, now dyscrease:
> So in this worlde there is no Sykernesse,
> But fallyble Flatery enmyxed with Bytternesse.

[4a] ⟨*Nowe hope, now feare, now Ioie now wofull case*⟩

Hand: same as the preceding. See the Note on No. 4.

[5] *Th'assaulted mynde, besett with thoughtfull throwse*

Hand: probably the same as that of No. 4. The "finis" is in a different secretary hand. Lines 37-39 are evidently copyist's errors.

I have found no other copy of this plaintive lament, which is in the manner of many of the poems among the Uncertain Authors of *Tottel's Miscellany*.

[6] *Now all of Chaunge, must be my song*

Hand: same as the two preceding. The "finis" is in the same hand as that after No. 5. The words "To Smithe of Camden" are written in contemporary italic.

Within a group of poems by Sir Thomas Wyatt, a longer version of this poem is written in *D*, fol. 81$^{r, v}$:

> Now all of chaunge
> must be my songe
> and from̃ mye bonde
> nowe must I breke
> sins she so strange
> vnto my wrrong
> doth stopp her eris
> to to [*sic*] here me speke

yet none dothe kno
so well as she
my greefe wiche
can have no restrainte
that faine wolde follo
nowe nedes must fle
for faute of ere vnto my playnte

I am not he
bye fals assayes
nor faynid faith cā bere in hande
tho most I see
that such alwaies
are best for to be vndrestonde

But I that truth ⟨hath a⟩
hath alwaies ment
dothe still ꝑcede to sɔue in vayne
desire pursuithe
my tyme mispent
and doth not passe vppon my payne

O fortunes mighte
that eche cōpellis
and me the most y^{t} dothe suffise
nowe for my right
to aske noughte ells
but to w^{t}drawe this entreprise

And for the gaine
of that good howre
wiche of my woo shalbe relefe
I shall refrayne
bye paynefull powre
the thing that most hathe bene my grefe

I shall not misse
to excersyse
the helpe ther of w^{c} doth me teche
that after this ⟨yn any wyse⟩
in any wise
to kepe right w^{t} in my reche
and she oniuste
wich ferithe not

yn this her fame to be defilyd
yett ons I truste
shalbe my lott
to quite the crafte that me begild/

Printing from *D*, Wyatt's editors (Nott, *Surrey and Wyatt*, ii, 256; Foxwell, *Wiat*, i, 337-39; Muir, pp. 146-48) have included the poem as his. Nott and Foxwell make no mention of another copy. Whether the Haringtons considered the poem as Wyatt's is doubtful, as it is not placed with the groups of Wyatt poems in *AH*, Nos. 96-145, 154-169.

I was at first of the opinion that the words "To Smithe of Camden" were intended as an ascription, perhaps to a Tobie Smith, or to Thomas Smith the ballad writer, who was publishing about 1540; but I now offer another explanation. George W. Marshall in *The Genealogist's Guide*, 1893, p. 566, under the name *Smith*, gives as a source, "Pedigree of Smith of Campden, [T.P.] Broadside." I regret that I have been unable to locate this broadside. I suggest, however, that "Now all of Chaunge" was to be sung to the tune used for the broadside "Smith of Camden." This supposition has further substantiation from the fact that the words "lerne but to syng yt" are written just above the poem in *D*, indicating that it was commonly sung. The pedigree of "Smyth of Campden in com. Glocester" is given in *The Visitation of Gloucestershire, 1623*, ed. Sir John Maclean and W. C. Heane, Harl. Soc., xxi (1885), 147. Anthony Smyth of Campden, living in 1593, was son of Thomas Smyth of Campden and grandson of the first-named Smyth, who may have been the one celebrated in the broadside. *Notices Relating to Thomas Smith of Campden, and to Henry Smith, Sometime Alderman of London*, by C. P. Gwilt, 1836, might throw light on the matter, but only twenty-five copies of this book were printed, and I have been unable to see it.

[7] *The good & euell fortune of all a mans life*

Hand: late Elizabethan secretary, probably the handwriting of Sir John's daughter Ellina, found again in No. 8. There is no apparent reason why the stanza was crossed out on fol. 16ᵛ (see No. 7a) and rewritten with almost no change on the succeeding folio.

Some one, perhaps a Harington, has put into verse and extended a philosophic observation made many centuries earlier. By the time of this manuscript it had become proverbial. Hesiod in *Works and Days*, lines 702-05, says (*Hesiod, the Homeric Hymns and Homerica*, ed. and trans. H. G. Evelyn-White, Loeb Library [London, Heinemann; New York, Macmillan, 1914], p. 55), "For a man wins nothing better than a good wife, and, again, nothing worse than a bad one." Similar is the dictum of Semonides in *Elegy and Iambus*, Fragment VI (ed. and trans.

J. M. Edmonds, Loeb Library, vol. ii [London, Heinemann; New York, Dutton, 1931], p. 217), "A man wins himself nothing whatsoever that is better than a good wife nor worse than a bad." John Heywood makes use of the saying in his *woorkes*, 1562, Pt. I, ch. ii (Spenser Society, i [1867], 4):

> The best or woorst thing to man for this lyfe,
> Is good or yll choosyng his good or yll wyfe.

John Davies of Hereford quotes this couplet in an epigram addressed to Heywood (*Works*, ed. A. B. Grosart, ii [1878], 41, Epigram 243). See also No. 51 and Note.

[7a] ⟨*The good and evill fortune of all a mans liff*⟩

Hand: late Elizabethan secretary, except for No. 8, not occurring elsewhere in the manuscript.

See No. 7 and the Note on it.

[8] *The good & bad happ that som women have had*

Hand: same as the preceding. This is clearly a companion piece to No. 7, and had it not been for the "finis" after that sixain, the two would have been considered as one composition. The crossed-out version on fol. 16^{v}, No. 8a, it may be noted, follows after No. 7a without a "finis." The versions differ but slightly.

[8a] ⟨*the good and bad hap that some women haue had*⟩

Hand: same as the preceding.

See No. 8 and the Note on it.

[9] *In lief and health yf I remayne*

Hand A. In contrast to the plaintive love notes of such poems as No. 5, this unknown "ballad" is a flippant satire, addressed with little respect for age to a fifty-two-year-old matron.

21. That is, perchance some people here who hear this song.

[10] *To men that know you not*

Hand A.

The first three stanzas, written in an ill-formed secretary hand, are in *D*, fol. 60^{r}, without ascription, but other poems in that manuscript are signed, "E K," or, "E Knyvet." Kenneth Muir has printed this poem from *D* in "Unpublished Poems in the Devonshire MS," *Proceedings of the Leeds Philosophical Society*, VI, iv (May, 1947), pp. 273-74. The chief differences in the two versions of these three stanzas are in the order of certain lines, as may be noted from the collation:

1 know you] knowes ye
2 you] ye
4 truly] sewarly
5 Suche] so
6 by] be; surely] sewarly
7 as] that
8 myne eyes] my nyes; myne owen] my ⟨nowe⟩ nowen
13 though I can] be that man
14 I . . . powre] that so shal the de ⟨ffo⟩ voware
15 be . . . man] not thowe I kan
16 not the devour] show my poore
17 am] ham; will] will ⟨will⟩
19 your] thy; your] thy
20 myne eyes] my nyes
21 blynding] blyndyd
22 that leadeth] w^{che} movethe
23 they] the; prove] proffe ⟨or fall when⟩
24 they] the

"E Knevet" the poet was one of two of the name Edmund Knevet, or Knyvett, who were living during the reign of King Henry VIII. The *D.N.B.* identifies the poet with Henry VIII's sergeant porter, second son of Edmund Knevet of Buckenham Castle in Norfolk, who married Joan, daughter of John Bourchier, second Baron Berners, the translator of Froissart's *Chronicle*, and settled at Ashwellthorpe. This Sir Edmund Knevet, who died May 1, 1546, could have been the poet who was writing contemporaneously with Sir Thomas Wyatt and Henry Howard, Earl of Surrey.

More probably, however, it was his nephew, Sir Edmund Knevet of Buckenham Castle, elder son of the sergeant porter's elder brother, Sir Thomas, and his wife, Muriel Howard, sister to Thomas, third Duke of Norfolk. (On the Knevet, or Knyvett, family see J. and J. B. Burke, *A Genealogical History of the Dormant, Abeyant, Extinct, and Forfeited Peerages in the British Empire*, 1883, under *Berners*; Francis Blomefield and Charles Parkin, *An Essay towards a Topographical History of the County of Norfolk*, i [1805], 369-81). This Sir Edmund was therefore first cousin to Surrey and approximately of an age with him. He it was who testified against Surrey at the trial which led to his death early in 1547 (deposition of Edmund Knevet, December, 1546, *Letters and Papers . . . of Henry VIII*, vol. xxi, part 2, ed. J. Gairdner and R. H. Brodie [1910], No. 555 [1]). The *D.N.B.* has identified the sergeant porter as Surrey's accuser, but the date given for his death is earlier than that of the deposition. Likewise the *D.N.B.* assigns to the sergeant porter the notorious crime, recorded by Raphael Holinshed,

Chronicles, iii (1587), 953, and by John Stow, *Annales*, 1615, p. 581, of striking Thomas Clere, Surrey's squire, in 1541 on a tennis court in the royal precincts. Punishment for this misdemeanor was loss of the right hand as well as loss of property. Edmond Bapst, *Deux Gentilshommes-Poètes de la Cour de Henry VIII*, 1891, p. 348, identifies this Sir Edmund Knevet as Surrey's cousin and conjectures, though without definite grounds, that the quarrel with Clere may have arisen over discussion of the relations of Surrey and Cardinal Pole. Edwin Casady, *Henry Howard, Earl of Surrey* (New York, M.L.A. of America, 1938), p. 71, connects the quarrel with Surrey's intervention over an election dispute between Knevet and Sir Richard Southwell in 1539. Holinshed (and Stow, who takes his account from the earlier writer) does not enlighten us about the cause of the crime but is concerned with the dramatic events connected with the punishment.

On the tenth of Iune, sir Edmund Kneuet knight, of Norffolke, was arreigned before the kings iustices (sitting in the great hall at Greenewich) maister Gage, comptroller of the kings household, maister Southwell, sir Anthonie Browne, sir Anthonie Winkefield, maister Wrisleie, and Edmund Peckham, cofferer of the kings houshold, for striking of one maister Clere of Norffolke, seruant with the earle of Surrie, within the kings house in the tenis court. There was first chosen to go vpon the said Edmund, a quest of gentlemen, and a quest of yeomen, to inquire of the said stripe, by the which inquests he was found giltie, and had iudgement to lose his right hand. Wherevpon was called to doo the execution, first the sergeant surgion with his instruments apperteining to his office: the sergeant of the woodyard with the mallet, and a blocke wherevpon the hand should lie: the maister cooke for the king, with the knife: the sergeant of the larder, to set the knife right on the ioint: the sergeant ferrer, with the searing irons to seare the veines: the sergeant of the poultrie, with a cocke, which cocke should haue his head smitten off vpon the same blocke, and with the same knife: the yeoman of the chandrie, with seare cloths: the yeoman of the skullerie, with a pan of fire to heate the irons, a chafer of water to coole the ends of the irons, and two formes for all officers to set their stuffe on: the sergeant of the cellar, with wine, ale, and beere: the yeoman of the yewrie in the sergeants stead, who was absent, with bason, ewre, and towels.

Thus euerie man in his office readie to doo the execution, there was called foorth sir William Pickering knight marshall, to bring in the said Edmund Kneuet; and when he was brought to the bar, the chiefe iustice declared to him his trespasse, and the said Kneuet confessing himselfe to be giltie, humblie submitted him to the kings mercie: for this offense he was not onelie iudged to lose his hand, but also his bodie to remaine in prison, and his lands and goods at the kings pleasure. Then the said sir Edmund Kneuet desired that the king of his benigne grace would pardon him of his right hand, and take the left, for (quoth he) if my right hand be spared, I maie hereafter doo such good seruice to his grace, as shall please him to appoint. Of this submission and request the iustices foorthwith informed the king, who of his goodnesse, considering the gentle heart of the said Edmund, and the good report of the lords, granted him his pardon, that he should lose neither hand, lands, nor goods, but should go free at libertie.

The man who had the wit for such graceful speech to the king would probably have the wit to write this poem. Furthermore, it seems to me that something of the same spirit appears both in the sudden striking of a companion on the tennis court and in the tone of this poem, and that the man who did one might do the other. The poem has a simplicity and forthrightness of personal expression, a deftness and surety of manner that place it far above much of the poetry of the period. In its independent note and its succinct style it compares very well with some of Wyatt's poems.

[11] *Our Lord in Heaven, whiche raigneth still*

Hand: the first eight lines of this metrical paraphrase of the Pater Noster are in Hand A, but the final couplet, which gives the doxology, and the "ffinis" are in another secretary hand. The ink is blacker than that of the first of the poem, and the commas are in this same black ink. The heading is in contemporary italic. The doxology couplet is clearly an addition, for not only is the hand different, but it is written over a partially erased "finis," and a period and a diagonal mark appear both after line 8 and line 10.

As is well known, the Lord's Prayer is given in Matthew vi, 9-13, and in Mark xi, 2-4; but only in certain texts of Matthew vi, 13, does the doxology ending appear. Although it occurs in some texts in the early centuries of the Christian era, it is generally conceded that this close was an interpolation arising from liturgical use (*Dictionary of the Bible*, ed. James Hastings and others [New York, Scribner's, 1909], p. 553; *The Catholic Encyclopedia*, ix [New York, R. Appleton, 1910], 356, article by Herbert Thurston on the Lord's prayer; *An Encyclopedia of Religion*, ed. Vergilius Ferm, New York: Philosophical Library, 1945, p. 451). The Vulgate omits it, ending, "Et ne nos inducas in tentationem; sed libera nos a malo. Amen." Despite the fact that King Henry VIII by an ordinance in 1541 decreed that a uniform translation of the Pater Noster should be adopted, usage in England in the sixteenth century was not uniform. English translations of the Bible showing influence of the Reformers introduce the doxology close. Thus it is given in the 1534 edition of Tyndale's New Testament, in Coverdale's Bible,

1535, Matthew's Bible, 1537, Taverner's Bible, 1539, the Great Bible, 1539, the Great Bible, 1541, and the Geneva Bible, 1557. The 1549, 1552, 1553 (?), and 1559 editions of the Book of Common Prayer, on the other hand, give the Lord's Prayer without the doxology. The Rheims Bible of 1582, made from the Vulgate for English Catholics, of course, omits it.

The inference for this metrical version of the Pater Noster seems to be that the last two lines were added by some one who had become interested in the "New Religion," but it is impossible to say just when that might have been. Possibly the elder Harington, who in 1551 was attending disputes on the sacrament led by John Feckenham for the Catholics and John Cheke for the Reformers, heard also discussions on the Lord's Prayer and so directed an addition to the version in *AH* (on these disputes see John Strype, *The Life of the Learned Sir John Cheke, K*[t]., rev. ed., 1821, pp. 69-70, from a manuscript in Corpus Christi College, Cambridge; also, Strype, *Memorials of the most reverend father in God Thomas Cranmer*, i [1812], 385-86). About the year 1550 Cheke was himself engaged in translating the gospel of Matthew from the Greek into English, and the doxology is included in his rendering (*The Gospel according to Saint Matthew and Part of the First Chapter of The Gospel according to Saint Mark, Translated into English from the Greek by Sir John Cheke*, ed. James Goodwin, 1843, p. 37). As a faithful servant to the Princess Elizabeth, with whom he was imprisoned at the beginning of Queen Mary's reign, Harington was identified with the Reformers (see the Note on No. 20). There is also the possibility that the last two lines were added as late as Sir John Harington's time, for the handwriting bears some resemblance to his.

[12] *The servis is vnsene*

Hand A.

John Harington may have addressed this poem to Isabella Markham, or even to Sir Thomas Seymour, but it has not sufficient distinction of style or subject matter to offer clear indication of authorship.

21. For this common proverb see, for example, John Heywood, *woorkes*, 1562 (Spenser Society, i [1867], 17), Pt. I, chap. ix, "How to wyn present salue for this present sore." For a recent scholarly edition of Heywood, see Burton A. Milligan, *John Heywood's "Works" and Miscellaneous Short Poems*, Illinois Studies in Lang. and Lit.: Vol. 41 (Urbana: Univ. of Ill. Press, 1956). George Gascoigne in his *Supposes*, 1566, has a similar expression (*Works*, ed. J. W. Cunliffe, i [Cambridge, Cambridge University Press, 1907], 200-01).

32-33. See No. 32 and Note.

38-40. Compare John Capgrave, *The Life of St. Katharine of Alexandria*, about 1450, ed. Carl Horstmann (E.E.T.S., c [1893], 94), ii, 253:

The gray hors, whyl his gras growyth,
May sterue for hung*er*, thus seyth the p*ro*ue*r*be.

See also Richard Hill, *Commonplace Book*, about 1530 (ed. Roman Dyboski, E.E.T.S., Extra Series, ci [1907], 128), "Diwe[r]s good prowerbis," No. 2, "While the grasse grwith, the hors sterwith."

[13] *Peace restfull plentie bringes*

Hand A.

This is probably a Harington version of an old saying, which, according to John Florio in *His firste Fruites*, 1578, fol. 39^{v}, was a

> prouerbe of that our Philosopher, that saith, that of peace cōmeth prosperitie, prosperitie bringeth plentie, plētie bringeth riches: riches lust: lust, contempt: contempt breedeth warre: of warre cōmeth pouertie: of pouertie, humilitie: of humility, peace: of peace, prosperity: and so the world goes about.

A version appears in British Museum MS. Harl. 629, fol. 97^{r}, a fifteenth-century manuscript of John Lydgate's "Life of Our Lady." I am indebted to Kathleen Tillotson for the following copy:

Peese maketh plente
Plente maketh pride
Pride maketh plee　　　And therefore
Plee maketh pouɔte
Pouɔt maketh pees

Grace growith after gouɔnaũce

Thomas Wright and J. O. Halliwell, *Reliquae Antiquae*, i (1845), 315, print from this and mention another copy in Bodleian MS. Douce 15. George Puttenham in *The Arte of English Poesie* (ed. Gladys Willcock and Alice Walker, Cambridge University Press, 1936, p. 208) quotes another version, attributing it to Jean de Meung:

Peace makes plentie, plentie makes pride,
Pride breeds quarrell, and quarrell brings warre:/
Warre brings spoile, and spoile pouertie,
Pouertie pacience, and pacience peace:
So peace brings warre, and warre brings peace.

George Gascoigne echoes the same idea in the ninth stanza of "Dulce Bellum Inexpertis," printed in *The Posies*, 1575 (ed. J. W. Cunliffe, Cambridge University Press, 1907, p. 142).

Plutarch in "The Education of Children," *Moralia*, 9 C (trans. F. C. Babbitt, Loeb Library, 1927), has an observation on the working of opposites in life, which furnishes an interesting parallel:

> We must bear in mind that our whole life is divided between relaxation and application. For this reason there have been created not only waking hours but also sleep, not only war but also peace, not only storm but also fair weather, not only periods of vigorous activity but also holidays. In short rest gives relish to labour.

Another is to be found in *The Secreta Secretorum* (*Three Prose Versions of the Secreta Secretorum*, ed. Robert Steele, E.E.T.S., Extra Series, lxxiv [1898], 10) in an account of the circuit of good and evil:

> Envye engendrith yville spekying, and of yville speche cometh hatrede: Hatrede engendrith vylenye, vylenye engendrith rankoure: Rankoure engendrith contrariete: Contrariete engendrith vnrightwisnes, vnrightwisnes engendrith batayle: Batayle yevith vp alle lawes and distroyeth citees, and is contrary to kynde and distroyeth mannys body. . . . And vndirstonde that trouthe engendrith desire; desire engendrith Iustice. Iustice engendrith good feith. Good feith engendrith largesse; largesse engendrith famulyarite, that is homelynes, ffamulyarite engendrith frendshipe. ffrendshipe engendrith counselle and helpe, and bi these thingis rehersid was all the world ordeynyd and the lawes made.

[14] *Syns I am dryven to geve assay*

Hand A. This is another poem which might have been included among the Uncertain Authors of *TM*.

[15] *Vnto my songe geue eare that wyll*

Hand A. The ascription is in contemporary italic. Words in the following lines are written over erasures: 12, "as toching love"; 16, "reckt no whit"; 20, "lyefe"; 39, "she was that."

A version (*T*) among the Uncertain Authors of *TM*, sigs. Q4^r-R1^r (ed. Rollins, No. 175), entitled, "The louer that once disdained loue is now become subiect beyng caught in his snare," differs considerably from this. Another version (*N*) in *NA*, 1769, pp. 91-92, headed, "SONNET *by* John Harington, 1554," has but six stanzas (ed. 1779, 1792, iii, 265-66; ed. 1804, ii, 334-36).

Lines 1-6 are wanting in N.

1 Vnto] To this; that wyll] who list
2 deeme my doinges] mine intent iudge; please] wyll
3 for . . . still] The tyme is cume, that I haue mist
4 what . . . ease] The thyng, wheron I hoped styll
5 how . . . best] from the top of all my trust
6 in . . . vnrest] Myshap hath throwen me in the dust
7 dayes . . . very] time hath been, and that of *T*

9 and . . . not] Nor were we *N*
11 any . . . did] what myghte greife, or did *N*
12 as . . . any] To rack the mynde with ceasless *N*
Lines 13-18 are wanting in N.
14 toke . . . laught] marked not, who lost, who saught
16 reckt . . . sought] forced not, who wept, who laught
17 ffrom . . . hart] My thought from all such thinges
19 tooke . . . nor] toke no hede to tauntes, nor *T*: heedede not or taunte or *N*
20 as . . . as] Nor pin'd to see them frown or *N*
21 their . . . mockt] Where fortune laught *T*; I skorn'd] and scorn'd *N*
22 fownd] shunn'd *N*; eu^{r}y] cunning *N*
23 and] Then *N*; oft tymes I] I often *N*
24 see] think *N*; them] such *N*
26 fourthe] styll *T*
30 I . . . and] In wanton waye I *N*
31 last] length *T*
33 saw] how *T*; who was] those were *N*
34 so that] If so *N*; lyve still] still liue *T*
36 cast] threw *T*
37 never nature] nature neuer *T*
38 but] saue *T*; she] her *N*
39 that wolde] as would *T*: as mighte *N*
40 an] A *T*
42 nature her] Her nature *T*
43 all in a Maze] euen in a maze *T*: in strange amaze *N*
44 Whan] All *N*; is a way] far awaye *N*
45 So I began] Did I begin *N*
46 and . . . without] Nor co^{ud} my folly brooke *N*
47 or that] Or euer *T*: For, 'ere *N*
Lines 49-60 are wanting in N.
49 greevythe] greues me
50 kyndes] sortes
51 heale] salue
52 save . . . alone] But onely she
53 health] life
54 heale . . . even] saue or slay me
55 Wherefore synce] But seeing
56 fest] bounde
57 you] ye; example] ensample
58 Whiche] That; fynd] fele
59 them not] not them
60 lack . . . the] be caught within his

With some assurance one may draw the conclusion that not one of the above copies was made from the other. The *NA* text must have been taken from some other copy than that in *AH*, even if we admit the possibility that Henry Harington omitted four stanzas and that he engaged in a little editorial polishing. The problems of the *NA* texts of poetry in relation to *AH* are discussed in detail in the Introduction (pp. 18-26). I see no way to resolve them without further evidence.

Neither can the question of John Harington's authorship be definitely determined. G. F. Nott in one of the incomplete copies of his unpublished edition of the *Songs and Sonnets* in the British Museum (C.60. 0.13, vol. i, p. 148) says in a manuscript note that it is his opinion that the ascription "huomo inconosciuto" is written in a later hand. It is my opinion, however, that the writing is contemporary italic, although it may have been entered some time after the poem was copied into the manuscript. If the Haringtons meant that the authorship of the poem was unknown, then on no account can the poem be considered as John Harington's. If, on the other hand, the words may be interpreted as meaning a man without fame or reputation, they might be applied to Harington. The title may be Henry Harington's addition, suggested by manuscripts of other poems with ascriptions to John Harington and dated from the Tower. In his note on this poem, H. E. Rollins does not accept the authority of the *NA*; but Charles Crawford (*Notes and Queries*, XI, iii [1911], 201, 322, 423) upholds the authority of the *NA* and Harington's authorship of this and other poems. The inference from the Nott note, referred to above, is that he accepts the *NA* heading. See also the Notes on Nos. 19 and 22.

From internal evidence one may conclude that the poem could have been written by Harington. There is a smoothness in the meter, which is one of the main characteristics of Harington's verse. Compare his poem "Whence comes my love" (*NA*, 1769, p. 129), which has the same stanzaic form and is built on the conceit of the heart of stone, which is mentioned in line 40 of No. 15. Of significance also may be the marked influence of two of Surrey's poems, "When youthe had ledd me half the race" and "Geue place, ye louers here before" (*Poems*, ed. Padelford, 1928, Nos. 15, 18).

Mary Queen of Scots appears to have applied lines 5 and 6 as given in *TM* to her own misfortune. George Ballard in *Memoirs of Several Ladies of Great Britain*, 1752, p. 161, says that she wrote these lines on a window in Fotheringay Castle, as follows:

From the top of all my trust,
Mishap has laid me in the dust.

This observation is repeated by Horace Walpole in *Royal and Noble Authors* (ed. Thomas Park, v [1806], 38), where the lines are quoted as above.

[16] *The care to compasse quyet rest*

Hand A. The following words are written over erasures: 20. "lyve"; 24. "speake."

I have found no other copy of this poem, which could have been written by John Harington during one of his two imprisonments in the Tower, 1549 and 1554 (see the Introduction, pp. 63-66), when he had no assurance that his life would not be taken. If in 1549 he had been willing to forego his loyalty to Admiral Seymour and cast his lot with Edward Seymour, Duke of Somerset, however dishonorably, he could have been assured for a time of peace and comfort; and if in 1554 he had chosen to declare himself a follower of Queen Mary, disowning his former attachment to the Princess Elizabeth, he might have been spared imprisonment and fear of death. An added reason for considering Harington as the most probable author comes from its inclusion in that part of the manuscript where there are poems known to be Harington's (for the discussion on the grouping of authors, see the Introduction, pp. 27-30).

From the content of No. 16 and No. 17 and from the form of the two, one may consider them companion poems, inspired perhaps by similar circumstances. For parallels on the theme, compare Publius Syrus, *Sententiae* (ed. Jules Chenu, 1835, p. 62), "Honestam mortem vitae turpi praefero"; and Juvenal, Satire VIII, ll. 83-84:

> summum crede nefas animam praeferre pudori
> et propter vitam vivendi perdere causas.

[17] *If right be rakt and over ronne*

Hand A. In line 10 "lyfe" is written over an erasure and in line 28, "all."

A copy (*A*) among the Uncertain Authors of *TM*, sig. Q2r,v, entitled, "They of the meane estate are happiest" (ed. Rollins, No. 170), differs but little from this. One published later (*B*) in *The Arbor of Amorous Devises*, 1597, sig. B2r,v (facsimile edition, with introduction by Rollins, Huntington Library Publications, 1936), has several changes.

1 be] were *B*
3 feare through force] fear by force *A*: force by feare *B*; yeld vpp] do yelde *AB*
4 my] The *AB*
5 for] sot *B*; vnplaste] vnplaced *A*
6 and] If *AB*; leese his due] lose his shape *A*: leaues his shape *B*
7 enbraste] embraced *A*: imbrac'd *B*
8 harme . . . sue] hurt . . . happe *AB*
12 rychesse] tiches *B*

13 ffor rychesse hates] Riches doth hate *B*
14 quyetnesse] quiet ease *B*
15 for . . . bent] is most part impacient *A*: for the most part is vnpacient *B*
16 lyve] llue *B*
17 herdman] Shepheard *B*
18 mo slepte] more sleepe *B*
19 moe] more *B*
20 the . . . kept] his Flock of sheepe *B*
23 nor] Ne *B*
24 rove] rowe *A*
26 good] well *A*
27 tyll my] till the *B*; shall] doth *B*; brest] bsest *B*
28 will] shal *B*; stay] ceasse *A*; all] you *AB*

Lines 9-12 are written in Queen Elizabeth's hand on the fly-leaf of a New Testament that once belonged to Anne Poyntz, now in the British Museum (C.45.a.13). The lines there run:

> Amonge good thinges
> I proue and finde, the quiet
> life doth muche abounde,
> and sure to the contentid
> mynde, ther is no riches
> may be founde,
> Your louinge ⟨friend⟩
> maistres
> Elizabeth

Anne Poyntz was daughter of Sir Nicholas Poyntz of Iron Acton, Gloucestershire. About 1556 she was married to Sir Thomas Heneage, who later became Vice-chamberlain of Queen Elizabeth's household, and he and his wife were on terms of great intimacy with the queen (*D.N.B.*; see also the Notes on Nos. 175 and 235).

The fact that Queen Elizabeth quoted the lines does not, of course, signify that she composed them. The poem may very well be another of John Harington's, a companion to the preceding, which it resembles in style and form, although it has not the same depth of feeling. G. F. Nott in the unique copy of his unpublished edition of the *Songs and Sonnets* at Arundel Castle (see the Introduction, p. 15) prints a tune for this poem, which he there assigns to "J.H.," i.e., John Harington. There may be some significance in the fact that the poem in *TM* follows after John Harington's elegy on "master Deuerox," beginning, "Who iustly may reioyce in ought vnder the skye?" Sir John Harington in *A Tract on the Succession to the Crown* (*A.D. 1602*) (ed. C. R. Markham, Roxburghe Club, 1880, p. 75), quotes lines 17-18 of the elegy, naming his father as the writer. No. 17 is followed in *TM* by a version of No. 19, which is assigned to Harington in *NA*.

[18] *All ye that ffrindshipp do professe*

Hand A. In line 11 "will" is written over an erasure, and in line 38, "that." In line 21 the revised reading, "raise," which agrees with the version in *TM*, is written in another secretary hand.

The copy among the Uncertain Authors in *TM*, sigs. Y4^{v}-Z1^{r,v} (ed. Rollins, No. 226), is entitled, "Of a louer that made his onelye God of his loue," and shows little significant variation.

1 ye] you
2 or] And; presentes] present
5 my . . . playne] the circumstance
6 well . . . payne] them selues that did auaunce
8 frindshipps] vertues
11 than] I
12 no] none
16 was] in
18 all] such
19 that was only] onely that was
21 one] Whom; ⟨please⟩^{raise}] raise
22 her] to
23 tearmes] wordes
25 had enioyed] did enioy
26 Lord . . . pleasant] Who liued Lord in such a
28 great] fowle
30 a] the
32 no . . . sett] by my selfe I set no
33 was so moche] so much was
34 creapt . . . part] clene orecome my hart
35 frindly thought] thought of her
36 care had never] neuer care had
38 that] Was; more] so
39 toke . . . her] carde for her so much
40 as] That
42 vnto hym] to them selues
43 my . . . sweete] So my swete graffe
44 that . . . is] Where I sowed mirthe I
46 transform'd] transformed; into] to
47 pleasd] pleased; now] *omitted*
48 hope] hart
50 must] may

53 for my more] the more to
55 you frynds] ye frendes

Since this poem is placed in *AH* with others which were probably written by John Harington, this may also be his. Lines 19-22, which emphasize the beauty of mind and character of the woman, should be compared with other poems which may be the work of Harington: Nos. 23, 177, 247, the first two poems in the Appendix, and the sonnet beginning, "Marvaylous be thie matcheles gyftes of mynde," attributed to Harington in *NA*, 1769, p. 198.

[19] *The lyf ys longe that lothsomly doth last*

Hand A.

Entitled, "Comparison of lyfe and death," the poem was printed in (*A*) *TM*, sigs. Q2^{v}-Q3^{r} (ed. Rollins, No. 171) among those of Uncertain Authors. In (*B*) *The Paradyse of daynty deuises*, 1576, sig. F2$^{r, v}$ (ed. Rollins, 1927, No. 47), it is entitled, "Thinke to dye," and is ascribed to "D.S." A copy in (*C*) Bodleian MS. Ashmole 48, fols. 24^{v}-25^{r}, is written without ascription in a mid-sixteenth century hand, immediately following "I loath that I did love," which is generally assigned to Lord Vaux. A shorter version in (*D*) *NA*, 1769, pp. 95-96 (eds. 1779, 1792, iii, 269-70; ed. 1804, ii, 332-33), is headed, "ELEGY *wrote in the* Tower by JOHN HARINGTON, *confined with the Princess* ELIZABETH, 1554."

1 that] whiche *B*
2 draw] drawythe *C*
3 panges and] pange or *D*; plage skarce past] plages forepast *A-C*
4 yeldes . . . thie estate] yelde . . . *A*: But some new greif, still green, doth marr our state *D*
5 so . . . fynde . . . great] . . . fele . . . *A-C*: In all we find 'midst this worlds *D*
6 that] The *A*: Sure *D*; shortyth] endeth *A*: shorteneth *B*: shortnythe *C*
Lines 7-12 are wanting in D
7 Yet] And *BC*
8 at] All *B*
9 my . . . thanck] The Lord be praysed *A-C*
10 wheareto] whens *B*
12 doth] doeth *B*; shall] doth *A-C*
13 seme] semes *B*: sow[n] *C*: some *D*; swiftlye] swift that *A*: swetely *B*
14 that flete] they flytt *C*

15 ioyfull . . . dawth] . . . daweth *A*: . . . wights . . . daies dawes *B*: . . . daws *C*: riot night which day draws on *D*
16 mo] more *D*; meete] hytt *C*
17 do] dothe *C*; as . . . agaynst] lyke snow kyss'd by *D*
18 makes . . . lyf] soon ends all that vain lyfe *D*
Lines 19-30 are wanting in D
19 lye] be *A-C*
20 shon͠ne] drede *A-C*
21 alway] allwayes *C*
24 thowh . . . only] Though how, or when, the lord alone doth *A*: The hower wherein onely hym self doeth *B*: but o^{r} whane onlye ye lord dothe *C*
25 doth] doeth *B*
26 he doth] he doeth *B*: yt *C*
27 greefes . . . dayly] plages, what panges, what perilles therby *AC*: *B as in A except* perill
28 safe] sure *A-C*; dayes] tyme *C*
29 as] and *B*
30 wear better] is happier *B C*
31 a porte] the doore *B*; passe] drawe *B*
33 deare] dole *B*: swet *C*; ceasyth] killeth *D*; anoy] awaie *B*
34 that . . . ys] yt yeldythe all in *C*
35 ffor] And *A-C*; to] in *B*; was] in *AB*
36 by . . . lykewyse wrought] likewise by death was fredome wraught *A*: by death is freedome . . . *B*: likewise *omitted C*: by deathe all freedom too was wroughte *D*
Lines 37-42 are wanting in D
37 Wherefore] therefor *C*; flesshe] men *A-C*
38 dissolv'd] disolued *B*; from] of *A-C*
40 they be] we may be *C*
42 to] And *B*

It is hardly possible to speak dogmatically about the authorship of this poem or the relative value of the versions. The variants indicate that *A*, *B*, and *C* are somewhat more closely related to each other than to the copy in *AH*. Such variants in *B* as "swetely," line 13, and "awaie," line 33, are probably copyist's errors. Rollins is of the opinion that the copy in *B* is less reliable than that in *C*, which closely follows *A* (see "Bodleian MS. Ashmole 48," *M.L.N.*, xxxiv [1919], 342).

The vexed question of authorship is tied up with the problem of the authority of the headings in *NA*, although in this instance the position of the poem in *AH* is of importance. In his note on the poem in *B*, Rollins accepts the ascription to "D.S.," identifying it as referring to D. Sand. G. F. Nott has two notes on the matter, which exactly oppose each other, but presumably the opinion of the later one may be accepted as final. In a manuscript note opposite this poem in one of the copies of his unpublished edition of the *Songs and Sonnets* in the British Museum (C.60.o.13), i, 144, he says: "NB This has no signature of John Harington: nor does it purport to have been written by him from the Tower, as it is said to have been in the *Nugae Antiquae*." Nott is here referring to the version of the poem in *AH*, which has neither ascription nor title. In a note in his published edition of the poems of Wyatt (*Surrey and Wyatt*, ii [1816], 550), which is later than the manuscript note just quoted, Nott says of this poem that in the *Paradise* it "bears for signature 'D. S.' whereas we know on positive authority that it was written by John Harrington. See Songs and Sonnets. Ed. 1816, p. 144, and the note upon it." Unfortunately, an 1816 edition of the *Songs and Sonnets* is not known to exist (see the Introduction, p. 57). It is possible that Nott had access to an authoritative manuscript among the papers of Dr. Henry Harington of Bath.

It is quite clear from the variants of No. 19 that the *NA* copy was not set up from that in *AH*, and that another copy of the poem, differing considerably from the *AH* version, was used. Henry Harington says that No. 2 was printed from a copy in John Harington's own hand, but he does not say that of this poem, as he does not of No. 15; so that we have no way of knowing just what his authority was for title and attribution. Nor do we know whether he simply omitted stanzas, or whether his version represents one older and shorter than the others. There is also the possibility that he may have edited his copy, whatever its authority. Thomas Park accepted the poem as Harington's, although he dropped others from his edition of the *NA* when he considered them doubtful. As indicated in the Note on No. 15, Charles Crawford supports the *NA* authority. Norman Ault, printing the poem in his *Elizabethan Lyrics* (London, Longmans, 1925, p. 25) from the version in *C*, assigns it to John Harington.

I think that the probability that Nos. 19 and 22 are Harington's is far greater than in the case of No. 15. The former could well have been written during Harington's periods of imprisonment (see the Introduction, pp. 63-66), when there was time and provocation for meditation on the significance of life and death. The fact that No. 19 immediately precedes in *AH* Harington's plea to Gardiner, written from the Tower in 1554, No. 20, further supports argument for his authorship. Finally, one cannot overlook the metrical smoothness of the poem, which is very much after Harington's style of writing.

The disputed authorship has nothing to do with the real poetic worth of the lines. That they were popular in their own day is attested not only by the several versions noted above, but also by adaptations, especially of lines 31-36. These are quoted by Allot in *England's Parnassus*, 1600, where they are assigned to Surrey (ed. Charles Crawford [Oxford, Clarendon Press, 1913], No. 282); but Allot was frequently wrong in his ascriptions. Elizabeth Grymeston makes use of a couplet in her *Miscelanea*, 1604, sig. C2^{v}:

> It is onely death that brings vs into harbour, where our repose is without trouble, our comfort without crosses, where our teares shall be turned into triumph, our sadnesse into ioy, and all our miseries into perfit felicitie.
>
> *Death is the salue that ceaseth all annoy.*
> *Death is the port by which we passe to ioy.*

Another adaptation is in Bodleian MS. Rawl. Poet. 172, fol. 6^{v}:

> Death is the salve y^{t} healeth all annoye
> Death is the port by wch we passe to ioye
> Life is a bubble blowne vp wth breath
> whose witt is weakenes & whose wage is death
> A flower a play, a blast, a shade, a dreame
> A living death a never turning streame.

For lines 3 and 4 of the above stanza compare Spenser, *The Shepheardes Calender*, "Februarie," lines 87-88 (ed. E. De Selincourt and J. C. Smith, London, Oxford University Press, 1937, reprint of ed. 1912, p. 424):

> For Youngth is a bubble blown vp with breath
> Whose witt is weakenesse, whose wage is death.

[20] *At least withdraw your creweltie*

Hand A. In line 2 "force" is written over an erasure and in line 21, "thān." The alterations in line 10 are written in another ink and secretary hand, probably Sir John's. Four later copies of the poem agree with these alterations. A later italic hand, perhaps Bishop Percy's, has made some unauthoritative additions: Title, "To Bishop Gardiner"; line 30, "whan," underlined, and "This," written in the left margin; line 36, "might," underlined, and "Pow'r" written beneath; line 40, "to wound," written above "and noye."

Copies of this poem by John Harington are in several Harington MSS. The one in (*A*) *P*, fols. 67^{v}-68^{r}, was made before line 10 was corrected. The poem was included by Sir John Harington in his essay on "Winchester" in "A Catalogue of Bishops," of which there are two autograph manuscripts: (*B*) the earlier (now imperfect) British Museum MS. Add. 46370, where the poem is on fols. 6^{v}-7^{r}; (*C*) the fair copy made from *B* for Prince Henry, now British Museum MS. Royal

17 B.XXII, where the poem is on pp. 39-41. John Chetwind, Sir John's grandson, used *B* for his edition of "A Catalogue of Bishops," published as *A Briefe View of the State of the Church*, 1653, where the poem is printed on pp. 47-49 (*D*). In his 1769 volume of *NA*, pp. 103-04 (*E*), Henry Harington printed this poem separately with the heading, "JOHN HARINGTON, *from the* Tower, *to* GARDENER, *Bishop of* Winchester, 1554." Here it agrees almost exactly with Chetwind. In the 1779 edition of *NA*, i, 54-56 (and in the reprint of 1792), where it is included in *A Briefe View*, there are a few minor changes. The poem also appears in Park's edition of *NA*, ii (1804), 70-71. Sir John quotes the third stanza as given in *B* in *A Tract on the Succession to the Crown* (*A.D. 1602*), (ed. C. R. Markham, Roxburghe Club, 1880, p. 101).

In the collation following, it can readily be seen that the *B-E* readings in lines 21 and 22 better fit the context than do those of *A* and *AH*, and that the variant "that" in lines 16 and 40 of *D* and *E* (corrected in the 1779, 1792 editions of *NA*) is a misinterpretation of "yt" as "y^{t}."

7 vse] doe *B-E*
8 offre] proffer *B-E*
9 Yet can not] nor can *B-E*
10 ⟨A⟩ Elevẽn mõnths ⟨full⟩ [past]] A leuin months full *A*: Eleavn months past *B*: Elev'n months past *C*: Eleven moneths past *D E*
11 endured] abid *B-E*
12 whylest] whil'st *A*: while *B-E*
14 with] in *B-E*
15 in] with *B-E*
16 it] that *D-E*
18 ought] can *B-E*
21 swarve] sware *B-E*; you] I *A*
22 sware] swarve *B-E*; I] you *A*
24 forgeates] forgat *A*; that Clerk] that a Clerke *D-E*
27 Wrestes] Wrest *A-E*
29 thoughe] if *E*
31 as] [as] ⟨when as so doth⟩ *B*
33 as] [whom] ⟨as⟩ *B*: Whom *D E*
34 weare] t'were *C*
38 Somtyme] somtimes *C*; bownds back] rebounds *A*
40 it] that *D-E*
43 yll] euill *A*

In his essay on "Winchester," Sir John tells us that his father addressed this impassioned plea to Stephen Gardiner, Bishop of Winchester, in 1554, when the latter was Lord Chancellor, and the elder Harington was a prisoner in the Tower. Sir John thus introduces the poem:

> . . . and I haue heard old Sr Mathew Arundell say that Bonner was more faultie then he [Gardiner], and y^{t} Gardener would rate him for yt, and call him Asse for following poore men so bloudily, and when I would maintaine the contrary, he would say that my father was worthie to haue layn a yeare longer in prison for the sawcie Sonnet he wrat to him from out of the tower, which sonnet both by cause it was written in defence of Queen Elizabeth, and because (if I bee not partiall) it is no ill vearse for those vnrefined tymes, and toucheth the matter I enforce, I do here sett downe. Presupposing that in the Eleven months before, hee had sent him many letters and petitions full of reason (that could not prevaile) for his liberty, the distressed Prisoner wryteth this Ryme [quoted from MS. Royal 17 B. XXII, p. 39].

Similar, though briefer, is the reference Sir John makes to the verses in *A Tract on the Succession to the Crown*, p. 101:

> But finding Gardiner as he thoughte his heavie freind and hearkning to no reason, he wrote a Ryme to him (in whiche kynde, if I were not a partiall praiser, I would say he was equall to the best of those tymes).

It is interesting to note that Harington evidently had at hand a copy of an unsigned poem in the *D* MS., fol. 4^{r}, which has been attributed to Wyatt by two of his editors, Foxwell (*Poems*, i [1913], 259; Muir, *Poems*, 1949, pp. 93-94). As may be seen from the first stanza quoted below, Harington took over the first and third lines, the unusual nine-line stanza and rhyme pattern, but his measure is tetrameter rather than the combined trimeter and tetrameter of the *D* MS. poem. The total effect of the two poems is quite different, as the *D* poem is a rather mediocre love plea, while Harington's is a passionate denunciation of a personal enemy. The *D* stanza follows:

At last w^{t}drawe youre cruelltie
or let me die att ones
It is to moche extremitie
Devised for the nones
To holde me thus alive
In paine still for to dryve
Whatt maye I more
sustayne alas that dye wuld fane
and cane not dye for paine

The circumstances connected with the writing of Harington's poem may be briefly outlined. Harington was apprehended by Gardiner for suspected complicity in the revolt led by the younger Sir Thomas Wyatt, the Duke of Suffolk, and others in protest against the proposed Spanish match. In a letter to Secretary William Petre, January 28, 1553/4, Gardiner says that he has "founde a letter lately wryten by Harington, which Harington cam to me this night, and, after examination, I have taken him tardy by occasion of that letter and kepe him with me as prisoner this night, entending in the mornyng to send him to the Towre" (as printed from the State Papers Dom., Mary, vol. ii, no. 20, in *The Letters of Stephen Gardiner*, ed. J. A. Muller, Cambridge, Cambridge University Press, 1933, pp. 459-60; also printed by J. G. Nichols in his edition of *The Chronicle of Queen Jane and of Two Years of Queen Mary*, Camden Society, xlviii [1850], 184, where it is dated January 27). According to an entry in the *Chronicle of the Grey Friars of London* (ed. J. G. Nichols, Camden Society, liii [1852], 53), Harington appears to have entered the Tower February 8, 1553/4. Harington himself in a letter to Gardiner, written from the Tower in 1554, says: "Why, my good Lord, must I be thus annoy'de for one deed as was sent from one that had such ryghte to gyve mee his commande and to one that had such ryghte to all myne hartie sarvyce" (*NA*, 1769, pp. 63-64). Nichols in *Queen Jane* (p. 53) suggests that the letter was from Suffolk, with whom Harington was closely associated. Sir John Harington in a letter to Prince Henry in 1609 says that his father was imprisoned by Gardiner for eleven months for "only carrying a letter to the Princess Elizabeth" (*NA*, 1769, p. 69; similarly in the essay on "Winchester," *NA*, 1779, i, 52). Sir John says further that his father sent many petitions to Gardiner and spent £1000 to gain his freedom. Not long after this poem was written, Harington was released. He was fined £100 by the Privy Council on January 18, 1554/5 (*Acts of the Privy Council*, ed. J. R. Dasent, v [1892], 90-91), and discharged the same day in company with other prisoners held for treason (John Stow and Edmond Howes, *The Annales, or Generall Chronicle of England*, 1615, p. 623).

13-15. Gardiner was charged with craft and subtlety and was popularly known as "Wily Winchester" (J. A. Muller, *Stephen Gardiner and the Tudor Reaction*, Cambridge, Cambridge University Press, 1926, p. 303).

19-27. Gardiner was prisoner in the Tower five years, 1548-53. He was given an open hearing December 15, 1550, to February 14, 1551 (the same ref., pp. 194-204; *D.N.B.*).

28-36. Harington is, of course, referring to the persecution of the Reformers in Mary's reign.

Gardiner died November 12, 1555. Sir John Harington in *A Tract* (p. 101) records that his father "prosecuted him with his penne after his death, that persecuted him by his power in his life, verefieng the old saeing, *Scribit in marmore læsus*; for this Epitaph I found in a book of my father's of his owne writing,

> Heer lye the bones of busy Gardiner dead
> That in five yeres spoiled more good lawes and love
> Then two great Kings with all the wittes they bred
> Could stablish sure in forty yeares before
> The Queen beguild, the Lordes like lymehoundes led,
> The usurping rules of Rome he did restore,
> Burne, head and hang, imprison, vex and spoile,
> The worthie sort of this declyning soile."

The *love* of line 2 should clearly be *lore*, in the sense of doctrine or creed, which thus agrees with the rhyme as well as the context.

[21] *Husband, yf you will be my deare*

Hand A. The following are written over erasures: line 8, the *S* in "Speache"; line 20, "And longe ffrome home"; line 26, "good." In line 20 the *d* in "stayd" is squeezed in, clearly added, although in the same hand.

This address to a husband is an answer to an address to a wife which was first printed in *NA*, 1775, p. 259 (eds. 1779, 1792, iii, 294-95; ed. 1804, ii, 395-96; printed from *NA* by David F. Markham in *A History of the Markham Family*, 1854, pp. 258-59), beginning, "Yf dutye, wyf, lead thee to deeme," and headed, "JOHN HARINGTON to his Wyfe, 1564." That poem was almost certainly written opposite No. 21 in *AH* on fol. 25, now missing, which no doubt provided the copy used for *NA* (see the Introduction, p. 24). Another Harington copy of the address to the wife occurs in *P*, fol. 69^{r}, written in secretary. A later italic hand has added a title, "Advice to his Wife," and has called attention to a few words in the right margin. The *P* text is as follows:

> If dutie wyf leade the to deeme
> that trade moost fytt I hold moost deere
> first god regarde next me esteme
> thy chirdrene [*sic*] then respecte thow neere
> o^{ur} howse both Sweete and clenlye see
> ordre o^{ur} fare thy maides kepe short
> thye mirth with meane well myxed be
> thy curtese partes in chast wyse sort
> in sober weede the clenly dresse
> when ioyes me rayse thy cares downe cast
> when gryeffes me grype thy solace sease
> who so me frendes frend them as fast
> in preasse gyve place what so I say
> apart complayne yf cause thow fynde

let liberall Lypps no trust bewray
no^{r} ielous humo^{ur} payne thy mynd
yf I the wronge thy gryef vnfold
yf thow me vex thyne erro^{ur} graunt
to seke straunge soyles be not to bold
the stryfles bedd no iarrs may haunt
smale sleap and tymely prayer intende
the Idle lyff as poyson hate
no credytt light nor much spech spende
in open place ⟨no⟩ cause no debate
no thwartes, no frowns, no grudge no^{r} stryf
eschew the badd embrace the best
to troth of worde ioyne honest lyff
and in my bosom buyld thy nest

The above is a better text than that in *NA*, as the variants show:

4 thy chirdrene] Our chyldren
11 sease] ceace
13 preasse] peace
17 gryef] greifes
19 soyles] toyles
21 tymely] early
24 ⟨no⟩ cause no] no cawse
25 no^{r}] no

There is no significance in the fact that this poem is not ascribed to John Harington in *P*; neither are the copies there given of Nos. 3 and 20, as they are not in *AH*. Sir John Harington happens to tell us that his father wrote Nos. 3 and 20, but he is silent about these addresses of the husband and wife. The style of the two poems is so like that we may reasonably conclude they were the work of the same person, and it may be that John Harington wrote them about 1564 for his wife, Isabella Markham, as the *NA* title indicates.

But what is the relation of the poems to Latin versions by the distinguished Reformer and Cambridge professor Dr. Walter Haddon (1516-72), who on Elizabeth's accession became Master of Requests? In 1567 Latin version of both poems were published opposite each other in Haddon's *Poëmata* (ed. T. Hatcher, sigs. K1^{v}-K3^{r}; ed. 1576, sigs. G5^{v}-G7^{r}). Through that ardent Reformer and friend of the Cambridge leaders in the movement Katherine, Duchess of Suffolk, to whom he dedicated *The booke of freendeship of Marcus Tullie Cicero*, Harington may have become acquainted with Haddon as early as the year of its publication in 1550; or, as the personal friend of the queen, Harington could easily have come into contact with Haddon at Court. The poems may, therefore, have been translated into English from Haddon's manuscript copies. Despite the fact that Harington's translation from Cicero is made from the French and that in his dedicatory epistle he professes himself to be ill versed in Latin, he may have become sufficiently proficient to handle the simpler Latin of Haddon's verses. It is, of course, possible that Haddon turned the English originals into Latin, but a comparison of the English with the Latin (given below from the 1567 text) indicates, I think, that the reverse method was followed. No. 21 parallels the Latin closely except in lines 17-20, where line 19 has no Latin parallel, and that for line 20 falls at line 24 in the Latin. Line 17 in the Latin is not in the English. The relationship in the address to the wife is not quite so close.

Præcepta Coniugii-Mariti Postulata.

Vxor, si cupias mihi placere,
Semper prima dei, secunda nostri,
Tum sit tertia cura liberorum.
Ædes fac sine sordibus nitére.
Mensæ prospice, prouide puellis.
Vultu sis hilari, tamen modesto.
Mores sint faciles, tamen pudici.
Vestis sobria sit, vacetq̃ labe.
Cum lætus fuero, dolero noli,
Nec cum tristis ero, decet iocari.
Et quemcunq̃ vides mihi placere,
Fac hunc esse tibi putes amicum.
Quicquid dixero, ne palam refelle.
Clam, quod displicet, admonere debes.
Arcanum tibi si reuelo, cæla.
Nec te suspicio sinistra vexet.
Si te læsero, vulnus indicabis.
Me si commoueas, fatere crimen.
In lectum veniat nihil querelæ.
Somnus sit modicus. Precare manè
Cum surrexeris, occupata viue,
Non credes nimium, parum loquêre.
Nec coram tibi disputare fas est.
Responsare caue, caueq̃ murmur.
Te coniunge bonis, malos relinque.
Sit vitæ probitas, fidesq̃ linguæ.
Morum deniq̃ sit pudor magister.
Hæc si feceris, in sinu iacebis.

Præcepta Coniugii-Vxoris Responsa.

Mi vir, si mihi charus esse curas:
Me solum colito quasi teipsum.
Sic tu proximus es deo futurus.
Sic nostros ego liberos fouebo.
Fac vt tuta domus sit, & salubris.
Nec desint ea, quæ requirit vsus.
Execere tuos stude ministros.
Sit comis tibi vox, sit os serenum.
Si vis temporibus tuis vt vtar:
Et tu tempora nostra scire debes.
Quantum vis tribui tuis amicis,
Tantum fac tribuas meis amicis.
Seruis iurgia dura fac reserues:
Et me leniter admoneto solam.
Mecum liberius licet iocari.
Nec me reijcies nimis seuerè,
Tecum lætior esse, si requiram.
Et me non satis est tibi placere,
Sed sciri volo te bonum maritum.
Me si non sinis esse suspicacem:
Causam suspicionis amoueto.
Quantumcunq̃ dies tulit laborum,
Nox secum placidam ferat quietam
Non absis temere domo, diuuè.
Quicquid pollicitus procus fuisti,
Nunc præstare maritus id memento.
Si me Penelopen habere speras,
Fac vt te mihi præbeas Vlyssem.

English versions, evidently translated from the Latin, were printed by Timothy Kendall in his *Flowers of Epigrammes*, 1577 (sigs. M2^{v}-M3^{v}), as "The husband's requests" and "The wife's answer" (available in the reprint of the 1577 edition, Spenser Society, No. 15 [1874], pp. 196-98). Kendall's verses fail to convey the spirit of playful domesticity and affection which is present both in the Latin and in Harington's English.

[22] *When I looke back and in my self behold*

Hand A. In line 7 "how . . . skill" is written in the same hand over "that . . . skyll," which in turn appears to be written over an erasure. Lines 8-10 and in line 18 "Cansell" are written over erasures. As indicated in the marginal numbering, which seems to be in Hand A, lines

25-30 were obviously intended to be rearranged in the order *2 1 4 3 5 6*. The order of the lines in other versions, however, is just as they are written here.

The poem appeared in (*A*) *The Paradyse of daynty deuises*, 1576, sig. B2$^{r, v}$ (ed. Rollins, No. 17), where it is ascribed to Lord Vaux and is entitled, "*Of the instabilitie of youth*." There is a version in (*B*) British Museum MS. Add. 26737, a commonplace book of the late sixteenth century, on fols. 108^{r}-107^{r} (*sic*). A version which was evidently used as a song is found in another late sixteenth-century commonplace book, (*C*) British Museum MS. Add. 30076, fol. 2^{v}. A tune by "Parsons" is in Bodleian MS. Music Sch. e.423, fol. 41^{r}. This is in all probability Robert Parsons, composer of church music and a gentleman of the Chapel Royal, who died in 1570. An abbreviated version of the poem is in (*D*) *NA*, 1769, pp. 97-98 (eds. 1779, 1792, iii, 271-72; ed. 1804, ii, 333-34), with the heading, "SONNET *wrote in the Tower*, 1554."

2 *left marginal note in B*: penitens de iuvenilibus

3 see] markt *A*: marke *B C*

4 I] youth *A-C*; strayed] strayd *B C*: stray'd *D*

6 O Lord] My God *D*; youthes] these *A*; fawltes] fawlte *D*

This line is expanded into a refrain of two lines in C:

o Lord, o lord, forgett youthes fottes & follyes all
follyes all, forgett youthes fauttes & follies all

Lines 7-12 are omitted in D.

how . . . skill

7 ⟨that . . . skyll⟩] howe voyde youth is of skill *A*: how voyde youth was of skill *B C*

8 I . . . payne] I see also his prime time and his end *A*: and know right well youthes prime tyde & his end *B C*

9 feele . . . still] doo confesse my faultes and all my yll *A*: do confesse my faultes & all myne ill *B C*

10 I . . . trayne] And sorrowe sore, for that I did offend *A*: And doe repent, that ev'r I did offend *B C*

12 *This line is expanded into a refrain in C:*

pardō, pardon I aske for youth ten thousand tymes
ten thousand tymes, pardō I aske ten thousand tymes

14 Knowledge] Eke wysdome *A*: And skill *C*; to] *omitted A D*; the] a *A*

15 Wysdome] And wit *A*; that] what *D*

16 his . . . his] her . . . her *A*: his captive, brought in *D*

17 wherefore] Therefore *A*; O] the *C*

18 Cansell] Pardon *A B*; the] those *D*; crymes] faultes *A*
This line is expanded into a refrain in C:

Pardō, pardon the crymes comytted in my youth
comytted in my youth, the crymes comytted in my youth

Lines 19-30 are combined into one stanza in D:

Thou that didst grant the wise kynge his request,
  Thou that of grace didst bring the blinde to sighte,
Thou that forgav'st the wounding of thy brest,
  Thou that in favour cam'st the worlde to lighte;
Thou only good dispenser of all grace,
Wype out the guilte that grew in youthe's green race.

20 thye] the *B C*
21 thy brest] the brest *B*
23 good and] God, the *A-C*
24 forgeve . . . greene] Wipe out of mind, the path of youthes vaine *A*
This line is expanded into a refrain in C:

fforgive forgive ye gyltes y^{t} grew in youths greene race
yn youths greene race, ye gyltes y^{t} grew in youths greene race

26 restoredst] restorest *A*: restored *B C*
27 for] of *B C*; lif and blood] life and love *A*: blood & life *B C*; bledd] shedd *B*
30 Wype . . . of] Forgeue the gilth, that grewe in *A*: Wipe out of mynde the vauntes of *B*
This line is expanded into a refrain in C:

Wype out, wypp out of mynd ye vantes of youthes vaine waies
of youthes vaine waies, wype out ye vantes of youthes *blurred*

31 And] But *D*; hope . . . with] I, with faith and *A B*; doubtlesse] dolefull *C*
32 doth preace] Doo fly *A B*: doth praie *C*; t'appease] to appease *A C*: to assuage *D*; thyne] thy *A*
33 with . . . I] that, thee, I onely seeke *A*
34 and wayte through] And hope by *A*: Waitinge, through *D*; t'attayne] to attayne *A C D*; this] my *A*; iust] *omitted C*
35 nor] and *A*: or *B C*
36 but] And *A*
Lines 35 and 36 are expanded into a refrain in C:

graunt lord, grant lord to age to do thy holy will
thie holy will, graunt age to doe thy holy will

Of the three long versions, that in *The Paradyse* shows most divergence and that not always for the best. The short *NA* version is so markedly different from that in *AH*, even in idiosyncracies of spelling, that it is unreasonable to suppose that it was copied from *AH*. In view of Bishop Percy's statement about the nature of the copy for the poems in the *NA*, we must suppose that another manuscript copy was available. It may be, of course, that some eighteenth-century editing was done, but many Elizabethan manuscript versions vary widely, omitting and combining stanzas, as in this *NA* version.

Who wrote the poem, Vaux, as *The Paradyse* has it, or John Harington, as the *NA* implies? Unlike D. Sand, mentioned in the Note on No. 19, Thomas, Baron Vaux, was a poet of some distinction. George Puttenham in *The Arte of English Poesie*, 1589 (ed. Gladys Willcock and Alice Walker, 1936, p. 239), describes Vaux, whom he confuses with his father, Nicholas, as "a noble gentleman, and much delighted in vulgar making . . . hauing herein a maruelous facillitie." At least two of his poems are in *TM*: "When Cupide scaled first the fort," and the more famous, "I lothe that I did love" (ed. Rollins, Nos. 211, 212), which has a theme similar to the one under discussion. Twelve undisputed poems are assigned to Vaux in *The Paradyse*, of which three, "The day delayed, of that I most doo wishe," "How can the tree but wast, and wither awaie," and "When I beholde the baier, my laste and postyng horsse" (ed. Rollins, Nos. 16, 71, 113), may be profitably compared with this poem in subject matter, rhythm, and phraseology. Yet, in subject matter they have even closer resemblance to *AH* No. 19, which *The Paradyse* (ed. Rollins, No. 47) assigns to Sand. I call particular attention to the sixth stanza of No. 16 in *The Paradyse*, which runs:

> The dayes be long, that hang vpon desert,
> The life is irke of ioyes that be delayed:
> The time is short, for to requite the smart,
> That dooth proceede of promise long vnpaid,
> That to the last of this my fainting breath,
> I wishe exchange of life, for happy death.

Or, consider the fourth stanza of No. 113:

> Loe here the Sommer floure, that sprong this other daie,
> But Winter weareth as faste, and bloweth cleane awaie:
> Euen so shalt thou consume, from youth to lothsome age,
> For death he doeth not spare, the prince more then the page.

Or, consider the refrain of No. 71:

> Is this a life, naie death you maie it call,
> That feeles eche paine, and knoweth no ioye at all.

On the basis of these comparisons one is forced to conclude that Vaux could have been the author of No. 22; yet no more so than of No. 19. A. B. Grosart accepts *The Paradyse* ascription for No. 22 and includes the poem in his edition of the poems of Lord Vaux in *Miscellanies of the Fuller Worthies Library*, IV, ii [1872], 367-69.

What of the implications of authorship in the *NA*? No. 22 in *NA* follows No. 19, which is there assigned to John Harington as a composition written in the Tower in 1554. The heading of No. 22 asserts the same place and date of composition and implies the same authorship. G. F. Nott has no comment on the authorship of this poem, as he does for No. 19. In his *Surrey and Wyatt*, i [1815], 294, in a note on Surrey's poem "When youth had led me half the race," Nott calls attention to this poem, which he thinks was written in imitation of Surrey, as it undoubtedly was. Harington, like Vaux, wrote with rhythmical facility and enjoyed making use of balance and alliteration. The theme could easily have been inspired by a stay in the Tower in 1554. In the end, however, there is no proof of authorship.

Popularity of the poem is indicated not only by the several versions mentioned above but by others written in imitation of it. William Hunnis wrote one beginning, "Alacke when I looke backe vpon my youth thatz paste," with the refrain, "Good Lorde with mercie doe forgiue, the follies of my youthe" (*The Paradyse*, No. 108). Another, less readily available, appears in *Songs of sundrie kindes* by Thomas Greaves, 1604, sig. L1, as follows:

The Dittie of the X. Song.

When I behold my former wandring way,
And diue into the bottome of my thoughts,
And thinke how I haue led that soule astray,
Whose safetie with so precious bloud was bought:
  With teares I cry vnto the God of truth,
  Forgiue O Lord, the errours of my youth.

A blessed Sauiour left his heauenly throne,
To seeke my straying soule, and bring it backe:
Himselfe the way, the way, I should haue gone,
The way I left, and sought eternall wracke,
  Which makes me crye in depth of bitter ruth,
  Forgiue O Lord, the errours of my youth.

Inestimable gaine he did propose
T'allure my erring fancy to retire:
But idle fancy would haue none of those,
Delighting still to wallowe in the mire,
  Wherefore I crye, vnto the God of truth
  Forgiue O Lord, the errours of my youth.

I saw the way, the way it selfe did cleare it,
I knew the way, the way it selfe did shew it,

I markt the way, but fondly did forbeare it,
I left the way, because I would not know it:
But now I cry vnto the God of truth;
Forgiue O Lord, the errours of my youth.

Iesu the onely way, most perfect true,
Iesu the onely truth of heauenly life,
Iesue the onely life, that doth renue
My sinne-sickle soule, halfe slaine by Sathans strife.
With teares I beg, teach me the way of truth;
Forgiue O Lord, the errours of my youth.

In another imitation Thomas Lodge turned a religious hymn into a Petrarchan poem, beginning, "When with aduice I weigh my yeares forepast," which was printed in *Scillaes Metamorphosis* in 1589 (see *Complete Works*, ed. Edmund Gosse, Hunterian Club, vol. i [1883], sig. F1^{v}-F2^{r}, reproducing the format of the first edition).

[23] *Amanza myne with heedefull eye beholde*

Hand A. The following are written over erasures: 7. "dothe"; 11. "cleare fa"; 33. "skill from"; 35. "Amydds."

So far as I have been able to discover the poem has not been printed before, and there are no other copies of it. The metrical and stanzaic form is the same as that of Nos. 19 and 22. The sentiment and phraseology of stanza 3 suggest comparison with Nos. 177, 178, 247, 262, the first two poems in the Appendix, and to a lesser extent with Nos. 2 and 21—all of which were probably written by John Harington. Addressed to "Amanza myne," that is, lover, clearly derived from *amans*, the poem may be another of those composed by Harington for Isabella Markham. See, "Whence comes my love, O hearte, disclose" (*NA*, 1769, p. 129), and "Alas! I love yow overwell" (*NA*, 1775, pp. 257-58).

EXPLANATORY NOTE ON NOS. 24-63

This group of verses, on fols. 27^{v}-30^{r}, is headed, "dyvers sentences." The handwriting is discussed in the Introduction p. 30. Numbers are written by the side of a good many of the sentences, suggesting that they were being arranged in an order, perhaps for publication. They represent the current proverbial and sententious wisdom popular in the sixteenth century. For some I have discovered definite sources; for others, parallels; and for a few, nothing at all close. I am convinced, however, that none of them is strictly original. For the most common I have pointed out but a few suggestive references. Several of the sentences have sources or parallels in Cicero's *De Amicitia*, translated by John Harington the elder in 1550; and others, in Ariosto's *Orlando Furioso*, of which occasional lines and stanzas were translated by the elder Harington and the whole by his son in 1591.

One may wonder whether the Haringtons would agree with John Florio in his sentiments about collecting proverbs. In his *Second Frutes*, 1591, "To the Reader," sig. A6r, he says:

> The Greeks and Latines thanke Erasmus, and our Englishmen make much of Heywood: for Prouerbs are the pith, the proprieties, the proofes, the purities, the elegancies, as the commonest so the commendablest phrases of a language. To vse them is a grace, to vnderstand them a good, but to gather them a paine to me, though gaine to thee.

Both the Haringtons and John Florio could have lessened the "paine" of the editor considerably by naming the sources from which they gathered their proverbs and sentences.

[24] *The Citie rear'de enriched with moche payne*

Hand A (?).

This is probably a translation, but I have not found the source. By way of parallel note lines in *Respublica*, 1553 (ed. L. A. Magnus, E.E.T.S., Extra Series, xciv [1905], 44), V, iii, 1341-46:

> but as meate & drinke & other bodylye foode
> is never founde to bee, so pleasaunte nor so goode
> As whan fretting hongre/ & thrifte hathe pincht afore;
> & as health after sicknes is sweeter evermore,
> so after decaye & aduersytee overcome
> welth and prospiritee shalbe double welcome.

Also compare lines from *The Dictes and Sayings of the Philosophers*, translated from the French of Guillaume de Tignonville, *Les Dicts moraulx des philosophes*, by Anthony Wydeville, Earl Rivers (facsimile, with preface by William Blades, 1877, p. [88]):

> And said the lordshippes wonne by study dangiers and peynes and so kept/ ought wele to contynne and prospere// And thoos yt be lightly wonñe & kept in Ioye and plesaunce/ comme to a littill prouffyt atte last/ & we se comonely the townes wherin the inhabitauntes take grete labour be wele maynteyned and encresse with grete richesses/ and the townes full of pleasaunce & delices fall to ruyne & distruction/.

More simply Thomas Howell puts it in his *Devises*, 1581 (ed. Sir Walter Raleigh, Oxford, Clarendon Press, 1906, p. 70): "Things hardly had, obtaynde, are holden deere."

[25] *To waite for that, which commith never*

Hand A (?).

I have found no source for this.

[26] *Theare be two thinges especiallye*

Hand A (?).

In No. 26 a sentence in John Harington's *The booke of freendeship of Marcus Tullie Cicero*, 1550, sig. F3v, has been put into verse form, possibly by John himself. There it reads:

> Yet these two thynges make mē for the most part to be noted of vnstedfastnesse and lightnesse, if either in their owne prosperitee they set their frēdes light, or in their frēdes aduersitee they cast theim of.

The Latin, *De Amicitia*, XVII.64, runs, "tamen haec duo levitatis et infirmitatis plerosque convincunt, aut si in bonis rebus contemnunt aut in malis deserunt."

In a somewhat similar vein Diogenes Laertius advises, *Lives of Eminent Philosophers*, I.97 (ed. and trans. R. D. Hicks, Loeb Library, vol. i [London, Heinemann; New York, Putnam, 1925]), "Be the same to your friends whether they are in prosperity or in adversity." Plutarch remarks in "A Letter to Apollonius," *Moralia*, 102.F (ed. and trans. F. C. Babbitt, Loeb Library, vol. ii [London, Heinemann; New York, Putnam, 1928]):

> It is the mark of educated and disciplined men to keep the same habit of mind toward seeming prosperity, and nobly to maintain a becoming attitude toward adversity.

In another passage Plutarch, *Moralia*, 68.E (same ref., vol. i [1927]), quotes Euripides, *Orestes*, 667, " 'When Heaven grants us luck, what need of friends?' "

[26a] *oft sarvice offred vn accepted*

Hand: contemporary italic. The *b* and *a* above "sarvice" and "offred" clearly indicate an intended reversal in order.

This couplet perhaps should be numbered as a separate sentence, but since it is written at the side of No. 26, I have assumed that it was intended as a comment on that sentence, and I have therefore numbered them as parts of one sentence.

The observation in John Florio's *Second Frutes*, 1591, p. 105, is more in accord with No. 26a than are those commonly given: "Fauours vnexpected, are most thankfully accepted." Contrast Richard Taverner,

Proverbes or adagies with newe addicions gathered out of the Chiliades of Erasmis, 1539, sig. D3^v:

Merx ultronea putet.

> Profered ware stynketh. Seruice y^t is wyllyngly offered is for most parte to be suspected.

Compare with Taverner, John Heywood, *woorkes*, 1562, No. 198 (Spenser Society, i [1867], 159):

> Proferde seruice stinketh, thou art deceiued else,
> Thy proferde seruice stinkth not: thou stinkst thy selfe.
> Otherwyse,
> Proferde seruice stinkth. more foole thou to profer it,
> Thou shuldest season thy seruice ere thou offer it.

In agreement with Heywood's counsel is that of Ariosto, which reads in Sir John Harington's translation of the *Orlando Furioso*, 1591, Book XLI, stanza 42, lines 5-8 (p. 345):

> Madnesse and follie tis (thus he replide)
> In you, or anie man that in such sort,
> Will counsell and aduise men what to do,
> Being not calld of counsell thereunto.

[27] *Thryse Happie thei, can cutt the winges*

Hand of No. 4. "Thryse" is written in the margin in another secretary hand; the "be" was obviously crossed out to take care of the meter.

Compare Publius Syrus, *Sententiae* (ed. Jules Chenu, 1835, p. 70), "Is minimo eget mortalis, qui minimum cupit." Also, p. 120, "Quis plurimum habet? is qui omnium minimum cupit."

[28] *In doing well vse no delay*

Hand of No. 4.

Sir John Harington in a letter to Thomas Sutton, December 21, 1609, quotes a slightly different version of this distich, saying that it had been taught him by his father more than forty years earlier:

> In doing good use no delay
> For tyme is swift, and slydes away.

The letter is printed, with some modernization of spelling, by Robert Smythe in *Historical Account of Charter House*, 1808, p. 148, taken, he says, from the original in the Charterhouse Evidence Room. James Peller Malcolm gives it in *Londinium Redivivum*, i (1803), 400, in the chapter on "Charterhouse," although without definite statement of the whereabouts of the original. Malcolm in his notes confuses Sir John Harington of Kelston with his kinsman Baron Harington of Exton. N. E. McClure, *The Letters and Epigrams of Sir John Harington* (Philadelphia, University of Pennsylvania Press, 1930), p. 139, prints from Malcolm.

Similar advice can be found in many of the classics. Compare Ovid, *De Arte Amatoria*, III, 65, "Utendum est aetate; cito pede labitur aetas"; and III, 79, "Nostra sine auxilio fugiunt bona. Carpite florem"; Virgil, *Georgics*, III, 284, "Fugit irreparabile tempus"; Seneca, *De Brevitate Vitae*, 9. 3, "Itaque cum celeritate temporis, utendi velocitate certandum est; and *Epistle*, I, 2, "Sic fiet, ut minus ex crastino pendeas, si hodierno manum inieceris. Dum differtur vita, transcurrit."

Nor were English writers lacking in reflections on the value of time. Compare Chaucer, *Troilus and Criseyde*, IV, 1283 (Skeat), "For time y-lost may not recovered be"; and *Canterbury Tales*, E. 118-9,

> For though we slepe or wake, or rome, or ryde,
> Ay fleeth the tyme, it nil no man abyde;

also John Heywood, *woorkes*, Pt. I, Ch. III (Spenser Society, i [1867], 6): "Take time whan time comth, lest time steale away"; and, Pt. II, Ch. I (p. 42), "And that tyme loste, again we can not wyn."

A stanza on the theme was set to music by Thomas Whythorne in *Medius, Of Songes*, 1571, sig. DD1[r, v]:

> Take time while time is, for time wil away,
> I haue ere this time heard many one say,
> take time while time is, for time will away,
> take time while time is, for time will away,
> which at their own will they may dispatch soon,
> lest they be far off whē they wold be sped,
> lest they be far off whē they wold be sped.
> Take time while, etc.

[29] *ffaire wordes, fowle deedes, do oftẽ vse*

Hand of No. 4. Compare *Iohn Florio, His firste Fruites*, 1578, fol. 27[v], "Fayre words, and yl deedes, deceiue both wise and fooles"; *Howell's Devises*, 1581 (ed. Sir Walter Raleigh, 1906, p. 16), "Fayre words foule deeds, pretended and foretought"; John Davies of Hereford, *The Scourge of Folly*, 1611 (*Works*, ed. A. B. Grosart, ii [1878], 46), "Vpon English Prouerbes," No. 228, "Good words and ill deedes deceaue wise and fooles."

[30] *Who so to do his best is fownd*

Hand of No. 4.

Alfred Henderson, *Latin Proverbs and Quotations*, 1869, p. 430, gives the following line, which may be compared: "Tantum, quantum quisque potest, nutatur." He does not name the source, and I have not discovered it.

[31] *Serve aie he shall with paine*

Hand of No. 4. Emendations are probably in the handwriting of Sir John Harington.

Compare, *The Mariage of Witte and Science*, 1570 (Tudor Facsimile Texts, 1909), sig. A3v, "The worthiest thĩgs ar wonne wt pain in tract of time alwaies"; Thomas Churchyard, *The Mirror of Man and Manners of Men*, 1594 (reprint by Alexander Boswell in *Frondes Caducæ*, vol. i [1817]), sig. A4v, "Nothing is gotten, without toyle and labor"; Randle Cotgrave, *A Dictionarie of the French and English Tongues*, 1632, "Peine: f. . . . Nul pain sans peine: . . . Prov. *Nor bread, nor ought is gotten without paines.*"

[32] *His fall is nye*

Hand of No. 4.

Compare Henry Bradshaw, *Saynt Werburge*, 1513, I, line 931 (ed. Carl Horstmann, E.E.T.S., lxxxviii [1887], 40), "Who clymbeth to hye/ often hath a fall"; also "The Assumption of the Virgin," l.32, *Ludus Coventriae* (ed. K. S. Block, E.E.T.S., Extra Series, cxx [1922], 356), "Whoso clyme ou*er* hie. he hath a foule fall." More elaborate is the expression of a similar idea in Sir John Harington's translation of the *Orlando Furioso*, 1591, Book XLV, stanza 1 (p. 384):

> Looke how much higher fortune doth erect,
> The clyming wight, on her vnstable wheele,
> So much the nigher may a man expect,
> To see his head, where late he saw his heele:
> *Polycrates* hath prou'd it in effect,
> And *Dionysius* that too true did feele:
> Who long were luld on high in fortunes lap,
> And fell downe sodainly to great mishap.

One may compare also somewhat similar expressions in the classics: Seneca, *De Brevitate Vitae*, XVII. 4, "Omne enim quod fortuito obvenit instabile est, quoque altius surrexerit, opportunius est in occasum"; Plautus, *Miles Gloriosus*, IV, iv, 14,

> Non tu scis, quom ex alto puteo sursum ad summum escenderis,
> Maxumum periclum inde esse ab summo ne rusum cadas?

Ovid, *Tristia*, III, iv, 5-6,

> Vive tibi, quantumque potes prælustria vita:
> Sævum prælustri fulmen ab igne venit.

Other examples could be cited both from the classics and from English works. See also the Note on No. 45.

[33] *The Scilent servant serving well*

Hand of No. 4.

Compare Wydeville, *Dictes* (see the Note on No. 24), p. [107]:

And sayd + The kynges seruauntis ought to shewe in seruyng hym their good vertues their feith the noblesse of their kynrede + to thentente that the kyng may bettir knowe hem and do to euery of them as he shal haue deserued.

[34] *No man can daunce amisse*

Hand of No. 4.

Compare *Iohn Florio, His firste Fruites*, 1578, fol. 27v, "He daunceth wel, vnto whom fortune pipeth." Thomas Fuller gives the proverb in his *Gnomologia*, 1732, No. 1832: "He dances merrily, whom Fortune pipes to."

[35] *Thei know not peace/ nor rightlie how to deeme it*

Hand of No. 4. Alterations are in the same hand.

These lines are a translation of the closing couplet of Book XXXI, stanza 2, of Ariosto's *Orlando Furioso*. Like No. 2 they probably represent some preliminary work on the *Orlando*, prior to Sir John's translation of the whole, and my supposition is that, like No. 2, the couplet was taken out by the elder John because it struck his fancy. This version in *AH*, which differs slightly from that in Sir John's translation, may have been his.

The stanza in Sir John's translation, ed. 1591, p. 250, reads:

For eu'rie other sowre that gets a place,
  To seate it selfe amid this pleasant sweet,
  Helps in the end to giue a greater grace,
  And makes loues ioy more gratful whē they meet
  He that abstaines from sustenance a space,
  Shall find both bread and water rellish sweet:
  Men know not peace, nor rightly how to deem it,
  That first by war, haue not bin taught t'esteeme it.

The copy in MS. Add. 18920, fol. 157v, in Sir John's autograph, agrees exactly with the above. It is not in MS. Rawl Poet. 125, also in autograph, which has the first twenty-four books only. In the 1634 edition of the *Orlando*, p. 250, the last line reads: "That have not first by war been taught t'esteem it."

A translation of these lines from Ariosto is included in *Iohn Florio, His firste Fruites*, 1578, fol. 44,

> None can esteeme or knowe what peace can be,
> Vnlesse he prooued haue, what warre is first.

[36] *Bewtie is seldome fownd*

Hand of No. 4.

Compare John Florio, *Second Frutes*, 1591, p. 193: "Because beawtie and honesty seldome agree, for of beautie comes temptation, of temptation dishonour." See also Thomas Fuller, *Gnomologia*, 1732, No. 954: "Beauty is the Subject of a Blemish."

[37] *The good and evill horsse the spurr doth crave*

Hand of No. 4. The *a* is written over an erasure.

Compare John Florio, *Second Frutes*, 1591, p. 183:

> and therfore Bocace saith wel:
> To make thy horse to runne, and thy wife to stop,
> Giue him the spurre, giue her the holly crop.

Also at p. 175:

> Wiues, Asses, nuttes, the more they beaten bee,
> More good and profite they will yeeld to thee.

See also Plutarch, *Moralia*, 139 B, "Coniugalia Praecepta" (ed. and trans., F. C. Babbitt, Loeb Library, vol. ii [1928]): "But, as one pays heed to the size of his horse in using the rein, so in using the rein on his wife he ought to pay heed to her position."

[38] *Vertue wheare wealth doth want, esteemed is but vayne*

Hand of No. 4.

In Sir John Harington's translation of the *Orlando Furioso*, 1591, Book XLIV, stanza 33, lines 7-8 (p. 377), there is a similar observation,

> Alas (quoth he) gentrie doth small auaile,
> And vertue lesse, if lands and riches faile.

The same idea is somewhat differently expressed in stanza 48 (p. 378). Its origin is ancient. Hesiod in *Works and Days* (*Hesiod, the Homeric Hymns and Homerica*, ed. and trans. H. G. Evelyn-White, Loeb Library, 1914), line 313, observes, "Fame and renown attend on wealth"; and, again, lines 319-20, "Shame is with poverty, but confidence with wealth." The Haringtons would almost certainly have known Horace's Satire III, lines 94-97:

> . . . omnis enim res,
> virtue, fama, decus, divina humanaque pulchris

> divitiis parent; quas qui construxerit, ille
> clarus erit, fortis, iustus.

Very probably they were also familiar with the comments of Plutarch in "How to Study Poetry," *Moralia*, 36.E (ed. and trans. F. C. Babbitt, Loeb Library, vol. i [1927]), "Who all [the father, mother, and nurse of youth] beatify and worship the rich, who shudder at death and pain, who regard virtue without money and repute as quite undesirable and a thing of naught." "Mr. G. H." (George Herbert?) in *Iacula Prudentum*, 1640, No. 509, puts it thus, "Health without money is halfe an ague." This is followed by Thomas Fuller in *Gnomologia*, 1732, No. 2479, "Health without Wealth, is half a Sickness."

[39] *The inward mirth of hart*

Hand of No. 4. The "ye" is inserted above the line in another secretary hand.

Compare Seneca, *De Tranquillitate Animi*, IX, iii, 6, "Nunquam enim quamvis obscura virtus latet, sed mittit sui signa"; also John Davies of Hereford, *The Scourge of Folly*, 1611 (*Works*, ed. A. B. Grosart, ii [1878], 46), "Vpon English Prouerbes," No. 224: "The ioy of the heart, fairly coulors the face"; and the *Book of Meery Riddles*, 1629, Proverb 54: "The hearts mirth doth make the face fayre."

[40] *Lyke as men deeme not that bread best*

Hand of No. 4. In line 5 "doe" is written over a word, possibly "can."

I have not discovered any exact source for these lines. Juvenal's Satire VIII, "Stemmata Quid Faciunt?" on the bootlessness of pedigree unless individual virtue and achievement are present, may be compared. Alfred Henderson, *Latin Proverbs and Quotations*, p. 269, without naming a source, gives one which is applicable, "Nobilitas morum plus ornat quam genitorum."

[41] *ffrom those I trust god me defend*

Hand of No. 4.

Compare Wydeville, *Dictes* (see the Note on No. 24), p. [127]:

> And ther was one that praied god to kepe him from the daunger of his frendis And it was asked him/ why he prayed not rather/ that god sholde kepe him from his ennemyes than fro hys frẽdes And he ansuerd/ for asmoche + as I may wele kepe me from myn ennemyes in whom I haue no truste/ but I may not kepe me from my frende whom that I truste/.

Note also Robert Crowley, "Of Flaterars," 1550 (*Select Works*, ed. J. M. Cowper, E.E.T.S., Extra Series, xv [1872], 30, lines 825-28):

Of an open enimie,
a man may be ware;
When the flatteryng frend
wyl worck men much care.

Alexander Copley, *Wits, Fits, and Fancies*, 1614, p. 50, quotes from the Italian: "The Italians vse to say, *De che me fio, me gaurde Iddio: De che me fio, me guardare Io*: That is, A fained friend God shield me from his danger, For well, I'le saue my selfe from foe and stranger."

[42] *Who so hath tyme at will*

Hand of No. 4.

Compare *Iohn Florio, His firste Fruites*, 1578, fol. 26ᵛ, "Who hath tyme, and tarieth for time, looseth tyme." Alfred Henderson, *Latin Proverbs and Quotations*, 1869, p. 368, gives the following pertinent line, but without naming the source: "Qui tempus proestolatur, tempus ei deest."

[43] ⟨*Submitt your selves wives wth care to accord*⟩

Hand of No. 4. The verses are crossed out by diagonal lines.

This is a metrical version of Ephesians v. 22-24:

Wives, submit yourselves unto your own husbands, as unto the Lord. For the husband is the head of the wife, even as Christ is the head of the church: and he is the saviour of the body. Therefore as the church is subject unto Christ, so let the wives be to their own husbands in every thing.

Compare No. 62.

[44] *No state can be more sownd, no lif more swete*

Hand of No. 4. Alterations are in the hand of the "dyvers sentences," written before No. 24.

Compare lines from Sir John Harington's translation of the *Orlando Furioso*, 1591, Book XXXI, stanza 1, lines 1-4 (p. 250):

What state of life more pleasing may we find,
Then theirs, that true, & heartie loue do beare?
Whom that sweet yoke doth fast together bind,
That mā in Paradice first learnd to weare:

Thomas Howell in his *Devises*, 1581 (ed. Sir Walter Raleigh, 1906, p. 70), has lines somewhat similar to this couplet,

What state more sweete, more pleasant or more hie,
Then loues delight, where hartes doe ioyntly ioye?

There is nothing new in the idea that goodness is essential to perfect friendship. Compare Aristotle, *Ethica Nicomachea*, 1156^{b}, 6-8 (trans. W. D. Ross, Oxford, Clarendon Press, 1925), "Perfect friendship is the friendship of men who are good, and alike in virtue; for these wish well alike to each other *qua* good, and they are good in themselves." Similarly, Diogenes Laertius, *Lives of Eminent Philosophers*, VII, 124 (ed. and trans. R. D. Hicks, Loeb Library, vol. ii [1925]), "Friendship, they [the Stoics] declare, exists only between the wise and good, by reason of their likeness to one another." Sallust, *Catilina*, XX. 4-5, emphasizes only similarity of interest, "Nam idem velle atque nolle, ea demum firma amicitia est." Cicero in his *De Amicitia*, XIV, 49-50, says:

> Nihil est enim remuneratione benevolentiae, nihil vicissitudine studiorum officiorumque incundius. Quid? si illud etiam addimus, quod recte addi potest, nihil esse quod ad se rem ullam tam illiciat et tam trahat quam ad amicitiam similitudo,

which John Harington in his *Booke of freendeship of Marcus Tullie Cicero*, 1550, sig. E2^{v}, translates thus:

> For there is nothyng goodlier, then requityng of benefites, nor any thing pleasanter, than thenterchangeyng of loue and dutie. And also if you putte this vnto it, which maie wel be added, that there is nothyng, whiche allureth and so draweth oughte vnto it, as lykenesse of condicions doeth one to freendship.

[45] *So moche more great, eache fault is deem'de to be*

Hand of No. 4. In line 1 "deem'de to" is written over an erasure, and in line 2 all words except "he" and "is" are written over erasures.

I have found nothing exactly like this, but many sayings that are somewhat similar. Perhaps the closest of these is in the *Sententiae* of Publius Syrus (ed. Jules Chenu, 1835, p. 148), "Esse necesse est vitia minima maximorum maxima." Similar comments appear in Wydeville's *Dictes* (see the Note on No. 24). Compare, for example, "Ther is nothing so euyl vnto a man/ as to be euil endoctrined/ and in especyal/ whan he is yssued of noble and good lignage" (p. [120]); again, "And another said the more y^{t} thastate of king Alexãder was grete & more exellent the more is thoccasion of his deth greuous & pytefull" (p. [97]); and, "And saide the hygher that a man is exaltid in his lordship/ the more greuous it shalbe to him to fall from the same" (p. [105]). A saying attributed to King Edward I about John, Earl of Atholl, a murderer, given by William Camden in his *Remaines*, 1605, carries the same idea as that expressed in the last quotation, "The higher his calling is, the greater must his fall be; and as he is of higher parentage, so he shalbe the higher hanged" (p. 206). Numerous examples could be given to illustrate popularity of the idea that the man who climbs too high is due a very great fall, or that the higher he rises, the lower he falls. Some of these apply perhaps better to No. 32 than to No. 45. See G. L. Apperson, *English Proverbs and Proverbial Phrases*, 1929, p. 301, and B. J. Whiting, *Proverbs in the Earlier English Drama*, Cambridge, Mass., Harvard University Press, 1938, pp. 44, 125, sqq.

[46] *When fortune doth faile, then frindship is gone*

Hand of No. 4.

Compare Richard Taverner, *Proverbes or adagies with newe addicions gathered out of the Chiliades of Erasmis*, 1539, sig. F7[r, v]:

Viri infortunati procul amici

The frendes of an infortunate person be farre of. When fortune ones beginneth to fayle the, anone thy frendes are gone.

Ovid, *Tristia*, I, ix, 6, expresses it, "Tempora si fuerint nabila, solus eris." Compare also Chaucer, *Canterbury Tales*, B.3431-6 (ed. Skeat):

For whan Fortune wol a man forsake,
She bereth awey his regne and his richesse,
And eek his freendes, bothe moore and lesse;
For what man that hath freendes thurgh Fortune,
Mishap wol make hem enemys, I gesse:
This proverbe is ful sooth and ful commune.

Cicero, *De Amicitia*, IX, 32, has an observation similar to the thought in the whole of this quatrain,

Nam si utilitas conglutinaret amicitias, eadem commutata dissolveret; sed quia natura mutari non potest, idcirco verae amicitiae sempiternae sunt.

John Harington in *The booke of freendeship*, 1550, sig. C7[v], Englished it thus,

For if profite shoulde fasten frendship, then the same beyng changed, shoulde vnlose it againe. But because nature cannot be chaunged, therefore true frendships be euerlasting.

A closer parallel, however, seems to be found in Anthony Wydeville's *Dictes* (see the Note on No. 24), "And sayd the frendes that be acquerid by good dedes ben better than tho that ben acquerid by force" (p. [101]). See also the Note on No. 61.

[47] *Woe, vnto whome, the poores small, moche doth seeme*

Hand of No. 4.

Compare Publius Syrus, *Sententiae* (ed. Jules Chenu, 1835, p. 68), "Instructa inopia est in divitiis cupiditas"; also, Wydeville, *Dictes* (see the Note on No. 24), "& he wrote thus to alexandre . . . nether is nothĩg so couenable to a king as to coueyte vnduely the goodes of his peple" (pp. [87-88]). Similar is a speech noted by William Camden in his *Remaines*, 1605, "When this *Caratacus* now enlarged was carried about to see the state and magnificence of *Rome*, *Why doe you* (saide hee) *so greedily desire our poore cottages, whenas you have such stately and magnificall pallaces?*" (p. 179).

[48] *Wolves be lyke Dogges flatt'rers lyke frends*

Hand of No. 4.

Compare Diogenes Laertius, *Lives of Eminent Philosophers*, VI.92 (ed. and trans. R. D. Hicks, Loeb Library, vol. ii [1925]), "Those who live with flatterers he [Crates] declared to be as defenceless as calves in the midst of wolves; for neither these nor those have any to protect them, but only such as plot against them." See also Plato, *Sophist*, sec. 231 (*The Dialogues*, trans. Benjamin Jowett, iv [1892], 357):

> Theaet[us]. Yet the Sophist has a certain likeness to our minister of purification.
>
> Str[anger]. Yes, the same sort of likeness which a wolf, who is the fiercest of animals, has to a dog, who is the gentlest.

[49] *Oft tymes good heede*

Hand of No. 4.

John Heywood, *woorkes*, 1562 (Spenser Society, i [1867], 72), Pt. II, Ch. VIII, says, "Take heede is a faire thing." This is repeated by John Florio, *Second Frutes*, 1591, p. 169. Thomas Fuller, *Gnomologia*, 1732, No. 6315, has, "Take-Heed/ Is a good Read." Chaucer, *Troilus and Criseyde*, II, 343 (ed. Skeat), expresses the idea a little differently, "Avysement is good bifore the nede."

[50] *A proverb olde, love those that loves agayne*

Hand of No. 4.

Compare lines from Sir John Harington's translation of the *Orlando Furioso*, 1591, Bk. V, stanza 54, lines 5-6 (p. 36):

> Loue those that loue againe if you be wise,
> For of my counsell this is the conclusion.

[51] *Whoe so a wyfe doth take*

Hand of No. 4.

This is an ancient lament. Compare the plaint of Semonides, Fragment VII, lines 99-100 (*Elegy and Iambus*, ed. and trans. J. M. Edmonds, Loeb Library, vol. ii [London, Heinemann; New York, Putnam,

1931]), "Whoso dwelleth with a woman, he never passeth a whole day glad." Similar is the cry of Alexis, as quoted by Athenaeus in "Concerning Women" (*Deipnosophistae*, XIII.558; ed. and trans. C. B. Gulick, Loeb Library, vol. vi [London, Heinemann; Cambridge, Mass., Harvard University Press, 1937]), "Leonides, spurning the very thought of marriage, cited this group of verses from *The Soothsayers of Alexis*: 'Oh, unlucky we, men who are married! We have sold our right of free speech and our comfort in life, and live as slaves to wives instead of being free.'" John Florio, *Second Frutes*, 1591, p. 189, includes an observation from Aretino which is closer to No. 51, "And as Aretine . . . was wont to say . . . vndone is he that must needes haue a wife." See also No. 7 and Note.

[52] *Other delight of mynde*

Hand of No. 4.

In "The Education of Children," Plutarch says (*Moralia*, 5.E, ed. and trans. F. C. Babbitt, Loeb Library, vol. i [1927]), "But learning, of all things in this world, is alone immortal and divine." See also Plato, *Laws*, Book II. 667 C (ed. and trans. F. G. Bury, Loeb Library, vol. i [London, Heinemann; New York, Putnam, 1926]), "Learning, too, is accompanied by the element of charm, which is pleasure, but that which produces its correctness and utility, its goodness and nobleness, is truth."

[53] *He that is an Asse, and Hart hym self doth weene*

Hand of No. 4.

This is an Englishing of an Italian proverb (Giuseppe Giusti's *Proverbi Toscani*, ed. Gino Capponi, 1873, p. 286):

Chi è asino e cervo si crede,
Al saltar della fossa se n'avvede.

I am indebted to Professor Margret Trotter of Agnes Scott College for this identification.

[54] *He whose faithe once hath suffred staine*

Hand of No. 4.

Sir John Harington made use of the phraseology of this couplet in his translation of the *Orlando Furioso*, 1591, Book XLVI, stanza 91, lines 7-8 (p. 401):

Saying, he readie was there to maintaine,
That yet his faith has neuer sufferd stane.

The idea expressed in No. 54 is found in Publius Syrus, *Sententiae* (ed. Jules Chenu, 1835, p. 54): "Fides, ut anima, unde abiit, eo nunquam redit."

[55] *He was frend never*

Hand of No. 4.

This maxim need not have a direct "source" anywhere, but one may compare Cicero, *De Amicitia*, XV. 55, "Amicitiarum sua cuique permanet stabilis et certa possessio," which was translated by John Harington in *The booke of freendeship of Marcus Tullie Cicero*, 1550, sig. E6r, as, "But freendship once gotten, abydeth with euerie man stedfast and surely." Similar is Proverbs XVII, 17, "A friend loveth at all times, and a brother is born for adversity."

[56] *blynde ffortune gevs tomoche to manye*

Hand of No. 4. The word "blynde" was clearly added in the margin in another secretary hand, possibly that of the heading before No. 24, and the same hand has changed "gevith" to "gevs." The numbers in the left margin seem to indicate that the couplet had first been numbered third in the series and later sixteenth.

The source for No. 56 is Martial, *Epigrammata*, XII.x, "Fortuna multis dat nimis, satis nulli," which is translated in the 1615 edition of Sir John Harington's *Epigrams*, sig. D2v, as,

> Fortune (men say) doth giue too much to many:
> But yet she neuer gaue enough to any.

Since these lines are not in the autograph manuscripts of Sir John's "Epigrams" (Brit. Mus. MS. Add. 12049, Cambridge Univ. MS. Add. 337, and Folger MS. 4455), one may suspect that the epigram was not Sir John's. Possibly it was his father's. A copy in Brit. Mus. MS. Sloane 1489, fol. 10r, differs from the reading of the *Epigrams* only in *did* for *doth* in line 1.

[57] *Wheare goodnes guydes the mynde*

Hand of No. 4. In line 3 "kynde" is written over an erasure.

To the right of the second line are seven Greek letters, apparently παγμτερ; these are clearly in the old ink. Nott's transcript omits them.

The idea of the harmony in outward and inward beauty, deriving ultimately from Plato, was, of course, commonly held in the Renaissance and was often expressed in both prose and poetry. Similar to the gnomic effect in these lines is the observation of Diogenes Laertius, *Lives of Eminent Philosophers*, VII.130 (ed. and trans. R. D. Hicks, Loeb Library, vol. ii [1925]), "And beauty they describe as the bloom or flower of virtue." Elizabethans would have been familiar with Ovid's verses in *De Medicamine Faciei Liber*, lines 44-46:

Ingenio facies conciliante placet.
Certus amor morum est; formam populabitur aetas,
Et placitus rugis vultus aratus erit.

[58] *Vse temperaũnce in feedinge*

Hand of No. 4.

John Florio in *His firste Fruites*, 1578, fol. 65v, gives similar advice to these verses: "The Philosopher perswadeth princes to be tẽperate in their life, sober in speaking, & to abstaine frõ much eating, to ouercome appetite and lust: and to suppresse pleasure, is a greate victorie." The philosopher should be Aristotle, but I have not discovered where Aristotle gives exactly such advice as this. Seneca, however, has a passage sufficiently like to be worth noting, *De Tranquillitate Animi*, IX, 2:

Cibus famem domet, potio sitim, libido qua necesse est fluat; discamus membris nostris inniti, cultum victumque non ad nova exempla componere, sed ut maiorum mores suadent; discamus continentiam augere, luxuriam coercere, gloriam temperare, iracundiam lenire, paupertatem aequis oculis aspicere, frugalitatem colere, etiam si multos pudebit, eius plus, desideriis naturalibus parvo parata remedia adhibere, spes effrenatas et animum in futura imminentem velut sub vinculis habere, id agere, ut divitias a nobis potius quam a fortune petamus.

[59] *Lend not to hym, whose state doth thyne exceade*

Hand of No. 4.

The heading should read "Ecclesiasticus" instead of "Ecclesiastes." The lines translate metrically verses 12-13 of Chap. VIII (*The Apocrypha and Pseudepigrapha of the Old Testament in English*, ed. R. H. Charles, i [Oxford, the Clarendon Press, 1913], 344):

Lend not to a man that is mightier than thou,
And if thou lend, (thou art) as one that loseth.
Be not surety for one who is more excellent than thou,
And if thou become surety (thou art) as one that payeth.

[60] *Eache man so ought to love his wif*

Hand of No. 4.

These lines paraphrase verses 28-31 of Ephesians V:

So ought men to love their wives as their own bodies. He that loveth his wife loveth himself.

For no man ever yet hated his own flesh; but nourisheth and cherisheth it, even as the Lord the church:

For we are members of his body, of his flesh, and of his bones.

For this cause shall a man leave his father and mother, and shall be joined unto his wife, and they two shall be one flesh.

[61] *When ffortune gave good wynde vnto my saile*

Hand of No. 4.

The stanza occurs twice in the manuscript. See No. 309, fol. 216r. It is taken from Ovid, *Ex Ponto*, II, iii, 23-28:

> diligitur nemo, nisi cui Fortuna secunda est:
> quae simul intonuit, proxima quaeque fugat,
> en ego, non paucis quondam munitus amicis,
> dum flavit velis aura secunda meis,
> ut fera nimboso tumuerunt aequora vento,
> in mediis lacera nave relinquor aquis.

Compare likewise *Ex Ponto*, IV, iii, 5-8:

> dum mea puppis erat valida fundata carina,
> qui mecum velles currere, primus eras,
> nunc, quia contraxit vultum Fortuna, recedis;

also, *Tristia*, III, v, 3-6:

> nec me complexus vinclis propioribus esses
> nave mea vento forsan, eunte suo.
> ut cecidi, cunctique metu fugere ruinam,
> versaque amicitiae terga dedere meae.

Thomas Blage in *A schole of wise conceytes*, 1572, p. 52, has a translation of the same passage:

> As Ouid complayneth not without cause
> When prosprous windes did driue my sailes,
> of Frendes I had good store,
> But all were gone, when raging Seas
> By blustring windes did rore.

Many parallels might be cited on the instability of friendship when adversity appears. Compare for example, Diogenes Laertius, *Lives of Eminent Philosophers*, V. 83 (ed. and trans. R. D. Hicks, Loeb Library, vol. i [1925]), "In prosperity friends do not leave you unless desired, whereas in adversity they stay away of their own accord"; also, Wydeville, *Dictes* (see the Note on No. 24), in the section on Diogenes, "One asked him whan he shulde knowe his frende/ he sayd in necessite for in prosperite euery man is frendely" (p. [45]). Note also, *Everyman*, sig. A6v (Tudor Facsimile Texts, 1912):

> It is sayd in prosperyte men frendes may fynde,
> Whiche in aduersyte be full vnkynde.

See also No. 46 and Note.

[62] *Men are borne to obay the lawse of their contrey*

Hand of No. 4.

Erasmus in his *Apophthegmes* (trans. Nicholas Udall, 1542, reprint of the 1564 edition, 1877, p. 43), says, referring to Socrates:

> It was also one of his saiynges, That menne were bounden, to be obedient to the lawes of the citee or countree: and wiues to the maners and facions of their housbandes, that thei liue in companie withal.

I cannot find such a saying by Socrates. Erasmus, writing perhaps from memory, may have attributed to Socrates the following remarks made by Meno to Socrates, *Meno*, 71. E (*Dialogues*, ed. and trans. W. R. M. Lamb, Loeb Library, vol. iv [1924]):

> First of all, if you take the virtue of a man, it is easily stated that a man's virtue is this—that he be competent to manage the affairs of his city, and to manage them so as to benefit his friends and harm his enemies, and to take care to avoid suffering harm himself. Or take a woman's virtue: there is no difficulty in describing it as the duty of ordering the house well, looking after the property indoors, and obeying her husband.

Compare also Aristotle, *Ethica Nicomachea*, 1160^{b}, 33-38 (*Works of Aristotle*, trans. W. D. Ross, vol. ix [1925]),

> The association of man and wife seems to be aristocratic; for the man rules in accordance with his worth, and in those matters in which a man should rule, but the matters that befit a woman he hands over to her;

and again, Plutarch, *Moralia*, 142. E, "Coniugalia Praecepta" (trans. F. C. Babbitt, Loeb Library, vol. ii [1928]),

> So is it with women also, if they subordinate themselves to their husbands, they are commended, but if they want to have control, they cut a sorrier figure than the subjects of their control.

See also No. 43.

[63] *A gratefull guift, from thanckfull mynd*

Hand of No. 4. The name "Iohn Harington" is written in sixteenth-century script in the right margin just below this sentence, which ends on the first half of the folio. The rest of the folio is torn away. Just above the torn edge are the words: "[dele?] hoc vt obscoenissimū," indicating that there had been a very improper drawing or sentence on that half of the folio.

With No. 63 one may compare Richard Taverner, *Proverbes or adagies with newe addicions gathered out of the Chiliades of Erasmis*, 1539, sig. D2^{r}:

Munerum animus optimus.

The mynde of gyftes is best, that is to saye, In ye gyftes or presẽtes of freendes the price or value of the thyng that is sent is not to be considered, but the mynde rather of the sẽder, as ye renoumed kyng Xerxes receyued thãkefully of an uplandish man an hãdful of water.

Compare also Cato, *Disticha de Moribus*, Lib. I, Dist. 20 (as given in *Sales Epigrammatum*, trans. James Wright, 1663, p. 135):

Animus in dono aestimandus
Exiguum munus cum dat tibi pauper amicus:
Accipito placide, plene & laudare memento.

The mind of the Giver is to be esteem'd in the Gift.
Thy poor Friend's gift though a small benefit
Receive, but render prayse surpassing it.

Parallels from the classics may be noted: Ovid, *Heroides*, XVII, 71:

Acceptissima semper
Munera sunt, auctor quae pretiosa facit;

Cicero, *Oratio pro Cn. Plancio*, cap. 33: "Haec [gratus animus] est enim una virtus non solum maxima, sed etiam mater virtutum omnium reliquarum."

[64] *I Scited once t'appeare/ before the noble Quene*

Hand A. This is a translation of the first thirty-eight lines of Petrarch's Canzone in Morte 7, beginning, "Quel antiquo mio dolce empio Signore." It should be compared with the same portion of Wyatt's poem "Myne olde dere En'mye" (No. 144), which has the same source.

No. 64 was printed from *AH* by Nott, *Surrey and Wyatt*, ii, 551-52, in his note on Wyatt's poem. Rollins, *TM*, ii, 178-79, prints it from *N*, fol. 17. It is also included in *The Sonnets, Triumphs, and Other Poems of Petrarch*, translated by Various Hands, with a Life of the Poet by Thomas Campbell, 1904, pp. 311-12.

[65] *ffower of Roses Angells ioy*

Hand: Sir John Harington's. 13. The "w" in "fawlte" is inserted above the line. 23. "mownt more hye" is written in pencil by the same hand in the right margin.

I have found no other copy of this hymn to the Virgin. I suggest that it was found in the books of Edmund Campion, which the elder John Harington had special permission to carry about with him. See the Note on No. 66.

[66] *Why doe I vse my paper ynke and pen*

Hand: Sir John Harington's. In lines 14, 121, and 152 the emendations are in Sir John's hand; but in lines 7, 36, 52, 69, 91, 115, 123, 139, 151, and 167 the emendations are in another ink and apparently in another hand. Some of these revisions were evidently made to accord with the printed copy, but others indicate a definite change from that text, as the collation shows. Much of the punctuation was added in another ink and was perhaps later.

Entitled, "Vpon the death of M Edmund Campion, one of the societie of the holy name of Iesus," this poem was first printed in (*A*) *A true report of the death and martyrdome of M. Campion Iesuite and preiste, & M. Sherwin. & M. Bryan preistes, at Tiborne the first of December 1581 Observid and written by a Catholike preist, which was present therat Wherunto is annexid certayne verses made by sundrie persons*, sigs. E2ʳ-E4ᵛ-F1ᵛ (British Museum copy 1370.a.38), a controversial pamphlet printed without designation of place or date as "the woorkmanship of a strainger" (sig. G2ʳ). According to *S.T.C.* 4537, this work was brought out at Douay in 1581, but the British Museum Catalogue correctly assigns it to the year 1583. "A caueat to the reader touching A.M. his discouery" (sigs. D4ᵛ-E1ᵛ) makes it clear that the pamphlet was brought out after January 29, 1582/3, when *A Discouerie of Edmund Campion, and his Confederates, their most horrible and traiterous practises, against her Maiesties most royall person, and the Realme* was published by Anthony Munday, printed for Edward White (date and "A. M." on title-page; "A. Munday" on Sig. G7ʳ; British Museum copy 860.d.3). That *A true report* was issued in February or the early part of the March following is evident from the fact that "A. M." had a reply to it ready by March 22, 1582/3. *A breefe Aunswer made vnto two seditious Pamphlets, the one printed in French, and the other in English. Contayning a defence of Edmund Campion and his complices, their moste horrible and vnnaturall Treasons, against her Maiestie and the Realme* by "A. M." bears the date 1582 on the title-page and the specific date "22. of March, 1582" for the address "To the Reader" (sigs. A7ʳ-A8ʳ; British Museum copy C.38.e.33). Thus, it is conclusive that *A breefe aunswer* was printed during the last few days of 1582/3. The second of the "seditious Pamphlets" answered is designated as *A true report* (sig. C7ʳ), and a parody of the verses of No. 66, ascribed to "Anthony Munday," is included (sigs. D7ʳ-E7ʳ). It is clear, then, that *A true report* was printed after January 29, 1582/3 and long enough before March 22 of that year for Munday to prepare his answer, including perhaps his parody of No. 66, although he may have had a manuscript copy of that poem, as did John Harington (see below).

In addition to the copy in *AH*, there are several other manuscript copies. That in (*B*) Bodleian MS. Rawl. Poet. 148, fols. 79^{v}-82^{v}, was obviously made by a Protestant since it is headed, "A good verse, vpon a badd Matter." It is unascribed. Too late to use I discovered another unascribed copy in British Museum Egerton MS. 2009, fol. 53^{v}. Still another unascribed copy is said to be in MS. Laud. Miscell. 755, No. 1, dated approximately 1582 (*Recusant Poets*, ed. Louise I. Guiney, New York: Sheed and Ward, 1939, pp. 176-77).

Collation with A and B follows:

1 my] *omitted B*
3 mortall] earthly *B*
4 shall] can *A B*
5 an⟨d⟩] an *A B*
6 on] in *B*
then
7 ‸ Pardon ⟨my⟩] Pardon my *A B*
11 base and lowly] lowe and homeli *A*: lowe & humble *B*
word
14 ⟨devell⟩] word *A B*; his] y^{e} *B*
15 spoyl ⟨e⟩] spoyle *A*: spoyles *B*
16 the . . . foe] His badg the Cross *B*; his] the *A B*
17 Hys triumphe ioy] The Divell his foe *B*
18 ever blessed] blessed euer *B*
21 feares] feare *B*
26 temper⟨e⟩d] tempered *A*: tempred *B*; wth] by *B*
27 a lowly] His lowly *B*
28 suger⟨e⟩d] sugred *A*
30 s⟨h⟩ow] sow *A*: lowe *B*
35 or] & *B*
then
36 ⟨as⟩] as *A B*; speeches] speech *B*
39 yet] but *A B*
41 Whome] When *B*
45 but] yet *A B*
47 wear] are *A*
49 This . . . enrag⟨e⟩d] This . . . enragde *A*: But this enrag'd *B*
57 had not beene] haue . . . *A*: haue not byn seene *B*
59 Cases] cawses *B*; bane] were bane *B*
60 ⟨a⟩] a *A B*
61 are] be *A*
63 mallis] on Mallice *B*
64 speak⟨e⟩st . . . those] speakst . . . them *A B*; giltlesse] guildless *A*
65 nowe] *omitted B*
for
69 ⟨in⟩] in *A B*

70 rare] straunge *B*
72 whyle] whiles *A*
75 have] hast *A B*; deathe] deaths *A B*; ⟨w⟩th] *omitted* *A B*
76 that] which *A B*
78 must . . . force] of force must needs *B*
81 w^{ch}] who *B*
86 that had] which had *A*: wth all *B*; booke] Bookes *B*
88 looke] doth looke *A*: lookes *B*
91 ⟨the eleven⟩ th'eleven] the leauen *A*: the rest *B*
92 wch was] *omitted* *B*: geven] giue *B*
93 Ioys of heaven] place of blest *B*
96 ⟨let him⟩] let him *A B*; that] this *B*
97 rymes] rime *B*
99 betymes] in time *A B*
103 yee] you *A*: thow *B*; would] wouldst *B*
105 revest her gresly] revert her greedie *B*
108 styll] skil *A B*
109 Yee] You *A*
111 forget] forgot *A*
112 or] and *A*
114 those] his *A B*; guiftes] death *B*
hee
115 Lyvinge ⟨he⟩] Liuing he *A*: Lightninge he *B*
116 theyre . . . the] the . . . their *B*
118 theyre] his *A B*
rope
121 Eng⟨land⟩] Europe *A B*
122 was] is *A B*
and
123 ‸ . . . ⟨nedes⟩] London must needs *A B*
125 steppes the stones] stones, the steps *A B*
126 Proclaymes] proclaime *A*
127 dothe tell] saith *A B*
129 did try] doth tell *A B*; pacient] goodly *B*
131 ye] you *A*
now
134 Iudgment⟨es for⟩] iudgments for *A*: iudgm^{t} for *B*
140 torture] Tortures *B*
141 reproche] reportes *B*
144 an ever durynge] a sempiternall *B*
145 wth] in *B*
148 for] And *B*
149 that] which *A B*
150 that] which *A B*

deeds
151 ⟨lyfe⟩] faith *A B*
feare
152 ys it] ist *A B*; ⟨that⟩ wee ⟨doe feere⟩] we feare *A B*
158 this] These *B*; hath moystned] doth moysten *B*
164 how] so *B*
166 that] to *B*
home
167 ⟨hope⟩] home *A B*; daunger] dangers *B*
170 provoketh vs to] prouoke vs for to *A B*
171 his] this *A*; our] a *A B*
172 his ⟨he⟩] his *A B*
173 agree] conspire *A B*
175 who] which *A B*
176 that] which *A B*
177 that] which *A B*
178 his] him *A B*
179 we be] be we *A*
180 whoe] which *A B*; saynt] man *A B*

Despite the number of variants, few of them change the essential character of the poem. The *B* version seems to be derived from *A*, perhaps by way of an intermediary manuscript.

A musical setting in five parts is in William Byrd's *Psalmes, Sonets, & songs of sadnes and pietie*, 1588, No. 33, where three stanzas are printed. The first stanza agrees exactly with the first stanza as printed in *A*, but the other two differ entirely from any of the stanzas in No. 66. Byrd's version is a song of praise for religious martyrs generally and is not related to religious controversy. For this version see *English Madrigal Verse, 1588-1632*, ed. E. H. Fellowes (Oxford, Clarendon Press, 1929, 2nd ed.), p. 48.

Edmund Campion, the Jesuit priest whose martyrdom is celebrated in No. 66, was tried November 20, 1581, and executed, on grounds of treason against the Queen, December 1, 1581 (*D.N.B.*). His apprehension and subsequent execution resulted in the publication of a series of bitter controversial pamphlets in prose and verse by Catholic and Protestant writers.

Traditionally No. 66 is said to have been written by Henry Walpole (1558-95) of Norfolk, who merely as an interested Protestant had gone to see the execution of Campion. According to the story, blood from the drawn quarters of the body splashed upon Walpole, and he felt at once compelled to follow Campion in his work. Walpole became a Jesuit and in 1595 was also executed as a traitor (Simpson, *Edmund Campion*, pp. 322, 385, where are given the manuscript authorities for the account of Walpole's conversion). In the account of Walpole in the

D.N.B. No. 66 is definitely attributed to him. Augustus Jessopp in *One Generation of a Norfolk House* (1878, pp. 97-102) prints the poem as Walpole's from *B.* J. H. Pollen in his edition of *The Death and Martyrdom of Father Edmund Campion* (London, Burns and Oates, 1908, pp. 26-31) includes it from *A.* Byrd's version is assigned to Walpole by Fellowes (p. 225, note). In the section devoted to Campion in *Recusant Poets* six stanzas are printed with the comment that the poem was probably written by Walpole (pp. 176, 178-79).

I have, however, discovered no contemporary authority who ascribes this particular poem to Henry Walpole. By inference one may suppose that a statement made by Father John Gerard, a Jesuit who returned to England in 1588 after a period in Rome, refers to stanzas 27-29 of No. 66:

> Yet he [Walpole] used to be at Court before the death of Father Campion, in whose honour he also wrote some beautiful verses in the English tongue, declaring that he and many others had received the warmth of life from that blessed martyr's blood, and had been animated by it to follow the more perfect counsels of Christ ["The Life of Father John Gerard," by John Morris in *The Condition of Catholics under James I*, 1871, p. xci].

In 1595 Father Henry Garnet, S.J., wrote that before Walpole left England in 1582 "he had made a poem upon the martyrdom of Father Campion which was so much taken notice of by the public, that, the author not being known, the gentleman who published it was condemned by the Council to lose his ears" (*Recusant Poets*, p. 176, quoted from Richard Challoner, *Memoirs of Missionary Priests*, rev. and ed. J. H. Pollen, New York, Kennedy, 1924, p. 225). Henry More, writing of Walpole in his *Historia Provinciae Anglicanae Societatis Iesu*, 1649 (ed. 1660, Book V, art. xxxiii, p. 202), says that legal action was first taken against Walpole because he had written a poem on Campion's death. Father Christopher Grene, writing about 1666, ascribes No. 66 to Walpole (*Recusant Poets*, pp. 176-77, 257-58, from information in Stonyhurst MSS., Collectanea I, fol. 3). His attribution may have been deduced from the remarks of Father Gerard. If we knew more about Walpole's poetry, we might be able to form a reasonable judgment by internal comparison. Two poems, "A Prisoner's Song" and "The Song of Mary the Mother of Christ," which were printed anonymously in 1601 under the title of the second, are included as his in *Recusant Poets* (pp. 257-67). The first of these is somewhat in the manner of the poetry of Robert Southwell, S.J. The second, written in the same stanzaic form as No. 66, is similar in its opening lines to the beginning of No. 66. Perhaps more like is an anonymous poem, "Calvary Mount," which the editors of *Recusant Poets* conjecture was written by Walpole (pp. 268, 274-75). As can be seen, we end with conjecture.

There is some reason for considering that the author of No. 66 may have been Stephen Valenger of Norfolk, B.A. from Caius College, Cambridge, in 1559/60, and tutor there until about 1568 (*Alumni Cantabrigienses*, compiled by John and J. A. Venn, Part I, vol. iv [1927]). In a letter addressed to the Lord Keeper in April, 1595, William Lee, who was foreman of the jury which tried Campion, writing as a prisoner in the Fleet, says:

> houbeit, I trust, to helpe, to trusse vppe, the rest of them first: allthoughe, that I have bene ꝑsecuted, by them, for my verdit, given in haste, (as Valenger Rymed) against Campion, and his trayterows cōpanions [Harl. MS. 6998, fol. 182ʳ].

Lee's reference to the hasty verdict refers to line 91 of No. 66 and indicates that Lee, at any rate, thought Valenger wrote the poem. The account of the trial and conviction of Campion given by John Bridgewater in *Concertatio Ecclesiae Catholiciae in Anglia Adversus Calvinopapistas Et Puritanos sub Elizabetha Regina* (1588, fol. 225) reveals that Valenger was the gentleman referred to by Father Garnet who was punished by having his ears cut off for his involvement in the bringing out of subversive matter relating to Campion's death. Further evidence is given in a letter written by Walton, the keeper of the Fleet prison, to Sir T. Walsingham on June 27, 1586:

> Here is now remaining one Stephen Vallenger, committed from the Starre Chamber by her Majestie's Privy Counsell for publishing certain libels of Edmund Campian, and hath been committed these iiij. years [as quoted in *Records of the English Province of the Society of Jesus*, ed. Henry Foley, S.J., iii (1878), 648, from the State Papers Domestic, vol. cxc, no. 55].

If records of Valenger's trial before the Star Chamber had not been lost (see comments by Richard Simpson in *Ballads from Manuscripts*, ed. W. R. Morfill, II, ii [Ballad Society, 1873], 157, note 1), it might be possible to know exactly what was meant by Valenger's "publishing." According to the *D.N.B.* (article on Walpole) and Augustus Jessopp (p. 92), Valenger printed *A true report of the death and martyrdome of M. Campion* at his private press, and for that reason was tried before the Star Chamber. Simpson in his 1867 study of *Edmund Campion* (Appendix IV, p. 350) expresses the opinion that Valenger printed the book and that the poems, of which there were four, were by Walpole, Thomas Pounde, and Valenger. In his later comments to these as they are printed in *Ballads from Manuscripts* (pp. 157-91), Simpson attributes No. 66 to Valenger. There is no doubt that Valenger was known as a writer of verse. He had even been recognized by Gabriel Harvey and Edmund Spenser, though not kindly (see the Note on No. 180). No. 180, "the Cockolds kallender," is Valenger's, and on first reading appears to offer only extreme contrast to No. 66, for it has characteristics of the kind of balladry for which Elderton is condemned in stanza 17 of No. 66. Closer study reveals a few points for comparison, notably the same religious bias. In No. 180 it is expressed as gross satire of the Anglican clergy. Especially pertinent for comparison are lines 209-21 with lines 91-96 in No. 66. Although elements of satire are also present in No. 66, the predominant note is one of exultation in the martyr's faith and death. We may also note that both compositions are written in six-line stanzas, but quite properly No. 66 has a pentameter line and No. 180 a tetrameter.

As with so much of the work connected with the religious controversies of the period, we are left only with surmises and inferences, and I think we shall never know who wrote the highly charged lines of No. 66, which the elder John Harington considered the best poetry he had ever read. In *A Tract on the Succession to the Crown, 1602* (ed. C. R. Markham, Roxburghe Club, 1880, pp. 104-05), Sir John Harington says:

> But of Campion, though he had the death of a traytor, yet there was an epitaph written fitt for a martyr, and in my father's judgement, who as I presume to say could bothe write well and judge well, it was the best Englishe verse, and I think the last Englishe verse, that ever he redd. Yet I will say for him, truely he misliked both the man and the matter. One stanza or two of it I will cyte, because it contains a summary of all those complaintes that I said the Papists make against our tyme.

After quoting stanza 10, Sir John introduces stanza 12 thus:

> And soone after in a patheticall manner directing his verse to hir Matie, though I think she hath not to this hower ever seen it, affirming they meant her no hurt (though the contrary was proved to plaine).

He then quotes stanza 12 and concludes:

> Now though this be neither so nor so, yet wordes so well coutched together, move much the vulgar eares, and the suffering side drawes still a compassion to it, and the known lewdnes of manie of their persecutors addes much unto it.

Since the elder Harington died July 1, 1582 (Heralds College MS. I.10, fol. 82^{r}), he must have gotten hold of a manuscript copy of No. 66 not long after Campion's death the preceding December. The copy in *AH* was probably made from it. John Harington had been given a special commission by the Council permitting him to carry about Edmund

Campion's books (*C.S.P.D., 1581-90*, vol. ii, ed. Robert Lemon, 1865, p. 150, vol. clxvii, art. 8). The permission must have included this poem, which also was forbidden to circulate. As late as March 21, 1594, one John Bolt was called before Solicitor General Edward Coke for having a copy of verses beginning, "Why do I use my paper, pen, and ink" (*C.S.P.D., 1591-94*, ed. Lemon, 1867, p. 467, vol. ccxlviii, art. 38).

As indicated earlier in this Note, notice of a different kind was given the poem by Anthony Munday, one of the leaders of the Protestant side in the controversy about Campion. In March, 1582/3, Munday brought out *A breefe Aunswer* containing "Verses in the Libell, made in prayse of the death of Maister Campion, one of the societie of the holie name of Iesus; heere chaunged to the reproofe of him, and the other Traitours" (sigs. D7^{r}-E7^{r}). The name *Anthony Munday* is printed in full on sig. E7^{r}, although this answer is sometimes attributed to Elderton (see the British Museum Catalogue and Simpson, *Campion*, p. 350; but in *Ballads from Manuscripts* Simpson assigns them to Munday). The nature of Munday's parody can be seen from the first three stanzas:

Why doo I vse my paper, inke and pen,
and call my wits in coũcell what to say?
Such memories were made for woorthy men,
And not for such as seeke their Realms decay,
An Angels trumpe, exalts ye Subiects trueth:
When shame rings foorth ye Traitors fearful rueth.

Pardon my want, I offer naught but will,
To note downe those, at whome the Skies do skowle:
Cãpion, his treasõs do exceed my skil,
The cause, his comming, & the deede too fowle.
Yet giue me leaue in base and homely verse:
His lewd attempts in England to rehearse.

He came by vowe, the cause, his Princesse foyle,
His armour, Treason, to his Countryes woe:
His comfort, blood, slaughter & greeuous spoyle,
The Deuill his Author had incenst him so.
His triumphe, *Englands* ruine and decay:
The Pope his Captaine, thirsting for it aye.

Explanatory comments on some of the lines of No. 66 are necessary.

38. Campion was imprisoned in the Tower in "Little Ease," July 17, 1581 (*D.N.B.*)

39, 43. He was put to the rack in July and October, 1581 (the same).

43-48. There were four disputations which Campion was forced to undergo without preparation: (1) August 31, 1581, against Dean Nowell of St. Paul's and Dean Day of Windsor; (2) September 18, against

William Fulke and Roger Goode, or Goaden; (3) September 23, also against Fulke and Goode; (4) September 27, against Dr. Walker and William Charke (Simpson, *Campion*, pp. 257-67; *Records of the English Province of the Society of Jesus*, iii, 652; *D.N.B.*).

79. The writer of *A true report* says:

> First he [Anthony Munday] writing vpon the death of Euerard Haunse, was immediately controled and disproued by one of his owne hatche, and shortely after seting forthe the aprehension of M. Campion, was disproued by George (I was about to saye) Iudas Eliot, who writing against him, proued that those thinges he did were for very lucers sake only, and not for the truthe, althogh he himself be a person of the same predicament, of whom I muste say, that if felony be honesti, then he may for his behauiore be taken for a laweful witnes againste so good men [sig. E $1^{r,v}$].

In 1581, before Campion's trial, Munday had brought out *A breefe Discourse of the taking Edmund Campion and divers other Papists in Barkshire*. This was followed by *A very true Report of the apprehension and taking of that arch-papist Edmund Campion . . . Containing also a controulment of a most untrue former book set out by A(nthony) M(unday) concerning the same, as is to be proved and justified by Geo. Ellyot, one of the ordinary yeomen of her Majesty's chamber, author of this book, and chiefest cause of the finding of the said lewd and seditious people* (quoted from Simpson, *Campion*, p. 350). The originals of both these pamphlets are in the Library at Lambeth Palace (*S.T.C.* 18264 and 7629, respectively). George Eliot was a witness against Campion in his trial (*Cobbett's Complete Collection of State Trials*, ed. T. B. Howell, i [1809], 1063).

81. In January, 1580/1, Thomas Norton became the official censor of Catholics in England. He conducted the examinations by torture of Alexander Briant and Edmund Campion and was consequently nicknamed, "Rackmaster General." At the time of the writing of this poem, he was held prisoner in his house in the Guildhall for disrespectful comments on English bishops. He was put into the Tower, January, 1583/4 (*D.N.B.*).

83. Sir Christopher Wray was the Chief Justice of the King's Bench at the time of Campion's trial (Simpson, *Campion*, p. 281).

85-86. Both Anthony Munday and Charles Sled had acted as spies and under the pretence of being Catholic converts had gained entrance into the seminary at Rome. On the title-page of *A Discouerie* (see above) A. M. is described as "sometimes the Popes Scholler, allowed in the Seminarie at Roome amongst them." At the trial of Campion, Munday "deposed that he heard the Englishmen, as the Doctor and others, talk and conspire of these Treasons against England, and that Campion and others afterward had conference with Dr. Allen" (*State Trials*, i, 1063). Concerning Sled's activities, Munday writes in *A Discouerie*:

> *Charles Sled*, who sometyme serued Maister Doctour *Moorton* in *Roome*, in whose house there was many matters determyned, bothe by Doctor *Allen* when hee came to *Roome*, and diuers other Doctours, lyuing there in the Cittie, as also diuers of the Seminarie: he lykewise vnderstoode of the prouision for the great daye, that it was generallie spoken of among the Englishe men, and to be more certayne, he kepte a Iournall or Booke, of theyr daylie dealinges, noting the daye, tyme, place, and personnes, present at theyr secrete conferences, and verie much matter hath he iustified against them [sig. E3^{r}].

For the deposition of "Sleidon," that is, Sled, against Kirbie, who was tried with Campion, see *State Trials*, i, 1068.

91. For the letter by William Lee written in 1595, see comments above. On the jury see Simpson, *Campion*, pp. 282-83.

97. H. E. Rollins, "William Elderton: Elizabethan Actor and Ballad-Writer," (*SP*, xvii [1920], 229), quotes this verse about Elderton and suggests that the specific ballad referred to was perhaps "A gentle Iyrke for the Jesuit," licensed February 13, 1581. Attributed also to Elderton (*S.T.C.* 7564) is "A Triumphe for true Subjects and a Terrour unto al Traitours: By the example of the late death of Edmund Campion, Ralphe Sherwin, and Alexander Bryan, Jesuites and Seminarie Priestes," 1581 (as given in the *Catalogue of a Collection of Printed Broadsides in the Possession of the Society of Antiquaries*, compiled by Robert Lemon, 1866, No. 76).

124. The names of those executed with Campion are given in the preceding comment.

[67] *The fyre to see my woes for anger burnethe*

Hand: Sir John Harington's, with the ascription in the same hand. Just beneath is Bishop Percy's note in pencil, "S^{r}. Philip Sidney."

Introduced in the Third Book of the revised version of *The Countesse of Pembrokes Arcadia* as a part of the musical entertainment provided by Amphialus ostensibly to honor Anaxius, yet really for "the beloved *Philoclea*," the poem is described as sung by five voices to the accompaniment of five viols. It is printed in the three sixteenth-century editions of the *Arcadia*: (*A*) ed. 1590, fol. 306$^{r, v}$; (*B*) ed. 1593, fols. 148^{v}-149^{r}; (*C*) ed. 1598, p. 289. It occurs also among "Certaine Sonets Written by Sir Philip Sidney" in (*D*) ed. 1598, p. 473, where it is directed to be sung "*To the tune of* Non credo gia che piu infelīce amante." The poem had first been printed in (*E*) Abraham Fraunce, *The Arcadian Rhetorike* [1588], sig. E1^{r}; and it was included without ascription in (*F*) *The*

Arbor of Amorous Devises, 1597, sigs. B3^{v}-B4^{r}, headed, "A Lovers complaint" (facsimile edition of the copy in the Huntington Library, with introduction by H. E. Rollins, 1936). A musical setting for it is given in (*G*) William Corkine, *The Second Booke of Ayres*, 1612, No. 9, sigs. C2^{v}-D1^{r}. Other manuscript versions are in: (*H*) Folger MS. 400903 (the Clifford MS. of the original version of the *Arcadia*), among "Dyuers and sondry Sonettes," fol. 216^{v}, with the tune indicated as in *D*, "avãnte" incorrectly substituted for "amante"; (*I*) Bodleian MS. Rawl. Poet. 85 (described by Mary Bowen, "Some New Notes on Sidney's Poems," *MLN*, x [1895], 235-46), fol. 9^{v}; (*J*) Harl. MS. 7392, fol. 39^{r}. I am indebted to Professor William Ringler for the variants of *J*. Collation with *A-D*, and *G* are given from copies in the British Museum; the variants of *A-D* have been checked with copies in the Huntington Library. *E* variants are from the unique copy in the Bodleian.

1 woes] wronges *B E F H-J*

2 rayne] teares *I*; my] mine *F I*

3 for woe to ebb] to ebbe for griefe *A-J*

4 wth] for *I*; dullde] dull *A-J*; the center] his . . . *A-C G*: his Centure *H*

6 runnes] flyes *I*; for] with *E*

7 Place] Prayse *H*

8 nyght] nights *F I*; woes] ils *A G*: ill *E*: euils *B-D H*: euill *F J*: griefe *I*; that] which *A-D F-J*; hathe] haue *F J*

9 alonely] all onely *A-C E G-I*: onely *F J*

10 see] know *A-E G H J*; mystryes] miseries *A-H*: myserye *I J*; but] *omitted I*

11 fall] tale *I*

12 yet . . . fuell] Yet still her eyes giue to my flames their fuell *A-D G I J*: Yet still her eyes giues to my flames their fuel *F*: Yet still her eyes giue to my flames the fuell *E H*

13 quyte] quick *F J*; me] *omitted F I*

14 noe more this brethe] thy breath no more *A-C F G*: my breath no more *F I*: . . . thy . . . *D E*: . . . my . . . *H J*

15 drownd] drowne me *F I*: drownde me *J*

16 my] these *F I J*

18 haste my dyinge] draw my dismall *F J*

20 fyre sea] Fire, aire, sea *A-J*

21 theyre] your *H I*; helps] helpe *A D*

22 I am hers] hers am I *A-H*: hers I am *I J*

23 fye] Oh *F I J*

24 she . . . me] . . . sets by . . . *A G H*: of me she makes *E*

The collation shows that *G* was probably set up from *A*, and that *F* and *I*, which frequently agree in variants, have the poorest readings. It is clear that the *AH* version is not taken from printed copies in the three editions of the *Arcadia*, but it may be noted from readings in lines 4, 9, and 14 that *AH* is closer to *D* than to *A-C*. The omission of the word *air* in line 20 of *AH* destroys Sidney's perfect use of the figure *collectour* (G. Puttenham, *The Arte of English Poesie*, ed. Willcock and Walker, 1936, pp. 236-37). The substitution of "mystryes" for *miseries* suggests another error, although *mistery* in the sense of personal secret (*N.E.D.* 5) might be acceptable. The *AH* readings for lines 3 and 12 are interesting even if they are probably without authority.

In *E* Fraunce quotes the poem in his chapter "Of Polyptoton" (Bk. I, Chap. ii), a figure which he thus defines (sig. D6ᵛ): "*Polyptoton*, often falling or declining of one word, is when as words of one ofspring haue diuers fallings or terminations." This appears to agree with Puttenham's *traductio* (pp. 203-04). It is difficult to see, however, that No. 67 is a very good illustration. No. 229, also by Sidney, offers excellent examples.

[68] *O heavenlye god, o father deare cast downe thie tender eye*

Hand: Sir John Harington's. The inserted *h* in line 22 and the ascription are in the same hand.

That this poem was popular may be inferred from the number of extant contemporary copies, most of which associate it with Walter Devereux, first Earl of Essex, though not necessarily as the composer. In the collation I have made use of one Bodleian MS., six British Museum MSS., and one printed version, as follows:

(*A*) MS. Gough Norfolk 43, fol. 41ʳ, where the poem is headed, "The songe of the Right noble Earle Walter Erle of Essex by hym songe yᵉ night before his disceace who died in Iearlonde In september Anno dñi 1576." This manuscript is the commonplace book of the Brampton family, referred to in the Note on No. 1. The copy of No. 68 is in the same handwriting as a statement signed by Thomas Brampton, fol. 54ᵛ, dated, 17 Elizabeth.

(*B*) MS. Cotton Vesp. A. XXV, fols. 143ᵛ-144ʳ (152ᵛ-153ʳ, old numbering), where the poem is headed, "A prayer of earle of essex death." Elizabethan secretary.

(*C*) MS. Cotton Vit. C. XVII, fol. 380ʳ, which is imperfect because of the state of the manuscript. Elizabethan secretary.

(*D*) MS. Harl. 293, fol. 120ʳ, which follows a prose account of the death of Essex and is headed, "The Songe of his Honoʳ songe the night before he died." Elizabethan secretary.

(*E*) MS. Sloane 1896, fol. 58ʳ⸴ᵛ, headed, "A godly & vertuous songe made by the hono^{r}able the Earle of Essexe—Late deceassde in an^{o} dñi. 1576." Elizabethan secretary.

(*F*) MS. Add. 15117, fol. 4^{r}, which has both words and music. Elizabethan secretary.

(*G*) MS. Add. 5845, pp. 345-46, ascribed, "E.L," which again follows a prose account of the death of Essex, and is headed, "The Song which his Ho: sung the Night before he dep̄ted this Life." This copy was made by William Cole, the antiquary, in 1773, but I have included it as he states on p. 337 that he took it from one in the handwriting of Thomas Churchyard.

(*H*) *The Paradyse of daynty deuises*, 1576, sig. L4 (ed. H. E. Rollins, 1927, No. 98), where it is headed, "The complaint of a Synner," and is ascribed, "F.K.", i.e., Francis Kinwelmarsh. Rollins in his note on the poem, says that this ascription appears in the succeeding editions of 1578, 1580, 1585, and that the leaf on which it was printed is torn out of the only copy of the fifth edition, ca. 1590. In the two editions of 1596 and in those of 1600 and 1606, the poem is printed without ascription. The heading in the edition of 1585 and in the last four editions has the addition, "and sung by the Earle of Essex vpon his death bed in Ireland."

1 O heavenlye] O ⟨father⟩ heavenly *A*: *torn off* *C*; o father] o *omitted* *A*: and . . . *C*; cast] bowe *F*; tender] *torn off* *C*: heavenly *E F*; eye] *torn off* *C*.

2 that] w^{ch} *D*

4 the] thy *D*

5 sinfull] simple *D*: siely *G*: fainting *H*; suppressed] oppressed *C-G*; clogge] cledges *B*

6 humble] symple *C*; sorte] wysse *B E F*; submyttes] submyttith *A C*; mercyes] mercye *A-H*; for] Lord *G*

7 o savoure] oh my Savio^{r} *F*; wretched] woofull *A-H*

8 mornefull] mindefull *F*; Cryes] crye *A-H*; o Lorde] alone *A C E F G*: o god *B*: about *D*; do styll] dothe . . . *A C-H*: to the *B*

9 wyll] name *E*; despised] displeased *D*

10 Vnto] & to *B-H*; wordlye, *copyist's error*] earthly *B F*: worldly *A C D E G H*

11 powre] powers *A C E H*: dome *B*: Things *G*; do] dothe *A D*

12 had] did *F*; walke] trode *A*: treade *B-H*; pathes] steppes *A D E*: pathe *B C H*; that] & *F*; leade] leades *A C E F H*: leadeth *D*

13 o my] my dere *A C G*: nowe my *B D H*; and Lodstarr] . . . loadestone *A*: my . . . *B H*

14 former] ffond *A*; melt] weepe *D*: bleed *E*
15-16 and 17-18 are transposed in order in D
15 sighe] sythe *A*; sobbe] and *D*; repent] Lament *B*
16 wyll] lyfe *E*
17 thus] this *A B*: that *G*; mornefull] Irefull *A*: earnest *B*: cheerfull *C*: dolefull *D E*: yearnefull *F H*: wofull *G*; playntes] playnte *A B D G*: plain *H*; I . . . mercye] thie mercy I do *A C G*
18 Good] o *A-H*; mercyes] mercy *B C*; let . . . mercye] thy mɔcy let me *D*; have] *wanting C*
19 this] the *A-E H*: that *F*: my *G*; whiche] that *A-H*
20 So . . . name] my voyce vnto yt name *B*; eternallye] continuallie *G C, where only* cont *appears because of torn leaf*
21 ar] were *B C D G*; done] *wanting C*
23 your] thie *A B E G H*: thyne *C F*: the *D*
24 restinge] dwelling *A-H—the* ing *wanting in C*

It will be apparent that the foregoing differences are not significant and that there is not a great divergence in the versions. Walter Bourchier Devereux in *Lives and Letters of the Devereux, Earls of Essex* (i [1853], 145, n. 1), prints the first stanza of No. 68 and adds that it may be found in full in MS. Add. 5830, fol. 122. Unfortunately this reference, which has been handed on in certain other accounts of Walter Devereux, including that in the *D.N.B.*, is a mistake. Nothing about him appears in that manuscript. A. B. Grosart prints No. 68 as a composition by Essex in *Miscellanies of the Fuller Worthies' Library* (iv [1872], 451-3), from MS. Sloane 1896, fol. 58, and he has included as a part of this poem, six verses which are written at the top of fol. 59. I am confident that these verses were not intended as a part of No. 68, which ends on fol. 58v and has three rows of lines after the last stanza, the same marking used to separate other poems in that manuscript. The point is of some importance, as Rollins points out in his note on "O heavenly God" in the *Paradise*, p. 252, that these six verses are part of a ballad that is preserved in *The Maitland Folio Manuscript* (ed. W. A. Craigie, Scottish Text Society, i [1919], 287-8), and that they could not therefore be of Essex's composition.

Of some special interest is the copy of No. 68 in the *Devereux Papers*, ed. H. E. Malden, Camden Miscellany, xiii (1923), 11, since it is there printed from the papers of Richard Broughton, man of business to Walter Devereux, Earl of Essex. But this copy is headed simply, "The songe his honor songe the night before he died," and does not tell us who wrote the song. Nor is the matter any further resolved by the heading to a version printed in *Notes and Queries* (IV, iii [1869], 361), from a manuscript said to be dated 1693: "Canticū Walteri Comitis Essex cantatū paulo ante mortem suam qui obiit mense Septembris anno Re^e^ Elizabethae viii^o^ anno dm̄ 1576."

Thus once again we have to consider the question of authorship, and again I think there is no means by which it can be categorically determined. Rollins, in his note on the poem in the *Paradise*, supports the attribution there given to F. K., identified as Francis Kinwelmarsh, a poet of the period. This view is held also by J. P. Collier in his introduction to "Ancient Biographical Poems" (*Camden Miscellany*, iii [1855], 9), where the poem is printed (pp. 19-20) from *A*. I have noted above that Grosart and W. B. Devereux considered it the work of Essex, as did Edward Farr, *Select Poetry of the Reign of Queen Elizabeth*, ii, 316-17 (Parker Society, 1845). Certainly Sir John Harington thought No. 68 was by Essex, as did, apparently, the writers of the copies in *A*, *D*, and *E*. Conceivably the ascription in *G*, "E.L." by transposition could mean "Lord Essex." Whether Essex himself, or the unknown E. L., or Francis Kinwelmarsh wrote the poem, I fear we shall never know; but there is no doubt from the many testimonies that have come down to us that Essex sang this song the night before he died in September, 1576, at the age of thirty-five. The touching prose account of his illness and death, written by a follower, leaves one with the feeling that Walter Devereux, Earl of Essex, was a man who might well have written a poetic prayer so simple as this. There are, by the way, several copies of this prose account, all unsigned: (1) MS. Top. Oxon. e.5, pp. 138-48; (2) MS. Harl. 293, fols. 115-19^v^; (3) MS. Sloane 303, fols. 18^v^-20^v^; (4) MS. Add. 5845, pp. 337-45. There are discrepancies in the dates of Essex's illness and death as given in these versions. The heading to (1) records that he became ill, August 21, 1576, and died, September 14; (2) says only that Essex fell sick the last of August, 1576; (3) gives the dates as August 21, 1576, and September 21; (4) puts the date of his illness as August 21, 1575. The *D. N. B.* states that he died, September 22, 1576. Thomas Hearne in the preface to his edition of William Camden's *Annales* (vol. i [1717], pp. lxxxix-xcviii), prints a version of this prose account of the illness of Essex, which is the principal source for the discussion of Essex by W. B. Devereux (i, 136-62). H. E. Malden, pp. 6-10, gives two extracts from the Broughton Papers of a prose account of Essex's death. Both Devereux (p. 138) and Malden (introduction, pp. viii-ix) attribute the authorship to Edward Waterhouse, who, according to the *D. N. B.*, was secretary to Essex. William Cole in his notes on the copy in MS. Add. 5845, p. 345, considers that Waterhouse could not have been the author because in the account itself he is spoken of as "Mr. Waterhouse."

Because of the light it throws upon the character of Essex, and, by inference, upon his possible authorship of No. 68, I quote extracts from the account of his illness and death as related in MS. Top. Oxon. e.5, pp. 138-48:

> Walter the noble Erle of Essex & Erle marshall of Ireland, knight of the most noble order of the garter, falling sick of a Laske as it was supposed called Dysenteria, through adustion of choler, on fridaie the xxith of August. 1576. or whether yt were of any other accident, the living god both knoweth, & will revenge it, was grevouslie tormented by the space of xxij daies . . . being both weakned in body, and naturall strength diminished, he addressed him selfe to that, wch his friends & servantes feared, y^{t} is to finish his life, to o^{r} great sorowe, but vnto his everlasting ioy: . . . so great was his faith, so ernest were his praiers, and petitions vnto god that Iob in his suffering, did not w^{t} les shewes of grief or grudging pas over his paine then this noble man: so thankfull was he to god, so ioyfull of his correction, and of so valiant a mynde, that although he felt intolerable payne yet he had so cheerfull and noble a countenaunce, that he seemed to suffer none at all, or elce very little: full often on his knees besought he mercie at the handes of god, and continually yelded most faithfull, and devowte praiers, w^{t} his owne mouthe . . . he made many tymes a livelie and open profession of his sownd faith . . . w^{t} such a noble and lively feeling of the mercies of god, & such a spirit of heavenly vnderstanding, as not only amazed vs to here, but brake o^{r} very harts, and forced oute abundaunt teares: ꝑtlie for ioy of his godlie mynde, ꝑtly for the doctrine & comfort we had by his words; but cheefly (I blur the paper with tears as I write) o^{r} sorowe was iustly augmented to remember o^{r} los of so worthie a noble peer; being to vs so carefull & loving a lorde: for to say the truth what was there in a noble man to be requyred, wch was not rife in him: what gifts of nature; what wisdom, policy, courage, bountie, iustice mɔcie, pity, and compassion? . . . Two daies before his death, there being present many both noble and worshipfull persons: he saied thus. o good Lorde haue mercie vpon me: and you all here, may take example by me to lerne howe vain and vncertain this world is: within this month, I was, as you sawe, well & strong, and nowe am redy to die. this life is vain; this worlde ys vaine: this worlde is vain: and therwth all Lamented the negligence of his lyfe in the service of god. Since I came into Ireland, god forgiue me, saieth he; for synce I came into Ireland, these iij yeres I haue liued very negligently, and haue not serued god, but haue lyved lyke a soldiour: & altho a soldiour should feare god and serue him: yet I haue not serued him, but spent my tyme vainely. I beseech god forgiue me: and therupon he desired to receiue the sacrament . . . many tymes begging mercie at godes handes, and forgiuenes of his synnes, he cried oute vnto god; lorde forgiue me, and I forgiue all

the worlde: all the worlde; lorde from the bottom of my hart, from the bottom of my harte . . . there being present, the L. Chauncelo[r], M[r] ffrauncis Agars; M[r] Edward Waterhouse, M[r] Iohn Trauers; Iohn browne preacher; Th. knell preacher, & the most pte of the gentlmen of his howsehold, and chamber . . . the night folowing the friday night w[ch] was the night before he died, he willed Hewes his musician to play on the Virginals, and to sing. Play, the my song (Will. Hewes) and I will sing it my self: so he did most ioyfully, not as the howling swanne, w[ch] still looking downe, bewaileth her ende; but as a sweet larke lifting vp his handes, and casting his eies vp to his god, w[t] his spirit mownting the christall skies, and reached w[t] his vnweeried winges the top of the highest heauens: who coulde haue herd and seen this valiant conflict, hauing not a stony harte withoute innumerable teares and watered plantes? . . . This hath he written w[ch] honored him and serued him in lyfe, w[ch] lamenteth his death, and besecheth god that all w[ch] here this piteous tragedie of this death of this noble peer, may thinke on godes iudgmentes.

In the same manner Nicholas White wrote to Lord Burghley, September, 1576 (MS. Lansd. 21, fol. 66[v]), of the death of Essex:

His [Essex's] fleashe and complexion did not decay, his memory and speeche was so pfitt that at the last yelding vpp of his breathe, he cryed, Couradge Couradge. I am a soylder that must fyght vnder the baner of my savior christe./ and as he prayed alwaies to be dissolued so was he lothe to dye in his bed.

For my part I am willing to concede the composition of No. 68 to Essex. It would be interesting to know whether the tune to which Essex sang this poem was that set by William Damon, musician to Queen Elizabeth. Music of his composition, with words of the first stanza, are in British Museum MS. Add. 29732, fol. 23[r]. Only three years after the death of Essex, Damon published *The Psalmes of Dauid in English meter with notes of foure partes set unto them* (1579).

[69] *A tale I once did heare a true man tell*

Hand: Sir John Harington's (?).

Whether the "Mr. Grevell," accredited with having put this "tale" into verse, is the well-known poet Fulke Greville, first Lord Brooke, is not known; but if he is, the fact adds nothing to his reputation. If Greville did write it, I suggest that it was a very early composition, perhaps belonging to his period at Jesus College, Cambridge, where he matriculated in 1568; or perhaps to the year, 1577, when he came up to Court with Sir Philip Sidney (*D. N. B.*). That being so, the Master of the Rolls would have been Sir William Cordell, who held the office from 1558 to 1581. He was succeeded by Sir Gilbert Gerard, who was in the office from 1581 until 1593 (Edward Foss, *The Judges of England*, v [1857], 410). The "S^r. M. A.," mentioned in the title may have been Sir Matthew Arundell of Wardour Castle, Wiltshire, friend of the Haringtons, referred to by Sir John Harington. See the Notes on Nos. 20 and 262. Sir Matthew was son of Sir Thomas Arundell of Wardour Castle and his wife, Margaret, daughter of Edmund Howard, third son of Thomas, Duke of Norfolk, and sister of Queen Catherine Howard (J. J. Howard, *Roman Catholic Families of England*, Part III [1887], p. 151).

[70] *I love a lady wondrows well*

Hand: Sir John Harington's.

I have found no other copy of this poem, which from its light, flippant tone, might well be a composition by Sir John Harington.

[71] *O deer lyfe when shall yt bee*

Hand: Sir John Harington's, though less carefully written than is usual. The ascription to Sidney is in the same hand.

With the caption "The tenth Sonnet," a shorter version of No. 71, wanting lines 17-28, was twice printed by Thomas Newman in 1591: (*A*) *Syr P. S. His Astrophel and Stella* (first edition), sigs. I 2^v-I 3^r, where it is the last of the Sidney poems following the sequence proper; (*B*) *Sir P. S. his Astrophel and Stella* (second edition), sigs. H 3^v-H 4^r. In the same year Matthew Lownes reprinted Newman's first edition "with a few trifling corrections and some new errors to counterbalance them" (*Sir Philip Sidney's Astrophel and Stella*, ed. Alfred W. Pollard, 1888, "Introduction," p. xxxv). Lownes' text of No. 71 agrees with that of *A*. In (*C*) *The Countesse of Pembrokes Arcadia*, 1598, the longer version of the poem is printed, pp. 561-62, as a part of the *Astrophel and Stella* sequence, following sonnet 92, in keeping with the general procedure adopted in that edition of interspersing the songs and longer poems among the sonnets proper. A musical setting for the poem was published in (*D*) William Byrd's *Songs of sundrie natures*, 1589, No. 33, sig. F4^v, where the first twelve lines are printed. The shorter version as in *A* with music also appears in (*E*) Robert Dowland's *A Musicall Banquet*, 1610, No. 5, where it is headed, "*D'Incerto*." An inferior version omitting lines 21-24 and ascribed to "Britton," is in (*F*) Bodleian MS. Rawl. Poet. 85, fols. 107^v-108^r (see the Note on No. 67 for reference on this manuscript). Thus only *AH* and *C* have the complete poem. In copies other than *AH* the poem is arranged in stanzas of six lines, the long lines of the *AH* version being given as two, but I have, of course, kept the numbering of lines in the collation according to the *AH* copy.

Collation with *A* is made from the copy in the British Museum; with *B*, *C*, and *D* from copies in the Huntington Library. For *E* I have used the text given by E. H. Fellowes in *English Madrigal Verse, 1588-1632* (Oxford, Clarendon Press, 1929, p. 456).

1 lyfe] loue *F*; shall] may *D*; may] shall *A-C*

2 thy thoughts] thy minde *A-CE*: my mind *D F*

3 have] hath *D E*

5 O] Or *C*; yf I] if that *F*; my] me *C*; by . . . absence] By thine absence *A B E*: After parting *C*: though my parting *D*: Throughe my partyng *F*; owght] oft *A B E*

6 nor] Not *D*; debard] yet bard *F*

7 what stately ioys] what high ioyes *A-E*: what ioyes *F*; I dwell] I shall dwell *A-E*: I do dwell *F*

8 measure] pleasure *A-F*

9 I must] will I *A B E*: I will *D F*; the] a *F*

11 Thear] Wher *F*; those] These *D*

12 that] Which *A-F*; hopes do] happs to *F*

The rest of the poem is wanting in D.

15 And] But *A-C E*; wilt] wouldst *A B E*: wouldest *F*; garded] garder *F*; from] Fearing *A-C E F*; then] *omitted A-C E*

Lines 17-28 are omitted in A B E. Lines 17-18 and 19-20 are reversed in order in F.

17 vppon] of *C F*; pleasaunt] most gratefull *C*: most happy *F*; would] will *C*: shall *F*

18 my] her *F*

19 Thear] And *F*; fayr] for *C*; to] do *F*; that] Which *C F*; breathe owt] do breath *C F*

Lines 21-24 are omitted in F.

21 vppon] of *C*; my princely] my most Princely *C*; most . . . I] I blessed shall *C*

23 sweetnes musyke] musicke, sweetnesse *C*

25 Thinke vppon those] Thinke, thinke of *C*: And if after these *F*; and those] When with *C F*

26 when] *omitted C*; pleasawnt] glad moning *C*: glad moned *F*

27 harts for harts] hart for hart *C*; then ymparts] do depart *C*: to imparte *F*

28 Ioys . . . languyshe] Ioying till ioy make vs languishe *C*: Ioye vntyll ioye makes one language *F*

29 Ah] O *A-C E*: *omitted F*; thoughts my thoughts] thoughte! my thoughtes *F*; surcease] now surcease *F*; yowr] thy *C*: These *F*; payns] woes *A-C E*

30 ah I dye] My life fleetes *A-B E*: My life melts *C*
31 Whearfore . . . bee] Thinke no more, but die in mee, Till thou shalt receiued bee *A C E*: . . . reuiued be *B*: Thoughte! therfore come sleepe wth me Vntill thou maist awaked be *F*
32 lypps] mought *F*

It is at once apparent that *F* presents a version often garbled in sense and needs no serious consideration. It is also evident that *E* was set up from *A*. Despite the fact that the *AH* version differs rather markedly from the supposedly authentic version of the 1598 folio, *C*, I submit the view that the *AH* readings are sometimes superior in poetic quality, or in sense. I call attention to lines 5, 8, 17, 19, 21, 27, and particularly I would stress the superiority of lines 30 and 31 in *AH*. Unfortunately, I cannot state that Sir John Harington took his copy from one in Sidney's handwriting, but there is no reason why he may not have done so. It is certain that Sir John had access to a copy of Sir Philip Sidney's unpublished version of the old *Arcadia*, for in his notes to Book XI of the *Orlando Furioso*, 1591, p. 87, he quotes some verses beginning, "Who doth desire that chast his wife should bee," of which he says, "And therefore that excellent verse of *Sir Philip Sidney* in his first *Arcadia* (which I know not by what mishap is left out in the printed booke) [i.e., *Arcadia*, 1590] is in mine opinion worthie to be praised and followed to make a good and vertuous wife." (For these verses in the old *Arcadia*, see *Complete Works*, ed. Albert Feuillerat, iv [Cambridge University Press, 1926], 236-37.) The verses were published in the *Arcadia* of 1593 (*ibid.*, ii [1922], 70). Evidence that Sir John also had access to the *Astrophel and Stella* sequence in manuscript is set out in the Note to No. 223.

[72] *Gyrtt in my giltlesse gowne*

Hand A. The copy shows some correction, both in Hand A and in at least one other hand, possibly two. Words in Hand A are written over erasures in three lines, and these I record for their possible future use: 1. "my gil"; 4. "Shall"; 17. "will." Another hand has also introduced readings written over erasures: 7. "kill . . . tryed"; 8. "they . . . see." G. F. Nott in a copy of his unpublished *Songs and Sonnets* (Brit. Mus. C.60.o.13), ii, 33, mentions the different handwriting in lines 7 and 8. In addition the following corrections occur: 8. the final *e* in "see" is clearly written over the caesura mark; 11. the first *o* of "goodlye" is an insertion, possibly made by the corrector in 7 and 8; 21. the *r* of "vntruth" is written over another letter; 32. the "ed" in "chardged" is written in another hand over the *e* of Hand A. There are three penciled notes in Bishop Percy's hand: (1) in the upper left-hand margin, "Printed in Surreys Poems fo. 13"; (2) heading, "On the story of

Susanna"; (3) along the left margin, as far as line 20, "only thus far printed in Surrey's Poems."

As Percy correctly noted, only the first twenty lines were printed in *TM*. In the first edition they appeared among the Uncertain Authors, sig. Aa3^{r,v} (ed. Rollins, No. 243), headed, "Of the dissembling louer." The editor evidently recognized from lines 14-15 that the poem was an answer to Surrey's satirical verses beginning, "Wrapt in my carelesse cloke, as I walke to and fro" (sig. D 1^{r,v}, ed. Rollins, No. 26), for in the second and succeeding sixteenth-century editions the *TM* version of No. 72 was printed with Surrey's poems (sig. D1^{v}, 2nd ed.), with the heading, "An answer in the behalfe of a woman by an vncertain aucthor." Many years later, in 1598, Sir Richard Barckley in *A Discourse of the Felicitie of Man*, p. 499, quoted lines 5-12, attributing them to Surrey (printed from Barckley by Rollins, *TM*, ii, 299). As I have explained in the Introduction (pp. 30-31), if folios 38-48 were not wanting in the *AH* MS. we should have a clearer indication as to whether the Haringtons intended Nos. 72 and 73 to be included with Surrey's poems, which are represented in Nos. 74-90.

It is interesting to note in the collation following that those parts of lines 7 and 8 which have been corrected by another hand do not agree with *TM*.

6 styckes not] seke for
7 skill . . . tryed] practise yf were proued
8 they . . . see] Assuredly beleue it well
10 that can] That could
13 flyttes] fletes
14 right] full
16 in will] With . . .
17 mett] ioynde
21-38 *Wanting in all editions of TM.*

F. M. Padelford in his edition of Surrey's *Poems* (2nd ed., 1928, pp. 79-80) prints the longer version from *N*, fol. 23^{r}, which he has curiously entitled, "Modern Saws and Ancient Instance." In his notes (p. 218), he questions whether the poem should be included as Surrey's but comments, "If written by another, he has succeeded in hitting off the style of Surrey to a nicety." With this opinion I agree. The longer version was first printed in modernized form from *AH* by G. F. Nott in his *Surrey and Wyatt*, i (1815), 31-32, with his own title, "*The Fair Geraldine retorts on Surrey the charge of artifice, and commends the person whom he considered to be his rival, as superior to him in courage and ability*." In his note, p. 314, Nott says: "There is no reason to suppose that it was written by the Fair Geraldine herself; at least we may hope it was not; for it breathes an air of such bitter insult as no one of the gentler sex, not wholly destitute of generosity, could be capable of shewing towards an unsuccessful lover. We may therefore attribute it to one of the lady's friends, perhaps to the very rival alluded to in Surrey's Poem."

As is well known, the "Fair Geraldine" was Lady Elizabeth Fitzgerald (1528?-1589), youngest daughter of Gerald Fitzgerald, ninth Earl of Kildare, by his second wife, Lady Elizabeth, daughter of Thomas Grey, Marquis of Dorset. "Geraldine" was married first to Sir Anthony Browne and second to Edward Clinton, Earl of Lincoln. These basic facts of her life are attested not only by Nott in his *Surrey and Wyatt*, vol. i, "Memoirs of the Earl of Surrey," pp. cxvii-cxxxiii, but also by several others, e.g., the Marquis of Kildare (Charles W. Fitzgerald, fourth Duke of Leinster) in *The Earls of Kildare, 1057-1773*, 1858, pp. 126 ff., by the Reverend James Graves in "Notes on an Autograph of the Fair Geraldine," *The Journal of the Royal Historical and Archaeological Association of Ireland: Originally Founded as the Kilkenny Archaeological Society*, 1849, vol. ii, series 4 (1874 for 1872-73), pp. 561-70; and by Sir Sidney Lee in his article on Lady Elizabeth Fitzgerald in the *D.N.B.* Surrey's name was first associated with that of "Geraldine" in print in the following sonnet published in *TM* (sig. B1^{r}, No. 8):

Description and praise of his loue Geraldine.

From Tuskane came my Ladies worthy race:
Faire Florence was sometyme her auncient seate:
The Western yle, whose pleasaunt shore dothe face
Wilde Cambers clifs, did geue her liuely heate:
Fostered she was with milke of Irishe brest:
Her sire, an Erle: her dame, of princes blood.
From tender yeres, in Britain she doth rest,
With kinges childe, where she tasteth costly food.
Honsdon did first present her to mine yien:
Bright is her hewe, and Geraldine she hight.
Hampton me taught to wishe her first for mine:
And Windsor, alas, dothe chase me from her sight.
Her beauty of kind her vertues from aboue.
Happy is he, that can obtaine her loue.

Some years later Richard Stanyhurst, who contributed "The Description of Ireland" to Holinshed's *Chronicles*, in his account of "Gerald Fitzgerald earl of Kildare" (ed. 1587, ii, 33), says, "The familie is very properlie toucht in a sonnet of Surreies, made vpon the earle of Kildares sister, now countesse of Lincolne." After quoting the sonnet, he comments on various forms of the name: "Some write Gerold, sondree Gerald, diuerse verie corruptlie Gerrot, others Gerard." Official records show that the Earl of Kildare's family used the corrupt "Garret" frequently. In the second edition of *TM*, Surrey's sonnet beginning, "The golden gift that nature did thee geue," reads in line 9, "Now certesse Garret," rather than, ". . . Ladie," as in the other editions (*TM*, No. 13, and note, ii, 141) and in the manuscript version, *P*, fol. 55r (see *Poems*, ed. Padelford, No. 29). Five years after the death of the Countess of Lincoln in 1589, fiction took over the story of "Geraldine" and Surrey, when Thomas Nashe published his highly imaginative romance, *The Vnfortunate Traveller. or, The life of Iacke Wilton*, in which Surrey is reputed while touring the continent to have seen Geraldine's image in a magic crystal shown him by Cornelius Agrippa, and at the lists in Florence to have challenged all and sundry in defence of his fair Geraldine. R. B. McKerrow in his edition of Nashe's *Works*, iv (London, A. H. Bullen, 1910), 252-55, says that Nashe's story is fictitious, but he cannot show whether or not it was original. Following broadly the plan of Nashe's narrative, Michael Drayton in *Englands Heroical Epistles* published a more sober story of Surrey and his love for Geraldine. Surrey's epistle to Geraldine appeared in the edition of 1598 (fols. 86v-90v), and Geraldine's answering epistle in the edition of 1599 (fols. 94v-97v). See Kathleen Tillotson's comments on these epistles in *The Works of Michael Drayton*, ed. J. W. Hebel, vol. v, ed. Kathleen Tillotson and Bernard H. Newdigate (Oxford, Shakespeare Head Press, 1941), pp. 130-33. There can be little doubt that Drayton's *Epistles* contributed much to the popularity of the tradition of Surrey's love for Geraldine and gave credence to a good deal of absurd fictitious material. G. F. Nott showed great ingenuity in bringing all Surrey's love poems, and some others, within the orbit of this romantic tradition, though Nott clearly does not accept Nashe's narrative account.

In contrast twentieth-century commentators take the position that Surrey addressed only the sonnet quoted above to Lady Elizabeth Fitzgerald, and that when she was a little girl of nine or ten. See Padelford's remarks in his edition of Surrey's *Poems*, 1920 (ed. 1928, pp. 219-20); J. M. Berdan's brief account in *Early Tudor Poetry* (New York, Macmillan, 1920), pp. 516-17; Rollins' summary of the tradition in *TM*, ii, 70-75; Edwin Casady's discussion in his biography, *Henry Howard, Earl of Surrey*, 1938, pp. 244-50. The interpretation that the sonnet was addressed to Geraldine as early as 1537 has its origin in the work of Edmond Bapst, *Deux Gentilshommes Poètes de la Cour de Henry VIII*, 1891, pp. 365-70. After giving his French version of the sonnet, Bapst has this to say:

> Quelle était cette Geraldine, objet de ce joli poème? et quelle influence eut-elle sur la vie de lord Surrey? Lady Elizabeth Fitzgerald était la fille du comte de Kildare, un des principaux chefs de clan

> irlandais; arrachée de son pays natal à la suite d'une révolte dirigée par sa famille contre la souveraineté anglaise, elle avait été placée, en raison des liens de parenté que par sa mère elle avait avec Henry VIII, dans la maison de la petite princesse Elizabeth et elle était élevée auprès de celle-ci. Surrey la vit pour première fois au château de Hunsdon dans le cours du printemps de 1537, et il la revit bientôt après, au commencement de juillet de cette même année, à Hampton Court, où elle avait accompagné Elizabeth mandée par son père. Lady Elizabeth Fitzgerald n'avait alors que dix ans; mais malgré son bas âge, sa beauté future se révélait déjà et l'imagination du poète pressentit, à la vue de l'enfant, ce que seraient un jour les charmes de la femme. L'impression qu'il éprouva fut même assez puissante et durable pour que, quelques jours après, alors qu'il était relégué à Windsor et peut-être, encore sous le coup d'une peine fort grave, il ait composé le poème que nous avons transcrit. Faire d'une enfant de dix ans l'objet d'un sonnet d'amour était bien l'oeuvre de cette imagination effrénée qui, au même moment, faisait dire à Surrey qu'à l'âge de douze et treize ans il avait, ainsi que son compagnon le duc de Richmond, connu tous les emportements de la passion.

Bapst's reference for the household of the Princess Elizabeth in 1537 is given as Cotton MS. Vespasian C.XIV, part 1, fol. 274 (p. 369). This is also Padelford's reference for his statement (p. 219), "In 1537 she entered the household of the Princess Mary." This manuscript is actually undated. Examination shows that fol. 274^r (old numbering, 245) has a list of "Parsons attending vpon the Lady Marys grace," and on the verso a similar list for "the Lady Elizabeths grace." On this second list is the name "The lady garet." The endorsement for the two lists on fol. 275^v has the added caption in another hand, "princes Howshold." Frederick Madden in *Privy Purse Expenses of the Princess Mary*, 1831, "Introductory Memoir," p. lxxxiv, says that in the period 1536-39 Mary and Elizabeth had only one household and one cofferer. The accounts indicate that the household of the Princess Mary moved about frequently, including a good many stops both at Hunsdon and at Hampton, and that the Princess Elizabeth was often with her (see Madden, pp. lxxvii-xxxiv, and pp. 88-90 of the text). Madden further calls attention to the Lady Mary's list mentioned above (p. lxxiv, using the old foliation he gives the reference as fol. 246 instead of 245), and points out that Dr. Michael, whose name is included, was not appointed physician until January, 1536/37. Consequently, the list could not be earlier in date, but it could be later.

Another reference which has been overlooked by investigators indicates that Lady Elizabeth Fitzgerald did not enter the service of the Princess Elizabeth until 1539. In *Letters and Papers . . . of Henry VIII*, vol. xiv, part 1, ed. J. Gairdner and R. H. Brodie (1894), No. 1145, under the year 1539, is the following quotation from a letter written about June 22 by John Husee to Lady Lisle:

> Mrs. Denny thanks you for your token. . . . I moved the matter concerning my lady Elizabeth. She answered that suit was made for Mrs. Hill, and the King answered that she should no more, for my lady Garrett's daughter was lately admitted, so that her Grace was full furnished, and he said she had too much "uthe" (youth) about her.

Thus, lines 7-8 of Surrey's sonnet must be interpreted as referring to a connection of "Geraldine" with the Princess Elizabeth which did not begin until 1539. Although he does not give his authority, Graves says that the Princess Mary received "Geraldine" into her house in 1538 and that Surrey first saw the young girl at Hunsdon in 1539. Surrey's eleventh line may refer to a time in 1539 when the Princesses were visiting at Hampton Court, or it could easily refer to a later period.

Statements about the future service of Elizabeth Fitzgerald to the royal family show some discrepancy. Bapst (p. 570, note 2) says that until her marriage to Sir Anthony Browne, Master of the Horse, in December, 1542, "Geraldine" remained attached to the household of the Princess Elizabeth, and that after the marriage she was at court by reason of the office of her husband. Nott ("Memoirs," p. cxxix, note b) mistakenly interprets references to Mistress Mary Browne, who served Mary Tudor from 1533 to 1558 (see Harl. MS. 6807, fol. 7ʳ, and Madden, pp. 9, 21, 28, 121, 215 on the identity of Mistress Browne; also, Harl. MS. 7376, fols. 4ʳ, 18ʳ for records of gifts after Mary became queen; Royal MS. App. 89, fol. 96ʳ for the record of "Mʳⁱˢ Browne" as one of nine ladies in the fifth chariot at Mary's coronation), as records of Elizabeth Fitzgerald after her marriage. Padelford and Graves both say, but without naming the authority, that Elizabeth Fitzgerald was transferred in 1540 to the service of Queen Catherine Howard, whose marriage to the king was announced in August of that year. Drayton, we may recall, described "Geraldine" as "*one of the honorable maydes to Queen* Katherine Dowager." Only Catherine of Arragon, who died in 1536, and Catherine Parr could properly be termed Queen Dowager, the latter after the death of Henry VIII in January, 1546/47. A tantalizing reference occurs in Royal MS. App. 89, fol. 104ᵛ (formerly Cotton MS. Appx. XXVIII, fol. 101ᵛ, from which it was printed in *Letters and Papers . . . of Henry VIII*, xxi, 2, ed. Gairdner and Brodie [1910], No. 1384 [ii]), where in a list of the "Quenes Privy Chamber," drawn up for festivities concerned with the reception of the French Admiral in July, 1546, is the name "Mastres Garet." It is thus certain that one Mistress Garett did serve Queen Catherine Parr, and it is not unknown in Tudor records for the lady to be referred to by her maiden name.

It is quite probable that Drayton thought that the "Mastres Garet" who served Catherine Parr was indeed "Geraldine." Graves and Padelford may have interpreted Drayton's statement to mean service to Queen Catherine Howard, but I have been unable to find a record substantiating this conclusion. Whatever her particular connection with the royal family may have been after 1540, it seems evident from the attention given by the king and the Princess Mary to Elizabeth Fitzgerald's marriage in 1542 that she was much in evidence at court. It would not be difficult for Surrey to become very well acquainted with her, especially during the halcyon days of Queen Catherine Howard's brief reign (August, 1540–February, 1541/42). In 1541 "Geraldine" was thirteen or fourteen years old, of an age to command the chivalric admiration of a young courtier, who might profess to serve her in the courtly love tradition. (On this point see the observations of W. J. Courthope, *A History of English Poetry*, ii [London, Macmillan, 2nd ed., 1904, reprint, 1935], 78-79.) Surrey's own marriage, which was made by his father's arrangement when Surrey was fourteen, should not be considered a deterrent to interests of this nature. I suggest that Surrey wrote this particular sonnet during his visit to Windsor in May, 1541 (note line 12), for the Feast of the Garter, following his election as a Knight of the Garter the preceding April 23 ([John Anstis] *The Register of the Most Noble Order of the Garter*, i [1724], 421-23). It was a compliment for a young girl who in a little more than a year would be married. To interpret Surrey's lines as written for a child of nine seems to me as wide of the mark as to incorporate the fantastic fiction of Nashe into the relationship. I fear that if Surrey's lines had not made it very clear that the sonnet was actually written for Elizabeth Fitzgerald many modern critics would have maintained that he wrote nothing at all for her. Perhaps some of his other courtly poems were addressed to her—and to other ladies about the court.

What does all this have to do with No. 72? There is reason to believe that it may have been written shortly after Elizabeth Fitzgerald's first marriage. In an elaborate ceremony, with a sermon by Nicholas Ridley, and with the king and the Princess Mary in attendance, Elizabeth was married on or about December 12, 1542, to Sir Anthony Browne, Master of the Horse. She was then fourteen or fifteen and he is said to have been about sixty. The vicissitudes of the Fitzgerald family undoubtedly were responsible for a marriage of this nature, which can only be looked upon as one resulting from necessity and not from romance (on the family, see *The Earls of Kildare*; Holinshed, iii, 943, 953-54; *D.N.B.*). Gifts presented by the Princess Mary are recorded in Royal MS. 17 B.XXVIII, fol. 113^{r} (old foliation, 137), as follows:

The xijth daye of Decem̃bre Anno xxxiiij^{to}
Reges Henrɔ VIII

Geuen to M^{rs} garet at hir mariage	Itm̃ a Broche of golde w^{t} oon Balace and of the history of Susanne
	Itm̃ A Broche of golde w^{t} oon emawraude of the story of Salomon/
Geuen to s^{r} Antony Browne drawing her g^{r}ce to his valentyne	Itm̃ a Brooche of golde enamyled blacke w^{t} añ Agate of the Story of Abrahām w^{t} iiij small Rocke Rubies

This account was printed by Nott, vol. i, "Memoirs," p. cxx, note a, but he mistakenly dates it "X^{o}. Decemb. XXXIII° H. VIII," and in his text interprets the year as 1543. Madden (pp. 175, 177) dates it correctly.

Now it is my suggestion that Surrey's satiric lines "Wrapt in my carelesse cloke" were written on the occasion of this ill-suited match, which he could very well deplore, especially since he had a special regard for the bride. I would further suggest that the answer, No. 72 in *AH*, which presents in the lines omitted in *TM*, the story of Susanna and the elders from the Apocryphal Book of Daniel, was a mocking reply written by Surrey himself, conceived from the knowledge of the brooch which the Princess Mary had given Lady Elizabeth. The applicability of the Susanna story to the circumstances is obvious. Is it unreasonable to suppose that the lines may have been omitted from *TM* out of deference to "Geraldine," who in 1557 was the Countess of Lincoln? If No. 72 is taken to be the work of another poet, it becomes a bitter rebuke to Surrey for his satiric criticism of a situation which he had so scathingly denounced. The tone of the satire is similar to that in Surrey's poem beginning, "To dearely had I bought my grene and youthfull yeres" (*TM*, sig. C3^{r}, No. 22; ed. Padelford, No. 25). While stressing the polished style of some of Surrey's poems, especially a few sonnets, critics have failed to emphasize sufficiently the strong satiric note, often expressed with a certain mirthless arrogance (quite in keeping with his temperament) which appears frequently in his poetry, e.g., in his sonnet on

Henry VIII and in the two sonnets on Wyatt (ed. Padelford, Nos. 40, 44, 45). See also Nos. 75 and 78 in *AH* as well as passages in his biblical paraphrases following.

[73] *Vnto thee lyving lord/ for pardon do I praye*

Hand A. Corrections appear in several lines as follows: 1. the *d* of "do" is written over a *t*; 5. the first *f* in "offendid" is written over another letter; 7. "race" is written over an erasure; 16. "tyme" and "place" are over erasures; 22. the whole line is written over an erasure; 33. "fayth" is made from another word; 34. "Stretche" and "the . . . save" are over erasures. In line 12 "dispaye" must be a copyist's error for "dispayre." Above the poem is Percy's penciled note, "See Surrey's Poems fo. 57," and another beneath the last line, "4 lines more in Surrey's Poems." Since fol. 38 is missing in *AH*, these four lines were probably written on that folio. Fol. 37^{v} is full, and there is no finis.

The longer version in (*A*) *TM* is printed among the Uncertain Authors, sigs. $R4^{v}$-$S1^{r}$ (ed. Rollins, No. 184), headed, "The repentant sinner in durance and aduersitie." Another copy of this longer version is in (*B*) Brit. Mus. Sloane MS. 1896, fols. 38^{r}-39^{v}, headed, "The repentaunt synner in aduᴐsity prayeth vnto god." In *B* the lines are written as in ballad measure. I am indebted to Kathleen Tillotson for the *B* variants.

1 thee] the *A B*
2 the shell] my youth *B*
4 grate] call *B*
5 thow . . . lorde] thee O Lorde alone *A B*
7 race] way *A B*
9 The . . . pursude] The throng wherin I thrust *A B*; brought] throwen *A B*
12 of] and *A B*; dispaye] dispayre *A B*
13 flye] flee *A B*
14 theare] *wanting in B*
16 no tyme no place/nor] no place no houre no *A B*
17 shall never] noe tyme shall *B*
18 to crave to call] to call to crave *A B*; that] which *A B*
19 you] it *A B*
21 And] For *A B*
24 receav'd] receiued *A*
26 the] me *B*; past] waste *B*
27 draw] draweth *B*
33 my hope, my trust] my trust, my hope *B*
34 the sowle to save] to saue the soule *A B*
36 saftye] all safety *A B*
37 eke confesse] knowledge eke *A B*

38 to . . . in] I ought to loue and dreade in *A B*
The last four lines added in A read:

> And with repentant hart do laude thee Lord on hye,
> That hast so gently set me straight, that erst walkt so awry.
> Now graunt me grace my God to stand thine strong in sprite,
> And let y[e] world thē work such wayes, as to the world semes mete.

The same lines are in *B* with the following variants: 2. "walked"; 3. "spirite"; 4. "walke" for "work."

Although No. 73 is placed among the Uncertain Authors in *TM*, its position in *AH* raises the question as to whether the Haringtons considered it to be Surrey's. No. 72 may be his and Nos. 74-90 have been attributed to him. Between Nos. 73 and 74, however, eleven folios are now missing in *AH*, but poems by Surrey may have been written on these missing folios, in keeping with the ordered arrangement of the original collection (see the Introduction, pp. 30-31). Furthermore, in support of Surrey's authorship of No. 73, it should be noted that it is written in poulter's measure, which he frequently used, that it reflects feelings which he must have had in 1546, and that it compares favorably with some of his biblical paraphrases. See especially Nos. 86, 87, and 89. Nevertheless, No. 73 is not in G. F. Nott's edition (*Surrey and Wyatt*, vol. i, 1815); nor is it in F. M. Padelford's (*Poems*, rev. ed. 1928).

In his note on the poem Rollins has pointed out some of the biblical expressions which occur. He has also called attention to Puttenham's quotation of lines 33-34 in *The Arte of English Poesie*, 1589 (ed. Gladys Willcock and Alice Walker, 1936, p. 215), as an illustration of the figure *sinonimia.*

[74] *vnto my self, vnlesse this carefull song* [The sonne hath twyse brought forthe the tender grene]

Hand A. The following are written over erasures: line 2, "good will"; line 5, "lyfe." All the commas are in another ink.

These six lines form the last part of Surrey's poem beginning, "The sonne hath twyse brought forthe the tender grene." They occur at the top of fol. 49[r]; the rest of the poem was written on the preceding folio, now missing. This might be surmised in any event, but it is certain from evidence left by G. F. Nott. In his note on this poem in his *Surrey and Wyatt*, i (1815), 233, Nott says, "In the Harington MS. only the first nine and the last fourteen lines are preserved. The leaf containing the other part of the poem has been destroyed." It is thus evident that when Nott used *AH* in the early nineteenth century (see the Introduction, p. 16), there was a small portion of the preceding folio still in it. This is proved by his transcript of *AH, N*, fol. 24, which is blank except at the bottom on both sides. The recto has the first nine lines of this poem, and the verso, on the back of the beginning, has eight lines and part of another, followed by the last six lines of the poem at the top of fol. 25^{r} (according with the six lines here given from the original). The parts of the poem on *N*, fol. $24^{r,v}$, show that they were made from a damaged folio. The beginning of No. 74 as given in *N*, fol. 24^{r}, follows:

The Sonne hath twyse brought forthe - - - -
and cladd the earthe in lyvely lustinesse
once have the wyndes the treese dispoyled cleene
and now agayne begyñns their crewelnesse
synce I have hydd vnder my brest the harme
that never shall recover healthfullnesse
the wynters hurt recovers with the warme
the pearched greene restored is with shade
what warmthe alas may serve for to disarme

That portion of the poem written on *N*, fol. 24^{v}, runs:

- - - - - - - - - - - - - - of the port
my sayles do fall and I advaunce right nought
as anchorde fast, my sprytes do all resort
to stand at gaze, and suck in more and more
the deadlye harme which she doth take in sporte
So yf I seeke how I do fynde my sore
and yf I flye, I carrye with me still
the venomde shafte, whiche doth his force restore
by hast of flyght and I may playne my fill

Following are the concluding six lines on fol. 25^{r} of the transcript, copied from the lines in *AH* as given in this text. It is clear that at some time after Nott's copy was made, the torn half of fol. 48 was lost from *AH*.

Fortunately a copy of No. 74 is in another Harington MS., *P*, fol. $50^{r,v}$, where it is ascribed, "H.S." In my earlier study of *AH* and related manuscripts I have discussed in detail the identification of the *P* MS. and the supposedly "lost" Hill MS. (Hughey, pp. 409-13). Since texts of other poems common to *AH* and *P* show few variants, it is probable that the text quoted below from *P* gives us essentially the text of *AH*.

The sonne hath twyse brought forthe the tender grene,
and cladd the yerthe in livelye lustynes,
Ones have the wyndes the trees dispoyled clene,
and now agayne begynnes their cruelnes;
sins I have hidd vnder my brest the harme

that never shall recover helthfulnes
the wynters hurt recovers w^{t} the warme;
the perched grene restored is w^{t} shade
what warmth alas may sarve for to disarme
the froosyn hart that my inflame hath made?
what colde agayne is hable to restore
my freshe grene yeres that wither thus & faade?
alas I see nothinge to hurt so sore
but tyme somtyme reduceth a retourne;
yet tyme my harme increseth more & more,
and semes to have my cure allwayes in skorne;
straunge kynd of death in lief that I doo trye
at hand to melt farr of in flame to bourne
eche thing alive that sees the heaven w^{t} eye
w^{t} cloke of night maye cover and excuse
him self from travaile of the dayes vnrest
save I alas against all others vse
that then sturres vpp the torment of my brest
to curse eche starr as cawser of my faat
and when the sonne hath eke the darke represt
it
and brought the daie ⟨yet⟩ doth nothing abaat
the travaile of my endles smart & payne
ffor then as one that hath the light in haat
I wishe for night more covertlye to playne
and me w^{t}drawe from everie haunted place
lest in my chere my chaunce should pere to playne
and w^{t} my mynd I measure paas by paas
to seke that place where I myself hadd lost
that daye that I was tangled in that laase
in seming slacke that knytteth ever most
but never yet the trayvaile of my thought
of better state could catche a cawse to bost
for yf I fynde somtyme that I have sought
those starres by whome I trusted of the port
my sayles do fall and I advaunce right nought
as anchord fast my sprites do all resort
to stand atgaas and sucke in more & more
she
the deadlye harme which doth take in sport
loo yf I seke how I do fynd my sore
and yf I flye I carry w^{t} me still
the venymd shaft which dothe his force restore
by hast of flight and I may playne my fill

vnto my self oneles this carefull song
prynt in yor hert some ꝑcell of my will
for I alas in sylence all to long
of myne old hurt yet fele the wound but grene
rue on me lief or elles yor crewell wrong
shall well appeare and by my deth be sene
ffinis. H. S.

Comparison of lines 48-53 with the fragment in *AH* shows a difference in two words only: line 49, "good" *AH*, "my" *P*; line 52, "my" *AH*, "me" *P*.

The poem was printed as the first of Surrey's poems in *TM*, sig. A2$^{r, v}$ (ed. Rollins, No. 1), where it is entitled, "Descripcion of the restlesse state of a louer, with sute to his ladie, to rue on his diyng hart." Using the text in *P* as a basis, collation follows with the version in *TM*.

1 the] his
4 now] new
10 my] mine
11 hable] able
13 to] hath
14 somtyme] in time
15 yet] In
17 kynd] kindes
19 eche] All; sees] seeth; heaven] heauens
Inserted between lines 18 and 19 in TM:
And like as time list to my cure aply,
So doth eche place my comfort cleane refuse
21 him self] It self
23 torment] tormentes
24 to] And
25 represt] opprest
26 ⟨yet⟩^{it}] it
27 travaile of my] trauailes of mine
31 in] my; pere] appere
32 w^{t}] in
33 that] the
35 that] the
38 fynde] found
42 atgaas *the t inserted*] agazed; sucke] sinke
45 flye] flee
49 will] tene
52 me] my

It should be noted that the differences are verbal, not metrical. The *TM* variant "tene" (line 49) is poor, as it is not in keeping with the demands of the rhyme. The poem represents one of the early attempts to introduce into English poetry the Italian *terza rima.*

Nott (i, 233) observes that Surrey appears to have had in mind Petrarch's sestina beginning, "A qualunque animale alberga in terra" (*Le Rime sparse e i Trionfi,* ed. Ezio Chiòrboli, Bari: Gius. Laterza and Figli, 1930, No. XXII). There the theme is on the despair of the lover, who finds no rest at night nor happiness in the day. Nott (i, 237-38) has also noted similarities to other passages in Petrarch. These, or others, are pointed out by F. M. Padelford in his edition of *The Poems of Surrey* (1928, No. 11, note), by Rollins in his note on the poem, and by Emil Koeppel, "Studien zur Geschichte des englishchen Petrarchismus im sechzehnten Jahrhundert," *Romanische Forschungen,* v (1889), 80.

[75] *London hast thow accused me*

Hand A. The following are written over erasures: 23. "aref"; 26. "ye dredfull"; 40. "lutt"; 62. "turrettes hye." In the upper right-hand margin is a penciled note by Bishop Percy, "Intended for Surrey's Poems New Edit^ion^."

A copy of the poem is also in *P,* fol. 52^r, v^, where it is ascribed "H S," and headed, in a later hand, "N° 3." It is the third in a group of Surrey's poems in *P,* the first being a copy of *AH* No. 74, and the second a copy of Surrey's elegy "So crewell pryson howe could betyde alas." The copy of No. 75 in *P* has but two variants: 61. "they" instead of "thie"; 66. "right wise" instead of "rightuous." On the relation of *P* and *AH,* see the Introduction, pp. 40-44.

The poem remained in manuscript until Thomas Park printed it from *P* in his edition of the *NA,* ii (1804), 336-38. G. F. Nott printed it, in modernized form and with emendations, from *AH, Surrey and Wyatt,* i (1815), 53-55. Padelford's text is from *P* (*Poems,* 1928, No. 32).

Like a good many other poems in *AH,* this satire on London was probably written in prison. On April 1, 1543, Surrey and two companions, Pickering and the younger Thomas Wyatt, were brought before the Privy Council on two charges: first, of eating meat during Lent, contrary to royal proclamation, and, second, of walking about the streets at night in an unseemly manner, and, most extraordinarily, breaking windows with stonebows (cf. lines 18-20, 44). In answering Surrey said he had a license for the eating of meat, but that he had not used it as privately as he should have. He admitted his guilt in using the stonebows and submitted to punishment. He was then committed to the Fleet. The date of his release is not given, but his companions, who were sent to the Tower, were free on May 3 (*Acts of the Privy Council,* ed. J. R. Dasent, i [1890], 104-05, 125; E. Bapst, *Deux Gentils-*

hommes-Poètes De La Cour De Henry VIII, 1891, pp. 267-73; E. Casady, *Henry Howard, Earl of Surrey*, 1938, pp. 96-101. Also, Nott, "Memoirs" in vol. i, pp. lii-liv; Padelford, pp. 22-24, and note on No. 32). Thus from this escapade and its punishment, with the enforced leisure giving opportunity, came Surrey's mocking defence of his own actions, for which he could cite scripture, as they are set forth as a means of scourging proud, sinful London, another Babylon.

It has not been pointed out, I believe, that in Jeremiah 50. 9, 14, 29, Surrey had scriptural authority for using the bow against the sinful city (cf. lines 20-44), thus:

> 9. For, lo, I will raise and cause to come up against Babylon an assembly of great nations from the north country; and they shall set themselves in array against her; from thence she shall be taken: their arrows *shall be* as of a mighty expert man; none shall return in vain.
>
> 14. Put yourselves in array against Babylon round about: all ye that bend the bow, shoot at her, spare no arrows: for she hath sinned against the Lord.
>
> 29. Call together the archers against Babylon: all ye that bend the bow, camp against it round about; let none thereof escape: recompense her according to her work; according to all that she hath done, do unto her: for she hath been proud against the Lord, against the Holy One of Israel.

With these verses as a starting point, Surrey could satirically turn his own misdemeanor into a righteous action, and at the same time denounce the city of evil which presumed to judge him, which would not be warned of its impending doom, and yet would come to utter ruin, as did Babylon. The Bible offers the poet many passages on proud Babylon and its fall. In addition to the verses quoted, Surrey seems to have drawn upon others in the same chapter; also upon Jeremiah 51 and Revelation 17.5 and 18. Although in lines 56-58, Surrey must have had in mind religious martyrs of his day, he had a parallel in Rev. 18.24: "And in her [Babylon] was found the blood of prophets, and of saints, and of all that were slain upon the earth." Padelford also notes that in lines 60-64 Surrey was indebted to Ezekiel 5.12-17, 6.11-14, which refer to the destruction of Israel. Ezekiel 7.12 might be added (cf. line 55).

Nott (pp. 364-65) calls attention to similarities in lines 53-68 with lines in Petrarch's sonnets addressed to the papal court at Avignon, which is compared to Babylon (Nos. CXXVI-CXXVIII, or sonnets 105-107). Nott believed that Surrey, as a zealous Protestant, was specifically attacking the evils of papal influence in London. This seems to me to give the satire a slant not intended. I should not, however, describe it as "waggish," as Padelford does, but rather as shrewd and clever. Surrey implies, I think, that the Council is giving its attention to minor offenses while heinous sins continue in secret. If he was guilty of eating meat publicly during Lent, London was gluttonous and drunken, though more discreetly so (lines 39-42).

Like No. 74, No. 75 is written in *terza rima*, except for lines 29-40, which are a modification, rhyming *a b a b a b c d c d c d*.

[76] *Laid in my quyet bedd, in study as I weare*

Hand A. In line 7 "pay" is written over letters not decipherable. In line 9 "sore" is written over an erasure. Above the poem at the right is Percy's penciled note, "In Surrey fo 18."

The only other contemporary copy of the complete poem seems to be that printed among the Surrey poems in *TM*, sig. D3^{r,v} (ed. Rollins, No. 33), which is entitled, "How no age is content with his own estate, & how the age of children is the happiest, if they had skill to vnderstand it." The text differs only in the forms of a few words from that of *AH*. In line 4 *TM* reads in the first edition, "doth ryse," but in the second and succeeding editions the reading agrees with *AH*. In lines 4 and 25 *TM* has "sighed" instead of the older "sight." In line 16, however, it is *TM* which gives the old "chewes," represented in *AH* by "Iawes." In his text of the poem, given in modernized form as usual, G. F. Nott retains the *TM* reading and in his note comments that the "jaws" of the manuscript seems to have been substituted for a word which was becoming obsolete. He notes that the substantive *chew*, or *chow*, or *chol*, is the same as the *jole*, or *jowl*, and that the form *chew* was in use in Scotland (*Surrey and Wyatt*, i [1815], 41-42, 328). It is not given in the *N.E.D.* In view of the colloquial nature of the diction in other lines (e.g., 12, 17, 26), it seems quite probable that Surrey wrote "chewes."

The first twelve lines of the poem, it may be noted, can easily be taken as an entity, and it is therefore not surprising to find two versions of these lines. The earlier, which was probably copied in the time of Edward VI or Mary, is in Brit. Mus. MS. Cotton Titus A. XXIV, fol. 83^{r}, and runs as follows:

Layde in my quiet bed ⟨in studie a⟩
in studye as hit were
I saue withe in my trubled hed
an heape of thowghtes apere

And euerie of them didde shew ⟨so⟩
so liuely in myne iees
that now I sighte and then I smilde
as cause of thowghte didde

I save the litel boy in ⟨thoughte⟩
in thowghte how ofte that he
didde wishe of god to skape the rode
a tall yonge manne to be

The Iownge mane eke that felte
his bones withe paynes opprest
how he wolde be a riche olde mâ
to liue and lye at reste

The olde man eke that sawe ⟨h⟩
his time to drawe onne sore
how he wolde be a boy agayne
to live so muche the more

Thus musinge as I lay
I saue how al thes thry
from boy to manne from mâ to boy
wolde choppe and chawnges degry

Late in the century this shorter version, considerably changed, appeared in *Brittons Bowre of Delights*, 1591, sig. G2$^{r, v}$, entitled, "*A pleasant sweet song*" (facsimile edition of the copy in the Huntington Library, with introduction by H. E. Rollins, 1933). Variants from the Cotton MS. version are as follows (disregarding crossed-out readings):

1 quiet] restlesse
2 in . . . were] In dreame of my desire
4 an] A
5-6 euerie] each; didde shew/ so liuely in] so strange,/ In sight before
7 sighte] sigh; smilde] smile
8 of thowghte didde] thereby doth rise
9 save the litel boy in] see how that the little boy
11 didde] Doth
13 The . . . felte] I saw the yong man trauelling
14 his bones withe] From sport to
17 eke that sawe] too, who seeth
18 time] age
19 how . . . a] Would be a little
20 muche] long
21 Thus . . . lay] Whereat I sigh and smile
22 I . . . thry] How *Nature* craues her fee

These two shorter versions obviously have no textual validity and are interesting only in showing how poems were changed as they were handed about.

Descriptions and reflections on the ages of man were common in classical literature, but the more usual division was ten, or seven, as in the familiar lines spoken by Jaques in *As You Like It* (II, vii, 142-65). As Padelford notes (*Poems*, 1928, p. 226), in the *Ars Poetica* (153 ff.) Horace comments on the three stages of man. Rollins thinks that the general idea of the poem may have been suggested by Horace's first satire.

The expression "trusse vpp thie pack and trudge" (line 26), connected with peddlers and their packs, here, of course, refers to binding up and marching on with the burdens of age. Compare "Thomas More to them that seke fortune" (*The English Works of Sir Thomas More*, ed. W. E. Campbell and others, facsimile of the 1557 edition, vol. i, London: Eyre and Spottiswoode, 1931, sig. 2#8^v):

> Then for asmuch as it is fortunes guyse,
> To graunt no manne all thyng that he wyll axe,
> But as her selfe lyst order and deuyse,
> Dothe euery manne his parte diuide and tax,
> I counsayle you eche one trusse vp your packes,
> And take no thyng at all, or be content,
> With suche rewarde as fortune hath you sent.

[77] *Suche wayward wayes hath love/ that moste part in discorde*

Hand A. The following are written over erasures: line 1, "that"; line 16, "truce"; line 34, "this I"; line 35, the *e* in "the," and the *r* in "Lover"; line 39, "helppe"; line 42, "self"; line 43, "a." In line 47 "thos" has been made from "the" in another ink. In the upper right-hand margin is Percy's penciled note, "Printed in Surrey fo. 3."

There is a copy, wanting two lines, in (*A*) *P*, fol. 53^r, designated in a later hand, "N°. 4," that is, fourth in the group of Surrey poems in *P*. F. M. Padelford's text is taken from *P* (*Poems*, 1928, No. 22). No. 77 was printed among the Surrey poems in (*B*) *TM*, sigs. $A3^{r,v}$-$A4^r$ (ed. Rollins, No. 4), entitled, "Description of the fickle affections panges and sleightes of loue."

wais
1 wayes] ⟨wailes⟩ *A*
2 doth stand] do stand *A B*; doth] doe *B*
4 whiche] whom *B*
5 and] he *A B*; causeth hartes] makes the one *B*
6 tothers] other *B*
10 the darke deepe well] a depe dark hel *B*
12 will that still] willes me that *B*: wooll that still *A*
13 and] he *A B*

14 spilt] lost *B*; er] or *A*
15 Lo . . . rules] So by this meanes *B*; can] may *B*
17 convert my will] content my self *B*
19 harme] harmes *B*; dissemblid] dissembling *B*
21 dead] dredd *A B*
24 know] wote *B*
25 be] by *B*
28 can] doth *B*
in
30 in] ⟨hys⟩ *A* *Padelford does not indicate the corrected reading. Lines 31-32 are wanting in A.*
31 lyke] list *B*; face] grace *B*
32 pleasure] pleasures *B*; delightes] delight B; doth] doe *B*
35 the Lover] that lovers *A B*; belov'd] beloved *A B*
36 could] would *B*; spirite] spryte *A B*; remov'd] removed *A B*
39 withouten] with others *B*
41 the] my *A B*
42 to . . . to . . . to] I . . . I . . . I *B*
43 a yolden] the yeldon *A*: a yelding *B*
44 an] a *A B*
45 whiche . . . seasoned] Or els with seldom swete to season *B*
46 glyntt] glyns *A*: glimse *B*
47 thos] the *A B*
48 may] wil *B*; will] may *B*
49 that] The *B*; those] the *B*
50 that . . . that] The . . . the *B*

Thus the *P* text stands between *AH* and *TM*, although it is closer to *AH*. It will be conceded, I think, that in lines 6, 14, 15, 17, 25, 39, and 45, the manuscripts, which agree, have better readings than *TM*. The latter is especially faulty in line 45. In line 10, however, the couplet rhyme is more truly maintained by the "hel" of *TM*. G. F. Nott, whose text is taken primarily from *AH* (*Surrey and Wyatt*, i [1815], 24-26; notes, pp. 297-303), introduces the *TM* reading, though on the basis of meaning. The independent readings of *AH* are probably Surrey's. In line 2 *AH* has the old syntax, a plural subject and a singular verb. In line 43 "yolden" is the older form of "yelden," i.e., submissive (see the Note on No. 89, line 54). In support of the *AH* reading in line 21, I call attention to lines 41-42 in Surrey's elegy on the Duke of Richmond (Padelford, No. 31):

And with this thought the blood forsakes my face,
The teares berayne my chekes of dedlye hewe.

Perhaps the corrections in lines 35 and 47 were made from Surrey's manuscript. The singular form is preferable in line 35.

Nott's notes on this poem are full and interesting, especially for the literary parallels to which he refers. He points out Surrey's indebtedness in his opening lines to Ariosto's *Orlando Furioso*, II, 1, and in lines 4-8 especially to Ovid's *Metamorphoses*, I, 466-71. Nott cites a number of passages in Petrarch, the most important being the *Trionfo d'Amore*, III, 151-57, which presents the general subject of the poem. Padelford adds lines 158-90 and a passage in Chap. IV, lines 139-53, and other parallels in Petrarch.

As Nott and Rollins have indicated, line 40 should be compared with Chaucer's *Squire's Tale*, F.490-91 (ed. Skeat):

> And for to maken other be war by me,
> As by the whelp chasted is the leoun.

Nott says, "Heraldic writers say, that the Lion is of so courageous a nature, that no compulsion or beating can make him couch; but that he is so gentle-hearted, that if he see a whelp beaten he will immediately become couchant, as if interceding to have the chastisement remitted." A pertinent comment on the magnanimous nature of the lion is given by the thirteenth-century authority Albertus Magnus in his treatise *De animalibus*, Lib. xxii, Tract 2, cap. 1 (Beiträge zur Geschichte der Philosophie des Mittelalters, herausgegeben von Baeumker, Band XVI, Hermann Stadler: *Albertus Magnus de Animalibus, Libri XXVI. Nach der Cölner Urschrift*, Zweiter Band, Buch XIII-XXVI [Verlag Aschendorff, Münster, 1920], p. 1406):

> Obviantes autem et provocantes discerpit et prostratis et veniam petentibus aliquando parcit: et cum raro formidet, scorpionem mirabiliter fugit et abhorret. Album etiam gallum multum timere dicitur: et quando domitus est, catuli percussione disciplinatur.

Albert's real treatise on zoology ends with lib. xxi. Libri xxii-xxvi treat of the birds, beasts, and fishes, real and fabulous, and their matter was largely borrowed from Albert's pupil and friend Thomas de Chantimpré (see Hieronymus Wilms, O.P., *Albert the Great*, English Version by Adrian English, O.P., and Philip Hereford, London: Burns, Oates and Washbourne, 1933, p. 27).

[78] *Eache beast can chuse his feere/ according to his minde*

Hand A. In line 7 "praũnced" is written over an erasure, and the line is added to fill space. In line 19 the *n* in "beforne" is written over an erased *e*; the word had been "before" (see collation). In line 53 the "st" of "wist" and the caesura mark are written over an erasure. Above the poem at the right is Percy's penciled note, "In Surrey's Poems fo 10."

The poem was printed among "Other Songes and Sonettes written by the earle of Surrey" in *TM*, sig. Cc4$^{r, v}$-Ddl^{r} (ed. Rollins, No. 264), entitled, "A song written by the earle of Surrey by a lady that refused to daunce with him." Nott's text is based on *AH* but with emendations (*Surrey and Wyatt*, i [1815], 26-29; notes, pp. 303-10); Padelford's is taken from the transcript, *N*, fols. 27$^{r, v}$-28^{r} (*Poems*, 1928, No. 34).

2 to] can

3 theare] late

5 this] the; lyked] pleased

6 it seemyd me] he semed well

9 whale his] whales

10 a fressher] of fresher

11 fearce] coy

12 toward] Vnto

17 Wheare with] With that

19 beforne] before

20 and] nor

22 but] Go; thow . . . oute] where thou mayst finde

23 fforthwith] With that; begoñne] began

25 rage] wrath

29 you] ye

35 dothe know] haue heard

37 both] *omitted*

39 who] whom

40 seeke his death] lese his life

41 lyfe to] liues doe

42 will . . . is] willes . . . ar; right] *omitted*

43 well I may] now I doe; movid] moueth

46 you] ye

47 my kynd] our kyndes

48 my frends] your frendes

49 fedd] fled; flee] slay

52 of] on

53 Coy] coyed

54 traynd] trapt; bye] with

55 list to bow] lust to loue

56 a Currant fawne] of currant fort

60 or] nor

63 Rew] ruse

64 thus] This; no] ne

65 in the] And for; wherof] therof

66 a] I

67 happ] luck
69 to low] and bow
70 you] ye; saile] sailes
71 Syns] Sith; woolfe] a wolfe
72 of . . . wrath] go slake your thirst on simple shepe
75 this] the
76 by] for

A good many of the differences in the *TM* and *AH* texts have no more than casual significance, but others result in a distinction of emphasis or meaning. It is obvious that in lines 19, 53, 63, and 66 the *AH* text is preferable. In the second and succeeding editions of *TM* line 63 agrees with *AH*. I should also say that the *AH* readings are preferable in lines 11, 40-42, 49, 54-56, although this is not so evident until the total meaning of the poem is considered.

Indication of the identity of the lady to whom Surrey addressed these caustic lines seems to have first appeared in the 1598 edition of Michael Drayton's *Englands Heroicall Epistles* (fols. 89^{r}, $91^{r,v}$; in *Works*, ed. J. W. Hebel from the 1619 text, ii [Oxford, Shakespeare Head Press, 1932] 281, 285, from which my quotations are taken). Surrey in his epistle to Geraldine, when speaking of her excellence above all others, says:

> Nor beautious STANHOPE, whom all Tongues report
> To be the glory of the *English* Court,
> Shall by our Nation be so much admir'd,
> If ever SURREY truely were inspir'd. (lines 145-48)

In his note on these lines (p. 285), Drayton says:

Of the Beautie of that Lady, he himselfe testifies, in an Elegie which he writ of her, refusing to dance with him, which he seemeth to allegorize under a Lion and a Wolfe. And of himselfe he saith:

> A Lion saw I late, as white as any Snow.

And of her,

> I might perceive a Wolfe, as white as a Whales Bone,
> A fairer Beast, of fresher hue, beheld I never none,
> But that her Lookes were coy, and froward was her Grace.

Thus Drayton has quoted lines 3, 9-11 of No. 78, according to the *TM* version. Since "That Lyon plac'd in our bright Silver bend" (Drayton, same epistle, line 96; notes, pp. 284-85) was the heraldic emblem of the Howard family, Surrey quite properly so designated himself. Similarly it is clear that the wolf was an emblem of the family of "beautious STANHOPE." Bapst (*Deux Gentilshommes-Poètes*, 1891, pp. 370-75) gives a good deal of attention to No. 78, and identifies this lady more specifically as Lady Anne, daughter of Sir Edward Stanhope, and second wife of Edward Seymour, Earl of Hertford (later Duke of Somerset), leading member of the family whom Surrey so much hated. Bapst points out that the wolf was an emblem of the Stanhope family, contrary to the claims of Nott, who attempted to connect the poem with Lady Elizabeth Fitzgerald. Since Lady Anne Seymour, born in 1497 (*D.N.B.*, under her husband), was twenty years older than Surrey, it is difficult to believe that his feeling for her was one of romantic passion, as Bapst supposes. Indeed the poem itself reveals the bold arrogance of the king of beasts, who prances up to the beautiful, proud mate of his enemy, and with mock show of humility, asks for a dance (lines 7, 13-14). Although, as Surrey insists, her looks may have encouraged this advance, if she accepted, she would be recognizing his lordly conquest of a foe, toward whom he could then be magnanimous (see lines 49-51; also the Note on No. 77). Consequently, she refuses with "scornfull cheere" (lines 11-15). Who better deserved this response than the lion (line 16, surely satiric)? She had checked him at his own game (line 75). Enraged (lines 23-26), he reminds her of the noble nature of the lion, which would not destroy "yelding pray," and contrasts the vicious nature of the wolf, which kills what it subdues (lines 50-52). Since lines 47-52 are concerned with this contrast, in line 48 the "your" of *TM* is better than the "my" of *AH*; but in line 49 the "fedd" of *AH* is preferable, i.e., I am kind to those who feed me, but you slay them. Lines 55-58 are somewhat puzzling, but the *AH* version is clear if, as Nott suggested, we understand "a Currant" as "accurrent," from the Latin *accurere*, to run toward. These lines then would mean: though there are some who wish to bow where they ought to blame, and running toward such beasts, fawn upon them instead of fighting—I instead will observe the law of my nature (the lion's) and conquer those who resist, including you (line 68), and in vengeance will harm many who are innocent (line 63). Thus in the end the lion ironically has admitted that the wolf is an adversary worthy of his strength.

To support his claims for the nobility of the lion, Surrey refers to achievements of his family. Lines 29-30 have reference to Surrey's grandfather, Thomas Howard, Earl of Surrey, and later second Duke of Norfolk, who defeated James IV of Scotland at the battle of Flodden Field in 1513. In lines 35-40 Surrey is speaking of his half-uncle, Thomas Howard, who was committed to the Tower in June, 1536, for having become engaged to Lady Margaret Douglas, the king's niece, without the royal consent. Lord Thomas died in the Tower, October 31, 1538. Poems expressing the affection of the lovers are in the *D* MS. (Nott and Padelford have full notes on this affair). Lines 41-42 are taken by Bapst (p. 371), who used the *TM* version, to refer to members of the Howard family who had been imprisoned in the Tower for being implicated in the affair of Queen Catherine Howard. Since they were released in August, 1542, Bapst thinks this poem was written shortly before that time. This is a possible interpretation, although it seems extravagant to believe that members of the family so imprisoned "wold have dyed right fayne." The lines in *AH*, with "to" instead of "doe" in line 41 could be interpreted to mean that there were others, of which the poet may have been one, who would rather die than live on in such mental torture as Lord Thomas suffered. Both Nott and Bapst (and apparently also Padelford) think the closing lines of the poem signify that the incident took place at an entertainment given by Surrey himself. Earlier in this note I have suggested an interpretation of line 75.

[79] *Thie name o Lord how greate/ is fownd before our sight*

Hand A. In lines 25 and 51 "light" and "within," respectively, are written by the same hand over erasures; but in lines 4 and 19 "it" and "marke," respectively, are written in another hand over erasures. The "cnfused" of line 49 is clearly an error.

No other contemporary copy of this paraphrase of Psalm 8 is known. It appears in modernized form in G. F. Nott's *Surrey and Wyatt* (vol. i [1815], pp. 85-86; notes, pp. 398-99); and in F. M. Padelford's edition of Surrey's *Poems* (1928, No. 53), where it is printed from *N*, fol. 28[r,v]. In his notes Nott says, "This paraphrase of the eighth Psalm is here printed for the first time from the Harington MS. upon the authority of which it is given to Surrey; it is found in that part of the volume, which seems to have been allotted to Surrey's poems exclusively," Nott's reasoning is sound, for it has been shown that an ordered arrangement prevails in parts of *AH* (see Hughey, p. 417; Introduction, pp. 29-34). Nos. 72-90 comprise the Surrey section as *AH* now stands. Of these Nos. 79-84 are paraphrases of Psalms, including two prologues, and Nos. 86-90 are paraphrases of the first five chapters of Ecclesiastes. Nott's texts of these paraphrases, all of which are accepted as Surrey's, are based on *AH*. With the exception of No. 79, versions of these biblical paraphrases occur also in the *P* MS. in an ordered arrangement, but with the Ecclesiastes chapters preceding (for foliation in *P*, see Notes on those poems). Unlike some other Surrey poems in *P*, the biblical paraphrases are not ascribed "H S." Thomas Park, who owned the *P* MS. in the early nineteenth century (Introduction, p. 8, n. 9), printed the paraphrases from *P* in his 1804 edition of the *NA* (ii, 339-71), attributing them to Surrey. No. 79 is, of course, not included. A penciled note written by Park on fol. 59[r] of the *P* MS., just beneath the closing lines of the paraphrase of Ecclesiastes 1 (*P* version of No. 86), reveals the authority on which his attribution to Surrey was made. This note reads, "These lines [i.e., the last two] are printed before Archb. Parker's

Psalms, as taken from the Earle of Surrie's Ecclesiastices, which denotes this coms'ion' to be his Lordship's." Similarly Park has noted at the head of this paraphrase, "By the Earl of Surrey—to page 145 [fol. 65, new numbering]. See Warton III." On turning to Archbishop Matthew Parker's work *The Whole Psalter translated into English Metre*, 1567 (?), we find that the prefatory remarks conclude (sig. G2^{v}) as follows:

> Henrie Haward Earle of Surrie/ in his Ecclesiastices
> All such as enterprise,
> To put newe thinges in vre:
> Of them that scorne shall their deuise,
> May well themselues assure.

Thus so good an authority as Parker quoted, though in a slightly different text, the last two lines of No. 86, thereby giving us a positive contemporary statement of Surrey's authorship of this paraphrase. This ascription was substantiated some years later by George Puttenham in *The Arte of English Poesie, 1589* (ed. G. Willcock and A. Walker, 1936, p. 73), who commented on the first line of this same paraphrase as follows:

> They do very wel as wrote the Earle of Surrey translating the booke of the preacher.
>
> *Salomon Dauids sonne, king of Ierusalem.*
>
> This verse is a very good *Alexandrine*, but perchaunce woulde haue sounded more musically, if the first word had bene a dissillable, or two monosillables and not a trissillable: hauing his sharpe accent vppon the *Antepenultima* as it hath . . . Iudge some body whether it would haue done better (if it might) haue bene sayd thus,
>
> *Robóham Dauids sonne king of Ierusalem.*
>
> Letting the sharpe accent fall vpon *bo*, or thus
>
> *Restóre king Dáuids sónne vntó Ierusálém.*

Puttenham's remarks are misdirected, however, since he has misquoted the line, or he may have had another version of the poem.

The earliest mention of Surrey's biblical paraphrases seems to have been made by John Bale in his *Index Britanniae Scriptorum* of 1548 and 1549 (ed. Reginald L. Poole, Oxford, Clarendon Press, 1902, p. 162), in which is the following entry:

> Henricus Howerd, comes de Surre, vir ingeniosissimus carminibus Anglicis elucidauit,
> Ecclesiasten, li. 1. 'Ego Salomon filius Dauidis regis'
> Quosdam psalmos, li. 1.

Unfortunately, it is again the same paraphrase which is specifically indicated, but it is evident that Surrey's contemporaries recognized that he wrote several paraphrases both from Ecclesiastes and from the Psalms. An entry on the paraphrases given by Thomas Tanner in his *Bibliotheca Britannico-Hibernica; sive de Scriptoribus*, 1748, p. 416, appears to be drawn from Bale and Parker and adds nothing more exact to our knowledge. Thomas Warton, who, as Park observed, discusses Surrey's biblical paraphrases in his *History of English Poetry* (iii [1781], 26), probably had access to the *P* MS., then in the possession of the Reverend Sayle (see the Introduction, p. 8, n. 9).

By the grouping of these other biblical paraphrases in the two Harington MSS. with No. 86, positively ascribed to Surrey by his contemporaries, we can thus reasonably conclude that they form the body of work to which Bale refers. In addition the content of some of the paraphrases, which frequently have personal interpolations, and the style substantiate further Surrey's authorship of Nos. 74-84 and 86-90.

Only on internal evidence can we conjecture when Surrey wrote his biblical paraphrases. No. 79 is of so impersonal a nature that it might have been composed at any time, although a poem of this kind is more likely to belong to maturity than to youth. The other Psalms and the two prologues undoubtedly were composed shortly before Surrey's execution on January 19, 1546/47, and were therefore written in the Tower, where he was confined after December 12. The five chapters on Ecclesiastes, which form a kind of commentary on the vanity of worldly riches and ambition, may have been written earlier in 1546, as Nott suggested (p. 377), after Surrey had been relieved of his command in France and had returned to England, a disillusioned young man, but not yet facing charges of treason. It is well to keep in mind that there were several periods in Surrey's life when he might have reflected on the vanity of worldly things. Bapst (*Deux Gentilshommes-Poètes*, 1891, pp. 360-61), Padelford (p. 42), and Casady (*Henry Howard, Earl of Surrey*, 1938, p. 209) assign the composition of the Ecclesiastes paraphrases also to the Tower period. I find it impossible to believe, as does Casady, that Surrey could have written these after the Psalms as an expression of calm philosophic resignation.

The paraphrases should not be described as translations, since they do not follow the biblical chapters closely. Nos. 81, 83, and 84 especially are a vehicle for the expression of Surrey's personal feelings, as is true in similar paraphrases written by the Dudley brothers in prison (see Nos. 289 and 290).

No. 79 illustrates very well Surrey's freedom, although the paraphrase remains impersonal. Psalm 8 in the Vulgate has ten short verses, but Surrey has expanded these to forty-six lines. The concluding five lines present what I should term a free rendition of the *Gloria*. It is quite possible, I think, that Surrey may have had a continental source for No. 79.

[80] *Wheare rechelesse youthe in a vnquyet brest*

Hand A. A penciled note by Bishop Percy in the right margin reads, "Intended for ye new Edit^n^. of Surrey's Poems."

A copy in *P*, fol. 63^r^, has no variants.

Thomas Park, who printed the poem from *P* in his 1804 edition of the *NA*, ii, 360, misread "deny" (the *P* spelling of "denny," line 5) as "devy," which he interprets as "deviation," referring to Surrey's failure to follow royal proclamations on religion. Thus by the misreading of one word, Park misconstrued the total meaning of this prologue to Psalm 88 (No. 81). Nott's text (*Surrey and Wyatt*, i [1815], 78; notes pp. 390-91) is taken from *AH*; Padelford's (*Poems*, 1928, No. 35), from *P*.

As has been pointed out by Bapst (*Deux Gentilshommes-Poètes*, 1891, p. 361) and Padelford, the lines of No. 80 were addressed to Sir Anthony Denny (1501-1549), a member of the Privy Council and a secretary of state during the last years of Henry VIII's reign. It was his duty to affix the royal signature to official documents. For sometime before the end of his life, Henry VIII was unable to sign his name, and a stamp was used. Surrey's enemies may have prevailed upon Denny to use the stamp upon the documents concerned with Surrey's conviction. Surrey here seems to forgive Denny for the act and to recognize his own blame.

An epitaph upon Denny is in *TM* (ed. Rollins, No. 227), which is mistakenly attributed to Surrey in John Weever's *Ancient Funeral Monuments*, 1631, p. 852. Denny, of course, died two years after Surrey was executed. Lines in the epitaph indicate that Denny was disliked because of the royal favor.

[81] *O Lorde vppon whose will/ dependith my welfare*

Hand A. There are a number of erasures in the copy, and in several instances the erased word is still visible: line 4, "as" over an erased "that"; line 9, "me cast" over an erasure; line 16, the "ai" in "appaire" formed over other letters; line 24, "praise" over an erased "faithe"; line 26, "nor" over an erasure; line 27, "blazed" over an erased "blasted"; line 44, "to" over an erased "for."

A copy in *P*, fol. 63^r, v^, is headed as in *AH*. A later hand has there indicated in the margin that it should read "Psal: 88" instead of 98. In the Vulgate it is Psalm 87.

Nott's modernized text is taken from *AH* (*Surrey and Wyatt*, i [1815], 78-79; notes, pp. 391-92); Padelford's is from *P* (*Poems*, 1928, No. 55). Park's is also from *P* (*NA*, ii [1804], 361-63), although he ill-advisedly printed this and the other paraphrases in half lines. He seems not to have understood poulter's measure, for he says, "For typographical convenience and uniformity the alexandrine couplet has been divided into the stanza measure" (ii, 340, note).

The corrections indicated above should be studied in relation to the *P* variants:

4 as] that
9 me cast/ headlong] cast me hedling
13 banisht] bannyshed
17 do] did
18 thyne] thy
24 praise] faith
26 nor] as
27 blazed] blasted
28 shutt] shitt
36 shuld'st] sholdest
44 to] for

It is interesting to find that in lines 4, 17, 24, 27, and 44 the *P* MS. agrees with the erased reading in *AH*. In lines 9 and 26 this is probably true also, but the erased words are not decipherable in *AH*. Evidence such as this suggests that copies of No. 81 in *AH* and *P* may have been made from a common source and that *AH* was then corrected, either by a reviser, or by another copy. In line 27 especially the *AH* reading is necessary to maintain the sense of the Psalm. For further discussion on the relation of these two manuscripts, see the Introduction, pp. 40-44; and for an introductory account of Surrey's biblical paraphrases, see the Note on No. 79.

It is not difficult to understand Surrey's choice of this Psalm, for it is directly applicable to his own situation. The mood of repentance and humility, so touchingly expressed here, is not repeated in the two other Psalms (Nos. 83 and 84) belonging to the period of his last imprisonment. We do not know the order in which the three were written, but this Psalm precedes the others in both *AH* and *P*, which indicates that it may have been done first. It is reasonable to believe that Surrey brought himself to a feeling of resignation shortly after his conviction, but as he brooded over his wrongs in prison, became more bitter toward his enemies when he realized that he was actually to die on unjust charges.

This paraphrase follows the Latin of the Vulgate fairly closely, although in some lines there is change either in sense or implication. For example, the Latin for lines 9-10 reads, "Posuerunt me in lacu inferiori, in tenebrosis, et in umbra mortis." In lines 13-14 Surrey places the blame for the defection of his friends directly upon them, not upon the Lord, as in the Vulgate, "Longe fecisti notos meos a me; posuerunt me abominationem sibi." Lines 19-30, which paraphrase very freely verses 11-13 in the Vulgate, seem also to draw upon a Protestant commentary (line 22). In lines 24 and 27 the *AH* readings, though not directly translations, convey the sense of the original better than those of *P*. I suspect the mistaken "blasted" of *P* occurred because the word was first written "blased." The implication in the Latin for lines 43-44 differs, "Elongasti a me amicum et proximum; et notos meos a miseria." It was not God who was keeping Surrey's loved ones from him.

[82] *The soudden stor̃mes that heave me to and frow*

Hand A.

A copy in *P*, fol. 63^v, has one variant, "well" instead of "will" in line 11. Either is possible, but I think the *P* reading better fits the context. Nott's modernized text is based on *AH* (*Surrey and Wyatt*, i [1815], 80; notes, p. 392); Padelford's on *P* (*Poems*, 1928, No. 36); and Park's on *P* (*NA*, ii [1804], 364).

As No. 80, addressed to Sir Anthony Denny, is a prologue for Surrey's paraphrase of Psalm 88, so this short poem, addressed to "my Blage" is a prologue for Psalm 73. Both prologues are written in a spirit of penitence, asking for forgiveness.

Since George Blage is the author of No. 295, an account of him is given on the Note to that poem. Here we need to consider only his relations with Surrey. Blage accompanied Surrey to France in October, 1543, shortly before the battle of Landrecy (Nott, same vol., Appendix XI; Bapst, *Deux Gentilshommes-Poètes*, 1891, p. 278, n. 3), when presumably they were on friendly terms. In using the address "my Blage," Surrey suggests that a warm personal relationship had once existed between them. The deposition of Edward Rogers, taken at the time of Surrey's trial in 1546, indicates that an altercation between Surrey and Blage had taken place some months previously, concerning the appointment of a protector in the event of Henry VIII's death. According to Rogers, Surrey "held that his father was meetest, both for good services done and for estate. Blage replied that then the Prince should be but evil taught; and, in multiplying words, said 'Rather than it should come to pass that the Prince should be under the government of your father or you, I would bide the adventure to thrust this dagger in you.' The Earl said he was very hasty and that God sent a shrewd cow short horns. 'Yea, my lord (quod Blage), and I trust your horns also shall be kept so short as ye shall not be able to do any hurt with them.' Afterwards the Earl, who at the time had no weapon, took sword and dagger and went to Blage's house 'and said unto him, that of late he had been very hasty with him' " (*Letters and Papers . . . of Henry VIII*, vol. xxi, part 2, ed. Gairdner and Brodie [1910], pp. 284-85, No. 555 [4]). The end of the dispute is not reported, but this testimony suited the purposes of Surrey's enemies, and indirectly made Blage one of those responsible for his conviction. No doubt, however, Surrey knew well enough that Blage was in reality not a leader in the conspiracy against him. Reflecting in the Tower upon the "soudden stormes" of the recent weeks, Surrey recognized the folly of his dispute with Blage, led thereto, so he tells us, by the seventy-third Psalm.

[83] *Thoughe Lord to Israell/ thy graces plentuous be*

Hand A. The following words or letters are written over erasures, indicating corrections: line 7, "payre" in "appayre"; line 10, "un" in "daunger," written over an erased *m*; line 16, "loftye lookes/ whyles they"; line 17, "handes"; line 44, "sleape"; line 54, the *d* in "dreede," written over an erased *t*. In line 11 the *c* in "sckornefull" has been squeezed in, probably by another hand.

A copy in *P*, fol. $64^{r,v}$, headed as in *AH*, has several variants. Nott's modernized text is based on *AH* (*Surrey and Wyatt*, i [1815], 80-82; notes, pp. 393-95); Padelford's is from *P* (*Poems*, 1928, No. 56); and Park's is from *P* (*NA*, ii [1804], 364-68).

7 appayre] appere
ed
14 gluttyd] glutt⟨en⟩ *correction written over letters*
18 skourdge] skourdge⟨s⟩
22 with] lyke
doth
25 doth know] ^ know
30 effectes] affects
35 whan] as
42 powres] power
43 dreames] dreme
fleece
47 fleece] ⟨fleshe⟩ *correction in another hand*
care
49 care] ⟨rare⟩
51 spirites] sprits
57 with'rid] withered
59 others] other; succours] succo^{r}

Since the corrected readings in five lines in *P* conform with *AH*, it seems probable that *P* was compared with *AH* and some changes made. I incline to think a common original, perhaps a bit difficult to read, lies behind both *AH* and *P*. An ignorant, or immature, copyist would not distinguish such differences as appear in lines 7, 30, 51, 57, and probably not those in lines 42, 43, and 59.

Surrey's paraphrase of Psalm 73 (Vulgate 72) is so free, with so many interpolations of the poet's thoughts, and so many departures from the strict sense of the Latin that it may be regarded as a poem, following generally the order of the Psalm, in which Surrey contrasts his own state with the well being of his enemies in this world and draws consolation from the expectation that in the next they will be herded with the goats, while he will be in glory among the sheep. Recognition of the error of his ways, to which he referred in the prologue (No. 82), is evidently to be interpreted only as regret for having accepted temporarily the standards of these wicked enemies. The tenor of the poem is not one of penitence but of self-righteousness.

I am indebted to my former student Nancy Blaicher Pollock, who prepared an M.A. thesis on Surrey's biblical paraphrases (Ohio State University, 1951), for calling my attention to *A Paraphrasis vpon all the Psalmes of Dauid*, 1539, by Johannes Campensis, which may have been known to Surrey.

In lines 13-18 Surrey is probably making a thrust at his diseased but ruthless sovereign, as he almost certainly did in his sonnet "Th'Assyrans king—in peas, with fowle desyre" (Padelford, No. 40). The Vulgate, verses 7-8, omits reference to those who fawn before such power:

> Prodiit quasi ex adipe iniquitas eorum; transierunt in affectum cordis.
>
> Cogitaverunt, et locuti sunt nequitiam; iniquitatem in excelso locuti sunt.

A suggestion for Surrey's passage is in Campensis "Euery man that meteth them, is afrayde of them by reason of theyr power, which is waxen so greate, that they gyue no force whether theyr wyckednesse and vyolence be knowne or no (wherby they oppresse the poore) . . ." (sig. K2^{v}).

Lines 21-22 may be compared with Campensis, "Soche thynges shall cause ye people of God to wauer, reuoluinge in theyr mynde now one thing nowe another, & these thinges lyke bytter waters in a full cuppe, shalbe set before them to dryncke" (sig. K3^{r}). Verse 10 runs, "Ideo convertetur populus meus hic; et dies pleni invenientur in eis."

Lines 23-34, which place emphasis on the "electe" and the "Chosen," depart freely from the Vulgate, verses 11-15,

> Et dixerunt: Quomodo scit Deus, et si est scientia in excelso?
>
> Ecce ipsi peccatores, et abundantes in sæculo, obtinuerunt divitias.
>
> Et dixi: Ergo sine causa justificavi cor meum, et lavi inter innocentes manus meas;
>
> et fui flagellatus tota die, et castigatio mea in matutinis.
>
> Si dicebam: Narrabo sic; ecce nationem filiorum tuorum reprobavi.

The biblical justification for the emphasis on the chosen is, of course, in the last verse.

Lines 43-48 have their basis in verse 20 of the Vulgate, "Velut somnium surgentium, Domine, in civitate Tua imaginem ipsorum adi nihilum rediges." Surrey's figurative language probably resulted from Greek, or Latin, myth.

Lines 55-58 re-introduce the figure of the voyage, mentioned in the prologue, which has no basis in the Latin. Compare Campensis, "And thorowe thy councell thou kepedest me euer company in my iourneye what waye so euer I went, And at the last thou shalt receaue me vnto the as partaker of thy magestie" (sig. K4^{r}).

Lines 63-66 twist the Latin to suggest that because the poet has put his trust in the Lord, he can be of the elect. Compare Campensis, "Wherfore when I had persuaded my selfe that it shulde be very profytable for me to come in to fauoure wyth the true GOD I set all my confydence in the Lorde God, trustynge that in tyme to come he wolde gyue me lycence to wrytte those dyuerse and most perfyte workes whyche he hath contynually in hande" (sig. K4^{r}). The closing verses in the Vulgate merely say that it is good to trust the Lord—a very different concept.

[84] *Geave eare to my sute lord, fromward hyde not thie face*

Hand A. In line 2 "herken" was probably originally copied as "herking" (see collation), as the "en" and line following are written over an erasure. In line 7 "overwhealm'the" is written over an erasure and in line 43, "whiche," where the preceding word, "Coales," is evidently a copyist's error for "Coates." The translation of the Latin ending, beginning with "id est" in line 48 and continuing through line 49, is written in another ink and in smaller script, though I believe it to be also Hand A. The smaller script was necessary because the "ffinis" had already been written. As the punctuation also indicates, it was clearly added later to the copy, and was probably not a part of the poem as Surrey left it.

The copy in *P*, fol. 65^{r,v}, to which I have referred, has the same heading as that in *AH*. Nott's modernized text is based on *AH* (*Surrey and Wyatt*, i [1815], 83-84, notes; pp. 395-98); Padelford's is taken from *P* (*Poems*, 1928, No. 54); and Park's is from *P* (*NA*, ii [1804], 368-71).

2 herken *altered from herking* (?)] herking
5 spirit] spryte
7 of dread, cleane] $^{\text{of dred}}_{\wedge}$ clene; overwhealm'the] ouerwhelmeth
11 speedie] sp$^{e}_{\wedge}$ady; they] the^{i}⟨n⟩ *correction in different ink*

⟨do⟩ e
15 kepe walles] ‸ kep⟨t⟩ ⟨the⟩ walles
ioyn'd ⟨ek⟩
16 myschief ioyn'de] ⟨whiles⟩ myschief *correction in a different hand*
ne
18 ne] ⟨then⟩ *correction in same hand as preceding*
for
20 en'myes] enemyes; for to] ⟨not⟩ to
21 coulde haue] cold ⟨not⟩ haue
ll
26 hym self] ⟨t⟩ hym he⟨e⟩
29 aulture] ⟨h⟩ aulture
30 moves] moueth
39 half] halfte
43 Coales] cootes
47 the other] the thother; psalme] phalme *obvious error*
The "id est" of line 48 and line 49 are omitted in P.

This collation from two Harington MSS. is interesting but difficult to interpret. Once more I incline to the opinion that a common original was used for both, but that there was a later check between *AH* and *P*. The handwriting of *P* seems to be that of Sir John Harington's daughter Frances, who probably did not always understand the sense of the lines. Possibly a tutor was responsible for some of the corrections. It may be that Frances was given the exercise of copying this poem from an original in so rough a state that it was difficult to decipher. Since the corrected readings in lines 7, 11, 15, 16, 18, 20, 21, and 29 of *P* accord with those lines in *AH*, we must recognize a positive connection in these two family manuscripts; but the variants in lines 2, 26, 30, and 43, especially, indicate another source. I offer the tentative suggestion that *AH* was copied from this source by a mature person and then used as a partial check for *P*. The reading of line 26 in *AH* was probably not adopted because it is contrary to the sense (see below).

Both manuscripts place this paraphrase of Psalm 55 (Vulgate 54) last in the order of the Psalms paraphrases, and in *P* it marks the end of Surrey's nine biblical paraphrases. We should not ignore this arrangement, although that alone would not give us sufficient reason for considering No. 84 the last in order of composition. It should be kept in mind, however, that the paraphrases of Psalms 88 and 73, believed to be written during Surrey's last imprisonment, are introduced by prologues and are more polished in style; whereas Psalm 55 is sometimes obscure and is left unfinished. Most significant, however, is Psalm 55 itself, which becomes the medium for Surrey's deepest expression of bitterness and despair, contrasting markedly from the assured superiority maintained in Psalm 88 and the somewhat calm attitude of penitence expressed in Psalm 73. There it is as if he felt that true penitence would bring him forgiveness—and life. That Surrey did not attain final resignation to his fate nor any lasting sense of forgiveness toward his real enemies is plainly revealed in the lines beginning, "The stormes are past these cloudes are ouerblowne" (*TM*, ed. Rollins, No. 34), with the title, "Bonum est mihi quod humiliasti me," which is taken almost verbatim from Psalm 118, verse 71 (Vulgate). According to Surrey's son Henry Howard, Earl of Northampton, this poem was the last thing his father wrote (as stated in the dedication to Queen Elizabeth of his "A dutifull defence of the lawfull regiment of Weomen," Bodleian MS. 903, fol. 6[r]). The last six lines of the poem, left imperfect, violently and bitterly contradict the mood of calm resignation and spiritual freedom expressed in the beginning lines:

> But when my glasse presented vnto me.
> The curelesse wound that bledeth day and nyght,
> To think (alas) such hap should graunted be
> Vnto a wretch that hath no hart to fight,
> To spill that blood that hath so oft bene shed,
> For Britannes sake (alas) and now is ded.

Lines 18-25 of No. 84, based on verses 13-15 of the Vulgate, are believed to refer to the "wretch" mentioned above, Surrey's old friend Sir Richard Southwell, who betrayed him (Bapst, *Deux Gentilshommes-Poètes*, 1891, pp. 346-55; Padelford, pp. 37, 40, and note on Psalm 55; Casady, *Henry Howard, Earl of Surrey*, 1938, pp. 190-95).

Surrey's trial was held January 13, 1546/47, and he was executed January 19. During these final days he must have suffered his darkest despair and endured his greatest struggles between bitterness and resignation. It was then, I believe, that he turned to Psalm 55, writing a close paraphrase, for the Psalm itself spoke for him. Perhaps with a prologue or epilogue in mind, he wrote his last poem. (Bapst, pp. 360-61, Padelford, p. 231, and Casady, pp. 208-09, take the view that Psalm 55 was written before Psalms 88 and 73. Casady holds that the Ecclesiastes chapters were composed last.) It is perhaps significant that Surrey abandoned poulter's measure, in which the other biblical paraphrases and most of his longer poems were written, and used a blank verse of unrhymed hexameters, which though less effective than the unrhymed pentameters which he adopted for the *Aeneid*, have more gravity and are more suited to the tragic state of mind than are the rhymed couplets of poulter's measure (for other examples of unrhymed hexameters, see Nos. 282-85).

Line 26 presents a problem as to what Surrey actually wrote or meant. The first part of verse 16 in the Vulgate has, "Veniat mors super illos; et descendant in infernum viventes." The reading in *P* is nearer to the Latin and conveys the idea, whereas *AH* does not. Perhaps Surrey meant, "May death him sudden surprise; quick (i.e., living) may him hell devour," which except for the change from "them" to "him," apparently intentional, would be very near the original.

Lines 32-33 depart from the sense of the Latin, verse 19, "Redimet in pace animam meam ab his, qui appropinquant mihi, quoniam inter multos erant mecum." The rendering of "qui appropinquant mihi" in the text must be taken as the passage "those that prelooked on, with Ire to slawghter me and myne." Nott suggests "pressed" for "prelooked," and the *N.E.D.*, quoting this line as the only example of the word, considers that there is "evidently some error" and suggests "prikked." But I think we can construe "prelooked" as one of Surrey's many coined words, having in it the idea of a preconceived scheme of attack as the enemy pushed forward. In 1535 Myles Coverdale had translated the passage as "them that laye waite for me" (*The Holy Scriptures . . . translated . . . by Myles Coverdale*, 1847), which conveys the idea of a previously set trap, as does this suggested interpretation of Surrey's line. Quite apart from the freedom of the paraphrase for all of verse 19, the tense is changed from the future to the past. It is as if Surrey had been freed from the toils of his enemies, whereas the whole of the rest of the poem shows that he did not so consider himself.

Surrey breaks off suddenly with verse 22 of the Vulgate and in lines 42-46 reproaches a "friour," some cleric whose identity is unknown, for an offence which he felt to be unforgivable, perhaps a breach of confidence.

Verses 23 and 24 of the Vulgate are left untranslated, and Surrey ends with the Latin of the first half of verse 23. Perhaps he had no time to complete the Psalm.

A paraphrase of Psalm 55 was written by John Dudley, Earl of Warwick, when he was confined in the Tower in 1553-54 (see No. 289).

[85] *Good Ladies you that have/ your pleasure in exyle*

Hand A. The name "Preston" below the poem is in the same hand. In the upper right-hand margin is Percy's penciled note, "Printed in Surrey's Poems fo 9."

Included among Surrey's poems in *TM*, sigs, C1^{v}-C2^{r} (ed. Rollins, No. 19), the poem is there entitled, "Complaynt of the absence of her louer being vpon the sea." The printed version has two more lines and shows a number of other divergences. Nott's text (*Surrey and Wyatt*, i [1815], 14-15; notes, pp. 264-67) is a combination of *TM* and *AH*; Padelford's (*Poems*, 1928, No. 33) is from *N*, fol. 31^{r,v}.

1 you . . . pleasure] ye . . . pleasures
5 you] ye
7 youe] ye
9 lord and love] loue and lord
11 That . . . myndes] Whome I was wont tembrace with well contented minde
12 wyndes] winde
13 Theare . . . send] Where God well him preserue, and sone him home me send

Between 14 and 15 TM adds two lines:

Whose absence yet, although my hope doth tell me plaine,
With short returne he comes anon, yet ceasith not my payne.

15 they] do
16 then] when; and stand] I lye; yf] where
17 they] do
18 that . . . lye] That my dere Lord (ay me alas) me thinkes I se him die
20 T. his] his faire
21 lyfesome] leefsom
22 thinckes] think; now . . . home] welcome my lord
24 betwixt] atwixt
28 breakes] Breake; dischardgeth] dischargen; great] huge
29 fyndes] finde
32 wheare . . . mynd] place, wherein to slake the gnawing of my mind
34 there is] I find; some] good
35 feele the] think, by
37 when that we two] when we
38 tyme] while; that] the
39 convart] coniure
40 you] ye
41 suche] this

The two most significant peculiarities of the *AH* copy of No. 85 are somewhat paradoxical, and, curiously, they have not been carefully considered by Surrey's editors. In the first place, we have a poem presumably ascribed to one "Preston" which nevertheless occurs in the midst of the Surrey group (see the Introduction, p. 27), thereby inferentially according with the *TM* attribution of Surrey's authorship. In the second place, the *AH* reading of line 20 by specifying "T. his lytle sonne" tends to connect the poem with Surrey, whose eldest son, Thomas, was born March 10, 1536 (Nott, "Memoirs," pp. xxx-xxxi; Padelford, p. 13; Casady, *Henry Howard, Earl of Surrey*, 1938, pp. 52-53. Bapst, *Deux Gentilshommes-Poètes*, 1891, pp. 232-33, gives the date as 1538). In

TM the child is left anonymously "faire." Nott, who used the *AH* original, does not refer to "Preston." Padelford, who used the transcript, merely notes the name in his textual variants, and says in his critical notes, "This poem was clearly written for the Countess of Surrey while Surrey was separated from her during his winter of military service in France." Rollins, dismissing the manuscript signature, continues, "Obviously, however, the poem was written for the Countess of Surrey by her husband during his military service in France, September, 1545-March, 1546." But these conclusions are not so certain for this editor; at least we must consider the use of Preston's name, and, further, recognize that even if the poem is Surrey's, it may have been written as early as 1543.

As I have suggested in the Introduction (pp. 30-31), "Preston" may refer to one Thomas Preston, who in 1533 wrote Thomas Cromwell as follows, "As it hath pleased the King through your Mastership's mediation to give me a living and a yearly pension, and I understand by my brother Barthelet that you would see my fashion of writing, I send you a specimen." Presumably he is the Thomas Preston who shortly before had been appointed as one of the Princess Mary's Gentlemen Waiters and is recorded as carrier of a letter from the princess to her mother. In 1536 Thomas Preston received a monetary award from the king, and in 1537 he was made clerk of the peace and of the Crown in Notts and Derby. In 1542 he was granted a lease of lands in Herts, which had belonged to Queen Jane Seymour. In 1544, described as "King's servant," he and his wife Agnes receive a lease in St. Botolph's parish, London (information taken from *Letters and Papers . . . Henry VIII*, ed. J. Gairdner, or Gairdner and R. H. Brodie, 1882-1903, *passim*, as follows: vol. vi, no. 1674; same vol., nos. 1199, 1522, respectively; vol. xi, no. 516; vol. xii, part 2, no. 411 [35]; vol. xvii, no. 1154 [38]; vol. xix, part 1, no. 1036). Our problem would be much simpler if we knew just what Preston meant by his "fashion of writing." It is possible that we do have the name of an unknown poet, who, if the author of No. 85, was exceptionally gifted. But in using such an expression Preston may have been referring to his handwriting, which in that case must have been worthy of such attention that he could have been employed as an amanuensis. We may then in the *AH* copy of No. 85 have a poem which was taken from a copy made by Thomas Preston. Since the poem is grouped with other Surrey poems in *AH*, it does appear that the Haringtons regarded it as Surrey's, although this circumstance cannot be taken as a certain guide. It is also possible that Preston, the "King's servant" in 1544 was the bearer of the poem from Surrey to his wife, and it was so marked, as was the letter carried for the Princess Mary (for other examples of letters marked with the names of the bearers, see my edition of *The Correspondence of Lady Katherine Paston, 1603-1627*, Norfolk Record Society, xiv [1941], 27, and notes on Nos. 53-80, *passim*). Since the poem itself has characteristics of Surrey's style, I find it difficult to believe that it was written by anyone else for the Countess of Surrey or another woman. In considering the question of Surrey's authorship of No. 85, the reader must, of course, compare it with other of his poems (e.g., Padelford, Nos. 1, 18, 21, 30, 31). The poem beginning, "O happy dames, that may embrace" (No. 21) is often associated with this one, but in the *NA* (ed. 1769, p. 187) that poem is attributed to John Harington (see the Introduction, p. 22).

It is evident from lines 10, 12, 17, 39 that No. 85 was conceived as written upon the high seas. Surrey first served in the war in France in the autumn of 1543, when he took part in the battle of Landrecy. He returned to England before Christmas, but in the summer of 1544 he was back in the campaign. During the early part of 1544 Surrey gave much attention to his family and was occupied in the building of a handsome new home, Mount Surrey. His son Thomas was just eight years old, and his father had more opportunity than usual to enjoy him. It must have been hard to leave this domestic felicity and return to another military siege. I suggest that Surrey wrote the poem as a letter for his wife as he crossed the Channel, and that the copy brought to Lady Surrey bore the name of Preston, as copyist, or carrier. (For Surrey's activities during 1543-44, see Bapst, pp. 274-308; Casady, pp. 102-26.)

In her discussion of Surrey's diction, Veré L. Rubel, *Poetic Diction in the English Renaissance* (New York, M. L. A. of America, 1941, pp. 57-82) calls attention to a number of examples in this poem. She points out that the expression "Stepp in your foote" (line 2), in the sense, "set your foot," antedates the first instance cited in the *N.E.D.* The Scottish origin, through Gawain Douglas of "lyfesome" (line 21), that is, pleasing, is noted. The Chaucerian words "saluith" (line 25) and "vnneth" (line 31) she thinks were given "a renewed existence through Surrey's use of them" (p. 67). We may also note "convart" in line 39, in the sense, "direct," for which the *N.E.D.* has no example after 1577.

[86] *I Salamon Davids sonne/ Kinge of Ierusalem*

Hand A. Lines 26-44 are in a different ink but in the same hand. The following are written over erasures: line 14, "Then" and the *t* in "fast," in the second ink; line 27, "all . . . the s"; line 38, "errours."

A copy in *P*, fols. 58v-59r, has the title, "Cap. 1. Eccles." Written in the hand of Sir John Harington's daughter Ellina, as are Surrey's five Ecclesiastes paraphrases in *P*, the *P* version shows that it was copied by an inexperienced amanuensis. In the Note on No. 79 I have referred to the *P* copy and have mentioned contemporary quotations from this paraphrase.

Nott's text is based on *AH* (*Surrey and Wyatt*, i [1815], 66-67;

notes, pp. 376-79); Padelford's is from *P* (*Poems*, 1928, No. 48); and Park's is from *P* (*NA*, ii [1804], 339-42).

5 Children] Childeren

9 Chaunges] chaung^{e}s

13 Hoarrye] h$_{\wedge}^{a}$orrey; blast] blast⟨s⟩ *s erased*

18 skarce] skace

22 As] A⟨ll⟩^{s}

24 even] Euen so

26 my voyce] $_{\wedge}^{my}$ voyce

27 all] ⟨straunge⟩^{all} *see line 29*

32 vayne myxed] $_{\wedge}^{uaine}$ mixed

35 gan] ⟨gall⟩^{gan}

37 And] ⟨that elders⟩ and *see line 36*

41 skoole] ⟨skolle⟩^{skoole}

The corrections in *P* appear to have been made by a comparison with *AH*. See the Introduction, pp. 41-42.

Surrey's paraphrase of Ecclesiastes 1 is reasonably close to the Vulgate, although the sense of the Latin is sometimes expanded or expressed in figurative language.

Lines 5-6 render freely the Latin, "Quid habet amplius homo de universo labore suo, quo laborat sub sole?" (verse 3).

Line 10, not in the Vulgate, adds a classic note. Lines 7-9 translate "Generatio præterit, et generatio advenit; terra autem in æternum stat" (verse 4).

Lines 13-14, which echo Chaucer, are Surrey's figurative Englishing for the sixth verse in the Vulgate.

Lines 33-34 depart curiously from the Latin, "Perversi difficile corriguntur, et stultorum infinitus est numerus" (verse 15).

[87] *ffrom pencife fancies then/ I gan my heart revoke*

Hand A. In the following lines words or letters are written over erasures: 9. "stormes"; 51. "To sharppe"; 56. "glories"; 71. "mple." In line 61 the *w* of "low" is written over an *o* or an *e*.

A copy in *P*, fols. 59^{r,v}-60^{r}, entitled, "Cap. 2. Eccles:", is written in the hand of Ellina Harington.

4 alwayes] ⟨When they most l⟩ Allways *see line 3*
9 I] of
22 tewnes] times
26 so] to
35 mye] myne
43 sheene] shine
51 sharppe] sha^{r}pe
55 even] eun
72 the broken] w^{t} broken
74 or with] of o^{r}
76 sheene] shyne
82 may] my

The *P* readings are preferable in lines 9 and 74 and *AH* is better in lines 22 (see below) and 82.

Nott's text is based on *AH* (*Surrey and Wyatt*, i [1815], 67-70; notes, pp. 379-82); Padelford's is from *P* (*Poems*, 1928, No. 49); Park's is from *P* (*NA*, ii [1804], 343-48).

In contrast to Surrey's paraphrase of the first chapter of Ecclesiastes, this of the second chapter is so free that it may be termed a poem developed from the original.

Lines 11-17, based on verses 4-6 of the Vulgate, have a peculiar autobiographical significance, for Surrey must surely have had in mind the handsome palace he had built on St. Leonard's Hill near Norwich. It was seized by Kett's rebel forces in 1549 and used as their main camp. See Nott, vol. i, "Memoirs," pp. lx-lxi; Francis Blomefield and Charles Parkin, *An Essay Towards a Topographical History of the County of Norfolk*, iii (1806), 225, and iv (1806), 427; Walter Rye, "Surrey House and St. Leonard's Priory, Norwich," *Norfolk Archaeology*, xv (1904), 194-95.

In line 22 the "tewnes" of *AH* is the correct reading, for this passage expands the Latin expression, "feci mihi cantores et cantatrices" (in verse 8).

Lines 77-82 bring us finally to Surrey's reflection on himself as an example of one who knows the folly of material gain, but the expanded paraphrase lacks the compelling assurance and power of the preacher's words: "Homini bono in conspectu suo dedit Deus sapientiam, et scientiam et lætitiam; peccatori autem dedit afflictionem et curam superfluam, ut addat, et congreget, et tradat ei, qui placuit Deo; sed et hoc vanitas est, et cassa sollicitudo mentis" (verse 26).

[88] *Lyke to the stearlesse boate/ that swarves with everye wynde*

Hand A. In line 8 "Sprayes" is written over an erasure.

A copy in *P*, fols. $60^{r,v}$-61^{r}, entitled, "Capitulo. 3.Eccles.," is written in the hand of Ellina Harington.

Nott's text is based on *AH* (*Surrey and Wyatt*, i [1815], 70-72; notes, pp. 382-85); Padelford's, on *P* (*Poems*, 1928, No. 50); Park's, on *P* (*NA*, ii [1804], 348-52).

1 boate/ that] $^{\text{boote}}_{\wedge}$ that
3 Skarce] Skace
10 revyves] re^{uiues}⟨ioyce⟩
13 springes] spring
16 travail'd] trauelid; vnlose] un⟨c⟩lose *see line 17*
30 searche] se$^{\text{r}}_{\wedge}$che
43 wand'rid] wanderyd; sore] ^{s}⟨h⟩ore
44 eke wheare/ as] $^{\text{eke}}_{\wedge}$ wher⟨as⟩ ^{as}⟨that⟩
51 This] His
53 that beast] the beaste
55 thath] hathe; geven to either man] ⟨ether⟩ geuen to $^{\text{ether}}_{\wedge}$ man
65 me] may
66 to fore know] to $^{\text{fore}}_{\wedge}$ know

As is obvious, the corrections in *P* conform with the *AH* readings. See Notes on Nos. 86 and 87 and Introduction, pp. 40-44.

As with Surrey's paraphrase of the second chapter of Ecclesiastes, this of the third chapter is so free that it is better described as a poem developed from the original. The first eight verses in the Vulgate are built on the figure of *epanados*. The topic is set out in the opening verse, "Omnia tempus habent, et suis spatiis transeunt universa sub cælo." In verses 2-8 *tempus* is taken as the key word for repetition and elaboration. Surrey in lines 1-20 has departed completely from this forceful method of the preacher, so that his paraphrase seems at first to have little connection with his source. In contrast the familiar verses in the King James version follow closely the Vulgate.

In lines 25-26 Surrey expresses beautifully, though not exactly, the Latin "Cuncta fecit bona in tempore suo" of verse 11. In continuing his paraphrase on the rest of that verse in lines 27-30, he remains close to the

Latin, but is more awkward in his rendering of "et mundum tradidit disputationi eorum, ut non inveniat homo opus, quod operatus est Deus ab initio usque ad finem."

Lines 43-46 are derived from verse 16 of the Vulgate, "Vidi sub sole in loco judicii impietatem, et in loco justitiae iniquitatem." Surrey is more concrete than the Latin here indicates and may have had in mind a passage in Revelation or one from medieval allegory.

Although lines 47-58 are fairly free, they nevertheless convey generally the thought in verses 17-21 of the Vulgate.

In lines 61-66 Surrey has introduced the classic concept of the mean as the desirable aim for man and has therefore changed the emphasis of the Vulgate, verse 22, "Et deprehendi nihil esse melius, quam laetari hominem in opere suo, et hanc esse partem illius. Quis enim eum adducet, ut post se futura cognoscat?"

[89] *When I bethought me well/ vnder the restles Sonne*

Hand A. The following are written over erasures: line 10, *w* in "wronges," over an erased *g*; line 11, *w* in "sawe"; line 44, "tracing." In line 20 "glutted" was first written "glutten." In line 42 *v* in "greeved" is written over a letter not decipherable.

A copy in *P*, fols. $61^{r,v}$-62^{r}, entitled, "Capitulo. 4. Eccles.," is in the hand of Ellina Harington.

Nott's text is based on *AH* (*Surrey and Wyatt*, i [1815], 73-75; notes, pp. 385-87); Padelford's, on *P* (*Poems*, 1928, No. 51); Park's, on *P* (*NA*, ii [1804], 352-56).

5 terrours] terroure

                    ease
13 and] of; ease] ⟨eache⟩
22 they] the

                    thre fould
34 brayded three folde may] brayded ^ may
40 Septer] sept⟨u⟩re
44 goe] groo

          deth
45 death] ⟨change⟩

                    g
54 golden ghoost] yolden ⟨h⟩oost *g written over h*

               re
58 vnsav'reth] unsaue ^ th

In the Note on No. 87 I have discussed a probable relation between these manuscript versions. The variants in lines 44 and 54 are mentioned below.

Lines 1-36 closely follow the Vulgate, verses 1-13, but in lines 37-58 Surrey writes very freely, sometimes departing almost entirely from the

Latin text. This point is at once apparent by comparing lines 37-44 with verse 14 of the Vulgate, "quod de carcere catenisque interdum quis egrediatur ad regnum; et alius natus in regno, inopia consumatur." Surrey has deliberately changed from the third to the first person and appears to be commenting on his own observations in prison. Is it possible that the "wofull wight" who "never knew what freedom ment" may refer to young Edward Courtenay (1526?-1556)? At the age of twelve Edward Courtenay was sent to the Tower with his father, Henry, Earl of Devonshire, who, as a cousin to the king, was arrested, attainted, and executed in 1538 on the charge of being an aspirant to the throne. Edward Courtenay remained in the Tower until Mary's accession in 1553, and he was therefore one of Surrey's fellow inmates in 1546. If Surrey does have Courtenay in mind, he is, of course, speaking of the despair that might be lifted if a scepter replaced the gyves. In lines 41-42 Surrey may be thinking of this conspiracy, or he could be reflecting on the death of his cousin Queen Catherine Howard, whereby any children she might have had were kept from rule, or perhaps he is thinking of himself and his father, who bore the arms of Edward the Confessor. Lines 44-45 offer another of the many comments on those who beg for favor at court. The *AH* reading in line 44 better suits the context.

Lines 45-50 derive from verses 15-16 of the Vulgate, but Surrey has reason to relate them to the impending death of Henry VIII. There were many, including himself, who would rejoice in a new reign, but with the preacher Surrey must admit that it will bring as much burden and dissension as the old reign.

The English Bible closes this chapter with verse 16, but the Vulgate includes as verse 17 the first verse of chapter 5. In lines 51-58 Surrey is paraphrasing freely both this verse and the second of the fifth chapter (i.e., Vulgate 5:1), with interpolations of his own reflecting the doctrine of love and mercy emphasized in the New Testament.

Particularly interesting is the use of "coniures" in line 41. The *N.E.D.* quotes this line as the only example illustrating the word used as a noun, in the sense of conspiracies. In line 54, however, Surrey used an old form in "yolden," the *P* variant, meaning submissive (see the Note on No. 77, line 43). The *AH* copyist evidently did not understand the line and was perhaps misled by the alliteration in "golden ghoost," but the sense clearly is: and simple faith the yolden (i.e., yelden) spirit his mercy doth require.

[90] *When that repentaunt teares/ hath cleansid cleare from yll*

Hand A. The following are written over erasures: line 18, "ne own"; line 38, "riche mãns." The reading in line 18 was probably first written in the form of the variant listed in the collation.

A copy in *P*, fol. 62^{r,v}, entitled, "Capitulo. 5. Eccles./", is written in the hand of Ellina Harington.

Nott's text is based on *AH* (*Surrey and Wyatt*, i [1815], 75-77; notes, pp. 387-90); Padelford's, on *P* (*Poems*, 1928, No. 52); Park's, on *P* (*NA*, ii [1804], 356-60).

4 sayth] fayth *copyist's error*; none] no^{ne}⟨t⟩
10 Chatt'ring] chattering
15 bet] bet⟨ter⟩
17 workes] wor^{ks}⟨ds⟩
18 thyne owne] thy nown
27 withouten] w^{t}out‸^{en}
28 suffreth] suffereth
29 to]⟨the⟩‸^{to}
30 mod'rate] moderat
31 greed'lye] gredely
32 the tillers hand] the ‸$^{\text{tillers ⟨toiling⟩}}$ hand
35 hordith] hurdeth
36 travailes] trau‸^{e}lls
40 thynne] thy^{n}ne
43 rightuous] ^{righteous}⟨gredy⟩
46 sparkled] sparkelid
48 Armes] clothes
50 boote] bote
51 men/ then that] men ‸^{then} that ^{then}⟨that⟩
55 Lyb'rall] liberall
56 poores] powres
61 No] ^{No}⟨Ne⟩
62 temp'ratte] temp⟨e⟩rat
64 seas'ned] season⟨e⟩d

A note in Thomas Park's handwriting following the poem in *P* reads, "The above variations marked H, from Dr. Harrington's copy, were inserted by Bp Percy." The "variations" from "Dr. Harrington's copy," i.e., *AH*, are written in the margin and are those of lines 35, 48, and 50, as noted above. Percy also gives "our" in line 28 of *AH* where *P* has "o^{r}," and "thirst," the last two letters now lost in the binding, in line 60, where *P* has "thurst."

The relation of the two versions is the same as has been pointed out for the first four chapters of Ecclesiastes, Nos. 86-89. Where the texts for No. 90 do not agree in a real variant, *AH* is preferable. Other differences are of spelling or rhythm.

Although Surrey's closing lines of the paraphrase of Ecclesiastes 4 include reference to the first verse of the fifth chapter in the Vulgate, he continues with that thought in the first eight lines of this paraphrase, emphasizing more than the Latin indicates the necessity for the contrite heart. Compare verse 1 in the Vulgate, "Ne temere quid loquaris, neque cor tuum sit velox ad proferendum sermonem coram Deo, Deus enim in cælo, et tu super terram; idcirco sint pauci sermones tui."

In the rest of the paraphrase Surrey renders some verses in the Vulgate closely and briefly and others freely and elaborately, or, one might say, not at all. Thus lines 9-13 treat briefly verses 2-4 in the Vulgate, but lines 14-20 are devoted to verse 5 alone. Again, in lines 21-32 Surrey closely follows verses 6-11, but in lines 33-44 he comments at length on verse 12, "Est et alia infirmitas pessima, quam vidi sub sole: divitiæ conservatæ in malum domini sui," no doubt meditating upon his own sumptuous living. Lines 45-46, which derive from verse 13 in the Vulgate, are ironically prophetic, for in 1549 Mount Surrey was sacked by Kett's rebels (see the Note on No. 87), and, of course, not long after this poem was written Surrey's "sparkled goods" were divided among his enemies, and his heirs were needy. Lines 47-52 follow closely the Vulgate, verses 14-16, but lines 53-64 freely paraphrase verses 17-18. Surrey introduces again, as in No. 88, the classic emphasis upon liberality and temperance, suggested but not so marked in the Vulgate. His closing lines do not touch the religious note of verse 19, "Non enim satis recordabitur dierum vitæ suae, eo quod Deus occupet deliciis cor ejus."

The reasonable, worldly tone of the end of the paraphrase would hardly have been achieved by a man doomed to die on the scaffold in a few days. It stands in sharp and tragic contrast with the close of his paraphrase of Psalm 55 (No. 84), which, as I have said, is an expression of bitter despair, the cry of a man whose only hope is not in temperate living but in the mercy of God in the face of death, unjustly decreed.

[91] *Owr belly-gods disprayse this Lenton faste*

Hand: Sir John Harington's secretary, with the ascription to himself in his italic script.

No. 91 occurs in three autograph manuscripts of Sir John's epigrams: (*A*) Cambridge University MS. Add. b.8.1, p. [27], written in Sir John's italic hand, and entitled, "In defence of Lent"; (*B*) British Museum MS. Add. 12049, the rough copy of the epigrams, pp. 103-04, written in his secretary hand, and headed as in *A*; (*C*) Folger Library MS. 4455, pp. 138-39, written in his italic hand, and headed as in *A*.

The *C* MS. is the fair copy of the book of epigrams made for Prince Henry. The dedicatory letter (first and second preliminary leaves, verso and recto) is dated June 19, 1605. N. E. McClure used *A* and *B* but not *AH* or *C* for his edition of *The Letters and Epigrams of Sir John Harington* (1930). Not included in the 1615 edition of the *Epigrams*, a version of No. 92 was first published in (*D*) *The most elegant and witty epigrams of Sir Iohn Harrington, Knight*, 1618, Book II, No. 90, with the title as in *A-C*. This edition was reprinted in 1625. Since copies of these two editions are not now available to me, I am using McClure's bibliographical descriptions, text (based on the 1618 edition), and collation (pp. 55-56, 222-23). According to *S.T.C.* 12778, a quarto edition of the *Epigrams*, printed by G. Miller, appeared in 1633. This edition is not mentioned by McClure, and I have not seen the unique copy in the British Museum. I have, however, examined the Ohio State University copy of Miller's folio edition with title-page dated 1633, which is appended with continuous signatures to the 1634 edition of Sir John's *Orlando Furioso*. This is described by McClure (p. 56) as a reprint of the 1625 edition. The text of No. 92, which appears on sig. Rr 4^{v} (in error for sig. Qq 4), agrees with that of *D*.

The collation following indicates that the version of No. 92 in *AH* represents the earliest writing of the poem. *A*, *B*, and *C*, which show revisions, are usually in agreement, but in lines 17 and 21 *B* is in accord with *AH*, suggesting that *B* gives the second stage. Since *D* was printed six years after Sir John's death, its variants, carried on in successive reprints, are of doubtful authority, unless evidence not now available should show that the changes were made by the author. The versions of *C*, carefully copied by Sir John, should almost certainly be taken as his final texts, although it is possible that between 1605 and 1612, the year of his death, he prepared the manuscript which was used by the printer.

1 this] the *A-D*
3 Swearing] And sweare *A-D*
6 only with] with naught but *A-D*
11 whome] home *D*; Heaven] heau'n *B D*
12 and] Yea *A-D*
13 scryptures doe] Scripture doth *D*
16 ev'ry] euery *A-D*
17 And] Are *A C D*; tast] tastes *D*
19 Sugar nor Currants] Both sugar, ginger *A-D*; nor] and *A-D*
20 Nor . . . nor] and . . . and *A-D*; any] ev'ry *A C*: every *B D*
21 Reasons [*i.e., raisins*] and] And Reasons *A*: And Raysons *C*: And Reysons *D*
23 shalbee] should be *D*

The poem, it should be noticed, is made up of one English sonnet plus two quatrains and the closing couplet of a second sonnet. The first quatrain presents the theme, and the third and fourth quatrains are balanced against the fifth and sixth quatrains, just as the first couplet balances the second.

5-6. Methuselah, who is referred to in Genesis 5:21, 25, 27, and I Chronicles 1:3, is said to have lived 969 years; but there is nothing in these verses about his feeding upon herbs and berries.

7-8. John the Baptist was but a few months older than Jesus, who was said to be about thirty when he was baptized by John (Luke 3:23). "And John was clothed with camel's hair, and with a girdle of a skin about his loins; and he did eat locusts and wild honey" (Mark 1:6).

9-10. See Exodus 2-16.

11. II Kings 2:1-11 gives the account of the translation of Elijah.

13-14. "Thease Three" are Moses, Elijah, and Jesus. When Moses went up on Mount Horeb to receive the tables of the covenant, he remained forty days and nights and "neither did eat bread nor drink water" (Deuteronomy 9:9). Elijah was fed by an angel in the wilderness and on the strength of that meat went forty days and nights (I Kings 19:4-8). When Jesus was tempted by the devil, he ate nothing for forty days and nights (Matthew 4:2; Luke 4:2).

[92] *fflye Sinne for sharp Revendge doth follow sinne*

Hand: Sir John Harington's.

In his notes to the twenty-second book of his translation of the *Orlando Furioso*, 1591, p. 175, Sir John Harington says:

> That wise and honorable counseller *Sir Walter Mildmay*, as in all other things he shewed him selfe an vncorrupt man to his end, so his writings and sayings were euer spiced with this reuerent feare of God: for *ex abundantia cordis os loquitur*: and among other of his (worth the noting) of which him selfe gaue me a little volume when I was a boy of Eton colledge (the which since his death haue bene published in print) but one speciall verse he had to that effect in Latin, and was by me put into English at the request of that honorable Gentleman his sonne in law, *Master William Fitzwilliams.*
>
> *Vltio peccatum sequitur delinquere noli,*
> *Nam scelus admissum pœna seuera premit:*
> *Quod si forte Deus, patiendo differat iram,*
> *Sera licet veniat, certa venire solet.*
>
> Flie sinne, for sharpe reuenge doth follow sinne,
> And wicked deeds, do wrathfull doomes procure

If God stay long ear he to strike beginne,
Though long he stay, at last he striketh sure.

A worthie saying of a most worthie man, and thus much for the morall.

Sir Walter Mildmay, 1520?-1589, was Chancellor of the Exchequer from 1566 until his death; in 1585 he founded Emmanuel College, Cambridge. The account of him in the *D. N. B.* mentions Sir John Harington's reference to Mildmay's book of Latin verses but states that it is otherwise unknown, and I have discovered nothing further about it.

The notes to Bk. XXII of Harington's *Orlando Furioso* are wanting in the two autograph manuscripts, Brit. Mus. MS. Add. 18920 and Bod. MS. Rawl. Poet. 125. There is a copy of No. 92 written in a seventeenth-century hand, in Sloane MS. 4454, fol. 61ᵛ, which the British Museum manuscript poetry index attributes to Katherine Austen. This copy agrees exactly with that given above.

[93] *With Petrarke to compare theare may no wight*

Hand A. In the right-hand margin is Bishop Percy's penciled note, "In Surrey's Poems fo. 71."

The only other contemporary version known is printed among the Uncertain Authors in *TM*, sig. Y1ᵛ (ed. Rollins, No. 219), headed, "That petrark cannot be passed but notwithstanding that Lawra is far surpassed." The printed copy is punctuated and some words are differently spelled, but there are no real variants. This sonnet and the preceding in *TM* are the only two in the miscellany written in praise of Petrarch. They were probably composed in competition or in sequence.

In the Introduction (p. 31) I have raised the question as to whether the Haringtons considered this sonnet to be Wyatt's. The large group of his poems in *AH* begins with No. 96, and it is possible that Nos. 93-95, all included among the Uncertain Authors of *TM*, were also regarded as his by the Haringtons. Since there are no other copies of these three poems, we have no additional external check on authorship, but we can consider the style of each poem.

To bring forward any points on rhythm is futile because we know that Wyatt's lines were edited both for *TM* and *AH* in order to produce a smoother metrical effect (Introduction, pp. 52-56). Of more significance, however, is the experimental six-rhyme pattern, *abba caac deed ff*. William R. Parker in "The Sonnets in 'Tottel's Miscellany'" (*PMLA*, liv [1939], 675) calls attention to the fact that this pattern varies only slightly from that of Wyatt's sonnet "Vnstable dreame, accordyng to the place" (Rollins, No. 42), which has the pattern *abba acca deed ff*. From this similarity as well as from the position of the sonnet in *AH*, Professor Parker tentatively suggests that No. 93 may be of Wyatt's composition. When we turn to the substance of the sonnet and its treatment, we are, I believe, in greater doubt of Wyatt's authorship, for although it is possible that Wyatt wrote this delicately turned compliment to Petrarch and his own lady, the manner is not characteristic. Except for his charming epigram "A face that shuld content me wonders well" (ed. Foxwell, i [1913], 61), Wyatt writes of the beauty of women only as it brings him pain or pleasure related to personal feeling. We are aware not so much of the looks of women as of their attraction or power in relation to the lover. This sonnet does have something of the manner of Surrey, as is evident by comparing "The golden gift that nature did thee geue" and "Geue place, ye louers, here before" (ed. Padelford, Nos. 8, 18), or of John Heywood as exemplified in "Geue place you Ladies and be gon" (*TM*, No. 199). No. 93 should also be compared with poems attributed to the elder John Harington. For example, "Marvaylous be thie matcheles gyftes of mynde" (*NA*, 1769, p. 198) also has a six-rhyme pattern, *abab cacd edef ff*, and has a similar emphasis in content on perfect proportion. Line 5 in No. 93 also reminds John Harington's reader of his sonnet on Admiral Seymour (*AH* No. 2), which has a curious five-rhyme pattern and has a touch of the same style. The felicitous line 8 of No. 93 is equalled by lines in Harington's beautiful poem beginning,

> Whence comes my love, O hearte, disclose,
> 'Twas from cheeks that shamed the rose. (*NA*, 1769, p. 129)

It may also be useful to compare three other poems in *TM*: "Lyke the Phenix a birde most rare in sight" (No. 260); "In court as I behelde, the beauty of eche dame" (No. 306); "Resigne you dames whom tikelyng brute delight" (No. 309). These poems have characteristics of Harington's style, but I cannot show that they are his.

It thus appears that I have argued against Wyatt's authorship of No. 93; but I do not deny that the Haringtons may have *known* that the poem was Wyatt's.

As a postscript I may add that I should like to know whether Sir Walter Ralegh was in any way influenced by No. 93 when he wrote his magnificent sonnet for Spenser's *Faerie Queene*, "Me thought I saw the graue, where *Laura* lay."

[94] *It was the day on whiche the Sonne depryved of his light*

Hand A. In line 13 the "aūn" of "vaūntt" is written over an erasure. In line 9 the final letter of "approche" may be a *t* instead of an *e* (see collation). Percy's penciled note is written in the upper right-hand margin, "In Surrey's Poems fo. 90."

This sonnet was first printed among the Uncertain Authors in the second edition of *TM*, sig. Z2^{r} (ed. Rollins, No. 277), where it is entitled,

"The louer sheweth that he was striken by loue on good friday." Variants are as follows:

3 my] mine
6 no] none
7 flight] plight
9 approche (?)] approcht
13 that flyeste] which fleest
14 vnweap'nyd] vnweaponed

Except for line 14 the *TM* version is preferable. *AH* is clearly faulty in line 7.

In his note Rollins prints Petrarch's sonnet "Era il giorno ch'al sol si scoloraro" (*Rime*, III), of which No. 94 is a translation (pointed out by Emil Koeppel, "Studien zur Geschichte des englischen Petrarchismus im sechzehnten Jahrhundert," *Romanische Forschungen*, v [1890], 88).

This experimental sonnet in rhymed heptameters has even less of the manner of Wyatt than does No. 93 (see Note).

[95] *I ne can close in short and conning vearse*

Hand A. In line 17 the *v* of "vayne" is written over an erased *f*; in line 21 "ame" in "fame" is written over an erasure. Percy's penciled note in the right margin reads, "In Surrey's Poems fo. 85."

The copy among the Uncertain Authors in *TM*, sig. Bb1^{r,v} (ed. Rollins, No. 247), is entitled, "Of one vniustly defamed." There is but one variant: line 9, by] thy. In the third and succeeding editions, however, the *TM* reading agrees with *AH*, clearly preferable.

I can discover nothing in the style or content of this mediocre poem to suggest that it was written by Wyatt (see the Note on No. 93). As Rollins has pointed out, it seems to be addressed to a man, "G.," who was perhaps the Gray who contributed to *TM*. The poem presents a curious rhyme pattern. There are six stanzas of iambic pentameter plus a closing couplet, perhaps written with the model of Surrey's "So crewell prison" (Padelford, No. 31) in mind, but the author experimented. The first four lines present the pattern of alternate rhymes, but the rest of the poem is erratic: *ccdcdefefgghghigigjjkk*. This is inartistic variety.

[96] *The piller pearisht is whearto I Lent*

Hand A.

This sonnet was printed among the poems of Sir Thomas Wyatt in *TM*, sig. I3^{v} (ed. Rollins, No. 102), entitled, "The louer lamentes the death of his loue." There are three variants:

8 Dearlye] Daily
11 wofull] carefull
14 cause] ease

It is probable that the copyist of *AH* made an error in line 11 since "wofull" occurs in line 10. Either reading in line 8 is acceptable, but I believe that of *AH* better fits the context.

Nott's modernized text is from *AH* (*Surrey and Wyatt*, ii [1816], 16-17; notes, p. 544); Foxwell's from *N*, fol. 37^{v} (*Poems*, i [1913], 41).

This sonnet, as has been several times noted, is adapted from Petrarch's sonetto in morte 2 (*Rime*, CCLXIX), beginning, "Rotta è l'alta colonna, e'l verde lauro" (printed in full by Rollins). Nott expressed the view, generally adopted, that Wyatt was using the material of the original sonnet to write a lament on the death of Thomas Cromwell in 1540, and that he consequently departed from Petrarch to suit his own purposes. Wyatt's final tercet is entirely his own, though inferior to his source. A closer translation of Petrarch's sonnet is in *P*, fol. 47^{r}, from which it was printed by Rollins in his note on the poem under discussion.

[97] *A Ladye gave me a gyfte she had not*

Hand A. As indicated, "whiche" in line 2 is crossed out, probably to make the line more regular metrically. Percy's penciled note in the right margin reads, "In Surrey fo. 42."

The copy printed among Wyatt's poems in *TM*, sig. DD2^{r} (ed. Rollins, No. 268), is entitled, "A riddle of a gift geuen by a Ladie." This agrees exactly with *AH* before it was corrected. A copy in Bodleian MS. Rawl. Poet. 172 fol. 3^{v}, also agrees with line 2 as first written in *AH* and has the following additional variants:

5 geve] gaue
6 And] *omitted*; it] *omitted*
7 this is] is this

The Rawl. MS. copy has so far not been used as a base text.

Rollins, who has a very full note on this poem, calls attention to a marginal note in the Bodleian copy of the 1587 edition of *TM*, "J think it is a Kysse." Presumably this is the note attributed to Selden by Nott (*Surrey and Wyatt*, ii [1816], 560). Nott, Foxwell (*Poems*, ii [1913], 63), and Rollins print the imitation by George Gascoigne in his *Posies* (*Works*, ed. J. W. Cunliffe, i [1907], 340). Gascoigne, however, fails to achieve the deftness of Wyatt's riddle, partly because he carefully avoids Wyatt's effective use of identical rhyme, which emphasizes the most important word in the little poem, *not*, and further contributes to the note of flippancy.

See Rollins for other examples of riddles and for mistaken attribution of the poem to Surrey.

[98] *Was never ffile yet half so well yfyled*

Hand A. In line 1 "ffile" is written over an erasure. Percy's penciled note in the right margin reads, "In Surrey's Poems fol. 37."

Another version of this sonnet, derived from the *E* MS., fol. 14^{v}, is closely followed in *AH* No. 108, and a still more distinctive version is in the *D* MS., fol. 19^{v}. As I have pointed out in the Introduction (p. 51), the first line of No. 98 may be derived from *D*. Collation with the *E* and *D* versions is given in the Note on No. 108.

The version as given in No. 98 was printed in *TM*, sig. E1^{r} (ed. Rollins, No. 39), among Wyatt's poems and headed "The abused louer seeth his foly, and entendeth to trust no more." The first edition of *TM* has one variant from *AH*: line 7, laste] lost; but in the second and succeeding editions the line agrees with *AH*. Since "laste" is a poor reading, suggesting a printer's mistake, it is reasonable to believe that No. 98 may have been copied from the printed version. No. 98 is metrically more regular than its sources, as can be seen by a study of No. 108, and is without doubt the result of editorial work.

[99] *The long love that in my thought doth harber*

Hand A. Percy notes in the right margin, "In Surrey's Poems," without giving, as usual, the folio reference.

This well-known sonnet by Wyatt is in (*A*) the *E* MS., fol. 5^{r,v}, where it is headed "Sonet" in contemporary italic. An added notation in another contemporary hand appears to read, "1 enↄ," which Nott (vol. ii, "Preface," p. iv) interprets as "1 enter," the first of six such divisions among the Wyatt poems in *E*, "made probably with a view to publication." As I have pointed out in my earlier study of *AH*, this is one of the nine Wyatt poems in *E* which have corrections in the hand of Nicholas Grimald, some of which illustrate his concern with spelling and punctuation (see Hughey, pp. 415-16, 427-29, 442-43). The sonnet was printed among Wyatt's poems in (*B*) *TM*, sig. D4^{v} (ed. Rollins, No. 37), where it is entitled, "The louer for shamefastnesse hideth his desire within his faithfull hart." In the Appendix to my earlier study (pp. 442-43), this poem is printed in full in the three versions so that Grimald's corrections in spelling and punctuation as well as in diction can be observed in relation to the *AH* and *TM* versions. For the convenience of the reader I print below the *E* and *TM* versions in that order. Grimald's corrections are noted in bolder type. It will be noticed that all the punctuation in *E* was added by Grimald.

The longe love, that in my thought doeth harbar:
The longe loue, that in my thought I harber,

and in my ⟨n⟩ hert doeth kepe his residence:
And in my hart doth kepe his residence,

a
intoo my face preseth, with bolde pretence:
Into my face preaseth with bold pretence,

lernz
She that mee lerneth too love, & suffre:
She that me learns to loue, and to suffer,

wyllz
and will: that my trust, & lustes negligence
And willes that my trust, and lustes negligence

be rayned by reason, shame, & reverence:
Be reined by reason, shame, and reuerence,

takis
with his hardines taketh displeasur.
With his hardinesse takes displeasure.

Where-withall vntoo the hertes forrest hee fleith:
Wherwith loue to the hartes forest he fleeth

leving his entreprise, with payne, & cry:
Leauyng his enterprise with paine and crye,

and there, him hideth: & not appereth.
And there him hideth and not appeareth

What may I doo: when my maist^{r} fereth?
What may I do? when my maister feareth,

i
but, in the f elde, with him too lyve, & dy⟨e⟩.
But in the field with him to liue and dye,

for, goode is the liffe, ending faithfully.
For good is the life, endyng faithfully.

It is instructive to observe that *AH* has incorporated Grimald's word corrections and some of those in spelling but pays no attention to the punctuation. *TM* also makes use of the word corrections and some of the spelling changes, but *TM* introduces other editorial revisions in lines 1, 4, 5, and 9, usually for metrical regularity. It appears that the spelling "long" in line 1 of *AH* indicates that the compiler of that manuscript, at any rate, thought that the final *e* in "longe" was not to be pronounced.

It has been frequently noted that No. 99 is a translation of Petrarch's sonetto in vita 91 (*Rime*, CXL), which begins, "Amor, che nel penser mio vive e regna." This was also translated by Surrey in the sonnet "Love that doth raine and liue within my thought" (*Poems*, ed. Padelford, 1928, No. 4). Inevitably the two translations have been frequently compared, and until recently Wyatt's sonnet has been judged inferior. See, for example, W. J. Courthope, *A History of English Poetry*, ii (1904, reprint 1935), 89-94; J. M. Berdan, *Early Tudor Poetry*, New York, Macmillan, 1920, pp. 520-23; Padelford in his Introduction to Surrey's *Poems*, pp. 47-49. This opinion is reversed in a valuable article by Hallett Smith, "The Art of Sir Thomas Wyatt," *Huntington Library Quarterly*, ix (1946), 332-37, where emphasis is given to the stronger, more vivid effect of Wyatt's imagery and rhythm. Although I agree with this critical view, I believe Professor Smith has perhaps done some injustice to Surrey's achievement. Helpful for a better understanding of the background of Wyatt's rhythm is C. S. Lewis' study "The Fifteenth-Century Heroic Line," *Essays and Studies by Members of the English Association*, xxiv (1938), 28-41. For further critical approaches to Wyatt's rhythm, see D. W. Harding, "The Rhythmical Intention in Wyatt's Poetry," *Scrutiny*, xiv (1946), 90-102; and Alan Swallow, "The Pentameter Lines in Skelton and Wyatt," *MP*, xlviii (1950), 1-11.

[100] *Whoe so liste to hunt I know wheare is an hynd*

Hand A.

This sonnet by Wyatt is found in the *E* MS., fol. 7[v], where it is headed in contemporary italic, "Sonet," and is designated in still another contemporary hand as, "2 entͻ." "Wyat" is written in the left margin, apparently in his handwriting. This is another of the *E* MS. poems with Grimald's corrections in diction, spelling, and punctuation, as indicated in No. 99. The facsimile reproduction in Hughey, between pp. 414 and 415, shows Grimald's distinctive handwriting but cannot make clear that the same ink was used for punctuation and for deletion of letters. Nor does it make certain, as does the original, that another corrector made a change in line 8. The complete *E* text follows, with Grimald's additions in bold type.

Who so list to h⟨o⟩unt⟨e⟩: I knowe, where is an hynde.
a
but, as for me: helas, I may no more.
the vayne travaill hath weried me so sore.
furdest cūme
I am⟨e⟩ of the⟨i⟩m, that farthest cōmeth behinde.
yet, may I, by no meanes, my weried mynde
drawe from the D⟨e⟩ere: but as she fleeth afore
faynting I folowe. I leve of therefore:
Sins
sithens in à nett I seke to hold the wynde.
Who list her h⟨o⟩unt: I put him owte of dowbte:
as well, as I: may spend his tyme in vain.
and, graven with Diamondes, in letters plain:
There is written, her faier neck rounde abowte:
noli me tangere: for Cesars I am⟨e⟩:
and wylde for to holde: though I seme tame.

A comparison shows that *AH* has incorporated Grimald's corrections in lines 2, 4, 7, 13, and 14, but has not adopted the change made by some one else in line 8. Nor are Grimald's changes in spelling and punctuation followed. In line 11 "grave" was probably used to secure greater metrical regularity.

Wyatt seems to have made use both of Petrarch's sonnet "Una candida cerva sopra l'erba" (*Rime*, CXC), and of Romanello's treatment of the same theme in "Una cerva gentil, che intorno avolto" (Sonetto 3). Both are printed in full by Miss Foxwell (*Poems*, ii, 188). Wyatt's sonnet, however, is very much his own. A stubborn tradition, with which I am sympathetic, associates this excellent poem with Anne Boleyn. See Nott, *Surrey and Wyatt*, ii, 517; Foxwell, *Poems*, ii, 31, 253-56; Sir E. K. Chambers, *Sir Thomas Wyatt and Some Collected Studies*, 1933, pp. 131-39; also, W. J. Courthope, *History of English Poetry*, ii (2nd ed., 1904, reprint, 1935), 45-46.

[101] *Was I never of your love yet greevid*

Hand A. In line 4 "me" is written over an erasure.

A copy in *E*, fol. 11^{r}, has the signature "Wyat" in the left margin, as by the copy of No. 100. Above the poem is the note, "2 Ento." This is the last of the poems in the *E* MS. with Grimald's corrections.

The sonnet was printed among Wyatt's poems in *TM*, sig. $D4^{v}$ (ed. Rollins, No. 38), entitled, "The louer waxeth wiser, and will not die for affection."

Since the *E* version of this complete sonnet has not been given in my earlier study of *AH* (see Notes on Nos. 99 and 100), I print it below, indicating Grimald's corrections in bold type, and following each line with the corresponding line in *TM*.

e
1 Was I never**,** yet**,** of yor love gr**‸**eved**:**
Yet was I neuer of your loue agreued,

2 nor never shall**:** while that my liff**e** doeth last**:**
Nor neuer shall, while that my life doth last:

3 but**,** of hating myself that date is past**:**
But of hatyng my self, that date is past,

4 and teeres continuell sore have me weried**.**
And teares continual sore haue me weried.

5 I will not yet in my grave be buried**:**
I will not yet in my graue be buried,

6 nor on my tombe yor name yfixed fast**:** [*y added in same hand*]
Nor on my tombe your name haue fixed fast,

7 as cruell cause**,** that did the sperit son hast
As cruel cause, that did my sprite sone hast.

e
8 ffrom thunhappy bon**⟨**y**⟩**s**:** by great sighes sterred
From thunhappy boones by great sighes stirred

9 Then**,** if an hert of amo**⟨**u**⟩**rous faith**,** & will**,**
Then if an hart of amorous fayth and will

e
10 may content you**:** withoute doyng gre**⟨**i**⟩**ff**e:**
Content your minde withouten doyng grief

e
11 please it you so**,** to this to do**o** rele**⟨**i**⟩** ff**e.**
Please it you so to this to do relief

12 yf**,** othrɔ wise**,** ye seke for to fulfill
If otherwise you seke for to fulfill

e
13 yor disdain**:** ye erre**:** & shall not, as ye we‸ne**:**
Your wrath: you erre, and shal not as you wene,
ow beene
14 and ye yor self the cause therof hath be^{e}ne
And you yourself the cause therof haue bene.

Thus *TM* has readings which differ from *E* in lines 1, 6, 7, 10, 13, and 14, and most of the differences result in smoother metrical lines in *TM*. In line 6 the old form "yfixed" is dropped. On comparing *AH* we find that it never agrees with the readings peculiar to *TM*, and that it differs from *E* only in line 1 by a transference of "yet," a change which lessens the emphatic use of the word. *AH* has adopted Grimald's spelling corrections in lines 1, 8, 9, 10, 13, and 14, but not his punctuation. In line 8 "bones" would presumably not be pronounced as the original "bonys," and a difference in rhythm would result. The "boones" of *TM* is essentially in accord with Grimald.

The poem is translated from Petrarch's sonnet "Io non fu' d'amar voi lassato unquanco" (*Rime*, LXXXII; printed in Foxwell, ii, 189). As Miss Foxwell has pointed out (ii, 31), in his second quatrain Wyatt has reversed Petrarch's expression of complete humility in love, even to a willingness to be buried that the lady's name be marked on the tomb:

e voglio anzi un sepolcro bello e bianco,
che 'l vostro nome a mio danno si scriva
in alcun marmo, ove di spirto priva
sia la mia carne, che pò star seco anco.

As frequently, Wyatt is here a rebel against the code of courtly love.

[102] *Eache man me tellithe I chaunge most my devise*

Hand A. In line one the *o* in "most" is written in the same ink over a *u*. Percy's penciled note in the left margin reads, "Printed in Surrey's Poems fo. 21."

A copy of this sonnet by Wyatt in *E*, fol. 11^{v}, has the signature "Tho" in the left margin. Above this Percy's note, as in *AH*, is written. The number "18," apparently contemporary, is in the right margin. At the top, "Sonet" and "2 entɔ" have been written over by a later hand. An unsigned copy of the poem is in *D*, fol. 75^{v}. It was printed among Wyatt's poems in *TM*, sig E2^{v} (ed. Rollins, No. 46), with the title, "Of change in minde."

1 me tellithe] tells me *D*: me telth *TM*; most] mooste *E*: of *D*
3 purpose] propose *E*: po^{r}pos *D*; lyke] even *D*

4 everye] ech *TM*
7 after a] after/ aftɔ a *D*
9 that . . . dyversnes] this diuersnesse that blamen *TM*
11 ye me] you me *TM*; ye in the] ye y[e] *D*: you in that *TM*
12 dothe] doeth *E*
13 worde] wordes *E D*; now] nor *E D TM*; not] never *D*
14 one you] as yo[r] *D*: one, your *TM*

AH is close to *E*, from which it was almost certainly taken. The *AH* copyist evidently misread the "nor" of line 13, resulting in a change in sense.

So far as is known, this sonnet is original with Wyatt.

[103] *Alas madame for stealing of a kisse*

Hand A. Percy's penciled note in the margin reads, "In Surrey fo. 23."

A copy of this poem by Wyatt in *E*, fol. 31[r], has the signature "Tho." in the left margin. A contemporary hand has noted above the poem "I entɔ." The text is written in the hand of an amanuensis, but there are revisions in Wyatt's hand made in two different inks, one faded and brown, like that of the copyist, the other black. Other revisions appear in what seems to be one unidentified contemporary handwriting, also in the faded ink. Miss Foxwell (i, 46) says there are two revisers in addition to Wyatt, but I cannot see a distinction in the handwriting. She is in error in supposing these secondary revisions were made "possibly by Harrington, but more probably by Nott" (*A Study*, p. 139). Fortunately, however, in her edition of Wyatt she has reproduced in facsimile the half page on which the poem is written in *E* (vol. i, facing p. 45), so that the reader can the more easily check readings.

The epigram was printed in *TM*, sig. E4[v] (ed. Rollins, No. 54), with the title, "To his loue whom he had kissed against her will."

Because of the nature of the *E* text, its relation to *AH* and *TM* can best be understood by setting it out in full with explanation following each line.

stelyng
1 Alas madame for ⟨robbing⟩ of a kysse/
The corrected reading made by Wyatt in faded ink was adopted both in *AH* and *TM*, both of which agree otherwise.

r in
2 have I somuch yo[r] mynd the⟨n⟩ offended?
The *r*, which is written over the *n*, is in Wyatt's black ink. The "in" is added by the second corrector. Both *AH* and *TM* agree with the revised line.

3 have I then done so greuously amysse/
AH and *TM* agree.

the matt^r may
4 that by no meanes ⟨it may⟩ be⟨a⟩mended?
The revision is in the hand of the second corrector.
AH has the line as revised.
TM reads: "That by no meanes, it may not be amended?"
Thus the original reading is reversed in sense.

the next way is this
5 then ⟨to⟩ revenge you/ ⟨then⟩ and ⟨sure, ye shall not mysse⟩
Revisions are by Wyatt in black ink. The "then ⟨to⟩" were added in the left margin.
AH agrees with the line as corrected.
TM reads: "Reuenge you then, the rediest way is this:"
TM thus keeps the first half as originally written, but changes for metrical reasons the second half as revised.

⟨throughe⟩
an other kysse shall have my lyf⟨f⟩e ^ endid throughe endid
6 ⟨to have my liff with an other ended⟩
The revised line written above the original is in Wyatt's black ink. I am not entirely certain that the first "throughe" is crossed out. The final "throughe endid" in the right margin is written in the hand of the second corrector, suggesting to me that the first "throughe" was not intended to be omitted.
AH takes the revised line, including "throughe."
TM reads: "Another kisse my life it shall haue ended."
TM's line is regular iambic pentameter.

first
7 for to my mowth the ⟨ton⟩ my hart did suck
AH and *TM* have the line as revised by Wyatt in faded ink.

next clene
8 the ⟨tother⟩ shall ^ oute of my brest it pluck
AH and *TM* have the line as revised in Wyatt's black ink.

In conclusion we find that *AH* incorporates all revisions in *E* and is clearly copied directly from it. *TM* appears to be printed from a copy made from the *E* MS., for some of Wyatt's corrections are included and that of the second corrector in line 2, but *TM* shows additional editorial revision. The texts of the three versions of this little poem offer us a rare and instructive lesson in sixteenth-century textual criticism, for it is not often that we have such an admirable opportunity to check versions with a manuscript showing both authorial and editorial revision. Particularly significant is *TM*'s relation to *E*, for we may justifiably suppose that many other poems which cannot be checked by an original were revised for the miscellany.

The epigram is effectively adapted from Serafino's strambotta "Incolpa donna amor se troppo io volsi" (printed in full by Miss Foxwell, ii, 214).

[104] *Myne ow̃ne I. P. sins you delight to knowe*

Hand A. In line 6 the last word seems to be "lowe," but it could be "lawe," which is clearly correct. In lines 50 and 88 the corrected readings, as indicated in the text, are in another secretary hand. In line 94 the same hand has corrected "plage" to "plague" by writing over the final *e*. In line 17 "nowe this" is written over an erasure, and in line 34, "scape." Percy has a penciled note in the right margin on fol. 64^{r}, "Printed in Surrey's Poems fo. 25. NB In the printed copy are several Lines omitted here." The collation shows that *TM* has five more lines.

There are several contemporary copies of this well-known satire by Wyatt:

1 *E* MS., fol. $49^{r, v}$, a fragment, which begins with line 48 of *AH*; designated *E*.

2 *D* MS., fols. 85^{v}-87^{r}; designated *D*.

3 *P* MS., fols. 30^{r}-31^{r}, with omission of the same lines as *AH*; designated *P*.

4. Corpus Christi College, Cambridge, MS. 168, item 22, folios not numbered, ascribed, "W"; designated *C*.

5. *TM*, among Wyatt's poems, sigs. $L3^{r}$-$L4^{r}$ (ed. Rollins, No. 125), entitled, "Of the Courtiers life written to Iohn Poins"; designated *T*.

The collation follows:

1 Myne ow̃ne] My nowne *D*; I. P.] Iohn poyntz *D C T*; you] ye *D C T*

2 cawse] causes *C*; do] *omitted* *D C T*

3 flye] fle *D P C T*; they] I *C*

6 lowe] lawe *D C T*

7 not] not for *D*

8 to] *omitted* *T*; powre hath] fortune hath *D P C*; fortune here hath *T*

9 to stryke the stroke] to stroke to strike to strik ye stroke *C correction in margin*

10 ever] allwaies *D P C T*

13 what dothe inward] that dothe inwarde *C*: what inward doth *T*

14 that of glorye] of glory that *T*

15 touche] twyche *D*; me . . . reporte] my lyst not to report *D*; and me lust not repent *C*

17 nowe this honour] this honour now *D C T*
Two lines are here omitted in AH and P. They read in D:
y^{t} cannot dy the coloure blake a lyer
My poyntz I cannot from me tune to fayne
T agrees in the first line; C has "colour of blak." *In the second line T has* "frame my tune to fayne," *and C has*, "frame my tonge to sayne."
19 list] lust *C*; vyce] vices *C*: nice *T*; for] *omitted C*
20 them] them them *C*; settes] sett *C T*
22 though that] allthoo *D C T*
23 to do so great] to such *T*: nor do suche *C*; a] *omitted C*
24 as] lyke *D P C T*
25 as] like *C;* woolves] wollffes *D C*
26 *This line is omitted in D.*
with wordes] with my wordes *T*: wth my worde *C*
Following line 26 C and T have two lines not in the other copies, quoted from C:
and suffer nought nor smart wythout cōplaynt
Nor torne the worde that from my mouthe is gone
D C and T then have a line not in AH and P; quoted from D:
I cannot speke and loke lyke a saynct
T has "like as a," *and C*, "wth loke ryght as a."
27 wyles] willes *D*; make] use *C*
28 and] *omitted T*; profitt] lucre *T*
31 my self] most *D P C T*; my self] most hellp *D C*: that most helpe *T*
33 of highe Cesar] off him Cesar *D C*; dampne . . . die] ⟨Catho deme to dye⟩ and deme cato to dy *C*
34 with] by *C*; his] is *D*
35 Livie] lyve *D*; do] can *D*: doth *P T*: did *C*
36 will] wolld *D C T*: ⟨will⟩ would *P* *correction in a different hand from the text*
37 his] is *D*; weale] wealth *C T*
39 Crowe singing] singing crowe *C*: crow in singyng *T*
40 lyon] lyond *D*; of Coward] of cowardes *D*: of coward $\overset{of}{\wedge}$ *P correction in another hand from the text*
42 the] *omitted C*
44 many folde] many a fold *C*
47 dronck] drounkin *D*; of ale] ⟨a sale⟩ of ale *P* *correction in hand of text*
48 laughes] laugheth *E C*; beareth] beres *C*; the] all y^{e} *E D C T*

49 frowneth] frownes *D T*; he] *omitted* *E*
50 lustes] lust *E D C T*; ⟨day and⟩ night and day] nyght and daye *E D C T*: day and night *P*
51 will] would *E D T*; ever] neu^{r} *D*; in] wyth *C*
52 to] the *E D C T*
54 aske] asken *E D C T*; to] of *E D C*
56 with the] With *T*; to cloke all way] ay to cloke *T*
57 it shall] may *C*
58 vertue] vertu ⟨to cloke⟩ *C*
Lines 57 and 58 are repeated in T.
60 his doble] his faire double *T*
61 he] this *C*
62 and that] and say that *E D C*: Affirme that *T*
67 to every] vnto ech *T*
71 nor it] no no it *E D C T*: no nor yet *P*
72 that] *omitted* *C*; wold] could *C T*
73 maist] may *D*
74 Chipp] ⟨ship⟩ chip *P*
75 and hawke] and to hawke *E*
76 in] in the *C*
77 with . . . stalk] ⟨at my book to Sitt⟩ w^{t} my bowe to stalke *C*
78 wheare that] where so *E D T*: wher to *C*
79 leases] lees *E D C T*
80 these] theire *D*; nother] nor *E C T*: no *D*; nor] ne *C*
81 that] of *C*; doth hang yet still] doeth hang yet *E*: dothe hang yet *D P T*: that yet doth hang *C*
83 dytche] dike *E T*
84 am not] ame not now *E D C T*
85 what] with *E C T*; saverye] saffry *E*; sawce] sawces *C*; these] the *E*: those *T*
86 one] ay *D*; hym] so *D*
87 outwardlye] vtterlye *D*
89 lettes] letteth *E C*; my] me *D*; wittes] syght *E D P T*: wyt *C*
90 nor] and *E C T*; takes] taketh *E*; wittes] wit *E D*
91 the beastes do so esteeme] they beestes do so esteme *E*: they bestes do esteme *D*: those beastes do esteme *C*: such do those beastes esteme *T*
92 I am not] am I *C*; Chryste] truth *T*
93 at Rome] of some *T*
94 plague] practise *E D C T*: place *P*
95 heare I am] I am here *T*
96 Mvses] ⟨musues⟩ muses *C*; read] do rede *C*

97 list] lust *C*; my] myne owne *T*; I. P.] poynz *E D C*: Iohn Poyns *T*; for] *omitted T*

98 do spende] do *inserted in another hand P*: dispende *C*

Since the *E* MS. has but little more than one half of this satire, the editor of Wyatt's poetry is faced with a difficult problem. The collation of lines 48-98 indicates that no single one of the other versions is in complete agreement with *E*, although *TM* again has more decided departures. Of special significance are the peculiar *TM* variants in lines 92-93, clearly adopted for political reasons, since *TM* was published during Mary Tudor's reign. In general the *C* MS. is closer to *TM* than are the others, and it has readings which are obviously corrupt. The two Harington MSS., *AH* and *P*, do not always follow *E* in the latter half as closely as we might expect from the study of Nos. 100-103, and extra revisions, not always identical in the two, were used. Although the *D* MS. also differs from *E* in a number of readings in the latter portion, it is probably, as Miss Foxwell decided (i, 135), the best source for the first part of the poem. I do not believe, however, that it can be determined that this was Wyatt's first satire, as she supposes.

Nott (ii, 562-64), Foxwell (ii, 100-04), and Rollins have very full notes on this poem, and I shall therefore give only a summary. The satire is freely adapted from Luigi Alamanni's "Satira X," beginning, "O ui dirò poi che d'udir ui cale," addressed to Thommaso Sertini and first published in 1532 (*Opere Toscane*, Lyons, 1532, pp. 400-04). The satire is printed in full by Foxwell (ii, 226-30) and by Rollins in his note. At the time Alamanni was an exile in France from his native Florence. Similarly, Wyatt's satire is addressed to John Poyntz, a courtier from Iron Acton in Gloucestershire (Nott, vol. ii, "Memoirs," p. lxxxiii, n. 3; see also the Note on No. 17 of this edition), and was written in all probability when Wyatt was exiled from the Court in 1536 and was spending time at his father's estate, Allington in Kent. Wyatt has also imitated Alamanni in the use of the *terza rima* form, though not with complete success. Wyatt, to an even greater extent than Alamanni, adopted the quiet, urbane tone of the Horatian satire, which was directly imitated by Wyatt in Nos. 141 and 142. This type of satire, one of Wyatt's influential innovations in English poetry, was frequently employed for court satire as the sixteenth century advanced. See, for example, Churchyard's satires on the Court, Nos. 171 and 321. By his references to Chaucer's Sir Thopas and the Knight's tale (lines 45-46), and in the closing lines of the poem, Wyatt introduces a distinctively English note, and in lines 75-82 a personal comment on his confinement. Nott (ii, 562) suggests that Wyatt took his reference to Livy on Cato's death (lines 33-34, not in Alamanni) from the Epitome of Book CXIV, which has been lost.

Since the above textual study was prepared, F. D. Hoeniger has called attention to a version of No. 104 in a contemporary commonplace book, Cambridge University MS. Ff. 5.14, fols. 5^{v}-7^{r}. See "A Wyatt Manuscript," *N & Q*, New Ser., vol. iv, no. 3 (1957), pp. 103-04. Collation is given, where possible, with *E*; otherwise with the text in K. Muir's *Collected Poems of Sir Thomas Wyatt* (1949), No. 196. Variants are not significant; the length agrees with *C*.

[105] *Yf amorous faithe an hart vnfayned*

Hand A. Percy's penciled note in the right margin reads, "In Surrey's Poems, fo. 36."

A copy of this sonnet by Wyatt in the *E* MS., fol. 12^{v}, is written in the hand of an amanuensis and, so far as I can see, has no corrections. The page was completely scribbled over by the seventeenth-century Haringtons. The sonnet was printed among the Wyatt poems in *TM*, sig. $I2^{v}$ (ed. Rollins, No. 98), with the title, "Charging of his loue as vnpiteous and louing other."

1 amorous] amours *E*; faithe an] fayth, or if an *TM*
5 depaynted] distayned *TM*
6 or ells in] Or if *TM*
7 now feare, now shame] fear and shame, so *TM*
8 a] *omitted* *TM*; Love hath] loue alas hath *TM*
10 Sighing] sighting *E*
12 fall] farre *E TM*
13 or] ar *E TM*; destroye] stroy *TM*

The *AH* copyist clearly followed *E*, but made mistakes in lines 12 and 13. *TM*, as usual, has more revision.

The poem follows closely Petrarch's sonnet "S'una fede amorosa, un cor non finto" (*Rime*, CCXXIV; printed in full by Foxwell, ii, 190).

[106] *ffarewell love and all thie Lawes for ever*

Hand A. Percy's note is in the right margin, "In Surrey fo. 37."

A copy in the *E* MS., fol. 13^{r}, has the signature "Tho." i.e., Wyatt, in the left margin, beneath another of Percy's notes on the location of the poem in *TM*. Like other sonnets in the *E* volume this is headed "Sonet" in another hand, and is marked, "2 entↄ."

A very different version of the sonnet is in the *D* MS., fol. 75^{r}, unsigned.

Printed among Wyatt's poems in *TM*, sig. $I3^{r}$ (ed. Rollins, No. 99), the poem there has the title, "A renouncing of loue."

1 ffarewell . . . thie] Nowe fare well love and thye *D*
3 Senec and Plato call] to sore a profe hathe called *D*

4 perfect wealthe . . . to] surer ⟨selth⟩ welthe my wyttes to *D*
5 when I] when last I *D*
6 aye] *omitted D*
7 Hath . . . store] Taught me in trifles that I set no store *TM*
8 and] but *D TM*; syns] for *D*: thence: since *TM*
12 theare on spend] thervpon go spende *D*; many] *omitted D*
13 thoughe] *omitted D*; loste] ⟨spend⟩^{lost} *E correction in hand of poem*; all] *omitted D TM*
14 lustithe] liste *D TM*; longer rotten] longe & rottyn *D*

It is obvious that *AH* was copied from *E*. The *D* version, which differs so much from *E*, may, of course represent a first draft of the poem; on the other hand, I think it should make us question whether we should in other instances always accept the *D* MS. as a base text unless necessity demands it.

This sonnet, presumably original with Wyatt, is one of several poems in which he expresses strong feeling against the lack of good faith in women. Thought and form are handled with a harmony not always found in Wyatt's sonnets. Effective is his introduction to the sestet by a repetition of his farewell to love, and the figurative final couplet expresses succinctly the disillusioned reason for the farewell.

[107] *My hart I gaue the not to do it payne*

Hand A.

A copy of this sonnet by Wyatt is in the *E* MS., fol. 13^{v}, without signature. It has been so completely scribbled over by the seventeenth-century Haringtons that it is all but undecipherable. Curiously they used only the part of the page on which the poem is written and left blank fol. 14^{r}. It seems they did not like the poetry.

Two copies of the poem, written in different secretary hands, are in the *D* MS. at fols. 3^{r} and 75^{v}, here designated *D*1 and *D*2. The two copies are imperfect and the ink of *D*1 is badly faded in the last three and one half lines. An interlaced "tv" is written in the left margin of *D*1. *D*2 is unsigned. Neither Foxwell (i, 20) nor Muir (p. 260) calls attention to *D*1.

The sonnet was printed among Wyatt's poems in *TM*, sig. $I3^{r}$ (ed. Rollins, No. 100), entitled, "The louer forsaketh his vnkinde loue."

2 it was to the] lo it to thee was *TM*: ⟨was⟩ yt was to the *D1*
3 not to be] not that I should be *TM*
4 be rewardid] receiue reward *TM*
6 payed vnder] repayd after *TM*; this] suche *D1,2*
7 no sens in the] nowe syns in the *E D1 TM*: now sins y^{t} in the *D2*; none other] no maner of *D1*: there none nother *TM*

8 Displayse] de displease *D1*; if that] tho if *D1*; refrayne] restraine *D2*
9 thie desyre] my desyre *D1*
10 *Line 10 is omitted in D1.*
by] be *E*; to excuse] texcuse *D2*: for to excuse *TM*
11 *Line 11 is omitted in D1, 2.*
please] pleaseth *TM*; a] *omitted* *TM*
12 parting] departing *TM*; this] the *E D1,2 TM*
13 belevith] doth beleue *TM*
14 *Imperfect in E; only* "weth in the sand" *remains. In D1* "and sowes in the sand" *can be deciphered.*
in water] in the water *TM*; in sand] in the sand *TM D1*

In evaluating the collation, we find that *AH* is, as frequently, closer to *E* than are the other texts. Through a fault of the editor or the copyist line 7 in *AH* disturbs the sense. If *E* is to be taken as the authoritative text, we must recognize that *D*1 and *D*2 are not as reliable as *AH*. *TM* varies characteristically for metrical reasons.

The sonnet is taken from two *strambotti* of Serafino. The first, beginning, "El cor ti diedi non che el tormentassi," is followed closely by Wyatt in the octave; the second, "La donna di natura mai si satia," is adapted in the sestet. Both are printed by Foxwell (ii, 191) and by Rollins. We may note that Wyatt's first line contains two words which occur often in his poetry, *heart* and *pain* (see Josephine Miles, *Major Adjectives in English Poetry*, University of California Publications in English, vol. xii, no. 3 [1946], p. 316).

[108] *There was never fyle half so well fyled*

Hand A. In the left margin "/twise/" is written in another secretary hand, undoubtedly in reference to the fact that No. 98 is also a version of this poem. Percy also has a note in this margin, "In Surrey fo. 29." His reference, however, should be for No. 98. At the top of fol. 66[r] is some extraneous matter.

A copy of No. 108 in the *E* MS., fol. 14[v], has the signature "Tho.," i.e., Wyatt, in the left margin, with another of Percy's notes above. The poem is headed "Sonet" in another contemporary hand. The text is in the hand of a scribe, and the corrected readings indicated in the collation are made in at least two other contemporary hands.

2 anye] any ⟨every⟩
4 other] othrↄs *the s added under the curve, possibly in hand of first corrector*
6 pardons] ꝑdons d *the d added in another ink and hand*

Thus with the exception of the one word in line 4, the *AH* copyist has closely followed *E*, including the revised reading in line 2, but he has ignored the *d* of line 6, suggesting that it was added after *AH* was copied. Nott (ii, 2), Foxwell (i, 21), and Muir (p. 16) are in error, as I read the *E* text, in failing to recognize that the *d* was added in another ink to "ꝑdons," not "ꝑdon."

The corrections in lines 2 and 6 of *E* may stem from *TM* (see No. 98), or from a copy of the poem in *D*, fol. 19ᵛ. The distinctive, and attractive, quality of the *D* version can best be appreciated by a complete reading:

To my

Was neuer yet fyle half so well fylyd
to fyle A fyle to any smythys intent
as I was made a fylyng instrument
to frame other/ whyle I was begylyd
But Reason at my foly hathe smylyd
And pardond me, syns yᵗ I me Repent
my lytyll ꝑseyvyng/ & tyme myspent
ffor yowthe dyd lede me & falshed ⟨be⟩ gylyd
But thys trust I haue by gret Aparans
syns yᵗ dyscayte ys ay Retournable
of very force yt ys A greable
that therwᵗall be done the Recompence
& gylys Reward is small trust for euer
gyle begyld shuld be blamyd neuer
ffynys tv [*Interlaced*]

The "gylyd" in line 8 (read as "gyded" by the editors named above) better fits the rhyme pattern than does the "guyded" of *E* and *AH*. Further, does not the closing couplet of *D* better fit the context of the poem than does that of the other versions? Presumably the *E* text is authoritative, but it is well to keep in mind that it was not corrected by Wyatt.

[109] *Some fowles thear be that haue so perfect sight*

Hand A. Percy's note above the poem reads, "In Surrey fo. 21."

A copy in the *E* MS., fol. 19ᵛ, has the signature "Wyat" in the left margin, with another of Percy's later notes above. The poem is headed in another hand, "Sonet," and marked, "2 entↄ."

The *AH* version as corrected in line 8 agrees exactly with *E*.

The sonnet was printed among Wyatt's poems in *TM*, sigs. E2ᵛ-E3ʳ (ed. Rollins, No. 47), headed, "How the louer perisheth in his delight, as the flie in the fire." There are several minor variants:

2 agayne] Against
4 do] *omitted*; peere] appeare
5 that] to; fyre] fire so
6 do] *omitted*
7 and] But; the] *omitted*
8 I maye] may I; ⟨of⟩ by] by
10 and yet] Yet can
11 remembrãnce so followith me] So foloweth me remembrance
12 So . . . tearry] That with my teary
14 Yet do I] And yet I

This is a translation of Petrarch's sonnet "Son animali al mondo de sí altèra" (*Rime*, XIX; printed by Foxwell, ii, 192, and by Rollins in his note). Another translation of the same sonnet is in the *P* MS., fol. 45^{v}, and still another by George Puttenham in *The Arte of English Poesie* (ed. Willcock and Walker, 1936, p. 242). Both are printed by Rollins.

[110] *Because I haue the still kepte fro lyes and blame*

Hand A. Percy's note in the right margin reads, "In Surrey fo. 21." A copy in the *E* MS., fol. 20^{r}, has the signature "Wyat" in the left margin, with another of Percy's later penciled notes above. As usual, the sonnet is headed "Sonet" in another contemporary hand and is marked "2 entↄ."

Printed among Wyatt's poems in *TM*, sig. E3^{r} (ed. Rollins, No. 48), the poem is there entitled, "Against his tong that failed to vtter his sutes."

1 haue . . . kepte] still kept thee *TM*
2 have] *omitted* *TM*; the] I the *E*
3 right well] ryght ill *E*: to yll *TM*
6 then . . . as] then standest thou like *E*: thou standst like *TM*
7 if . . . worde] if thou speke towerd *E*: if one word be sayd *TM*
8 it . . . a] it is as in *E*: As in a *TM*; and lame] is the same *TM*
9 agaynst] againe *E*
10 fayne] *omitted* *TM*
12 you] ye *TM*
14 my Love declareth] my loke declareth *E*: doth my loke declare *TM*

In this sonnet *AH* departs considerably from *E*. Evidently the compiler of *AH* did not understand the sense in lines 3 and 14 and so altered the lines in such a way as to destroy the point. In both lines, however, *TM* conveys the sense of *E*.

No. 110 is a translation of Petrarch's sonnet "Perch' io t'abbia guardato di menzogna" (*Rime* XLIX; printed by Rollins and by Foxwell, ii, 193).

[111] *Thoughe I my self be brydelid of my mynde*

Hand A.

A copy written by a scribe in the *E* MS., fol. 21r, is signed "Tho.," i.e., Wyatt, in the left margin. It is headed "Sonet" in another contemporary hand and again marked "2 entↄ." There are no corrections.

The two versions differ only in spelling and punctuation. The most important spelling variant is "maisteres" in line 13 of *E*, thereby giving the *E* line an added syllable. Miss Foxwell (i, 25) has mistakenly omitted "dere" in that line and gives it as a variant. Also in *E* a colon follows "maisteres," which, if accepted as authoritative, makes a difference in the meaning.

In his note on the poem Nott (ii, 572) says, "This sonnet is designedly obscure, and probably was never corrected. It might have been a fine composition. It alludes probably to Wyatt's unfortunate passion for Anne Boleyn, and intimates, that if she preferred, as she ought to do, honour to ambition, she was still free to refuse the magnificent proposals which the king had then laid before her." Whether or not the sonnet does refer to Anne Boleyn (see No. 100 and Note), we can hardly deny that it is obscure. I should like to suggest, however, that it is highly dramatic and is conceived as addressed to his own heart (line 4); that this address continues through line 13; and that line 14 is a comment on a crisis only implied. The meaning thus interpreted would be:

Lines 1-4: although my mind, or will, is held in check by force, thereby making me reverse my course in love, who (or what) can hold you in check, my heart, even though you are seeking honor by keeping a promise made to my mind, unless you unbind yourself in love?

Lines 5-13 continue the address: sigh then no more, my heart, since no way can be found to prevent your remaining true in love, although I (i.e., my will) am held back by fortune; there are others, my heart, but you are not entirely behind. Suffice it then that you be ready at all times with time, truth, and love to save you from any offence, crying, "I burne in a lovely desyre with my deere mystres," but that lovely desire may not follow. Without the colon, of course, "that" refers to "mystres."

Line 14 is a comment by the poet on the sorrow of the heart by the absence of the following desire; or, the sorrow of the heart on his own absence from the heart of the beloved.

We could wish that Wyatt had revised a line or so.

[112] *My Gallye chardged with forgeatfulnes*

Hand A. The corrected readings in lines 6 and 8 are in another ink and secretary hand. Percy's note in the right margin reads, "In Surrey fo. 22."

A copy written by a scribe in *E*, fol. 21^{v}, is signed "Wyat" in the left margin, where above is another of Percy's notes. The poem is headed "Sonet" in another contemporary hand and marked, "2 entɔ."

Printed among Wyatt's poems in *TM*, sig. E3^{v} (ed. Rollins, No. 50), it is there entitled, "The louer compareth his state to a shippe in perilous storme tossed on the sea."

2 throughe] thorrough *E*; doth] doeth *E*
3 myne enemye] my fo *TM*
4 stirreth] sterith *E TM*
5 houre] owre *E*
    lif
6 ⟨light⟩] light *E TM*
7 doth] doeth *E*
    sighes
8 ⟨sightes⟩] sightes *E*
11 Wreathid] Wretched *E*; eke] *omitted* *TM*
12 ledd] leade *TM*
13 Drowñed] Drownde *TM*; me] be my *TM*; compforte] confort *E*: comfort *TM*

The *AH* version is clearly copied from *E*, with the changes in lines 6 and 8 made later. By changing spelling the copyist has disturbed the rhythm in lines 2 and 7 and the sense, probably in line 4, and certainly in line 5, where the "owre" of *E* should be interpreted "oar." There is a difference of opinion about the *E* variant of "compforte" in line 13. As noted above, I read it as a variant in spelling only. Foxwell, i, 26, erroneously has "comfort." Nott, i, 10, has "consort," with which Muir, p. 23, agrees. R. C. Harrier in "Notes on the Text and Interpretation of Sir Thomas Wyatt's Poetry" (*N and Q*, cxcix [1953], 234) finds Muir in error and reads, "confort." In Muir's answer (p. 236) he maintains the correctness of "consort." After a careful examination of the *f's* and the long *s's* of the scribe, I read the word as "confort."

The poem is a translation from Petrarch's sonnet "Passa la nave mia colma d'oblio" (*Rime*, CLXXXIX; printed by Rollins and by Foxwell, ii, 195). There line 5 runs, "a ciacsum remo un penser pronto e rio," the "remo" making definite that "oar" was intended. Line 6 continues, "che la tempesta e 'l fin par ch'abbi a scherno," which Wyatt has not followed, and therefore the reviser in *AH* was evidently merely seeking a direct contrast to "deathe" when he changed "light" to "lif." Nor is Wyatt sufficiently close to his original to determine the correct reading of line 13. Lines 12-14 in Petrarch run:

> Celansi i duo mei dolci usati segni;
> morta fra l'onde è la ragion e l'arte,
> tal ch'i' 'ncomincio a desperar del porto.

[113] *Advysing the bright beames of theis faire eyes*

Hand A. In line 3 "frõm the" is written over an erasure. Percy's note in the right margin reads, "In Surrey fo. 22."

A copy in the hand of a scribe in *E*, fol. 22^{r}, is signed "Wyat" in the left margin, with another of Percy's notes above. The poem is there headed, "Sonet," and marked, "2 entↄ."

Printed among Wyatt's poems in *TM*, sig. E3^{v}-E4^{r} (ed. Rollins, No. 51), it is entitled, "Of douteous loue."

1 Advysing] Auysing *E TM*; theis] those *TM*
2 is] abides *TM*; moystethe] moistes *TM*
3 parteth] depteth *E*: departeth *TM*
4 for] *omitted TM*; in] within *TM*; worldlye] woroldly *E*
5 fynd . . . bitter] bitter findes the swete *TM*
6 webb] webbes *E TM*; he hath] there he hath *TM*
7 whearby] Wherby then *TM*
8 spurrith] spurs *TM*; brydelith] brydleth *TM*
9 Thus . . . extreamytie] In such extremity thus is he *TM*
10 in . . . standith] Frosen now cold, and now he standes *TM*
11 myserye] wo *TM*; twixte earnest] betwixt earnest *TM*
12 but few] With seldome *TM*
13 with] In *TM*
14 Roote] roote lo *TM*

Despite the fact that *AH* differs from *E* in lines 1, 3, and 6, there is no doubt that it was taken from *E*. In line 10 the *AH* copyist has followed the senseless "though" of *E*, which should have been written "thought." The *TM* reviser has attempted to bring meaning to the line. The *AH* copyist misunderstood "Auysing," i.e., gazing at, in line 1 of *E*, and curiously has made less smooth the meter of line 3. It is interesting to notice that *TM* agrees with *E* against *AH*, although *TM* has many other variants from *E*.

The poem is translated from Petrarch's sonnet "Mirando 'l sol de' begli occhi sereno" (*Rime*, CLXXIII; printed by Rollins and by Foxwell, ii, 196). There line 10 runs, "or con voglie gelate, or con accese," making clear that "thought" must have been intended in *E*.

[114] *Ever my happ is slacke and sloe in commynge*

Hand A. In line 9 "or" is written over an erasure. Percy's note in the right margin reads, "In Surrey fo. 36."

A copy in the hand of a scribe in *E*, fol. 22^{v}, is signed "Wyat" in the left margin, and another of Percy's notes is written above. The poem is headed "Sonet" and marked "2 enↄ" in the same contemporary hand used previously for these notations.

Printed among Wyatt's poems in *TM*, sig. I1^{v}-I2^{r} (ed. Rollins, No. 94), it is entitled, "How vnpossible it is to finde quiet in his loue."

1 my] myn *E*
2 my] myn *E*: ay my *TM*
3 leave it] loue *TM*; doth me like] doeth . . . *E*: alike doth me *TM*
4 swifte] so swift *TM*
5 shall be black] black shal it be *TM*
6 fisshe] and fishe *TM*; in] vpon *TM*
7 returne back] backe returne *TM*
8 take] take his *TM*
9 that] *omitted* *TM*
10 rightuouslye] rightwisely *E TM*
11 againe] against *TM*
12 that] *omitted* *TM*

Once more it is evident that *AH* was taken directly from *E*. The four differences in lines 1, 2, 3, and 10 are in the nature of later forms of words in *AH*, although in lines 3 and 10 the changes lead to differences in rhythm. The variants in *TM* accord with the usual practice of the miscellany in presenting more regular meter.

No. 114 is translated from Petrarch's sonnet "Mie venture al venir son tarde e pigre" (*Rime*, LVII; printed by Rollins and by Foxwell, ii, 197). Lines 6-8 in Petrarch read:

> e 'l mar senz'onda, e per l'alpe ogni pesce,
> e corcherassi il sol lá oltre ond'esce
> d'un medesimo fonte Eufrate e Tigre.

To adapt his sonnet to the English setting, Wyatt did not name the mountain and substituted the Thames for the Tigris and Euphrates. Neither the original poem nor the translation could be described as having very much poetic merit.

[115] *Love and fortune and my mynde remembre*

Hand A. Percy's note in the right margin reads, "In Surrey fo. 36."

A copy in the hand of a scribe in *E*, fol. 23^{r}, is signed "Wyat" in the left margin. Another of Percy's notes is in the right margin. The poem is headed as in No. 100.

Printed among Wyatt's poems in *TM*, sig. I2^{r} (ed. Rollins, No. 95), it is entitled, "Of Loue, Fortune, and the louers minde."

1 and fortune] Fortune *TM*; remembre] which do remember *TM*
2 of that that] Eke that *TM*; with that that] and that that once *TM*
3 Do . . . I] Torment my hart so sore that *TM*
4 envie] I hate and enuy *TM*; them] theim *E*
5 sleithe] sleeth *TM*; fortune] while Fortune *TM*
8 in] & (in written above) *E* *correction in a different hand*; rest] rest. *TM* *period erroneously changes meaning*
10 but] And *TM*; yet the yll dothe] yet the ill doeth *E*: doth myne yll *TM*; into] into the *E*: to the *TM*
11 and . . . ron̄ne] While more then half is runne now *TM*

AH has as usual followed *E*, but in lines 4 and 10 the more modern spelling of *AH* changes pronunciation and rhythm. The *TM* version is in accord with the metrical principle of the miscellany.

No. 115 is translated from Petrarch's sonnet "Amor, Fortuna, e la mia mente schiva" (*Rime*, CXXIV; printed in Rollins and Foxwell, ii, 198). Wyatt's first quatrain does not convey the desire for death as given in the original, where lines 2-4 run:

> di quel che vede, e nel passato volta,
> m'affligon si, ch'io porto alcuna volta
> invidia a quei che son su l'altra riva.

Rather curiously in line 12 Wyatt substitutes "not of steele" for Petrarch's "non di diamante."

[116] *How ofte have I my deere and cruell foe*

Hand A. Percy's note in the right margin reads, "In Surrey fo. 36."

A copy in *E*, fol. 23^{v}, is written in the hand of a scribe. The entire page is closely written over by the seventeenth-century Haringtons, but fortunately the ink of Wyatt's poem is clearer than theirs. I do not, however, detect any heading to the poem. As in No. 115, the ascription "Wyat" is written in the left margin.

Printed among Wyatt's poems in *TM*, sig. I2^{r} (ed. Rollins, No. 96), it is entitled, "The louer prayeth his offred hart to be receiued."

2 those . . . and] my great pain to get som peace or *TM*
3 profferd . . . hart] Geuen you my hart? *TM*

4 among] In *TM*
5 ye] you *TM*
6 weite] weke (?) *E word not decipherable but see below*: weake *TM*
7 thus . . . ye] that thus I disdayne, that you *TM*
8 may nomore] can ^{no} more *E TM*
9 I then] you *TM*; nor] that *TM*

AH has again followed *E* but with a slight difference in line 8 and very probably one in line 6.

No. 116 is a translation of Petrarch's sonnet "Mille fiate, o dolce mia guerrera" (*Rime*, XXI; printed by Rollins and Foxwell, ii, 199). Petrarch's line 6 runs, "Vive in speranza debile e fallace," and thus "weak," translating "debile," was probably the word used by Wyatt, as given in *TM*. The "weite" of *AH* is either a copyist's error or an unusual spelling for "white." Foxwell (i, 30) and Muir (p. 25) both have "weke." In his fine closing couplet Wyatt characteristically introduces the note of personal pain in love, not indicated in Petrarch's lines 13-14:

che grave colpa fia d'ambeduo noi,
e tanto piú de voi, quanto piú v'ama.

As Nott has said (ii, 543), in his fourteenth line Wyatt adapted another line from Petrarch, "vostro, donna, 'l peccato, e mio fia 'l danno," which is the closing line of the sonnet Englished in No. 105. The mood expressed in No. 116 differs, however.

[117] *Lyke to theise vnmeasurable mountaynes*

Hand A. In line 4 "teares" is written over an erasure. Percy has the right marginal note, "In Surrey fo. 36."

A copy in the hand of a scribe in *E*, fol. 24^{r}, is signed "Tho." i.e., Wyatt, in the left margin. The sonnet is headed as in No. 100. In the right margin Percy has another penciled note on the *TM* location.

AH follows *E* exactly except in spelling. In line 6 *E* has "doeth" and in line 9, "boyseus," in both instances adding a syllable not in the *AH* lines.

Printed among Wyatt's poems in *TM*, sig. I2^{v} (ed. Rollins, No. 97), it is entitled, "The louers life compared to the Alpes." *TM* has the following variants:

1 to] vnto
2 is] So is
3 of great height be they] hye be they
5 full] *omitted*
8 small effecte with] With small effect

10 from] in
11 Cattell] Wilde beastes; and in me Love] fierce loue in me
12 Immoveable] Vnmoueable; they are full] they
13 that restlesse] singing
14 that passe] passing

No. 117 is a translation of Sannazaro's sonnet beginning, "Simile a questi smisurati monti," which was first published in 1531 (*Le Rime Di M. Giacobo Sannazaro*, Nicolo d'Aristotile, sig. G8^{r}). This is printed in full both by Rollins and by Foxwell (ii, 200). Both editors call attention to the translation by Mellin de Saint-Gelais, beginning, "Voyant ces monts de veuë ainsi lointaine," which was formerly thought to be Wyatt's source. For discussion of these versions, see Arthur Tilley's article in *MLQ*, v (1902), 149, and that by L. E. Kastner in *MLR*, iii (1908), 273-74. The sonnet is an excellent example of the studied intellectual conceit, which is carefully worked out in the details, but the total poetic effect is mediocre.

[118] *The lyvelye sparckes that yssue from those eyes*

Hand A. In the right margin Percy has noted, "In Surrey fo. 19."
A scribe's copy in *E*, fol. 32^{v}, is signed "Tho.," i.e., Wyatt, in the left margin, in which is written also another of Percy's notes. The sonnet is headed as in No. 100.

An unsigned copy is in *D*, fol. 36^{v}.

The sonnet was printed among Wyatt's poems in *TM*, sig. E1^{r} (ed. Rollins, No. 40), with the title, "The louer describeth his being striken with sight of his loue."

2 ne] there *TM*
3 prest] perst *TM*; my] myn *E D*
6 the] *omitted* *TM*
9 ystreeken] I stricken *E D*: striken *TM*
10 blyndid] Blind *TM*; erring] and erryng *TM*
11 ne] Nor *TM*
12 fall] fal⟨s⟩ *E*: faute *D*
13 after] streight after *TM*
of dedly naye
14 of deadly nay] ⟨Geue I the nay⟩ *D*: Of deadly noyse *TM*

There is a difference of opinion on the *E* variant of line 12. According to my reading, as noted above, the *E* MS. has "fals," round *s*, with a line drawn through the *s* in the ink of the poem. Miss Foxwell (i, 32) and Muir (pp. 36, 262) read "falt" and comment that the *t* was changed to an *l* by a later hand. Nott, on the other hand (ii, 3), uses "fall" in his modernized text. The word *fall*, it may be observed, better suits the context than does *fault*. I should say that it is the "faute" of *D* which is the erroneous reading.

The poem was suggested by Petrarch's sonnet "Vive faville uscian de' duo bei lumi" (*Rime*, CCLVIII; printed by Rollins and by Foxwell, ii, 201). The freedom of Wyatt's adaptation is evident by a comparison with the recent translation of Petrarch's sonnet by Anna Maria Armi (*Petrarch Sonnets and Songs*, New York: Pantheon Books, 1946, p. 363):

> A living radiance shone out of the beam
> Of two eyes scintillating toward me,
> And a wise heart lamented destiny
> With the high eloquence of such sweet stream,
>
> That memory itself makes me break down
> When I come back to that day and recall
> How all my spirits then began to fall
> Under the change of her habitual frown.
>
> The soul nourished in continuous pain and grief,
> (How great the power of a strict routine!)
> Struck by the double pleasure felt so ill,
>
> That in tasting the unusual relief,
> Now from hope, now from terror trembling still,
> Was about to desert me in between.

Wyatt has in reality written another poem. There is nothing in the original to compare with his fine closing line.

[119] *Right true it is and said full yore agoe*

Hand A. Percy noted in the right margin, "In Surrey fo. 23." As indicated in the text, Nos. 119 and 120 are erroneously copied into *AH* as one poem, probably because as two seven-line epigrams they come to sonnet length.

A scribe's copy in *E*, fol. 33ʳ, is signed "Tho." in the left margin, where also is another of Percy's notes. The epigram is mistakenly headed "Sonet" and marked "2 entɔ," as are many of the sonnets in *E* (see No. 100). Miss Foxwell (i, 48) thinks this heading caused the *AH* scribe to copy Nos. 119 and 120 as one poem, since the latter follows on fol. 33ᵛ of *E*. I believe, however, that the italic hand in which "Sonet" is written is too late for such an influence on *AH*.

No. 119 was printed among Wyatt's poems in *TM*, sig. F1ʳ (ed. Rollins, No. 57), with the title, "Of the fained frend."

4 thoughe they] Thought he *TM*
6 oft . . . fyre] such fier oft *E*: such fire oft times he *TM*
7 beard singethe] berd him self he singeth *TM*

The *AH* departure from *E* in line 6 is curious, for the line is less smooth than in *E*. Rollins notes that the error "Thought he" of line 4 in *TM* is a misprint peculiar to the first edition.

[120] *what worde is that that chaungethe not*

Hand A. Percy has noted in the right margin, "In Surrey fo. 22." As indicated in the preceding Note, Nos. 119 and 120 are mistakenly written as one poem in *AH*.

A scribe's copy in *E*, fol. 33v, is signed "Tho." in the left margin, on which Percy has left another note on the location in *TM*. A later hand has written "Anna" above the poem.

No. 120 was first printed among "*Other Songes and sonettes written by sir Thomas wiat the elder*" in *TM*, sig., DD2r (ed. Rollins, No. 266), with the title, "*Of his loue called Anna*," which is distinguished from other titles by the use of italics.

The versions differ significantly:

3 yf . . . answere] it is myn aunswer *E*: It is mine Anna *TM*
4 and the cause] and eke the causer *E*: The only causer *TM*
5 A Love] a love rewardeth *E*: My love that medeth *TM*
6 wold ye] would ye *E*: will you *TM*
7 health eke and] salue, and eke *TM*

Miss Foxwell's variants from *N*, fol. 45r, are erroneous in lines 6 and 7 (i, 48), for *N* follows *AH*.

The *TM* version obviously connects the poem with Anne Boleyn (see the Note on No. 100). The *AH* version is clearly edited and results in a different meaning from that given in *E*, which the *AH* compiler may not have understood. Line 5 in *AH* stands in apposition to "answere" in line 3, depending on "Yf." The word "that chaungethe not," then, is "a love with disdayne," which is nevertheless loved. This may not be what Wyatt wrote, but the meaning is clear enough.

[121] *Suche vayne thought as wonted to mislead me*

Hand A. Percy noted in the right margin, "In Surrey fo. 20."

A scribe's copy in *E*, fol. 38r, is signed "Wyat" in the left margin. There is no heading, but the same secretary hand used for notations on previous sonnets in *E* has marked it "2 entɔ." Another of Percy's notes is written in the right margin.

An unascribed copy is in *D*, fol. 31r.

No. 121 was printed among Wyatt's poems in *TM*, sig. E1^{v} (ed. Rollins, No. 41), in a version which differs considerably, with the title, "The wauerying louer wylleth, and dreadeth, to moue his desire." In *TM* line 5 of *AH* is line 8, and therefore lines 6 and 7 of *AH* are 5 and 6 in *TM*. The rhyme pattern, of course, differs.

3 maketh] Makes *TM*; lyve] leyff *D*
4 bid] bids *TM*
5 she fleeith as fast] She flyeth as fast *D*: So fleeth she *TM*
6 my] myn *E D*
7 do] doth *D*
8 lacking] lockyng *TM*; libertie] ⟨lib⟩ libertie *E*
9 disdaynfull] ⟨that scornfull⟩ disdaynfull *E revision by Wyatt*: the skornfull *D*
10 pittie] ruth *TM*
11 compforteth] comfortes *TM*
12 and thearwithall . . . how] That bolded straight the way then seke I how *TM*
13 vtter the] vtter forth the *TM*; that I suffer] I bide *TM*
14 it] ⟨y⟩ ytt *D*

It is evident that *AH* was copied from *E* after line 9 was revised by Wyatt. The *AH* copyist has, however, substituted "my" for "myn" in line 6. *D*, on the other hand, agrees with the first reading of line 9. In line 3 the "leyff" of *D*, presumably to be taken as a noun, is acceptable as far as sense is concerned.

No. 121 is a fairly close translation of Petrarch's sonnet "Pien d'un vago penser, che me desvia" (*Rime*, CLXIX; printed by Rollins and by Foxwell, ii, 202).

[122] *Vnstable dreame according to the place*

Hand A. Percy has noted in the right margin, "In Surrey fo. 20."

A copy without ascription is in *E*, fol. 54^{r}, with heading notations as in other sonnets of *E* (see the Note on No. 100). Percy's penciled note is repeated here in the left margin.

Printed among Wyatt's poems in *TM*, sig. E1^{v} (ed. Rollins, No. 42), the sonnet is there entitled, "The louer hauing dreamed enioying of his loue, complaineth that the dreame is not either longer or truer."

6 broughtest] broughtes *E*; this tossing mewe] these tossing seas *TM*
7 lyve] to liue *TM*; to renewe] tencrease *TM*
8 succour to enbrace] delight timbrace *TM*
10 th'other] the other *TM*
12 Returning] But thus return *TM*

13 it] *omitted TM*
14 they] do *TM*

AH follows *E* except for the difference in the verb forms in line 6. The transcript of *AH*, *N*, fol. 43^{v}, omits *a* in line 5 (noted by Foxwell, i, 38). As Nott pointed out (ii, 538), a mew was a place for keeping hawks, and it is used in line 6 to represent figuratively the lover's bed, on which he tosses restlessly. But this meaning was evidently not appreciated by the *TM* editor, who altered the line conventionally, necessitating change for rhyme in the following line. Other revisions in *TM* follow the usual metrical principle.

Miss Foxwell (ii, 50, 205) and Rollins note that the sonnet is taken from Marcello Filosseno's strambotto beginning, "Pareami in questa nocte esser contento," printed in full by both editors from the 1507 edition of his *Sylve*, sig. I2^{r}. Wyatt's sonnet, however, freely adapts and expands the original eight-line poem, ending typically with the note of "deadlye payne." I need not remind the reader of the many similar cries of restless lovers in Elizabethan poetry.

[123] *You that in love fynd luck and habundãnce*

Hand A. Percy's note is in the right margin, "In Surrey fo. 21." The *AH* version of this sonnet, it will be noticed, is imperfect, lacking one line.

A copy of the complete sonnet is in *E*, fol. 64^{v}, where it is signed "Tho.," i.e., Wyatt, in the left margin. It has heading notations previously described (see the Note on No. 100) and another of Percy's notes in the right margin. The text of the poem is written in a careless secretary hand, the same as that used in the *E* copy of No. 168.

The sonnet was printed among Wyatt's poems in *TM*, sig. E2^{r} (ed. Rollins, No. 43), with the title, "The louer vnhappy biddeth happy louers reioice in Maie, while he waileth that moneth to him most vnlucky."

1 You] Ye *TM*; and habundãnce] and swete abundance *TM*
2 luste and] lust of *TM*
3 awaye] way *TM*
5 in mischaũnce] of . . . *TM*
E and TM here have the following line, quoted from E, then TM:
let me remembre the happs most vnhappy
Let me remember my missehappes vnhappy
8 Sephances] Sephane [?] *E*: Stephan *TM*
9 Mischaunce] mischaunced *E TM*
10 of . . . prove] ⟨of⟩ I prove of that *E*: (I proue) of that *TM*

11 life] wittes *TM*; my wealth] my ⟨self⟩ welth *E*
13 Reioyce] Ioye *TM*

The omission of the line in *AH* was no doubt an accident, caused by the fact that the preceding line begins with the same two words. By dropping the *d* from "mischaunced" in line 9, *AH* changes the meaning, introducing a personified "Mischaunce," but the grammatical connection with the preceding line is destroyed. *TM*, of course, has a good deal of independent revision.

The name of the person to whom Wyatt attributes the interpretation of his horoscope, whether real or feigned, is still in doubt. As written in the *E* MS., the name is not clear. The *AH* scribe, who presumably was using the *E* text, has "Sephances," and the *TM* editor, or printer, "Stephan," a more usual name. Editors of Wyatt's poems who have used the *E* MS. differ in their readings. Nott (ii, 5, 539) has "Sephane"; Miss Foxwell (i, 39), "Sephanes"; Muir (p. 75), "Sephame." Thus no two readings agree, indicating the lack of clarity in the *E* handwriting. On the basis of Muir's reading of the word, William H. Wiatt has recently suggested an identification of the person to whom Wyatt refers ("Sir Thomas Wyatt and 'Sephame,'" *Notes and Queries*, cxcvii [1952], 244). Wiatt calls attention to one Edward Sepham, who took his M.A. at Oxford in 1528, lectured in logic at Cardinal's College in 1530, took orders in 1539, when he obtained the living of Reculver in Kent, and was dead in 1554. It is, of course, possible that he practiced astrology, but there is no proof of it.

The Chaucerian quality of this original sonnet has been commented on by Nott, Foxwell, and Rollins, who call attention to lines in *Troilus and Criseyde* (II, 111-12) and *The Knightes Tale* (A. 1042-45) to which Wyatt was indebted in lines 3 and 4. To this same tradition belongs Shakespeare's beautiful song "Hark! hark! the lark" (*Cymbeline*, II, iii, 22-30). But of this "ioyfull iolytie" commonly associated with May, the poet can only dream, for May is for him the month of mischance, as illustrated by his arrests in May of 1534 and 1536.

[124] *If waker care if suddaine pale coulour*

Hand A. Percy noted in the right margin, "In Surrey fo. 20."

A copy in *E*, fol. 66v, is signed "Tho.," i.e., Wyatt, in the left margin, and contains some corrected readings in Wyatt's hand. The heading notations are the same as previously described (see the Note on No. 100). Another of Percy's notes is in the left margin.

Printed among Wyatt's poems in *TM*, sig. E2r (ed. Rollins, No. 44), the sonnet is there entitled, "The louer confesseth him in loue with Phillis."

5 to slake] or slack *TM*; pase] pace to *TM*
6 by] Be *TM*
brunet my welth such
8 Brunet . . . rore] ⟨her⟩ y^{t} ⟨did⟩ set ⟨o^{r} country⟩ in a rore *E Wyatt's revision*

AH follows *E*, incorporating Wyatt's revisions in line 7, and these *TM* has also but adds three minor changes.

The opening lines of the sonnet were probably suggested by Petrarch's sonnet (*Rime*, CCXXIV):

S'una fede amorosa, un cor non finto,
un languir dolce, un desiar cortese;
s'oneste voglie in gentil foco accese,
un lungo error in cieco laberinto;

se ne la fronte ogni penser depinto,
od in voci interrotte a pena intese,
or da paura, or da vergogna offese;
s'un pallor di viola e d'amor tinto.

s'aver altrui piú caro che se stesso;
se sospirare e lagrimar mai sempre,
pascendosi di duol, d'ira e d'affanno;

s'arder da lunge et agghiacciar da presso,
son le cagion ch'amando i' mi distempre,
vostro, donna, 'l peccato, e mio fia 'l danno.

But Petrarch does not relate the symptoms of the lover to a new love, as does Wyatt in line 6, and in lines 7-14 Wyatt departs completely from the Italian. It is generally believed that the "Brunet" of the sonnet was Anne Boleyn. This conclusion is the more reasonable from the first writing of line 8 in *E*, which Wyatt may have altered to hide her identity (on Anne Boleyn, see No. 100 and Note). The identity of "Phillis" is uncertain, but she may have been Elizabeth Darrell, Wyatt's mistress in his later years (see Sir E. K. Chambers, *Sir Thomas Wyatt*, 1933, pp. 141-45). Whoever the ladies were, the poet has expressed an attitude of graceful flippancy in love, the more artistically effective because it is only implied, even through denial.

[125] *Whoe hath heard of suche crueltie before*

Hand A. Percy notes, right margin, "In Surrey fo. 28."

A copy in *E*, fol. 29^{v}, is signed "Tho." in the left margin and has three corrections in Wyatt's hand. Another secretary hand has marked above the poem, "1 entↄ."

An unsigned copy is in *D*, fol. 73ʳ.

The epigram was printed among Wyatt's poems in *TM*, sig. G2ʳ (ed. Rollins, No. 68), with the title, "Of the same," referring to the preceding poem, beginning, "She sat, and sowed" (*AH* No. 127).

1 Whoe] What man *TM*; of] *omitted TM*; crueltie]
  crueltye   tyranny
  ⟨tyranny⟩ *E Wyatt's correction*: ⟨crultye⟩ *D*
                        prykt
5 pricked my] ⟨pricked⟩ myn *E Wyatt's corrections, n added*: prickt my *TM*
8 hard] her *D*

It is interesting to find that both *AH* and *TM* include Wyatt's revised reading in line 1, but that *D* has curiously reversed the revision. It is, of course, possible that Wyatt first wrote *cruelty*, changed to *tyranny*, and then returned to *cruelty*. Only *TM* incorporates Wyatt's careful change from the dissyllabic "pricked" to the monosyllabic "prykt" in line 5, but no one of the other versions takes account of his change from "my" to "myn," which, as Miss Foxwell says (i. 45), is more euphonius.

Her suggestion (ii, 58-59) that Wyatt took the idea of No. 124 from a passage in John Skelton's "Phyllyp Sparowe" (*Poetical Works*, ed. A. Dyce, i [1843], 57-58) seems to me quite reasonable, although Rollins in his note on the poem questions it. Both editors quote Skelton's lines.

For a slightly different, and more polished, treatment of the theme in No. 125, see No. 127.

[126] *What needes theise threatning wordes and wasted wynde*

Hand A. Percy noted, right margin, "In Surrey fo. 23."

A copy in *E*, fol. 33ʳ, is signed "Tho." in the left margin, where also is written another of Percy's notes. The poem is marked "1 entɔ."

The epigram was printed among Wyatt's poems in *TM*, sig. F1ʳ (ed. Rollins, No. 56), with the title, "To his loue from whom he hadd her gloues."

1 needes] nedeth *E*; threatning] threning *E*
5 mete] finde *TM*
7 toke from me an] reft my *TM*
8 now] then *TM*; thone] one *TM*; th'other] the other *TM*

Once more *AH* closely follows *E*, with but two changes in line 1, both in the nature of more modern forms of the words, as in *TM*, although the use of "needes" results also in a more regular metrical line. *TM* revises further to the same effect, and in addition emends the rhyme word in line 5 to bring the poem into the perfect *ottava rima* pattern, which necessitates at least secondary emphasis upon the final weak syllable in line 8. Wyatt, of course, has many such rhymes as the latter, but an unrhymed verse such as line 5 is extraordinary, particularly so since it has no special emphasis.

Editors have pointed out that the source for the poem is Serafino's strambotto "À che minacci, à che tanta ira e orgoglio" (*Opere*, 1516, fol. 170$^{r, v}$; printed by Rollins and by Foxwell, ii, 215). This, it should be noted, is written in *ottava rima*.

Wyatt's pointed antithetical couplet could scarcely be improved.

[127] *She satte and Sowede that hath done me the wronge*

Hand A. Percy noted, right margin, "Surrey fo. 28."

A copy in *E*, fol. 37^{r}, is signed "Tho." in the left margin, and another of Percy's notes is in the right margin. The poem is marked for entry as in the preceding. Three lines of the text have corrections in Wyatt's hand.

An unsigned copy is in *D*, fol. 73^{r}.

Printed among Wyatt's poems in *TM*, sigs. G1^{v} - G2^{r} (ed. Rollins, No. 67), it is there entitled, "Of his loue that pricked her finger with a nedle."

                                            in
3 whylest] while *D*; in] ⟨&⟩ *E*
4 Wisshed] She wisht *TM*
5 ⟨so⟩] so *E D TM*
              Made   do
7 Made] ⟨With⟩ *E*: W^{t} *D*; doe] ⟨did make⟩ *E*: did make *D*
          in
8 in] ⟨a⟩ *E*

Thus *AH* follows *E* except in line 5, where the "so" was evidently crossed out because "servid" was read as a dissyllable. *TM* also incorporates Wyatt's corrections but makes one further change in line 4. The *D* text is curiously in between, having Wyatt's minor changes in lines 3 and 8, but keeping his first writing in line 7. The *D* text was probably not derived from *E*, or, if so, we must suppose it was made between two periods of correction by Wyatt.

No. 127 is another epigram on the theme of No. 125. There is a marked distinction between the two, for in No. 125 the lady herself brings about her ironic hurt, whereas in No. 127 it is the "blynde master" who rewards the lover's faithful service by causing the cruel lady to prick herself. Miss Foxwell (ii, 60) and Rollins call attention to a similarity between No. 127 and a dizaine by Maurice Sève, beginning, "Ouvrant ma Dame au labeur trop ardente" (printed by Rollins from *Délie*, 1544, ed. E. Parturier, 1916, p. 227).

[128] *Some tyme I fledd the fyre that me brent*

Hand A. Percy noted, right margin, "Surrey fo. 29."

A copy in *E*, fol. 40^{r}, is signed "Tho" in the left margin and has a corrected reading in Wyatt's hand. Another of Percy's notes is in the right margin, and an entry notation, as in the preceding, is above the poem.

An unsigned copy is in *D*, fol. 38^{v}.

The first four lines only are in Brit. Mus. MS. Harl. 78, fol. 23^{r}, where they are headed, "Tho. w." They agree with these lines in *AH*.

Printed among Wyatt's poems in *TM*, sig. G2^{v} (ed. Rollins, No. 71), the poem is there entitled, "The louer that fled loue now folowes it with his harme."

1 me brent] me so brent *TM*

sea by
2 by Sea by lande] by ⟨hilles⟩ l and ⟨dales⟩ *E corrected by Wyatt, the l prefixed to original "and."*: by hyllys by dales *D*
3 I . . . Coales] the coales I folow *TM*
4 agaynst my mynde] with willing minde *TM*
5 both sprõnge] both furth sprong *TM*
7 now he laughe] laughes he now *TM*
8 all to] onely *TM*

Again *AH* follows *E*, including Wyatt's corrections in line 2, which are also incorporated by *TM* and the Harl. MS. copies, but *D*, as we have seen in Nos. 121 and 127, has the first reading, though with a slight variant. *TM* as usual shows more change. In lines 4 and 8 the *TM* meaning is contrary to that in the other versions. Commenting on line 8, Miss Foxwell (ii, 65) says, "Wiat is now merely caught by the 'briars that formerly had torn him severely,' 'to-torn' (with old intensive prefix 'to') meaning 'torn to shreds.' "

As line 4 plainly indicates, the poem was written either on board ship between Dover and Calais, or after arrival in the French port. It may have been composed in 1528, when Wyatt began his two years of duty in the port of Calais. The "fyre that me brent" and the "Coales that be quente" may very well refer to his affair with Anne Boleyn, which he presumably confessed in 1527. His assignment to the French post served the king's purpose in removing him from court (see Sir E. K. Chambers, *Sir Thomas Wyatt*, 1933, pp. 137-38). Rollins thinks the poem may have been written in 1532, when Henry VIII visited the court of Francis I.

[129] *The furyous gon̄ne in his raging yre*

Hand A. Percy noted, right margin, "Surrey fo. 29."

A copy in *E*, fol. 40^{v}, is signed "Tho" in the left margin and has several corrections by Wyatt. Another of Percy's notes is in the right margin, and the poem is marked for first entry, as is No. 128.

A version among Wyatt's poems in *TM*, sig. G3r (ed. Rollins, No. 73), is entitled, "The louer compareth his hart to the ouercharged gonne."

the furyous gonne
(bombard)
1 The furyous goñne] ⟨Like as the cannon⟩ *E*; raging] most ragyng *TM*
2 when the] When that the *E TM*
3 and it the same] and that the flame *E TM*
4 Cracketh] Crackes *TM*; doth] doeth *E*: doe *TM*
5 right] *omitted* *TM*; doth] doeth *E*
Whose flame
6 whose flambe] ⟨Which daily⟩ *E*; from] ay from *TM*
Wych to lett owt
7 whiche to lett out] ⟨Whose flame to open⟩ *E*
8 that of force] now hard force *E*: inward force *TM*; doth] doeth *E*

Both *AH* and *TM* incorporate Wyatt's revisions, but both have independent readings. Exceptionally *AH* shows considerable variation from *E*, differing in lines 2, 3, and 8 in ways that indicate an editorial hand, but these differences do not accord with *TM*. The *TM* addition of "most" in line 1 was clearly added to bring the line from tetrameter to pentameter. Puttenham in *The Arte of English Poesie*, 1589 (ed. Willcock and Walker, 1936, p. 126), quotes the *TM* line as a strange illustration of a dactyll in the first foot, thus: "*Thē fŭrĭ ous gone in his most ra ging ire.*" But Puttenham's accent is, of course, hopelessly distorted. Spelled "furyous" in both *E* and *AH*, it is quite probable that the word was pronounced as a dissyllable.

As with many of Wyatt's short poems in *ottava rima*, his source is from Serafino, the *strambotto* beginning, "Se una bombarda è dal gran foco mossa" (*Opere*, Firenze: per Philippo di Guini, 1516, fol. 145v; printed by Rollins and by Foxwell, ii, 216).

[130] *ffansye doth know how* [If fancy would favor]

Hand A. The *n* in line 9 seems to be inserted in another hand. Because of the folios missing between Nos. 129 and 130, the latter is a fragment, which begins with line 9 of the poem "If fancy would favor," generally attributed to Wyatt.

A complete copy of thirty-six lines is in *E*, fol. 30r, v, where it is written in the hand of an amanuensis and is marked "1 entͻ," as are the short poems just considered. Here it is placed between the *E* versions of Nos. 125 (*E*, fol. 29^{v}) and 103 (*E*, fol. 31^{r}), with the three poems written by the same hand. The other two, however, are signed "Tho" (i.e., Wyatt) in the left margins, and it is curious that the signature is omitted from the *E* version of No. 130. As may be seen from the *E* text printed below, the *AH* fragment follows the *E* text, lines 9-36, except for spelling differences and for the omission of the word *gladly*, *AH*, line 13; *E*, line 21. This was no doubt an unintentional error on the part of the copyist.

An unsigned copy in *D*, fol. 34^{v}, omits one stanza, the third, lines 13-16, according to the *E* numbering.

That a version of this poem was published by 1551, and possibly earlier, was unknown to scholars until 1928. In that year Professor R. H. Griffith announced the dramatic discovery of two leaves from *A Boke of Balettes*, which had been by chance used in the binding of the copy of Ralph Robinson's translation of More's *Utopia* (1551) in the Miriam L. Stark Collection of the University of Texas Library. On the four pages thus preserved, with the running title as given above, are printed in black letter three complete poems and two fragments, these latter being the first and the last items. The first fragment consists of the last fifteen lines (*E* numbering, as given below) of a version of No. 130 (*B*). This is here reprinted from the text given by R. H. Griffith and R. A. Law in " 'A Boke of Balettes' and 'The Courte of Venus,' " (University of Texas *Studies in English*, No. 10 [1930], p. 7). This article (pp. 5-12) gives an account of the discovery, the condition of the leaves, and a reprint of the five texts, which are sometimes undecipherable. Professor Law has recently sent me an off-print of the article, corrected after he had studied the texts with the help of a microscope. No change was made in the lines from "If fancy would favor." In order that his corrections on the other texts may be generally known, I include them here, as follows: (1) p. 7, "L[oue] w[home ye] lyst," line 3, "whom" has a final *e*; (2) p. 8, "Shall she neuer," line 14, "will" should be "wyll"; (3) p. 9, "My penne take payne," line 14, "Hens" should be "Sens"; (4) p. 10, ". . . wake perfourme the last," line 12, an *s* can be detected before "continuallye"; (5) hands with pointed fore fingers are printed opposite "I neuer told her of my mynde" (p. 8) and "And then may chance the to repent" (p. 11).

Professors Griffith and Law brought up the question of a possible relationship between *A Boke of Balettes* and another fragmentary collection, *The Courte of Venus*. Unfortunately, they relied for their textual comparison upon texts printed by Mrs. C. C. Stopes in *Shakespeare's Industry* (London, G. Bell, 1916, pp. 325-33), as being from *The Courte of Venus*. Her texts appear to be drawn from the *E* and *D* MSS., and, consequently, a comparison between them and those in *A Boke of Balettes* has nothing to do with *The Courte of Venus*. This poetry collection is extant in two printed fragments, one in the Douce collection at the Bodleian Library, and the other (formerly in the Britwell collection) in the Folger Shakespeare Library. Both are described by Sir E. K. Chambers in *Sir Thomas Wyatt and Some Collected Studies* (1933), pp. 207-08, and the Folger fragment is reprinted, pp. 209-27. He sets out reasons for dating the fragment between 1561 and 1565.

Russell A. Fraser in his recent edition of *The Court of Venus* (Durham, N.C., Duke University Press, 1955), presents a carefully detailed study of the Douce and Folger fragments of the *Court* and of the Stark fragment of *A Boke of Balettes*, arguing convincingly that Douce should be dated between 1535 and 1539, Stark between 1547 and 1549, and Folger between 1561 and 1565 (see pp. 3-26, 36-46).

Included in the Folger fragment is a thirty-six-line version of No. 130, fols. 6^{v}-7^{r} (*C*). With the permission of officials at the Folger Library I print below my transcription of this version made from photostats of the original; and with the consent of Professors Law and Griffith I reprint the fragment of the poem as it exists in *A Boke of Balettes*. This complete presentation of the several texts of this lyric will make their relationships more readily understood.

Texts are given in the order: *E*, *D*, *B*, *C*. It should be kept in mind that *B* lacks lines 1-21 and *D* lacks lines 13-16, *E* numbering.

If fancy would favo^{r} 1
Iff fansy would favoure

If fantasy would fauour

as my desɔuing shall 2
as my deservyng shall

As I deserue and shal

my love my p̱amo^{r} 3
my love my paramore

My loue my lady paramour

should love me best of all 4
shuld love me best of all

should loue me best of al

But if I cannot attain 5
Butt yff I cannott attaỹn

And if I not attayne

the grace that I desir 6
the grace y^{t} I desyer

The grace that I desire

then may I well complain 7
then may I well complay͠n/

Then may I wel complayne

my sɔuice & my hier 8
my servyce and my hyer

My seruyce and my hier

As noted above AH begins with the following line and, as pointed out, follows the E text except in line 21, E numbering.

ffansy doeth knowe how 9
ffansy doth knowe howe

Fantasy knoweth how

to fourther my trew hert 10
to furder my trew hart

To forbeare my true hart

if fansy myght avowe 11
yff fansy myght avowe

If fantasye might auow

with faith to take ꝑt 12
W^{t} fayth for to take parte

Wyth fayth to take part

But fansy is so fraill 13

But fantasy is frayle

and falling still so fast 14

And fletynge styl so fast

that faith may not prevaill 15

that faith may not preuail

to helpe me furst nor last 16

To helpe me fyrst nor last

ffor fansy at his lust 17
ffor fansye att hys luste

Since fantasy at his luste

doeth rule all but by gesse 18
doth rule all but by gesse

Doth rule al by gesse

Whereto should I then trust 19
wherto shuld I then truste

wherto shoulde I put trust

in trouth or stedfastnes 20
in trowgh or stedfastnesse

In truth and stedfastnes.

Yet gladdely would I please 21
Yett gladly would I please

Yet gladly would I please

the fansy of her hert 22
the fansye of her hart
The fantasy of my harte
That fantasy of my hart

that may me onely ease 23
that may me only ese
That may me only ease,
That may me onely ease

and cure my carefull smart 24
and cure my carefull smarte
And helpe my careful smarte
and helpe my careful smart.

Therefore my lady dere 25
Therfore my lady dere
Therfore my lady dere
Ther[f]ore my lady deare [broken *f*]

set ons your fantasy 26
Sett ones yow^{r} fantasye
Let se your fantasye
Let se your fantasy.

to make som hope appere (fol. 30^{v}) 27
to make some hope Apere
To make some hope appeare
to make some appeare

of stedfastnes remedy 28
off stedefast remedye
Of helpe and remedy
Of helpe and remedy

ffor if he be my frend 29
ffor yff he be my frend
For if ye be my frende
For if ye be my frend (fol. 7^{r})

and vndertake my woo 30
and vndertake my woo
And vndertake my wo
And vndertake my wo

my greife is at an ende 31
my greeff ys att an ende
My grefe is at an ende
My gryefe is at an end

if he continůe so 32
yff he contynew so
Yf ye continew so
If ye contynew so.

Elles fansy doeth not ryght 33
Elles fansy doth not ryght
Els fantasy doth not ryght
Els fantasy doth not ryght.

as I desɔue and shall 34
as desɔve and shall/
As I deserve and shall
As I deserue and shal

to have you daye & nyght 35
to haue yow day and nyght
To haue her day and night
To her day and night

to love me best of all 36
to love me best of all
To loue me best of all
To love me best of al.

Clearly, *D*, as well as *AH*, has a close relation to *E*, which in keeping with others in that manuscript, is very probably the text best representing the author's intention. The *D* variant in line 34 may be disregarded as a mere copyist's error, and the omission of a stanza may have the same cause; but the *D* variants in lines 12 and 28 are probably intentional, the first for rhythm and the second for meaning. Actually no revision is necessary in line 28, as the "stedfastness" and "remedy" of *E* are in apposition. It is evident that *B* and *C* are closely related, with textual changes affecting the sense common to these two texts. Not only is line 28 made more certain in meaning, but, indeed, the same type of revision is given for the last three stanzas. In *E* it is not the lady who is "my frend," but "fantasy," who is then referred to by the masculine pronoun in lines 29 and 32. The lady is asked to set just once her fantasy in such a way that some hope may appear for the lover. If her fantasy will continue the lover's friend, then woe is gone. Less subtle are the *B* and *C* texts; likewise their roughness I would judge to be that of a reviser, hardly that of Wyatt.

Something must be said about the attention given the poem by Wyatt's editors. Nott (ii, 162) gives a modernized text and in his note (p. 576) makes no mention of any but the *E* source. Line 28, however, is emended to accord with *D*, and in line 14 "flitting" is used instead of "falling," which suggests influence of *The Courte*. Miss Foxwell's text (i, 96) is based on *E*, with "flitting" in line 14, but with line 28 as in *E*. She gives variants from *D* and the *AH* transcript but not from *C*. She does, however, print some poems from *The Courte* (i, 357-60; ii, 171-75). Neither Nott nor Miss Foxwell knew anything about *A Boke of Balettes*. Muir also prints this poem from *E* (No. 43, pp. 33-34), but he gives "flitting" in line 14 and adopts the *D* reading in line 28. He records variants from *D* and *AH* only (p. 262) and says nothing about the texts of *B* and *C*. He mentions *The Courte of Venus* (p. 257) and reprints five poems from it as they are given by Chambers, but he makes no use of *A Boke of Balettes* except to refer to "minor variants" as given by Chambers (see Muir, pp. 236-40, 283). It is to be regretted that Wyatt's most recent editor has not considered newly discovered texts and their significance, particularly as they throw light on the way Wyatt's contemporaries read his poetry.

[131] *Patience thoughe I have not*

Hand A.

A copy in *E*, fol. 28^{r}, is signed "Tho." in the left margin and is marked for first entry as is the version of No. 130 in *E*.

A copy in *D*, fol. 13^{v}, is ascribed at the end, "q^{d} Wyatt."

2 requyre] desyryd *D*
4 my moste desyre] y^{t} I Requiryd *D*
5 can] $\overset{\text{can}}{\langle\text{not}\rangle}$ *E* *corrected in hand of poem*
7 they] she *D*
10 both . . . night] y^{t} ons I myght *D*
13 without] w^{t}outen *E D*

15 they know] she knows *D*
16 they . . . their] she . . . her *D*
18 hate that] hat⟨h⟩^{e} that *E* *corrected in hand of poem*: hate where *D*
22 heale] ease *D*

Quite clearly again *AH* was copied from *E*, the only difference occurring in line 13, where *AH* has the later form "without," which does, of course, change the rhythm. *D* may have been written from memory. Variations of this nature in the Wyatt poems of *D*, where it is possible to check against *E*, tend to make us question the validity of the *D* texts; that is, it can hardly be argued that they always give us the texts as Wyatt wrote them.

No. 131, for which No. 132 is a companion poem in the three manuscripts, presents the point of view of the courtly lover up to the final two lines, when the rebellious voice of Wyatt breaks forth, as happens so frequently in his poetry. Nott (ii, 578) speaks of No. 131 as having "little merit," but Sir E. K. Chambers included it in his edition of the *Oxford Book of Sixteenth Century Verse*, Oxford: Clarendon Press, 1932, p. 52.

[132] *Patience for mye devyse*

Hand A. Because fol. 76 is now missing in *AH*, No. 132 remains as a fragment of the first eight lines only.

The complete poem of twenty-four lines is in *E*, fol. 28^{v}, unsigned, but it follows its companion poem, the copy of No. 131 in *E*, which is signed "Tho."

A different version of the complete poem is in *D*, fol. 71^{r}, where it is introduced as a companion to No. 131 in the following manner:

> patiens tho I had nott th etc/ to her y^{t}
> saide this patiens was not for her but y^{t}
> th cōt^{ra}rye of myne was most metiste for
> her pv^{r}posse/

Collation for the first eight lines is as follows:

3 contraries] contrarye *D*
4 Ys ever the] must nedes be *D*
5 true] ⟨tr⟩yt^{r}ue *D*
8 you have] y^{r}os hathe *D*

As we might expect, *AH* agrees exactly with *E* in these lines, and in all probability the rest of the poem followed *E* closely. The poem is therefore continued from *E*, with *D* variants given on the right.

therefore you standeth awry	truste me that standes awrye
ꝑchaunce somtyme to fall	perchaunce maye some time fall
paciens then tak him up	patiens the saye and supp
and drynk of paciens cupp	a taste of patiens cupp
Paciens no force for that	
but brusshe yor gowne again	yet brushe yor gowne againe
paciens spurne not therat	
let no man knowe your payne	let folkes ꝑceyve yor payne
pacience evyn at my pleasure	patient at my plesure
when yo^{rs} is owte of mesure	when yo^{r}s hath no measure
Thother was for me	the tothr was for me
this pacience is for you	
chaunge when ye list let se	
for I have taken a new	for I have tane a newe
pacience wth a good will	
is easy to fulfill	

Wyatt is, of course, lightly satirizing the lady for her lack of response to the devoted patience expressed in No. 131. The *D* version is somewhat harsher. Wyatt expresses a similar attitude in other poems, e.g., "In eternum I was ons determined," "There was never nothing more me payned," and "I have sought long with stedfastnes" (Foxwell, i, 125-26, 88-89, 121-22).

[133] *Yf then I burne to playne me so* [To wish and want and not obtain]

Hand A. Because of the missing fol. 76, the first part of this poem, which was evidently written on the verso of that folio, is now wanting. The poem begins, "To wish and want and not obtain" and consists of nine three-line stanzas plus refrain. The *AH* fragment begins with the third line of the third stanza.

A copy of the complete poem is in *E*, fol. 39^{r,v}, where it is signed "Tho.," i.e., Wyatt, in the left margin, and marked in another secretary hand for first entry.

An unsigned copy is in *D*, fol. 71^{v}.

The first three stanzas are quoted below from *E*:

To wisshe and want and not obtain
to seke & sew esse of my pain
syns all that ever I do is vain
What may it availl me

All tho I stryve boeth ‸dey & howre *inserted in another hand*
against the streame w^{t} all my powre
if fortune list yet for to lowre
What may it availl me

If willingly I suffre woo
if from the fyre me list not goo
if then I burn to plaine me so
What may it availl me

The refrain in *D* is, "What may that availe me." In line 5 *D* has "night" instead of "howre," and in line 11, "my foo," corrected to "me soo." Using *AH* as a base, the collation then follows:

7 heares] hereth *E*: heris *D*
8 Pitieth] pitis *D*
15 doth] doeth *E*
17 releace] relef *D*; entreat] tret *E*
20 moves not her] moveth her not *E D*
21 dothe] doeth *E*

[134] *My hope alas hath me abused*

Hand A.

A scribe's copy is in *E*, fol. 41^{r,v}, marked in another hand for first entry. This is signed "Tho."

An unsigned copy is in *D*, fol. 74^{v}.

The collation shows a close relationship between the three.

8 Wheare to] Whereof *D*
12 wonderlye] wonderuslye *D*
13 thought] though *E*
17 wheare] were *D*
19 from] for *D*; trothe] trouth *E D*
20 trothe] trouth *E D*; mye] me *E*
23 lead] leds *E*
29 doth] do *E*

Wyatt has written this personal lyric in a modified form of rhyme royal, using tetrameter instead of the usual pentameter. His rhyme pattern is *a b a b b c c*, which often depends upon a final weak syllable, as is not uncommon in his poetry. The first stanza, however, demands a little juggling with pronunciation, either in line 2 or in lines 4 and 5. In *E* the final words in lines 4 and 5 are spelled, "stede" and "spede," rhyming, presumably with a short *e*, with "fed" of line 2. We would then have *a a a a a b b*. The *D* MS. accords with this. The *AH* editor may have changed the spelling to "steed" and "speed" to indicate the long vowel and thus bring the rhyme pattern to harmonize with the others, but the "fedd" in line 2 of *AH* remains out of line.

Nott (ii, 576) speaks of this poem as having much merit and calls attention to the figure of fortune's forge. It has the plaintive note found in many of Wyatt's personal lyrics.

[135] *Wheare shall I have at myne owne will*

Hand A. In line 29 a blank space was left as if the copyist did not understand, or could not read, the passage (see collation). Percy noted, right margin, "In Surrey fo. 27."

A scribe's copy in *E*, fol. $36^{r, v}$, is signed "Tho." in the left margin and is marked for first entry (see preceding poems). Another of Percy's notes is in the right margin. The text has revisions in another contemporary hand. Miss Foxwell (i, 103-05) is mistaken in supposing these revisions were made by a "later hand."

The poem was printed as Wyatt's in *TM*, sig. $G1^{r, v}$ (ed. Rollins, No. 66), with the title, "The louer complaineth himself forsaken."

3 as] that *E TM*
4 playntes] plaintes ⟨to⟩ *E* *crossed out in same ink*
12 all] stil *TM*

rue
14 shuld rue vppon] should ‸ vpon *E* *correction in another contemporary hand*

that
17 since that I] syns ‸ ⟨for you⟩ I *E* *corrected in hand of text*
22 thie] yor *E TM*
23 return'de] retorned *E TM*; vnto] to *TM*
24 saith] saieth *E*: sayeth *TM*
25 advaũnce] avaunce *E TM*

hir of
29 withe [*blank*] of crewelnes] with ⟨yor owne⟩ cruelnes *E*: with her of cruelnesse *TM* *E* *correction in same hand as in line 14*

is
34 wheare is your] Wher ‸ your *E* *correction in same hand as above*
35 dothe] doeth *E*

syns so moche
37 since so moche] ⟨for bicause⟩ *E* *correction in same hand as above*; doth] doeth *E*

naught
39 trouthe nought shall] trouth ‸ shall ⟨not⟩ *E* *same hand as above for correction*
40 verye] wretched *TM*

Except in line 29 of *AH*, both *AH* and *TM* have incorporated the corrections made on the *E* text both in the hand of the poem and in another contemporary hand. We have observed that it is characteristic of the *AH* text to follow the *E* text as revised by Wyatt or another. Here both *AH* and *TM* have a few extra changes. Line 23 furnishes an illustration of the ways in which *AH* and *TM* independently make slight changes to accord with the iambic measure.

Nott (ii, 547) suggests that the idea for the opening verses may have come from lines in Giusto de' Conti's *La Bella Mano*. In the edition of Giuseppe Gigli, 1753, p. 73, these are as follows:

> Chi darà a gli occhi miei sí larga vena
> di lacrime, ch'io possa il mio dolore
> sfogar piangendo sí che poi m'attempre?
> E per quietare il tormentoso core,
> chi darà al petto sí possente lena,
> che, siccome convien, sospiri sempre?

Veré Rubel (*Poetic Diction in the English Renaissance*, 1941, p. 290) quotes lines 41 and 42 to illustrate the figure *synathroesmus*, or the "heaping figure."

[136] *Thoughe I cannot your crueltie constrayne*

Hand A. Because fol. 79 is now missing, the *AH* copy of this poem is a fragment, though a long one, wanting the last three lines.

A copy of the complete poem in *E*, fol. 38^{v}, is signed "Tho" in the left margin and has revisions in Wyatt's hand. It is marked for first entry (see preceding Notes).

Another copy is in *D*, fol. 37^{v}.

9 vouchesave] voytsave *D*
11 obtayne] optayne *D*
12 so highe rewarde but] so $\overset{\text{hey}}{\wedge}$ reward *D*
16 But] $\overset{\text{but}}{\langle\text{ffor}\rangle}$ *E* *Wyatt's revision*: for *D*
17 Will] Wull *E D*

Thus again *AH* proves to be a copy of *E* as revised. The last three lines in *E* are:

> yet ye must graunt att the laste
> this my powre and small request
> reioisse not at
> ⟨to rew vpon⟩ my pain *Wyatt's revision*

As is true in line 16, *D* keeps the unrevised passage in the last line. But Wyatt's revision is significant in that the change of the refrain from the positive request for pity to the negative plea, "reioisse not at my pain," implies drama during the poem, thereby increasing the feeling of the lover's subjection. At the same time the poem is ended with an artistic finality which would not have been achieved through repetition.

Rhythmically the poem is interesting: pentameter couplets in the first two lines of the stanza; trimeter couplets in the next two lines, with anapests in the first foot of each; the refrain in simple, lilting iambic trimeter. Nott (ii, 578) calls attention to the variety in the rhythm, but he would turn the third and fourth lines into octosyllabic couplets, which necessitates either some emendation or a distortion of accent.

[137] *Proces of tyme worketh suche wonder*

Hand A.

A copy in *E*, fol. 55^{r}, is signed "Tho." in the left margin and, like the preceding, is marked for first entry.

2 softe] ⟨fest⟩ soft *Wyatt's correction?*
3 Dothe] doeth
8 soundes] ⟨sends⟩ sowndes *corrected in hand of poem*
12 meanes of wylde] mens the w⟨h⟩ild
20 treadist] ⟨doest excede⟩ tredis *copyist's error; see next line*
21 Eache] ⟨Eche⟩ Eche *E*; doste] doest *E*

AH follows the corrected *E*, differing only in one word, "of" instead of "the" in line 12, which, it appears, the *E* scribe did not understand. Both manuscripts omit the rhyme word in line 18. Nott (ii, 186) reasonably supplied "boot," which Miss Foxwell (i, 156) and Muir (p. 62) have accepted.

Nott is undoubtedly right when he says (ii, 578) that the "thought in this piece is common." Nevertheless, Antonio Cecchini in *Serafino Aquilano e la Lirica inglese del '500* (Aquila, Vecchioni, 1935, p. 109) points out that this poem is drawn from Serafino's *Sonetto* CIII, which in *Opere*, 1516, fol. 26^{v}, is as follows:

Col tempo el uilanello al giogo mena
El tor si fiēro, e si crudo animale
Col tempo et falcon susa à menar lale
E ritornare à te chiamando à pena,
Col tempo si domestica è in chatena
El bizarro orso, el feroce cinghïale,
Col tempo lacqua che è si molle e frale
Rompe il dur sasso come fosse harena,
Col tempo ogni robusto arbore ars cade
Col tempo ogni alto monte si f' á basso
Et io col tempo non posso à pietade

Mouer un cor dogni dolceza casso
　Vnde auanza dorgoglio e crudeltrade
　Orso, toro, leon, falcone, e sasso.

[138] *After great stormes the calme retournes*

Hand A. A penciled note, "not printed," apparently in the hand of G. F. Nott, is written above the poem.

An unsigned copy is in *E*, fol. 55^{v}, where as in *AH*, it follows immediately after No. 137.

5 The heaven] Thevin
11 thoughte] though
16 vnhappie] happy

Miss Foxwell (i, 157), using the *AH* transcript, *N*, fol. $48^{r,v}$, mistakenly gives "demgour" as a variant of the *E* "langour" in line 7; but *N*, like *AH*, reads "langour." In line 11 the *AH* "thoughte" is essential to the meaning, but in line 16 the *AH* editor evidently misunderstood the point of the poem by reversing the sense of the refrain. Line 10 was regarded as corrupt by Nott (ii, 156), who emended it to, "My trust alway in her did lie," which was adopted by Muir (p. 63). In "Notes on the Text and Interpretation of Sir Thomas Wyatt's Poetry" (*N and Q*, cxcviii [1953], 234) Richard C. Harrier, commenting on Muir's emendation, aptly says:

> An old idiom has been lost in l. 10 of "After great stormes" (83), where the emended line reads: "My trust alway in her did ly." The manuscript reads: "My trust alway *in hid ly*." The concluding phrase is for *in occulto* or "in hiding lay." The scribal spelling *ly* for "lay" is not the oddest in the MSS. If the scribal phrase is unacceptable the proper emendation is clearly: "My trust alway in hiding lay."

[139] *So feoble is the threde / that dothe the burden stay*

Hand A. Words or letters are written over erasures in the following lines: 3, "hathe"; 5, "ffor"; 11, "mayste ones"; 15, "perceyve," "how they bend"; 17, "dothe"; 18, "Butt"; 23, "space" written over an erasure and the word "space" following erased; 38, the third "the"; 39, "shyning"; 40, "speare"; 42, "howe"; 43, whole line; 54, "eke"; 55, a portion of "men reioyce"; 57, "those"; 70, "streames"; 72, "W^{ch}"; 74, "gave to me," the end of "Curteist." Most of these have significance in relation to the collation given below. Percy noted by the beginning lines of the poem, right margin, "Printed in Surrey's Poems fo. 38."

In *E*, fols. $67^{r,v}$-$68^{r,v}$, the poem is written in Wyatt's hand and signed with an interlaced "T V." There are numerous revisions in his hand, indicating that the *E* version is a first draft, representing the poem in the process of composition. A heading, "In Spayne," is also in his hand. The poem is marked "3 entɔ" in the same secretary hand used for these notations in previous Wyatt poems. An italic hand, probably of the late sixteenth or early seventeenth century, has written "Petrark" above the poem. Also, Percy left another of his penciled notes on the *TM* location on fol. 67^r. It is obvious that the *E* version of No. 139 is of great significance. Unfortunately some of the words, particularly in revised passages, are difficult to determine.

An unsigned copy is in *D*, fols. $49^{r,v}$-$50^{r,v}$.

The poem was printed as Wyatt's in *TM*, sigs. $I4^{r,v}$-$K1^{r,v}$ (ed. Rollins, No. 104), with the title, "Complaint of the absence of his loue."

In the collation revisions noted in *E* are in Wyatt's hand.

2 in heavie] ⟨y^t⟩ In ⟨sory⟩ hevy *E*; in decay] ⟨w^t his sway⟩ in dekay *E*
3 hathe] have *E D TM*; ells] ⟨frome⟩ elles *E*; some] ⟨some⟩ some *E*; or some] or ‸ some *E*
5 ffor sens] ⟨ffore⟩ sins *E*: syns *D*; that] *omitted D*
6 and] one *E D TM*; staid] ⟨held?⟩ staide *E*; my] *inserted D*
7 whiche] ⟨That⟩ wych *E*; suche wordes] ⟨w^t such life⟩ ‸ such wordes *E*; sored] ⟨wofull⟩ sory *E*: sory *D*
8 wight] spryte *E D*
10 more] most *E D*
11 mayste ones] ⟨maist⟩ ons ‸ maist *E*: ons must *D*
12 wrapp] ⟨w⟩rape *E*: rape *D*; thee] y^e *E not* "ye"
13 This is the] Thus is this *TM*; as] y^t *E D*; that] *omitted E D*: it *TM*
14 but] and *E D*; I by] by *D*
15 fleete] ⟨passe⟩ flete *E*; perceyve] se *TM*; the howres how they] thowrs . . . *E*: how the howers do *TM*; bend] ⟨flye⟩ bend *E*
16 that] ⟨alas⟩ y^t *E*
17 the easte] thest *E D*; dothe scantlye shew] skant doth shew *E D*: scant shewes *TM*
18 Butt] when *E D TM*; streight] ⟨selff⟩ straite *E*
19 as fast] ⟨agayne⟩ as fast *E*; he] *omitted D*
20 from] ⟨comest⟩ from *E*; to easte] to thest *E D*; iourney] ⟨voiage⟩ Iornei *E*

22 bodies] body *E D*
24 desyred] desird *E D*
26 my waight] me vp *TM*; I] it *E D*; flye] fle *E D*
27 as yet] *omitted* *E D TM*; lyf sustayne] lyff some thing sustayne *E D TM*
28 feele] fle *D*
29 my] me *E D TM*
30 lovelye] lyvely *E D TM*; whiche] wich ⟨y^{t}⟩ *E*
31 enioyed] enioy'd *E D*
32 when] wher ⟨y^{t}⟩ *E*: wher *D*; well] *omitted* *D*
33 But] And *TM*
34 and sleepe] in slepe *E D*
35 syns] *omitted* *D*
36 I . . . hart] I neuɔ saw the thing y^{t} myght my ‸ faythfull hert *E D*: Was neuer thing that mought in ought my woful hart *TM*
38 Landes the Hilles] land and hilles *E D*: land, the hylles *TM*
39 shyning] shene *TM*; for to] to *E D*
40 darked] darke *E D*; speare] spere *E D TM*
41 also] also ⟨vnknow⟩ *E*
42 feele] sele *D*
43 my͠nde] ⟨my⟩ mynd *E*
44 Whiche] wich ⟨that⟩ *E*; the daye] y^{t} day *E D TM*
46 did] doth *E D TM*
48 all . . . still] all thing forgott still ⟨to think on nowghte and⟩ *E*: all thyng forgott styll *D TM*
49 that] the *E D TM*; transplendant] transparãt ū *E D*
50 bewraye] bewray ⟨declare⟩ *E*; coulour] colours *TM*; vnderneithe it] vnder neth it *E*
51 now] ⟨&⟩ *E*: *omitted* *D*: the *TM*
53 shewethe] shewth *E*
54 of] and *E D TM*; and eke] & that ⟨to seke⟩ *E*: & y^{t} *D*
55 new] *omitted* *TM*; kynde] kyndes *E D TM*; whearin most] wherein most ⟨all⟩ *E*: most wherein *TM*
56 sighes] sightes *D*
57 those] them *E D TM*
58 for to] me to *E*; ‸ me to *D*

59 to geve assaye] for to'assay *E*: for to assay *D*: tassay *TM*; myne] my *D*

lyke as
60 Lyke as] ⟨sins y^{t}⟩ *E*; my] myn *E D*; above] ⟨o-ed (?)⟩ above *E*; payne] pa *E* *rest of word cut off from page*

63 toucheth] towches *E*: toucheht *D*

65 do] shall *TM*

67 my harte] min hert *E*

68 weare] wher *D*; guydes] gooides *D*; the smarte] smart *D*

70 streames] strenes *E D*

71 dothe so] doth still *E D*: doe styll *TM*; heate] hete *E*: hete *D*

72 me so] so *D*

74 gave to me] did me gyve *E D*; Curteist]courtese *E D*:
such
curteis *TM*; earste] ⟨earst⟩ *E*: suche *D*

be
75 be] ⟨are⟩ *E*

76 it that] that y^{t} *E*: y^{t} I *D*: this that *TM*

lingred
77 lingred] ⟨all my⟩ *E*: linger *D*

in to
78 whiche] and *E D TM*; in] ⟨w^{t}⟩ *E*; to] ⟨in⟩ *E*

79 dryven] forst *TM*

80 renewes] renewe[s] *E* *letter cut off page*

mone
81 mone] ⟨playne⟩ *E*: morn *D*

fermely
82 that fermlye do] y^{t} ‸ do *E*

83 stearne] streme *D*

84 eke the lovelye] ye eke louyth *D*

well
85 well] ⟨offt⟩ *E*

86 rage] Charge *D*

87 Craggie] craggyd *E D*; ragged *TM*

at othrs ⟨will⟩ wyill
88 att others will] ⟨my faintyng hope⟩ *E*: at other will *D*;
long abode
my longe abode] my ⟨brytill lyff⟩ *E*; my deepe dispaire]
my diepe
⟨willing⟩ despaire *E*; fulfills] fulfill *E* *letters cut off from page*

89 But] And *TM*; somtyme] some tymes *D*

suche
90 suche excesse] such exs *E* *letters cut from page*: ‸ express *D*

sort
91 sorte] ⟨fere⟩ *E*

92 whearbye . . . truste] ^ [wherby I fere] and yet I trust *E*: And yet I trust ere that I dye *TM*

93 lyves] dwelles *TM*

94 Wheare] There *TM*; wearyd] wery *E D TM*; somtyme maye] ^ [also all] may sometyme *E*: also may somtyme *D*

96 may chaunce] ⟨p⟩ [may] chaunce *E*; to have] ⟨she shew⟩ [to haue] *E*: the have *D*

97 dreede] grief *TM*; serve] sterve (?) *E D*

99 tell her that] ⟨say⟩ [tell her y^t] *E*: tell her *D*; shee shall me shortlye see] ⟨for here I may not tary⟩ [she shall me shortly se] *E*

100 and yf for] yff y^t for *E D*; the Sowle] ⟨my⟩ [thie] sowle *E*: y^{is} soule *D*; flye] fle *E TM*

On analysis this complicated collation is unusually interesting. It is evident that *AH*, *D*, and *TM* stem from *E*, for the three copies present the text in most lines according to Wyatt's revised readings, but, at the same time, the three have independent variants. Contrary to the relation which has usually existed in the Wyatt texts previously examined in this study, the *D* text does not follow the unrevised line, but usually incorporates Wyatt's revisions and is closer to *E* than are *AH* and *TM*. When *D* is independent, the variant is of a casual nature, as in lines 11, 19, 32, 35, 68, 81, 84, 100. The *D* text gives no indication of any editorial principle in such differences. The *AH* and *TM* texts, on the other hand, do show clearly the supervision of editors, and in the texts of this poem there is more agreement between *AH* and *TM* in their variants from *E* than is true of the preceding Wyatt poems in *AH*.

Examination of Wyatt's revisions in *E* shows that some were made to obtain different rhythmical or sound effects, usually of a more varied nature. For example, the alterations in line 2 relieve the excess number of *s* sounds in the first three lines, and in line 15 by the substitution of "flete" for "passe" the same result is achieved for lines 15 and 16. Further, alliteration with the closely following "pceyve" is avoided. In line 19 Wyatt first wrote, "And now agayne where/ he began," thus giving a rhyme within the line, but this is eliminated by the use of "as fast" for "agayne." In line 81 the change from "playne" to "mone" was probably made because the next line has "cōplaine." Revisions of this type are accepted by *AH* and *TM*, but those which tend to reduce the iambic regularity are usually not incorporated, and, further, both make some independent revisions for metrical reasons. As D. W. Harding has very rightly pointed out ("The Rhythmical Intention in Wyatt's Poetry" *Scrutiny*, xiv [1946], 94), Wyatt sometimes altered verses away from iambic regularity. This principle is illustrated in the revision made in line 5 in the *E* text, where the deletion of the initial "ffor" gives the line an introductory trochee. *AH* and *TM*, however, retain *for*, and from the fact that the word is written over an erasure in *AH*, we may conclude that it was deliberately used no doubt after the line had been started with *since*. Again, in line 11 Wyatt carefully changed the position of "maist," clearly for a difference in rhythmical emphasis, but *AH* and *TM* retain the original order, which is smoother but less emphatic. The *E* text also affords examples of changes made by Wyatt to bring his lines up, or reduce, to the metrical length required by the poulter's measure he was using. For example, he reduces line 7 from seven to six feet, but he lengthens line 92 from five to seven feet, and line 99 from five to six feet. *AH* incorporates these exactly, but *TM* revises line 92. In line 40 both *AH* and *TM* alter Wyatt's "darke" to "darked," thereby gaining regular iambic measure. The *AH* "spheare" at the end of the line was deliberately substituted for "spere," as the erasure indicates, probably because the editor was thinking in terms of the moving sun. In line 38 of *AH* so slight an alteration as "the" for "and" brings a more exact parallelism into the line, again revealing the thoughtful attention of an editor; but by changing "one" to "and" in line 6, if deliberate, he destroyed both meaning and emphasis. Possibly he intended "an." In line 70 both *AH* and *TM* (and later editors), but not *D*, misread the word "strenes," i.e., strains, referring to light from the stars, for "stremes." Much more might be said about the variants, but these illustrations are, I hope, sufficient to indicate the relationship of the texts and particularly the character of *AH*.

That Wyatt should have chosen the so-called poulter's measure for this poem may seem strange to us, who connect it with the verses put out by mediocre writers in the mid-sixteenth century, though its beginnings were at least two centuries earlier. It is well to keep in mind that it had not been so degraded when Wyatt wrote. Both he and Surrey, who used it for all but one of his biblical paraphrases and also in long secular poems, appear to have considered these alternate lines of six and seven feet, rhyming in couplets, as a dignified form, suited to long poems presenting serious themes. In using it, Wyatt has succeeded in maintaining a high level of poetic excellence, for unlike the common versifiers, he does not descend to a sing-song jog trot.

It is not without interest that while he was in Spain on an embassy for the king from 1537 to 1539, Wyatt should have selected a native form into which to cast his translation of an Italian poem. Nor can it be accidental that Wyatt Englished at this time Petrarch's beautiful canzone beginning, "Sí è debile il filo a cui s' attene" (*Rime*, XXXVII), with its expression of the pain in exile from that which is loved. In his note on the poem Rollins has printed the seven stanzas of the canzone, with the indications of the accompanying lines in Wyatt (see also Foxwell, ii, 124-25, 221-25). Rollins also mentions (from Nott, ii, 553) Wyatt's departures from the canzone by the occasional inclusion of another line in Petrarch or in other writers. Among these is a note on line 84, which Nott pointed out was taken from Petrarch's line "Dolci durezze, e placide repulse" (*Rime*, CCCLI), but Wyatt probably also had Chaucer in mind. Chaucer enjoyed this figure of contraries, or the *synoeciosis*, as is illustrated in *Troilus and Criseyde* (II. 1099), "I have a joly wo, a lusty sorwe."

[140] *When Dido feasted first/ the wandring Troian knight*

Hand A. Words are written over erasures in the following lines: 23, "discryde"; 59, the "ye" in "Mercurye."

In *E*, fols. $100^{r,v}$-101^{r}, this unfinished poem, entitled, "Iopas Song," is written in Wyatt's hand, with his revisions, as in No. 139. It is marked for third entry and another of Percy's penciled notes is in the left margin of fol. 100^{r}.

In *TM*, sigs. $M1^{v}$-$M2^{r,v}$ (ed. Rollins, No. 127), among the Wyatt poems, it is entitled, "The song of Iopas vnfinished."

1 wandring] wanderyng *TM*
2 light] lygh[t] *E* *letter cut off page*
3 taught] did teche *E*
on
4 on] ⟨and⟩ *E*; his *omitted TM*
repugnāt
8 Repugnant] ⟨the dyuɔse⟩ *E*; alone alo[ne] *E*
liuing
9 lyving] ⟨lyvely⟩ *E*
11 and] *omitted* *E*
firmamēt is next containīg
12 firmament . . . conteyning] ⟨stery ‸ skye vnder the wich that movith⟩ *E*
that same
13 that same] ⟨this sky⟩ *E*
therin
14 thearin] ⟨therto⟩ *E*
the first his
15 the first] ⟨thys hevin⟩ *E*; with his restles sours] w^{t} restles
sours
⟨recours⟩ *E*
eight
16 eight] ⟨seven⟩ *E*
pointes
18 Two . . . be] There be ij ⟨signs⟩ *E*; place] pla[ce] *E*

obiect
19 obiect] ⟨direct⟩ *E*
20 grownd] round *E*
21 the one to th'other] ton to tothr *E*

touchith
22 Touche the ⟨S⟩] ⟨passeth⟩ the *E*: Toucheth the *TM*; for] ⟨for⟩ *E*; none other] no nothr *E*

discribd by sterres not bryght
23 be] bene *E*; discryde . . . bright] ⟨as axell is the light⟩ *E*

northward
24 the one] the tone *E*; Northwarde we se] ⟨y^{t}⟩ we ⟨do⟩ se *E*; thother] tothir *E*
25 thone to th'other] ton to tothr *E*

⟨the hole⟩
26 the heavens] ⟨thevin⟩ *E*; do] doth *E*

thevins
27 have] ⟨hath⟩ have *E*

those
28 those] ⟨the⟩ *E*

but thei ben
29 But they bene] ⟨ffor it is⟩ *E*; simple . . . vnmixt] ⟨vnmixt⟩ symple and pure v̄mixt *E*

all those
30 all those] ‸ those *E*; those same] ⟨the⟩ same *E*; bene] be *TM*

erryng
31 erringe] ⟨wandryng⟩ *E*; circle] cyrcles *E*

t first
32 that first] y⟨e⟩ ⟨heven⟩ *E*
35 nyne above] nyne ⟨y^{t}⟩ above *E*
39 betweene] by twene *E*; two] tow *E* *note rhyme*

sli so slake name it not
40 slye so slacke] ⟨slow to prove⟩ *E*; name it not] ⟨let it passe⟩ *E*

next to
41 Seventhe] sevent *E*; nexte . . . skye] ⟨vnder⟩ the ⟨firmament⟩ sterry skye *E*
⟨y^{t} mouethe vnder that⟩

complete
44 yeares compleat/ and] yeres/ ‸ and *E*

all
46 of all lyvinge] of ‸ lyving *E*; and with] and ⟨eke⟩ w^{t} *E*

viage
48 thothers vyoage was] tothrs ⟨Iorney⟩ was *E*
49 is it that beares] in it doth bere *E TM*

frendly
50 men/ frendlye defending] men deffendĩg ⟨and frendly⟩ *E*

berthe in iij Hunderd dayes
51 beares] ⟨hath cruell⟩ *E*; in . . . dayes] ⟨movithe all this warre⟩ *E*

53 A] A ⟨the⟩ *E*; and howres thearto] and howres therto ⟨howres⟩ *E*
54 daye his] dayes *TM*; he] her *TM*
55 governs me] govrneth me *E*
57 that . . . tother] y^{t} ‸ \did the/ tother *E*
58 So] ⟨and⟩ so *E*; vnto] to *E*
61 fyxte] first *E*; next . . . gone] ⟨and⟩ next ‸ \vs those ways hath gone/ therwith *E*
64 now bent] no bent *E*; oute] ou[t] *E*
65 of . . . they] have thei of ⟨them selffes⟩ \there owne/ *E*: haue they of theire owne *TM*; theise] those *E*
67 them selves] hym selffes ⟨his body⟩ \⟨as he⟩/ *E*; be] ben *E*
69 still] lest *E TM*
71 to east] to thest *E*: to the east *TM*
72 a loft] ⟨thevin⟩ \a lofft/ *E*
74 east to east] est to thest *E*
75 the] these *E TM*
76 about the] ⟨ap⟩ bout that *E*
77 to the tother] tone to tother *E*: tone to the tother *TM*

At the bottom of fol. 100^{v} in *E*, that is following line 52 but separated by considerable space, there is another couplet in Wyatt's hand, though it was obviously written at a different time and is now faint and barely decipherable:

> Nor is it lyke y^{t} ma[n] may think thes steres all
> streyis ther pathe as thei do passe w^{t}[in] that hevinly hall

These lines do not seem to belong between lines 52 and 53. The collation shows that *AH* and *TM* carefully incorporate Wyatt's revisions, indicating that both copies stem from *E*, although both have independent and common variants from *E*. As pointed out in the Note on No. 139, the *AH* text does not follow the *E* text as closely as we might expect from the relationship observed in previous Wyatt poems in the *AH* MS. But this does not mean that *AH* copies *TM*, or vice versa. In a number of lines in No. 140 where *AH* departs from *E*, *TM* accords with *E*, e.g., lines 22, 49, 65, 69, and 79.

Disregarding differences in forms and spelling, *AH* and *TM* do agree, however, in distinctive variations from *E* in lines 3, 11, 12, 18, 22, 23, and 67, thereby leading to the inference that some comparison was made between the two copies. I should suppose that the *TM* editor made use of both *AH* and *E*, and then made some further revision, although less than appears in a number of Wyatt's poems. It is quite possible, I think, that Wyatt's lines in this poem were not entirely understood by the editors, for his matter tortures his mode of expression.

Despite the lack of poetic excellence, this fragment based on the Ptolemaic system reveals Wyatt's interest in theories that were beginning to be brought to question. Although the great work of Copernicus, *De revolutionibus*, was not published until 1543, after Wyatt's death, his preliminary commentary on the celestial movements had appeared about 1530. This introductory work may have stimulated advocates of the Ptolemaic system to bring these theories to public attention. In 1538 Theon of Alexandria's commentary on Ptolemy's *Syntaxis* was published at Basle, where in the same year the Greek text itself was printed. George of Trebizond's Latin translation had been published at Venice in 1528. Miss Foxwell (ii, 126-28) calls attention to a small popular treatise on Ptolemy's theories, *The Compost of Ptolemy Prynce of Astronomye*, which was translated from the French and published in England in 1536. Consequently, a cosmopolitan and intellectually inclined courtier and ambassador, such as Wyatt was, could scarcely fail to be aware of the renewed interest in astronomical speculation. We should like to know whether this poem was left unfinished because Wyatt had come across the introductory treatise of Copernicus, or the explanation of the new theory given by Georg Joachim, or Rheticus, which was published in 1539 (see Preserved Smith, *A History of Modern Culture*, New York: Henry Holt, 1930, pp. 18-22). Of course, Wyatt's death in 1542 may have prevented completion of the poem.

Wyatt arbitrarily introduced his "song" of heaven and earth (lines 1-4) by using the setting of the banquet given by Dido for Aeneas, when Iopas, said to have been taught by Atlas, entertained the guests (Virgil's *Aeneid*, I, 723-47, with particular reference to lines 740-47).

[141] *A spending hand that alway powreth out*

Hand A. Letters or words are written over erasures in the following lines: 2, "as fast"; 9, "Bryan"; 21, "So, on"; 40, the *r* and *v* in "far vnmeete." Percy noted in the upper right margin, fo. 99^r^, "Printed in Surrey's Poems fo. 49."

A copy in *E*, fols. 56^r, v^-57^r^, is written in the hand of a scribe and is marked for third entry as are Nos. 139 and 140. Another of Percy's penciled notes is in the left margin of the first page.

The poem was printed as Wyatt's in *TM*, sigs. L4^v^-M1^r, v^ (ed. Rollins, No. 126), with the title, "How to vse the court and him selfe therin, written to syr Fraunces Bryan."

3 doth] doeth *E*
4 growes] groweth *E*: groweth *TM*
8 stand'st] standes *E*

14 doste] doest *E TM*
15 mightest] myghtst *E*
16 nones] noyns *E*
19 in] Inj *E apparently an error*; donge] the tordes *E*
20 pearells with] perilles the *E*: pearles with *TM*
21 So, on] then of *E*: So of *TM*; dothe] to *E*
22 fild . . . Courtyer] filled vp in the cloyster *E*
23 So] that *E*
24 withouten moisture] w^{t}oute moyster *E*
25 will] woll *E*
27 lyve to feede] fede to lyve *E*
29 doste] doest *E*
30 wolde] would *E TM*
32 knowest] knowst *E*
34 for] boeth *E*: both *TM*
35 have] hath *E TM*
37 adayes] a daye⟨s⟩ so *E scribal error?*
39 thie] the *E TM*
44 calf] dogge *E*
45 but yf thow can] by which retorn *E TM*
46 I] it *E TM scribal error in AH?*
47 the Ladde] Kittson *E*
48 withouten] w^{t}oute *E*
49 knowes] knoweth *E*
51 ryche age also] also riche age *E TM*; begynnes] begynneth *E*
55 what] When *E*
59 thow] you *E*
60 payne disbursse] charge deburse *E TM*
61 than] ⟨then⟩ (than) *E alteration in same hand*
64 maist] mayest *TM*
65 moyle] mule *E TM*
66 Whylest] Whilst *E TM*; dothe] do *E TM*: thye] thyn *E TM*
67 that thow] ⟨thou⟩ (you) *E alteration in same hand*: thou *TM*
68 Cosen . . . doughter] cosyn thy sister or thy doghter *E TM*
69 be] by *E*
71 Advaunce] avaunce *E TM*
72 thow] *omitted E TM*
75 As] ⟨and⟩ (as) *E alteration in another hand*
81 would'ste] Wouldest *E TM*
85 thow] you *E*

89 guifte] thing *E*
90 worlde] worould *E*

It is again evident that *AH* and *TM* both stem from *E*, but *TM* has fewer changes than does *AH*. Notice, for example, lines 4, 14, 45, 51, 60, 66, 68, and 72, where *TM* agrees with *E*, but *AH* is independent. On the other hand, in such significant lines as 22 and 47, and in others where the readings are not so striking, *AH* and *TM* agree and *E* is independent. Certainly, therefore, there is a direct relation between *AH* and *TM* as well as between *E* and the other two, but the editors of *AH* and *TM* exercised "discretion" in their copies. It is, of course, impossible to say whether the marked changes in lines 22 and 47 appeared first in *AH* or *TM*, but the same procedure may have been followed here as I have suggested for No. 139. When Wyatt wrote his satire, probably shortly before the dissolution of the monasteries in 1538, lines 22 and 23 as given in *E* presented a point of view on the cloistered houses of the Catholic church which would have accorded with governmental policies directed by Thomas Cromwell; but such a criticism was not acceptable during Mary Tudor's reign. Whether made first in *AH* or in *TM*, the emendation of line 22 must belong to the years 1553-57. Reason for the alteration in line 47 is not so clear. Nott (ii, 565) suggests that the "Kittson" of *E* refers to Sir Thomas Kitson, Sheriff of London in 1533, but Rollins thinks the wealthy bookseller Anthony Kitson may have been intended as the butt of Wyatt's jibe. Does "the Ladde" of *AH* and *TM* refer to an inn or tavern?

In his comments on this satire, Nott ("An Essay on Wyatt's Poems," vol. ii, p. cxliv) speaks of it as "evidently an imitation of Horace's fifth Satire of the second book," and then very justly continues:

> But it is one of those imitations which entitle to all the praise of originality. Wyatt is indebted to Horace for little more than general ideas. The particular subject to which the Satire is applied is different, and so likewise are the actors. In fact Wyatt cannot be said to have borrowed any one thought distinctly from Horace. His thoughts seem to have been rather excited by reading the Latin Satirist than taken from him.

We who read No. 141 are in no doubt that the real stimulus for the biting lines of the poem was the court of Henry VIII, with which Wyatt and his friend and fellow courtier Sir Francis Bryan were well acquainted. Dramatically presented in dialogue form between these two servants of the king who spent their lives in trotting "still vpp and downe," running "ffrom realme to realme," wearing their bodies "to the bones," and compelled to spend more money than the government was willing to supply its ambassadors, the satire nevertheless unequivocally upholds those who so serve prince and country and denounces those who remain snugly at home heaping up "pound bye pound," as "Swyne so groines/ in stie and chaw donge mowlded on the grownde." Lines 30-79, purportedly spoken by the poet, reveal Wyatt's realistic perception of man's predilection for practices so foul that we can almost smell them as we read his lines. Yet despite this awareness of human frailty, Wyatt ends his poem on the firm note of the belief in honesty, even though it means a life of adversity. Rollins calls attention to an article by J. P. Collier (*Archaeologia*, xxvi [1836], 446-53), who thinks that lines 60-79 were intended as a reproof for Bryan, whose first wife was the widow of John Fortescue. If so, it is, indeed, an outspoken reproof, which hardly seems in keeping with the friendship for Bryan evident in the epigram Wyatt addressed to him from prison, "Sighes ar my foode: drynke are my teares" (ed. Foxwell, i, 62).

The Chaucerian influence in the poem is marked. With lines 21 and 75-77, compare *Troilus and Criseyde*, I, 731, and III, 260-63. For the account of the "diligent knave that pykes his masters pursse" and still pleases him (lines 56-58), Wyatt probably remembered Chaucer's account of the reve in "The Prologue" to the *Canterbury Tales* (A. 587-622). The word "cantt" (line 45), i.e., portion, appeared in "The Knightes Tale" as "cantel" (*Cant. Tales*, A. 3008). It is possible that the *AH* use of "I" in line 46 is a deliberate emendation, meaning the whole; i.e., win at least half a portion, for it is not good to lose the whole.

Like No. 104 this satire is written in *terza rima*. For critical comments on Wyatt's use of this Italian form, see the divergent views expressed by George Saintsbury in *A History of English Prosody*, i (London, Macmillan, 1906), 311-12, and by J. M. Berdan in *Early Tudor Poetry*, 1920, p. 479.

[142] *My mothers maydes when they do Sowe and Spinne*

Hand A. Letters or words are written over erasures in lines as follows: 7, "fur" in "furrowes"; 17, "Slepe"; 41, "ua" in "language"; 51, "stra" in "straunger"; 70, "Alas (my P." Percy noted in the right margin of fol. 100^{r}, "Printed in Surrey's Poems fo. 45."

A copy in *E*, fols. 50^{v}-52^{r}, is written in the hand of a scribe and is marked for third entry as are Nos. 139-41. Two interlaced letters above the poem may be intended for "T V." Another of Percy's notes is written in the right margin of fol. 50^{v}.

An unfinished copy, consisting of the first eighteen lines and the first word of line 19, is in *D*, fol. 87^{v}.

The poem was printed as Wyatt's in *TM*, sigs. L1^{v}-L3^{r} (ed. Rollins, No. 124), with the title, "Of the meane and sure estate written to Iohn Poins."

1 do] did *E D*; and] or *D*
2 sing . . . mowse] sang sometyme a song of the ffeld mowse *E*: sang somtyme a sonng of the fildy mowsse *D*
4 se] seke *E D*
5 greevous] much *E*: myche *D*
7 furrowes] forowse *E D* *note erasure in AH*
12 bothe] boeth *E*
13 when] whilest *E*: whylst *D*: while *TM*
14 when her store] wher stoore *E*
17 cowlde] myght *E D TM*
18 quod] *omitted* *D*
The rest is wanting in D; see above.
22 labours] laboureth *E*
23 feedes] fedeth *E*
24 neede] nydes *E*: nedes *TM*
25 of delicates] of the delicates *E*
27 she . . . roste] she fedeth on boyled bacon meet and roost *E*: She fedes on boyle meat, bake meat, and on rost *TM*
28 therfore . . . of] therof neither *E*; travayle] trauell *TM*
30 Doth] doeth *E*
31 makes she] she maketh *E*
32 goethe] goes *TM*
34 theare] *omitted* *E*
35 doth] doeth *E*
37 scrapes] scrapeth *E*
38 well appeare] well scarse appere *E TM*
40 At last] At ⟨the⟩ last *E* *deletion in same ink*
43 Towne] town⟨[e]ysshe⟩ *E* *deletion in same ink; "e" formed over the "y"*; speak'st] spekest *E TM*
45 by] [by] my *E* *correction in same hand, no deletion*; roode] rode *TM*
46 ioye was] Ioy it was *E TM*
50 Amyd] amyddes *E*
53 stoole] stole *E TM*; espyed] spied *E TM*
55 so fearde] ⟨fe⟩ so ferd *E*; the] tho *E*; vnwyse] *omitted* *E*
59 Towne] towney *E*; whyther] whether *E*
60 The other] thothr *E*
61 wisht] wyshed *E*
63 The heaven] thevyn *E*
65 recover it agayne] ⟨it⟩ recover ‸[it] again *E* *correction in same hand*

68 forgote] forgotten *E*
69 seeking] semyng *E TM*
71 worsse] wourst *E TM*
73 blyndes] blynde *E*
76 you] ye *E*
77 hoope] howpt *E*: hoopt *TM*; of] with *E TM*
78 withe] *omitted twice* *E*; hawlberd] hawbart *TM*; or] nor *E*
79 That can] cannot *E TM*
81 delightes] delight *E TM*
82 thee . . . please] doeth moost the please *E*: doth most thee please *TM*
84 is it] it is *E*
85 you] ye *E*;
86 for] *omitted* *E*; on brambles] vpon brambles *E*; or on] or *E*
87 a] his *E TM*
89 Nor ye sett] ne ye se *E*
91 You] ye *E*; myslyke] myseke *E TM*; travaile] trauell *TM*
92 thye] thyn *E TM*
94 ffor] ffrom *E TM*; never] euer *E TM*
95 assynde] assigned *E*
99 stickinge] sitting *E*
100 Made] Madde *E TM*
102 thie] yor *E TM*; travaile] trauell *TM*
105 his Dome] his high dome *E*
107 dothe] doeth *E*; them] then *E*
108 backward, they] backward vertue they *E TM*

Thus *AH* has a number of independent readings, with *E* and *TM* agreeing not infrequently against *AH*. In no single instance do *AH* and *E* agree against *TM*, but *AH* and *TM* agree against *E* many times. The relationship of the texts approximates that existing in Nos. 141 and 139 (see Notes). In the instance of No. 142 the *AH* editor has disturbed the sense in lines 77-79, 91, 94, and 100. The word omission in line 108 is probably a copyist's error. It would be interesting to know just why the *AH* editor followed the *E* texts so closely in the sonnets and in some of the other shorter poems and departed so noticeably in the satires and other of the long poems.

For a brief account of John Poyntz, to whom this satire is addressed, see the Note on No. 104, which is also written to him.

Wyatt drew upon Horace, Book II, Satire 6, for this fable of the town and country mouse. G. F. Nott (ii, 561) calls attention also to the possibility of Wyatt's having known Robert Henryson's "The Taill of the uponlandis Mous and the burges Mous" (printed in full by Nott, ii, 451-57), a longer poem which relates an exchange of visits between the sisters and permits the chastened uplandish one finally to escape the clutches of Gib Hunter the cat, and to return gladly to the "kith" from which she came, there to dwell in peace and quiet. Each sister is contented with her own abode. Deftly told, Henryson's story may have been another suggestive influence upon Wyatt. As in No. 141, however, Wyatt's poem, though based ultimately on Horace, is his own, made all the more delightful by the Chaucerian flavor of some of the lines. See the notes by Nott (ii, 560-62), Foxwell (ii, 104-08), and Rollins. The serenity and playful lightness of this satire are in marked contrast to the caustic, bitter tone of No. 141.

[143] *In Greece somtyme theare dwelt a man of worthie fame*

Hand A. In line 4 "fyled" is written over an erasure. Percy noted, right margin, "Printed in Surrey's Poems fo. 52."

In *TM*, sig. Q3[r, v] (ed. Rollins, No. 172), the poem is printed among the Uncertain Authors, with the title, "The tale of Pigmalion with conclusion vpon the beautye of his loue."

10 wandringe] wandering
12 mov'd] moued
14 wolde] might
18 toucht] coucht
21 envious] curious

The first three variants have significance only if we suppose an extra syllable was pronounced in lines 10 and 11 of *TM* and in line 12 of *AH*. The three word variants are acceptable as far as sense is concerned.

That this pedestrian poem in a jogging poulter's measure should be grouped with the Wyatt poems in *AH* is puzzling. That circumstance does suggest that the Haringtons considered this one of Wyatt's compositions. Nevertheless, neither in subject, rhythm, nor diction does it give evidence of Wyatt's individual characteristics, and without more evidence I should on no account accept it as his. For his use of poulter's measure, see Nos. 139 and 140, the latter admittedly of a low poetic level but not commonplace. In *An Analytical Index to the Ballad Entries (1557-1709)*, 1924, No. 2087, Rollins suggests that this was the ballad "Pygmalyon," entered to Richard Jones in 1568-69.

[144] *Myne olde dere En'mye/ my froward master*

Hand A. Words or letters are written over erasures in lines as follows: 1, the "E" of "En'mye"; 29, "lesse," "oughte." A note by Percy is in the upper right-hand margin of fol. 102^{r}, "In Surrey fo. 25." Since fol. 103 is missing in *AH*, No. 144 is now a fragment of the first seventy-nine lines of a poem of 147 lines by Wyatt. According to G. F. Nott (ii, 551), the complete poem was in *AH* when he used it. Both fols. 103 and 104 were evidently lost shortly after that, however, for when the manuscript was bound under Nott's direction, blank leaves were used to indicate the missing folios (see the Introduction, pp. 14-16); and, further, Nott's transcript of *AH*, MS. Add. 28635, also has blank leaves for these two folios.

A scribe's copy in *E*, fols. 8^{r}-10^{v}, lacks the first twenty-one lines, which were evidently written on the verso of fol. 7, now missing. Some of Grimald's corrections in spelling and punctuation appear in the lines of the *E* copy (see the Introduction, pp. 44-45, also Notes to Nos. 99-101). The text of this poem in *E* is especially difficult because the seventeenth-century Haringtons used these pages for closely written matter.

The only complete contemporary version of the poem is that in *TM*, sigs. F3^{r}-F4^{v} (ed. Rollins, No. 64), where it is entitled, "wiates complaint vpon Loue, to Reason: with Loues answer."

In the collation following, the *E* variants begin with line 22. Grimald's corrections are indicated in bold type whenever they appear in the variants; otherwise they are not noted.

3 of nature] of our nature *TM*
22 So] O *E*
23 my . . . hath ytasted] have my blynde lyfe taisted *E*
24 semblaunce] swetenes *E*
25 faire and] the *E*; made me be] have made me *E*
26 araced] a taced *E*
27 ffrom earthlye] from all erthely *E*; and from vayne] & vain *E*
28 Me . . . toke] he toke me from rest *E*; sett in] set me in *E*
29 God . . . lesse] He hath made me regarde god**,** muche lesse *E*
30 take lytle] take right litle *E TM*

t

34 Whetting . . . desyre] alwayes**,** wheting my youthely desyere *E*
35 On cruell] on the cruell *E*

ə

36 oh *omitted* *E*; alas] (helas) *E*; wheare had] where, nowe, had *E*
37 Or other] or els any othr *E*; geven me] geuen to me *TM*
38 be chaunged] chaunge *E*
40 be my freedom̃e] my libertie *E*
42 hath turned in] have torned me in *E*
43 hath me hasted] hath chased me *E*; throughe] thorough *E*
44 Throughe] thorough *E*

45 Throughe] thoroughe *E*; and through bitter passions] & straite pressions *E*
46 Throughe] thorough *E*; and] *omitted* *E*
47 travaile] trauell *TM*; and with] & *E*
49 All in] in all *E*
52 my] *omitted* *E*
53 me as] as *E*; hath me not] hath not *TM*

Goddz

54 gods] good❮er❯es *E* *insertion above line is Grimald's; deletion to make "goodenes" into "goodes" may be in hand of poem, but I think the ink is Grimald's*: goddes *TM*; slake]

l

s❮h❯ake **slake** *E*

55 they] *omitted* *E*; cruell] cruell extreme *E*

e

56 feedes] fedeth *E*
58 to do] for to do *E*
59 in] *omitted* *E*
60 by . . . sprites] by decepte and by force over my sprites *E*
61 syns whiche bell never] and syns there never bell *E*
62 That . . . renewe] Where I am❮e❯**:** that I here not : my playntes to renewe *E*
63 My . . . say] and he himself**,** he **e** knoweth **:** that ❮that❯ I saye *E*
64 olde . . . have] have an old **e** stock **e** *E*
65 is resydent] is alwaye resident *E*
67 thence] *omitted* *E*
69 noye bothe] annoye boeth *E*
70 the . . . tother] thone & thothr *E*
71 adversarie] aduersair *TM*; suche] *omitted* *E*; reprofe]

reproofe

reprouff *E* *Grimald's spelling correction, adopted in* *TM*

Heare, Lady, thoother part

72 Heare Ladye, thother parte] here lady thothr part *E* *Grimald's corrections in spelling and capitalization, partially adopted in AH and TM*
73 trothe] trueth *E*
74 Thus] this *E TM*; may] shall *E* err]❮h❯ere *E*
75 his] *omitted* *E*; toke] take *E*
76 makes] maketh *E*; clatt'ring] clattering *E TM*
77 my delight] the delight *E TM*
78 shames] shameth *E*

This concludes the collation for the part of the poem in *AH*. The collation of these seventy-nine lines of No. 144 indicates a very close relation between *AH* and *TM* as opposed to *E*. It is therefore reasonable to assume that the rest of this long poem as once written in *AH* would have agreed substantially with that portion as printed in *TM*. See the text in Rollins's excellent edition. A collation of lines 80-147 in *TM* and *E* shows the same type of divergence as appears in lines 1-79. What is the significance of the differences revealed in the collation of these seventy-nine lines in the three texts, *AH*, *TM*, and *E*? We may note that in a few instances of minor import *TM* retains the *E* readings where *AH* departs, e.g., lines 30, 43, 74, and 77; and in lines 37, 53, and 71 *AH* and *E* agree in minor readings against *TM*. The major conclusion remains, however, that in No. 144 there is a direct connection between *AH* and *TM*. Since both of these texts make use of some of Grimald's corrections, notably in lines 54 and 72 of *E*, we may conclude that the *E* MS. was, as for other Wyatt poems, accessible for the preparation of the *AH* and *TM* versions; but it is certain that a considerable amount of deliberate extra revision was given the text of the poem before these copies were made. A study of the variants indicates, as might be expected, that *AH* and *TM* were emended usually for rhythmical purposes, that is, to bring the lines to a scansion of iambic pentameter according to the rule for rhyme royal, which is the stanzaic pattern of the poem. As written in *E*, the poem has an exceptional number of lines in a free rhythm, which does not accord with iambic pentameter, or, if they are so read, the accent is wrenched. For example, line 23 in *E* can be made into iambic pentameter:

u — / u — / u — / u — / u —
in bit / ter nes / have my / blynde lyfe / taist ed

But if the normal stress of a free rhythm is permitted, we should probably read:

u — / u u / — u / — — / — u
in bit / ter nes / have my / blynde lyfe / taist ed

As emended in *AH* and *TM*, the line is smoother metrically. Again, line 25 in *E* must surely be read with two anapests, resulting in a catalectic line:

u u — / u u — / u — / u — / u
With the am / our ous dawnce / have made / me trac / ed

But *AH* and *TM* could not accept such irregular variety. Line 29 in *E* has two anapests, two trochees, and only one iambic foot:

u u — / u u — / — u / — u / u —
He hath made / me re garde / god muche / lesse then / I ought

The *AH-TM* revision destroys Wyatt's emphasis on "god." Line 34 in *E* scans as a tetrameter verse of two trochees, one iamb, and an anapest:

— u / — u / u — / u u —
al wayes / whet ing / my youthe / ly de syere

The emendation of *AH* and *TM* does permit the introductory trochee so frequently found in the poetry of Surrey. Line 35 in *E* has an introductory anapest:

u u — / u — / u — / u— / u —
on the cru / ell whet / stone temp / er ed / wth fire

But *AH* and *TM* deliberately drop "the," and the line becomes iambic. This illustrates very well why it is necessary to consider articles and prepositions and other apparently small variants which seem to have no meaning—and, of course, sometimes they have little. This is not the place to enter into an analysis of the far-reaching results of emendations of this kind, but there can be no doubt that the various rhythms of late sixteenth-century poetry would have been attained generally much earlier had it not been for the popular influence of *TM*, a printed book, widely circulated. Nevertheless, it cannot be denied that the lines of this poem as written in *E* suggest frequently that Wyatt was struggling for the control of his rhythm, whether "pausing," as D. W. Harding terms it ("The Rhythmical Intention in Wyatt's Poetry," *Scrutiny*, xiv [1946], 96-102), or metrical. Although I know of no basis for Miss Foxwell's claim that the poem was written in 1529 (ii, 83), it is reasonable to believe that it does precede the satires, where Wyatt shows himself the master of his form.

As has been several times pointed out, the poem is a fairly close translation of Petrarch's *canzone* beginning, "Quel antiquo mio dolce empio signore" (*Rime*, CCCLX; printed in full by Foxwell, ii, 208-13). Frequently Wyatt adapts the form as well as the content of his original, but here he has attempted to express Petrarch's matter through a native medium. This may account for some of the roughness of the poem.

A partial translation of the same *canzone* is also represented in *AH* No. 64.

[145] *But Lorde how straunge is this/ that to the iust befall*

Hand A. In line 7 the final *h* in "myrth" is faded out in the manuscript.

These lines, of which I have found no other copy, evidently form the latter part of a poem which was begun on the now missing fol. 104. Since the poem was written at the end of the large group of Wyatt's secular poetry, it may be that the Haringtons regarded it as his. Although not distinguished, the verses compare very well with portions of Wyatt's paraphrases of the Penitential Psalms, which, however, are written not in poulter's measure but in *terza rima*. The style and content of the fragment suggest a closer relation with Surrey's biblical paraphrases than with Wyatt's poetry. Muir (pp. 240-41) includes this as one of Wyatt's Doubtful Poems, but he has no critical comments. He emends "for" in line 12 to "from."

EXPLANATORY NOTE ON NOS. 146-153

This group of poems is headed, "Certayne verses made by vncertayne autors wrytten out of Charleton his booke." They are all in the same handwriting, an unidentified secretary, and they could not have been written into *AH* before 1572, as Nos. 147 and 148 and probably 149 were composed about that time.

I cannot identify "Charleton" exactly. He may have been John Charlton, who translated *The Casket of Jewels* by Cornelius Valerius, published in 1571. At the end of the book John Charlton is described as late fellow of Exeter College and schoolmaster of Worksop. According to the *D.N.B.* the name is thought to be a form of *Chardon*, and the translator may, therefore, have been John Chardon, Bishop of Down and Connor, a native of Devon, who received his B.A. degree at Exeter College in 1567 and was later a fellow there. In 1571 he was living near Exeter; he died in 1601. Another possibility for the identification of "Charleton" is George Carleton, 1559-1628, Bishop of Chichester, son of Guy Carleton of Carleton Hall in Cumberland. He entered St. Edmund Hall, Oxford, in 1576, and was a fellow at Merton in 1580. He had a high reputation as a poet and theologian (*D.N.B.*). Still a third possibility is Richard Carleton (or Charleton), 1560?-1638?, the musical composer, who was educated at Clare College, Cambridge, where he took his B.A. degree in 1577. In 1601 he published a collection of madrigals, to which he contributed one, "The Triumphs of Oriana" (*D.N.B.*). He was contemporary at Cambridge with Sir John Harington, who matriculated at King's College in 1576. This fact is of some significance, as John Harington might have got hold of Charleton's book during his stay at Cambridge. If, on the other hand, we suppose that the poems were collected by the elder Harington, I should give the preference in the identification to John Charlton.

[146] *Whye would yow frende that I my selfe should wreake*

Hand: unidentified secretary. 13. "The" is written over a word, perhaps "So."

I have found no other copy of this sonnet, directed against drinking, particularly drunkenness in the Court.

[147] *If fortune good could awnswer p^r^sent ill*

Hand: unidentified secretary, as in the preceding, with the correction in line 33 in the same hand. The two Latin lines at the end and the ascription are in contemporary printed script. Lines 13 and 14 are written in the right margin opposite and below line 12, evidently added by the copyist. The sense and the structure demand that they follow stanza 3, as every third quatrain is followed by a couplet.

Nos. 147 and 148 are companion poems having to do with the assistance of Sir Henry Goodyer (1534-95) to Mary Stuart, Queen of Scots. No. 147 was written by Goodyer when he was a prisoner in the Tower, about 1572; No. 148 is a direct answer, line by line, by Thomas Norton. They appear as companion poems also in Bodleian MS. Gough Norfolk 43, fol. 53^{v} (see the Notes to Nos. 1 and 68 for some description of that manuscript), from which they were printed by J. P. Collier in "Ancient Biographical Poems" (*Camden Miscellany*, iii [1855], 13-16). Sir John Harington refers to both poems in *An Apologie*, 1596 (sigs. CC1^{v}-CC2^{r}):

> I will no Stoickes of my Iury; of the two extreames, I would rather haue Epicures. Besides that I would haue no such blacke fellowes, for we shall haue some of these Poetrie men say, as one said of Sir Harry Goodyeare when hee wrote *Candida sint comitum Goodyeery nil nisi nigrum*, he wrate vnderneath it *Hic niger est, hunc tu Regina caueto*, a good yeere on him for his good *caueat*, for hee hath had since some young scholers that haue learned to put in the like *caueats.*

For No. 147 collations follow with two contemporary manuscript copies. That in (*A*) MS. Gough Norfolk 43, fol. 53^{v}, is headed, "Verses sett forthe in the faver of y^{e} ⟨Duke⟩ Duke of norff his causes." Below the title, apparently in a different contemporary hand, is the puzzling word "Relesses." At the end of the poem, in printed script, are the words, "Godyeri nill nisi nigrum̃." Lines 13 and 14 are combined with lines 15 and 16 to make a stanza, thus changing the rhyme scheme. The next two stanzas consequently have no rhyme at all. The rhyme is restored at line 29 through the second couplet, lines 27 and 28, but the pattern is again destroyed with the omission of line 40. The copy of No. 147 in (*B*) Marsh Library (Dublin) MS. 183 Z 3.5.21, fols. 2^{r}-4^{r}, has no heading. Below the poem is written, again in printed script, "Goodier nil nisi nigrum," and beneath that in the handwriting of the poem, "Goodyer the pencyon beinge prisoner in the tower." See the Preliminary Note on Nos. 201-21 for some further account of this manuscript. The collation shows, I think, that *AH* has the best version and *A* the poorest.

1 fortune] fformer *A B*
2 amend] mighte mende *A B*; once] on *B*
3 truthe] loue *B*
4 m^{a}y] mighte *A B*; the sore] this favlte *A B*
5 they] then *B*; theare] such *B*; princes] p^{r}inches *B*; soe] see *B*
8 yll] evell *A*; a] teen *A*: ten *B*
9 Is] If *B*

10 fa⟨wl⟩te] fate *A B*
11 heerin] therin *A B*
13 my] *omitted A*
15 An] a *A B*; sinns] sin *B*
18 myne] my *A B*
20 selfe] will *A B*
22 &] a *A B*
24 out] oughte *A*
26 feele] byde *A B*
29 compassion] passion *A*
30 the] that *B*
31 conveyed] conceved *B*; that] whiche *A B*
foes
33 ⟨frends⟩] foes *A B*; can] will *A*
35 my] any *B*
36 in] be *A*
37 brought] wrought *A B*
39 my] any *B*; as] so *A B*; yll] evell *A*
40 *Wanting in A*
41 englandes] England *B*

Sir Henry Goodyer, son and heir of Francis Goodyer, succeeded his father as lord of the manor of Polesworth in 1547 and later married the daughter of Hugh Lowther, a connection which seems to have brought upon him most of his subsequent troubles, which, in turn, led to the writing of these verses. His brother-in-law Richard Lowther, a Catholic, was deputy warden of the west marches and sheriff of Cumberland at the time Mary Stuart crossed the Solway, May 16, 1568, on the first stage of her flight into England. Lowther escorted her safely from Workington to Carlisle, and, like many others, was captivated by her charms, refusing to release her to the Earl of Northumberland, the lord warden, and permitting Thomas Howard, fourth Duke of Norfolk, to hold conference with her a few days later (F. C. Cass, *Monken Hadley*, 1880, p. 145; *D.N.B.*, under Goodyer and Lowther). According to the testimony of Lawrence Bannister, a follower of Norfolk, in his examination, October 13, 1571, the acquaintance between Goodyer and Mary Stuart was brought about by Gerard Lowther, younger brother of Richard (*Calendar of the Manuscripts of the Marquis of Salisbury*, i [1883], 536; printed in full by Thomas Murdin, *A Collection of State Papers Relating to Affairs in the Reign of Queen Elizabeth, 1571-1596 . . . Left by William Cecill Lord Burghley*, ii [1759], 144). Goodyer appears to have been drawn actively into the machinations concerning the proposed marriage of Norfolk and Mary after Norfolk was sent to the Tower, October 8, 1569, where he remained until his execution, June 2, 1572, except for a short period from August 3 to September 5, 1570, when he was held at his own house because of the plague (*D.N.B.*). Mary was hastily removed from Tutbury Castle to Coventry in November, 1569, on account of the Catholic uprising, sometimes called "the rising in the North," in her behalf, in which Richard and Gerard Lowther took part (*D.N.B.*). Gerard Lowther then came to London, where he acted as agent for the delivery of letters from Mary to Norfolk, sent, it appears, by Goodyer. According to Lawrence Bannister (I quote from Murdin, reference above):

> . . . Aboute the Tyme that the Quene of *Scotts* dyd lie at *Coventrie*, or verie shortlie after, Mr. *Goodgier* sent to *London* by a Boye of his, a Letter from the Quene of *Scotts* to *Gerrarde Lowther*, who then dyd lie at *London*, to be delyverid to my Lord in the *Tower*; the whiche I conveyed to him. And afterwardes, at dyvers Tymes, before my Lord came out of the *Tower*, by *Goodgier's* Meanes, ther was Letters conveyid frome the Quene of *Scotts* to my Lord, and from my Lord to the Quene of *Scotts*, and most comenlie the same Boye was the Conveyer of the Letters: And as I thinke, ther was a Cypher betwene the Quene of *Scotts* and him, but the Alphabete of that Cypher I never had; neyther was there anie Cypher betwene him and me. . . .
>
> Mr. *Goodgier* dyd write dyvers Tymes to the Byshop of *Rosse*, and dyd write onse, as I remembre, to my Lord in Cyphre, whiche was dissiphered by the Byshop of *Rosse*, and sent in to my Lord by me. The Cypher for *Goodgier's* Name was, as I remembre, ⊙ .

Thomas Norton in line 21 of No. 148 refers to the "cyphringe sleyghte" which Goodyer had used. Bannister's testimony is largely substantiated by that of William Barker, October 11, 1571, another of Norfolk's followers (*Salisbury MSS.*, i, 534; Murdin, pp. 113-14). Robert Higford, servant to the Duke of Norfolk, testified, October 13, 1571 (*Salisbury MSS.*, i, 536; Murdin, p. 85), that the duke caused him to write a letter of thanks to Goodyer for the intelligence which he had given the duke. Norfolk himself, upon being questioned, October 13, 1571, admitted that Goodyer wrote once to him in cipher, "the which he would never take Paynes to decifre; but many other Letters *Goodier* wrote out of Cyfre, but with so high and glorious a Stile, and of so litle Mater, that this Examinate wrote to *Banister* to rede them over, and not send but such Parts as was materyall. And *Banister* him self wold write that the said *Goodier* was so busy with hym, that he was very wery of hym" (quoted from Murdin, p. 161; summarized in *Salisbury MSS.*, i, 535). At another examination, September 8, 1571, Norfolk said that the alphabet of the cipher was written in his Bible and then torn out with his consent, and its whereabouts were unknown to him (*Salisbury MSS.*, i, 522; Murdin, p. 151).

When Goodyer was questioned, October 12, 1571, he at first maintained that he had not dealt in any way in the matter concerning the Queen of Scots and the Duke of Norfolk, but he said he had heard by common report that the Queen of Scots had practised against the Queen's Majesty in stirring up the last rebellion and in seeking to marry with the Duke (*Salisbury MSS.*, i, 535; not printed by Murdin). On October 13 Goodyer said that he had spoken with the Queen of Scots but once in his life, on the day she removed from Coventry to Tutbury, when she spoke of a spaniel, the weather, the redness of her hand, and "'lastly somewhat as the time served of her innocency touching the matters whereof she is commonly charged'" (*Salisbury MSS.*, i, 536; not in Murdin). Perhaps this was the time she gave him the buttons of gold which he wore on his cap and doublet, according to the testimony, October 6, 1583, of John Somerfeld, one of Goodyer's helpers at Coventry (*C.S.P.D.*, *1581-90*, ed. Robert Lemon, 1865, p. 124, vol. clxiii, art. 4; see also Cass, p. 146). Goodyer finally confessed at length to Burghley, October 27, 1571, admitting his communications with the Queen of Scots, the Bishop of Ross, and the Duke of Norfolk, even to the correspondence with Norfolk in cipher; but he protested his innocence of any part in a plot of treason. He had evidently been accused of pretending that he was descended from King Edward IV, as he says, "for the alledginge of my discente from Ed. the 4th, I assure yor L. upon my faythe & credytt I never did it" (Cass, p. 146; *C.S.P.D.*, *1547-80*, ed. Lemon, 1856, p. 426, vol. lxxxi, art. 56). The accusation about his descent from Edward IV probably arose from a connection between Goodyer's ancestor Sir Thomas Hawte and the Woodviles (see the letter by the younger Sir Henry Goodyer to Buckingham, quoted later in this Note). It will be remembered that Edward IV married Lady Elizabeth Grey, formerly a Woodvile.

As a result of his activities on behalf of Mary Stuart and Norfolk, Goodyer was made a prisoner in the Tower. William Camden in *The History of Elizabeth, Queen of England* (1688, p. 163), under the date September 7, 1571, in an account of the trial of Norfolk, says:

> Afterwards *Banister*, who was the Duke's Counsellour at Law, the Earls of *Arundell* and *Southampton*, the Lord *Lumley*, the Lord *Cobham*, and *Thomas* his Brother, *Henry Percy*, *Lowder*, *Powell*, *Goodyer*, and others, were committed to Prison, who every one of them in hopes of Pardon confessed what they knew.

The names of Goodyer and Norfolk are included in a list of prisoners in the time of Sir Owen Hopton, Lieutenant of the Tower (John Bayley, *The History and Antiquities of the Tower of London*, Part II [1821], Appendix, p. lvii). Goodyer's name is also in a list of the prisoners, compiled June 14, 1572, twelve days after the execution of Norfolk (Lansdowne MS. 14, No. 16; the same list is printed in *Miscellanea*, the Catholic Record Society, i [1905], 59-60, as from Lansdowne MS. 73, No. 16, but this reference is an error). On July 18, 1572, Goodyer wrote at length from the Tower to Burghley (Lansdowne MS. 15, fol. 165^{r}), first apologizing on behalf of his brother Thomas, who had been suing for his release, and then continuing:

> If it please hir ma^{tie} to contynue this my imprysonmente, for my offence or for anye other cause knowen to hir H^{nes} hir selfe/ I doo moste humblye submytt my selfe whollye to hir m^{ties} wylle, and pleasure in that behalfe: and will moste willinglye, and gladlye accepte of this punishment, or of anye other that it shall please hir H^{nes} to laye vpon me, yf my sufferinge of the same in anye sorte maye be the meane to satisfye hir ma^{ties} heauye displeasure conceyued agaynste me, for whatsoeuer hathe bene said heretofore by my selfe or by any other for me, of my myserye, of my extreme wante, and necessitye, allthoughe I haue so greate cawse still to complayne, as no manne can̄ haue more, yett make I lytell accompt, or no reckonynge at all thearof, in respecte of hir ma^{ties} good grace & fauoure, wch is the onelye thinge in effecte that I haue hitherto soughte, and sued for, by all the dutyfull meanes, that I possiblye colde deuyse. And I assure yor L. it shall mooche better contente me to lyue at lybertye hereafter, (when it shall please hir ma^{tie} to graunte me the same,) in the pooreste estate that I may be, wth hir H^{nes} fauoure, then to lyve in mooche better case then I did before I cam̄ to this place, wth hir ma^{ties} displeasure: the heauye burthen whearof hathe bene, and is so greuous to me, as I am forsed to sinck vnder the weighte tharof: hauinge borne it, (to my extreme grefe, and Loss manye wayes/ nowe allmoste theas nyne yeres, not allwayes for the greatest cawses, (god he knowethe) though nowe soom waye (I muste confess) iustelye for my desartes. . . .

Something of Goodyer's "so high and glorious a Stile" may be gleaned from this letter. He may have written No. 147 about this time. Just why he should have been in Elizabeth's ill graces for nine years is not clear; certainly he seems never to have regained her good will. Sir John Stanhope wrote Viscount Cranborne in March, 1605, that although Goodyer was delivered out of the Tower after some time, he never recovered the good opinion of the late queen (*Salisbury MSS.*, xvii [1938], 120). His nephew and heir, also Sir Henry Goodyer, seeking redress of the family estate, wrote Cecil December 31, 1604, reminding him that his uncle had suffered imprisonment, disgrace, and loss of fortune because of the zeal he bore to the house of King James I (Cecil Papers 189, fol. 124, from a copy lent me by Mr. Bernard H. Newdigate). In much the same vein the younger Goodyer wrote the Duke of Buckingham February 24, 1619/20, referring to his ancient family "who by my greate grand father Sr Tho: Hawte can justly derive my selfe from Woodvile Earle of Rivers, w[ch] blood wheresoever it moves is for ever dignifyed, and enobled in having some dropps of it in y[e] sacred person of his Ma[ty]" (Sackville Papers 2451, from a copy also lent me by Mr. Newdigate).

Despite Queen Elizabeth's dislike of him, the elder Sir Henry Goodyer had a fairly distinguished career after his release from prison. He was knighted by the Earl of Leicester in Holland in 1586 (W. A. Shaw, *The Knights of England*, ii [London, Sherratt and Hughes, 1906], 85), and was a colonel in the army against the Armada in 1588 (*C.S.P.D. 1581-90*, p. 519, vol. ccxiii, arts. 86-87). Goodyer is remembered today chiefly for his patronage of the poet Michael Drayton, whom he is said to have sent to Oxford and who later was a witness to his will (Cass, p. 147). His death in 1595 inspired the following epitaph, given by William Camden in his *Remaines* (ed. 1614, p. 377):

To the honour of Sir Henry Goodyer of Polesworth
An ill yeare of a Goodyer vs bereft,
Who gon to God, much lacke of him here left
Full of good gifts, of body and of minde,
Wise, comely, learned, eloquent, and kinde.

It is indicative of the age that the imprisoned petitioner set out his plea for redress in verses, which were very probably intended for Queen Elizabeth herself. In No. 147 we have another example of "Tower literature."

[148] *Good ever due distroyed wth present yll*

Hand: same as the preceding, with the emendations in lines 33 and 37 in the same hand. As in No. 147 lines 13 and 14 are written in the right margin, opposite and below line 12. The Latin line at the end and the crossed-out ascription to "Dier" are written in printed script. The ascription "M[r] Norton" is in a different ink and possibly a different handwriting. An illegible word is scratched out after this.

Since No. 148 is an answer to No. 147, the two poems and their Notes must be read together. In MS. Gough Norfolk 43, fol. 53[v], No. 148 is headed, "An Aunswere to y[t] first is wretin." There is no ascription, but below the poem, in printed script, are the words, "Hic niger est hunc tu Regina Caueto." No. 148 is not in the manuscript in Archbishop Marsh's Library, Dublin, as is No. 147. The collation shows considerable difference between the two versions of No. 148. Neither copy appears to be reliable, but that in *AH* more closely answers the lines of No. 147.

4 may] can; the] yo[r]
5 wyked] wretched; theyre] soche
6 the] yow

7 guerdon] gwerdo; her] here
9 mishap] yor hap; hathe] had
12 lefte] leste
13 sinne] synnes
14 fayn'd . . . &] self vnsene ought moste offend one
22 of neyboure] a neighbo^{r}
23 good] true
25 now guiltye] who gilteles
26 and many] or any; thease] your
s
27 What] w^{ch}; ray⟨e⟩'d] raysed
32 ⟨of⟩ our] o^{ur}
let . . . they
33 now . . . can] now glose it as yow can
36 may . . . the] new graft maye lyve with changed
Whoes . . . wonted
37 Now . . . to ‸ be broughte] on heade stocke no more to be so wroughte
as
39 thy Queene] her; think] pursue; so] so; yll] fowle
40 breede . . . happye] wynne to perell of her lief or
41 grãnt . . . see] an aged quene make to remayne
42 to . . . thee] beyond her lief y^{t} made yow erre in vayne

The *D.N.B.* gives a fairly full account of the part played by Thomas Norton (1532-84), the zealous Protestant, in the religio-political conflict of the period. Before No. 148 was written, Norton had published pamphlets concerned with the Catholic "rising in the North," which rallied about the figure of Mary Stuart as the future ruler of England. In 1569 he published *To the Quenes Maiesties poore deceiued Subiects of the Northe Contrey, drawen into rebellion by the Earles of Northumberland and Westmerland*, which went into three editions within the year (*S.T.C.* 18680-18682; title quoted from the British Museum copy of the second). Later in the same year he brought out *A warning agaynst the dangerous practises of Papistes, and specially the parteners of the late Rebellion*, which went into two editions, the second probably in 1570 (*S.T.C.* 18686, 18687; title and quotation following taken from the British Museum copy of the second). A passage in the second pamphlet may refer to an earlier time when Mary Stuart and her first husband, the Dauphin of France, took to themselves the titles of King and Queen of England:

> Let not be forgotten their [the Papists] glorienge in their champion of Guise. It is yet fresh and raw in remembrance, how openly they vttered their as it were applaudinges, gratulations, and cherefull significations of fauor to that side, euen when, as it is well knowen, the

> same familie of Guise sought, vnder color of his kinswomans title, and by that foren title which was made the title and fundation of this last rebellion, to inuade this land, to ouerthrow the Queenes maiesties estate, and to transport the crowne of our countrey to strangers (sig. F4^r).

The *D.N.B.* attributes to Norton *A discourse touching the pretended match betwene the Duke of Norfolke and the Queene of Scottes*, also under the 1569 date. But the British Museum Catalogue, describing the copy from which the title is here quoted (press mark 1724.5) makes no attribution of authorship and assigns it tentatively to the year 1571, which is followed in *S.T.C.* 13869, with the statement that it is sometimes attributed to Thomas Sampson.

Norton's religious zeal and legal ability were recognized by the authorities, and he was appointed to take notes at the trial of the Duke of Norfolk, January 10, 1571/2 (*Cobbett's Complete Collection of State Trials*, ed. T. B. Howell, i [1809], 958). It is not surprising, therefore, to find Norton writing a satiric reply to Goodyer's plea for mercy. Norton's answer should be compared with Anthony Munday's parody of No. 66 (see the Note on that poem). Like Munday, Norton went to Rome, in 1579, to gather information about English Catholics there, and in 1581 he became official censor of Catholic subjects in England (for a brief account of his activities after that time, see the Note on No. 66, line 81). He was well regarded as a poet. Jasper Heywood in "The Preface" to *The Seconde Tragedie of Seneca entituled Thyestes*, 1560, sig. *7^v, praises him. Heywood has been urging Seneca to seek a more learned translator for his tragedies and has suggested that Seneca go to the Inns of Court:

> There Sackuyldes Sonettes swetely sonste,
> and featly fyned bee,
> There Nortons ditties do delight,
> there Yeluertons doo flee
> Well pewrde with pen: suche yong men three,
> as weene thou mightst agayne,
> To be begotte as Pallas was,
> of myghtie Ioue his brayne.

Norton is the author of No. 300 (No. 289 in *TM*) and of No. 257 in *TM*, but I fear they no longer delight, nor, indeed, does *Gorboduc* (1565), written in collaboration with Sackville, despite the fact that it has the distinction of being the first English tragedy written in blank verse.

[149] *He that his myrthe hath lost whose comfort is dismayde*

Hand: same as the preceding. Emendations are in the hand of the poem, but in line 30 "be" is inserted in another ink. Line 22 is written over an erasure, and in line 54 the *t* of "to" is written over *d*. The manuscript was torn at lines 45-50 and is now mended; therefore the first part of lines 46, 48, and 50 are now wanting and are supplied in brackets. Line 41 consists only of catch words for the next page. The name of the author, Sir Edward Dyer (1543-1607), is revealed through the pun in line 74 and by the monogram "E.D." in the left margin by that line.

Collation is given with five contemporary manuscript copies, all written in late Elizabethan secretary.

(*A*) Bodleian MS. Ashmole 781, pp. 140-42, ascribed, "S^{r} Ed: Dyer," presents the longest of the versions, although not always the best. The manuscript is so illegible that photostats cannot be made from it. Ralph M. Sargent in his book *At the Court of Queen Elizabeth*, which has as its sub-title, "The Life and Lyrics of Sir Edward Dyer" (London: Oxford University Press, 1935, pp. 184-87, notes, pp. 205-07), uses *A* as his base text, with emendations from other versions.

(*B*) Bodleian MS. Tanner 306, fol. 173^{r,v}, has the ascription, "qth Dier."

(*C*) Bodleian MS. Rawl. Poet. 85, fols. 109^{r}, 110^{v}, 111^{r,v}, 112^{r,v}, is written in double lines and is ascribed, "E. dier," following the line, "Miserū est fuisse."

(*D*) British Museum MS. Harl. 6910, fols. 158^{v}-159^{r}, which has no ascription, is the shortest and probably the latest of the versions.

(*E*) Huntington MS. HM 198, vol. ii, fols. 43^{r}-45^{r}, is written in double lines and has no ascription.

comfort
1 his] is *A*; ⟨sorrow⟩] comfort *A-E*

2 hope ys vayne] feare is fallen: hope's in . . . *E*; faythe ys scorne] succoure voyd *D*: . . . scornd *A-C E*

3 have] hath *B E*

5 the] his *E*

6 *The line occurs twice in D, the first written between lines 4 and 5 and crossed out.* Yf . . . yeere] But if in day, or moneth, or yeare *Da*: If either day, or moneth, or yeare *Db*: . . . moneth the day . . . *E*; lightninge] lightsome *A*: lightening *D*: happy *E*

7 wth] by *C D*; he ys] he he is *E*

help his
8 feare] hope *C*: cheare *E*; hurt his] ⟨succour voyde⟩ *C*

9 w^{ch}] that *A B E*; noe] ne *E*; or] nor *A-D*: ne *E*

keepinge backe
10 making] makinge *C*; free] the *C*; wracke] lacke *A*: wrackes *D*

11 Oh] no *B*; well] good *C*; greefe] death *A-C E*; the mynde] that kinde *E*

12 whiche] That *E*; allways yeeldes] brynges allwayes the *C*; extreamest payns] extreame gref *A*; but] yet *A*: and *B C E*; leaves] keepes *A B E*; worst] leste *B*

13 but] yet *B*

14 knowledge] knowledg, *with an illegible word above* *C*; helpe] hope *C*: helpes *E*; doth] doe *E*

his
15 his] whose *A-C E*: ⟨whose⟩ *D*; spyrit] sprite *E*; to] the *A-C E*

17 My] whose *A*; fancies] senses *D*

18 Myne] whose *A*; an] a *A*; whose] that *A-C E*: which *D*; force] feare *B*; ys] hath *A-E*

19 My . . . thought] whose sense whose thoughte whose passions *A*: my sences passions are my thoughtes *B*: My sence is my passions spye My Thoughtes *C*: . . . thoughts *D E*

20 of famous Carthage] of Carthage *A*; or the towne w^{ch}] or the famous towne that *A*: or the towne that *B C*: . . . townes w^{ch} *D*: & of Troy that *E*

Lines 21-24 are wanting in D and lines 21-26 are wanting in E.

21 myne eyes] my face *A*; fall dothe] fall doe *B*: fales do *C*

22 &] But *C*; have] hath *B C*

23 thought . . . thought] thoughtes . . . thoughtes *B C*; ⟨who⟩] *omitted* *A-C*; somtyme] sometimes *A B*

24 somtyme] Sometymes *A C*; store] seate *B*: sore *C*; of rest] of quiet rest *A-C*; the nourse] *omitted* *A-C*

26 I eat] I ate *A*: did reape *C*; that] which *D*; did] doth *B*

27 To nettles now my corne my feelde] . . . my feelde My corne *C*: my Corne to nettles now . . . *E*

28 reade] reape *B*; this] the *A-C*; hiacinthe] Hiacintes *C*

29 peace . . . lyfe] ioy, the rest, the life *A*: reste, the lif the peace *B*: peace, the ioy the life *D*; that] w^{ch} *C D*; tofore] *omitted* *A-E*

⟨my⟩ my
30 Came] Come *C*; ⟨the⟩] my *A-D*: the *E*; the losse] my losse *A C E*; my smarte myght ^{be} the more]

. . . smarte the more *A C*: . . . stinge the more *B*: my hurt . . . *D*: they might stinge mee noe more *E*

Lines 31 and 32 are wanting in D.

31 So] Thus *A*; me⟨ enne ⟩] man *C*; best] last *C*; for] to *A-C E*

32 then deere] dere then *A-C E*; but] and *B*

33 stands] stood *A D*

34 Myne] my *A-E*; horror] sorrowe's *E*; fastned in] . . . on *C*; yea] yees *E*; hope hangde] . . . hanges *A-C*: hopes hange *E*

35 noe releefe] . . . delight *A*; would] will *A D*: dothe *B*

36 (well) soone] well *A-E*; myne] my *A C-E*

Lines 37-40 are wanting in E.

37 what pleasure] & nothing *A C*: what thing may *D*; ys] be *D*

38 Ah] wher *B*: Oh *D*; cares and playntes] plaintes & cares *A*: care and plainte *B*: playnte and care *C*: plaints and moane *D*; dothe] may *B*

Lines 39 and 40 are wanting in D.

39 am I] was I *B*; yea] then *A-C*

40 they] he *A B*: ⟨the⟩ he *C*; neere] to *B C*; are] hath *A-C*

41 Then] nowe *A*; ys] are *A*; thie sawce] thy souces *A*: the cause *C*: the sauce *D*: . . . fauour *E*; tormentes] tirementes *E*

42 wheare] what *A*; some] men *E*; have thowghte theare deathe for the but] through the have thought ther death but *A*: . . . through the but *B D E*: . . . Thy deathe for thee most *C*

43 The . . . the] Thy . . . thy *A B*; thankfullness] shamefastnes *C*

44 The . . . the] Thie . . . thie *B*; light] (lighte) ⟨knyght⟩ *corrected in a later hand* *C*; that] wch *B D*; in] through *E*

45 that] would *D*; I yt coulde] that I could *A B*: I could it *C*: I it might *D*

46 [Oh] that] or that *C*: O would *D*; wrathe] ronges *B*; iudgment myght] Iudgments did *D*

Lines 47-50 are wanting in D.

47 frayle] false *C*; vnconstant] inconstant *C E*; Kinde] sex *E*; oh] & *A C*; sure] safe *A-C*: faith *E*; in] & *E*; trothe] truste *A-C E*; to no man] in none *E*

48 [No w]omen] No women *A-C E*; be] are *E*; but] and *B C*

49 hate] had *A*; and] *omitted A*; fawlty one] faultie bene one *A*

50 [Nor]] nor *A C*: ne *B E*; [c]anne] can *A-C E*; frome me] me of *A B E*: me from *C*; the] those *B*; in whiche] Wherin *C*

51 Alone] I love *E*; in love] by love *B D E*: ⟨by loue⟩ (found out) In loue *C*; never yet] never sene as yett *B*: neuer yet *C*

52 The . . . or] nor in prince nor poore nore young nor old nor fond nor *A*: . . . the old the younge the fonde nor *B*: . . . are *C*: The yong, the old, the riche the poore, the fonde the *D*: . . . the ould the yong . . . *E*

A, B, C, and E here have the following four lines, quoted from B, with variants beneath:

Hurs still remayne must I by death by wrong by shame
Here *E* wronge by death *CE*

I cannot blot out of my brest that love hath wroughte hur nam
love wrought in her name *A E*
mynde What loue wroughte in her name *C*

I cannot set at nought that once I held so de^{a}re
held hast soe deare *A*
I haue held so deere *C E*

I cannot make it seme so farr that is in dede so nere

Lines 53-56 are wanting in D.

53 Nor that I] not . . . *B C*: I doe not *E*; this] such *E*

54 As . . . trothe] I never will betray such trust *A*: as on that wold betray such truth *B*; ⟨d⟩o (t)] & *A C*: to *B E*

55 But . . . never] nor shall it ever *A*; faythe bare word . . . *A*: word gave *B*

56 guift] dede *B*

57 Sithe . . . be] Sithe that . . . *B*: But since that it is *D*: Since . . . *E*; this] thus *C D*; yll] ⟨ill⟩ (evall) *B*

58 yeelde] hould *C*; curse] corse *B D E*

59 woodes] wood *B D*; becom⟨me⟩ (e)] remaine *A*

60 den] mines *E*; in wch I reste or rome] wherto noe light shall come *A*: to which no light shall com *B*: In wch Ile rest {alone / or run} *C*: wherin I . . . *D*: . . . runne *E*

61 feast] meate *A*

62 Whearwth] On which *D*; carcase] body *E*; vntill they] till they doe *A D E*

63 My] ⟨bed⟩ wyne of Niobe] my pillow . . . *A*: My {wine / coyne} . . . *C*: of Niobe my wine *E*; of Craggie] a cragged *D*

64 the . . . myne harmonye] my harmony the serpentes hisse *A*: . . . my hermonie *B-E*; shreekinge] schreeching *E*; clocke] rocke *A*

Lines 65-68 are wanting in D.

65 Myne] My *C E*

66 spytefull . . . or] . . . & *A E*: fortune spitfull foyles & *B*: . . . spoylles And *C*; dreery] dolefull *E*

67 walke] walkes *A E*; pathe] pathes *A*: parkes *E*; of] to *C*; playnt] plaintes *E*; my] the *B*

68 wheare] With *A*; Sisiphe] Sisiphus *A*; wretched] *omitted A E*; his] all his *A E*; in endles torment] in all endles paines to *A*: . . . payne doe *B*: . . . paynes do *C E*

Lines 69-72 are wanting in E.

69 fayninge poetes] Poets fained *A C*: fayned poets *D*

70 rufull] ruthfull *B D*; flyght] plight *A B D*; playnte *C*; fall] fate *D*; or] & *A B C*

71 are] is *A-D*; greefs] greefe *A B D*: woe *C*; whearin] in which *D*; sterue or] strive or *A*: starve and *B C*: serue & *D*

72 feelethe] feele it *B*: fyndeth *D*; yt] tis *C*; yf his compare] comparinge his *A*: . . . compars *B*: if he compare *D*

73 songe] verse *D*: Muse *E*; greevous case] hevie case *B*: wrathfull state *E*; ys] was *D*

74 thowe let] that lest *A*: . . . lettst *E*; folly] follyes *C*

Lines 75 and 76 are wanting in D and E.

75 yt is] were this *A*: is the *B*: it were thee *C*

76 one the earthe] in the world *A C*; may] can *A C*; I] thee *A*; the] these *A*: this *B C*; accente] accents *A*: actaon *B*

A adds two lines:

And soe an end my tale is tould his life is but disdaind
whose sorrowes present paine him soe, his pleasures are full faind.

It is painfully evident that the versions differ considerably, indicating how much an Elizabethan poem might be changed as it was passed about from one collector to another. Unfortunately, it is very probable that no one of these versions presents the poem as the author wrote it. Sargent (work cited, pp. 202-03) discusses the difficulties in the editing of the poetry of Dyer, who did not collect his poetry, and who left no manuscripts in his own handwriting. The *AH* and *E* texts have not been previously collated. *E* is peculiarly interesting as it undoubtedly was the source for the first printed copy of the poem. The younger John Donne included No. 149, erroneously, in an edition of *Poems, Written by the Right Honorable William Earl of Pembroke. Whereof Many . . . are aunswered . . . By Sr Benjamin Ruddier*, 1660, pp. 29-30. A. B. Grosart in his edition of *The Writings in Verse and Prose of Sir Edward Dyer, Knt.* (*Miscellanies of the Fuller Worthies Library*, iv [1872], 25-32) prints No. 149 from *A*, collated with *B*, *C*, and *D*, and mistakenly refers to the above printed copy as of date 1620. The printed text omits and adds the same lines as does the *E* text; readings peculiar to *E* are, with but two or three exceptions (e.g., lines 30 and 60), found also in the printed copy. Common to the two are such striking differences as "that kinde," line 11; "& of Troy," line 20; "fauour" and "tirementes," line 41; "sex," line 47; "Muse" and "wrathfull state," line 73.

Even without the ascription to Dyer in *A*, *B*, and *C*, and the "E.D." monogram of *AH*, the play on the name in line 74 would lead to the supposition that he wrote the poem. Confirmation of his authorship is given by his younger friend and Somerset neighbor Sir John Harington, who in 1591 praised Dyer as "a man euer of great wit and worth" (*Orlando Furioso*, 1591, Book XVI, Notes, p. 126). Their relations were peculiarly close when Sir John was a student at Cambridge, as is sufficiently evident from a letter Sir John wrote Dyer in 1580 (see *Letters and Epigrams of Sir John Harington*, ed. N. E. McClure, 1930, pp. 61-62, and Sargent, pp. 74-75, who says that Dyer was at this time acting as guardian for the queen's godson). Alluding to line 44 of No. 149 in the Notes to Book VIII of his *Orlando Furioso* (ed. 1591, p. 63), Sir John says:

> But to proceede in the Allegorie these impediments that disturbe men in their good course are all but like owls or batts driuẽ away with the sunne shine: for the light of vnderstanding and the shining of true worthines, or (as *M. Dyer* in an excellent verse of his termeth it) the light that shines in worthines, dissolueth and disperseth these dustie impedimẽts, that let a man in his iorney to *Logestillas* Court, that is to the court of vertue, of temperance, of pietie, where all good lessons are taught, as shalbe showed more playne in that part of this booke, where *Rogero* comes to *Logestilla.*

These comments are interesting also in that they reveal the philosophic significance which the poem might have for an Elizabethan reader. They need not dispute Sargent's view that the poem refers immediately to Dyer's disfavor with Queen Elizabeth in 1572-75 (see p. 207, and for this period in his life, pp. 23-35). Nor is Sargent's view necessarily contrary to the appropriateness of the *AH* title if we interpret "his love" as the queen.

A close imitation of No. 149 was written by the Jesuit martyr Robert Southwell before his death in 1595, entitled, "A Phansie turned to a Sinner's Complaint," or, "Dyer's Phancy Turned to a Sinner's Complaint" (see *Complete Poems*, ed. A. B. Grosart, The Fuller Worthies Library, 1872, pp. 96-103). Fulke Greville, first Lord Brooke, in Sonnet LXXXIII of "Caelica" (*Certaine Learned and Elegant Workes*, 1633, pp. 228-33) follows somewhat the pattern of No. 149. John Davies in *Microcosmos* (1603, p. 17) answers the closing lines of No. 149, with perhaps a reference to the passage quoted from Sir John Harington, as follows:

> Thou virgin *Knight* that dost thy selfe obscure
> From *Worlds* vnequall *eies*, and faine wouldst *dy*
> *Er'* thy name should be knowne to *Worlds* impure,
> Now shew thy selfe, thou canst not hidden lie
> From our new *Worlds desert*, out-searching *EIE*.
> Great *Sidneies loue* (true proofe of thy great *worth*)
> Liue now, for now thou maist not living die;
> *Vertue* must vse thee, then (*Dyer Knight*) come forth
> To haile thy vertues *Loadstarre* from the *North*.

[150] *A withered plant, wth storim and lightninge blasted*

Hand: unidentified secretary. In line 13 the line under "hell" may indicate deletion, as the meter would seem to suggest.

I have found no other copy of this sonnet. Although the rhyme pattern is that of the ordinary English form, there is no division of thought to accord with the quatrains. It is, however, an excellent example of the figure *hirmus*, which George Puttenham in *The Arte of English Poesie* (ed. Gladys D. Willcock and Alice Walker, 1936, p. 176) calls "the long loose":

> Ye haue another maner of speach drawen out at length and going all after one tenure and with an imperfit sence till you come to the last word or verse which cōcludes the whole premisses with a perfit sence & full periode, the Greeks call it *Irmus*, I call him the [*long loose*] thus appearing in a dittie of Sir *Thomas Wyat* where he describes the diuers distempers of his bed.

The anonymous poet also, of course, makes use of *parison* and *anaphora.*

[151] *All women have vertues noble & excellent*

Hand: unidentified secretary.

An anonymous Scottish version of No. 151, plus an added comment on the double meaning, occurs on p. 356 of Magdalene College, Cambridge, MS. Pepys 2553, which is printed as *The Maitland Folio Manuscript Containing Poems by Sir Richard Maitland, Dunbar, Douglas, Henryson, and Others*, ed. Sir William A. Craigie, 2 vols., Scottish Text Society, New Series, vii, xx (1919, 1927). With the permission of the present General Editor of the Scottish Text Society, James Craigie, I give variants from the printed text, vol. i, p. 433:

1 have vertues] Ar guid
2 prove] say
3 god] thair god
6 in . . . shrewdnes] man can feind in yam bruikilnes
7 Commonly] *omitted*; have women] thay vse

Added in the Maitland text:

Reid this werss acording to ye meitter
& It is guid of wemen bot reid it to
ye nott ewin the contrair

Francis L. Utley in *The Crooked Rib* (Columbus, The Ohio State University Press, 1944), p. 107, refers to a copy in the manuscripts of the Marquis of Bath, Longleat, 258, which I have not seen. Mr. Utley has called my attention to the listing of this copy in *The Index of Middle English Verse*, ed. Carleton F. Brown and R. H. Robbins (New York, Printed for the Index Society by the Columbia University Press, 1943), p. 38, where the poem is said to occur on fol. 32^{v}.

A copy of No. 151 in *D*, fol. 18^{v}, with two additional stanzas, is attributed to Richard Hatfield. Ewald Flügel's transcription of this version is printed in *Neuenglisches Lesebuch*, 1895, p. 39; that by F. M. Padelford is in *Early Sixteenth Century Lyrics* (Boston, D. C. Heath, 1907), pp. 94-96. My transcription, which differs somewhat, is as follows:

All women have vertues noble & excelent
Who can ꝑceyve that/ they do offend
dayly/. they s^{ɔ}ve god w^{t} good intent
Seldome/ they dysplease there husbandes to theyr lyves end
Always/. to plese them they do intend
neu^{r}/ man may fynd in them srewdnes
comonly/. suche condycyons they haue more & lese.

What man can ꝑceyve that women be evyll
eu^{r}y man that hathe wytt, gretly wyll thē prayse
ffor Vyce: they Abhorre w^{t} all theyre wyll
prudence m^{r}cy & pacyence: they vse always
ffoly wrathe & cruelte. they hate As men says
meknes & all vertue. they practyse euer
syn. to Avoyde vertues they do procure

Sum men speke muche evyll be women
truly. therfore they be to blame
nothyng. A man may chekk in them
haboundantly. they haue of g^r^ce & good fame
Lakking. few vertues to a good name
in them fynd ye. All constantnes
they lak ꝑde. All srewdnes As I gese.
fynys q^d^ Rychard hattfeld

Nothing seems to be known about the Richard Hatfield who was a poet in the time of King Henry VIII. It seems probable that he came from Hatfield in the East Riding of Yorkshire. George Poulson, *The History and Antiquities of the Seigniory of Holderness in the East Riding of the County of York*, i (1840), 442, gives information about the Hatfield family of Hatfield. A Richard Hatfield of the time of Henry VII, Henry VIII, and Edward VI is named. He was son of John, lord of Hatfield, and his wife, Margaret, or Elizabeth, daughter of Rydnes. Richard died without issue. In *The Visitation of Yorkshire, 1563, 1564*, ed. C. B. Norcliffe, Harleian Society, xvi (1881), 157, two Richard Hatfields are given. One was third son of William by his wife, Margaret Stanton; the second Richard was nephew of the first, being fourth son of Robert by his wife, Margaret Boynton; but I judge this Richard was too late. Both the uncle and nephew are given as dying without issue. British Museum MSS. Add. 24436, fol. 63^v^, and 34106, fols. 88-89, have pedigrees of the Hatfield family, but the records begin with the early seventeenth century.

As the comment in the Maitland Folio MS. points out, the poem may be read in two ways, one exactly contradicting the other. Some examples of this device are noted by James R. Kreuzer, "Some Earlier Examples of the Rhetorical Device in *Ralph Roister Doister* (III. iv. 33 ff.)," *RES*, xiv (1938), 321-23; R. H. Robbins, "Punctuation Poems—A Further Note," *RES*, xv (1939), 206-07. Neither of these writers calls attention to Sir John Harington's epigrams, based on the lines of No. 151, which he wrote for his mother-in-law, Lady Rogers, and his wife. I quote from the *Epigrams* appended to the 1634 edition of his *Orlando Furioso*, sigs. Pp1^v^-Pp2^r^:

33 *Of writing with double pointing.*

It is said, that King Edward *of Carnarvan lying at Berkly Castle prisoner, a Cardinall wrote to his Keeper,* Edvardum occidere noli, timere bonum est, *which being read with the point at* timere, *it cost the King his life. Here ensues as doubtfull a point, but I trust, not so dangerous.*

Dames are indu'd with vertues excellent,
What man is he can prove that they offend?
Daily they serve the Lord with good intent:
Seld they displease their husbands, to their end
Alwaies to please them well they do intend:
Never in them one shall find shrewdnesse much,
Such are their humours, and their grace is such.

34 *To my Lady Rogers.*

Good Madame, in this verse observe one point,
That it seemes the Writer did appoint
With smoothest oyle of praise your eares to noint;
Yet one his purpose soon may disappoint.
For in this verse disparting but a point,
Will put this verse so clearly out of joynt,
That all this praise will scant be worth a point.

35 *To her Daughter upon the same point, reading the same verse with another point.*

Dames are indu'd with vertues excellent,
What man is he can prove that? they offend
Daily: they serve the Lord with good intent
Seld: they displease their husbands to their end
Alwayes: to please them well they do intend
Never: in them one shall find shrewdnesse much.
Such are their humours, and their graces such.

36

My *Mall*, the former verses this may teach you,
That some deceive, some are deceiv'd by showes,
For this verse in your praise so smooth that goes,
With one false point or stop did over-reach you,
And turn the praise to scorne, the rimes to prose,
By which you may be slanderd all as Shrowes:
And some (perhaps) may say, and speak no treason,
The verses had more time, the prose more reason.

[152] *The earthe and Sea a sunder shall*

Hand: unidentified secretary.
I have found no other copy of this sixain.

[153] *Ingratitude the greateste vice*

Hand: unidentified secretary.
For this, the last of the verses taken from Charlton's book, I have

found no other copy. This ten-line poem, with the rhyme scheme, *ababcdcdee*, and the meter of iambic tetrameter, was probably called a sonnet at the time it was written. For some further expressions on the theme of ingratitude see No. 63 and the Note on it.

PRELIMINARY NOTE ON NOS. 154-67

Nos. 154-67 are introduced to the *AH* reader by one of Bishop Percy's notes, written in ink at the top of fol. 108^r: "The 7 Penetential Psalms by Sr Thos Wyat (to pag. 118 inclusive) Printed 1549—12 mo." As indicated in the Introduction (pp. 46-50) and more fully in the Notes following, the *AH* copy of these Psalms is an edited text derived from the *E* MS., fols. 86^r-98^v, where the paraphrases are written in Wyatt's hand, with numerous revisions also in his hand. Another of Percy's notes introduces the Psalms in *E* (fol. 86^r), and that text of No. 154 is contemporaneously headed, "4 entͻ." The *AH* copy usually incorporates Wyatt's revisions. Some of the *AH* departures from *E* are clearly copyist's errors; others show that the copyist did not understand the author's meaning; still others were clearly introduced to regularize the measure.

Also derived from *E*, but with more changes than occur in *AH*, is the printed text of 1549 (*PC*), *Certayne psalmes . . . by Sir Thomas Wyat* (see the Introduction, p. 50). Nott and Muir do not give variant readings from this edition; Miss Foxwell's variant readings are taken from the Percy-Steevens printing of the work rather than from the 1549 edition itself (see Foxwell, ii, 133). The collation following, which includes variant readings from the copy of the 1549 printed text in the Cambridge University Library (Syn. 8.54.156), substantiates the point made in the Introduction that *PC* is an edited text, derived from *E*, but not through *AH*. *PC* has many poor readings, some of which are undoubtedly the fault of the printer.

Still a third derived text is extant in British Museum MS. Royal 17 A. XXII (*R*), a small vellum-bound volume of thirty-seven leaves, containing only Wyatt's Psalms, which are written in a careful text hand. The paraphrases are on fols. 3^r-36^r. The title of the *R* version of No. 154 is on fol. 2^v, "The prologue to the sixt psalme of Dauid." The collation shows that the *R* text also stems from *E*, with influence from a text close to *PC*. There are, however, independent readings in *R*.

Mr. Arundell Esdaile, formerly of the British Museum, discovered that a major source for Wyatt's metrical paraphrases of the Psalms was the prose version by Pietro Aretino, *I Sette Salmi De La Penitentia Di David*, first published in Venice in 1534 and in three other editions by 1540. Of his search for this source Mr. Esdaile wrote me, "I found Wyatt's source by the simple method of comparing every paraphrase of the Penitential Psalms in the B. M., of a possible date that is." In her *Study*, pp. 90-99, Miss Foxwell discusses in some detail the nature of

Wyatt's dependence upon Aretino's version, from which passages are quoted. In the Notes following I make no attempt to repeat this analysis. In summary it should be noted that although Wyatt departs frequently from passages in Aretino, he is significantly indebted to the Italian writer for the romantic concept of the Psalms as repentant laments uttered by David for his sin with Bathsheba (II Samuel 11, 12), with the dramatic and psychological progression secured through the prologues. In his article on "English Metrical Psalms in the Sixteenth Century and their Literary Significance" (*Huntington Library Quarterly*, ix [1946], 262-63), Hallett Smith says that in Wyatt's paraphrases "David is made the author of a kind of *de remedia amoris*," and, further, that "the mind of the courtier has turned divine poetry to its own use." We may, however, question the decorum of this procedure.

Wyatt's paraphrases should not be referred to as translations from Aretino, for he frequently leaves Aretino's elaborate passages to follow the Vulgate, or the simple but dignified translations in the 1530 Psalter or the Great Bible.

From passages in Nos. 159 and 167 especially we may suppose that Wyatt was at work on the Psalms in 1540 and 1541, after the fall of his friend Thomas Cromwell, and possibly during and after his own imprisonment in 1541.

Critical opinion of the paraphrases varies, but I am convinced that a more careful study than has yet been made, especially in connection with the revisions as given in the *E* MS., would bring us to a better understanding of Wyatt's poetics. The lack of understanding of his contemporaries is illustrated in the three derived texts.

[154] *Love to geve lawe vnto his subiectes hartes*

Hand A. In line 16 a portion of "thinges best" is written over an erasure.

See the preliminary note on Nos. 154-67.

Collation is given with the following texts: *E*, fols. 86^{r}-87^{r}: *PC*, sigs. A3^{r}-A6^{r}; *R*, fols. 3^{r}-5^{v}.

1 subiectes] subiect *E R*
3 hym self] hymselfes *PC*
4 Davides] David *E*
5 David] dasdd *E R*
venemed
6 venemd] ⟨poyson⟩ *E*; venmed *PC*
7 Towch't . . . ranne] towcht his sensis/ and ouↄ ronnis *E*: Touche his senewes, and ouer runnes *PC*
creping
8 creaping] ⟨sparplyd⟩ *E*; spark'led] sparplid *E*: sparkeled *PC*

moyst
10 moiste] ⟨warme⟩ *E*: noysome *PC*; hart] hert he *E PC R*

11 his] the *E PC R*

he
12 this] his *R PC*; he] ⟨at⟩ *E*

that had
15 that] ⟨wheroff⟩ *E*; love had printed] love prⁱntyd *E*

16 honoreth] honorth *E*; a] *omitted* *E R*

17 that forgott] that he forgotte *PC*; the . . . cast]
the wisdome ⟨and all⟩ and forecast
⟨and owt off mynd clene cast⟩ *E*

to
18 to] ⟨the⟩ *E*; this kinges do] the kynge dothe *PC*: . . . doth *E*

forth wᵗ
20 Yea and] ⟨and⟩ ye and *E*; forthwith] ⟨honors⟩ *E*

Vrye to go in to the feld
21 Vrye . . . field] ⟨vnder ꝑtence off victorye⟩ *E*

I say
22 I saye] ⟨to go⟩ *E*; Idolls] Ieweles *PC*

24 en'myes] enemyes *PC*; dye] be *PC*

owt of dowt
25 out of doute] ⟨all alone⟩ *E*

more then god/ or ⟨elles⟩
26 more . . . or] ⟨he doth owe more then⟩ *E*;

myndyth
he ⟨loveth⟩
he myndeth] ⟨or god⟩ *E*

after
27 after] ⟨when⟩ *E*

that ⟨his⟩ lust
28 that luste] ⟨this delyght⟩ *E*

from
30 from] ⟨and⟩ *E*

31 his] this *E R PC*

32 thinge] thynges *PC*; nought] nothing *PC*

trecherye
33 this] his *R*; trecherye] ⟨grete⟩ *E*

34 ruthfull] rufull *E PC*; set] settes *E PC R*

from
38 hym] *omitted* *PC R*; from] ⟨how⟩ *E*; threates alas]
thretes alas
⟨sore menace⟩ *E*

agid
40 this aged wofull] this ‸ woofull *E*: thys wofull aged *PC*

41 mete] metes *E*: meateth *PC*

42 heate] ⟨colour⟩ hete *E*; lymbs] lymyttes *PC*

43 drowpith] droppeth *PC R*

his er
44 his fyre] ⟨the⟩ fy⟨re⟩ *E*
45 heat] helth *R*; and] his *PC*; fyre] fere *E PC R*
pall
47 purple palle his] ⟨pall his⟩ purpull ‸ his *E*: purple pauler, hys *PC*; letts] letteth *PC*
48 throwthe] throweth *PC*
49 The pompous] Then pompious *PC*; of state and] & statelie *R*
50 rebates] rabates *E*: rebate *R PC*
vile
51 Th'inner vile clothe] ⟨a thyn cloth⟩ thynner vyle clothe *E*: Thinner vyle clothe *PC R*
fayre
53 His faire hore] his ‸ hore ⟨his⟩ *E*; of] w^{t} *R*
54 hears] here *E*: heyre *PC*; knowinge his wickednes]
knowyng wykednes
⟨repentyng⟩ his ⟨excesse⟩ *E*
he ū
55 was he] ⟨he⟩ was ‸ *E*; self] *omitted* *PC*; repentante] repentance *E PC R*
th
57 takes] ⟨hath⟩ take⟨n⟩ *E*: takethe *PC R*; in hand] in ⟨his⟩ hand *E*
his
58 offerith] offerth *E*: offreth *PC*; his playntes] ⟨the⟩
his sowle
plaintes *E*: playnts *PC*; his soule to save] ⟨and the
to save
Cryes⟩ *E*
59 distills] dystylleth *PC*
60 hym] hym selfe *PC*; depe] *omitted* *E PC R*
61 grownds] grownd *E PC R*; wheare in] wher *PC*:
hym
whence *R*; might hym] myght ‸ *E*
as
62 fflyeng] fleing *E*: flyinge *PC*; as in] ‸ in *E*: or] or ⟨in⟩ *E*
did make
64 did make] ⟨mad⟩ *E*
or
65 he] *omitted* *PC*; or] ⟨of⟩ *E*
rof that
66 Of that] ⟨the thinge⟩ *E*; that] whyche *PC*
67 ffalleth] fallth *E R*
68 yfraughted] frawtyd *E PC R*
69 his . . . claye] depe draughtes of hys decaye *PC*: and touching of the stringes *R*

sekyng to
70 Dressid] dressing *R*; sekinge to counterpayse] ⟨he tunes his
cōterpese
god to plese⟩ *E*
71 songe] songes *PC*

Analyzing the collation, we find that the three subsidiary texts, *AH*, *PC*, and *R*, stem from Wyatt's own text as written and corrected by him in the *E* MS., for despite differences they tend to follow Wyatt's corrected readings. The *AH* text has several independent readings, which, with two exceptions, indicate editorial change. Thus the *AH* readings in lines 1, 11, 34, 45, and 55 appear to have been made for a supposedly better meaning in sense, and those in lines 57, 60, and 68 to effect a smoother metrical line. The omission of "he" in line 10, thereby making the line less regular, and the use of "David" in line 5 must be the result of copyist's errors. *AH*, it may be noted, does follow *E* in line 69, where *PC* and *R* depart, each with marked independence. *PC* has more independent readings than do the other two derived texts. Some of these, as in lines 42 and 47, were no doubt due to the printer, but deliberate change is indicated in *PC* in lines 10, 18, 22, 24, 60, and 69. Although the *R* text agrees with *PC* against *E* and *AH* in lines 38, 43, and 50, it is independent in lines 45, 49, 53, 61, 69, and 70. The distinctive reading in line 69 alone shows that it is not a mere copy. Clearly no one of the manuscripts served as copy text for the printed edition, or, if so, considerable change was introduced.

I am indebted to Richard C. Harrier for calling my attention to the *E* MS. reading in line 66. In my collation I have accepted the reading "rof" recently put forward by Harrier in "Notes on the Text and Interpretation of Sir Thomas Wyatt's Poetry" (*N and Q*, CXCIX [1953], 234). I agree that there is an *r* before "of" at the beginning of the line. Harrier points out that the object of "rof," i.e., took, is David's harp, mentioned in line 67. Wyatt's modern editors, however, have followed the other contemporary texts, which have *of*. See Nott, ii, 106; Foxwell, i, 208; Muir, p. 205. Muir, answering Harrier's "Notes" (p. 236), maintains that "of" is preceded by an accidental mark, not an *r*.

[155] *O Lorde sence in my mowthe thie mightie name*

Hand A. Letters or words are written over erasures in the following lines: 17, "kte" in "provokte," probably over an erased "eth"; 31, "d" in "trowbled," over an erased "th"; 35, "in"; 36, "as" in "assayle"; 38, "che" in "wretche"; 49, the final "h" in "hathe"; 71, "esse" in "confesse"; 96, "them byd." As indicated in the text, the "finis" for this paraphrase, which belongs after line 111, was written by the copyist after the first stanza of the second prologue. This error may have come from the *E* MS. See below.

See the preliminary Note on Nos. 154-67.

Wyatt's draft of the paraphrase in *E*, fols. 87^{v}, $88^{r, v}$, now lacks lines 28-80. The leaf on which they were evidently written, old numbering pp. 173-74, is now missing. In the British Museum more recent folio numbering, this missing leaf is not taken into account. In *E* the heading is, "Domine ne in furore. Psal. 6." A "finis" at the end of the paraphrase is crossed out, but the interlaced initials "T V" remain.

Complete texts of No. 155 are given in *PC*, sigs. $A6^{r}$-$B2^{v}$, and in *R*, fols. 6^{r}-10^{r}.

1 in] ⟨off⟩ *E*: *omitted* *PC*; mowthe] mowght *E*
2 Sufferth] Suffereth *PC*; call] to call *PC*
hope taken
3 harte] harpe *PC*; hope taken] ⟨cawght cōfort⟩ *E*: he taken *PC*
mercy as the
5 mercye as the] ⟨euↄ the same⟩ *E*
6 Onlye comforte of] Of onely comfort to *PC*; wretchid]
wrechid
⟨vs⟩ *E*
8 thie] the *PC R*; this] *inserted* *E*
open
13 thee for] the the *E R*: Thee *PC*; open] ⟨knolege⟩ *E*
15 it in] it not in *E PC R*; lardgenes] ⟨lengh⟩ largenes *E*
17 provokte] provok⟨eth⟩t *E*: prouoked *PC*; mye] myne *R*
for recompence
19 for recompence] ⟨p^{r}pare agayne⟩ *E*
is the I have
22 More . . . remedye] ⟨And have⟩ more ‸ nede ‸ of ⟨the for⟩ remede *E*
es
24 straieth] strays *R*; sekes] sek⟨th⟩ *E*
25 I seeke] and seke *PC*
fele
26 ffeele] ⟨for⟩ *E*
in onles
27 in] ⟨for⟩ *E*; vnlesse] ⟨of⟩ *E*; me assure] me ⟨not⟩ assure *E*

Lines 28-80 are wanting in E.

30 Threateth] Tretith *R*
33 worldlye] worlds *R*; vanytie] vanities *PC*
34 weyke] *omitted* *PC*
37 vse] pleasure *PC*
38 shadowe] shade *PC R*
44 o . . . beseche] I beseche thee o lorde *PC*
45 thie] thine *R*
48 hath] had *PC*; tane] had *PC*

51 sharp'the] sharpeth *PC*
53 great] *omitted R*; turnes] turneth *PC R*
55 rightuous] rightwise *R*
Between lines 58 and 59 of AH, PC and R have the following line; quoted from PC:
For that in deathe there is no memorye
66 for] *omitted PC*
68 In momente] In a moment *PC*
72 done] denne *PC*
73 it] hym *PC*
74 suffers] suffreth *PC*: sufferth *R*; nowe] none *PC*
75 mightye] nightly *R*
78 stirr] stere *PC*
81 besettes] bysett *E PC R*
82 trappes] ⟨gye⟩ trapps *E*
som to my weping
83 some do] ⟨the and⟩ do ⟨th⟩ *E*; to my weeping] ⟨vnto myn⟩ *E*: to me, my wepinge *PC*; lo] *omitted R PC*
84 the maner] manere *R*; bewtie] bea^{u}te *E read by Foxwell and Muir as "bealte"*; and] or *PC*
87 Those] These *PC*
88 shew] shewe *E illegible word above*; my] myne *R*
89 my] myne *R*
90 the] *omitted PC*
ryches
91 riches] ⟨glory⟩ *E*
92 theise] the *PC R*
93 my] mine *R*
94 comes] comth *E*: commeth *PC*: cometh *R*
95 hart those] harpe these *PC*: . . . these *R*
herd I say &
99 herd I say and] ⟨pitid for to⟩ *E*; sene] seme *R*
100 pittieth] pitith *E*
102 therefore] the rule *E R*: thee rule *PC*
the
103 the] ⟨by⟩ *E*: that thee *PC*; glawncynge bayte] glosinge
baite
⟨venem⟩ *E*: glosing bayte *PC R*
made them
104 Made them] ⟨that had⟩ *E*; vsurpp] vsurpt *E Wyatt neglected to delete final "t" when revising*
so
105 that so lye in] y^{t} ‸ ly in ⟨&⟩ *E*: that so do lye in *PC*

107 decaye] decayte *E*: dysceyte *PC*: deceite *R*

i
108 as] ⟨a⟩s *E* *the "i" written over "a"*

sugestion
109 suggestion] ⟨entreprise⟩ *E*

Independent readings are fewer than in No. 154, but the relation of the texts is essentially the same, with *AH*, *PC*, and *R* showing derivation from Wyatt's text in *E*, as indicated by the portion still extant in that manuscript. *PC* is again the least reliable of the three subsidiary texts. Although *AH* usually follows Wyatt's corrected readings, it is occasionally independent, as in lines 15, 94, 102, 103, 107. In the last instance the *AH* "decaye," which is probably a copyist's error for the "decayte" of *E*, curiously disturbs the *terza rima* rhyme pattern. Presumably the additional line found in *PC* and *R* (following *AH* line 58) was originally in the *E* text, for without it the rhyme pattern is again disturbed and a part of verse 5 in the Psalm is omitted. Nevertheless, the very closeness of the line to the Vulgate and to the Great Bible is unlike Wyatt's general method in the paraphrases. The Latin runs: "Quoniam non est in morte, qui memor sit Tui," which is translated in the Great Bible, "For in death no man remembreth the" (ed. 1541, sig. Aa 2^{v}). But seldom does Wyatt speak with the moving simplicity of Psalm 6, which has only ten short verses. With lines 1-30, which derive from Aretino (Foxwell, i, 209), contrast the two opening verses in the Great Bible:

> O Lorde, rebuke me not in thyne indygnacion: nether chasten me in thy displeasure. Haue mercye vpon me, O Lorde: for I am weake: O Lorde heale mee for my bones are vexed.

Wyatt's line 50 echoes the latter part of the second verse. As Miss Foxwell has noted (i, 213-14), in lines 79-80 and 96-97, which refer to verses 7 and 8 of the Psalm, Wyatt seems to have been influenced by the 1530 Psalter, which reads:

> My face is wrinkled and dried vp with kare and anger; my enymes have made it full thirme with trouble.
> Avoide from me ye workers of wikednes: for the lorde hath harde my complaintis powerd oute with wepinges. (sig. $A8^{v}$)

Lines 81-95, with the reference to David's sin with Bathsheba and the baits of mermaids, lead us far from the Psalm to the prose of Aretino (Foxwell, i, 213).

No. 155 well illustrates, I think, the criticism I have made in the preliminary Note on the lack of decorum in the Psalms paraphrases by Wyatt.

[156] *Who so hathe sene the sick in his feaver*

Hand A. On the "ffinis" following line 8, see the Note on No. 155. In line 6 "downe rolde" is written over an erasure.

Wyatt's draft, signed "T V," is in *E*, fols. 88^{v}-89^{r}. Texts are also in *PC*, sigs. B3^{r}-B4^{r}, and in *R*, fols. 10^{v}-11^{v}.

fevour
1 feaver] ⟨dolour⟩ *E*
the hete
2 After] afftre ⟨the⟩ *E*; heat] ⟨thete⟩ *E*: the heate *PC*; wth] *omitted* *E PC R*
3 furour] faruour *E R*: fevour *PC*
let hym I say behold
4 let . . . beholde] ⟨wth sobbyng double fold⟩ *E*
5 Sorowfull] ⟨let hym⟩ sorowfull *E*
6 the] his *PC*; eyes] eyen *PC*; downe] *inserted* *E*
7 adowne] downe *PC*
11 errour] terrour *PC*
13 willd] wyll *PC*; his] *inserted* *E*
beknowyng
14 by knowing] ⟨and knoleging⟩ *E*: be knowynge *PC R*
15 to] for to *E*
16 Easyd] esdd *E*: Eesd *R*: And *PC*; helde] healed *PC*; filleth] felith *E PC R*
17 Semethe] ⟨Now⟩ semyth *E*: Nowe semeth *PC*; horrible] fearefull *PC*
for tremble
18 for to tremble] ‸ to ⟨be adrad⟩ *E*
19 or] of *PC*
20 doth] dyd *PC*
him
21 hathe] had *E PC R*; so . . . grave] so ‸ knele w^{t} in th grave *E*: so kneeling with in the graue *PC*
22 Th'ebrues] the hebrewes *PC*
26 a whyle hym self] himself a while *R*; besought] bethowght *E PC*
27 Gatheringe] gadryng *E R*; sprytes] spirites *PC R*; weare] where *E*
28 agayne] agayne ⟨&⟩ *E*; into] vnto *PC*; caught] rowght *E PC R*
strained agayne
32 strayned] ⟨lowd⟩ *E*; agayne] ⟨lo⟩ *E*; Cryethe] ⟨ ⟩ cryth *E*: cryed *PC*

This prologue to the second of Wyatt's Penitential Psalms is based on Aretino (see Foxwell, i, 215; *Study*, p. 93).

Commenting on the phrase "With vapourd eyes" in line 25, Nott (ii, 567) points out that it was "adopted by Surrey"; and Miss Foxwell (ii, 138) that it is one "of the many phrases imitated by Surrey." Actually, it was almost certainly Surrey who first used the expression which appears in line 12 of his sonnet "When Windesor walles," written in 1537 (see Padelford, No. 30 and note). Further, lines 27, 31-32 in No. 154 are suggestive of lines 41-42 in Surrey's poem "In winters iust returne, when Boreas gan his raigne" (ed. Padelford, No. 24).

[157] *Oh, Happie are they that have forgevenesse gott*

Hand A. In line 60 "alone this" is written over an erasure.

See the preliminary Note on Nos. 154-67.

Wyatt's draft in *E*, fols. 89^{r}-90^{v}, is signed, "T V," and is headed, "Psal: 32 beati quoR remisse sũt." Texts are also in *PC*, sigs. B4^{v}-B7^{v}, and in *R*, fols. 12^{r}-15^{r}.

1 that] ⟨that⟩ y^{t} *E*

and
7 and] ⟨y^{t}⟩ *E*; coverthe] couert *PC*

w^{t} in a marcifull discharge
8 within . . . dischardge] ⟨vnder the mantell off m^{r}cy⟩ *E*

and / the willfullnes
9 And] ⟨oh⟩ *E*; the wilfullnes] ⟨forgeffe⟩ *E*

of ⟨wt⟩
13 Of] ⟨off⟩ *E*; others fault] other faultes *PC*; to . . .

to suffer the Dolour
Dolour] ⟨examplid theire errour⟩ *E*

was / execute
14 was] ⟨did⟩ *E*; execute] ⟨it extend⟩ *E*

16 he] *inserted* *E*

18 But] And *PC*

19 fresshe] *inserted* *E*; and] *omitted* *E PC R*; stripped] ⟨y⟩ stryppid *E*

owght
20 spryte] spirite *R*; ought] ⟨nothing⟩ *E*

by cause
21 I, for becawse] I⟨I⟩ for ⟨that⟩ *E*; had] hidd *E PC R*

thy^{n} kinge by state in
22 Thyncking . . . preferd] ⟨and for to shew my⟩ fawte

to be ⟨deberd⟩ ꝑferd
⟨haue bene aferd⟩ *E*

⟨and⟩ do
23 Do fynde] ⟨do⟩ fynd⟨es⟩ *E*

24 feeles . . . hynderd] fyndeth, hys healthe hyndered *PC*: feleth . . . *R*

26 Leathis] lechis *E R*

and
27 And] ⟨Dyd⟩ *E*

rage ⟨did skill⟩ roryng in excesse
28 radge . . . excesse] ⟨plaint y^{t} I by force expresse⟩ *E*
29 Thie] ⟨And for⟩ thy *E*; The *PC*; was so encreaste]
⟨did⟩ was
⟨hath⟩ so encreast *E*
priking
31 pricking] ⟨restles⟩ *E*
32 That] y^{t} ⟨I am⟩ *E*
33 hathe] haue *R*
from
37 from] ⟨to⟩ *E*
38 confesse] ⟨bemon⟩ cōfesse *E*
⟨to⟩ for
44 for] ⟨for⟩ *E*
stormes
45 stormes] ⟨waves⟩ *E*; hym mysse] *omitted* *PC*
49 Ioye] Ioyes *PC*; scapes] scapeth *PC*; en'myes] enemyes *PC*
50 bondes] bandes *PC*; his] *omitted* *PC*
51 ioye mye] is my *PC*
53 light] syght *PC R*; porte] lyghte *PC R*
55 looke] boke *PC*: booke *R*
58 redresse] adresse *E PC*
59 Myne] My *PC R*; eyes] eye *PC R*
60 I] ⟨be⟩ I *E*; alone] onlye *PC*
61 moyle] mule *E R*; man dothe] men do *PC*
62 not his] his *PC R*
63 hym must] muste hym *PC*
64 bryd'led] brydeld *E*: brideled *PC*; least] ⟨yt⟩ lest *E*; guide] maister *R*
65 are the] there are *PC*
67 in watche] and watche *PC*
69 ffilld] Feld *R*; that] ⟨but⟩ y^{t} *E*
hert
70 hart] ⟨mynd⟩ *E*; so] to *E R*; blynde] bynd *E R*
I say
73 saye] ⟨o⟩ *E*: I saye *PC R*; ye] you *PC*; be] be⟨ne⟩ *E*
makth & holdyth
74 makethe and holdethe] ⟨doth cōtynew⟩ *E*
alwey set
75 In . . . must] in hym ⟨I say set all⟩ yor glory ‸ yow must *E*
76 All] All ye *E R*: All you *PC*; an] *omitted* *E PC*

The greater part of the collation shows, of course, that *AH*, *PC*, and *R* usually follow Wyatt's corrected text. The *AH* reading of "Leathis" for "lechis" in line 26, though not authoritative, is interesting. The copyist may have been uncertain about Wyatt's handwriting, which is often crabbed. "Leathis Cure" would refer to forgetfulness and would make sense. In line 70 the *AH* copyist does not make sense. Strangely enough, in line 76 *AH* does not adopt Wyatt's regular iambic line.

Following Aretino (see Foxwell, i, 217), Wyatt's opening lines, 1-16, expand very considerably the first verse of Psalm 32, which is simply given in the Great Bible, "Blessed is he, whose vnright'ousness is forgyuē: & whose synne is couered" (ed. 1541, sig. Aa6^{v}). Verses 2-11 of the Psalm are less elaborately developed, and in some lines Wyatt is close to the original. Compare lines 21-33 with verses 3 and 4, which read in the Vulgate (Psalm 31):

> Quoniam tacui, inveteraverunt ossa mea, dum clamarem tota die.
> Quoniam die ac nocte gravata est super me manus Tua, conversus sum in ærumna mea, dum configitur spina.

It is interesting to find that in line 29, translating "dum clamarem tota die," Wyatt is close to the King James version, "through my roaring all the day long." The Great Bible has, "thorow my dayly complaynynge."

Several lines in No. 157 are suggestive of Surrey's poetry. With line 10 compare Surrey's, "The adder all her sloughe awaye she slinges," in the sonnet "The soote season" (ed. Padelford, No. 2). Lines 23-24 and 32-33 are strikingly like lines in Surrey's poem "The sonne hath twyse brought forthe the tender grene" (ed. Padelford, No. 11, lines 1-2, 5-6, 27; *AH*, No. 74, Note). With lines 32-33 compare also Surrey's "Set me wheras the sonne dothe perche the grene" (ed. Padelford, No. 6). As in No. 156 it is quite probable that these similarities reflect influence of the younger poet upon Wyatt, for the references to nature are common in Surrey's poetry but rare in Wyatt's, and the manner of expression is Surrey's.

[158] *This songe endid, David did stynte his voyce*

Hand A. Letters over erasures occur in lines as follows: 7, "es hand"; 15, "Carved in Rock."

See the preliminary Note on Nos. 154-67.

Wyatt's draft of this prologue to the third Penitential Psalm is in *E*, fols. 90^{v}-91^{r}, signed, "T V." Texts are also in *PC*, sig. B7^{v}-C1^{r} and in *R*, fols. 15^{r}-16^{r}.

1 songe] *inserted* *E*; David] ⟨did y^{t}⟩ David *E*; did stynte] ⟨held⟩ [did stynt above] *E*: did skant *R*; voyce] ⟨pees⟩ [voyce above] *E*

2 a boute he] ⟨did seke⟩ [abowte he above] *E*: he aboute *PC*

3 Did seeke] *inserted* *E*; Cave] darke Cave *E*: darcke caue *PC R*

4 His] ⟨ye⟩ his *E* *written over "ye"*; seem'de] semid ⟨his⟩ *E*: semed *R*

pees this pees y^{t}
5 Vppon . . . that] Apon this ⟨marcy wheron he⟩ *E*: Vppon hys harpe . . . *PC*

sowle
6 The Soule] the ⟨hert for⟩ *E*: crye] cal *R*

plentifull
7 plentifull mercyes] mercy full *E*: plentifulles *R*
8 wheare] whi *R*
9 As] ⟨And⟩ as *E*; that] *omitted* *PC*
10 the] *omitted* *PC R*

yt
13 that seemyd] ⟨and⟩ semid *E*: did seme as *R*; that] thee *PC*

marble
14 Marble] ⟨and⟩ ‸ ymage *E*: a marble *PC*
15 in Rock] in the rokke *E*: in the rocke *PC R*; handes]

on hygh
hande *PC*; on highe] ⟨lyfft vp⟩ *E*

made as
16 Made as] ⟨semÿge⟩ ‸ by *E*: Made is *PC*; playne]

plaine
⟨syghe⟩ *E*; sighe] ⟨supp⟩ sygh *E*
17 The] This *E PC R*; beame] beme *E PC R*; that brighte

bryght
sonne] ⟨down from⟩ that ‸ sonne *E*; forthe sendes]

forth
⟨dis⟩sendes *E*: forthe sendeth *PC*
18 theare] *omitted* *E PC R*; clowde] sonne *PC R*; could] *inserted* *E*
19 his] the *E PC R*; descendes] descendethe *PC*

whose ⟨small⟩ glawncÿg light
20 Whose . . . lighte] ⟨and w^{t} the lustre on⟩ *E*; cordes]

did ouD
world *PC*; did over] ⟨it⟩ *E*
21 glister] luyster *E PC R*; extendes] extendethe *PC*
23 starte] stette *PC*

affect
25 then] more *PC*; affecte] ⟨desire⟩ *E*: effecte *PC*

⟨erst⟩ he was erst off
26 he . . . of] ⟨off his Idolle⟩ *E*
27 lefte] list *R*; the earthe] therthe *R*
28 And] *omitted* *PC*; the tother] the other *PC*
29 his] thee *PC*; lefte] lift *R*

sure
30 Sure] ⟨assured⟩ *E*: For *PC*; and] hys *PC*
31 eke] *omitted* *E PC R*
32 looke] voyce *E PC R*

In two lines of the poem Wyatt's intentions as given in *E* are not clear. Thus, in line 3 he did not delete "darke" after inserting "did seke," and *PC* and *R* accordingly retain the word, thereby giving the line six feet. Again, line 7 as it stands in *E* appears to read, "and fownd m^{r}cy at plentifull mercy full hand," which was surely not intended, and the subsidiary texts are emended. Nott (ii, 116) has accepted the *AH* reading. Foxwell (i, 221) has, "And fownd mercy at mercyes plentifull hand," which is followed by Muir (p. 212).

For the opening lines from Aretino's third prologue, see Foxwell, i, 221.

[159] *O Lorde as I thee have bothe prayde and praye*

Hand A. Letters over erasures occur in the following lines: 19, "shrinck"; 36, "my"; 42, "me fayle"; 57, "Abyde."

See the preliminary Note on Nos. 154-67.

Wyatt's draft of his paraphrase of the third Penitential Psalm in *E*, fols. 91^{r}-92^{r}, which is unsigned, has the heading, "Psal: 38. dñe ne in furore tuo arguas me." Texts are also in *PC*, sigs. C1^{r}-C4^{r}, and in *R*, fols. 16^{v}-19^{r}.

1 thee have] have y^{e} *PC*

no
2 in] ⟨be⟩ in *E*; no] ⟨no such⟩ *E*: none *R*; alteracon̄] alleration⟨s⟩ *E*

lyke as
3 lyke as] ⟨as we⟩ *E*
4 Measuring] ⟨And⟩ mesurȳg *E*; our mutacon̄] ⟨the⟩ o^{r} mutation⟨s⟩ *E*
6 castigacon̄] castigation ⟨s⟩ *E*
7 thie] thine *R*

famine fyre
8 of famȳne, of fyre] off ⟨derth⟩ & ⟨of deth⟩ *E*: a famin & fire *R*

stikkes diepe lo
9 Stickes deepe] ⟨as stykyd⟩ *E*; loe] ⟨now⟩ *E*
10 plounged] plucked *PC*; as] like *R*

terrour
12 terrour] ⟨fere⟩ *E*; thye] thine *R*
13 ffyrme] ⟨helthe⟩ ferme *E*

drede
15 dread] ⟨fere⟩ *E*

frailefull
16 frailefull] ⟨sinfull⟩ *E*

for why
17 ffor whye] ⟨By cawse⟩ *E*; above . . . bownd] ⟨ar clene⟩

hed ar bownd
a bove my ⟨hed crownd⟩ *E*

18 waighte] weightes *PC*

to
19 shrinck] stoppe *E*: stoupe *PC R*; to] ⟨a⟩ *E*: to the *PC*

Line 20 in E is preceded by a deleted line:
by force wheroff the evill Curid skarris

whilow plant
20 willowe plant] ⟨doth a bow⟩ *E*

and not well
21 And] ⟨y^{t}⟩ *E*; not well] ⟨evyll⟩ *E*

is
22 festerd is by] festred‸ by *E*

vnder skynn
23 rancklyd] ranked *PC*; vnder skynne] ⟨styll w^{t} sin w^{t}in [?]⟩ *E*

26 his] *omitted* *PC*

gruging
27 grudging] ⟨gnawyng⟩ *E*; worme] wounde *R*

29 mye] myne *PC R*

welth
30 the] my *PC R*; hathe] *omitted* *PC*; wealth] ⟨helthe⟩ *E*

32 wond'rous] wonderous *PC*

it hath forst
33 it hathe forste] ⟨forcyd hath⟩ *E*: it forsced *PC*; to

to crye
crye] ⟨for to⟩ *E*

34 know'ste the inward] knowest, thinwarde *PC*: knowest . . . *R*

35 know'ste] knowest *PC R*

36 know'ste] knowest *PC R*

quaile
38 hart] ⟨force⟩ hart *E*; quayle] ⟨faile⟩ *E*

39 my eyes] myn Iyes *E R*

40 mye] myne *R PC*

frendes most sure most
41 Mye . . . sure] my⟨n⟩ owne vɔtues *E*; my] ⟨my⟩ *E*: most *PC R*

my̅ owne v^{r}tues acquaintance
42 Myne . . . vertues] ⟨as frendes most sure⟩ *E* "*acquaintance*" *in a later hand*; me] *omitted* *E PC R*

&
43 And] ⟨did⟩ *E*; stond] stode *PC*

⟨naturall⟩ fardest
44 kynne] kyn *E*; fardest gone] were ‸ gone ⟨farr off⟩ *E*; were fardeste gone *PC R*

reproche
47 reproche] ⟨decyte⟩ *E*; wittes] wit *PC*

knowyng y^{t} from thi hand
50 One] Not one *PC*; knowing . . . hande] ⟨ffor that to the O lord⟩ *E*: . . . thyne hands *PC*

thes thinges procede ⟨but⟩ and o lord shalt
51 Theise . . . supplye] I ⟨me dyrect⟩/ thow ⟨shalt my hope⟩ supplye *E*; Lord] *omitted* *R*; supplye] replye *PC*

my in
52 my] ⟨the⟩ *E*; in thee] ⟨off⟩ the *E*: in that *PC*; whear in] where *R*

to
53 to] ⟨to off⟩ *E*

y^{u} woldst gyve my foos
54 thow . . . foes] ⟨thyn enmyes shold have⟩ *E*; thou wouldeste . . . *PC*

suche plesant
55 shew] shewed *R*; suche pleasant] ⟨reioycing⟩ *E*
56 And] That *PC*
57 Abyde] a byd *E*
58 and] y^{t} *E*: that *R*
59 my faulte confesse] ⟨confess⟩ my fawt cōfesse *E*
60 all] *inserted* *E*
61 en'myes safe] enemies styll *PC*

provokars
62 provokes] ⟨evill willers⟩ *E*: prouokers *PC* *R*; moche] *omitted* *E PC R*

hurt
63 hurt] ⟨harme⟩ *E*

be bent
64 be bentt] ⟨shall assent⟩ *E*

god seist
66 god, that] ⟨lord my⟩ y^{t} *E*; seiste] ⟨knowst⟩ *E*

lord
67 Lord] ⟨god⟩ *E*; well] *omitted* *PC*

farr
68 be . . . gone] ⟨nor⟩ be not ‸ from me ⟨farr⟩ gone *E*

The *AH* copy is closer to *E* than are *PC* and *R*, but in lines 19 and 62 *AH* has distinctive changes. The word "shrinck," written over an erasure in line 19, was probably introduced because the "stoppe" of *E* made no sense to the copyist, but the "stoupe" of *PC* and *R* surely gives the intended reading. Line 62 in *AH* appears to have been deliberately altered to obtain a smoother rhythm, but the meaning is also incorrectly changed, for the Latin has "inimici" (verse 17). It should be observed that Miss Foxwell in her note on line 42 (ii, 139) is mistaken in saying, "The insertion of 'acquaintance' is probably Nott's, following the A Version." The word is, of course, not in the *AH* version, and the handwriting is not that of Nott.

This paraphrase is fairly close in spirit and content to the twenty-two verses of Psalm 38 (Vulgate 37). After a brief preamble of four lines, following Aretino (Foxwell, i, 223), in lines 5-6 Wyatt translates the Latin almost exactly, "Domine, ne in furore Tuo arguas me; neque in ira Tua corripias me." Although lines 7-11, 17-20, and 25-28 amplify verses 2, 4, and 6 of the Psalm, particularly by the use of vivid similes, nevertheless the meaning is closely followed:

> Quoniam sagittæ Tuae infixæ sunt mihi; et confirmasti super me manum tuam.
>
> Quoniam iniquitates meæ supergressæ sunt caput meum, et sicut onus grave gravatæ sunt super me.
>
> Miser factus sum, et curvatus sum usque in finem; tota die contristatus ingrediebar.

In lines 41-44 the classic concept of friendship as a virtue is introduced, thereby giving a somewhat different interpretation to the words of verse 12, which reads:

> Amici mei, et proximi mei adversum me appropinquaverunt, et steterunt.

The closing prayer, lines 66-70, is a moving paraphrase of the Latin:

> Ne derelinquas me, Domine Deus meus, ne discesseris a me.
> Intende in adjutorium meum, Domine Deus salutis meæ.

[160] *Lyke as the pilgrym that in a longe waye*

Hand A. In line 21 "the . . . vncowthe" is written over an erasure, thereby deliberately giving *AH* an independent reading.

See the preliminary Note on Nos. 154-67.

Wyatt's draft in *E*, fol. 92^{v}, is signed, "T V." Texts are in *PC*, sigs. C4^{r}-C5^{v}, and in *R*, fols. 19^{v}-20^{v}.

  in
1 in] ⟨hath⟩ *E*
2 wynde] ⟨shaade⟩ wind *E*
  shaade lith downe ⟨the⟩ off
3 shade . . . daye] ⟨wynd restyth⟩ at ‸ mydes ‸ day *E*: . . . of the day *PC*
4 weried] wery *PC*
  still myndes
7 the . . . myndes] the tone ⟨it sekys still⟩ *E*: the tone . . . *PC R*
8 the other] the tother *ER*; still to marcye] to mↄcy still *E PC R*
  on sonour cordes his fingers he extendes
9 On . . . extendes] ⟨His ffingers sticke a pon the sonour cordes⟩ *E*: On foure . . . pretendes *PC*: On sono^{r} . . . *R*
11 from] of *PC*; streame] storme *R*
13 bayne] vayne *PC*

thalteryd
14 Th'alterid sensis] ⟨his sensis sparplid⟩ sensis *E*; so that] to y^t y^t *E*: to that, that *PC R*
15 sighe] syght *E*; weepe] slepe *R*
16 vppe] ⟨on⟩ vp *E*; the heavens] the heauen *PC*: theuins *R*
w^t owt
17 so] *omitted* *R*; had] hath *PC*; without] ⟨forth at⟩ *E*; Caves] caue *PC*
teris syghes did
18 teares] ⟨syghes⟩ *E*: sighes] ⟨terys⟩ *E*; did] ⟨powrd out⟩ *E*; he] hym *PC*
21 the . . . eke] so close the Cave was and *E PC R*; vncowthe] vnkoweth *PC*
23 blowne] blowen *PC*; in] in ⟨to⟩ *E*; Isr'ells] Israelles *E*: Israell *PC*: Israels *R*
24 The . . . teares] Of theyr Kynge, the wofull playnte and teares *PC*
vpp
25 some] sonne *PC*; vpsupped] ⟨had⟩ suppyd *E*: vp sapped *PC*
27 seemythe] semed *PC*
29 vyolence] vyolente *PC*
stertyng
30 Stertinge] ⟨he stertes⟩ *E*; feare dismayes] dispayre dismayde *PC*
31 His] ⟨w^t⟩ his *E*; voyce] herte *PC R*; his harte] the same *R*
32 that] *omitted* *R*; note] not *E R*; cryes] cryeth *PC*

Lines 24-25 appear to owe something to lines 42-44 in Surrey's elegy on the Duke of Richmond, written in 1537:

The teares berayne my chekes of dedlye hewe;
The which, as sone as sobbing sighes, alas!
Vpsupped have, thus I my playnt renewe: (ed. Padelford, No. 31)

[161] *Rewe on me Lorde for thie goodnes and grace*

Hand A. In line 5 the *r* is added in another ink. In line 42 "as yet decaye" is written over an erased "yet decaye," which is the reading of the other texts.

See the preliminary Note on Nos. 154-67.

Wyatt's draft in *E*, fols. 93^r-94^r, is signed, "T V," and is headed, "Psal: 51. Miserere mei dñe." Texts are in *PC*, sigs. $C5^v$-$C8^v$, and in *R*, fols. 21^r-24^r.

1 Lorde] goode Lorde *R*
in
3 in] ⟨all⟩ *E*; the worlde] thy worde *PC*
8 those marcyes] hys mercye *PC*

9 waye] a way *PC*; synnes] synne *PC*; so] *omitted PC*

agayne

10 Ofte tymes] Offttymes *E neither deleted*: Ofte tymes agayne *PC*

11 synne] synnes *PC*; makes] makth *E*

12 aye]euer *PC*

13 no nombre] nowe, none *PC*

14 remissions of offence] remysyon of synne *PC*

15 hartes] harte *PC*

16 faulte my] faulte, and my *PC*

17 And] *omitted PC*; synne] synnes *PC*; is fixed fast]

is fixid fast

⟨shall still remayne⟩ *E*

18 Thearfore] theroff *E PC*

19 alone] aboue *PC*

20 measure] cure *PC*

24 mynde] sight *PC*

shalt kepe still

26 thow . . . stable] thow ‸ ⟨hold farme and fast⟩ thie word ⟨still &⟩ stable *E*

pure

27 pure] ⟨stable⟩ *E*

then

28 then] ⟨and⟩ *E*; iustlye able] iusticiable *PC*

I ame

29 I am] ⟨to be⟩ *E*

31 fform'de] fourmed *R*

from my natyvite

32 from my nativitie] ⟨by corrupt nature⟩ *E*

Line 33 is preceded by a deleted line in E:

yet lo y[u] loves so the hertes trowgh in Inward place

33 this] these *PC*; myne] my *E*; alace] ah alas *PC*

34 necessitie] necessitie inwarde *PC*

35 lov'ste] loves *E*: louest *PC*; inward] the *PC*

36 my] mooste *PC*

37 frailtie overthwarte] frayle ouerthawrte *PC*

no the

38 led . . . waye] ⟨hath not⟩ led me ⟨a⟩ way *E*

42 my] my ⟨to⟩ *E*; as] *omitted E PC*

43 Iuyce] Iuyz *E PC R that is, "Jews"*

45 Thow] ⟨do⟩ thow *E*

48 when] when ⟨he⟩ *E*

50 afore] before *PC*; consum'de] consumed *PC R*

53 a] *inserted E*; the] *inserted E*; myddes] middell *PC*

spryte

54 with spryght vpright] w[t] ‸ vpryght ⟨spryte⟩ *E* . . .

voydyd
spyryte . . . *PC R*; voyde] ⟨purged⟩ *E PC R*; all filthie]
fylthye
⟨all vile⟩ *E*: fylthye *PC R*

55 thye] thyn *E PC R*

56 thie] thee *PC*; spryte] spyryte *PC*

rendre to
57 Render to me] ⟨retorne⟩ me *E*: reste] heste *PC*

my will
58 My will] ⟨And me⟩ *E*; with] wyth the *PC*; spryte] spirite *PC*

60 wayes] waie *R*

61 Theise] They *E PC R*

63 prayses] prayse *PC*

64 operation] ⟨reputa⟩ operation *E*

68 at] *omitted E PC R*

69 hadd'st] haddeste *PC*

72 delyghtest] delyghtes *E*

the lord likythe
74 the Lorde lykethe] ⟨plesith god⟩ *E*

75 spryte] spirite *PC*

78 goste] hoste *PC*

79 Hierusalem] ⟨I⟩ Hierusalem *E*; the] thy *PC*

80 theise] the *PC*

81 As] Of a *PC*

Line 82 is wanting in PC.

It is evident from the collation that Wyatt's draft of No. 161 has fewer revisions and seems to have been more easily written than were the first three paraphrases. *PC* continues to present an unsatisfactory text, although in line 43 *PC* and *R* follow *E* in giving the correct word, i.e., *Jews*, not *juice*. The *AH* copyist was evidently confused by the *E* spelling. Also in lines 42 and 68 *PC* follows *E*, but *AH* makes slight changes which regularize the measure. In line 10 *AH* and *R* have followed Wyatt's first reading, which is not deleted, but *PC* in confusion uses both. Nott (ii, 123) emends to "Oh! again"; Foxwell (i, 230) and Muir (p. 216) adopt "agayne."

Miss Foxwell (*Study*, p. 94) has pointed out the way in which Wyatt has made use of Aretino's paraphrase of Psalm 51 (Vulgate 50), that is, by omitting passages in which Aretino interprets the glory of God as revealed in nature. Aretino's influence is evident in the paraphrase of the first verse, lines 1-10. Compare the Latin:

> Miserere mei, Deus, secundum magnam misericordiam Tuam, et secundum multitudinem miserationum Tuarum, dele iniquitatem meam.

Verses 2-19 of the Psalm are more closely followed by Wyatt, particularly in lines 51-79, which relate to verses 9-18. The paraphrase of verse 7, lines 43-46, is amplified by brief reference to the law followed by the Jews in the cleansing of lepers (Leviticus 14); and the paraphrase of verse 8, lines 47-50, is expanded by inference of the doctrine of remission of sins through the coming of Jesus Christ. In paraphrasing the closing verse of the Psalm, Wyatt relates the significance of the meaning to his own time by translating the sacrificial bullocks and burnt offerings of the Jews into "theise outwarde deedes" (line 80), which may accompany the contrite heart.

[162] *Of deepe secreates that David heare did singe*

Hand A.

See the preliminary Note on Nos. 154-67.

Wyatt's draft of this prologue to the fifth Penitential Psalm is in *E*, fol. 94^{v}, signed, "T V." Texts are in *PC*, sigs. $D1^{r}$-$D2^{r}$, and in *R*, fols. 24^{v}-25^{v}.

1 Of] ^{off}⟨The⟩ *E*; heare] ^{here}⟨ther⟩ *E*: ther *PC*
2 of] ^{off}⟨and⟩ *E*
3 eke] *omitted* *E PC*
4 The . . . astoūn̄] ⟨did w^{t}⟩ the ⟨wonder⟩ ‸ $^{\text{⟨whe⟩ grettnes dyd so}}$ astonne *E*: The goodnesse . . . astony *PC*; hym sef a space] hym ‸ ^{selff} a space *E*: hym apace *PC*: himself . . . *R*
5 expreste] expressed *PC*
6 alas] ah alas *PC*
7 withine my] w^{t} ‸ ^{in} my ⟨me⟩ *E*
9 not exprest] expressed *PC*
11 earste] *omitted* *PC*; forthe aforde] foorde abrode *PC*
12 poyntes . . . wonders] pōiteth . . . wōdreth *PC*
13 hydes] hydethe *PC*
14 complisshethe] accomplysheth *PC*
16 That] ⟨so⟩ y^{t} *E*; his] ⟨doth⟩ his *E*; graces] grace *PC*; dothe] *inserted* *E*
18 measurelesse] ⟨this⟩ mesureles *E*; marcies] mercye *PC*; to] ^{to}⟨&⟩ *E*; faulte] fautes *PC*
19 Synnes] sin̄ers *E R*; infinite] Infinitye *PC*; treasure] mercie *R*
20 tearmelesse] celestyall *PC*
21 dure] endure *PC*

22 gaynste] gaine *E R*: agayne *PC*; not] no *E*
25 David] ⟨y^{t}⟩ David *E*; hathe] had *PC*; ponderid well]
ponderd well
⟨considerd this⟩ *E*: ponderd well *R*
26 depryv'de] deprived *E PC R*
dark of
27 ffrom] For *PC*; that dark of synne] y^{t} ‸ sinn ⟨had mad hym mis⟩ *E*: that dirke . . . *R*
28 fyndes] fyndeth *PC*; moche] ⟨so⟩ muche *E*; all] *omitted* *E PC R*; revyv'de] revivid *E PC R*
29 He Dare] *inserted in margin* *E*; importune the] Importune ⟨the he⟩ the *E*: importeth on the *PC*
30 know' the] knowethe *PC R*; to] that to *PC*; ascryb'de] ascrybid *E PC*
32 beginnithe] begynth *E*

For Wyatt's use of Aretino, see Foxwell, i, 235, and ii, 140.

[163] *Lord Heare my prayer and lett my crye passe*

Hand A. In line 68 "lawds" is written over an erasure, possibly of "laudes," as in *E*; in line 72 the "pl" of "Sample" is written over an erasure, probably of "bl," as in *E*. The copyist evidently misunderstood the line. Also in line 69 "one" is written over an erasure, and in line 88 the "pre" of "pretende."

See the preliminary Note on Nos. 154-68.

Wyatt's draft in *E*, fols. 95^{r}-96^{r}, is signed, "T V," and is headed, "Psal: 102. dne. exaudi orationem meam." Texts are in *PC*, sigs. D2^{v}-D5^{r}, and in *R*, fols. 26^{r}-29^{v}.

impediment
2 without impediment] w^{t}owt⟨en stopp or lett⟩ *E*
4 my self] meself *R*
6 to] vnto *PC*; thye . . . thie] thyn . . . thyn *E PC R*
7 when] when ⟨so⟩ *E*; helpp my necessitie] ⟨ffor⟩ help
my necessitye
⟨vnto the⟩ *E*
8 my] myne *PC*
9 Theise . . . do] Boldelye too *PC*
11 as smoke] a synke *PC*; bene] are *PC*
12 dry'de] dryed *PC*; as] as a *PC*
14 Because] But *PC*; bread] ⟨food⟩ brede *E*
brede
15 bread] ⟨foode⟩ *E*
16 playntfull] paynfull *PC*; sighes] ⟨my⟩ syghes *E*; for] *omitted* *E PC*: eke *R*

17 of] & *R*

18 Cleav'd] cleved *E PC R*; the sprite] y^{i} spirit *R*

as a

19 I, as desp'rate] I ⟨in diepe⟩ dispair⟨e⟩te *E*: As desperate *PC R*

20 me] am *PC*; solemne] soden *PC*: solaine *R*

ruyne

23 To ruyne life] to ‸ lyff ⟨alone⟩ *E*

was

25 was I] ⟨I ame⟩ I *E*

26 eaves] effes *E*

27 fooes] *something inserted before* "foes" *E*; conspyr'de] conspyred *PC R*

ꝓvoke

28 provoke] assaute *E*

29 me] *omitted* *R*

of thi iust word the tast not

30 of . . . please] ⟨In trowgh I fownd no tast y^{t}⟩ myght ‸ me ples *E*; me not] not me *PC R*

31 Whearefore] W^{t} ⟨in⟩ her fore *E*; temp'rid] tempered *PC*

32 Of] ⟨Of⟩ off *E*; from mye] ⟨haile downe⟩ from myn *E*: from myne *PC R*; downe] do *E*: dyd *PC R*

34 Provokte] Prouoked *PC*

35 didest] didst *E R*

36 my self] meself *R*

37 knew] knowe *R*

39 crowne] drowne *PC*

doth

40 doth] ⟨shall⟩ *E*

frailte all

41 frailtie] ⟨misery⟩ *E*; all] ⟨euɔy⟩ *E*

f

43 fynde] ⟨as⟩ fynd *E*

is

44 ys] ⟨ffor⟩ *E*

46 doth] *omitted* *PC*; servantes] seruaunt *R*

sins

48 Synñs] ⟨the⟩ *E*: his *R*

in

50 In] ⟨off⟩ *E*; lowre] ⟨lye⟩ lowr *E*: lore *PC*

then

51 Then] ⟨And so⟩ *E*

52 thie . . . honour] ⟨shall honour⟩ thy glory shall honour *E*

i Grace

53 thie grace] y⟨u hast⟩ *E*; this] thi *R*; thus redeamythe]

thus

⟨thus savid⟩ redemith *E*

54 declarde] declar⟨i⟩d *E*: declared *PC*

lord wishis so
55 Hee Lord] ⟨Th⟩ He ⟨lord hath⟩ *E*; wisshes so] ⟨cryes⟩ *E*: wishes and so *PC*
56 turn'the] turneth *R*
or discent to be wrytten
57 our discent] ⟨all mankynd⟩ *E*; to be wrytten] ⟨publysht me⟩ *E*
58 consolacōn] ⟨conffor⟩ cōsolation *E*
59 And] ⟨wherb⟩ and *E*
61 th'height] the heyght *E R*: the high *PC*
vs
62 vs] ⟨vs men⟩ *E*
64 fowle] soche *PC*
66 gracous] glorious *PC*
67 his] ⟨t⟩ hys *E*: thys *PC R*; name] ⟨to⟩ name *E*
68 in] *inserted* *E*; his] ⟨t⟩ hys *E*
bene gaderd
70 Realmes] remes *E*; bene gatherd] ⟨shall ranged⟩ *E*; to
to
praye] ⟨&⟩ pray *E*
aboue
71 above] ⟨y^{t} is⟩ *E*: that is above *PC*: y^{t} aboue *R*
72 to] *omitted* *R*; this] these *PC*; Sample] samble *E*: feble *PC*: semble *R*
74 abridg'd] abredged *PC*
that
75 see that] se ⟨the⟩ *E*
76 hartie] hart *PC*
77 Pray'de] Prayed *PC*; lord take me not] take me not lord *E R*: take me not *PC*
78 In] In the *PC*; of yeares] off my yeres *E PC*
80 wrought'ste] wroughteste *PC*; the heavens] thevyns *E*
81 alwaye] ay *R*
82 Age] aye *PC*
83 chaunge] *inserted* *E*; them] the *R*
tourne
84 Turne] ⟨torne⟩ *E*
85 the] thy *PC*; well] hole *PC*
86 waste] was *PC*; shalt] shall *PC*; thie yeares]
thi yeres
⟨w^{t}outen⟩ *E*: . . . yere *PC R*
90 thie worde] the world *PC*
91 stablishte] stabisht *E*: stablyshed *PC*

In his collation of this poem, Muir (p. 280) comments on the words "In diepe dispaire" in line 19 of *E*, "*the line deleting these words misses the initial* I"; but I see no reason to suppose that *I* must be deleted, as its inclusion makes good sense. Miss Foxwell (i, 238) curiously reads *E*, line 23, as "kuyut lyff," interpreting it as "quiet life," but the *E* MS. clearly has "ruyne lyff," as in the other texts.

In this paraphrase of Psalm 102 (Vulgate 101) Wyatt follows closely the Psalm itself, omitting digressions and elaborations introduced by Aretino. For some illustration of this comparison see Foxwell, *Study*, pp. 96-97, and *Poems*, ii, 140. In the latter reference the Psalm is unfortunately designated as No. 103. Wyatt's paraphrase in many lines is little more than a metrical translation of the Latin. For example, the Latin for lines 11-12 reads, "Quia defecerunt, sicut fumus, dies mei, et ossa mea sicut cremium aruerunt." In line 38 Wyatt is briefer than the Latin, "Dies mei sicut umbra declinaverunt; et ego sicut fœnum arui." By his omission, dictated by metrical necessity, Wyatt has left a peculiarly awkward line. More successful is the brevity of line 80, for which the Latin is, "Initio Tu, Domine, terram fundasti; et opera manuum Tuarum sunt cæli." Sometimes the meaning is slightly changed, as in lines 25-31, which are based on the following passages in the Vulgate:

> Vigilavi, et factus sum sicut passer solitarius in tecto.
>
> Tota die exprobrabant mihi inimici mei, et qui laudabant me, adversum me jurabant.
>
> quia cinerem tanquam panem manducabam, et potum meum cum fletu miscebam.

Lines 19-24 expand moderately the Latin passage, "Similis factus sum pellicano solitudinis; factus sum sicut nycticorax in domicilio." Miss Foxwell (*Study*, p. 97) points out, however, that Wyatt is not following Aretino in this passage. Wyatt's expansion may be in the nature of interpretative comments, as in lines 36-37 and 41, for which the Vulgate, verses 10, 12, Englished in lines 33-35 and 39-40, respectively, has no suggestion. The closing five lines of the paraphrase expand the last verse of the Psalm in such a way that an alien note of authoritative fear is introduced. The Latin reads simply "Filii servorum Tuorum habitabunt; et semen eorum in sæculum dirigetur."

[164] *When David had perceyved in his brest*

Hand A. Words written over erasures occur in the following lines: 17, "But . . . faulte"; 18, "He . . . deede"; 19, "A tweene them twoe." See the preliminary Note on Nos. 154-67.

Wyatt's draft of this prologue to the sixth Penitential Psalm is in *E*, fol. 96^{v}, signed, "T V." Texts are in *PC*, sigs. D6^{r}-D7^{v}, and in *R*, fols. 30^{r}-31^{r}.

2 spryte] spyryte *PC*; returnde] retourne *PC*

by cause ... he hath alone

3 Because] ⟨ffor y^{t}⟩ *E*; he hathe alone] ⟨off hym were not⟩ *E*

y^{t} spryte
4 same] *omitted E PC R*; that] ⟨by⟩ *E*; spryte] ⟨thinge⟩ *E*: spyryte *PC*
7 this] that, I wys *PC*
8 Spryte] spirite *PC*
11 have] hathe *PC*
13 our] ⟨he⟩ o^{r} *E*
16 gynneth] begynneth *PC*
17 he wayethe the] ⟨y^{t}⟩ he weyth ⟨tho⟩ the *E*
18 dam̃pnethe] damth *ER*; this] *omitted E PC R*
19 whytt] what *PC R*
all owtward dede in
20 takes] takethe *PC*; all . . . in] ⟨all recõpense as⟩ *E*: . . . dedes in *PC*
wich
22 Whiche] ⟨that⟩ *E*; returnde] returned *PC*
23 that] hart *PC*
the sygne or
24 the . . . fruite] ⟨is⟩ ^ fruyt ⟨theroff⟩ *E*; signe] synne *PC*
26 worde] voyde *ER*: owne *PC*
glory
27 glorye] ⟨meryt⟩ *E*
28 god] good *E*
30 whyl'ste] whyles *PC*; pondreth] ponder^{d} ⟨th⟩ *E*: pondered *PC*: ponderd *R*
knee
31 knee] ⟨arme⟩ *E*
32 his] ⟨th⟩ his *E*

As R. C. Harrier has pointed out ("Notes on the Text and Interpretation of Sir Thomas Wyatt's Poetry," *N. and Q.*, cxcviii [1953], 234), in his reading of the *E* text in line 28 Muir (p. 223) mistakenly has "sole" instead of "hole." Foxwell (i, 243) has "hole," and Nott (ii, 133) modernizing, of course, has "whole."

On Aretino's version, see Foxwell, i, 242, and ii, 140. In the second reference Miss Foxwell comments on line 31 and says that it was imitated by Surrey in "When Windesor walles sustained my wearied arme/ My hand, my chyn" (ed. Padelford, No. 30). As I have explained in the Note on No. 156, however, Surrey wrote this sonnet in 1537, and is the originator of the expression.

[165] *ffrom deapthe of synne and from a deepe dispaire*

Hand A. In line 16 "Dreade" and "not" are written over erasures. See the preliminary Note on Nos. 154-68.

Wyatt's draft in *E*, fol. 97^{r}, is signed, "T V," and is headed, "Psal: ⟨129⟩ 130 De profundis clamavi." The deleted "129" is in accord with the Vulgate numbering. Texts are in *PC*, sigs. D7^{v}-D8^{v}, and in *R*, fols. 31^{v}-32^{v}.

1 a] *inserted* *E*: *omitted* *PC*; deepe] dirk *R*

off diepe
3 of . . . deepe] ⟨whoe⟩ . . . ⟨doth⟩ *E*; dispayre] repayre *E PC R*

4 Thee . . . o Lord] ⟨To⟩ the ⟨o lord⟩ have I cald olord *E*

8 intende] attende *PC*

that it not
9 that . . . neare] ⟨but⟩ to the ‸ is ‸ nere *E*

ere
11 Thyne eare] thin ‸ ⟨selff⟩ *E*: Thyne eare sette *PC*: Thine eare self *R*

12 Lorde] *inserted* *E*; observe] do obsɔve *E PC*; offende] doo offende *PC*

13 And . . . marcye] & putt [*added in margin*] ⟨Th⟩y^{i} natyff mɔcy ⟨to put⟩ *E*: . . . the natyue . . . *PC*: . . . thi natif . . . *R*

14 a] *omitted* *E PC R*

A
16 At] ⟨a⟩t *E*; Dreade and not] dede, and no *PC*

17 raigne lardge] runne at large *PC*; seekest] sekes *E R*

in thi hand
18 in thie hand] ⟨mɔcy is w^{t} the⟩ *E*; mercye] mɔcyes *E PC R*

st
19 doste] do⟨th⟩ *E*: doeste *PC*; eke] *omitted* *E PC R*

20 have . . . confydence] have ⟨euɔ⟩ set my ⟨trust⟩ cōfydence *E*

eterne
22 etearne excellence] ⟨excellence⟩ excellence *E*

⟨puv⟩ mercyes
23 marcies promesse] ⟨Iust⟩ promesse *E*; alwaye iuste]
alway iust
⟨infallible⟩ *E*

man ing
26 watche man loking] wach ⟨y^{t}⟩ loky ⟨th⟩ *E*

by thy
27 By this his] ⟨for⟩ his *E*: By thy *PC*: By y^{e} *R*; of sleepe] of ⟨the⟩ slepe *E*; thurst] thrust *E PC R*

vnto
28 Let] Let ⟨all⟩ *E*; vnto] ⟨in⟩ *E*: to *PC*; alway] ⟨I say⟩ alway *E*

29 are] arn *R*

us shall come
30 Plentuouse] plente ⟨fful⟩ *E*; shall come] ⟨is⟩ *E*

redeme
31 shall redeme] ⟨he⟩ shall ⟨ranzome⟩ *E*

In this paraphrase the first seven verses of Psalm 130 are moderately expanded in lines 1-30. Thus lines 1-11 amplify the first two verses in the Vulgate (129):

> De profundis clamavi ad Te, Domine;
> Domine, exaudi vocem meam; fiant aures Tuae intendentes in vocem deprecationis meæ.

In contrast line 31 is briefer than the closing eighth verse of the Psalm, "Et ipse redimet Israel ex omnibus iniquitatibus ejus."

[166] *This worde redeeme that in his mowthe did sownde*

Hand A.

See the preliminary Note on Nos. 154-68.

Wyatt's draft of this prologue to the seventh Penitential Psalm is in *E*, fol. 97^{v}, signed, "T V." Texts are in *PC*, sigs. E1^{r}-E2^{r}, and in *R*, fols. 33^{r}-34^{r}.

did
2 Did] ⟨hath⟩ *E*; it . . . me] ⟨in to a diepe as⟩ it semyth vn to me *E*
4 height] ⟨hyg⟩ heyght *E*
conf
5 confownde] ⟨res⟩ ownd *E*
6 sworde] worde *PC R*; humble eare] humilitie here *PC*
8 Eternall lyfe] Eternallye *PC*
full rype sholde
9 full rype] ⟨plenne⟩ *E*; shulde] ⟨was⟩ *E*
Do way
10 Do waye] ⟨shake off⟩ *E*: Doo awaye *PC*
13 in ayre] in th Ayre *E*: in the ayre *PC R*
manne
14 Man] ⟨sine⟩ *E*; redeemed] redemeth *PC*
16 David] Too Dauid *PC*
his sonne
18 his sonne] ⟨the deth⟩ *E*: his some *R*
from deth for me
19 ffrom . . . me] ⟨of his dere sonne⟩ *E*
my
20 Mye] ⟨o^{r}⟩ *E*
can
21 can] ⟨c may⟩ *E*
23 have his] have ⟨then⟩ his *E*: have thys *PC*
25 moste do crave] ⟨aske hym⟩ most do crave *E*
suyte w^{t}owt respect
26 he] *omitted* *R*; sute . . . respecte] ⟨forceable request⟩ *E*
27 to the grave] ⟨w^{t} his ost⟩ to the grave *E*
28 Sufferd] Suffered *PC*; synne] synnes *PC*
29 synne] synnes *PC*; my pardon] may pardon *PC*

30 pursuite] suyte *PC*
31 sured] sure *PC*
32 begynnethe] begynns *E R*: begynne *PC*

Miss Foxwell, *Study*, p. 95, and *Poems*, ii, 141, points out that Wyatt does not follow Aretino in this prologue. From lines 27-30 it is evident that Wyatt sets the dramatic time as the interval just preceding the final battle with the hostile forces led by David's son Absalom (II Samuel 18). Wyatt may have had in mind the account of David's ascent, with covered head and bare feet, to the top of Mount Olivet, where he wept in sorrow (II Samuel 15:30). Shortly after he was cursed by Absalom's follower Shimei, who said, ". . . and the Lord hath delivered the kingdom into the hand of Absalom thy son: and behold, thou *art taken* in thy mischief, because thou *art* a bloody man" (II Samuel 16:8). In the reflections of David on his sin and forgiveness Wyatt introduces the New Testament teaching of humility and redemption through Jesus Christ. The spirit is in marked contrast to David's proudly exultant song of thanks to God for his victories over his enemies (II Samuel 22).

[167] *Heare my prayer o Lorde heare mye request*

Hand A. In line 16 "fforreỹne Realmes" is written over an erasure, almost certainly of the phrase in the *E* MS. See collation and comment below. In line 34 the *d* of "bend" is written in another hand over an *e*. In line 36 "that do" is written, apparently in another ink and hand, over an erasure. In line 37 "me" is corrected to "be" in another ink and possibly another hand. The correction accords with *PC*. In line 40 the letters "e to worke the same in" are written over an erasure, with "in" squeezed in. At the conclusion of this paraphrase there is a note in ink by Bishop Percy, "Here end the 7 Penitential Psalms by S^{r}. Thos Wyat."

See the preliminary note on Nos. 154-68.

Wyatt's draft of this paraphrase in *E*, fols. 98^{r,v}, is signed, "T V," and headed, "Dñe exaudi orationem meam. cxliij." Texts are in *PC*, sigs. E2^{r}-E4^{r}, and in *R*, fols. 34^{v}-36^{r}.

answere to
2 awnsweare to] ⟨supply y^{u}⟩ *E*: supply thou *PC R*
3 bye] for my *PC*
4 In] In⟨w⟩ *E*
after
5 after thie] ⟨for⟩ thy⟨n own⟩ *E*
6 the] that *PC*
Off ⟨Iustise⟩ aftre ⟨such⟩ the
7 not] *omitted* *PC*; of . . . and] ⟨acordyng to Iust right In
forme &
the⟩ *E*

thrall
8 thie thrall] thy ‸ *E*: thee thrall *PC*

⟨my⟩ his
9 his] ⟨thy⟩ *E*
10 Before] By fore *E*
11 my self] me self *R*; rightuousnes] ryghtwisenes *E R*

prykyng spurrs
12 pricking sourrs] ⟨suffrans that⟩ *E*: prickynge spurres *PC R*; have] I haue *R*

e rysen
13 Scante rysyng] skant⟨ly rysen⟩ *E*: Scant rysē *PC R*
14 myne enmye] my enmy *E*: myne enemyes *PC*
15 foyled] soyled *PC*
16 fforrey͞ne Realmes] ffor that in heins *E*: for in hernes *R*;

rage
to fle his ⟨furyes stry⟩ so ryff
to . . . rife] ⟨as man in mortall stryff⟩ *E*: to flee hys rage so ryfe *PC R*

me forst as ded
17 me . . . dead] ⟨constrained me for⟩ *E*: me forste, as deade *PC R*
18 because] by cause *E*; my self] meself *R*
19 harte and spryte] harte, spirite *PC R*

to
20 to] ⟨vnto the⟩ *E*: two *R*; have] *omitted* *PC*

dedes
21 deedes] ⟨workes⟩ *E*
23 knewe] knowe *PC*; those] these *PC*

were
24 weare] ⟨ar⟩ *E*

did
25 did] ⟨doth⟩ *E*
26 barren] bare *PC*
28 sure . . . spryte] euer . . . spiryte *PC*: . . . spirite *R*

that I be layd
29 that I be layde] ⟨to make me seme⟩ *E*: y^{t} I be layede *PC*
30 headlonge] hedlyng *E PC R*
32 I whollie do] I [*inserted*] holly do ⟨I⟩ *E*

and in thi hand
33 And . . . hand] ⟨do me to know⟩ *E*: And in thy handes *PC*
34 wilt] wolt *E*
36 Ridd] ⟨Do⟩ Rydd *E*; those that] that y^{t} *E R*: them that *PC*

be to
37 to ⟨m⟩e] ⟨on⟩ me *E*: to be *PC*: to me *R*; me

me
assinde] ⟨bene⟩ assind *E*: assigned *PC*
38 within] ⟨vnto⟩ w^{t}in *E*

39 Theache . . . will] Teche m⟨y[e] w⟩ thy will *E*

41 blessed vpright spryte] blyssyd ^[vpryght] spryte ⟨shall guyde⟩ *E*: blessed spirite vpryght *PC R*

42 lawde of trouthe] loud off trowght *E*: . . . & trouth *R*

43 lord] *inserted* *E*; spryte] spiryte *PC*

Between lines 45 and 46 E has the following deleted lines, which were Wyatt's first draft for lines 46-49:

There whilst thow shalt off thi benignite
confownd my foes/ & then destroy that seke
to hunt my lyff by theyre iniquite
thus
sins I thi sɔvant humbly the besek

46 their] the *PC*

47 also] y^u shalt also *E PC R*

49 aye] *omitted* *PC*

The collation shows that the subsidiary texts, *AH*, *PC*, and *R*, are peculiarly faulty in this paraphrase. As usual *PC* has many poor variants, some undoubtedly caused by the typographer, but the *AH* and *R* copies are but little better, though they may differ. Thus in lines 12, 13, and 17 the *AH* variants destroy the sense, and in line 47 the omission disturbs both sense and rhythm. The editors and copyists did not understand Wyatt's Yorkshire expression in line 16, "in heins"; i.e., in hedge, or, figuratively, in refuge. The *R* reading "in hernes," i.e., in harness, indicates an independent relation between *R* and *E*, evident also in line 36. *AH* and *PC* agree on the radical revision in line 16 of "fforreỹne Realmes." I have pointed out above, however, that these words are written over an erasure in *AH* and that the first writing almost certainly had followed the *E* MS. The correction in *AH* was probably made to accord with the *PC* reading, which was better understood. Evidence of influence of *PC* on *AH* occurs in line 37, where "me" was corrected to "be," as in *PC*.

In this paraphrase of Psalm 143 (Vulgate 142) Wyatt follows the biblical verses somewhat less closely than he tends to do in his paraphrase of Psalm 130 (No. 165). Thus lines 1-17 amplify considerably verses 1-3 of the Vulgate:

> Domine, exaudi orationem meam, auribus Percipe obsecrationem meam in veritate Tua; exaudi me in Tua justitia.
>
> Et non intres in judicium cum servo Tuo, quia non justificabitur in conspectu Tuo omnis vivens.
>
> Quia persecutus est inimicus animam meam, humiliavit in terra vitam meam.

Lines 43-45 change the Psalmist's plea to a statement of expected certainty. Verse 11 reads in the Latin:

> propter nomen Tuum, Domine, vivificabis me in æquitate Tua.
> Educes de tribulatione animam meam.

Lines 46-49 are almost in the nature of an epilogue; i.e., the Lord has punished his enemies because of his faithful service. But verse 12 of the Psalm continues as a plea:

> et in misericordia Tua disperdes inimicos meos,
> et perdes omnes, qui tribulant animam meam, quoniam ego servus Tuus sum.

It seems to me very probable that Wyatt wrote these lines after his release from prison in 1541.

[168] *Althoughe thow see th'owtragious clyme alofte*

Hand A. Letters written over erasures occur in the following lines: 3, "it seem"; 83, "the"; 109, "vnto." Beneath the "ffinis" is an ascription in ink in the handwriting of G. F. Nott, "By S^{r}: Thomas Wyatt."

A scribe's copy of the first thirty-six lines is in *E*, fol. 65^{v}, where it is headed, "Noli ⟨malignare⟩ emulare in maligna Psalm. 37," and is marked for fourth entry. It is unascribed.

3 seemythe] senith
4 thie] thi⟨s⟩
8 earthe] yerth
14 eke] *omitted*
15 trouthe] trowgh
16 as] all; rightuousnes] rightwisnes
22 sendes] sende
25 all] all ⟨a⟩; eschew] estewe
28 abydes] abid
32 eke] *omitted*; straunge] starūng

According to my interpretation of the last *E* variant, it is merely a copyist's error for "straung," but Muir (p. 198) reads the word as "scaring." The *E* copyist was careless in line 3 with "senith," in line 16 with "all," and in line 22 with "sende." Line 23, imperfect both in *E* and *AH*, may have been left incomplete by the author, who almost certainly was Sir Thomas Wyatt. Unfortunately he did not correct the *E* copy.

Although this paraphrase of Psalm 37 (Vulgate 36) does not have Wyatt's signature in *E*, its grouping with other Wyatt poems both in *E* and *AH* and its similarity to the style of Wyatt's Penitential Psalms support the ascription of the paraphrase to Wyatt by Nott, who first printed the poem (ii, 198-202). In his note (ii, 580) Nott makes no mention of the copy in *AH* and merely says, "In the MS. p. 128," which refers to the old page numbering of *E*. It is clear that *E* did not have the rest of the poem when Nott used it, for the poem "from thes hye hilles as when a spryng doth fall" is written in Wyatt's hand on p. 129 (so numbered). Nott's modernized, emended text reveals that he made use both of *E* and *AH* in lines 1-36. Thus in line 14 he retains the "eke" of *AH* but not in line 32. His line 16, which reads, "Bright as the sun, and thy rightwiseness shall," is constructed from *E*, *AH*, and his own emendation. In lines 22 and 28 Nott adopts the plural forms of the verbs as in *AH*. He leaves line 23 incomplete in accord with the manuscripts. For lines 37-110 Nott followed *AH*, indicating the missing portion of line 43 by asterisks and in the same way calling attention to the omission of two lines between lines 69-70. This omission is evident not only by the sense, which refers to verse 25 in the Psalm, but by the imperfection in the *terza rima* pattern. Miss Foxwell includes this paraphrase in her edition of Wyatt's poems (i, 197-202). She emends line 23 to read, "To wicked folke—[so prosper the untrue;]." Commenting on lines 19-23, she says, "The 1530 Psalter reads, v.7, 'Be not angry with hym that prosper in his way, which is the man that is geven to desayte.' The completion of l. 23 is to bring out the sense of *prosper in his waye*." The Latin for verse 7 runs:

> subditus esto Domino, et ora eum.
> Noli æmulari in eo, qui prosperatur in via sua, in homine faciente injustitias.

Muir, who also includes the paraphrase in his edition of Wyatt (pp. 197-200), accepts Miss Foxwell's addition to the line. Miss Foxwell completes line 43 "from the context of the [1530] Psalter," giving the line as, "To overthrowe the [just; stretched forth their honds,]" (i, 199; ii, 132). Muir accepts this emendation also. Verse 14, to which lines 41-44 refer, reads in the Vulgate:

> Gladium evaginaverunt peccatores, intenderunt arcum suum,
> ut dejiciant pauperem et inopem; ut trucident rectos corde.

Miss Foxwell notes the omission of the two lines between lines 69-70, according to my numbering. She does not give tentative readings but refers to the missing lines as numbers 70-71 (i, 200). Muir (p. 199) suggests as readings for these lines:

> [The righteous yet, though age has stolen on me,
> Forsaken by the Lord I ne'er have seen,].

Verse 25, to which these lines and line 70 in No. 168 refer, reads in the Vulgate:

Junior fui, etenim senui; et non vidi justum derelictum, nec semen ejus, quærens panem.

Despite the imperfections just noted, the paraphrase tends to follow closely the forty verses of the Psalm. A somewhat different emphasis or shade of meaning may be given in the paraphrase, as in lines 1-4. The first verse in the Vulgate is simpler, "Noli æmulari in malignantibus; neque zelaveris facientes iniquitatem." Again, lines 90-94 introduce a Messianic note, not present in the Latin, verse 34, "Exspecta Dominum, et custodi viam ejus; et exaltabit te, ut hæreditate capias Terram; cum perierint peccatores, videbis."

[169] *Somtyme the pryde of mye assured trothe*

Hand A.

In his note on the text of No. 168, G. F. Nott (ii, 580) suggests that No. 169 might be the proem for it, as "the subject is one to which that proem would apply." This may be, although more probably it was written as the proem for the paraphrase of another Psalm by Wyatt, which was copied on the now missing fol. 120. Nott prints No. 169 from *AH* in a note in the same volume (pp. lxxxvi-lxxxvii), with the suggestion that the address in line 6 was to Surrey. He further points out that Surrey imitated the lines in his proem for Psalm 88 (No. 80). Muir (p. 200) has included No. 169 in his edition of Wyatt.

[170] *but rest in doute as I began*

Hand A.

If the poem of which these are the closing lines is elsewhere known, I have not been able to identify it.

[171] *Among the Craggye Rockes/ bothe roughe and hard*

Hand A; ascription in the same hand. The changes in lines 1 and 12 are in another ink and hand. 2. "by" is clearly written over "for." A number of words and phrases are written over erasures: 4. "markettes"; 5. "for"; 8. "packstaff . . . bee"; 16. "am . . . mylke"; 18. "plaine fare"; 22. "knowen"; 25. "at all"; 26. "esteemes . . . hall"; 27. "cleare"; 28. The *d* in "goolden"; 33. "hym selffe"; 34. "I wolde be"; 35. "the . . . disdaine," where the last two words of the erased passage are discernible as "lif best"; 36. "thowgh . . . remayne." As is evident from the collation below, these corrections in *AH* were not made from the printed copy.

With the title "Of the quietnesse that plaine Countrey bryngeth" No. 171 was published in *Churchyardes Chance*, 1580, sigs. F1^{v}-F2^{r}. Collation with the unique copy in the Huntington Library follows:

1 Craggye] rustie; ⟨by⟩ [of]]by
2 by] for

3 ne] ndr *misprint for nor*
4 nor] Where
5 for] of
6 ne] Nor
8 packstaff . . . bee] in the twoo pickt staffe
11 me] I
delightes nowe
12 moche] moste; ⟨now⟩ me ⟨delightes⟩] now me delites
14 fieldes . . . and] feeld but asks a
16 better . . . with] Courtly fare, maie learne to feede on
17 easlye] easily
18 plaine fare] in deede; hath] haue
19 doth] doe
21 speake and laughe] laugh and speake
22 knowen] namde
23 hawltie] hautie
24 feathers] fether
25 Dales at all] dale likewise
26 esteemes . . . hall] doe princely halls despise
27 cleare] sowre
28 goolden] gilted
30 th'assured] the sured; knowe] troe
33 mightie] might; hym selffe] with tong
34 I wolde be] make me
35 the . . . disdaine] would change their states & holds the meane life best
36 me . . . remayne] not me where I doe like, I seeke to finde some rest

The printed copy, brought out under the author's supervision, as is noted below, presumably offers the preferred version. The *AH* copy probably represents a much earlier writing of the poem.

In one of the better known of his many works, *The Worthines of Wales*, 1587, Thomas Churchyard, 1520?-1604, writes of his native Shrewsbury in the Marches of Wales with nostalgic pride (sigs. K1^{r}-L2^{r}), a feeling no doubt enhanced by the fact that he left the West Country when still a youth to seek his way at Court and returned only at intervals during his long, wandering life as a soldier of fortune and a courtier of sorts. With equal pride he writes of his service to Henry Howard, Earl of Surrey. In the epistle dedicatory to *A light Bondell of liuly discourses called Churchyardes Charge, presented as a Newe yeres gifte to the right honour*^{able}*, the Earle of Surrie*, 1580 (sig. *2^{v}), he says:

> And honoryng in harte the Erle of Surrie, your Lordshipps graundfather, & my master (who was a noble warriour, an eloquent Oratour,

and a second Petrarke) I could doe no lesse but publishe to the worlde somewhat that should shewe, I had lost no time in his seruice.

Included in the *Charge* (sigs. A1^{r}-B2^{v}) is an autobiographical poem fictitiously entitled, "A storie translated out of Frenche," in which after further high praise of his master and a curse upon "those crooked crafts" wrought "To chop of sutche a chosen hed," Churchyard thus refers to his time of service:

As told I haue, this yong man seru'd, this maister twise twoo yere,
And learnd therein sutche fruitfull skill, as long he held full dere:
And vsd the penne as he was taught, and other gifts also,
Whiche made hym hold the capp on hed, where some do croch full lo.
(sig. A2^{r})

For many years Churchyard was a soldier. In "A Tragicall Discourse of the vnhappy mans life," first printed in *The Firste parte of Churchyardes Chippes*, 1575 (sigs. H1^{r}-H8^{v}-I5^{v}), he writes sadly of his thirty years service to the state in England, Scotland, Ireland, France, and Flanders; of his betrayal and imprisonments; of his often losing blood; and of his unhappiness on returning to Court. Despite this melancholy account four years later in *The Miserie of Flaunders* (sigs. E1^{r}-E4^{r}) he published his lyric lines on "The Blessed state of Englande":

Here haue wee scope to skippe or walke,
to ronne and plaie at base:
Still voide of feare, and free of minde,
in euery poincte and cace.
Here freends maie meete and talke at will,
the Prince and Lawe obaied:
And neither straunge, nor home borne childe,
of Fortune stands afraied.
Here hands doe reape the seeds thei sowe
and heads haue quiet sleeps:
And wisedome gouerns so the worlde,
that reason order keeps.
Here mercie rules, and mildenesse raigns,
and peace great plentie bryngs:
And sollace in his sweetest voice,
the Christmas carrowle syngs.
Here freends maie feast, and triumphe too,
in suertie voide of ill:
And one the other welcome make,
with mirthe and warme good will. (sig. E2^{r,v})

His *Chippes* is the first of several attempts on the part of the poet to bring out his various compositions in collected form. In the *Chance* of 1580, a sizeable volume in which both Nos. 171 and 305 appeared, Churchyard sets out his intention very clearly:

> Here endeth the booke called Churchyardes *Chance*, and beginneth an other booke named his *Charge*: and so in one volume shall followe, his *Choice*, his *Chippes*, and all the rest of his bookes that here tofore hath bin sette out, and written by *Churchyarde*, sauyng a booke of *Meta incognita*, and some other small volumes, whiche cannot be bound in quarto, yet hereafter (by Gods grace) shalbe sette out in a large volume . . . whiche booke shalbe called Churchyardes *Challenge*. . . . [sig. K4^{v}].

The *Charge*, which included No. 241, was out the same year, 1580, but the *Challenge*, in a different form from that planned, not until 1593. Like the *Charge*, described in the epistle dedicatory as having "emong some newe laces & odde trifles, a greate deale of old ware and little rēnantes" (sig. *4^{r}), the *Chance* and the *Challenge* also contain both old and new material. Thus "Dauie Dicars Dreame," brought out many years earlier in broadsheet, is reprinted in the *Chance* (sig. K4^{r,v}), described as "Written in the beginnyng of Kyng Edwardes raigne." It cannot be assumed, therefore, that Nos. 171, 241, and 305, which were printed in the two 1580 volumes, were of recent composition. No. 171 resembles in style and content another poem in the *Chance*, entitled, "Written from the Countrey twentie yere agoe, to one that poorely remaines at the Courte yet" (sigs. E3^{r}-E4^{v}). Likewise it is similar to one in the *Charge*, headed, "Churchyardes farewell from the Courte, the seconde yere of the Queenes Maiesties raigne" (sigs. B3^{r}-C3^{v}). The fact that these three poems in *AH* are written in Hand A and are grouped with the older poetry indicates further that they were composed some years before 1580. The fourth Churchyard poem in *AH*, No. 321, was published as a broadsheet about 1566. It was not reprinted in the collected works, possibly because, as in the instance of other compositions, Churchyard could not recover a copy (*Chance*, sig. B4^{r}; *Challenge*, sigs. *^{v}-**^{r}).

Despite his yearning desire for fame and his own abortive efforts to bring out all his work under his own name (touchingly expressed in the *Challenge*, sig. A3^{r,v}), Churchyard has been all but forgotten, except perhaps for "The Tragedy of Shore's Wife," first printed in the 1563 edition of *The Mirror for Magistrates* (ed. Lily B. Campbell, Cambridge University Press: 1938, pp. 373-86). No one has attempted a complete edition of his prose and his many poems. Of the works referred to in this Note there are editions by J. P. Collier of the *Chippes* and the *Charge* (1870?). Reprints in facsimile are available for *The Worthines of Wales* (Spenser Society, 1876) and *The Miserie of Flaunders* (Adnitt and Naunton, Shrewsbury, 1876). Pertinent selections are given in *Collectanea Anglo-Poetica*, ed. Thomas Corser, Part IV (Chetham Society, lxxvii [1869]), 354-89; also in Anthony à Wood, *Athenae Oxonienses*, ed. Philip Bliss, i (1813), 730-31. The most complete study of Churchyard is that by Henry W. Adnitt, "Thomas Churchyard," *Transactions of the Shropshire Archaeological and Natural History Society*, iii (1880), 1-68. A future editor should find useful, as I have, an M.A. thesis "Thomas Churchyard: A Descriptive Bibliography," presented at the Ohio State University in 1948 by one of my former students Richard B. Looser. Copies of the Churchyard poems in *AH* show few of the peculiarities in orthography pointed out by M. St. Clare Byrne in "Thomas Churchyard's Spelling" (*The Library*, Fourth Series, v [1924], 243-48).

The lines of No. 171 are representative of many Churchyard wrote in praise of the mean estate—to be found not in town or Court among the "peacockes prowde" with "platters full of bribes," but among the honest country folk who live on homely fare and seek to be good neighbors. It is, of course, the theme and somewhat the manner of Wyatt's satire "Myne owne I. P." (No. 104), which Churchyard certainly knew, as he did Surrey's translations from Horace and Martial on the mean estate (*Poems*, ed. Padelford, 1928, Nos. 42, 43). But Churchyard is not merely a literary imitator. His criticism of the Court reflects personal disappointment, often bitter in its note of disillusionment, as in No. 321. The setting which he describes as desirable for the good life is that of his native West Country, "Among the Craggye Rockes," which he eulogizes in "A Discourse of Mountaynes" (*The Worthines of Wales*, sigs. M1^{r}-M3^{r}):

> These ragged Rocks, brings playnest people foorth,
> On Mountaine wyld, the hardest horse is bred:
> Though grasse thereon, be grosse and little worth,
> Sweete is the foode, where hunger so is fed.
> On rootes and hearbs, our fathers long did feede,
> And neere the Skye, growes sweetest fruit in deede:
> On marrish meares and watrie mossie ground,
> Are rotten weedes, and rubbish drosse vnsound. (sig. M1^{v})

1-2. Compare lines in his description of Yale:

> This Soyle is cold, and subiect vnto winde,
> Hard duskie Rocks, all couered ore full dim:
> Where if winde blowe, ye shall foule weather finde,
> And thinke you feele, the bitter blasts full brim.
> (*ibid.*, sig. M3^{v})

According to the *N.E.D.* the north country word *brim*, i.e., *breme*, in the sense of the raging storm or sea, was taken from Lydgate by Spenser (*The Shepheardes Calender*, Feb., 42) and adopted by later writers from Spenser. If, however, No. 171 was written before 1579, as I think probable, Churchyard's use of the word would be independent of Spenser's influence.

8. "playne as packstaff." This was a common proverb. The staff on which the peddler supports his pack when resting is the packstaff, or pikestaff, and its use is obvious. The variant in the printed version evidently refers to the double pronged staff.

16, 27. For the fare of milk and whey, compare lines in "A Discourse of Mountaynes":

> Sowre Whey and Curds, can yeeld a sugred tast,
> Where sweete Martchpane, as yet was neuer knowne:
> When emptie gorge, hath bole of Milke embrast,
> And Cheese and bread, hath dayly of his owne,
> He craues no feast, nor seekes no banquets fine,
> He can digest, his dinner without wine:
> So toyles our life, and likes full well this trade,
> Not fearing death, because his count is made. (sig. M3r)

[172] *The Sillie bird that dreads no guyle/ is sone brought into thrall*

Hand A; ascription in the same hand.

I have found no other copy of this sonnet, which represents a peculiar kind of experimentation. The iambic hexameters and the rhymed couplets are, to say the least, rare.

"Cordall" was probably Sir William Cordell, the son of John and Eva Cordell, born at Edmonton, Middlesex. He was educated at Cambridge, although his college is unknown; later he had a part in the founding of St. John's College, Cambridge. He was admitted to Lincoln's Inn, April 15, 1538, and became a barrister in 1544. In 1553 he was appointed Solicitor General, and in 1557 he was made Master of the Rolls, an office he continued to hold after Queen Elizabeth came to the throne. He was also a member of Queen Mary's Privy Council, but Elizabeth did not retain him in that capacity. He was evidently a man who played his parts with care. He was active in the trial of the younger Sir Thomas Wyatt in 1554; but in 1569 he subscribed to the Act of Uniformity, and in 1578 he entertained Queen Elizabeth at his manor of Long Melford in Suffolk. He died in 1581 (*D.N.B.; Alumni Cantabrigienses*, compiled by John and J. A. Venn, I, i, [1922]).

Thomas Fuller in *The History of the Worthies of England*, 1662 (ed. John Nichols, ii [1811], 345-46), in the chapter "Suffolk," quotes the epitaph engraved upon the tomb of Sir William Cordall in the church at Long Melford:

> *Hic* Gulielmus *habet requiem* Cordellus, *avito*
> *Stemmate qui clarus, clarior ingenio.*

Hic studiis primos consumpsit fortiter annos,
Mox & Causarum strenuus actor erat.
Tanta illi doctrina inerat, facundia tanta,
Ut Parlamenti publica Lingua foret.
Postea factus Eques, Reginae arcana Mariae
Consilia, & Patriae grande subibat opus:
Factus & est Custos Rotulorum, urgente senecta
In Christo moriens cepit ad astra viam.
Pauperibus largus, victum vestemque ministrans,
Insuper Hospitii condidit ille domum.

Fuller's English version runs:

Here *William Cordal* doth in rest remain,
Great by his birth, but greater by his brain.
Plying his studies hard his youth throughout,
Of causes he became a Pleader stout.
His Learning deep such eloquence did vent,
He was chose Speaker of the Parliament.
Afterwards Knight Queen Mary did him make,
And Counsellor, State-work to undertake:
And Master of the Rolls. Well worn with age,
Dying in Christ, Heaven was his utmost stage.
Diet and clothes to poor he gave at large,
And a fair *Almshouse* founded on his charge.

No. 307 in *AH* is ascribed to "Cordall"; but, so far as I have discovered, he is otherwise unknown as a versifier. I have not the temerity to call him a poet, although his verses compare quite well with many of those in the early miscellanies of the period.

[173] *Syns by examples daylye we are taught*

Hand A; ascription to Vaux in the same hand.

I have come across no other copy of these verses assigned to Vaux, who must be that same Thomas Vaux, second Baron Vaux of Harrowden, 1510-1556, eldest son of Nicholas Baron Vaux, whose poems were published in *Tottel's Miscellany* and in *The Paradise of Dainty Devices.* No. 173 is not included by A. B. Grosart in his edition of the poems of Lord Vaux, *Miscellanies of the Fuller Worthies Library*, IV, ii (1872), 364-92. See also Nos. 22, 298, 299, and Notes.

[174] *My pen̄ to base, my skill but bluntt and bare*

Hand A.

I have found no other copy of this poem, which might well have been published among the Uncertain Authors of *Tottel's Miscellany.* The theme on love and disdain is typical of the period. The ten-line stanza with the experimental rhyme scheme, *ababccddee*, should be noticed.

[175] *Graunt that thie goodes, excead the treasures cleene*

Hand: the same secretary as appears in No. 185.

"Hennage" very probably refers to Sir Thomas Heneage (d. 1595), who is mentioned by Sir John Harington in *A Catalogue of Bishops* in connection with the appointment of Dr. John Still to the see of Bath and Wells in 1592, after it had been vacant for three years:

> During the vacancy I can well remember, there was great enquiring who should have it; and, as if all Bishops should now be sworn to follow *usum Sarum*, every man made reckoning that the mannour house and park of Banwel should be made a reward of some courtier; it encreast also this suspition, that Sir Thomas Hennage, an old courtier and a zealous Puritan, was said to have an ore in the matter, whose conscience, if it were such in the clergy, as that was found in the dutchy, might well have digested a better booty than Banwell [quoted from *NA*, 1769, p. 24].

Sir John's unflattering implications refer to Heneage's high office as Chancellor of the Duchy of Lancaster, to which he was appointed in 1590 (see the *D.N.B.*, from which this brief account is taken). It was one of the last of many appointments which he had received in his years of general service to the state and personal service to the queen, who marked her favor by many lucrative land grants, especially in the county of Essex. Shortly after Elizabeth's accession, Heneage was made a member of the Privy Chamber, and in January, 1569/70, was appointed treasurer of the queen's Chamber. In 1587 he became Vice-Chamberlain of the royal household and a member of the Privy Council. His first wife, Anne Poyntz, daughter of Sir Nicholas Poyntz of Acton, was also a favorite of the queen (in this connection see the Note on No. 17). In 1585 Heneage was associated with Sir Walter Ralegh in an inquiry into a dispute about the ransom of English captives in Barbary. It may have been about this time that Ralegh wrote No. 235, said to have been composed in answer to a poem by Heneage (see the Note), probably represented in the fragment No. 236. Since his name is given as the heading rather than as the subscription to No. 175, it is impossible to determine on present evidence whether he wrote the poem, or whether it was addressed to him. Sir John Harington uses the names of authors in headings to Nos. 201 and 223, but ordinarily they are written as subscriptions. The name heading for No. 199, however, presents another instance of the possible designation of authorship.

Harington's opinion of Heneage seems not to have been shared by Thomas Newton, who in 1581 submitted his edition of *Seneca, His Tenne*

Tragedies, Translated into English to the "learned Censure" of this gentleman of "Heroicall mynde," who is praised as a "zealous Professor" of God's truth, a "most loyall seruitour" of the queen, and a "most worthy Ornament" to his country ("The Epistle Dedicatory," *The Tenne Tragedies of Seneca*, Part I, Spenser Society [1887], pp. 1, 3).

Perhaps pertinent to the significance of lines 2-4 and 34-40 in No. 175 is the fact that in 1581 Heneage invested 200£ in Edward Fenton's expedition to Cathay. Heneage's fortune was gained, however, in England rather than by trade investments. It is evident from Sir John's remarks that Heneage was known to have an eye to the making of money. Although the general theme of No. 175 is the familiar one of praise for the quiet, virtuous life, free from thoughts of worldly gain, it also reflects briefly the Elizabethan interest in commerce with the East. Unusual is the reference to the desirably simple life of the Geats.

3. "Seas of Pontus and Tirhene," used figuratively to represent ancient trade routes; literally, the Black Sea and the seas used by the Phoenicians, whose main city was Tyre, in their extensive commerce.

9. "fyldye," i.e., given to life in the fields. The *N.E.D.* records no example after 1598.

51. "to Toppe and scourdge," i.e., to fight and whip. The last example quoted in the *N.E.D.* of the verb *top* in this sense is dated 1440.

[176] *Since shunninge payne I ease can never fynde*

Hand: the same as in Nos. 151-53. Inasmuch as this sonnet is attributed to Sidney on good authority, it is curious to find the initials "J. H.," i.e., John Harington, written on the margin in pencil in the handwriting of George F. Nott.

This poem was first published without attribution in (*A*) the 1594(?) edition of Henry Constable's *Diana*, sig. C5^{v}, Sonnet 6 of Decade 3. Nevertheless, in 1598 it was included in (*B*) *The Countesse of Pembrokes Arcadia*, p. 472, where it is the first of the poems in the section headed, "Certaine Sonets. Written by Sir Philip Sidney: Neuer before printed." Seven others among these "Certaine Sonets" had previously appeared in the *Diana*, which Sidney's sister, Mary Herbert, Countess of Pembroke, who authorized the publication of the 1598 *Arcadia*, should have known. From the collation following, one could conclude that the text of *B* was set up from *A*, but a valid opinion on this textual relationship for No. 176 should take into account that of the other seven poems, whose texts are not always so close (see *The Complete Works of Sir Philip Sidney*, ed. Albert Feuillerat, ii [1922] 386-87). Copies used for *A* and *B* are in the Huntington Library and British Museum, respectively.

2 harmed] harmd *A*
3 woomd] wonne *A*: won *B*; charmed] charmd *A*
5 shall] still *A B*
6 Whear] since *A B*; armede] armde *A*: armed *B*
7 ease] Ice *A B*; warmede] warmd *A*: warmed *B*
8 thoughtes] thought *A B*
10 whose lawe] . . . rule *A B*
11 hard'lyste] hardly *A B*; whome . . . ever] who euer pryson *A B*
13 Wheare . . . may] Whereas if I *A B*

A. W. Pollard in his edition of *Astrophel and Stella*, 1888, prints this sonnet (p. 151), in his section "Certain Sonets," made up of fourteen sonnets and songs taken from pp. 472-90 of the 1598 *Arcadia*. He holds that it is "a tenable theory that in all the poems on these pages there is some reference to Sidney's love for Stella, certainly this is the case with those here selected. The reason for their exclusion from the *Astrophel and Stella* series is matter of conjecture. It is possible that by some accident Sidney's own copies were destroyed, and that we owe these additional poems to the fortunate preservation of duplicates in the possession of the Countess of Pembroke" (p. 227). This statement does not, of course, take into account the 1594 printing of the poem.

[177] *A body chast, a virtuous mynd, a temperat toung, an humble hart*

Hand: Sir John Harington's. The emendation in line 2 is also in his hand.

These verses in honor of his mother were included by Sir John Harington in the notes to Bk. XXIX of his translation of the *Orlando Furioso*. They are found in the autograph manuscript, Brit. Mus. Add. 18920, fol. 147^{v}, and in the edition of 1591, p. 239 (they are also in the editions of 1607 and 1634). There is a copy in Bodleian MS. Rawl. Poet. 84, fol. 45^{r}, headed, "An Epitaph on a Lady." There are no variants, except that all the copies agree with the crossed-out reading "trew" in line 2 in *AH*.

In the notes to the *Orlando Furioso*, referred to above, Sir John prefaces this poem as follows (quoted from the edition of 1591):

> In the death of *Isabella* is a notable example of chastitie, which I must confesse I haue endeuored to set forth to the vttermost of my poore skill, of a speciall loue and reuerẽce I bare to the name, hauing had an *Isabell* to my mother, and such an *Isabell*, as if nature did not make me to parciall a praiser, I would boldlie affirme (both for the honorable place she liued in, and for the vertuous sort she dyed in) to be worthie to whom the prophecie in the 31. staffe of this 29. booke may

be worthylie applied: As a better pen then mine, approued by this Epitaph made and intytled in this sort.

The poem, with the heading as in *AH*, follows. The stanza to which Sir John refers reads (p. 236):

That for her sake that dy'd of this name last,
Who euer shall hereafter beare that name,
Shal be both wise and continent and chast,
Of faultlesse manners, and of spotlesse fame;
Writers shall striue to make their glorie last,
And shall in prose and verse record the same,
Hellicon, Pindus, and Parnassus hill,
Sound *Isabella*, *Isabella* still.

It seems evident that No. 177 was inspired by lines 3 and 4 of this stanza. I am of the opinion that the elder John Harington was the author, of whom his son might aptly say that he had "a better pen then mine." It is quite possible that John the elder translated the above-quoted stanza, as he did stanza 1 of Bk. XIX (see No. 3 and Note), and then made use of it for a little poem of his own.

Isabell Markham, who became the second wife of John Harington the elder about 1559, was a Maid of Honour to the Princess Elizabeth at Hatfield, and in 1558, on Elizabeth's accession to the throne, she became a Gentlewoman of the Privy Chamber (see the Note on No. 262), to which Sir John no doubt had reference when he spoke of the "honorable place she lived in." In 1572 Thomas Palfreyman, a Gentleman of the Chapel Royal, dedicated his *Diuine Meditations* to Isabell Harington, addressing her as follows:

To the righte Worshipful, Maistresse Isabel Harington, one of the Gentlewomen of the Queenes Maiesties most honorable priuie Chamber, Thomas Paulfreyman hir dayly Orator wisheth (with continuance) the increase of Gods eternal grace and fauour. . . .

To the ende therefore, this small and moste simple volume, may vnder youre godly protection) gather thē rather some estimation and credite, & passe forth for good to the vse of the godly, I moste humbly beseeche youre worship, so to accepte it in the simplicitie thereof, and graunt thereunto your Christian furtherance, that some good for Goddes glory, may growe thereby to some, that some liues at the least may be somewhat amended, the furies of God the sooner preuented, and the bright lighte of the sonne of god shine with more power amongst vs, to ouerthrowe vs in his feare, to beate flatte to the earth, our earthie and proude fleshe, and to waste soone or consume, for good and most happie chaunge, our most damnable works of darknesse. I shall (as of bounden duetie, for this and for other the like causes deserued) most humbly pray for you, that God in mercie may euer blesse, both you, your moste worthy beloued in Christe, your ofspring, and whole familie.

Your humble Oratoure,
Thomas Paulfreyman

[quoted from the unique copy in the Bodleian Library, sigs. x2^{r}, x8^{r,v}; *S.T.C.* 19136].

Isabell Harington died May 20, 1579. Her funeral certificate, signed by her husband, is preserved at the Heralds' College, MS. I.10, fol. 144^{r}. I was permitted to examine this document and given permission to quote it through the courtesy of E. N. Geijer, esq., Rouge Dragon Pursuivant. It reads:

1579. Mrs Isabell Harington, Doughter to Sr Iohn Markham, Knyght, & wiff to Mr Iohn Harington, esquier, died at her house in London on Wensdaye, beinge the xxth daye of Maye, & was buryed at the parishe Churche of S^{t} gregories in poules churcheyarde the xxvth daye of the same monthe, & by him had yssue Iohn Harington, sonne & heire, frances Harington, 2 sonne. the offycer of armes that served their was Edmond Knyght al's Chester herault. In witnes of the truthe herof the said Mr Iohn Harington, Esquier, hathe here unto sett his hande the xxvith daye of Maye A^{o} d'ni 1579.

Io. Haryngton.

[178] *A boy that should content me wondrous well*

Hand: Sir John Harington's secretary, with the ascription in his italic hand.

In this instance does "Io Har." refer to Sir John or to his father? It is true that Sir John signed in this same way No. 91, which was included in his collection of epigrams. It is also true that one charming little poem is written "to a Daughter of nine yeere olde" (*Epigrams*, I, 75), and several, which reveal an abiding affection, are addressed to his wife, "Sweet Mall." See especially I, 38; II, 72, 81, 87, 96; III, 24. Yet even when he is speaking most tenderly, something of the jester will out, as in III, 24, "*To* Mall, *to comfort her for the losse of her Children.*" Another, I,38, which ends on an affectionate note, takes its point from his interrupting a grace begun by his "little sonne" in order to tease the child's grandmother, Lady Rogers, for the lateness of her dinner hour. A letter written in December, 1602, to Richard Langley, Schoolmaster at Eton, is unquestionably an expression of fatherly pride in his young son's proficiency in the writing of "latten verses." The fond parent, who has been keeping the boy at court, employing him "in exercyses to the queen and some of my Lords," which may seem "a litle to rype for a boy of the fift forme," desires that his son not be "much addicted to them least yt hinder him (as yt hath done mee) of better studies" (McClure, *Letters and Epigrams*, 1930, pp. 95-96, 394). The letter concerns his eldest son, John (1589-1654), for whom No. 178 may have been written a few years earlier.

Doubt arises from the tone and style of the sonnet itself. The first line is an adaptation from Wyatt's epigram "A face that shuld content me wonders well" (*Poems*, ed. A. K. Foxwell, i [1913], 61), and we may recall that the elder Harington modeled the beginning lines of No. 20 on a poem by Wyatt. Again, the style suggests comparison with No. 2, the elder Harington's experimental sonnet on Admiral Seymour. Lines 9-11 of No. 178 echo lines in Nos. 23, 177, 248, and the first two poems in the Appendix, which are probably, though not certainly, compositions by John the elder. It is possible that he wrote No. 178 when Sir John was quite small.

G. F. Nott printed the poem from *AH* in the note on Wyatt's epigram in his edition of *Surrey and Wyatt*, ii (1816), 554. H. E. Rollins printed it from *N*, fol. 72^{v}, in his edition of *TM*, ii, 194, in a note on Wyatt's poem. Neither of these editors comments on the probable authorship, although both refer to the ascription.

[179] *Syttinge alone vppon my thoughte in melancholye moode*

Hand: Sir John Harington's secretary. The ascription to "E. Veer. count d'Oxford," in printed italic, is written also, I think, by Sir John. Beneath is a line, crossed out, of some five words, which I have been unable to decipher satisfactorily. Sir John was probably responsible for the change in line 21 from "an oracle" to "meracle." A line is drawn through "an" and *m* written above, and the *o* of "oracle" has been changed to an *e*, thus resulting in "meracle," which agrees with the reading in other copies. The *a* in "an" should not have been crossed out, as the article is needed for euphony and rhythm.

I have come across three other contemporary manuscript copies. A copy in (*A*) Bodleian MS. Rawl. Poet. 85, fol. 11^{r}, written in late sixteenth-century secretary, is headed, "Verses made by the earle of Oxforde ⟨and Mrs Ann Vauesor⟩." A copy in (*B*) Archbishop Marsh's Library (Saint Patrick's Cathedral, Dublin), MS. 183 Z 3.5.21, fol. 20^{v}, headed, "Verses made of ye Earle of Ox^{en}forde And Mrs Ann Vauesor," is written in a small late secretary hand and is placed with a group of poems by Oxford. For some account of this little known manuscript, see the Preliminary Note on Nos. 201-21. A copy in (*C*) Folger MS. 1.112, fol. 12^{r}, has the name "Vavaser" at the end, apparently intended as an ascription.

1 thoughte] Thoughtes *B*
3 greefs] feares *A*: teares *B C*

4 a] an *A*; Vaer] Nun *A B*: bowe *C*; one her face] couered wth *A-C*
5 cleere] callme and cleere *A B*: Clere & Calme *C*
6 thoughe hid withe] hid vnder *A B*
7 softe] lefte *A*
8 syghed] syghted *A*: sighte *C*; would] myghte *A B*; mercie] pittye *A B*
10 And] When *A B*

Written and underlined between lines 10 and 11 in A and B are the words: Añ. Vauesor. eccho, *first written* Vauesors *in A, but the last* s *has a line through it.*

11 qu^{od} she] *omitted* *A*: quothe . . . *C*
13 cruell] tyrant *A-C*; harmes] harme *A*; the] thy *A B*
15 yea] oh *A-C*
16 nymphe] nymphe ⟨so⟩ *A*; sorrows] sorrowe *A C*
17 regarde] rewarde *A B*; remorse] rewarde *A*
19 bewty] fauour *A B*
20 dye. I] dye. Dye *B*
21 sayd] ⟨sade sy⟩ sayde *A*; yt ys ⟨an^{m} o^{e}⟩racle] howe great a myrackle *A-C*
22 heere this] her how *A B*: . . . the *C*; truethe to tell] toulde ⟨toulde⟩ the truthe *A*: tolde the truthe *B*: tell her truthe *C*; tweare Apolloes] true as Pheobus *A B*

The most interesting reading peculiar to *AH* occurs in line 4 with the word "Vaer," which is a pun on the author's name, as the star emphasizes. From the context, the word is evidently to be interpreted not as *ver*, spring, but as *vair*, referring to a squirrel with gray and white fur, which was frequently used on garments of the nobility in the thirteenth and fourteenth centuries. Thus the lady in her mourning pose, as she laments over the lost love of the noble Edward de Vere, Earl of Oxford, is appropriately clad in gray and white, the "colour of a Vaer," which also has its association with the apparel of the nobility. There is no particular reference to *vair* as used in heraldry, for this fur does not appear in the arms and crest of the Earl of Oxford (James E. Doyle, *The Official Baronage of England, 1066-1885*, ii [1886], 137-39). I suggest, however, that the pun may signify also the Old French *vair*, truth. As indicated below, the circumstances connected with the subject matter of the poem and its mocking tone imply that the lady is acting and speaking only with the "colour" of truth.

It is evident from *A*, *B*, and *C* that Anne Vavasour's name was associated with the composition of the poem, even though the copyist in *A* later crossed out the attribution to her. Sir John Harington assigns the poem only to Edward de Vere, Earl of Oxford, and the comment at the head of the poem suggests that Sir John knew Oxford's poetry well. This was not so easy to do, if we may judge by the remarks of George Puttenham in *The Arte of English Poesie*, 1589 (ed. G. Willcock and A. Walker, 1936, p. 61):

> And in her Maiesties time that now is are sprong vp an other crew of Courtly makers Noble men and Gentlemen of her Maiesties owne seruauntes, who haue written excellently well as it would appeare if their doings could be found out and made publicke with the rest, of which number is first that Noble Gentleman *Edward* Earle of Oxford.

Edward de Vere, 1550-1604, seventeenth Earl of Oxford, whose mother, Margaret, was sister of Arthur Golding, became a prominent figure at court during his boyhood. Upon his father's death in 1562, Edward became a royal ward and was taken into the house of Sir William Cecil, an association which resulted in 1571 in Edward's marriage to Anne Cecil. He soon became involved in a plot to rescue Thomas Howard, fourth Duke of Norfolk, from the Tower (see Nos. 147 and 148 and Notes), but escaped severe punishment. He spent the winter of 1575-76 in Italy, a sojourn which affected his character and his literary interests. On his return he became alienated from his wife and professed Catholicism (Sir E. K. Chambers, *Sir Henry Lee*, Oxford, the Clarendon Press, 1936, pp. 154-55; *D.N.B.*), steps which led to further quarrels and difficulties, not the least of which arose from his indiscreet relations with Anne Vavasour, a gentlewoman of the bedchamber to Queen Elizabeth, who came to court in 1580. Sir E. K. Chambers in his book on *Sir Henry Lee* (pp. 150, *passim*) gives a very full account of Anne Vavasour, the daughter of Henry Vavasour of Copmanthorpe, Yorkshire, by Margaret Knyvet, daughter of Sir Henry Knyvet of Buckenham, Norfolk. Anne became the mistress of Sir Henry Lee about 1590, but before that time she had bestowed her affections upon others, of whom Oxford was one. By March 23, 1580/1, she had scandalized the court by giving birth to a son, and Oxford was said to be the father. Sir Francis Walsingham, writing to the third Earl of Huntingdon on that date, says:

> On Tuesday at night Anne Vavysor was brought to bed of a son in the maidens' chamber. The E[arl] of Oxeforde is avowed to be the father, who hath withdrawn himself with intent, as it is thought, to pass the seas. The ports are laid for him and therefore if he have any such determination it is not likely that he will escape.
>
> The gentlewoman the selfsame night she was delivered was conveyed out of the house and the next day committed to the Tower [*Reports on the Manuscripts of the Late Reginald Rawdon Hastings, Esq.*, ed. Francis Bickley, Hist. MSS. Comm., ii [1930], 29].

Although the cause of detention, save that it was not "treason or anie criminall cause," is not named, the records show that Oxford himself was released from the Tower on June 8, 1581, and that he was not given full liberty for about two years (*Acts of the Privy Council*, ed. J. R. Dasent, New Series, xiii [1896], 74; B. M. Ward, *The Seventeenth Earl of Oxford, 1550-1604*, London, J. Murray, 1928, pp. 211, 223-24; Chambers, p. 156). Ward interprets Oxford's imprisonment and further restraint as arising from his involvement with Catholics; but Chambers attributes the cause to the affair with Anne Vavasour. Probably both reasons contributed to Oxford's general disfavor. At any rate, the Knyvet family, who were prominent at court, sought further vengeance on Oxford for the dishonor of their kinswoman. On March 3, 1581/2, the Reverend Richard Madox wrote in his diary:

> My Lord of Oxford fought with Master Knyvet about the quarrel of Bessie Bavisar, and was hurt, which grieved the Lord Treasurer so much the more for that the Earl hath company with his wife since Christmas [Ward, pp. 227-28, as quoted from Cotton MS. Appendix 47].

The "Bessie" is undoubtedly Madox's mistake. Thomas Birch in *Memoirs of the Reign of Queen Elizabeth* (i [1754], 22) records a pertinent passage in a letter from Nicholas Faunt to Anthony Bacon on March 17, 1581/2:

> In England of late there hath been a fray between my lord of Oxford and Mr. *Thomas Knevet* of the privy chamber, who are both hurt, but my lord of Oxford more dangerously. You know Mr. *Knevet* is not meanly beloved in court; and therefore he is not like to speed ill whatsoever the quarrel be.

With Thomas Knyvett and his men, Oxford and his followers were destined to have other meetings of like nature (see Ward, p. 231; Chambers, p. 157; Sir N. H. Nicolas, *Memoirs of the Life and Times of Sir Christopher Hatton*, 1847, pp. 256-61, 321-24). As late as January 19, 1584/5, Anne's brother, Thomas Vavasour, sent a challenge to Oxford, which, although arising apparently from more than one cause, seems certainly to have had its root in Oxford's dishonorable relations with Anne. Thus Vavasour wrote:

> If thy body had been as deformed as thy mind is dishonourable, my house had been yet unspotted, and thyself remained with thy cowardice unknown. I speak this that I fear thou art so much wedded to that shadow of thine, that nothing can have force to awake thy base and sleepy spirits. Is not the revenge taken of thy victims sufficient, but wilt thou yet use unworthy instruments to provoke my unwilling mind? Or dost thou fear thyself, and therefore hast sent thy forlorn

> kindred, whom as thou hast left nothing to inherit so thou dost thrust them violently into thy shameful quarrels? [Ward, p. 229, as quoted from Lansdowne MS. 99, No. 93].

Vavasour proposes a meeting at Nunnington, but the outcome does not appear. Chambers says that Anne had to leave the court after her disgrace, and he quotes a libel of the year 1584 on the Earl of Leicester, in which the Earl is accused of having made dishonorable overtures to Anne Vavasour (pp. 159-60).

Possibly all of these unfortunate developments had something to do with the fact that No. 179 was not contemporaneously published. There is the added consideration that because of the inclusion of the name "Vere" in the poem itself, there could have been no possibility of an anonymous printing. So far as I have discovered, No. 179 was first printed by A. B. Grosart from *A* in his edition of the poems of Oxford, included in *Miscellanies of the Fuller Worthies' Library* (iv [1872], 63-64), where the name "Vavesors" is mistakenly given as "Vanefors."

There is no doubt that Oxford was regarded as a writer of merit by his contemporaries. Not only do we have Puttenham's praise of him, but William Webbe in *A Discourse of English Poetrie*, 1586, says:

> I may not omitte the deserued commendations of many honourable and noble Lordes, and Gentlemen, in her Maiesties Courte, which in the rare deuises of Poetry, haue béene and yet are most excellent skylfull, among whom, the right honourable Earle of Oxford may challenge to him selfe the tytle of ye most excellent among the rest [*Ancient Critical Essays*, ed. Joseph Haslewood, ii [1815], 34].

And Francis Meres in "A comparatiue discourse of our English Poets, with the Greeke, Latine, and Italian Poets," published in his *Palladis Tamia*, 1598, names the Earl of Oxford among those "best for Comedy amongst vs" (ed. Haslewood, ii, 154). See also No. 189 and Note. According to Sir John Harington, No. 179 was Oxford's best poem, an opinion that is of interest to us in our understanding of Elizabethan taste. The frequent plays upon the author's name, both in sound and sense, would appeal to any Elizabethan, as would no doubt the pastoral lament. Probably a lesser number would enjoy with Sir John the ironic mockery of the poem, which reverses the role of the suffering Petrarchan lover and skilfully presents the author as scorning himself for his pride and unfaithfulness in love. As indicated above, however, line 4 suggests criticism of the lady and the closing couplet by innuendo mocks her.

[180] *Some soile doth scortche, keepe rutt at home*

Hand: a late, careless secretary, which occurs in other Harington MSS. and elsewhere in *AH*. See the Introduction, p. 32. The marginal notation by lines 31-36 is in another ink and probably another hand. In line 184 "Sable" is clearly a copyist's error for "Stable." In the notation by lines 203-08, omitted in Nott's transcript, "whytegifts" is all but obliterated, but I believe that to be the correct transcription.

No. 180 is a long fragment, lacking the first five stanzas because of the missing fol. 131. I have not located any other copy, but I suspect that there may be more than one in libraries at Cambridge University.

From lines 267-68 we learn that this "Cockolds kallender" was "devysed by vaine valenger." In the Note on No. 66 something has been said about Stephen Valenger, the recusant ballad writer, who had his ears cut off for the printing, and perhaps the writing, of that poem on the death of Edmund Campion in 1581. The son of Robert Valenger of Watlington, Norfolk, he took his B.A. degree from Gonville and Caius College, Cambridge, in January, 1559/60. He was granted the M.A. in 1562, and he is said to have remained as a fellow and tutor until about 1568 (John Venn, *Biographical History of Gonville and Caius College: 1349-1897*, i [1897], 49; *Alumni Cantabrigienses*, compiled by John and J. A. Venn, Part I, vol. iv [1927], 293). The lines of No. 180 indicate, however, that he was certainly in close contact with Cambridge for several years longer. By 1580 he had gained sufficient notoriety as a ballad writer, and perhaps as an experimenter in quantitative verse, to call forth an ironic comment from Edmund Spenser, to which Gabriel Harvey referred when writing Spenser his opinions on quantitative verse: "Indeed I remember, who was wont in a certaine brauerie, to call our *M. Valanger* Noble *M. Valanger*. Else neuer heard I any, that durst presume so much ouer the Englishe, (excepting a fewe suche stammerers, as haue not the masterie of their owne Tongues) as to alter the Quantitie of any one sillable, otherwise, than oure common speache, and generall receyued Custome woulde beare them oute" (*Three Proper, and wittie, familiar Letters*, 1580, in *The Poetical Works of Edmund Spenser*, ed. J. C. Smith and E. De Selincourt, 1912, reprint, 1937, p. 630). Harvey, who took his B.A. at Christ's College in 1570 and remained as student then lecturer, and Spenser, who was in residence at Pembroke College from 1569 to 1576, were quite possibly acquainted with "Noble *M. Valanger*." Although there is no doubt that the verses of No. 180 are not always to be literally interpreted, they nevertheless lend support to Harvey's lament over the low level of learning and morals at Cambridge in 1580 (same ref., pp. 621-22), and indicate further that this state of affairs had existed when Spenser was a student there. Sir John Harington, who was at King's College, Cambridge, from 1576 to 1581, no doubt took a copy of Valenger's calendar from one then current in the university.

As No. 181 is called a libel of Oxford, so No. 180 could very well be described as a libel of Cambridge, for with few exceptions the men designated in the margins or in the verses (usually by puns) were connected with Cambridge in the 1560's and 1570's. From the number of prominent clergymen who are included, it is evident that the Catholic Valenger was not merely compiling a "Cockold's kallender" as such, but that he was using this as a means for making a scurrilous attack on some of those in high places in the university community, with particularly vituperative thrusts at the Anglican clergy. Verses in the libel make it clear that he was mainly concerned with the critical period from 1570 to 1573.

As is mentioned in the comment below on lines 97-102, the reference to Mr. Cressey of Jesus College would be pertinent only some time after 1568 and before August 18, 1573, when he migrated to Caius. The scathing denunciation of Dr. John Whitgift, then Master of Trinity College and Vice-chancellor of Cambridge, in lines 209-20, with the emphasis upon his leading role in the displacement of the Puritan Thomas Cartwright, must have been written some time after December 11, 1570, when Cartwright was removed from the Lady Margaret Professorship (James B. Mullinger, *The University of Cambridge from the Royal Injunctions of 1535 to the Accession of Charles the First*, 1884, pp. 225-26; Charles H. and Thompson Cooper, *Athenae Cantabrigienses*, ii [1861], 361, 369-70; John Strype, *Annals of the Reformation . . . during Queen Elizabeth's Happy Reign*, I, ii [1824], 376-82). Among those who openly championed Cartwright and his views were several to whom reference seems to be made in No. 180: Robert Some, Edmund Chapman, Edward Dering, and Roger Kelke (Mullinger, pp. 209, 215, 228; Cooper, i [1858], 355, 382; ii, 511; Strype, *Annals*, I, ii, 373; Strype, *The Life and Acts of Matthew Parker*, iii [1821], 219-25; M. M. Knappen, *Tudor Puritanism*, Chicago: University of Chicago Press, 1939, p. 225; see lines 55-60, 109-14, 159-72 of No. 180). In September of 1571 Cartwright, on the ruling of Whitgift, was deprived of his longstanding fellowship at Trinity College (Mullinger, pp. 226-27). In both instances Whitgift proceeded by means of the increased authority given the heads by the new statutes of 1570, framed under his initiative and "enacted 'on account of the again increasing audacity and excessive licence of men' " (Mullinger, p. 222, where the Latin of the original is given in note 3). Adoption of the statutes led to formal protest and rebellious acts in the university. Whitgift's arbitrary actions, based on these unpopular regulations, served to fan opposition to them and to those in authority, increasing dislike of Whitgift and evoking partisanship for Cartwright and his fellows, even from those who, like Valenger, were not sympathetic with Puritan views (see Mullinger, pp. 222-40, for discussion of the statutes and the ensuing reaction against them; see also Dering's letter of protest to the Chancellor, William Cecil, in Strype, *Parker*, iii, 219-25). It is, of course, true that both

Catholics and Puritans were at a disadvantage in the face of established authority, but Valenger is by no means always kind to "precisians." The conflict between Whitgift and Cartwright was openly renewed in 1572 and later in pamphlets written by each following the publication of the Puritan manifesto, *An Admonition to Parliament.* On this controversy, see, for example, W. H. Frere, *The English Church in the Reigns of Elizabeth and James I (1558-1625)* (London, Macmillan, 1904), pp. 178-85; Knappen, pp. 234-45; William Pierce, *An Historical Introduction to the Marprelate Tracts* (London, Constable, 1908), pp. 36-53, favoring the Puritans; Donald J. McGinn, *The Admonition Controversy*, New Brunswick: Rutgers University Press, 1949, favoring the Anglicans. Libels, which had been circulating for some time, increased (Strype, *Annals*, I, ii [1824], 374). In 1572 Archbishop Parker wrote to Lord Burghley " 'That the Puritans slandered them with slanderous books and libels, lying they cared not how deep' " (Strype, *Parker*, ii, 192). At Cambridge "there was a slanderous libel set upon the outer door of the schools, against Dr. Whitgift and Dr. Pern. Some were not without cause suspected for it; but the author was not certainly known" (Strype, *Parker*, ii, 194-95; Knappen, p. 239). The author could have been Valenger. Whitgift himself complained that the followers of Cartwright " 'thought it a heinous offence to wear cap or surplice; but they slandered and backbit their brethren, railed on them by libels, contemned superiors, discredited such as were in authority; in short, disquieted the church and state' " (as quoted by Strype, *Annals*, II, i, 7). If so eminent a continental authority as Beza, whose opinion was greatly respected by the Puritans, could compare those who wore " 'square caps, tippets, surplices, and the like' " to " 'priests of Baal' " (Strype, *Annals*, I, ii, 172; see also Strype, *The History of the Life and Acts of the Most Reverend Father in God, Edmund Grindal*, 1821, pp. 167, 175), and could declare that some bishops were of the devil (Pierce, p. 258), it is not surprising to find similar views set forth at Cambridge. In 1572 William Chark, a fellow of Peterhouse, openly declared "that bishops were introduced into the church by the devil" (Knappen, p. 239; Strype, *Parker*, ii, 194). Somewhat earlier an extremist among the laity heckled square-capped Edmund Grindal, Bishop of London, with cries of "horns" (Knappen, p. 211). In 1565 William Turner, who, though Dean of Wells, was aggressively puritanical and opposed to vestments, made some one accused of adultery wear the square cap in penance, thus openly ridiculing the cap as a symbol of cuckoldry (Cooper, i, 257). These were Puritan taunts, but in 1572 a Catholic might relish them when they were directed toward the Anglicans. From the Roman point of view none of these clergymen had the right to wear the square cap, which on them might be derided as "horns" of the cuckold or the devil. Valenger was one who seized upon these implications.

As a Catholic associated with Gonville and Caius College, which remained predominantly of that faith, Valenger had additional reasons for denouncing Anglican authority (see John Venn, *Gonville and Caius College*, vol. i, pp. xiv, xviii-xix). After the excommunication of Elizabeth in 1570, the Ridolfi plot of 1571-72, and the 1572 Hugenot massacre, a reaction set in against Catholics and efforts were intensified to hunt them out and bring them into conformity (Mullinger, pp. 242-46; Frere, pp. 148-55, 176-77; see also the comments of Sir John Harington in *A Tract on the Succession to the Crown (A.D. 1602)*, ed. C. R. Markham, Roxburghe Club, 1880, pp. 102-03). In December of 1572 Whitgift and several others in authority built a bonfire and burned the " 'popish trumpery' " of Dr. Caius, who had been allowed to remain as president of Caius College. Such things as would not burn were hacked up (Mullinger, p. 244; Cooper, i, 313-14; Venn, *Caius College*, iii [1901], 53-54). Despite this "discipline," Dr. Caius was permitted to name his successor, Dr. Thomas Legge, who was installed June 27, 1573 (Cooper, ii, 455). Later charged with being " 'anhorryble papist,' " Dr. Legge appears to have had difficulty in controlling recalcitrant fellows, among them Edmund Hound, a fellow from 1573 to 1576, who was evidently regarded as a spy by Valenger (see line 224). Dr. Legge was said to have " 'suffred very greate and continuall disorder in Mr. Howndes chamber, as black sanctus, and singinge of lewde ballades, with heades out of the windowes, and so lewde voyces as that all the house wondred thereatt, to the very evill example of the youthe' " (Cooper, ii, 235). In 1573 Parker, writing to Burghley, observed, " 'Both Papists and Precisians have one mark to shoot at, plain disobedience' "; and Burghley in a letter to Parker described himself and the Lord Keeper, Nicholas Bacon, as " 'beaten with a viperous generation of traitorous Papists; and I fear of some domestic hidden scorpion.' " In the same year a proclamation was issued against the libels of Catholics (Strype, *Parker*, ii, 324, 298, 316-22, respectively).

In the midst of this slanderous raillery and backbiting, Valenger wrote his "Cockolds kallender," in all probability increasing the scurrility of his attack by mixing fact and fiction, using *cuckold* both in its primary and its figurative senses. Included are certain precisians. Religious hypocrisy, including that signified by the acceptance of vestments on the part of some who had been actively opposed to them, meets with general denunciation. It should be kept in mind that the irregular state of the married clergy in Elizabeth's reign, enforced by the queen's open preference for a celibate clergy, provoked jibes against them. Regulations forbidding women and children residence in the colleges and prohibiting marriage of fellows further encouraged this attitude and undoubtedly contributed to irregular relationships as well as immorality (see Frere, pp. 68-69, 107; Knappen, pp. 168, 170, 182;

Documents Illustrative of English Church History, compiled by Henry Gee and W. J. Hardy [London, Macmillan, 1910], pp. 431-32); also on the queen's attitude, see Sir John Harington, *A Briefe View of the State of the Church of England* (*NA*, i [1779 and 1792], 1, 4-5, 30-32, 130-32, 139-40).

In the commentary following on the verses I have indicated such identifications as I have been able to make and I have suggested interpretations of some of the stanzas. It is hardly possible to be certain at all times as to the author's meaning. As a guide for identification I have used Venn's *Alumni Cantabrigienses*, Part I, 4 vols. (1922-27), with such other references as are noted. I am grateful to Professor Kenneth M. Abbott of the Department of Classical Languages at the Ohio State University for assistance on the Latin glosses. References are to line numbers.

1-6. Since the first five stanzas are missing, it is impossible to say whether these verses have any significance. Augustine Dyke of King's College took his B.A. in 1567/8, his M.A. in 1571, and remained as a fellow until 1572/3. George Dyke of St. John's was B.A. in 1571/2 and M.A. in 1575. Conceivably this has a bearing upon the religious war then going on in the Low Countries against Spain. If the date of the libel were a little later, I should suppose this might relate to John Stubbe and *The Discoverie of a Gaping Gulf*, published in 1579, the pamphlet which caused its author to lose his right hand because he opposed the marriage of Elizabeth and the Duke of Anjou. Negotiations for this marriage began as early as 1570 (see Cooper, ii, 111-12; Pierce, pp. 28-30).

7-12. These verses probably refer to Barnabe Googe, who is said to have studied at Christ's College some time before 1562, when he became one of Chancellor Cecil's retainers. In 1570 Googe published *The Popishe Kingdome, or reign of Antichrist. Written in Latine verse by Thomas Naogeorgus and Englyshed by Barnabe Googe.* "Naogeorgus" was Thomas Kirchmeyer (*S.T.C.* 15011; Cooper, ii, 39-40; *Biographical Register of Christ's College, 1505-1905*, compiled by John Peile, i [1910], 56).

13-18. I cannot explain "Iaskell" and "gentle will" in lines 14, 16.

19-24. From the mention of the staff in line 21, it may be that this refers to Sir James Dyer (1512-82), a fellow at Jesus College at an earlier period, who became Judge of the Common Pleas in 1556 and of the Queen's Bench in 1557. He was recorder of Cambridge and counsel to the university (*D.N.B.*). Less likely is the James Dier who matriculated at Clare in 1570 and in 1571 was admitted to the Middle Temple. "Droncken donne" may refer to John Dunne, who matriculated from Jesus in 1568. He appears to have applied for ordination as deacon in 1574 but was rejected. A John Dune matriculated from Queens' in

1570. There were several Taylors. James Taylor of St. John's was M.A. in 1569 and B.D. in 1576. He was a fellow in 1566 and in 1573 was University preacher. Francis Taylor was M.A. from Trinity in 1570. Richard Taylor was B.A. from Christ's in 1568/9. William Taylor was admitted at Christ's in 1567 and at Caius in 1571.

25-30. I suspect that this is a slur upon Dr. John Pedder, one of the Marian exiles, who became Canon of Norwich in 1558 and Dean of Worcester in 1559/60. He was earlier at Cambridge (Cooper, ii, 1-2).

31-36. "More gayne" may refer to William Morgan, who was admitted at St. John's in 1563. He was B.A. in 1567/8; M.A. in 1571; B.D. in 1578; and D.D. in 1583, when he became chaplain to Archbishop Whitgift. He may have been one of Whitgift's "men" when this libel was written. In 1595 he was made Bishop of Llandaff and in 1601, Bishop of Asaph (Cooper, ii, 393-94). Sir John Harington in *A Briefe View* makes this same pun on his name (*NA*, i [1792], 192). Thomas Preston was B.A. from King's College in 1557-58 and M.A. in 1561. On the visit of Elizabeth to Cambridge in 1564, he took part in the play *Dido* and was the successful opponent of Cartwright in the philosophical orations. In 1569 his play *Cambises, King of Percia* appeared. Line 32 may relate to his dramatic activities. From 1584 to 1598 he was Master of Trinity (Cooper, ii, 247-48; Mullinger, pp. 190, 193).

37-42. I do not find a "Whytclyf." Peter Wyclyffe matriculated from Corpus Christi in 1568; Thomas Wyclyffe matriculated from Trinity in 1567 and took his B.A. in 1571/2.

43-54. Although the marginal notation does not so indicate, it is clear enough that these verses refer in part to Richard Fletcher, who in 1594 became Bishop of London. He matriculated from Trinity in 1562 and was B.A. in 1565/6. On the recommendation of Archbishop Parker, he was made a fellow at Corpus Christi College in 1569 and took his M.A. in the same year. In 1573, again on Parker's recommendation, he became chaplain to the queen (Cooper, ii, 205). The verses of No. 180 may refer to this patronage and appointment. Line 47 was later echoed by Sir John Harington in *A Briefe View*, where Fletcher, who is not presented as a very religious man, is called "a comely and courtly Prelate" (*NA*, i [1792], 26). John Archer took his B.A. from King's College in 1565/6 and his M.A. in 1569. He was a fellow from 1564 to 1575 and was ordained priest in 1569. Richard Bird took his B.A. from Trinity in 1568/9, his M.A. in 1572, and his B.D. in 1580. In 1590 he was Canon of Canterbury. I think, however, that "Richard" refers to Fletcher.

55-60. Robert Some, or Soame, mentioned above as a supporter of Cartwright, took his B.A. from St. John's in 1561/2, after which he became a fellow at Queens'. He took his M.A. from that college in 1565, his B.D. in 1571/2, and his D.D. in 1580. In 1567 he was University preacher. On the visit of the queen in 1564, he composed Latin verses in her honor and was appointed to welcome her; he was then in "the sonne." The lines here probably refer to the censure passed upon him after his outspoken sermon at St. Mary's in 1570, when he preached against pluralities, non-residence, and authority of bishops. Although on Whitgift's recommendation Some became Master of Peterhouse in 1589, he continued to preach openly on points to which the primate was opposed (Cooper, ii, 510-13; Mullinger, p. 209).

61-66. Robert Grace was chaplain of St. Andrew's, Cambridge, in 1567 and was rector from 1570 to 1578. John Fryer matriculated from St. John's in 1567, took his B.A. in 1570/1, and his M.A. in 1574. It is possible, however, that these verses refer to the John Fryer, or Frere, who was B.A. from Jesus College in 1544/5 and M.D. in 1555. He disputed before the queen on her visit in 1564. Some time after that he became a Catholic and went to Padua (Cooper, i, 302).

67-72. I have not identified the "Clearke of katherine hall."

73-79. Edmund Prise, or Prys, took his B.A. from St. John's in 1567/8 and his M.A. in 1571. He was ordained priest in 1568 and in 1575 served as University preacher. He also became chaplain to Sir Henry Sidney.

79-96. In these verses Avery and Welch make a cuckold of Smith, but Avery, in turn, is made a cuckold by Myles More. I cannot identify Avery, but Thomas Welch was admitted at King's College in 1559. He was B.A. in 1563/4; M.A. in 1567, and fellow from 1562 to 1578. In 1571 he is said to have turned to the study of medicine. Miles Moore of Christ's matriculated from that college in 1568. Quite tentatively I make the suggestion that Valenger may be referring to some activities of Sir Thomas Smith (1514-77), who was connected with Cambridge at an earlier period. In 1571 as a member of the Privy Council he acted as one of the examiners at the trial of the Duke of Norfolk and by his own words used the rack. Valenger's sympathy would, of course, have been with Norfolk, and lines 85-88 could apply. Also, there is the record of Smith's curious interest in alchemy in 1570, which led to the forming of a company in 1573-74, which included Burghley and Leicester. Known as "The Society for the New Art," the purpose was to turn iron into copper. The failure of the costly venture left Smith disillusioned, and he blamed those who were supposedly carrying out the undertaking. Whether Welch's interest in medicine was in any way connected with this, I do not know, but I should say that lines 79-84 could refer to this venture. It is also possible that the implications in lines 89-90 refer to the controversy about the pronunciation of Greek, in which Smith had a leading role (Cooper, i, 369-73; Mullinger, pp. 55-63, 374-76; *D.N.B.*).

97-102. Hugh Cressy matriculated from Queens' in 1568, migrated to Jesus, and then on August 18, 1573, to Caius. Consequently, he could be referred to as of Jesus College only before this date in 1573 and after 1568. He was rector of Wilford, Notts, from 1581 to 1590.

103-108. "A marke by name" may refer to Thomas Marker, who matriculated from St. John's in 1568; or it could refer to John Markham, who was at Pembroke in 1565.

109-114. A glance at Venn shows that eleven men of the Chapman name were connected with Cambridge in the 1560's and 1570's. Consequently, no identification can be certainly made. As I have said earlier, however, Valenger may very well be referring to Edmund Chapman, who matriculated from Gonville Hall in 1554. He migrated to Trinity, from whence he had his B.A. in 1558/9, his M.A. in 1562, and his B.D. in 1569. He was then made a canon of Norwich, and the following year, about the same time he was supporting Cartwright, he and others entered the choir of the cathedral, broke up the organ, and committed other destructive acts. Dr. William Chaderton of Queens' in a letter to Chancellor Cecil, June 11, 1570, described a sermon by Chapman as an example of the "licentious tone and dangerous doctrine" in Cambridge (Mullinger, p. 215). In 1573 he was prohibited from preaching at Bedford, and in 1576 he was deprived of his canonry at Norwich (Cooper, i, 382). The implication of the stanza may be that the established church (St. George), which has taken care of other Chapman men (e.g., Thomas Chapman of Clare, canon of Lichfield, and William Chapman of Queens', rector of Therfield, Herts), will do so no longer. I know of nothing significant about "m^r^ wilford." Two John Wilfords were at Christ's, one in 1560 and the other in 1565. James Wylford was B.A. from St. John's in 1571/2, fellow in 1573, and M.A. in 1575.

115-120. Gabriel Argall was B.A. from Trinity in 1572/3 and M.A. in 1573. This stanza may have reference to an amusing incident related in 1569 by Dr. Bartholomew Clerke of King's, then a proctor in the university. Disparaging the emphasis placed upon vestments, Clerke in a letter to Cecil tells the story of a young student who went to chapel without his surplice. On being summoned by the dean, he said he would do violence to his convictions if he put on the surplice. It turned out that he had pawned it to help pay for a feast (Mullinger, p. 206). As proctor, Clerke may have administered punishment. Clerke himself was charged with unsoundness in religion (Cooper, ii, 70-72).

121-126. Adam Rose, admitted at King's in 1567, took his B.A. in 1571/2 and his M.A. in 1575. He was a fellow from 1570 to 1577 and later held a living in Yorkshire.

127-138. Edward Ball was at King's College from 1556 to 1558. He was town-clerk of Cambridge from 1557 to 1596 and was a churchwarden of St. Mary the Great. In 1575 he obtained a grant of arms. In 1583 he was in conflict with Cambridge authorities and may have been earlier (Cooper, ii, 301-02). The "Collier knight" may refer to James Cole, B.A. from King's in 1561/2 and M.A., 1565. He was vice-provost in 1575. In 1565 and 1569 he and other fellows made charges against the provost, Dr. Philip Baker (Cooper, i, 383). Or this may refer to Robert Cole, M.A. from King's in 1550, who at first opposed the vestments but complied and was exhibited by Grindal as an example of the properly dressed priest (Cooper, i, 364; Knappen, p. 193, note 16). This Cole, however, was in London when Valenger was writing.

139-150. John Murton, or Morton, took his B.A. from Christ's in 1565/6, his M.A. in 1569, and his B.D. in 1577. He was a fellow from 1567 to 1577 and was probably the one ordained priest at Ely in 1567. Edmund Barwell was B.A. from Christ's in 1567/8, M.A. in 1571, and B.D. in 1578. He was a fellow from 1570 to 1581 and in 1570 was ordained deacon at Ely. In 1582 he was elected Master of Christ's and in 1586 was accused of maladministration (Peile, i, 83-84; Mullinger, p. 472; Cooper, ii, 522-23).

151-56. The name "Philoe" does not occur in Cambridge records of this period. I suggest that it is here used as a pseudonym to signify Dr. Lawrence Humphrey. As is pointed out in the Note on No. 181, Humphrey's academic career was for the most part connected with Oxford, but in March of 1568/9 he was incorporated D.D. at Cambridge. Although he had earlier aggressively opposed use of the vestments and other matters upheld by the established church, he nevertheless agreed to conform when he accepted the appointment as Dean of Gloucester in March of 1570/1. He was notorious for his opposition to Catholics. His "Philo de judice" in Greek and Latin was published at Basle in 1559 at the end of his volume *De ratione interpretandi authores*. In 1560 his "Philonis Iudæi de nobilitate," translated from the Greek, was printed at Basle at the end of his *Optimates, sive de nobilitate*. In 1563 an English version of this work appeared, called, *The Nobles, or of Nobilitye*, with the "small treatyse of Philo, a Jewe" attached. According to Knappen (pp. 177-78), *The Nobles* was an appeal to Protestant landlords to take the lead in carrying on the Reformation, emphasizing that the upper class of society should direct the movement. I suggest that Valenger is attacking Humphrey both for his concession in wearing the vestments and for his play to the nobility (Cooper, ii, 80-85, from which the titles are quoted; Frere, pp. 112-13, 115, 121; *D.N.B.*). I do not know who Gryggs was.

157-66. Lines 157-58 appear to be a series of glosses bearing upon the English stanza: "Regnum imperium regale civitatis genus Rex princeps"; i.e., Kingdom, royal power, a variety of state, King chief. Perhaps of more significance for the interpretation of the stanza is line 165: "Illud suum regnum iudicale opposuit Catelina"; i.e., That judicial tyranny of his Catiline opposed. Line 166 gives a reference which, unfortunately,

I cannot explain. The Latin must refer to Catiline's opposition to Cicero, but I have been unable to spot the exact line. The "ad etti," or "elli," probably refers to an editor. Estienne, who brought out an edition of Cicero's works in 1555, comes to mind, but the Latin form of his name is Stephanus. Professor Abbott has pointed out to me a pertinent passage in Cicero's *Pro Sulla*, VII.21: "Hic ait se ille, iudices, regnum meum ferre non posse"; i.e., He [Torquatus] says, iudges, that he cannot bear my [Cicero's] tyranny. This passage continues with the implication from Cicero that Torquatus considers him a tyrant because those against whom he has testified have been condemned and the one he supports hopes to be free. Even with the directive of the Latin, we cannot be certain of the author's meaning in the English stanza. I offer two suggestions, but I believe the second is to be preferred. (1) The stanza may have to do with the opposition to Matthew Parker, Archbishop of Canterbury, led by Robert Dudley, Earl of Leicester, which reached a crisis late in 1573 and in 1574. Parker could be "Rex princeps," the king of the herrings, who it should be noted, was said to be taken when in pursuit of other herrings in shoals. The expression "red herring" did not then signify nothing, as it now does (*N.E.D.*). Leicester would be equated with Cateline and with the one "whose Ore did row the bardge." As primate Parker was active in the pursuit of both Puritans and Catholics. The derisive reference to "the musterd pot of kent" is easily understood, but the meaning of line 161 is not clear in this interpretation. In 1570 Laurence Nowell, Dean of Lichfield, was accused of making seditious speeches against Leicester and the queen (Cooper, i, 358), but I am not prepared to say whether that has any special bearing upon Leicester's attack on Parker. It should be remembered that Parker was a graduate of Corpus Christi College, Cambridge, and that he maintained a close connection with the university (see Cooper, i, 327-37; Strype, *Parker*, ii, 393-96, 414-18, 489-92, 529-30; Frere, p. 185). (2) It may be that the stanza has reference to the final suspension in 1573 of Edward Dering, to whom reference was made earlier in this Note. A native of Kent, he was educated at Christ's College, where he was a fellow from 1560 to 1570. In 1567 he was Lady Margaret preacher. In 1568 on the recommendation of Parker, who called him "the greatest learned man in England," he was appointed to the rectory of Pluckley in Kent. In the same year, in reply to one of the pamphlets issued by the Catholic Thomas Harding, he published *A Sparing restraint of many lavish untruthes* (from Cooper, i, 356). His conflict with the established church began in 1569, when he preached a sermon before the queen, declaring her responsible for the irregular lives of the clergy. This led to suspension (Peile, i, 55-56). Reference is made above to his support of Cartwright in 1570, though he himself seems to have conformed on vestments. In 1572, on the request of Parker, he wrote another treatise against Catholics, *Responsio ad Nic. Sanderi librum de visibili monarchia* (from Cooper), and in the same year was appointed divinity reader at St. Paul's, Alexander Nowell then being Dean. Early in 1573 Dering was suspended by the Privy Council for slanderous sayings uttered at St. Paul's, among them a prophecy that Parker would be the last Archbishop of Canterbury. Restored on the intervention of Edwin Sandys, Bishop of London, Dering through lack of proper gratitude and respect so alienated that worthy that he secured the queen's intervention for a second suspension in July. Although Dering attempted to enlist the aid of Burghley, he was brought before the Star Chamber on November 27, 1573. He was not re-instated and died two years later. He lost the support of Parker and other bishops by his insistence that "*the lordship or civil government of bishops is utterly unlawful*" (see Strype, *Annals*, II, i, 400-17 for an account of Dering's activities in 1573; also, Strype, *Parker*, ii, 240-41, 270; Cooper and Peile, as noted above). Dering then is "Redd hearing," caught when he is in pursuit of both Catholics and Anglicans. He is the Catiline who has opposed the judicious tyranny of Parker and others. "Ho-well" I take to be Nowell of St. Paul's, the square-capped "Cuckow," an agent in "the musterd pot of kent." The one whose name could not be mentioned could be Burghley, even the queen. I should say that the Latin of lines 157-58 may derive from Dering's criticism of the civil government of prelates.

167-72. The "Kelkes" of line 171 probably refers to Roger Kelke, B.A. from St. John's in 1543/4, and fellow there in 1545. During Mary's reign he was in exile. In 1559 he was appointed Master of Magdalen College, but his administration was notoriously poor. As preacher at Ipswich in 1562 he was accused in court of being a liar and of preaching untrue doctrine but was acquitted. In 1563 and again in 1569 he was a candidate for the Mastership of St. John's but failed to secure the post. In 1572-73 he was engaged in disputes with his fellows, which were finally settled through the intervention of Whitgift (Cooper, i, 341-42; Mullinger, p. 286).

173-78. Anthony Alcock matriculated from St. John's in Lent of 1564/5. The only Nicholas Rust listed by Venn was admitted from Caius in 1592, which is too late. A Thomas Rust took his B.A. from Caius in 1573/4, his M.A. in 1578, and was ordained priest in 1577.

179-184. Henry Sadler, son of Sir Ralph, Knt., of Herts, matriculated from Gonville in 1557/8. From 1572 to 1604 he was Clerk of the Hanaper. "Gefferey Smythe" is not identified.

185-96. "Brave Ellis" may refer to James Ellys, who matriculated as a sizar from Queens' in 1554. He was B.A. in 1557/8; M.A. in 1561, and L.L.D. in 1568. He was chancellor of the diocese of Peterborough and canon there (Cooper, ii, 208). Edward Ellis, son of Lyon, mayor of Lincoln, took his B.A. from Christ's in 1565/6. In 1567 he was a fellow of St. John's and took his M.A. there in 1569. John Ellis, B.A. from Jesus in 1532-33, became a canon of Worcester in 1570. In convocation of 1562 he is said to have been one who favored removal of organs and music from the churches, disuse of vestments and of the cross, etc. (Cooper, i, 363).

197-208. The most promising candidate for the doubtful honor of being "Goodwyn the fensere" seems to be Vincent Goodwin, who matriculated as a sizar from Gonville in 1554. Ordained priest in 1562, he was rector of Oakington, Cambs., in 1564. He was preacher at Yarmouth from 1570 to 1584, when he was suspended. He also held other livings in Norfolk. Line 199 may be explained by the fact that Valenger was a Norfolk man. Goodwin was evidently a religious hypocrite, in reality subject to Whitgift and his followers, and so "horned." If "Challis" refers to an actual person, I have not identified him.

209-21. The main significance of these lines denouncing Dr. John Whitgift for his deprivation of Thomas Cartwright has been discussed earlier. The "Toye" in line 214 refers to the stationer Humphrey Toy, who brought out several of Whitgift's pamphlets on the Admonition controversy, published from 1572 to 1574, and a sermon preached by Whitgift before the queen in 1574 (*S.T.C.* 25427-25431). Toy and John Day acted as spies in hunting out the secret press of the Puritans during the period of the Admonition controversy (Pierce, p. 43), and this undoubtedly explains the "stollen flessh" of line 209. Toy matriculated as a sizar from Queens' in 1551 but did not take a degree (Cooper, ii, 4). I find nothing to justify charges of immorality against Whitgift. Sir John Harington in *A Briefe View* speaks well of him and has only the following anecdote to contribute:

> While he was Bishop of *Worcester*, though the revenew of that be not very great, yet his custom was to come to the Parliament very well attended, which was a fashion the Queen liked exceeding well. It happened one day Bishop *Elmer* of *London*, meeting this Bishop with such an orderly troop of Tawny Coats, and demanding of him, how he could keep so many men, he answered, it was by reason, he kept so few women [*NA*, i (1792), 9].

Cooper (ii, 369-79) has a useful record of Whitgift's activities in relation to Cambridge especially. See also Strype, *The Life and Acts of John Whitgift, D.D.*, 4 bks. in 3 vols., 1822. The Latin of line 221 serves as a satiric commentary on Whitgift's emphasis upon observances of ritual as essential to religion and piety. The last two words should be, "cærimoniæ auspicia."

222-30. The Latin reference in line 222 is to Cicero: "de nat[ura] de[orum] p[rimus liber] 1ª [prima capitula]. The passage quoted is taken from Cicero's first sentence but with an omission which leaves the subject of "est" unexpressed. As it stands, the meaning is: it is very attractive in regard to the nature of the soul and necessary for the regulation of religion. In Cicero that which is so attractive and necessary is inquiry into the nature of the gods, which is also described as very obscure and difficult. The reference to the second Latin quotation is to Cicero: "Tusc [ulanarum Disputationum] lib[er] 1, fol. 178"; i.e., in a modern edition, I.32. Translated the passage runs: Such old stories have for a long time been consecrated by religious feeling. Cicero is referring immediately to Hercules, who joined the gods after he had aided mankind. Cicero then relates the matter to his own state. The glosses stand in ironic contrast to the English stanza, which continues to reflect the bitterness of religious controversy and persecution. It is quite possible that the English stanza has a bearing upon the destruction of the "popish trumpery" of Dr. Caius by Whitgift and others in 1572 (see above). I have referred earlier to Edmund Hound, or Hownde, who caused difficulties at Caius after he became a fellow there in 1573. Hound had matriculated from Trinity as early as 1558, was B.A. in 1563/4, and M.A. in 1567, the year Whitgift became Master of Trinity. Richard Wood matriculated from Trinity in 1562, was B.A. in 1565/6, and M.A. in 1570. His later record shows close association with Whitgift, who, as Archbishop, appointed Wood licenser of the press. Wood is supposed to have written for the bishops in the Marprelate controversy (Cooper, ii, 523-24). "Hodge Cooke" may refer to a John Cooke who was at Trinity, B.A., 1559/60; M.A., 1563; B.D., 1569/70 (Cooper, ii, 86). If the stanza was written as late as 1575, the reference might be to the John Cock of St. John's, who was publicly reprimanded for a commonplace delivered against Dr. John Still. In this both Whitgift and Bishop Cox of Ely (see next stanza) took part (Cooper, ii, 445; Mullinger, p. 265). "Huntley called my lord" presents a problem. A Thomas Huntley was at Queens' in 1544, but I find nothing to connect him with these activities. Somewhat more plausible is John Hunt, who was at King's in 1565 and in 1571 held a lease under Cox of Ely (Cooper, iii, 59). Indeed, the "hunt and Lay" seems to refer back to Whitgift. There is, however, the possibility that the stanza is concerned with some activities of the Puritan supporter Henry Hastings, third Earl of Huntingdon (1535-95), Leicester's brother-in-law, who was avid in the hunting out of Catholics. In 1569 Mary Stuart was committed to the care of Huntingdon, and in January, 1571/2, he was one of the peers who sat in judgment on the Duke of Norfolk (Cooper, ii, 200-02; Knappen, pp. 194, 200; *D.N.B.*). Hound was later patronized by Leicester, whom he served as chaplain (Cooper, ii, 235), but the connection of Wood is uncertain. Another John Cooke, fellow at King's in 1536, was headmaster of St. Paul's School from 1559 to 1573, and was later presented to the rectory of North Cadbury in Somerset by the Earl of Huntingdon (Cooper, ii, 86). Whatever the particular references, it is clear from the stanza and the Latin lines, especially the second, that Valenger is concerned with the opposition to Catholic beliefs and symbols, the "vetera" which have long been consecrated by religious feeling.

231-36. This is an attack on Richard Cox (1500?-1581), who was elected Bishop of Ely in 1559. He was a member of the commission which arbitrated in favor of the new statutes in 1572. As visitor to St. John's he suggested that a new code be drawn up for that college in 1573. These lines are probably a slur on his second marriage to Jane Ander of Cambridge, widow of the Puritan William Turner (see above). In 1568 he asked Cecil to intercede with the queen in favor of his marriage. He had caused offence on his first marriage, and in 1561 he had incurred the queen's further displeasure by protesting the order that wives should not remain in colleges and cathedrals (Cooper, i, 437-45; Mullinger, pp. 237-38, 262, 267; Frere, pp. 48, 69; *D.N.B.*). Sir John Harington's account of him in *A Briefe View* explains why he might be called "a noble Cheat" (*NA*, i, 1779 and 1792, 91-92).

237-42. If the marginal notation is correct, this stanza refers to Nicholas Horne, B.A. from King's College in 1565/6, M.A. in 1569, and B.D. in 1577. He was a fellow from 1564 to 1579 and in 1573 was University preacher. I suspect, however, that the verses really have to do with Robert Horne, elected Bishop of Winchester in 1561. The "ringe" and the "Iewells" suggest the bishop's attire, and it was this Horne who ran "at Tillt." Educated earlier at St. John's College, Cambridge, he was Dean of Durham in Edward's reign and was one of the Marian exiles. After he became Bishop of Winchester, he had charge of several deprived Catholic bishops and was engaged in controversy about them. In 1568 he was one of those empowered to correct troubles at St. John's and in 1571 was engaged in a dispute about his rights as visitor there. Described as a religious fanatic, he was active in purging Catholics from Cambridge and resorted to such extreme measures as destroying painted windows at Durham and cutting away a part of the altar screen at New College, Oxford (Cooper, i, 407-12; Frere, p. 136). Nevertheless, in 1572 Horne defended the established church against Puritan attacks (Knappen, pp. 155-56, 229).

243-248. From the context "Gybbins musicõn" evidently refers to William Gybbon, or Gibbons, who matriculated from Clare in 1566. He must be the William Gibbons of Cambridge who is noted as father of the famous Orlando, who was at King's from 1598 to 1606.

249-260. The marginal notation appears to be misplaced and should be written opposite lines 249-54. Martin Crosfield, or Crofyld, matriculated from Christ's College in 1567. Ordained priest in 1569, he was vicar of Bracebridge, Lincolnshire, from 1569 to 1594 and rector of Claypole from 1576 to 1606 (Peile, i, 99). Lines 255-60 must refer to the John Sanderson who was B.A. from Trinity in 1557/8, fellow, 1560, and M.A., 1561. In 1562, when he was logic reader of the university, his commonplaces given in chapel provoked charges of superstitious doctrine. Although he made a revocation, he would not recant and was expelled from his fellowship. Alexander Nowell wrote to Parker that it was a question " 'whether the truthe shall obteine, or papistrie triumphe' " (as quoted by Cooper, ii, 352). He left England and in 1570 was a student at Douay. In 1580 he was divinity professor at Rheims. Valenger may be criticizing Sanderson for not supporting his case more fully, perhaps for taking refuge abroad.

269. "Sr Iohn de Gecke" is probably to be interpreted as Sir John the Derider, or Scorner, from the verb *geck*, rather than as Sir John the Dupe, or Fool, from the noun.

[181] *And thinkes thow I have nowght to load*

Hands: four in secretary and three in italic. The title is impressively set out in heavy black ink, written in printed italic script, probably by Sir John Harington; the sub-title and lines 1-5 are in Sir John's secretary; lines 6-64 are in the hand of No. 180. Lines 65-66, and 68 are in a third secretary hand; lines 69, 74, and 76 are in a fourth. Lines 67, 70-73, 77-83 are written in pencil in a seventeenth-century italic script and were clearly added later. The few marginal notations are written in red ink in another italic hand. The corrections in lines 57 and 65 are in the fourth secretary hand.

This fragment represents Sir John Harington's unsuccessful attempt to obtain a copy of "Mr Buckley's Libell of oxon: made about ye yeare 1564" (title of a copy in Bodleian MS. Tanner 465, fols. 105[r]-109[r]). In his account of Thomas Cooper (1517?-1594), Bishop of Winchester, Anthony à Wood in the *Athenae Oxonienses* refers to verses in the libel satirizing Cooper's wife, which were printed by Philip Bliss in his edition of the *Athenae* from a manuscript then in the possession of Mr. Gilchrist and there entitled, "*Mr. Buckley's libell of divers persons in Oxford, an 15 . . . or thereabouts*" (vol. i [1813], col. 610). Mr. Buckley soon learned that such writing on "divers persons," some of them the most distinguished in Oxford, was a dangerous pastime. In his *Fasti Oxonienses*, commenting on Thomas Buckley of All Souls' College, who was awarded the B.C.L. degree in 1566, Wood says, "He was now much in esteem among the academians for his poetry, but being given to libelling was forced to leave the university" (ed. P. Bliss, vol. i [1815], col. 171). Notes in the *Fasti* connect him with Thomas Bulkeley, LL.B., who was instituted to the rectory of Llandensant in 1543, and upon the death of Bishop Bulkeley in 1552, was made one of the guardians of the spiritualties of Bangor (vol. i, col. 55, note 5; col. 171, note 8). I question this identification, as it is reasonable to believe that the libeller was more directly associated with Oxford at the time of the writing. According to the *Alumni Oxonienses* (compiled by Joseph Foster, vol. i [1887]), Thomas Bulkeley, or Buckeley, who was awarded the B.C.L. degree in 1566, was a fellow at All Souls' in and before 1564. He may have belonged to the Bulkeley family of Cheshire (see *Cheshire Visitation Pedigrees, 1663*, ed. Arthur Adams, Harl. Soc., xciii [1941], 21-22). At any rate, on being forced to leave Oxford, Buckeley appears to have given up his concern with poetry and libelling.

Nevertheless, the libel on Oxford continued to circulate in manuscript. I have come across four copies among the Bodleian MSS. and another in the Marsh Library of St. Patrick's Cathedral, Dublin.

Rawl. Poet. MS. 172, fols. 16^r-18^v (*A*), consists of sixty-five stanzas with marginalia, headed, "Buckleye." It is written in a careless secretary hand, which is occasionally illegible.

Tanner MS. 465, fols. 105^r-109^r (*B*), has sixty-two stanzas and marginalia, with the title quoted above. The handwriting is italic, probably of the early seventeenth century.

Rawl. Poet. MS. 212, fols. 118^r-123^r (*C*), has forty-eight stanzas with explanatory matter following the stanzas and is entitled, "Mr Buckley his Libell: Oxōn." It is written in a neat secretary hand. This is followed, fols. 123^v-126^r, by "Bastards Libell cal'd Martin marre p^r^lates bastarde," in the same handwriting, which incorporates thirteen additional stanzas of the Oxford libel. This last is a copy of the libel referred to by Wood in his account of Thomas Bastard (1566-1618), who was admitted as a perpetual fellow at New College in 1588, from which he took his B.A. in 1590 (*Athenae*, ii [1815], 227-29). Wood says:

> In my collection of libels or lampoons, made by divers Oxford students in the reign of Q. Elizabeth, I meet with two made by this author. One of which is entit. *An Admonition to the City of Oxford: Or his Libel entit. Marprelate's Basterdine.* Wherein he reflects upon all persons of note in Oxon that were guilty of amorous exploits, or that mixed themselves with other men's wives, or with wanton huswives in Oxon. Another also, was made after his expulsion, wherein he disclaimeth the aforesaid libel, beginning thus: 'Jenkin why man? Why Jenkin? fie for shame.'

Regarding the expulsion of Bastard, Wood comments, "But this person being much guilty of the vices belonging to poets, and given to libelling, he was in a manner forced to leave his fellowship in 1591." A. B. Grosart in the "Introduction" to his edition of *The Poems, English and Latin, of the Rev. Thomas Bastard*, 1880, after quoting the first twelve lines from another copy of Bastard's libel, says:

> The satire is mild and toothless and eke formless enough. Bastard's disclaimer of it I feel disposed to accept. Be this as it may, I modify the harsher term of "expulsion" by the earlier phrase "he was in a manner forced." Probably he was simply for a time subjected to discipline. The subsequent M.A. testifies to restoration [pp. xi-xii].

However, Bastard did not take his M.A. until 1606 (*Alumni Oxonienses*, vol. 1). It seems evident that Buckeley's verses, which Bastard used and imitated, were again responsible for severe action on the part of the Oxford authorities. His libels were not printed in his *Chrestoleros: Seuen Bookes of Epigrammes*, 1598, and they are not included in Grosart's edition. The epigrams resemble those of Sir John Harington, who addressed three of his own epigrams to their author (*Letters and Epigrams*, ed. N. E. McClure, 1930, Nos. 160, 180, 358).

Since Bastard's libel, which shows influence of the Martin Marprelate controversy, was written about 1590 or 1591, it is evident that both it and the copy of the Oxford libel in *C* were not entered into that manuscript until some time thereafter.

Another copy of the Oxford libel is in Rawl. Poet. MS. 85, fols. 72^{v}-75^{v} (*D*), consisting of but forty-one stanzas with such indistinct marginalia that I have not attempted to decipher them. Written in secretary, it is entitled, "The libell of Oxenforde," but the sub-title is omitted.

Similar to *D* is the copy in Marsh MS. 183 Z 3.5.21, fols. 7^{r}-11^{r} (*E*), which also has forty-one stanzas, though no marginalia. It is entitled, "The Libell of Oxforde," with the sub-title omitted. Written in secretary, it was probably copied into the manuscript around 1588 (see the Preliminary Note on Nos. 201-21).

In dealing with these versions of No. 181, which is, of course, the poorest of all, and quite unsatisfactory as a basis for comparison, I have decided not to proceed in the usual manner with a complete collation, but rather to print a transcription of *A*, the longest text, and to make comparisons with the other versions. As might be expected in a "ballad" of this kind, the versions differ considerably, and I doubt that any one of these copies represents the libel just as Buckley wrote it. Variations, or errors, in the explanatory matter lead to the inference that the libel may have been written without any marginalia, and that these notes were deduced by others from the puns in the verses. Indeed, it is quite probable that some stanzas were also added by others.

The *A* version follows. For the sake of convenience I have numbered the stanzas.

BUCKLEYE

I

Iohn a dogges one appoynted to carte whores

What newes Iohn a dogges what newes?
And doe you think I haue nought abode
because I seeme a carelesse clowne
I goe and heare the newes abroade
And sitt and see ye trickes in towne

2

or Sr Diuel a bachelor of arte

The Diuels dead in Deuonshire late
a hapie ta⟨y⟩le if it be trewe
he giues the cecke but not ye mate
and are you dead Sr Diuell adue

3

A maid and a minister in Deuon als Dr Squire keepth a maid in mans apparell

Pope Ioane hath plaid a prittie cast
the clarke hath popt her bellie full
there was a minister made in hast
beshrew ye bishoppes bearded scull

4

Mr Hobbie had a red head Mrs Marbecke was called ye lark

A hobbie hufferinge in the winde
for wante of foode laye longe vnfed
I iudge him of some costrell bread
His flickeringe featheres war soe redd

5

he gott his maid bountinge wth childe.

He lay a loft longe for a larke
but brought a bountinge to ye baye
wch flight did cause each dogge to barke
and soe for shame he sored awaye

6

M^{rs} ⟨reiec⟩ Noble reiected forage

Nobilitie is sett a nought
noe man cares for xx^{tie} groates
the fine some finer still hath soughte
they list not blend wth liuery coates

7

Marbecke for saketh her be cause shee is cōmon to seruinge men

Nothinge more base then noble blod
whome double dealinge doth deface
for eloquence hath thought it good
to giue ye sword & buckler place

8

Marbeckes name was Laurance

Att laurance lane there dwelleth shee
the curtayle cares of Rethorik still
A broylinge gridion might shee bee
A moatheaten Iacke for a mangie gill

9

Mrs Warde & her daughter grace

A greate way hence ther was a warde
had special grace against a word
wth buckler bente both soft and hard
and foine there at they might y^{t} lyk

10

Mrs Crabbe wth her

But out of ward now beatten quit
driuen as drie as cryshed crabbe
noe man delightes wth her to fight
great worke hath she to ward ye scabbe

11

Mr Lambe vseth the maide at home kindly his weif vseth her frend abroad

The lambe y^{t} longe hath liued at large
and laft these louinge ones to scorne
hath bent herselfe to such a charge
as well to giue as take the horne

12

hee is offended wth her husband for vsinge ye maides

ffor duetie bindes y^{t} debtes be paid
the scoare and tayl kepes reckenings trewe
when wiues waxe ould well fare ye maides
close play will well, but how say you

13

Mr Body of Mag: Col: wth her.

Packe saddle pincheth at this geare
shall ⟨cud⟩ madge o^{r} maide matche my good man
wth y^{t} mee thought I heard one sweare
by the bodie of mee Ile pay her home

14

m^{rs} wake lynne

The wake y^{t} lyes while red nose winkes
tis pittie age her tayle should tayme
her season somewhat past he thinkes
yett beares she good will to the same

15

Mrs Crouch of ye Crosse Inne

But Papistry still doth patch this geare
that some to crosse doe creepe & crouch
and to such Idols as be there
they offer moste parte in theire pouch

16

A saddleres twoe daughters

Neare to ye crosse standes marie and Ioane
wth each ofe them an offering boxe
you wear as good let them alone
for best spedes he y^{t} scapes ye poxe

17

by ye bayliffe is ment m^{rs} Spencer

But to this prittie ⟨plil⟩ pilgrimage
some offer heire some offer wolle
the offerers ar of lawfull age
the bayliffe hath her bellie full

18

Dr Bayliffes weife wth her veale

yet syllie cloune what can I tell
vnto Physitiones I appeale
whether it be kindly that they swell
wch for the most ꝑte feed on veale

19

Mr Becke wth Mrs Ashlow et Mrs Dodwell

The becke wch feared some full soare
did well ꝑceaue old frendes to fainte
And seinge it at so loue a shoare
did intertayne a solemne saint

20

Mrs Noble wth m^{r} Dodwell

wch thinge displeasd ye nobles much
the ꝑties to ioyne themselues were loath
Lett goe sayeth one, since lucke is such
alas they be but leauinges both

21

Woodes weif

On hasell wood hanges ye browner sorte
of nutes whose tast doe some delight
the kernell tastes as sweete and shorte
as doth ye filbard faire and white

22

Westlake et Loue-lace wth m^{rs} woodes

Westward to wood then leapes ye lake
to loue ye nutes y^{t} hanges on lace
where cosen Craftes comes for her cake
to faine wth frendes he hath a face

23

Casterdene the Clowne of christ church wth Genings weife

Perchance you thinke I passe a cloune
of genesis matter to distroye
howe casterdein did laye her downe
Clownes be deuines and why not I

24

a Dr Thanker lookinge thro: a hole of his studdie into his garden sawe on Deringe weife

More wordes were written in ye text
but lik an asse I dare not tell
this chapter done beware ye next
fie holes in walles did neuer well

25

The good weife of ye angel whose name is vertue and her daugh. grace

Vertue and Grace dealt both at a place
the Angell keepes ye doare
If you wille speed goe thither to bed
and you shall not miss of a whore

26

Mrs Roes gott wth child by m^{r} Paintor of christ church

I will not tell what I heard saye
who hath of Roes ye garland wonne
but sure I am some doe her paie
shee beare a bellie lik a tunne

the same

27

The fruite was fetch from christ his flock
in christ begott in christ church bore
In christ church some did gett a knocke
I tould you not soe much before

Dr Humpheries weife & ye Lord Russell then schol: in Mag: col:

28

Duke Humphries dame loues well her lord
yett lieth to longe a bed I feare
All princes pride she doth abhore
and loueth russells for to weare

The same

29

The scripture sayeth we must forgiue
o^{r} brotheres faultes till seauen times
we preacheres must precisly liue
forgiuinge our bed fellowes there crimes

Do^{r} Cop: his weife wth Dr Daye

30

But he y^{t} all our tubbes coould trimme
can neuer keepe his vessell staunch
but he well venture life and limb
to haue a snatch at euerie haunche

Dr Day was bound in 300 pound not to come to m^{rs} Coper

31

The day will come else god defende
y^{t} best beloued shalbe vnbound
day by day shall filtch his freind
for lesse then for a hundred pound

the same

32

The greedie hauke must haue her praye
though shee it seeke in everie place
while some be angrie all ye daye
yett to agree they hade some grace

Mrs Coper to ye Clowne

33

But vse those wordes no more you clowne
yes masse chill tell what I doe heare
tis said abroad in feild and towne
the whoded whore she hath no peare

the authors name Buckley

34

While Bucke did lay his hornes in vewe
soe farre in place as Oxford shewes
his cockes did followe their masters crewe
still crying Cockoldes all a rewe

m^{r} Samon found a bed wth m^{rs} Sayer by ye proctor

35

A Samon in a sawyers pitte
did seeke to scape ye fisheres ginne
to hide him selfe he had no witt
the candle light bewraied his finne

36

the same once lost his gowne a cardes

O arrant asse thou shamest vs all
thie frindes abroad and here in towne
by this thou hast a greater fall
then when a cardes thou lost thy gowne

37

the same

Then once more forfit thou became
for cloathing then thou lernest to late
A silogisme reduced wth shame
from Brasen nose to bocardo gatt

38

Mr Watkins wth mrs miller

The wily wat or ladies kinne
a fellowe clark is plainly sped
he thinkes of right to entↄ in
wher holy church oft here hath bedd

39

the same

Although the miller be awaye
some can ye stones wth coning conch
there grist to grind they will not staye
& tole free will not passe ye hutch

40

Mr Dighs wth mrs Cogan

In buffen gownes some cog some foyst
turninge all earnest into game
Madg hundsdon taught her dame to royst
there some at dore speak soft for shame

41

mr Merick and Hilles weife

The meacocke mericke mountes ye hill
to pleasure them yt serues his neid
noe hurte it is to merrie will
to strike the gill yt will not bled

42

Morris ye coblers weife

Then to refresh it is delight
his mind wth musicke doth aduance
and doth vsurpe ye countries right
the cobler leades ye morrice daunce

43

Horbrand and Tilers weife

The herbrand yt her beard berent
ye silly soule to tylters thinge
she litle knows the knaues intente
wch shortly her to ende will bringe

44

the same

this brand attire ye ende of late
pretendeth to a greatter lacke
he serueth but her present state
her present is vppon her backe

45

Dr Whithingeton wth m^{rs} Hamon

The towne of withie worthie is
  that hauing plight his best behest
Defild Ioane on bed amisse
  a beastly knaue a knauish beast

46

Hamon was a taylor

And horned Hamon will not see
  but prickes his cloutes in carlesse case
His copsmate nowe againe is free
  and runnes againe his wonted race

47

Anne Mather reiected m^{r} Lancaster chose m^{rs} Leech

ffrom Annis mowth and eyes at once
  Duke Lancaster did take ye foyle
he was not p̱fect in his stones
  but lett ye dog leach gett ye spoyle

48

the same

And now in brotheres bondes ar knitt
  theire might they liue as if by stealth
They did intend by will and witt
  to plucke away the vidowes wealth

49

Mr Scot with ffurnices weife ye baker

When darknesse changeth vnto light
  the craftie scott will mend his life
And shall not need a cunninge wight
  to make a cage for furnace wife

50

the same wth m^{rs} Grate her dogges name was symnell

Within a grate they shall her laye
  the fine bread from her shalbe shutt
wth simnell may shee dayly playe
  soe cunningly she keepes ye cutt

51

m^{r} Key a common whore monger

There is a key of longe time knowen
  it cannot ruste ye vse is greate
Yeat entreth in where seed is sowen
  in everie locke it playeth feate

52

He frequented m^{rs} Furrs at ye beare

His flight is all about at head
  nought for ye bull wch sighes soe lowe
Yeat at ye beare he standes in stedd
  best game on him they there bestowe

53

Mr Bridgwater wth a plum̄er his weife

Through the bridge we see ye water runne
  A gulfe wch bottomles is thought
the shipmans markes ar mone & sunne
  the plumer hath the bottome sought

54

The same

He ledd ye larke to his lodginge gaye
wch rose before ye daye appears
by chirpinge fast and prettie playe
beshrewe your knaues pace were you there

55

Mr Key wth m^{rs} fynnel

In lente greate fynneles be full rife
the ale is nought w^{t} out a tost
keyes open lockes in paine of life
this bellie fortie powndes hath cost

56

D^{r} yealder feild[?] from relig: fell to couetousnesse

And he whome conscience once did cause
from deadly vice awaye to fly
must now be clapt in ye same clause
wth yealding voice doth error crye

57

Danyes weife

A laundresse nowe whome boyes doe vse
that thought to pick her husbandes patch
there cloakes to make did not refuse
ofe to drinke at Danyes hatch

58

Mr Griffith wth m^{rs} Flandon

The knaue of Clubbes wth some in hand
doth hould the cardes in handes aright
the tremblinge tub wch still doth stand
in griffetes gripes as one affright

59

the same

The husband he doth feed on fatt
and shee her bellie still doth stuffe
she playes as doth the vilie cat
and prateth still though others snuffe

60

Griffithe leaues for feare of kinde
& all y^{t} come of britishe bloud
in absence yet she hath assigned
to be in sheete of finer food

61

⟨Mr Coxe⟩ Mr Baker wth m^{rs} Coxe

The baker he did cram the cockes
wth bread well baked for ye nonce
and she her meatie mouth well stoppes
wth pleasinge meate quite free from bones

62

Mrs Conrade careth not for her Irish husband she hoisteth her white cloathes when others may

The Englishe hoy flyes irish stoanes
& setteth her full sayle to vewe
haste beare to Corke come all at once
at harrow hill my timber grewe

63

com y^re^ she was burnt on a pile of faggotes

Since I am built of English wood
shall I serue only Irish turne
Noe lett mee doe my countrie good
or else on faggotes lett me burne

64

Mr Barker a preacher

The strumpetes now most playn appeare
nowe barkinge preacher none abate
the children must the fathers heare
that loue to feed on other cates

65

And now you Dames wch ar not here
wch many times haue here been nought
Leaue of in time and doe you feare
least of Sr Diuel you be cought.

All of the copies, including *AH*, keep the stanzaic order through stanza 13, but *B* omits stanza 1. In the *AH* copy we may note that lines 53-60 present a version of stanzas 19-20 in *A*; lines 61-64, of stanza 14; lines 65-68, of stanza 16; line 69, of the first of stanza 30; lines 70-73, of stanza 28; line 74, of the first of stanza 34; lines 76-79, of stanza 23; lines 80-81, of the first and last lines of stanza 62, to which line 75 also refers; lines 82-83, of the beginning of stanza 35. Clearly the latter part of the *AH* copy represents the efforts of several people to remember lines from the libel.

The *B* version, though somewhat more polished than that of *A*, and differing in many readings, is more closely related to it than are the others. In addition to stanza 1, *B* also omits stanzas 25, 44, and 48, but it adds a stanza, as do *C*, *D*, and *E*. Here it follows the version of stanza 28 and is quoted in the comments on those lines. In *B* stanzas 16-17 and 31-32 are reversed in order.

In *C* stanzas 16-17 and 31-32 are reversed in order and stanzas 22, 25, 35-50 are omitted. One stanza is added as in *B*. Versions of stanzas incorporated in Bastard's libel, which follows in *C*, are 35-43, 45-47, 49-50.

D and *E* omit stanzas 25, 37, 40-61, 64-65. Versions of stanzas 62-63 follow after stanza 24. Versions of stanzas 34, 35, 36 are in the order 35, 36, 34. The same stanza added in *B* and *C* here follows the version of stanza 29.

In the comments on particular passages, given below, some of the variant readings are noted.

Like that of Cambridge (No. 180), the Oxford libel reflects the "increasing audacity and excessive license of men" in the universities during the early years of Elizabeth's reign and affords further evidence of the virulent nature of some of the attacks stemming from the religious dissension. In this connection see Charles E. Mallet's account of Elizabethan Oxford in *A History of the University of Oxford* (ii, [New York, Longmans, Green, 1924], 104-54, with the quotation above taken from p. 134, as given in a criticism directed toward Cambridge but here related to Oxford). Mallet (i [1924], 393-94) discusses the disorder at Magdalen College under the presidency of Dr. Lawrence Humphrey, 1561-1589, but we may doubt that Humphrey, who in 1564 was actively allied with the Puritan cause and later became Dean of Winchester, was guilty of the personal immorality mentioned in the *B-E* versions of the libel (see the comment on stanza 28 below). Oxford, notably sympathetic toward Catholicism, did not welcome men who had but recently returned from Geneva. Buckley, however, seems quite willing to make jibes at Catholics also (as in stanzas 15 and 16). To a greater extent than is evident in No. 180, this libel appears to have been provoked more by license than by intensity of feeling arising from religious controversies, which grew more acute after 1570 (see the Note on No. 180).

In the commentary following reference is to stanza numbers of the *A* text as quoted. Oxford men are identified from the *Alumni Oxonienses*, compiled by Joseph Foster, Part I, 4 vols., 1891-92, with other references as noted.

1. As stated above, this stanza is omitted in *B*. The first line in *C* reads, "And think y[o] I heare none abroad." In *D* and *E* it is closer to *AH*, "And thinke you I haue nought a loade," which better fits the context.

2. "The devil is dead" is a proverbial expression for which John Heywood in his *woorkes*, 1562 (Spenser Society, i [1867], 141) gives six variations, but without reference to Devonshire. According to the marginal note in *B*, "A backe in Deuons: hanged was thought y[e] diuell." Presumably, then, men could act without fear of being caught. An interesting quatrain built on the proverb is contained in Huntington Library MS. HM 116, fol. 65[r], written in early seventeenth-century italic:

O y[e] L. Rich Earls of Deuonshire
The Diuell men say is dead in deuonshire Late
Of Late did deuonshire live in rich estate
Till Rich wth toyes did devonshire bewitch
That Deuonshire died & left y[e] Diuell rich.

This was probably written in 1606 after the death of Charles Blount, Earl of Devonshire, and before the death in 1607 of Penelope Rich, then Countess of Devonshire, with a satiric thrust at the earlier liaison between the two.

3. According to the *A* marginal note, the reference is to Henry Squire, B.A. from Magdalen in 1551, fellow, 1552-55, and canon of Exeter

in 1562. In the *B* and *C* marginalia, however, Devon is not specified, and the reference may be to Dr. Adam Squire, M.A. from Balliol in 1564, fellow there from 1560 to 1568, and Master from 1571 to 1580. He was made canon of St. Paul's in 1577, the year his father-in-law, John Aylmer, was elevated to the see of London. In the account of Aylmer in *A Briefe View of the State of the Church of England* (*NA*, 1779, reprint 1792, i, 23-25) Sir John Harington tells how Aylmer was led to discipline his son-in-law, who both preached and practiced the text, "It is not good for *Adam to be alone*," even when his wife was away.

4-7. The third line of stanza 4 in *A* misses the rhyme pattern. Other versions agree with *AH* in having "kinde." Mr. Hobbie may refer to Anthony Hobby, B.A., 1560, who was perhaps in the prebendary of Cyro in the collegiate church of Brecon. *B* and *C* identify the woman of stanzas 4 and 5 as "M^ris^ Larke," but it is quite probable that *A* is correct. The reference is perhaps to the wife of Dr. Roger Marbeck, M.A. from Christ Church in 1558, senior proctor, 1562-64, canon, 1565. He was provost of Oriel, 1564-66. According to the *D.N.B.*, his discreditable marriage was discovered about 1566, and he was forced to give up all university appointments. He took the degree D.Med. in 1573 and later became chief physician to the queen. In stanzas 6 and 7 he is himself derided for association with "Mrs Noble," said in *B* and *C* to be of Carfax. The reference to his "eloquence" in line 3 of stanza 7 quite accords with his reputation as public orator. He spoke before Queen Elizabeth when she came to Oxford in 1566. The *B* caption wrongly connects him with New College.

8-9. These stanzas quite possibly refer not to Marbeck, whose first name was Roger, but to Dr. Lawrence Humphrey, who is mentioned also in stanza 28. Humphrey, D.D. from Magdalen in 1562, was Regius Professor of Divinity, 1560-89, and President of Magdalen, 1561-89. In 1564 he was cited by Archbishop Parker for refusing to wear vestments and is said after the hearing to have retired to the home of a widow named Warcup, who lived near Oxford. This may explain stanza 9 (see the *D.N.B.* and *Athenae*, i, 557-61). This stanza in *A* is defective in the rhyme, and *AH* gives the version generally in accord with the others.

10. The marginal note clearly should refer to Mr. Crabbe, as in *B*, but I cannot identify him.

11-12. Mr. Lambe seems to refer to William Lambe of Lincoln College, B.A., 1559/60; M.A., 1563; B.Med., 1568. *B* and *C* interpret stanza 11 as referring to Mrs. Bennett, whose first husband was Mr. Lambe, and stanza 12 is explained in *C* thus, "Mr Bennett trieth quittance wth his wife & vseth her maid." Hugh Bennett of Christ Church had his B.A. in 1564/5 and his M.A. in 1567, but William Lambe was alive in 1568.

13. John Body of Magdalen College had his B.A. in 1554 and his

M.A. in 1562. In 1564 he was rector of Burnet, Somerset. The other versions have "him" instead of "her" in the last line, which seems to fit the context.

14. According to *B*, Mrs. Wakline's husband was called "Brasenose" because of his red nose.

18. In *C* the explanatory note reads, "D[r] Baylye y[e] Physicians wife with M[r] Calfe." This refers possibly to the wife of Dr. Henry Baylie of New College, who took the D.Med. degree in 1563. I find no Dr. Bayliffe. A Richard Veale was B.A. from Magdalen in 1538. This may, however, be a slur on Dr. James Calfhill, canon of Christ Church in 1561, Margaret Professor of Divinity, 1564-5, and D.D., 1565/6.

19. The version of this stanza in *B* and *C* makes better sense (quoted from *C*):

> The faire whome folly long had fedd
> Did well pceive ould frends to fainte
> And being at so low an Ebbe
> Did entertayne a holy sainte.

B and *C* identify the "sainte" as Mr. Marbeck, to whom reference was made in stanzas 4-7.

20. Mr. Dodwell was perhaps John Dodwell, fellow of New College, 1559-76; B.A., 1563; M.A., 1566/67; B.Med., 1570. He later held a living in Dorset.

22. Westlake evidently refers to Remund Westlake, fellow of Exeter College, 1564-80; B.A., 1566; M.A., 1569. I do not find a Lovelace who was his contemporary at Oxford.

23. John Costerdine was B.A. from Christ Church in 1558 and M.A. in 1562. He became rector of Lutterworth, Leicestershire, in 1576.

24. The *A* copyist clearly did not understand the marginal notation, which in *B* reads, "The author spieth Casterdine through y[e] chinck of a wall." *C* also attributes the spying to the author.

26-27. Thomas Paynter was a student at Christ Church in 1564; B.A., 1567/8; M.A., 1570. He later held a living in Dorset and became canon of Sarum. *B* designates him as "Payton" and *C* as "Paton," but I do not find any one of those names at Christ Church at this time.

28-29. Edward, Lord Russell, eldest son of Francis, Earl of Bedford, took his B.A. from Magdalen in 1567. In the comment on stanzas 8 and 9 something has been said about Dr. Lawrence Humphrey, whose wife is mentioned in the marginalia for stanza 28. Humphrey married Joan Inkfordby early in Elizabeth's reign, but, according to Wood, was not happy with her (*Athenae*, i, 557-61; *D.N.B.*). *B*, *C*, *D*, and *E* add a stanza to the jibes on Humphrey. In *C* it runs, with the comment following:

Divines have Concubines & yet offend
It was not well but w[t] of that
Doe so no more seeke to amend
Take heed least papists laugh thereat.
Dr. Humphrey a Devine & great enemy to the Papists./

Perhaps closer to the author's writing is the stanza in *E*:

Divines Cↄubines & yet offende
tush twas not well but what of that
Doe soe noe more & ther an end
keepe Close, Lest papistes laugh therat.

During his exile abroad during Mary Tudor's reign, Humphrey became imbued with Calvinistic teachings and after his return to England was active in his opposition to Catholic influence.

30-33. These satiric stanzas are directed against the wife of Dr. Thomas Cooper, to whom reference was made at the beginning of this Note. They were written during Cooper's second period as Master of Magdalen College, an office he held from 1549 to 1557 and from 1559 to 1568. He was also Dean of Christ Church in 1567 and Vice-chancellor of the University from 1567 to 1570. He later was elevated to the see of Lincoln and then to the see of Winchester, when he became involved in the Martin Marprelate controversy. In his account of Cooper, Wood (*Athenae*, i, 608-13) speaks of his lowly origin and his saint-like qualities, and then says that he "did unhappily marry an Oxford woman, who proved too light for his gravity, and in the end became so notorious for her ill living, that the libels that then came forth, did sound out her infamy; especially that made by Th. Bulkley of Alls. coll." As indicated previously, Bliss prints thirteen stanzas from the libel: versions of 1, 23, 24, 26-34, and the added stanza quoted above. Sir John Harington in *A Briefe View* (*NA*, eds. 1779 and 1792, i, 71-73) gives an account of this unfortunate marriage and says that the whole university wanted Cooper to secure a divorce but his conscience would not permit it. By using "he" instead of "she" in line 3 of stanza 18, the *A* version erroneously seems to direct criticism against Cooper. Other copies have "she," which carries through the point. Dr. Day, who is named as Mrs. Amey Cooper's lover, is identified by Bliss in the *Athenae* as Thomas Day, B.C.L. from All Souls' College in 1521. He was made canon of Christ Church in 1547 (see also *Fasti*, i, col. 59). The date of his death, 1567, makes it certain that these verses were written before that time and support the date 1564 as given in *B*. The explanatory comments of *B* and *C* agree with the text of stanza 31 that Day was bound in a bond of 100£, not 300£, to keep away from Mrs. Cooper, and this is confirmed by Sir John Harington. By using more dialect for the speech of the clown, the *E* version of stanza 33, with which *D* substantially agrees, subtly conveys the sense of Mrs. Cooper's status as known to all and sundry. The last two lines in *E* run:

> Iche zay itz zed in feilde & towne
> the hoded hore had neuͻ peere.

34. For comment on the author, see above.

35-37. Rumbold Salmon is said to have been a chorister at New College in and before 1564. Proctor Fisher, so designated in *B*, was perhaps John Fisher, of New College from 1562 to 1573, B.A., 1565. *A* is inferior in stanza 37, as the *B* version shows:

> Then once more sophist y^{o} became
> ffor rayment wch was sent of late
> A syllogisme reduced with shame
> ffrō Brasnose to Bocardo gate.

The marginal note reads, "Salmon imprisoned in bocardo for Cosoning another Scholler of a Borrowed gowne."

38-39. John Watkins, fellow of All Souls', was M.A. in 1559 and B.D. in 1569/70. He was proctor in 1564, and in 1568 was canon of Sarum.

40. "Mr Dighs," i.e., Digges, may refer to Thomas Digges (d. 1595), the distinguished mathematician, to whom Wood gives a good deal of attention (*Athenae*, i, 636-39). Wood mentions this slur in Buckley's libel, but says he does not know whether it is directed against Thomas Digges.

41-42. John Merick, or Meyrick, was a fellow of New College in 1557; B.A., 1558; M.A., 1562; proctor, 1564 or 1565. Later he was Bishop of Sodor and Man (see *Fasti*, i, 154, 161, 166; *D.N.B.*).

43-44. I cannot explain "Horbrand." In *B* stanza 43 differs but is scarcely more informing. There it runs:

Mr Hayrbrayne with Mr Totters wife Toldernes wife.	The haire brayne y^{t} her berd be brent A silly soule to Totters thinges Shee little knows ye Cranes intent He bears his p^{r}bend ō his winges

45-46. "Dr Whithingeton" may refer to William Whittingham, a fellow of All Souls' in 1545 and a fellow of Cardinal College in 1547. As an exile during Mary's reign, he assisted in the translation of the Geneva Bible. He returned to England in 1560 and in 1563 was made Dean of Durham (see *Athenae*, i, 446-50; *D.N.B.*). The reference may, however, be to Robert Whittington the grammarian who flourished at Oxford during an earlier period. The date of his death seems to be unknown (*D.N.B.*). The anti-clerical bias of the libel suggests that Whittingham was the one in the writer's mind.

47-48. The *B* version, which omits stanza 48, suggests another jibe at Mrs. Amey Cooper:

Math: Lancaster wooed Amy but Leech sped	ffro Amies mouthe and eyes at once Duke Lancaster did take ye foyle He was nō ꝑfect in his stones But let ye horse leach win ye spoyle.

James Leche was B.A. from Christ Church in 1553, fellow of Merton, 1557-67, from which he had his M.A. in 1559. I find no Mathew Lancaster, but one John Lancaster was B.A. from Christ Church in 1560/1, and another was at Queen's in 1564. The *A* version mixes the relationships by referring to Mrs. Leech.

49-50. Alan Scott of Queen's was M.A. in 1556, fellow in 1559, and provost from 1565 to 1575. Michaell Scott, also of Queen's, was M.A. and fellow in 1563.

51-52. Thomas Kay (Caius) was fellow of All Souls' in 1525 and M.A. in 1530. He was Master of University College in 1561 and rector of Tredington, Worcester, from 1563 to 1572, when he died. Wood (*Athenae*, i, 397-401) mentions his election as registrary in 1534 but says he did not perform his duties well and was deprived in 1552. Wood further says he was "besotted with a certain crime which he could not avoid until old age cured it."

53-54. John Bridgewater took his M.A. from Brasenose in 1556. He became rector of Lincoln College in 1563 and held the office until 1574, when he joined the English Catholics abroad (Wood, *Athenae*, i, 625-27; *D.N.B.*). In *B* the plumber's wife is said to be named Rose Lark, but this mention of the lark may be another reference to Mrs. Marbeck (see above on stanzas 4-7).

56. In *B* the marginal note for this stanza reads, "Dr Yilder of Trin: Coll: who fled for religion and after became a wanton." *C* has, "D^r yeeldar who flyeng for religion became a wanton." These statements illustrate quite well the erroneous nature of some of the explanatory matter. From 1559 to 1598 Dr. Arthur Yeldard was president of Trinity College, where a Catholic movement was under way, but there is no indication that Dr. Yeldard attempted flight (see Wood, *Athenae*, i, 674-75; *D.N.B.*; H. E. D. Blakeston, *University of Oxford, College Histories, Trinity College*, no date, pp. 76-99). Referring to Yeldard, Mallet (ii, 160-61) says, "Libels accused him of 'deadly vice,' but those who knew him best spoke well of him." It is possible that the comment about flying for religion refers back to John Bridgewater, but I know of nothing to justify the slur on his character.

58-60. The Griffins and Griffiths who were at Oxford are too numerous to permit any attempt at identification.

61. Equally numerous were the Bakers.

62-63. The usual version of stanzas 62-63 is represented by *B*:

Mris Conradine wife wife to a flemming loued 2 schollers one called Irish ye other English	The fflemish hoy Lades Irish stones And hoists her fickle sayles to uiew Hoist sayles she saith come all at once On harrow hill my timber grew
She was wanton uppon a pile of faggotts & there burnt with a winch fire	Since I am built of Engl: Blood Shall I but seeme a fleminge burne O let me doe my Country good or else ō fagots let me burne.

64. William Barker was fellow at Magdalen from 1554 to 1555 and took his B.D. degree in 1573.

[182-183] *I know not how it comes to passe*
My maisters you yt read this ryme

These two are considered together because No. 183 is an epilogue for No. 182.

Hand: a careful, neat secretary, which appears also as the second hand of No. 238. It is similar to Sir John Harington's handwriting as exhibited in one of the manuscripts of his epigrams, Brit. Mus. Add. 12049, but I hesitate to say that this is his hand. The title, all proper names, and the Latin words in the text are written in printed italic. Line 106, in another secretary hand, is squeezed in between lines 105-107.

A copy of the two in (*L*) Brit. Mus. MS. Lansd. 740, fols. 87r-91r, with the same title, has few variants, and the same method is used to distinguish proper names and Latin words. Line 106 is added in the margin. There can be no doubt that *AH* and *L* are taken from the same source. In the latter No. 183 is entitled, "Lenuoy."

Another copy in (*R*) Bodleian MS. Rawl. Poet. 85, fols. 66r-72r (also numbered in an older hand, 63-69), entitled, "libell agaynst Bashe," is written without differentiation of names or Latin in a careless secretary hand. The *R* version of No. 183 is presented as an address "to the Reader," and "The lybell" follows. The text differs considerably and is even more outspoken than that in *AH* and *L*, but the rhyme pattern and meter are sometimes disturbed.

Samuel A. Tannenbaum in "Unfamiliar Versions of Some Elizabethan Poems" (*PMLA*, xlv [1930], 821) calls attention to a version of this libel in a manuscript then belonging to the Rosenbach firm of New York. I have not seen this manuscript.

In the collation following variants are from *R* unless otherwise designated.

4 I . . . how] me whye or howe
7 *line omitted*
9 dashe] rashe
11 tyed] bound
12 spava vade] spa=va=vade *L*
17 and though he] Perhapps you
18 yet] butt
21 will] would; w^{ch}] what
22 or els it] For else all
23 yt] Thys
26 Butcherlike] butcherlye
29 Albeif, namd] all Beeues made
31 Countie] And Countye
32 this] that
35 doe] trye
37 for . . . great] oft his birth and countryes
38 this . . . born] Borne he was
39 as] for
40 showing horns] shoynge-hornes
R here has two lines not in AH and L:

Ofe truth it was his misterye
To ⟨ ⟩ proue his soñes antiquitye

43 wandring . . . there] wanderynge bothe fare and neere
44 sundrie] manye a
45 seeke the fortune] take the vantage
Lines 47-48 are reversed in order in R.
47 In] Att; Vale] dalle
51 lucke] looke
52 y^{t}] a
53 came] scapte
54 after] for him
55 but . . . went] And then he came
56 climing] clyme
57 in] of
59 & brothells] brothells
60 in chaunters] enchanters *L*: theeues *R*
62 Privie] powlers *R*
63 Bribes] brybers
65 withall] And all
66 at the last] in fewe yeares; such] so much *L*
67 grew] gene; by Cuckolds] wth cuckould
68 now he gan] he began
69 twas] was

Lines 70-75 are omitted in R.

74 Cockhorse] Horsback *L*
76 but] yet
79 his] such
80 once was] was once
81 Synior] Seigniour *L*: Sqyre *R*
82 The walls of] His walles at; to] so
83 &] That; then must they] they muste now
85 great] foulle
86 shall] will; last] lengthe
87 M^{r}] Mas'; did] do
88 be as] now be
89 yet] But
90 Cope] coate
91 this howse] his house *L R*; needs must] muste needs
92 must] will
93 rapto] raptore
96 bee may] maye be that
97 skant worth] not worth the *R*: notworth *L*
98 could] woulde
99 spent] vsed
100 in the] vnder
102 for] No
103 strumpett] harlott
104 were] was; sore] whole; were] was
105 would] durste

Line 106 is written in the margin in L.

107 then] sir
108 y^{t}] this; among] amongst

Following line 109 R has four lines not in AH and L:

Ye muche good do it him lett him take hir
He bowghte his hornes euen of the makar
His dad could mak his hornes good cheape
And therefore since he could not leape

110 Alas] God knoweth
111 pull] pluck; owne] *omitted*
113 were] be
114 of] one
115 Surelie . . . pain] He myghte well do one of these twayne *R*; should] would *L*
117 & . . . haue] Or ells to lende him some
119 then might] myghte once
122 worke] corcke

123 abroad . . . for] He neadeth not abroade *R*; needs] need *L*
125 doubt] dowbte sir; hath] *omitted*
127 sore] longe
128 was] is
129 y^t, y^t] that it
130 pincheth] pinch't *L R*
131 of w^{ch}] Wher-of
132 although &] For trulye
133 assure] afforde
135 proper] tothesom
137 alas alas] Alas
138 whie . . . heard] she was I here men
139 she was] *omitted*
141 wot yow what] what of that
142 how] But how; the] *omitted*
144 of] bothe of
145 there] that; a] hir
147 would] Myghte; haue marid] marrye
148 t'haue . . . good] to do double good
149 help] serue
151 then] nexte
152 pownds & pence] pence and powndes
153 but . . . haue] And since I haue this game
154 assaie] assaylle
156 it] he
157 a] to a
158 well doth] doth well
159 which is as] Thoughe it be
160 then . . . doubt he] Yet since he playnelye
162 or] But

Lines 163 and 164 are transposed in R and read:

Firste if his heade were cutt of quyte
And than his body sett vp ryghte

165 shite] $\bar{\bar{7}}\ \dot{7}\ 3\ \bar{\bar{8}}\ 2$
166 sitt . . . necke] Maghte make his neycke a double ⟨Iakes⟩ $3\ 1\ \dot{8}\ 2\ \bar{\bar{7}}$
167 &] That; wth out all checke] by gobbs and flakes
168 would fall] myghte dropp
170 durt] dongue; did] doth
172 putrified] puryfyed; of] of the
174 or . . . haue] An other question haue I
175 feltred] feathered
176 bee] were; for] for to serue

177 master on a] Masker on his *L*: masker with a *R*
178 Another] And then this
180 of . . . of] for alle or noughte for
182 &] or *L*; troth] truthe
183 there . . . a] agayne will mone this
184 whether] As; whether; Turkie coullord] colored Turkye
185 mouth] moughte
187 this I boldlie] I perceyue and
189 And] Made; in] of
Line 193 is omitted in R.
193 skinks] stinks *L*
195 to] for to
196 she] she doth
197 yes indeed] yea surelye
198 with tongue & mouth] wth nose, chekes, tongue
200 it] I
204 hee rydeth] And he syttes; deniee] demye *L R*
205 or if I do] Si^{r} if I neede
206 like] *omitted*; on] vpon
207 but] And; and] for
208 let . . . or] hange to east or hange to
209 and on] vpon; wilbe] shall be
210 the] A
214 faire . . . fatt] Thyck fowle and fatt
Lines 215-16 and 217-18 are transposed in R.
215 some . . . great] And some by Calues tongue take moste
216 some . . . vnto] And some saye lykewyse to; tis] it's *L*
217 &] Some; it y^{t}] it; fine] *omitted*
219 this . . . to] if that I shall ryghtlye
221 clatter] chatter
223 cogg] bayle
224 sneake] speake
Lines 225-26 are omitted in R.
228 tawnt] check
229 to] vnto
230 falser tonge . . . man] fowlyer knaue you cannote
233 I thinke] Me thynke
237 beares] geues
238 but] For
239 the . . . of] His . . . att
240 they . . . guesse] And playnly did perceyue
241 must] would
Lines 242-44 are omitted in R.
244 herald] Harrolds *L*

245 assigned] appoynted
246 a] the
247 it] he
248 Marybone] marrow bone
249 do] *omitted* *L R*
250 But sir] Now tell me
252 nor] ye; y^{t}] the
253 did . . . the] Could neuer spye thys
254 takes] toke
255 forsooth . . . mine] Now suer and by me
256 Herrald] Herralds
257 had bene] is allwayes
258 among] amongste
259 of] for
260 herralds] Harrold *L*: Heraulde *R*
261 except I would of] But if I should for
263 what] these; he . . . should] than should he
264 wth] *omitted*
265 neck] cheife
266 two] 3; all] y^{e}
269 imbroydered] bordered
272 showing] shoynge; should] myght; the] his
273 yt] the
R has here eleven lines not in AH and L:

Sett one wreath of oken bowghe
Least if the horson heauy cowe
Shoulde strayne his haulter by the stress
This withe myghte be in redynes
Or in his hel'me this myghte be borne
A pretye thymble made of horne
And one a thumbe it must [?] stande
A sharpe knyfe and a nymble hande
Mangled, manngy, and lyned with lyce
Thys should be brave by my deuyse
As for his worde he should applye

275 et peccora] et vniversa pecora
276 A] For a; so shall] a kn: he shall
277 for sooth to] Mass Bashe I
278 I think tis] Me thynkes hyghe
279 scabby] scabbed
280 and] Butt; or ere] before
281 I must] must I
283 a] on

285 what] Not; ys] yes *L R*; sure] surlye
286 thinke . . . word] trow I did not vse yt
287 loe] Se; soone one maie] one may soone *L*: a mā may sone *R*
288 well] why; sith . . . vse] it was a small requeste
R inserts a line:
To tell what tourd myght please you beste
Lines 289-90 and 291-92 are transposed in order in R.
289 and . . . leaue] Take euen which turde you lyste to chuse
290 then . . . yow] And see you do
294 take all] vse it; a] your
295 tord] A tourde

The collation for No. 183 follows:
1 you] all *L*; this] my
2 take] count
R inserts two lines between lines 2 and 3:
Allthough I vse some brauery
In playne termes of knauerye
3 why . . . haue] thys surely haue I
4 keepe] obserue
5 Mr] Master
6 this pretty] A noble
7 should] would
8 not like] vnlyke
9 so . . . rym'd] wherfore if I wryte
12 are] be
13 yf . . . I] Ill fauored if I wrytten
14 Bashe] why Bashe
16 &] But; lie] laye

Many of the above variants, of course, have little significance, but others indicate that the libel underwent a good deal of change as it circulated. I cannot say which copy is earliest.

The object of this venomous attack was Edward Bashe, or Baesh (died, 1587), who in 1559 was granted the Crown manor of Stanstead in Herts. The inscription of him in the church at Stanstead proudly calls him "general surveyor of victuals for the royal navy and marine affairs in England and Ireland during the reigns of Henry VIII, Edward VI, Mary, and Elizabeth" (*The Victoria History of the County of Hertford*, ed. William Page, iii [London, A. Constable and Co., 1912], 369). Although an order of August, 1562, directed that this office of "General Surveyor of Victuals for the Navy, formerly granted to him [William Holstock] and Edw. Baesh," should cease, it appears to have had little real significance as far as Bashe was concerned, for he continued to discharge duties of purveyor for the navy. In January, 1565/6 he and John Ellyot (see lines 77, 80), described as "victuallers of the Navy," received a warrant from the Exchequer for 165£ 2s per month. Other official documents attest his continued activity as "victualler" for the navy (*CSPD . . . 1547-1580*, ed. Robert Lemon [1856], pp. 205, 268, *passim*). Bashe's concern with food and the "kitchen" was grist for the mill of our anonymous author in his railing invective against the "new made squier" of Stanstead, whose rise in the world was also recognized by grants of a coat of arms, first in 1550 and again early in 1572 (*Grantees of Arms Named in Docquets and Patents to the End of the Seventeenth Century*, ed. W. Harry Rylands, Harl. Soc., lxvi [1915], 11, 17). Satiric lines in the libel (see especially 83-85, 233-74) are illuminated by the description of the arms and crest:

Arms,—Quarterly—1 and 4, Per chevron Argent and Gules, in chief two moor-hens Sable beaked and legged of the second, in base a saltire Or; 2 and 3, Per chevron Argent and Sable, three towers triple-towered counterchanged.

Crest—A griffin segreant per pale Argent and Sable, holding in the beak a broken spear of the first.

[*The Visitations of Hertfordshire, . . . 1572, . . . 1634, with Hertfordshire Pedigrees from Harleian MSS. 6147 and 1546*, ed. Walter C. Metcalfe, Harl. Soc., xxii [1886], p. 125]

In the pedigree drawn up by the heralds, Edward Bashe is named as eldest son of Alexander, but nothing is said of his coming from "Worster town" (line 38), nor of any other forebears. Alexander's second son, Nicholas, was probably the brother whom Edward is said to have wronged (lines 106-18). Edward's young wife, whom the author evidently desired for himself, must refer to his third wife, the daughter of one Baker. Since the libel could not have been written before 1559, and perhaps not for several years after, the reference could not be to the second wife, Thomasia Abbott, to whom he was married by 1545 (the same ref., p. 125; *Letters and Papers . . . of Henry VIII*, Vol. XX, Part i, ed. J. Gairdner and R. H. Brodie [1905], p. 667, Grant 1335 [42]).

Although the author shows some influence from his acknowledged "M[r] Chawcer," particularly from parts of the Prologue to the *Canterbury Tales* and such tales as the Reve's and the Miller's, it is obvious that he is equally indebted to John Skelton. Lines 221-27 closely imitate lines at the beginning of *Colin Clout*, first published about 1545 (*S.T.C.* 22601). A less direct but evident influence can be detected in other parts of *Colin Clout* as well as in *Why Come Ye not to Court* and *Elinor Rumming*, which were in print by 1545 or 1550 (see *The Complete Poems of John*

Skelton, ed. Philip Henderson, London, Dent, 1931, pp. xxxvii, 99-118, 282-321, 338-75).

The vivid descriptive epithets of this libel on Bashe do not offer pretty reading, but they do give reality to Bashe, "victualler" of the navy and squire of Stanstead, especially in an olfactory sense.

[184] *Thryse had the sickle cut the harvest downe*

Hand: the first stanza and "I craved muche" of the first line of the second stanza are written in Sir John Harington's hand; the rest of the poem is in the hand of No. 180 and the greater part of No. 181.

I have found no other copy of this anonymous poem. It may be significant, however, that the word "deleaved," used in line 4, is noted in the *N.E.D.* as occurring only in Sir John's *Orlando Furioso*, 1591, Book XXXVII, stanza 31, which I quote (p. 308):

Thrise have the trees with winter been deleaued,
Since we haue been into this place confind,
Of husbands, fathers, and of sonnes bereaued,
So sore the tyrant hateth all our kinde;
And if that any chaunce to be perceaued,
(as some perhapps there be, that are so kinde)
To come but once to looke vpon his wife,
The man and woman both, shall loose their life.

The elder Harington used the word "degrace," not found in the *N.E.D.*, in No. 262, line 47, and he is probably the author of No. 246, where this word again occurs in line 11. It is possible that he is responsible for a similar coinage in the "deleaved" of No. 184. The contents of the poem link it with the earlier writers of the Tottel period rather than with Sir John's contemporaries. Sir John's line was no doubt suggested by this poem in *AH*.

[185] *Vnhappye verse the witnesse of my vnhappie estate*

Hand: the same secretary as appears in No. 175. "This was im̃erito" in line 21 is written in italic.

As every one knows, No. 185 is a copy of Edmund Spenser's contribution to Elizabethan quantitative verse. The poem was included in a letter written by Spenser to Gabriel Harvey in 1579. This was published the following year in (*A*) *Two Other, very commendable Letters, of the same mens writing: both touching the foresaid Artificiall Versifying, and certain other Particulars: More lately deliuered vnto the Printer*, where the poem entitled, "*Iambicum Trimetrum*," appears on p. 56. The earlier book was *Three Proper, and wittie, familiar Letters: lately passed betweene two Vniuersitie men: touching the Earthquake in Aprill last, and our English refourmed Versifying*, 1580, which contained one letter by

Spenser and two by Harvey, written later than the two mentioned above. These five letters are easily available, e.g., in the Oxford *Spenser*, ed. J. C. Smith and E. De Selincourt (1912, reprint 1937, pp. 609-43), where may be read Spenser's introductory remarks on this poem and Harvey's later comments (pp. 636, 639-40).

Abraham Fraunce quoted Spenser's poem in (*B*) *The Arcadian Rhetorike* [1588], sig. C4[r], with the heading, "*Immerito: Spencer*," as an example of "*Iambikes* . . . which admitteth also *Spondaeus*." In 1602 Francis Davison included it in (*C*) *A Poetical Rhapsody*, sig. L5[r] (ed. H. E. Rollins, 2 vols., 1931-32, No. 173), where it is entitled, "*An Elegie in Trimeter Iambickes*," and is attributed to Spenser. According to Rollins, it is in all succeeding editions of the *Rhapsody*.

1 estate] state *A-C*
3 thought] *given as the last word of line 2 in C*: thoughts *B*
7 myne] my *A B*
8 eate no meate] taste no food *C*
13 her her] hir, that hir *A-C*
18 allwaye] alwayes *A-C*; my] thy *A B*

It is evident that the texts of *AH* and *C* are inferior to those of *A* and *B*.

For the commentary on Spenser's quantitative verse, see *The Works of Edmund Spenser A Variorum Edition*, ed. E. Greenlaw, C. G. Osgood, F. M. Padelford, Ray Heffner: *The Minor Poems*, ed. C. G. Osgood and H. G. Potspeich, assisted by D. Mason, ii (Baltimore, Johns Hopkins University Press, 1947), 509-10 (textual notes, pp. 709-10); *Spenser's Prose Works*, ed. Rudolf Gottfried, 1949, pp. 249-55. For other references on English quantitative verse, see the Note on No. 229. Of interest is the quotation in *Prose Works*, p. 255, from Herbert D. Rix, *Rhetoric in Spenser's Poetry* (Pennsylvania State College Studies, No. 7, [1940]), pp. 63-64, where after analyzing the rhetorical pattern of the lines, Rix says:

> In short, not only do these verses "varie not one inch from the Rule" of metrics; they are equally perfect from the point of view of rhetoric. The "Iambicum Trimetrum" has, of course, no poetic value whatever, but it is worth attention as showing how serviceable Spenser regarded the "art of schoole."

[186] *Atteyned he hathe the deapthe who fyndes*

Hand: unidentified Elizabethan secretary, possibly the same as that in Nos. 146-53.

It may be that we have two separate poems here, the first ending with line 21, as there is no reason for the space separating this part from the other lines. I incline to think, however, from the content, somewhat confused at best, and the unrhymed tetrameters in which the ninety-four lines are written that the verses are to be considered one composition. From lines 51-66 it appears that the writer has been led to these ruminations on life and death by the untimely death of a woman whom he loved; but lines 67-68 offer a curious comment. It also seems that the writer became aware of the depth of his love only after the death of the beloved. At any rate, we have more confusion than poetry here, but the experiment with unrhymed tetrameters is worth some notice.

[187] *I hard a voyse and wyshed for a syght*

Hand: the first seven lines are in Sir John Harington's hand; the rest of the poem is in another carelessly formed secretary handwriting, which appears also in Nos. 188-194, 196, 198-199.

There are contemporary copies of this song in: (*A*) Bodleian MS. Rawl. Poet. 148, fols. 67^{v}-68^{r}; (*B*) MS. Rawl. Poet. 85, fol. 45^{v}; (*C*) Thomas Bateson's *Second Set of Madrigales*, 1618, sig. $D1^{v}$, No. 18, where, so far as I can discover, it was first printed. The collation with *C* was made by Kathleen Tillotson from the British Museum copy. The collation shows, I think, that *AH* gives the best reading.

1 voyse] noyse *A-C*
2 asyde] for life *A*
3 sonne] summe *C*
4 which] It *C*; away . . . flee] did goe from me *A*: was gone from me *B*: it went from me *C*
5 yet hath] But yet *C*; mee content] my . . . *A B*: my entent *C*
6 the] this *B*
8 did see] did not see *A C*
9 knowe] knew *C*
11 sawe] spyed *B*; passinge] glanceinge *A*
12 glawnce] glimse *A*; somwhat] somethinge *A C*
13-16 *Wanting in C*
13 as yeat] alas *A B*
14 because indede] Because of it *A*: For that indeed *B*; not] no *A B*
17 wether] whither *A*
18 blessed] Blest *A B*; shape] thinge *A-C*; hether] thether *B*

[188] *Blushe Phebus blushe thy glorye is forlorne*

Hand: see the Note on No. 187.

I have found no other copy of No. 188, which, I think, was intended to be sung. It is placed with a group of songs, and is written in the same handwriting, which occurs nowhere else in *AH*. It undoubtedly belongs, as do the rest of the songs in the group, to the late sixteenth century.

[189] *When weare you borne desire*

Hand: same as the preceding.

A version with four additional lines and with some reversal in order, as indicated in the collation, occurs in two late sixteenth-century poetry manuscripts: (*A*) Bodleian MS. Rawl. Poet. 85, fol. 15^{v}, with attribution to the "Earle of Oxenforde"; (*B*) British Museum MS. Harl. 7392, fols. 18^{v}-19^{r}, with the ascription, "Lo. OX." Another contemporary version in (*C*) Harl. MS. 6910, fol. 145^{r}, without ascription, includes the additional lines of *A* and *B* but omits lines 13-16, the whole copied as poulter's measure in twelve lines. George Puttenham in (*D*) *The Arte of English Poesie*, 1589 (ed. G. Willcock and A. Walker, 1936, p. 206), printed "some part of the verses," that is, the first twelve lines as given in *A* and *B* (agreeing exactly with *B*), with attribution to Oxford. The longer version of *A* and *B* was printed two years later in (*E*) *Brittons Bowre of Delights*, 1591, sig. F2^{r} (ed. H. E. Rollins, 1933, facsimile of the copy in the Huntington Library), where it is headed, "Of the birth and bringing vp of desire," and attributed to "E. of Ox." It is also included in the 1597 edition of the *Bowre*, sig. E3^{r}.

1 weare you] werte thou *A B D E*: were ye *C*
2 pompe and prime] pryde and pompe *A*: . . . pride *C*
3 boye . . . thowe] babe were you *C*; begotten] begott *A-E*
4 good] self *A*; conceites] conceyte *A-E*
5 thy] the *C*
7 thy] yor *C*
8 sad] sore *E*; sithes] syghes *A-E*; wth] and *A*
Inserted between lines 8 and 9 in A-E, quoted from A:
What haddest thou than to drincke: [. . . had you . . . *C E*]
Vnfeyned louers teares.
What cradlle werte tho^{u} rocked in? [. . . were you . . . *C E*]
In hope deuoyde of teares [. . . ffeares *B-E*]
The rest of the poem is not given in D.
9 broughte then a sleepe] . . . the to thy sleepe *A*: . . . the then . . . *B*: . . . you then . . . *C E*
10 speche that] thoughtes w^{ch} *A*; me] men *E*
11 yor] thy *A B*
Lines 13-16 and 17-20 are reversed in order in A B E; lines 13-16 are omitted in C.
13 thy] y^{r} *B E*
15 Whom . . . yor] . . . fynd'ste thou moste thy *A*: What

findste thou most to be thy *B*: Who find you most to be your *E*
18 in] to *C*; one] a one *B C*
19 dothe] woulde *A-C E*
20 likes] loues *A*; muse] be *C*
21 dothe ether] Will euer *A B E*
22 thee] you *C E*
24 ten] A *A*

The *AH* text is, of course, not a good one. There is no evidence that any one of these texts is certainly authoritative, but since the poem is adapted from the Italian or the French, as indicated below, it is probable that *B* most nearly represents the author's writing.

Rollins in his edition of *E*, pp. 94-98, has very full notes on No. 189. I have nothing to add to the information there given, but for the convenience of readers I repeat the main points here. Indication of a foreign source is found in Thomas Watson's *Passionate Centurie of Loue*, 1582, sig. C3^{v}, where he prints a sonnet of his own on the theme, with the statement that it "is taken out of *Seraphine* sonetto 127," which begins, "Quando nasceti amor? quando la terra." This sonnet attributed to Serafino Aquilano de' Ciminelli (*Le Rime*, ed. Mario Menghini, i [1894], 221, Sonnet xv) is actually by Panfilo Sassi. Desportes made use of it in his *Amours de Diane*, I, xxxvii (*Oeuvres*, ed. Alfred Michiels, 1858, p. 28), which begins, "Amour quand fus-tu né? Ce fut lors que la terre." A translation of the Italian sonnet into Latin, entitled, "Amor," was made by George Buchanan (*Poemata*, 1687, p. 377). A version of Oxford's poem, with added introductory and closing stanzas, which have no basis in the foreign originals, was introduced into a late edition of Thomas Deloney's *The Garland of Good-Will*. It is included in the Percy Society edition of *The Garland*, which is based on the 1678 edition, among the poems added in the edition presumably of 1709 (see *The Garland*, ed. J. H. Dixon, Percy Soc., xxx [1851], 105-06). The poem is not in the 1602 edition of *The Garland*, an omission which indicates that it was attached to Deloney's name at a much later date. Bishop Percy adopted *The Garland* text, with a few alterations of his own, in *Reliques of Ancient English Poetry*, 1765 (ed. H. B. Wheatley, ii [1887], 186-87), which, as Rollins points out, have curiously been followed by A. B. Grosart in his edition of Oxford's work in *Miscellanies of the Fuller Worthies' Library*, iv (1872), 407-09; by John Hannah in *The Poems of Sir Walter Raleigh . . . and Other Courtly Poets*, 1875, 1892, pp. 142-43; and by J. T. Looney in *The Poems of Edward de Vere Seventeenth Earl of Oxford* (London, Chapman, 1921), pp. 10-11. There appears, however, to be no contemporary authority for this text.

In the Note on No. 179 mention has been made of the high esteem accorded Oxford's poetry by his contemporaries. This judgment is further attested by Puttenham's introductory remarks on the lines which he quotes from No. 189. Oxford, "a most noble & learned Gentleman," is praised "for his excellencie and wit" in this composition, which is cited as an example of the figure of "responce," or *Antipophora*, which is described as "a figure of argument and also of amplification" (see p. 204).

[190] *The lowest trees have toppes ye aunt her gaule*

Hand: see the Note on No. 187.

If the number of extant contemporary copies is a good indication, No. 190 was one of the most popular of Elizabethan poems. Collation is given with the following eleven copies, of which the first three appear to belong to the late sixteenth century, the others to the early seventeenth century:

(*A*) Bodleian MS. Rawl. Poet. 148, fol. 50^{r} (103, new numbering), where the poem is ascribed to "Mr Edward Dier," with the "M^{r}" later changed to "S^{r}."

(*B*) Bodleian MS. Malone 19, fol. 50^{v}, headed, "A Louers conceipt."

(*C*) British Museum MS. Harl. 6910, fol. 140^{v}, with the stanzas reversed in order.

(*D*) British Museum MS. Add. 22602, fol. 19^{r}, headed, "A Louer."

(*E*) Bodleian MS. Tanner 169, fol. 192^{v}, an entry in the commonplace book of Sir Stephen Powle, with an introductory comment dated September 7, 1618, "Verses given as I suppose by Mr Lea to Laut; intimating that secret Loue speakes little, but sithence I did vnderstande that they weare Sr W. Rawleighs verses to Queene Elisabeth: in the beginninge of his fauoures" (the latter portion apparently written later).

(*F*) Folger MS. 2071.7, fol. 198^{v}.

(*G*) Folger MS. 1.27, fol. 43^{r}, headed, "A Louer."

(*H*) Folger MS. 452.4, fol. 37^{r}, headed, "A Louers conceipt."

(*I*) Francis Davison's miscellany, *A Poetical Rhapsody*, 1602, ascribed, "Incerto" (ed. H. E. Rollins, i [1931], 186, No. 128).

(*J*) With musical setting in John Dowland's *The Third and Last Booke of Songs or Aires*, 1603, sig. LI^{v}, No. 19. Collated by Kathleen Tillotson from the copy in the British Museum.

(*K*) *The Dr. Farmer Chetham MS.*, ed. A. B. Grosart, Chetham Society, lxxxix (1873), 89, headed, "Th' effects of loue." This manuscript is a commonplace book of the reigns of Elizabeth, James I, and Charles I.

The collation shows a number of important variations.

1 lowest] smallest *C*

2 her] his *K*; &] the *A-C E G-K*: a *D*; sparkes] sparke *A-E G H J K*; ther] his *A-C E J K*: it's *D H*: haue *F*: her *G*

3 and] *omitted* *B D G H*: The *I K*; heares] slender hears *A F I-K*; caste] haue *C*: casts *F*: cast their *B D G H*; shadowes] shade *F*; thoghe] although *F*; they be] *omitted* *A F I-K*

4 and] the *F*

sourse
5 shours] ⟨surge⟩ *A*: sourse *C I J*: course *B D-H K*; shollowe] shallow *A B D G-K*: litle *C F*

6 is] his *E*; as] and *A B D F-H J K*
Another stanza is inserted here in B, E, and H, quoted from H (see Rollins' note in I, vol. ii, p. 166, for quotation from B with variants in E):

The Ermin hath the fairest skin on earth
Yett doth shee chuse the wezell for her peere
The Panther hath a sweet perfumed breath
Yett doth shee suffer apes to draw her neere
  Noe flower more fresh, then is the damaske rose
  Yett next her side the nettle often growes.

7 waters] riuers *I*: water[s] *K*; depe are] y^{er} deepest are *A*: deep'st are *B G H*; are deepest *C*: deepst is *D*; the] *omitted* *C*: ther *H*; fordes] floodes *A B F G H*: flud *D*

8 thoghe] yet *A C E I-K*; pceve] perceiues *A E I-K*: can see *C*; move] Moues *D*

9 firmeste] fairest *B D G H*; faythe is in the] fayth, is fownd in *A*: faith should bee in *C*: Faith's not in y^{e} *D*: faith's in the *G*: fewest] sweetest *B H*: fairest *C*: cleerest *D G*

10 &] The *A-E G-K*; cannot singe] doe not singe *A*: sing not loud *B*: sing not Loue *D H*: cannot *omitted* *G*

11 Trewe] Trees *C*; eies & eares] ears & eyes *A E F*; tonges] tongue *C G H*

12 they] the *F*; sighe] sight *C*; then] so *F*
K adds the following stanza:

Ladye, since first my hart became yor thrall
fowre faultes there were y^{t} made you seeme vniust,
straunge in yor choice & coy to choose at all,
hard to beleue & easy to mistrust.
With these fowre faultes fowre vertues still did shine,

an angells face, sweete speaches, bewty, witt;
W[ch] makes me yours, though you ar never mine
and so fast yours y[t] I shall never flitt.

It does not take much critical ability to perceive that this added stanza is not in keeping with the rest of the composition and was probably added by some one who was making use of the poem for personal reasons.

As late as 1682 the two stanzas which appear in most of the copies were included by John Forbes in *Cantus, Songs and Fancies*, sigs. G1^v-G2^r, as "The XXVII Song." Following is "The Answer," beginning, "Bushes have tops, but the Cedar greater." Professor Rollins told me that there is a version of "Bushes have tops" in the 1612 edition of Thomas Deloney's *Strange Histories*, sigs. L1^v-L2^r, but I have not seen this. Another version of the answer in Harl. MS. 6910, fol. 153^r, differs somewhat, beginning, "The lowest trees have toppes the Cedars higher." This text of the answer and that in Forbes are reprinted in full by Rollins in his notes in I (ii, 167). Davison includes "An Answere to the first Staffe, that Loue is vnlike in Beggers and in Kings" in the *Rhapsody*, sigs. I6^v-I7^r. There is also a copy of an answer of five six-line stanzas in Rawl. Poet. MS. 148, fol. 53^r, headed, "The aunswe[re] to Mr: Diers ditie, in fol. 50" (the poem on fol. 50 is *A* of the collation given above), which there begins, "Though lowest trees haue topps, y[e] Ante some gall." Rollins (ii, 169-70) prints the first stanza entire and gives variants with the version in the *Rhapsody*. R. W. Bond in *The Complete Works of John Lyly* (iii [Oxford, Clarendon Press, 1902], 482-83) prints No. 190 and the answer, assigning the latter to Lyly, with the comment, "My belief is that these five stanzas, the refrain of which embodies an opinion expressed by Alexander in *Campaspe*, ii.2.80 sqq., are Lyly's reply to Dyer's verses, elicited partly by the fact that the latter were practically a cento from *Euphues* . . ." (p. 443). This dependence of lines in No. 190 on passages in *Euphues* has been pointed out in detail by Bond (pp. 442-43), by Rollins (pp. 168-69), and by R. M. Sargent in his book on Dyer, *At the Court of Queen Elizabeth* (London: Oxford University Press, 1935, p. 211), in which the poem is printed as Dyer's on p. 197. The suggestion of Ralegh's authorship, given in *E* as noted above, has not been considered by Agnes M. C. Latham in her edition of *The Poems of Sir Walter Ralegh* (London: Routledge and Kegan Paul, 1951, revised edition).

The proverbial and sententious cast of the lines in No. 190 no doubt contributed to its popularity. Compare, for example, lines in *The Three Lords and Three Ladies of London by R. W.*, 1590 (Tudor Facsimile Texts, 1912, sig. B3^v):

> Yea, haue ye not heard that the fly hath her spleene
> And the Ant her gall?

And Robert Greene makes a similar reference in *Greenes Neuer Too Late*, 1590 (*The Life and Complete Works in Prose and Verse of Robert Greene, M.A.*, ed. A. B. Grosart, viii [1881-83], 218):

> But *Mirimida*, meane men haue frownes as well as kings; the least haire hath his shadow, the Flye her spléene, the Ant her gall, and the poorest Peasant his choller.

Obviously, however, the poem itself could be responsible for both these quotations.

[191] *locke vp faire liddes the treasurs of my harte*

Hand: same as the preceding.

This popular song by Sir Philip Sidney is found in Book III of *The Countesse of Pembrokes Arcadia*, where it is sung by Musidorus to lull Pamela to sleep. Very appropriately Abraham Fraunce in *The Arcadian Rhetorike* [1588], uses it as an illustration in his chapter "Of the application of the voyce to seuerall affections" (Book II, Chap. ii). Introduced with the comment, "In ioy, gladnes, or pleasure, tender, mild, sweetlie flowing," Fraunce quotes the first four lines (sig. I5^r), which differ from the *AH* readings only in the use of "her" for "the" in line 4.

The sonnet was included in the original version of the *Arcadia*, of which there are a number of manuscript copies. I give collation with the following:

(*A*) Huntington Library MS. HM 162, fol. 101^v
(*B*) British Museum MS. Add. 38892, fol. 100^r
(*C*) British Museum MS. Add. 41204, fol. 90^v
(*D*) British Museum MS. Add. 41498 (containing sixty-six poems and two passages from the original *Arcadia*), fol. 21^v
(*E*) Queen's College, Oxford, MS. R.38/301, fol. 71^{r,v}
(*F*) Bodleian MS. è Mus. 37, fol. 115^r
(*G*) St. John's College, Cambridge, MS. I.7, fol. 109^r.
(*H*) Folger Library MS. 400903, fol. 98^v (printed from this manuscript by Albert Feuillerat in his edition of the original *Arcadia* in *The Complete Works of Sir Philip Sidney*, iv [1926], 189).

Although not printed in the 1590 *Arcadia*, the poem appeared in:

(*I*) *Arcadia*, 1593, fol. 180^{r,v} (copy in the Huntington Library)
(*J*) *Arcadia*, 1598, p. 350 (copy in the British Museum)

Copies occur also in two other contemporary manuscript poetry collections:

(*K*) Bodleian MS. Rawl. Poet. 85, fol. 9^r, where it is ascribed, "S.P.S." (see the Note on No. 67)

(*L*) British Museum MS. Harl. 7392, fol. 38^{v}, where it is ascribed, "Syd."

There are two early seventeenth-century musical settings, which include the text:

(*M*) Thomas Vautor, *Cantus. The First Set: Beeing Songs of diuers Ayres*, 1619, where the first eight lines are printed in No. VIII, sig. B4^{v}, and the concluding six in No. IX, sig. D1^{r}.

(*N*) Martin Peerson, *Priuate Musicke, or the First Booke of Ayres and Dialogues*, 1620, No. XIII, sigs. D2^{v}-3^{r}.

I am indebted to Professor W. R. Parker for the variants from *E* and *F*, and to Kathleen Tillotson for the variants from *M* and *N*, made from British Museum copies. To Professor William Ringler I am indebted for the variants from *L* and for the information that this poem does not appear in still another manuscript of the original *Arcadia*, Jesus College, Oxford, MS. 150, which derives from the same original as *E*. The Jesus MS. is defective, and the place where this poem would occur is represented by a blank leaf.

1 locke] Looke *H*; treasurs] treasure *E I L N*
2 pserve] preserues *F*; those] these *B*; this] these *A*; lighte] ⟨night⟩ light *A*
4 to] ⟨but⟩ to *A*; the] her *A-E G-L*
5 her] the *L*
6 her sighte where love] Wher cunninge Love *L*: Her light ... *N*; did] doth *M*; faireste] finest *L*; darte] darke *A*
7 ptes] sence *K*
8 dreame] Dreames *L*
9 but] and *M*
10 in] from *M*; faire] rare *A-N*; frame] from *A-L N*: of *M*; thy] the *I*; commone] wonted *K*; righte] ⟨syghte⟩ ryghte *K*
11 suche a] so sweet *K*
13 ⟨spirite⟩ sprighte] sprite *A E G I-K*
14 her] thes *K*; darkest] darkenes *E*; nyghte] lighte *D H*

The *AH* text differs noticeably in line 10, disturbing the sense in the word "frame" and agreeing with no other copy in the use of "faire" instead of "rare." It should be emphasized that the poem is carelessly written and is not in the handwriting of Sir John Harington; nevertheless, the text in *AH* shows fewer independent readings than do those in the poetry collections of *K* and *L*. In line 13 *AH* rightly corrects "spirite" to "sprighte," demanded by the measure and rhyme.

For discussion of Sir John Harington's access to a manuscript version of the original *Arcadia*, see the Note on No. 71.

[192] *All thy scence my sweetenes gained*

Hand: same as the preceding. In line 11 "greater" is crossed out in pencil, no doubt by a later hand.

No. 192 was printed among the "Certaine Sonets Written by Sir Philip Sidney" in (*A*) the 1598 edition of the *Arcadia*, pp. 486-87, directed to be sung "To the tune of a *Neapolitan Villanell*" (copy in the British Museum). A manuscript copy is in (*B*) Folger MS. 400903 (see the Note on No. 67), fols. 224^{v}-225^{r}, among the "Dyuers and sondry Sonettes" which follow a copy of the original version of the *Arcadia*. Directions for singing are given as in *A*. A musical setting with text appears in (*C*) Robert Jones, *The Muses Gardin for Delights*, 1610, No. 17 (copy in the Huntington Library). After each four lines of the poem in *A-C* the following of the music for the voice is indicated by variations on "Fa la dan dan deridan." These are not indicated in the collation.

1 thy] my *A-C*; scence] Senses *B*; my] thy *A C*: the *B*
4 loved] prooved *B*
5 thy] the *A-C*
6 of inwarde] of my . . . *B*
8 heare worthe] haire not worth *A C*: *contraction sign for* nought *inserted after* worthe *B*
9 reason . . . removed] While to my minde the outside stood *C*
11 greater] faire *A-C*
12 that] that the *A-C*; substance] Inne *B*; faile] do fayle *B*
13 is] in *A-C*
15 yee] thee *A-C*
17 thy coulowrs more] the Coloure fayre *B*
18 thy] the *A-C*
21 blaspheme] blasphemie *C*
22 I . . . soule] my soule I haue *A-C*
23 but] And *A-C*
26 me] my *C*; here] haire *A C*; holy] solly *C*
29 wilst I live] all my life *A-C*; muste] will *A-C*

It is obvious that the *AH* text, which, like that of No. 191, is not of Sir John's copying, has readings contrary to the sense in lines 1, 8, and 20, and probably also in line 26. The poem, of course, plays with the lady's "knitting hair," and in *AH* the "heare" of lines 2, 8, and 14 is merely a variant spelling of *hair*; but I take it that the "here" of line 26 should not be so interpreted, and the meaning would be: tie me here with your knitting hair. In *B* also the reading in line 26 is "here," and the spelling of *hair* in other lines is "hayre." Mona Wilson in her edition of *Astrophel and Stella*, 1931, p. 159, points out that Sidney normally wrote "me self" for "my self"; consequently the "me haire" of *A* probably expresses his intention in the line. The copyists of *AH* and *B* did not understand the form, and the copyist for *C* emended it to the more conventional "my hair."

George Puttenham in *The Arte of English Poesie*, 1589 (ed. Willcock and Walker, 1936, p. 203), quotes the last two lines as given in *A-C* as an example of *prosonomasia*, or the "nicknamer," as illustrated by the play upon *love* and *live*. A. W. Pollard includes this song in his edition of *Astrophel and Stella*, 1888, pp. 167-69, taken from *A*, as another of the poems which has reference to Sidney's love for "Stella" (p. 227).

[193] *Shorte is my reste whose toyle is overlonge*

Hand: same as the preceding, the careless secretary of No. 187. Thus, in line 6 "weepe the" was quite probably intended to be read "weepethe," as in other copies. In line 14 "ende" is, I think, correct, not "eide," as copied in *N*, fol. 86^{v}.

Contemporary copies are found in: (*A*) Bodleian MS. Rawl. Poet. 85, fol. 50^{v}, where it is ascribed to "A.H."; (*B*) Brit. Mus. MS. Harl. 6910, fol. 148^{r,v}; (*C*) MS. Harl. 7392, fol. 73^{r}, where it is ascribed "R all"; (*D*) *The Phoenix Nest*, 1593, sigs. N2^{v}-N3^{r} (ed. H. E. Rollins, 1931, pp. [100]-[101]); (*E*) William Barley, *A new Booke of Tabliture*, 1596, sig. D4^{r}. I am indebted to Kathleen Tillotson for the collation with *E*, made from the copy in the British Museum, *S.T.C.* 1433. This poem is not in the copy in the Huntington Library.

2 my . . . darcke] Darke are my Ioyes *B*; is seene] I see *A-D*
3 In] My *B D*; throughe] thorough *B*: by *D*
4 happ] hope *E*
5 and] a *C*; soule] harte *A-D*
6 laffethe] Ioyeth *B*
7 of] for the *A D E*: of the *B*
9 be] are *A-E*; pathes] pathe *A E*; be] is *E*; righte] light *B*
10 bould] bond *B*; my] and *C D*
11 lyf] ⟨lf⟩ life *B*
12 rare] care *C*
13 doulfull] ceasles *A*: restlesse *B*; clocke] Bell *C D*; w^{ch}] that *A-D*
14 myne] my *B D*; happes be] hap is *E*
15 falles] fall *B*; hopes] happes *C*
16 w^{ch}] that *A-D*; have] hath *B D*
17 truste] seke *C D*; not] none *C*
18 be . . . of Cesars fate] You are the starr: that guydes and rulles my fate *A*: You are the starre that rules & guides my state *B*: . . . have Caesars state *D*: . . . have Caesars fate *C E*

I do not know that authority can be claimed for any one of these texts, but the structure and apparent point of the poem seem more consistently set out in *D*. *A* and *B* may have been revised in line 18 for more obvious clarity.

The "R all" ascription in *C* refers to Robert Allot, to whom other poems in that collection are assigned. See the comment by H. H. Hudson in *M.L.N.*, xlvi (1931), 388. In view of Allot's interest in compilations, it is possible that the ascriptions in *C* signify only that the poems were taken from his collection. He was the editor of *England's Parnassus*, 1600 (ed. Charles Crawford, 1913), and was very probably connected with the edition of *Wits Theater*, 1599 (see comments by Rollins in his edition of *England's Helicon*, ii [1935], 48-49, 60).

With little reason R. W. Bond includes this poem in his edition of *The Complete Works of John Lyly*, iii (1902), 477, taken, with seven others, from *The Phoenix Nest*. In his introduction to "Poems (Doubtful)" (pp. 440-41), he says, "For the first seven [No. 193 is the seventh] of these eight, I can allege no very special likeness. They present a general resemblance both to each other and to Lyly. . . . I acknowledge their similarity also to much other ideal love-verse written about this time: they show, for instance, considerable likeness to the work of Lyly's friend, Thomas Watson." A review of Bond's edition in *The Athenaeum*, 1903 (i, 199-200), speaks of his dangerous habit of assigning "on little or no evidence beyond a few parallelisms of phrase, a whole number of anonymous pieces gathered from the miscellaneous literature of the sixteenth century." This criticism is continued by H. Littledale in the same volume, pp. 274, 435-36, and answers from Bond, with some reconsiderations, are given on pp. 594-95, 626. No. 193 is not mentioned specifically as are Nos. 194 and 199.

[194] *Lyke to hermite poore in pensive place obscure*

Hand: see the Note on No. 187.

No. 194 was one of the most popular of Elizabethan poems, and the popularity extended to the end of the seventeenth century. It was composed by 1591, and probably earlier, as it was printed in the first edition of *Brittons Bowre of Delights*, which appeared in that year; but not until 1644 was it published as a composition by Sir Walter Ralegh. Collation is given with the following late sixteenth or early seventeenth-century copies, all anonymous:

(*A*) British Museum MS. Add. 38823, fol. 58[v], headed, "Incerti Authoris." This is the commonplace book of Sir Edward Hoby, but the poem may be in the handwriting of Sir Henry Goodyere, as a summons signed by him, dated 1585, immediately precedes. This date suggests that the poem may have been written into the book about that time.

(*B*) Bodleian MS. Rawl. Poet. 85, fol. 25^{v}, written in late Elizabethan secretary.

(*C*) British Museum MS. Harl. 6910, fol. 139^{v}, also in late secretary.

(*D*) Folger MS. 621.1, fol. 10^{v}, written in contemporary italic, probably of the early seventeenth century. This was evidently taken from a musical setting, as the sonnet is broken up into a poem of three stanzas of four lines each and a refrain. The second and third stanzas, i.e., lines 5-8 and 9-12, are reversed in the order given in *AH*, thus according with the order of the printed version of 1644 (see below). The refrain, i.e., lines 13 and 14, is indicated after the first and second stanzas only.

(*E*) *Brittons Bowre of Delights*, 1591, sigs. B4^{v}-C1^{r}, headed, "A Poem" (facsimile edition of the copy in the Huntington Library, with Introduction by H. E. Rollins, 1933, pp. 20-21). Omitted in the 1597 edition of the *Bowre*.

(*F*) *The Phoenix Nest*, 1593, sig. K3^{r,v} (ed. Rollins, 1931, pp. 77-78).

(*G*) Alfonso Ferrabosco, *Ayres*, 1609, sig. B1^{r}, No. 1, lines 1-4 and 13-14 only. Collated by Kathleen Tillotson from the copy in the British Museum.

1 to] *omitted* *A C G*: to an *B E*: to a *F*; pensive] *omitted* *B E F G*
2 meane to] will go *A*; in] of *A C D F G*
3 wayle] wreake *A*
4 none] naught *C*; ever] *omitted* *G*
Lines 5-12 are omitted in G.
6 falne] fallen *A C*; myne] my *A*
7 suche] this *D*
8 flames] flame *D*; shall] maie *A C D*; w^{ch}] that *B C E*; arise] doth rise *D*
9 grife] graye *A D F*
10 of . . . staye] my staffe of broken hope wheron I staye *A F*: And broken hope the staff of all my staye *B E*: And broken hope shalbe my strenght and stay *C*: my staffe of broken hope whereon I'le stay *D F*
11 of] And *C*
12 y^{e} . . . framd] . . . made *B E*: Shall be the couch *C*; wheron . . . lim̃es] wherin . . . bones *B*: . . . bones *E*; Ile] I *A D*: do *B*: to *E*
13 and . . . gate] . . . gates *A G*: *repeated* *D*; despaire shall] *repeated* *G*
14 to . . . dethe] *repeated* *D*; when . . . fortune] *repeated* *G*

There are almost as many copies of No. 194 belonging to the mid-seventeenth century. In 1644 there appeared *Today a man, To morrow none: Or, Sir Walter Rawleighs Farewell to his Lady, The night before hee was beheaded: Together with his advice concerning Her, and her Sonne*, which included No. 194, sig. A4^v, with the ascription, "Walter Rawleigh," beneath the poem (*Occasional Fac-simile Reprints of Rare and Curious Tracts of the 16th and 17th Centuries*, ed. E. W. Ashbee, ii [no date], No. 6 in the Ralegh section). As printed in this pamphlet, the poem reads:

Like Hermite poore in pensive place obscure
 I mean to end my dayes with endlesse doubt,
To waile such woes as time cannot recure,
Where none but love shall ever finde me out
 And at my gates despair shall linger still
 To let in death when love and fortune will.

A Gowne of gray my body shall attire,
 My staffe of broken hope whereon I stay
Of late repentance linkt with long desire,
The couch is fram'd whereon my limbs I lay.
 And at my gates, etc.

My food shall be of care and sorrow made,
 My drink nought else but tears falne from mine eies,
And for my light in this obscured shade
The flames may serve which from my heart arise.
 And at my gates, etc.

Agnes M. C. Latham in her revised edition of *The Poems of Sir Walter Ralegh* (London: Routledge and Kegan Paul, 1951, p. 104) refers to a copy in "A manuscript in the Edinburgh University Library, mentioned in *The North British Review* (1870, LII, 543), with the title 'Sir Walter Rayleye's last Eligie.' " I have not seen this manuscript, but it is obvious that these lines printed in 1591 were not Ralegh's last elegy. Such a heading suggests a connection with the 1644 printed copy. It should perhaps be pointed out that the reference to *The North British Review* is unfortunately an error. No mention of this manuscript occurs in the review of John Hannah's edition of *The Courtly Poets from Raleigh to Montrose*, 1870, which is printed on pp. 543-45 of this number of the journal.

Nicholas Laniere included the poem with music in his *Select Musicall Ayres and Dialogues*, 1653, sig. B1^r, from which it was reproduced by E. F. Rimbault in *A Little Book of Songs and Ballads, gathered from Ancient Musick Books*, 1851, pp. 99-100. The stanzas follow the order of the 1644 printing. Rimbault says that No. 194 was printed as a song in *The Academy of Compliments*, 1650, with the title, "A Lover's Melancholy Repose," but I have not seen this. A copy was included by Lady Catherine Aston, wife of Herbert Aston, in her collection of poems made about 1658 (*Tixall Poetry*, ed. Arthur Clifford, 1813, pp. 115-16). It has the refrain, after each four lines, which follow the order of *AH*. I believe that no one has called attention to a copy which is written as No. 15 by John Gamble in his manuscript collection of songs with music, dated 1659, which is preserved in the New York Public Library, Drexel 4257. This also has the refrain and the order of stanzas as in the 1644 printing. The text differs as follows from that of 1644:

2 with] in
5 And . . . gates] *repeated*
6 To . . . death] *repeated*; when] where
8 hope] hopes
10 I] I'le
11 mine] my
15 may] shall; from] on

Further indication of the popularity of the poem in the seventeenth century is shown in references to it by various writers of the period, as was noted by Rimbault (pp. 98-99) and others, recently by Rollins in his notes in *The Phoenix Nest* and by Miss Latham in her revised edition of Ralegh's poems.

H. Littledale in "The Lylyan Apocrypha," *Athenaeum*, 1903, i, 436, pointed out that No. 194 is a translation from Desportes, *Amours de Diane*, II.8, beginning, "Je me veux rendre hermite et faire penitence" (*Œuvres*, ed. Michiels, 1858, p. 71). Thomas Lodge also made a translation of this sonnet, which first appeared in his *Scillaes Metamorphosis*, 1589. Both the Desportes and the Lodge poems are printed by Rollins in *The Phoenix Nest*, pp. 170-71, and by Miss Latham in her 1951 edition of Ralegh's poetry, pp. 107-08. Although No. 194 is freely translated, an examination of the French sonnet may be of some help in evaluating the versions. This comparison indicates that the poem was probably written as a sonnet of the English pattern, not as a song in stanzas with refrain, nor with the misleading division of *AH*, and that the proper order of the lines is that of *AH*. It should be noted that the felicitous closing couplet of No. 194, which could so easily be used as a refrain in song, has no basis in the French poem, which ends:

> Et tousjours, pour prier, devant mes yeux j'auray
> La peinture d'Amour et celle de ma dame.

Omission of "pensive" in line 1 of several versions has justification in the French, which reads, "en un lieu deserte" (line 3), but the English line is poetically more effective with the word. On turning to line 9, where the variant of "grife" is "gray," we find the latter supported in the French "gris." I suggest that the author of No. 194 wrote "grise," using it in the sense of "gray," as in Middle English, and that the copyists did not understand the word, which became "grife," the long *s* being read as an *f*. The word "grief" does, of course, fit the context.

No. 194 is another of the poems which R. W. Bond assigned to John Lyly, stating that it is "Possibly the missing song of Geron, in *Endim.* ii, 4.1" (*Works*, iii [1902], 470); yet Bond claims "no very special likeness" to Lyly in the lines of the poem (p. 440). Littledale (reference above) maintains that the usual ascription to Ralegh is not shaken. The earlier editors of Ralegh, Thomas Birch (1751) and Sir Egerton Brydges (1813), did not include No. 194. John Hannah, however, prints it as Ralegh's in *The Courtly Poets from Raleigh to Montrose*, 1870, pp. 12-13, and in *The Poems of Sir Walter Raleigh . . . with those of Sir Henry Wotton and Other Courtly Poets from 1540 to 1650*, 1875, 1892, 1910, pp. 12-13. Miss Latham includes it in her first edition of *The Poems of Sir Walter Ralegh* (London, Constable, 1929), p. 35, No. 7, and, as noted, in the revised edition of 1951, pp. 11-12, No. XI. For the letter, dated 1592, purporting to link Ralegh's name with the poem, printed by J. P. Collier in *Archaeologia*, xxxiv (1851), 161-62, see Rollins, *The Phoenix Nest*, pp. 169-70, and Latham, p. 105.

In my own opinion the poem has qualities both in thought and phrase that are peculiarly indicative of Ralegh, as is apparent from a comparison with the lines beginning, "GIUE me my Scallop shell of quiet/ My staffe of Faith to walke vpon" (ed. Latham, pp. 49-50). It is hardly too much to say that Lodge translated the French sonnet, but that Ralegh used the French for a poem of his own.

[195] *Helen was fayre, yet liued most vnchast*

Hand: unidentified contemporary italic.

The four lines of No. 195 are crossed out in *AH*. They appear to form a fragment of a longer poem, which the copyist decided not to include in the manuscript. I have not succeeded in finding any other copy of these lines.

[196] *Ringe out the bells lett morninge shewes be spred*

Hand: see the Note on No. 187.

No. 196 was first published in (*A*) *The Countesse of Pembrokes Arcadia*, 1598, p. 489, among the "Certaine Sonets Written by Sir Philip Sidney." An important copy is in (*B*) British Museum MS. Add. 28253, fol. 3^r, written in a careless Elizabethan secretary hand. On the verso, in another secretary hand, is the following note:

1584
Ringe owte yor bells Lett mowreninge
shewes be spredde for Love ys dedd//
A dyttye mad by S^{r} phillip sydnye
gevene me att pvttenye// In surrye
Decembris x^{o} Ann^{o} 1584

S^{r} phillyppe Sydnye//

Mona Wilson in her edition of *Astrophel and Stella*, 1931, p. 184, says, "Putney may mean Barn Elms, where Sidney was living at this time."

Other copies of the poem occur in: (*C*) *England's Helicon*, 1600, sigs. B3^{v}-B4^{r} (ed. H. E. Rollins, 2 vols., 1935, No. 3), where it is headed, "Astrophels *Loue is dead*," and is ascribed to Sidney; (*D*) Harl. MS. 7392, fol. 35^{r,v}, ascribed, "q^{d} S^{r}. Ph. Syd."; (*E*) Cambridge University MS. Dd. 5.75, fol. 27^{r}.

I am indebted to Professor William Ringler for the variants of *D* and *E*. The copy used for *A* is in the British Museum.

1 out] forth *D*; the] your *A B D E*; shewes] tunes *D*
3 plage] rage *D*
Added between lines 3 and 4 in A-E, quoted from A:
Worth as [is, *D*] nought worth reiected,
And Faith faire [fowle, *B*] scorne doth gaine
6 them] them that *A-E*
8 have] do *A C E*; hard] heare *A C E*
10 his] Whose *D*; Pracockes] peacocks *A-E*; his wynding] whose shrodinge *D*; his] is *A-E*
11 his will] Whose witt *E*; soules] sole *A-E;* exector] Executors *B*: executor *D E*
12 *C D E give the refrain in full after each stanza.*
13 dirge] diridge *E*; rightly] richly *C*
15 S^{r}] And *C*
16 his epitaphe] Which . . . *A C D*: whose . . . *B*; onn] once *A-E*; his] my *D*
18 rage] Wronge *B*; beredd] bred *A-E*
21 is] his *A-E*
22 then] Therefore *A C E*: Wherfore *B D*; vile] vild *E*; a] *omitted* *A-D*
23 fransy] frenzy *D*
24 whom] Who *A C E*: that *B D*

It is evident that the *AH* copy is not a particularly good text. Like Nos. 191 and 192, also Sidney poems, No. 196 has not the authority of

Sir John Harington's handwriting, which we find in Nos. 67, 71, 223, and 229.

Several biographers and critics of Sidney associate the writing of No. 196 with the marriage of Penelope Devereux to Robert, Baron Rich, e.g., H. R. Fox Bourne, *A Memoir of Sir Philip Sidney*, 1862, pp. 288-89; John A. Symonds, *Sir Philip Sidney*, 1887, pp. 106-07; A. W. Pollard, ed., *Astrophel and Stella*, 1888, pp. xiii, xxiv-xxv; Mona Wilson, *Sir Philip Sidney* (New York, Oxford Univ. Press, 1932), p. 183. Pollard implies that the poem may have been written when Sidney heard of the arrangements for the marriage which was being proposed in March, 1581, by one of Penelope's guardians, the Earl of Huntington (on these proposals, see also M. W. Wallace, *The Life of Sir Philip Sidney* [Cambridge Univ. Press, 1915], p. 246). The marriage did not take place until late in October of 1581. See Lisle C. John, "The Date of the Marriage of Penelope Devereux," *PMLA*, xlix (1934), 961-62, and *The Elizabethan Sonnet Sequences* (New York, Columbia Univ. Press, 1938), pp. 188-89; also, James M. Purcell, comment, *MLN*, xlv (1930), 310. Pollard interprets the last stanza as a "palinode," inspired by a realization that "Stella's" heart was not in her marriage. On the identification of Penelope Rich as "Stella," see No. 223.

Whether or not the poem has biographical significance, it is a superb example of poetic wit, attained by the deft reversal of the invective thrust in the lyric close. For examples of courtly invective against women, Sidney, of course, had only to look to the poetry of his immediate predecessors Wyatt and Surrey, but neither offers an illustration of the dramatic transference of the invective. See Wyatt's "Ffarewell Love and all thy lawes for ever," "They fle from me," "In eternum," "Gyve place all ye," and "Tanglid I was in loves snare" (*Poems*, ed. Foxwell, i [1913], 19, 86, 125, 310, 329); also, Surrey's "To dearly had I bought my grene and youthfull yeres," "Wrapt in my carelesse cloke," and "Eache beeste can chuse his feere" (*Poems*, ed. Padelford, 1928, Nos. 25, 26, 34). For the vaunting tone of the poem Sidney may also have learned something from Surrey's "Geue place, ye louers, here before" (*Ibid.*, No. 18).

[197] *A godly father sitting on a draught*

Hand: Sir John Harington's.

The *AH* copy of these cloacal lines by Sir John appears to represent an earlier version which was somewhat revised for his collection of epigrams and for use in *The Metamorphosis of Aiax*, 1596. Collation follows with: (*A*) British Museum MS. Add. 12049, the earlier autograph manuscript of the epigrams, p. 38; (*B*) Folger MS. 4455, the fair copy, also autograph, of the epigrams made for Prince Henry about 1605 or 1606, pp. 50-51, with the heading, "A dishe of daynties for the Deuill";

(*C*) *The Metamorphosis of Aiax*, 1596, *S.T.C.* 12779, copy in the Brit. Mus.), sig. C6r,v. This edition was set up by Richard Field directly from the author's manuscript, now British Museum MS. Add. 46368. See Hughey, p. 403. On the other two editions in 1596 (*S.T.C.* 12780 and 12781), see A. E. Kirwood, "'The Metamorphosis of Aiax' and its Sequels," *The Library*, 4th Series, xii (1932), 208-34. No. 197 was not included in the 1615 edition of Sir John's *Epigrams*, but it was printed in the 1618 edition, Book I, No. 48, from which it was reprinted in the editions of 1625, 1633, and 1634 (see the Note on No. 91). My variants for the 1618 version are taken from (*D*) N. E. McClure's edition of *The Letters and Epigrams of Sir John Harington*, 1930, p. 166, where the text is that of 1618. The verses are also in the edition of *Ajax* edited by Peter Warlock and Jack Lindsay [1927], pp. 34-35.

2 that] as *A-D*
3 Sayd . . . prayre] mumbled as was his manner certen prayers *A-D*
4 And . . . repayre] and vnto him the devill strayght repayres *A-D*
5 doth begin] he beginns *A-D*
6 it . . . sinne] such prayres wer deadly sinns *A B*: such praiers are deadly sins *C D*
7 it show'de] it provde *A B D*: he shewd *C*
8 from] in *D*; vnfitt] vn meet *C*
9 ffather . . . speeche] rev'rent man though at the first *A-C*: reuerend, though at the first *D*
10 thus to the divell said] thus to the De'ull he sayd *B*: to Satan thus he said *C*
11 Nurse . . . lying] damned spirit wicked false and lyeng *A-D*
13 Take . . . owne] each take his dew *A-D*
14 My . . . befall] to god my prayre I meant to thee *A-D*
15 Vpp . . . god] Pure prayr ascends to him *A-D*
16 dunge] filth *A-D*; most] more *B C*

In *C* the verses are illustrated by a woodcut in keeping with the subject, and are introduced by a reference to Arius:

But hee that woulde indeed call to minde, howe *Arrius* that notable and famous, or rather infamous hereticke, came to his miserable end vpon a iakes; might take iust occasion euen at that homely busines, to haue godly thoughts; rather then as some haue, wanton, or most haue, idle. To which purpose I remember in my ryming daies, I wrote a short Elegy vpō a homely Emblem, which both verse and Embleme, they haue set vp in *Cloacinas* chappell, at my house very solemnly. And I am the willinger to imparte it to my friendes, because I protest to you truely, a sober Gentleman protested to me seriously, that the conceit of the picture and the verse was an occasion to put honest and good thoughts into his minde [sig. C5v].

The copy in *AH* probably represents the lines as they were written in Sir John's "ryming daies."

[198] *Away wth these self lovinge laddes*

Hand: see the Note on No. 187.

The name of the author was not attached to No. 198 in print until the publication of (*A*) *Certaine Learned and Elegant Workes of the Right Honorable Fulke Lord Brooke*, 1633, pp. 197-98, where the poem appears as "Sonnet LI" in the "Cælica" series (copy in the Brit. Mus.). Geoffrey Bullough in the Introduction to his edition of *Poems and Dramas of Fulke Greville First Lord Brooke*, i (London, Oliver and Boyd, 1945, reprint of the edition of 1939), 34, notes that two items were numbered XXVII in the 1633 edition, and he accordingly prints the poem as Sonnet LII (i, 104). An important copy is in (*B*) the manuscript of "Cælica" at Warwick Castle, which Bullough describes as "A scribal copy much revised by the author" (i, 29). The variants here given are taken from Bullough's collation (i, 255), where the poem is said to be written on p. 50 of the Warwick MS. No. 198 was first printed in (*C*) John Dowland's *The first Booke of Songes or Ayres*, 1597, No. 21, sig. L1^{v} (copy in the British Museum). In (*D*) *England's Helicon*, 1600, sig. X^{r,v} (ed. H. E. Rollins, 2 vols., 1935, No. 121), it is headed, "*Another of his* Cinthia," and is the second of "*three ditties*" said to be taken from Dowland's book, "*the Authours names not there set downe, & therefore left to their owners.*" In the "Catalog of ye Poems contayned in Englands HELICON" (Harl. MS. 280, fol. 100^{v}), the first line is entered with ascription to "F Greuill."

2 arrowes] arrow *A-D*
3 sittes] sigh *A-D*
4 those] them *C-D*; a sleepe] & sleepe *C D*
5 the] a *A-D*
6 fɔcethe] forceth *A-D*; the rodde] ⟨his . . .⟩ the . . . *B*
7 Since] Sweet *A B*: God *C D*; shaftes] shaft *C D*
8 doo] Doth *C D*: ⟨doth⟩ Doe *B*; cawsles] either *C D*
9 borene] borne *A-D*
10 feete] wing *A*: winges *B*
13 songe] songs *A BD*; shalbe] they be *A-D*; Cynthyghs] *Cynthia's* *A-D*
14 gold] her *A-D*; holly days] Holy dayes *A*: holy daies *B*: hollidaies *C*: Holly-dayes *D*
15 in] On *C D*
17 Cupid] *Cupids* *A-D*
22 welfare] well-fare *A B*: well fare *C*
23 runes] runne *A-D*

25 the worthines] that . . . *A-D*
26 as] Is *A-D*; that] which *C D*; bond] bow *A-C*: due *D*
27 the foster] thee foster *A B*: the Sheepheard *D*
29 sayncte] Nimph *D*

The contraction "fↄcethe," i.e., forceth, in line 6 of *AH* is, I think, correct, although I first read the word as "ferthe," agreeing with *N*, fol. 147^{r}. If the spelling "thee" in line 27 of *A* and *B* is taken literally, the clause reads: and love can nourish thee as well. In the other versions it is: and the forester (or shepherd, as in *D*) can love as well. Bullough (i, 41-42) sets out reasons for believing the first seventy-six poems in "Cælica" were written before 1586, and it is possible that the version in *AH*, which differs considerably, stems from an early draft. It is clear that it was not taken from Dowland or from *England's Helicon.*

[199] *his golden lockes tyme hath to silver turned*

Hand: see the Note on No. 187. Corrections are in the hand of the poem.

Collation is given with four manuscript copies, of which three, *A-C*, appear to be later than that in *AH*.

(*A*) A copy in British Museum MS. Stowe 276, fol. 2^{r}, is headed, "Sr Henry Lee," and ascribed, "St John." The writing in seventeenth-century italic is said by Sir E. K. Chambers (*Sir Henry Lee*, 1936, p. 142) to be that of Oliver St. John, first Earl of Bolingbroke, who was born about 1580. Since No. 199 was composed in 1590, the ascription to St. John can signify only that he was the copyist.

(*B*) A copy in British Museum MS. Add. 33963, fol. 109^{r}, is written in contemporary italic on a small page which has been pasted to the larger page of the manuscript volume. The origin of the copy is explained by an introductory note, written in a later hand, "The following Lines I found on the fly leaf of Mornay's Work 'of the trewe Relligion' printed at London in the year [left blank]." Another hand, approximately of the same period, has added, "? 'a woorke of the trewnesse of the Christian Religion' By Philip of Mornay, Lord of Plessie Marlie: Begun to be translated into English by Sir *Philip Sidney*. Knight *London* 1587."

(*C*) A copy in the early seventeenth-century Folger MS. 1.28, fol. 99^{r}, is headed, "Sr Henry Lea his Farewell to the Court."

(*D*) The copy in British Museum MS. Add. 36526, fol. 9^{r}, has the first five lines only, written in a crabbed secretary hand beneath a line of music. According to Kathleen Tillotson, who sent me a copy of this version, the lower part of the folio has been cut away, but there would hardly have been room for more than the rest of the first stanza.

Collation is also given with three printed versions.

(*E*) The poem was first printed in George Peele's *Polyhymnia*, 1590, sig. B4^{v}, entitled simply, "A Sonet," and without any definite ascription of authorship. Variants are given from the copy in the Huntington Library.

(*F*) A musical setting for the poem appeared in John Dowland's *The first Booke of Songes or Ayres*, 1597, sig. I 2^{v}, No. 18. This collation was made for me by Kathleen Tillotson with the copy in the British Museum.

(*G*) Sir William Segar in *Honor, Military, and Ciuill*, 1602, pp. 198-99, printed a version written in the first person, whereas all the other copies are in the third person (copy in the New York Public Library).

1 his] my *G*

2 O swiftnes] in . . . *C*: & . . . *D G*

3 his] My *G*; age and tyme] age and *omitted* *D*: Time and Age *E F*: age and age at youth *G*; ever] alwayes *A*: *omitted* *G*

4 spurned] but spurnd *A C E-G*: yet spurned *B*: but all *D*

5 Beuty . . . youth are] youth bewty strength ar *B*: . . . and youth *G*; flowres] *omitted* *B*; but] euar *B*: *omitted* *G*; seene] beene *G*
D lacks the rest of the poem

6 deuty, fayth, love] fayth dwtie loue *B*: . . . faith and love *G*; and] but *C*; ev^{r}] allwayes *B*

7 his] My *G*; shall make] must make *A*: must be *B*; a] an *G*

8 sonett] sonnets *A-C E F*: songs *G*; turned] turne *A C F*: shall turne *G*

9 nowe] *omitted* *C*; serve] sit *G*; on] w^{t} *B*

10 w^{ch}] that *G*; ages] Louers *B*: Age his *E*: old ages *G*

11 but] and *B G*; though] so *G*; cotage] Countrye *A*; he] I *G*

12 his . . . his vnspotted] his saint shall kepe her shrine in spotles *B*: My . . . mine . . . *G*

13 he] I *G*; saddest sits] sittes at home *B*: sadly sit *G*; cowntry ⟨hevenly⟩] homelye *A-C E-G*

14 heill] I'le *G*; his] my *G*

15 blest] blessed *B*; the hartes] theire . . . *A*: they *B*; wishe] thinke *G*

16 curste] cursed *B*; the soules] theire . . . *A*: they *B*: the soule *F*; thynke] wisht *A*: wyshe *B*; her . . . wronge] to doe her wrong *G*

17 alove] allowe *A C E F*: vouchesafe *B G*; this] an *B*

18 yor . . . yor] thy . . . thy *B*

Sir Henry Lee, 1533-1611, whose name is superscribed to No. 199 in *AH*, was the son of Anthony Lee and Margaret Wyatt, sister of the poet Sir Thomas Wyatt (for a detailed account of him, see Sir E. K. Chambers, *Sir Henry Lee*; records of the birth of Lee are discussed on pp. 19, 27). About 1570 Henry Lee established the annual tilt on November 17, celebrating Elizabeth's accession to the throne; and as a result of his fame as a champion of the tilt, about 1578 he was appointed Master of the Armory (Chambers, pp. 37-8, 109, 129, sqq.). By 1590 he had reached an age when tilting was too arduous for pleasure, and he therefore decided to make a public farewell to his championship. He chose as the occasion the Accession tilt of November 17 in that year. To his opponent George Clifford, Earl of Cumberland, he presented his arms and his place of honor, petitioning the queen to accept the Earl as her knight. George Peele in his *Polyhymnia*, 1590, relates in verse the events of this impressive occasion, and William Segar, King of Arms, in his *Honor Military, and Ciuill*, 1602, Bk. III, chap. 54, which is entitled, "The Originall occasions of the yeerely Triumphs in England," gives an account of the affair, prefaced by a brief history of the Accession tilt, with due praise to the originator:

> Here will we remember also (and I hope without enuie so may) that these annuall exercises in Armes, solemnized the 17. day of November, were first begun and occasioned by the right vertuous and honourable Sir *Henry* Lea, Master of her Highnesse Armorie, and now deseruingly Knight of the most noble Order, who of his great zeale, and earnest desire to eternize the glory of her Maiesties Court, in the beginning of her happy reigne, voluntarily vowed (vnlesse infirmity, age, or other accident did impeach him) during his life, to present himselfe at the Tilt armed, the day aforesayd yeerely, there to performe in honor of her sacred Maiestie the promise he formerly made . . . true it is, that the Author of that custome (being now by age ouertaken) in the 33. yeere of her Maiesties reigne resigned and recommended that office vnto the right noble *George* Earle of *Cumberland*. The ceremonies of which assignation were publiquely performed in presence of her Maiestie, her Ladies and Nobilitie, also an infinite number of people, beholding the same, as followeth.
>
> On the 17. day of Nouember, *Anno 1590.* this honourable Gentleman together with the Earle of *Cumberland*, hauing first performed their seruice in Armes, presented themselues vnto her Highnesse, at the foot of the staires vnder her Gallery window in the Tilt yard at *Westminster*, where at that time her Maiestie did sit, accompanied with the *Vicount Turyn* Ambassador of *France*, many Ladies, and the chiefest Nobilitie.
>
> Her Maiesty beholding these armed Knights comming toward her,

> did suddenly heare a musicke so sweete and secret, as euery one thereat greatly marueiled. And hearkening to that excellent melodie, the earth as it were opening, there appeared a Pauilion, made of white Taffata, containing eight score elles, being in proportion like vnto the sacred Temple of the Virgins Vestall . . . Before the doore of this Temple stood a crowned Pillar, embraced by an Eglantine tree, whereon there hanged a Table, and therein written (with letters of gold) this prayer following [p. 197].

The prayer quoted can be read in No. 200, and the collation with Segar's version is given in that Note. Following the Latin poem, Segar continues:

> The musicke aforesayd, was accompanied with these verses, pronounced and sung by M. *Hales* her Maiesties seruant, a Gentleman in that Arte excellent, and for his voice both commendable and admirable.

There follows Segar's version of No. 199 (see collation). Segar then concludes his narrative of the day's events:

> The gifts which the Vestall maydens presented vnto her Maiesty, were these: A vaile of white exceeding rich and curiously wrought: a cloke and safegard set with buttons of gold, and on them were graven Emprezes of excellent devise: in the loope of every button was a noble mans badge, fixed to a pillar richly embrodered.
>
> And here (by way of digression) let vs remember a speech which this noble Gemtleman vsed at such time as these buttons were set vpon the garment aforesaid: I would (quoth he) that all my friends might have bene remembred in these buttons, but there is not roome enoughe to containe them all; and if I have them not all, then (said hee) those that are left out, may take exception. Wherevnto another standing by, answered: Sir, let as many be placed as can be, and cause the last button to be made like the Caracter of etc. Now Godamercie with all my heart (quoth the Knight), for I would not have given the Caetera of my friends for a milion of gold.
>
> But to returne to the purpose, These presents and prayer being with great reverence delivered into her Maiesties owne hands, and he himselfe disarmed, offered vp her armour at the foot of her Maiesties crowned pillar; and kneeling vpon his knees, presented the Earle of Cumberland, humbly beseeching that she would be pleased to accept him for her Knight, to continue the yeerely exercises aforesaid. Her Maiesty gratiously accepting of that offer, this aged Knight armed the Earle, and mounted him vpon his horse. That being done, he put vpon his owne person a side coat of blacke Velvet pointed vnder the arme, and covered his head (in liew of an helmet) with a buttoned cap of the countrey fashion.

After all these ceremonies, for divers dayes hee ware vpon his cloake a crowne embrodered, with a certain motto or device, but what his intention therein was, himselfe best knoweth.

Now to conclude the matter of assignation, you shall vnderstand, that this noble gentleman, by her Maiesties expresse commandement, is yerely (without respect vnto his age) personally present at these military exercises, there to see, survey, and as one most careful and skilfull to direct them; for indeed his vertue and valour in Arms as deserveth to command [p. 198].

Chambers, p. 142, referring to the verses of No. 199, says, "it is not inconceivable that they are Sir Henry Lee's own." A poem which has some similarity to No. 199, although of less poetic merit, is ascribed to Lee in MS. Rawl. Poet. 148, fol. 75^v (as quoted by Chambers, pp. 142-3):

Times eldest sonne, olde age, the heyre of ease,
  Strengths foe, loves woe, and foster to devotion,
Bids gallant youthes in martial prowes please,
  As for himselfe hee hath no earthly motion,
But thinks sighes, teares, vowes, praiers and sacrifices
As good as shewes, maskes, justes or tilt devises.

Then sit thee downe, and say thy *Nunc demittis*,
  With *De profundis*, *Credo*, and *Te Deum*,
Chant *Miserere*, for what now so fit is
  As that, or this, *Paratum est cor meum?*
O that thy Saint would take in worth thy hart,
Thou canst not please hir with a better part.

When others sings *Venite exultemus*,
  Stand by and turne to *Noli aemulari;*
For *quare fremuerunt* use *Oremus*
  Vivat Eliza for an *Ave Mari;*
And teach those swains that lives about thy cell,
To say *Amen* when thou dost pray so well.

These verses are said to have been given "in yeelding up his Tilt staff." Chambers also quotes, pp. 143-4, the poem, "Farre from triumphing Court and wonted glory," attributed to Lee in Robert Dowland's *A Musical Banquet*, 1610. If Lee was the author of No. 199, I think we may reasonably suppose that he wrote it in the first person, as given by Segar. It must be borne in mind, however, that Segar's book appeared twelve years after the occasion when the poem was publicly sung;

whereas George Peele's *Polyhymnia*, in which a third-person version was printed, came out the same year. And the *Polyhymnia* was concerned in subject matter only with the Accession tilt of 1590. Because of its presence at the end of the *Polyhymnia*, No. 199 is usually considered to be Peele's composition; but the manuscript of the *Polyhymnia*, which is in the Library of St. John's College, Oxford, according to the Librarian, S. L. Grenstede, does not include this poem. David H. Horne in *The Life and Minor Works of George Peele* (New Haven: Yale University Press, 1952), pp. 169-73, appears to agree with Chambers that Lee may have been the author of this and other verses, perhaps in collaboration with Richard Edes of Christ Church.

[200] *Piæ, potenti, fœlicissimæ virgini*

Hand: Sir John Harington's.

No. 200 is the prayer which was written in letters of gold on the table hanging from the eglantine tree as mentioned in the quotation from Segar in the preceding Note. Another contemporary manuscript copy is in (*A*) Brit. Mus. MS. Add. 41499A, fol. 11ᵛ, headed, "Elisae," and written in ten lines only. This is the former Ditchley MS., which is described by Sir E. K. Chambers in *Sir Henry Lee*, 1936, Appendix D, pp. 268-75. The prayer was printed in (*B*) Sir William Segar's *Honor, Military, and Ciuill*, 1602, p. 198, with the introduction as given in the Note on No. 199, and headed, "Elizae, etc." The lineation differs somewhat from that in *AH*.

1 potenti] reginæ *A*
5 et ludicra] *omitted B*;
6 certamina] Triumphos *B*
10 quietam] quietem *A*: quetam *B*
11 æternum] externam *A*: Æternam *B*; quam] *omitted B*
13 suo] so suo *A* *probably a copyist's error*
14 Sic] *omitted B*
16 superit] superet *A B*
17 vt] ⟨yut⟩ vt *A*
19 Coronam dedit] coronan ⟨dedill⟩ dedit *A*
21 æterne] eternea *A*; Audi] aude *A*
22 exaudi] exaude *A*

In all probability Sir John Harington saw the pageant described in the preceding Note and made his copy of this prayer at the time.

PRELIMINARY NOTE ON NOS. 201-21

Sir John Harington's designation of these twenty-one sonnets as written by Henry Constable to the Lady Rich in 1589 is of exceptional importance. Other contemporary copies, described below, attribute them merely to "H.C.," and specifically associate only one of these with Lady Rich (No. 210). Furthermore, of the other copies only *E*, which has not been used by editors, assigns the date of composition to a time preceding the publication of Sidney's *Astrophel and Stella* in 1591. Circumstantial evidence, discussed below, supports the claim that some of Constable's sonnets were circulating in the late 1580's. That Sir John Harington was in a position to speak with authority about Constable's sonnets is indicated in the notes to Book XXXIV of his *Orlando Furioso* (ed. 1591, p. 288). He quotes a sonnet to King James VI of Scotland, "Where others hooded with blind loue do fly," introducing it as a composition by "the well learned Gentleman, and my very good frend *M. Henry Constable*." This personal association and the quality of the *AH* texts of Nos. 201-21 suggests a close connection with the author's manuscript.

These twenty-one sonnets are all found in three other contemporary sources:

(*A*) *Diana. The praises of his Mistres, in certaine sweete Sonnets. By H. C. London, Printed by I.*[*ohn*] *C.*[*harlewood*] *for Richard Smith . . . 1592.* 4°; sigs. A-D[4], signed in 3's, except A2, title page. Sig. D4 is blank.

I am indebted to Dr. Lisle C. John for permitting me to use her photostats of the unique copy in the Huntington Library (*S.T.C.* 5637). I am also indebted to Dr. E. K. Edmonds of the Huntington Library for information that sig. D3[v], on which is printed the "*Ultimo Sonnetto*" (*AH* No. 220), has the catchword "Blame" with a cancel clip pasted over it, and that the blank sig. D4 is genuine. This catchword, it may be noted, correctly appears on sig. B1[v], for the sonnet "Blame not my hart" (*AH* No. 2) is printed on sig. B2[r]. It is not necessary to suppose, as has been said, that the copy is incomplete (see J. P. Collier, *A Bibliographical and Critical Account of the Rarest Books in the English Language*, i [1866], 189, and Edward O'Brien's account of Constable in *Recusant Poets*, ed. Louise I. Guiney, i [1939], 306).

A has introductory material not found in other contemporary sources: a sonnet addressed "*To his absent Diana*," beginning, "Seuer'd from sweete Content, my liues sole light" (sig. A3[r]); a prose address "To the Gentlemen Readers" (sig. A4[r]), in which the sonnets are significantly described as "sonnes of no partiall Iudge, whose eies were acquainted with Beauties Riches" and "are now by misfortune left as Orphans." The *A* text of the *Diana* proper is made up of the twenty-one sonnets found in *AH* plus one additional sonnet, "*Sonnetto nono*," beginning, "Thine eye the glasse where I behold my hart" (sig. C1[r]), clearly a companion to *AH* No. 205. This missing sonnet in *AH* presents a breach in the curious but definite correspondence in the order of the sequence in *AH* and *A*, where its twenty-two sonnets are printed one to a page.

Using the *AH* numbering of the sonnets, we find that the *A* order is 201, 211, 202, 212, 203, 213, 204, 214, [additional sonnet], 215, 205, 216, 206, 217, 207, 218, 208, 219, 209, 221, 210, 220. What is the meaning of this relationship by jumps of ten, disturbed only by the missing sonnet in *AH* and by the reversal of order in the last two sonnets? If we suppose that the printer's manuscript of twenty-two sonnets had the first eleven written on the rectos and the second eleven on the versos, but that they were marked up for printing in the usual way, recto and verso, the printed book would have the order of *A*; whereas the author's manuscript would have an order close to that of *AH*. A study of the sequence reveals that the *AH* arrangement is in general more logical, although Nos. 220 and 221 are probably better in reverse, and No. 210 hardly belongs in the sequence itself. As is indicated below, the *AH* order of its twenty-one sonnets is followed with a few exceptions in the 1594 edition of the *Diana*. From the introductory material in the 1592 edition, it is evident that the book was brought out without the author's supervision. Reasons for the orphan state of Constable's poems in 1592 are discussed later.

As the collations show, the *A* texts of Nos. 201-21 are very close to those in *AH*, though with sufficient difference to make it clear that neither copy could have been made from the other. Nevertheless, this similarity in the texts themselves, considered with the peculiar but definite relationship in order and number, leads to the conclusion that *A* and *AH* stem from the same source, perhaps the author's manuscript. Evaluation of particular readings is given in the Notes.

William C. Hazlitt mentions *A* in the Preface to his edition of *Diana: The Sonnets and Other Poems of Henry Constable*, 1859, pp. v-viii. Evidently, however, he had not seen the book, for he states (p. vii) that he has printed the introductory sonnet (p. 19) from a transcript made by J. P. Collier, who formerly owned the copy. There is no indication that *A* was used by John Gray for his unannotated edition of *The Poems and Sonnets of Henry Constable*, 1897, which does not include the introductory sonnet and prose address of *A*.

(*B*) *Diana. or, The excellent conceitful Sonnets of H.C. Augmented with diuers Quatorzains of honorable and lerned personages. Deuided into viij Decads. . . . At London, Printed by Iames Roberts for Richard Smith 1594.* 16° in 8's, sigs. A^2, B-E^8, F^6, with A1, title page, unsigned, A2 signed, the remaining signed in 3's.

I am again indebted to Dr. Lisle John for use of her photostats of the Huntington Library copy of this edition (*S.T.C.* 5638).

This problematical volume contains seventy-six sonnets in a sequence by Constable and others, of whom Sidney is one. The last Decade is incomplete, having but six sonnets. *B* drops the introductory sonnet and prose address of *A* and substitutes a sonnet by the publisher, in which the ensuing sonnets are referred to as "these Orphan Poems." With three exceptions the *B* texts of Nos. 201-21 appear in the first two Decades, and the order in *B* is generally close to that of *AH*. Following the *AH* order, the *B* arrangement by Decades is: I, 1-4, 6-9; IV, 3; VIII, 6; II, 2, 3; III, 1; II, 1, 4-8, 10, 9. Thus *AH* Nos. 220 and 221 are reversed as in *A*, and No. 210 is printed as the last sonnet in *B*. The fifth sonnet of Decade I is "Thine eye the glasse," mentioned in the discussion of *A* as missing in the *AH* sequence. Significantly, the tenth sonnet of Decade I, not found either in *AH* or in *A*, beginning, "Heraulds at armes doe three perfections quote" (sig. B5v), plays upon the word *rich*, and was addressed to Lady Rich in *C* (see below). Even though the order has been changed, the *B* texts of the twenty-two sonnets common to *A* are clearly set up either from the first edition or from the manuscript used for it. A few corrections appear in the *B* variants.

The *B* text of the *Diana*, omitting the eight Sidney sonnets, was printed in *An English Garner*, ed. Edwin Arber, ii (1879), 225-64, and in *An English Garner, Elizabethan Sonnets*, ed. Sir Sidney Lee, ii (New York, Dutton, 1904), 75-114. Hazlitt, pp. 1-18, prints only twenty-seven sonnets from *B*, on the basis that the other sonnets are not Constable's (Preface, p. vii). In Gray's edition the *Diana* texts appear to come from *C*, but a few variants indicate that *B* was consulted.

(*C*) Dyce MS. 44.25.F.39 (South Kensington Museum, London), a miscellany chiefly in Elizabethan poetry, of 117 folios, written in one hand of late sixteenth or early seventeenth-century italic. It is sometimes referred to as the Todd MS. because it belonged to Henry J. Todd in 1801 (*The Poetical Works of John Milton*, ed. Todd, v [1801], 443-45). Since Thomas Park, to whom Todd presented the manuscript before 1812, printed his transcription of its Constable material, with an introductory account of the author and of the manuscript in *The Harleian Miscellany*, ix (rev. ed., 1812), 489-517, it is necessary here to call attention only to the most important features of *C*. On fols. 12r-44r are sixty-three sonnets headed, "H.C. sonets/ To his Mistrisse," followed by a separate sonnet addressed to Arabella Stuart and by two anonymous sonnets addressed to "H.C." The sixty-three sonnets are divided into three parts, each part containing three arguments, and each argument seven sonnets. Part I is "of variable affections of loue"; Part II is "the prayse of perticulars"; Part III is "tragicall, conteyning only lamentations" (for further account of the divisions, see Park, p. 492). Texts of Nos. 201-21, as shown in the Notes following, are included in the sixty-three sonnets. Not only do the *C* texts differ considerably, but the arrangement differs to such an extent that there is very little relationship. Following the *AH* order, texts of Nos. 201-21 appear in *C* in the following position: 1, 7, 2, 19, 61, 14, 57, 15, 5, 41, 6, 21, 47, 62, 9, 59,

44, 45, 17, 20, 16. Thus only the sequence of *AH* Nos. 217-18 is kept in *C* Nos. 44-45.

C contains five sonnets which are particularly concerned with Lady Rich. Two have to do with the birth and death of her daughter (see the Note on No. 210). One is addressed "To Mr. Hilliard, vpon occasion of a picture he made of my Ladie Rich," beginning, "If Michaell the archpainter now did liue" (fol. 31^v). Two sonnets are addressed to Lady Rich: "O that my songe like to a ship might be" (fol. 29^r; also in *E*), and "Heralds in armes doe three perfections coate" (fol. 29^v; also in *B* and *D*). It may be significant, however, that the final Constable sonnet in *E*, beginning, "My Mistrisse worth gaue wings vnto my Muse," appears to lay all before Arabella Stuart, for it is headed, "To the diuine protection of the Ladie Arbella the author commendeth both his Graces honoure and his Muses eternity" (fol. 43^r). It is possible that sonnets of the *Diana*, addressed at one time by Constable to Lady Rich, were later transferred to the protection of the Lady Arabella, for whom two other sonnets in *C* are particularly written. There is some reason to believe, indeed, that *C* may derive from a later revised manuscript of Constable's, for a recantation of his secular sonnets, written in the first person, appears at the end of the sequence (see Park, p. 517).

The *C* text, which contains thirty-eight sonnets not printed in *B*, offers a valuable addition to the Constable canon. Both Hazlitt and Gray made use of it for their editions of Constable.

Two other contemporary manuscripts contain versions of several of the *AH* Constable sonnets:

(*D*) Bodleian MS. Ashmole 38, one of the poetry collections formed by Elias Ashmole. On pp. 52-55, written in one hand of mixed secretary and italic, are fourteen unascribed Constable sonnets. The first, numbered 63 in the collection, is a version of No. 210; the second, numbered 64, is addressed to Margaret Countess of Cumberland and Anne Countess of Warwick, beginning, "Yee sister-muses, doe not you repine" (also in *C* and *E*). Entered as No. 65 the other twelve sonnets are addressed "To the Fairest that hath bine." Among these are version of *AH* Nos. 201, 202, 204, 205, 207, 214, 215, and 218, in the order, 1, 2, 3, 6, 8, 11, 4, 5. In addition *D* has copies of: "Thine Eye the Glass" (see *A* above), numbered 7; "Needes must I leaue & yett needes must I loue" (in *B*, sig. C8^r), numbered 9; "Hearaulds att armes" (see *B* and *C* above), numbered 10; "Each day new prooffs of new Dispayre" (in *B*, sig. D2^v), numbered 12.

There seems to be no reason to attribute any special authority to the *D* versions, which, as the collations show, frequently have unique variants of doubtful value. I find no evidence that *D* has been used by editors of Constable.

(*E*) Marsh Library MS. 183 Z 3.5.21 (Saint Patrick's Cathedral,

Dublin), a late sixteenth-century collection which was briefly noticed by Edward Dowden in "An Elizabethan MS. Collection: Henry Constable," *Modern Quarterly of Language and Literature*, ii (1898-99), 3-4. On fols. 25^{r}-28^{v}, written in one secretary hand, which appears in many other entries in the volume, are fifteen sonnets with ascription at the end to "H.C." Nine of these, in the order 4, 8, 13, 2, 15, 3, 14, 11, 2, present versions of *AH* Nos. 205, 206, 208, 209, 210, 215, 216, 219, 221. Of the remaining six sonnets in *E*, two, printed by Dowden, do not occur in the other sources. One of these is the first in the series, headed, "To his mistris turtuously intertayning him after hard & disgratious wordes," and beginning, "My hope laye gasping on his dying bed" (fol. 25^{r}). The other, the seventh in the series, is addressed "To the same Ladyes in imitation of Petrarch, riminge only w^{t} two wordes in eight significations," and beginning, "In Eden grew many a pleasant springe" (fol. 26^{v}). This follows the sonnet addressed to the Countesses of Cumberland and Warwick beginning, "Yee sister Muses doe not ye repine (see *D* above). In addition *E* has copies of: "The love wherwth your vertues chaine my spright," addressed to the queen, numbered 5 (also in *C*); "O that my songe lik to a shipp," numbered 9, addressed to Lady Rich in *C*; "Bloome of ye rose," addressed "To the kinge of Scotts," numbered 10 (also in *C*).

From the heading to the *E* version of No. 210 (see Note), it is evident that it was copied into the manuscript in 1588, and since that is the last sonnet in the *E* series, it is probable that the others were entered about the same time. If this is correct, and I see no reason to doubt it, *E* presents the earliest Constable source here described. On this account peculiar interest is attached to the *E* versions, which sometimes differ considerably from the others. Note especially the *E* version of No. 206. On the other hand, the *E* text of No. 215 agrees exactly with that in *AH*, and in other instances there are indications of a relation with the later *C* MS. While no one of the *E* sonnets is there addressed to Lady Rich, it is interesting that *E* variants in Nos. 205 and 216 afford further examples of puns upon the word *rich*.

Like *D* and *AH*, *E* has not been used by editors of Constable's poems, but, as can readily be understood from the above account, it should not be ignored. Some of its readings, it is true, appear to be of doubtful value, but it adds two sonnets to the Constable canon, and it supports *AH* in assigning the composition of some of Constable's sonnets to a date preceding the publication of the *Astrophel and Stella* in 1591.

Letters concerning Constable's political activities in 1589 present further evidence that some of his secular sonnets were circulating in that year, prove conclusively that he was then closely associated with Lady Rich, as well as with others to whom he addressed particular sonnets, and may explain why it was that his sonnets had become "orphans" by

1592. This material, preserved at Hatfield (*Calendar of the Manuscripts of the Most Hon. the Marquis of Salisbury, K.G.*, Hist. MSS. Comm., iii [1889], 438-42), has been dealt with by O'Brien (ref. above, pp. 304-05), but it may be well to review the main points here. A letter from Thomas Fowler to Lord Burghley, dated October 20, 1589, reveals that Constable was then on a secret mission to King James VI of Scotland, acting in the service of the Earl of Essex and Lord and Lady Rich. Constable is said to have brought Lady Rich's picture (perhaps the one done by Hilliard). He also brought messages from the Countesses of Warwick and Cumberland and a special one from Lady Mary Talbot, who seemed to suspect that he might be on the side of Lady Arabella Stuart rather than on that of James VI. It is highly significant that Constable addressed sonnets to all of these ladies, as well as to the king of Scotland, and it is reasonable to believe that some of these sonnets, at any rate, as well as those to Lady Rich, were written about this time, or earlier. Two letters written by Richard Douglas, a confidante of James VI, on November 2, 1589, after Constable's return to London, throw some further light on Constable's literary and political activities. In a letter to Constable, after mentioning an unsuccessful interview with the king, Douglas wrote, "I am busy here with one of your books which I received yesternight from Mr. Hilman. I see perfectly therein the draughts of the spirit of my *Sconsolato* (?), which I honour." Though somewhat cryptic, it appears that Douglas was referring to Constable's love poems. Douglas' second letter, written in French to "V.S.P.," reveals that Constable had made reports to the French about affairs in Scotland. O'Brien reasonably infers that these letters were intercepted by Cecil (since they are at Hatfield), and deduces further "that Constable fled the country because he was suspected of treasonable dealings with James VI, and that he remained abroad because he had meanwhile become a Catholic." He seems to have been converted to Catholicism in 1591. He appears not to have returned to England until 1604, although he came to Scotland on a religio-political mission in 1599. After he became a Catholic, Constable was engaged in various plans and efforts to bring about a reconversion of the English and the Scottish to the Catholic faith (see O'Brien, pp. 305-15). On his return to England in 1604, he was imprisoned in the Tower. It is, therefore, not difficult to understand why his "orphan" poems were published without his full name and without any dedication to Lady Rich, or to other ladies. Despite this comparative anonymity in publication, Constable's poetic achievements were well known to many of his literary contemporaries, who accorded him high praise (see Hazlitt, "Biographical Notice," pp. xv-xviii, and O'Brien, p. 316).

Insufficient attention has been given to Constable's work by modern scholars. Perhaps the fullest discussion of the *Diana* is the chapter in

Janet G. Scott's *Les Sonnets Élizabéthains* (Paris: Librairie Ancienne Honoré Champion [1929], pp. 129-42), where his use of foreign source materials is related to a brief analysis of his style as represented in the 1594 *Diana*. A table of his sources is appended (pp. 314-17). The conventional themes and conceits in the *Diana* are considered by Lisle C. John in *Elizabethan Sonnet Sequences* (1938). In her conclusion she very appropriately remarks, "As for Constable, so much work remains to be done in the matter of the authenticity of the text that it is impossible to speak definitely of his style" (p. 176). Perhaps the lack of such a text prevented Rosemond Tuve in her study of *Elizabethan and Metaphysical Imagery* (Chicago: University of Chicago Press, 1947) from elaborating more fully her few suggestive comments about characteristics of Constable's style which are prescient of the manner of the metaphysical poets (see the Notes to Nos. 205 and 212).

It is to be hoped that some one will soon undertake a definitive study of Constable and his work.

I wish to express my thanks to my former student, Mr. Ivan Schreiber, for assisting me with the preparation of some parts of my notes on Constable.

[201] *Resolvd to love, vnworthye to obtayne*

Hand: Sir John Harington's. The numbering is contemporary.

See the preliminary Note on Nos. 201-21.

Collation is given with the following copies:

A, sig. B1^r^, where it is "*Sonetto primo.*"

B, sig. B1^r^, where it is "SONNET .1." under "The first Decad."

C, fol. 12^v^, where it is "Sonet. 1," under Part I, Argument I, "The first 7 only of the byrth and beginning of his loue."

D, p. 52, numbered "I" of twelve sonnets addressed "To the Fairest that hath bine."

2 not] no *A-D*
3 syghs] sigthes *D*
5 myne] my *A-D*
8 sustayne] ⟨sh⟩ sustayne *D*
9 thyne ey bred] thy lookes broed *D*; myne] my *C*
10 for] with *D*
11 be] are *A-C*
12 favors] favoure *C*
14 yowr] thyne *C*; geveth] bringeth *D*; the] my *D*

Although the variants are not striking, they present a few points that should be noticed. Only the two printed versions, *A* and *B*, agree entirely, but this indicates only that *B* was probably set up from *A*, which did not have the author's supervision. Consideration of the readings leads to the conclusion, I believe, that *AH* has the best text, with the possible exception of "yowr" in line 14, where "thyne" as given in *C* only is in keeping with usage in the rest of the poem. *C*, however, fails in line 9 to use the customary *mine* rather than *my* before words beginning with a vowel sound. This principle is evidently followed by *AH* in line 5, where "myne hart" indicates the dropping of the *h* sound. In line 12 of *C* the singular "favour" does not retain parallelism with "wonders" in line 11. In the same line *AH* and *D* employ the older "be" rather than "are"; but *D* is exceptionally poor in "lookes" of line 9, which is not in keeping with the context. There seems to be no doubt that this was the first sonnet in the series, for all copies concur on that point.

In Martin Peerson's *Priuate Musicke, or the first booke of Ayres and Dialogues*, 1620, the second song, set for four voices, is made up of the first quatrain of No. 201 and the first two quatrains of No. 7, as follows:

Resolu'd to loue, vnworthy to obtaine,
I doe no fauour craue, but humble wise,
To thee my sighes in verse I sacrifice,
Onely some pitty and no helpe to gaine.

Much sorrow in itselfe my loue doth moue,
More my dispaire to loue a hopelesse blisse:
My folly most to loue when sure to misse,
Oh helpe me but this last griefe to remoue.

All paine is you command it, ioy shall praie;
And wisdome to seeke ioy: then say but this,
Because my pleasure in thy torment is,
I doe command thee without hope to loue.

Since the British Museum copy of *Priuate Musicke* is imperfect, the song is here quoted from a copy made by Kathleen Tillotson from the Bodleian copy of the book.

[202] *Blame not myne hart for flying vp to hye*

Hand: Sir John Harington's. The numbering is contemporary.
See the preliminary Note on Nos. 201-21.
Collation is given with the following copies:
A, sig. B2r, where it is "*Sonnetto terzo.*"
B, sig. B1v, where it is "SONNET .II." of "The first Decad."

C, fol. 15^{v}, entitled, "An excuse to his Mistrisse for resoluing to Loue so worthye a creature. Sonet. 7," in Part I, Argument I.

D, p. 52, sonnet "2," addressed "To the fairest that hath bine."

1 myne] my *A-D*; to] so *C*
2 his] this *A-D*
4 become] begin *A*: begun *B D*
5 Myne] My *C*; thyne] thy *A-D*
6 drawn] Drawen *C*
7 thow] then *A B D*; myne] my *A-D*
8 may] shall *D*
9 I . . . not] Blame not I say againe *C*
12 drawth] drawes *A B D*: doth draw *C*; other] others *C*
13 a so] and so *A-D*

It is evident that *AH* and *C* have the best reading in line 4 and also, I should say, in "thow" of line 7. The *AH* "a so" in line 13 is clearly a copyist's error. For comment on the use of *mine* and *my*, see the preceding Note. It should be noted that *D* agrees with *AH* and *B* in giving this as the second sonnet.

Janet G. Scott, p. 136 (see preliminary Note) points out that lines 3 and 4 may have been suggested to Constable by two lines in the *Complainte* of Desportes (p. 49, ed. Michiels):

> Tous les astres divins qui dans le ciel ont place
> Sont nourris des vapeurs de ceste terre basse.

The conceit of the sonnet is nicely developed by means of parallelism and contrast.

[203] *ffly low my Love, thy Sonne dost thow not see*

Hand: lines 1-4, Sir John Harington's; lines 5-14, another secretary hand, not appearing elsewhere in *AH*, which continues through No. 221. The second hand is written in a different ink. The numbering is contemporary.

See the preliminary Note on Nos. 201-21.

Collation is given with the following:

A, sig. $B3^{r}$, where it is "*Sonnetto quinto.*"

B, sig. $B2^{r}$, where it is "SONNET .III." of "The first Decad."

C, fol. 13^{r}, entitled, "Of the byrth of his Loue. Sonet. 2.," in Part I, Argument I.

1 my] deare *A-C*
2 asp⟨a⟩yre] aspire *A-C*
3 wreakfull] kindled *C*
5 haply] happely *C*; saiest] saist *A-C*

6 so] *omitted* *C*
9 made] caus'd *C*
11 by] of *C*
14 art thou] thow art *C*

As frequently, the *C* version shows a divergence which could not be accepted without further investigation into its authority.

The sonnet as a whole reflects a common Platonic influence, and again the idea is deftly handled by Constable by the device of antithesis. Janet Scott (p. 315, ref. above) calls attention to analogues in Desportes, *Cléonice*, II, and Ronsard, *Astrée*, I.

[204] *A frind of myne pitying my hopeles love*

Hand: the second of No. 203.

See the preliminary Note on Nos. 201-21.

Collation:

A, sig. B4^{r}, "*Sonnetto settimo.*"

B, sig. B2^{v}, "SONNET .IIII." in "The first Decad."

C, fol. 21^{v}, "Of his Mistrisse vpon occasion of a friend of his wch disswaded him from Louing. Sonet 5," Part I, Argument III.

D, p. 53, No. "3" of the sonnets "To the Fairest that hath bine."

1 pitying] moaning *C*; hopeles] helplesse *C*
2 love] hope *A*
4 hart] mynde *D*
5 sith] since *D*
6 as long] soe long *D*; stay] sway *D*
9 impossibillitie] impossibilities *A B D*
11 the powr] the power *A B*: the powers *C*: thy power *D*; thy] *omitted* *C D*; divinitie] diuinities *A B*
12 me] my *D*

A study of the variants shows, I think, that *AH* has the best text, especially evident in lines 9 and 11, opposing *A B D*, and in line 1, opposing *C*.

[205] *Myne eye wth all the deadlie synns ys fraught*

Hand: the second of No. 203; contemporary numbering.

See the preliminary Note on Nos. 201-21.

Collation:

A, sig. C2^{r}, "*Sonnetto vndeci.*"

B, sig. B3^{v}, "SONNET .VI." in "The first Decad."

C, fol. 41^{v}, "Sonet. 5" in Part III, Argument III, which is entitled, "Of the end and death of his Loue."

D, p. 53, No. "6" of the sonnets "To the Fairest that hath bine."

E, fol. 25^{v}, the fourth sonnet by "H.C."

F, that is, *A Poetical Rhapsody*, 1602, sig. L6^{v} (ed. Rollins, No. 174), "SONNET," ascribed, "H. C."

2 sith . . . looke] because it is cause y^{t} *E*
3 a watchman being stood gasing bye] . . . being made stood . . . *A-D F*: my loue p^{r}sumd: & Slothfull is for why *E*
4 and . . . caught] save only gaze about it, it doth ⟨not⟩ naught *E*
5 bears envie that] wch envith y^{t} *E*; my] by *B F*
7 myne eye] my Eye *D*: it hath *E*
8 consent gave] was accessarie *C*
9 And] Then *D*; yt neuer should remove] . . . would . . . *A-D F*: whose only god is this *E*
10 from . . . sight] beawtyes ritche treasure hourded in my hart *E*
Lines 11-12 are transposed in A B D F.
11 drunck euery night] wch drunken is *E*
12 vnchast . . . love] A Baude vnchast betwene my thoughte and loue *D*: and all these sins shew how Vnchast y^{u} art *E*
13 these . . . haue] Thus haue thes sinns procured *D*: And therfore y^{u} deserust *E*
14 wherfore . . . ys] & therfore I am *E*; loves fire] Loues sweete fire *A-C F*: Loue hir fire *E*; damned] dampnd *E*

A, *B*, *D* and *F* number the seven sins in the margins, and since lines 11 and 12 are transposed in these texts, gluttony is the seventh sin. Although this order in the lines results in the rhyme pattern *c d c d*, often used by Constable in the third quatrain, it also destroys the climactic effect gained in *AH* and *C* by making the line "vnchast a bawd betweene my hart and love" the end of the analysis of the sins, which better fits the context of the poem. *E* also has the order of *AH*, but it differs to such an extent that it reads like a copy written from memory, or one deliberately changed by the copyist. In line 10, however, it has an interesting pun upon *rich*. *D* is as usual mediocre and *C* is doubtful in line 8. With the exception of the two words omitted in lines 3 and 14, *AH* presents a good text. If the transposed order of lines 11-12 is preferred, *A* offers the best text, followed by *B*, which has a mistaken variant in line 5. *F* was evidently printed from *B*.

As I have pointed out in the preliminary Note, *AH* lacks two of the twenty-three sonnets first printed in *A*: the sonnet of address and one other. This second sonnet, which begins, "Thine eye the glasse where I behold my hart," is clearly a companion to No. 205, which it immediately precedes in *B*, "SONNET V," sig. B3^{r}. In *A* it is printed on the preceding recto, sig. C1^{r}, as "*Sonnetto nono*." For the text of this missing sonnet, see *Diana*, ed. Hazlitt, p. 4.

No. 205 is a good example of the figure *prolepsis*. In a discussion of division by "a general with his specials," Rosemond Tuve (*Elizabethan and Metaphysical Imagery*, 1947, p. 307) calls particular attention to this sonnet, commenting that Constable "starts up images which are quite radical and subtle enough for the next century." She thinks this effect is not noticed because the images "are not sufficiently brilliant to outshine certain uses of conventions." The conceit of the war between the eye and the heart is, of course, conventional (see Lisle C. John, *Elizabethan Sonnet Sequences*, 1938, pp. 93-102).

[206] *ffalslie dothe envie of your prayses blame*

Hand: the second in No. 203.

See the preliminary Note on Nos. 201-21.

Collation:

A, sig. C3^{r}, "*Sonnetto tredeci.*"

B, sig. B4^{r}, "SONNET .VII." in "The first Decad."

C, fol. 19^{r}, "Of the slander envye giues him for so highlye praysing his Mistresse, Sonet. 7" in Part I, Argument II.

5 sayth] sayd *C*; hath] had *C*
7 that . . . flatterer] needs my heart a flatterer must *C*: . . . flattrer *A*
9 thee I] I thee *C*
10 sith . . . sunn] sith sun in world *C*
11 thee I] I thee *C*
13 in] is *C*
14 seen thee] thee seene *C*

Lines 7 and 10 in *C* suggest a reviser's hand. A version in *E*, fol. 26^{v}, differs to such an extent that it must be quoted in full. It is the eighth of the sonnets attributed to "H. C." in that manuscript.

ffalse the report, & vniust is ye blame
that envye of your praise imputes to mee
when it arreastes my penn of flatterye
for honoringe too muche thy sacred name.

And calls my tonge y^{e} ꝑciall trompe of fame
for saying that ther is no sūne but thee
and eke would burne my hart for heresye
sithe obstinate it doth beleve the same

No, no, I flatter not when thee I call
the sūne, the sūne was never suche
but when the sūne the I compard wth all
doubtlesse the sūne I flattered too muche

And thoghe I erd, my hart cañ not for this
be burnt, for it already burned is.

[207] *Much sorrowe in yt self my love dothe move*

Hand: the second in No. 203.
See the preliminary Note on Nos. 201-21.
Collation:
A, sig. C4r, "*Sonnetto quindeci.*"
B, sig. B4v, "SONNET .VIII." in "The first Decad."
C, fol. 39v, "The last 7 of the end and death of his Loue. Sonet. 1" in Part III, Argument III.
D, p. 54, No. "8" of the sonnets "To the Fairest that hath bine."

3 whom] where *C*
5 payne] paines *A B D*; shall] doth *C*
9 sorrowe] sorrowes *C D*
10 myne] my *A B*; folly] pleasure *D*
11 shall] will *D*
13 your] my *C*; and] but *D*; my] youre *C*

A study of the variants indicates, I think, that *AH* presents the best text. The readings of *C* and *D*, especially in lines 10 and 13, are inferior, even to the extent of missing the point in these particular lines. Other variants are slight, and *AH* and *B* differ in two instances only, in lines 5 and 10. It is impossible to know whether Constable used the singular "payne" in line 5, but it is surely more effective than the plural, and, further, is parallel with singular forms used in other lines of the sonnet. In the Note on No. 201 I have commented on the common use of *mine* before vowel sounds; hence we might expect to find it here in line 10. *A* differs from *AH* and *B* in line 3 with "where" instead of "whom." Either reading is acceptable, but presumably *B* gives a corrected line.

For use of a portion of this sonnet in Martin Peerson's *Priuate Musicke*, see the Note on No. 201.

[208] *My ladyes presenc makes the roses redd*

Hand: the second of No. 203.
See the preliminary Note on Nos. 201-21.
Collation:
A, sig. D1r, "*Sonnetto decisette.*"
B, sig. B5r, "SONNET .IX." in "The first Decad."
C, fol. 19v, "The thyrd of seuerall occasions and accidents happening in the life tyme of his Loue. Of his Mistrisse vpon occasion of her walking in a garden. Sonet. 1" in Part I, Argument III.
E, fols. 27v-28r, the thirteenth in the sonnets by "H.C."

4 and] and her *A-C E*
5 the leavs abrode dothe] abroad the leaues did *C*: hir . . . *E*
6 sunn] sunnes *A-C*; powr] power *C*
8 wth] in *A B*
9 flowrs] flowers *C*; vertue] virtues *E*
11 do] doth *A B*
12 quyckeneth] quickneth *C*
13 the] these *C E*

AH is lacking a word in line 4, but other than that gives a good text, probably the best. More euphonious than the possessive form and quite as logical is the "sunn" of line 6, which is equated with "her powr."

Although conventional, this is one of Constable's most charming sonnets.

[209] *When your pfections to my thoughts appeare*

Hand: the second of No. 203.
See the preliminary Note on Nos. 201-21.
Collation:
A, sig. D2^{r}, "*Sonnetto decinoue.*"
B, sig. D1^{r}, "SONNET .III." in "The fourth Decad."
C, fol. 14^{v}, "Of the discouragement he had to proceed in Loue through the multitude of his Ladies perfections and his owne Lownesse. Sonet 5" in Part I, Argument I.
E, fol. 25^{r}, the second of the sonnets by "H. C."

1 thoughts] thought *C*
2 amonnge] amongst *E*; we] he *C*
5 cost] ost *B* *printer's error*
6 love] hope *C*
10 heaps] heape *C*
13 out gold] not loue *A B*: out Loue *C E*
14 drowned] damned *C*

It is paradoxical that *C*, which has poor variants in lines 1, 2, 6, and 10, and *E*, which is often unreliable, should have in line 13 the reading which almost certainly expresses the author's meaning. That is, if the comparison of the sestet is logically developed, the word *love* is preferable to *gold*. *A* and *B*, however, destroy the sense by having *not* instead of *out*.

[210] *ffaire by inherytanc whome borne wee see*

Hand: the second of No. 203.
See the preliminary Note on Nos. 201-21.
Collation:

A, sig. D3^{r}, "A calculation vpon the birth of an honourable Ladies daughter, borne in the yeare, 1588. & on a Friday," not numbered, but follows the *A* text of No. 221, which is the twentieth sonnet in the numbered series of *A*.

B, sig. F6^{v}, headed as in *A*, not numbered, but is the last sonnet in the volume, that is, the sixth sonnet in "The eyght Decad."

C, fol. 32^{v}, "A calculation of the natiuitye of the Ladie Riches daughter borne vpon friday in the yeare 1588. comonly call'd the yeare of wonder. Sonet. 6," Part II, Argument III.

D, p. 52, "A Calculation vppon the birth of the Ladye Riches Daughter, borne Anno 1588, & on A friday," the first of the Constable sonnets in *D*, but not in the numbered series (see the Note on No. 201).

E, fol. 28^{r,v}, "A sonnet in manner of a calculation on ye natiuitye of a yonge Ladye borne on a friday, in this yeare, 1588," the last of the Constable sonnets in *E*, with the ascription "H.C." following.

2 on] in *C*; the day] that day *D*
3 fairest beare the] fairest Planet beareth *A-E*
4 the . . . do decree] . . . doth decree *A D*: The wonders loe of beautyes destinye *C*: to thee the heavens this destenye decree *E*
5 shalt] shall *D*
7 hoastes] hoste *E*; thy face] thyn Eye *D*
8 as] That *D*; rest] worth *D*
12 so . . . mother] Thy mother so shall *C E*
13 already she hathe] she hath alreadie *C E*
14 as] That *D*; behynd] for the *D*; shall] doth *C*: will *D*: do *E*

The *AH* text is obviously faulty in line 3. Omission of the word *planet* results not merely in a shortened line but in a failure to designate clearly the day of birth as that under the sovereignty of Venus, i.e., Friday. Otherwise the *AH* text agrees with *B*, which has properly corrected the "doth" of *A* in line 4 to "doe." Mention of Lady Rich's name in the title of the poem was probably deliberately withheld from the two printed copies, just as the *Diana* sonnets as a whole were not published as addressed to her. The variants of lines 4, 12, and 13 suggest a possible relationship between *C* and *E*. From the title of the latter, the only one of the manuscripts not naming Lady Rich, it is clear that the *E* copy was made in 1588, and, therefore, it must be the earliest of the copies.

The child for whom this "Calculation" was made was probably born on Friday, November 22, 1588, for "the Lord Rich his child" was christened on Tuesday, November 26, 1588, when Queen Elizabeth presented a bowl with a silver gilt cover (John Nichols, *The Progresses and Public Processions of Queen Elizabeth*, ii [1823], 115). No doubt Constable's sonnet, which is a deftly turned compliment to Lady Rich, was written shortly thereafter, and before March 25, 1588/89, had been copied into the *E* MS. On the early death of this child, Constable skilfully retracted his "Calculation" in another sonnet, "He that by skill of stars doth fates foretell," which again compliments the mother (printed by Thomas Park in *The Harleian Miscellany*, ix, 514, from the *C* MS., where it is Sonnet 7 in Part III, Argument II; also in W. C. Hazlitt's edition of Constable's poems, p. 45; and in Gray's edition, p. lxxxiii).

[211] *It may be love my death dothe not pretend*

Hand: the second of No. 203.

See the preliminary Note on Nos. 201-21.

Collation:

A, sig. B1v, "*Sonnetto secondo.*"

B, sig. B6v, "SONNET .II." in "The second Decad."

C, fol. 15r, "How he encouraged himselfe to proceede in Loue and to hope for favoure in the ende at Loues hands. Sonet 6," in Part I, Argument I.

1 my . . . not] doth not my death *C*
2 shoote] shootes *A-C*
7 part where] place that *C*
8 partie] parties *A-C*; his] the *C*
11 suffering] suffring *A B*
13 picture] pictures *A-C*
14 picture] pictures *A-C*; thy] my *A B*

The *AH* use of the nominative instead of the possessive forms in lines 8, 13, and 14 is, of course, in accord with frequent Elizabethan usage, and since the added *s* is less euphonious in these lines, it is probable that Constable deliberately chose the nominative forms. *AH* is probably wrong in use of the singular "shoote" in line 2, since the parallel "thinks" follows immediately. In line 14, however, "thy," as in *AH* and *C*, is essential to the point of the sonnet.

Janet Scott (p. 135) calls attention to a sonnet by Desportes, *Hippolyte*, XXII, to which Constable may have been indebted for the general idea and final point in No. 211. So deftly is the rather involved and antithetical conceit handled in this sonnet that we may wonder just how well John Donne knew Constable's poetry.

[212] *The sunn his iorney ending in the west*

Hand: the second of No. 203.

See the preliminary Note on Nos. 201-21.

Collation:

A, sig. B2^{v} "*Sonnetto quattro.*"

B, sig. B7^{r}, "SONNET .III." in "The second Decad."

C, fol. 22^{v}, "Of the thoughtes he nourished by night when she was retired to bed. Sonet. 7," in Part I, Argument III.

3 eyes] sightes *C*
5 sunn] same *C*
6 to] so *C*
11 beame] beames *A-C*; night] nights *A B*
14 my] the *C*; his] the *C*

In line 11 "nights," as in *A* and *B*, is required to rhyme with "lights" in line 9. I see no reason why the independent variants in *C* need serious consideration.

Rosemond Tuve (*Elizabethan and Metaphysical Imagery*, 1947, p. 134, n. 21) comments on the "cosmological detail" in this sonnet, which illustrates use of learned language "supposedly typical of the later poets," i.e., the "metaphysicals." We may also note that the logical development is in keeping with recognized methods of the later school. Janet Scott (p. 315) calls attention to parallels in Desportes and A. di Costanzo.

[213] *Vncyvile sycknes hast thou no regard*

Hand: the second of No. 203.

See the preliminary Note on Nos. 201-21.

Collation:

A, sig. B3^{v}, "*Sonnetto sesto.*"

B, sig. C3^{r}, "SONNET .I." in "The thyrd Decad."

C, fol. 35^{v}, "Complaynt of his Ladies sicknesse. Sonet. 5," Part III, Argument I.

5 then] thou *A-C*; hath not] neuer *C*
6 my] myne *C*
7 thought] thoughts *C*
8 wronngs] thoughts *C*; they] but *C*
9 then] for *C*
12 payne] paynes *C*
13 that] if *C*; revenged] rewarded *C*
14 shold] might *A B*; her] my *C*

The *C* variants result in an inferior text, especially marked in lines 13 and 14, where the sense is reversed and the point lost.

This treatment of the conventional theme of illness of the beloved by means of ingenious antithesis is typical of Constable. Contrast Sidney in *Astrophel and Stella*, CI.

[214] *yf true love might true loves reward obteine*

Hand: the second of No. 203.
See the preliminary Note on Nos. 201-21.
Collation:
A, sig. B4^{v}, "*Sonnetto ottauo.*"
B, sig. B6^{r} "SONNET .I." in "The second Decad."
C, fol. 42^{r}, "Sonet. 6," Part III, Argument III.
D, p. 55, No. "11" of the sonnets "To the Fairest that hath bine."

2 could] might *A B D*
4 sigh'd] sighe *D*: lou'd *C*
7 mights] mightst *A-D*
8 sight] praise *B D*
11 love] loues *D*
12 wold'st] wilt *C D*

The *AH* text is superior except perhaps for "mights" in line 7, which may be the fault of the copyist. In line 2 "could" and in line 8 "sight" better fit the sense than do the variants; further, the accent in the third iambic foot falls with more appropriate emphasis on "could" than on "might." Line 11 is interesting. By the juxtaposition of strong accents in the middle of the line, the dramatic conflict between pain and beauty is heightened.

[215] *Lady in bewtie and in favor rare*

Hand: the second of No. 203.
See the preliminary Note on Nos. 201-21.
Collation:
A, sig. C1^{v}, "*Sonnetto decimo.*"
B, sig. B7^{v}, "SONNET .IIII." in "The second Decad."
C, fol. 16^{v}, "Sonet 2," Part I, Argument II.
D, p. 53, No. "4" in the sonnets "To the Fairest that hath bine."
E, fol. 25^{r,v}, the third sonnet by "H. C."

5 nor] *omitted* *A*: And *C*; on me] on poore mee *A*;
bestow'd] bestowed *C*: you bestowed *D*
8 deare] great *D*
10 then] than *A B*; should vnto] that myght to *D*
13 do] may *C*: doth *D*

It is unusual to find such close agreement among the several copies, for *D* only shows any marked difference. Exceptionally *E* offers a good text, which agrees exactly with *AH*.

Built on the word *favor*, the sonnet is a graceful compliment, which becomes more formal in the *D* version by the substitution of *great* for *dear* in line 8.

[216] *My reason absent did myne eyes requyre*

Hand: the second of No. 203.
See the preliminary Note on Nos. 201-21.
Collation:
A, sig. C2^{v}, "*Sonnetto dodeci.*"
B, sig. B8^{r}, "SONNET .V." in "The second Decad."
C, fol. 40^{v}, "Sonet. 3," Part III, Argument III.
E, fol. 28^{r}, the fourteenth sonnet by "H.C."

1 My] *omitted* *E*
3 they . . . hart] neare my heart they should *C*
5 hopes guyfts] ritch hope *E*
6 and] yet *E*
7 was] were *A-C*
8 w^{ch} . . . quench'd] thoghe not to quenche, yet to asswage *E*
9 retorned] returnd *A B*
11 my] mine *E*
12 wished] wicked *E*
13 sithe] since *E*

AH gives the best text, for the context demands "was" in line 7, and the rhythm pronunciation of *ed* in line 9. It is doubtful that the independent *E* variants have authority, although line 5 of *E* may be another example of a play upon the name of Lady Rich. The variant "wicked" in line 12 is perhaps possible but hardly in keeping with the author's meaning.

Although this treatment of the war between the eyes and the heart may have been suggested to Constable by Desportes, *Diane* II, XLVII, as Janet Scott points out (p. 315), the legal imagery, logically developed, is prescient of the later metaphysical school.

[217] *Wounder yt ys and pittie ys that she*

Hand: the second of No. 203.
See the preliminary Note on Nos. 201-21.
Collation:
A, sig. C3^{v}, "*Sonnetto quaterdeci.*"
B, sig. B8^{v}, "SONNET .VI." in "The second Decad."
C, fol. 34^{r}, "Sonet. 2.," Part III, Argument I.

1 ys that] ist that *A B*: tis that *C*
3 or] and *A B*
6 yf bewty] if that Beautie *A-C*
7 then] than *A*; he] I *C*

9 pore] yonge *C*
12 sithe] for *C*
14 then] than *A B*

Clearly in lines 7 and 9 the meaning requires "than," for which the spelling "then" was used interchangeably. Omission of "that" in line 6 of *AH* was perhaps the fault of the copyist, just as the "ist" of line 1 in *A* and *B* may well have been a typographical error; but the *C* readings in lines 7 and 14 must surely be contrary to the author's meaning. It is probable that in line 3 Constable is once more playing upon the name of Lady Rich.

[218] *Pitty refusing my pore love to feed*

Hand: the second of No. 203.
See the preliminary Note on Nos. 201-21.
Collation:
A, sig. C4^{v}, "*Sonnetto sedeci.*"
B, sig. C1^{r}, "SONNET .VII." in "The second Decad."
C, fol. 34^{v}, "Sonet. 3," Part III, Argument I.
D, p. 53, No. "5" in the sonnets "To the Fairest that hath bine."

2 help] food *D*
3 youre] thy *D*
4 thenc] *omitted* *C*; graunts] grace *D*; might] may *C*: would *D*
5 but] There *D*; some] an *D*; almouse] almes *A-D*
Line is omitted in D.
8 two onely] One Cherrye *D*; may saue liefe] life may saue *C*: may giue helpe *D*; in this] to all *D*
10 my love] me (Deare) *D*
11 neuer] onlye *D*; but on] but of *C*: vppon *D*
13 for] And *D*; this] that *D*
14 cann] May *D*

In line 5 with the independent "almouse," that is, alms house, I suggest that *AH* has the authoritative reading, for the image of the house is indicated in lines 3 and 6. The inferior *D* version must have been written down from memory.

It is evident that Nos. 217 and 218, both dealing with the Anacreontic Cupid, are companion sonnets, and that the sense demands the order as given in *AH*, *B*, and *C*. Although comparison of the lips to cherries is conventional with Elizabethan poets, the figure here is distinctively treated and a sense of the dramatic is introduced by the dialogue.

[219] *The fowler hides as closslie as he may*

Hand: the second of No. 203.

See the preliminary Note on Nos. 201-21.

Collation:

A, sig. D1^{v}, "*Sonnetto deciotto.*"

B, sig. C1^{v}, "SONNET .VIII." in "The second Decad."

C, fol. 20^{v}, "Of his Ladies vayle wherewth she covered her. Sonet 3," Part I, Argument III.

E, fol. 27^{v}, "To his Ladye wearing a vaile ouer hir heade," the eleventh sonnet by "H.C."

3 least he] least that *C*: that it *E*; should but] it should *C*: should not *E*
4 for . . . forc'd] be forst for feare *E*
7 putts] put *B*; flee] see *C*
10 that] w^{ch} *C*; tame] tane *A B*
11 yt may] maie it *A-C E*
13 need] needs *C*

The question of the superior text rests with *A* and *AH*, which differ only in lines 10 and 11. In the former "tame," as in *AH*, is demanded to rhyme with "same" in line 12. The reversed order in line 11 is unimportant.

The conceit of the net as a device for snaring the lover is common among the Petrarchans. See Janet Scott (p. 315) for some references to parallels.

[220] *ffaire sunn yf you would haue me prayse you^{r} light*

Hand: the second of No. 203.

See the preliminary Note on Nos. 201-21.

Collation:

A, sig. D3^{v}, "*Vltimo Sonnetto.*"

B, sig. C2^{v}, "SONNET .X." in "The second Decad."

C, fol. 22^{r}, "Of his Ladies goeing over earlye to bed, so depriving him to soone of her sight. Sonet. 6," Part I, Argument III.

4 as I haue] That I had *C*
9 but] and *A B*
11 though] if *C*
13 dothe] doo *A-C*
14 be] is *A B*

Although the variants are slight, *AH* consistently presents the preferable readings. Since the subject matter of No. 220 rather than that of No.

221 makes a fitting close to a sequence, or to a division within the sequence, it would appear that *A* and *B* correctly reverse the order of these two sonnets.

No. 220 presents a deft antithetical treatment of the conventional theme of bestowing immortality upon the beloved through verse. The poet's compliment is even more extravagant.

[221] *Sweet hand the sweet but cruel bowe thou art*

Hand: the second of No. 203.

See the preliminary Note on Nos. 201-21.

Collation:

A, sig. D2^{v}, "*Sonnetto vinti.*"

B, sig. C2^{r}, "SONNET .IX.," in "The second Decad."

C, fol. 20^{r}, "To his Ladies hand vpon occasion of her glove wch in her absence he kissed. Sonet. 2.," Part I, Argument III.

E, fol. 27^{v}, "To his Ladyes hand," the twelfth sonnet by "H.C."

1 but] yet *C E*
4 my] in *C*: in my *E*
8 five] same *C*
10 that shoot] that shot *A B E*: wch shotte *C*
11 the] thy *E*; the] a *E*
13 some] I *C*
14 this . . . this] Thy . . . thy *C*: those . . . these *E*; shrine] shine *C*

Thus *AH*, *A*, and *B* agree except in the variant "shot" of line 10, which gives the required tense. Line 4, unsatisfactory in these three texts, may have been written, "bear in my brest . . . ," or as in *C* or *E*, although the latter results in a line of six feet.

Janet Scott points out that in this sonnet Constable has taken as his model Desportes, *Divers Amours* XVIII (quoted, p. 134, by Scott), but, further, that Constable has departed from his exemplar in the second quatrain to introduce St. Francis. She does not find it necessary to see in this a reminiscence of Mellin de Saint-Gelais, as does Sir Sidney Lee (*Elizabethan Sonnets*, vol. I [1904], p. lxiii), and pertinently comments, "Pourtant Constable, qui était fort pieux, était capable d'imaginer cette comparaison tout seul. En tout cas, elle vient ajouter une note d'independance à l'imitation." But surely it is this comparison of the wounded lover with the wounded St. Francis which makes the sonnet. I need not say that the Elizabethan poet would not look upon such a comparison as sacrilegious. Compare, for example, Spenser, *Amoretti*, XXII and LXI.

[222] *To lyve in lust I make not my professyon*

Hand: Sir John Harington's. The heading is in italic, the poem in secretary.

With some revisions copies of this translation out of Ovid by Sir John are in two autograph manuscripts of his epigrams: (*A*) British Museum MS. Add. 12049, pp. 99-101, headed, "Ovids confession translated into English for generall Norris 1593," and with revisions in the same hand; (*B*) Folger MS. 4455, the fair copy made for Prince Henry in 1605, pp. 134-36, with the heading as in *A*. Not included in the 1615 edition of the *Epigrams*, it was first printed in (*C*) the 1618 edition, Book II, No. 85, and is in the reprints of 1625 and 1633-34. Since a copy of the 1618 edition is not available to me, I have used N. E. McClure's text, based on that edition, with reference to his collation in *The Letters and Epigrams of Sir John Harington* (1930), pp. 219-21. See my Note on No. 91. As there indicated, I have consulted Miller's folio edition of the *Epigrams*, appended to the 1634 edition of Sir John's *Orlando Furioso*. The text of No. 222, which appears on sig. Rr $4^{r,v}$ (in error for Qq 4), differs from the text of *C* in four instances only, as noted below. Catchwords are disregarded in the collation following.

4 yt known] men know *A-C*
5 the thing] that most *A-C*: most that *1634*
7 runns my] ⟨runns myn⟩ doth runn *A*: runns mine *B*: runnes my *C*
8 my] *omitted 1634*
9 fancye] fancies *A-C*
10 my] myne *A B*
11 lookes] looke *A-C*
12 strayght . . . subiection] ⟨straight to⟩ those eyes to take my soule ⟨ys⟩ in theyr subiection *A*
13 my] myne *A B*
15 lyke . . . feerce] like Sabynes sharp and fierce *A-C*: *Sabine 1634*
19 sweet] myld *A-C*
20 vearses] writings *A-C*
22 the] their *A-C*
23 some] my *A-C*
25 not I thinck] yll perhapps *A-C*; myght] would *A-C*
26 Yf . . . cunning singer] Ys she with well tun'd voyce a lerned singer *A B*: Is shee well tun'd in voice, a cunning singer *C*
27 from . . . have] eu'n then I feele *A B*: eu'n thus I feele *C*
28 Yf . . . wth] Playes she one Lute wth sweete & *A-C*

29 could] can *A-C*
30 art] heart *C*
Corentoes
31 Quarantos] ⟨Carantoes⟩ *A*: C'urrentoes *B*: Carantoes *C*; stately] comly *A-C*
32 easely] quickly *A-C*
33 thear] *omitted* *A-C*; take] ⟨giue⟩ take *A*: haue *B C*
34 auncyent] th'auncient *A-C*; Heroyns] *Heroyes* *C*: *Heroes 1634*
35 good lardge] ⟨brave⟩ goodly *A*: braue *B C*; in] in ⟨the⟩ *A*: in the *B C*
36 nimbler] ⟨comlier⟩ nimbler *A*: comlier *B C*; proceed from] are found in *A-C*
37 tall . . . fedd] long & short haue ay my liking bredd *A-C*
39 weare she] ⟨wear she⟩ in riche *A*
the
40 ffayre . . . comes] Fayre, nut-brown, sallow, none do looke *A B*: Fayre, nut-browne, sallow, none doth looke *C*
47 love] like *A-C*; or] for *C*
48 or] and *C*
prove
49 ⟨make⟩] prove *A-C*

The collation, as I interpret it, tells the following story: the copy in *AH* is the earliest version; the poem was revised for *A*, from which with slight change it was copied into *B* in 1605; *A* was again revised with some reference back to *AH*, as in lines 33, 35, 36, but these revisions were not used in *C*. The latter, which has a few peculiar variants, normally agrees with *A* and *B* against *AH*, but in lines 7, 10, and 26 it shows a relation to *AH*, indicating further preparation for the published edition. Since Sir John died six years before the 1618 edition appeared, it is possible that someone else was responsible for the manuscript revised for the printer; but it is also quite possible that Sir John may have had still another manuscript which presented the texts as printed in *C*. I do not refer to obvious errors. The study of the three manuscript texts, all in the author's handwriting, is especially instructive in that it indicates how much authentic change might take place in copies of poems. Hence, we may well conclude that variants in copies of some poems *not* in autograph may also be authentic. In these instances, unfortunately, we cannot know.

General Norris, for whom the translation was made in 1593, must refer to the distinguished military commander, Sir John Norris, 1547?-1597, who in 1593 is said to have been in Brittany leading forces against the Holy League (*D.N.B.*). The translation may have been written shortly before or after this expedition.

McClure's brief note (p. 418) is disappointing in that it fails to identify the poem in Ovid or to give any evaluation of the translation. Sir John's poem is an English version from Ovid's *Amores*, Book II, Elegia IV, and he has succeeded remarkably well not only in translating into English metrical verse the sense of the original, but in conveying the Ovidian spirit and tone. The Latin which Sir John had before him undoubtedly differed in some readings from a modern text. Thus in line 23 was Sir John translating "Culpantis cupiam sustinuisse femur" (quoted from *Amores*, Verona: Bodoni, 1932, p. 58)? Instead of *femur* did he have a form of the verb *fenero*? In some instances he probably "modernized" to suit his own purposes. Thus, the Latin for lines 19-20 reads:

Est, quae Callimachi prae nostris rustica dicat
Carmina: cui placeo, protinus ipsa placet.

But Sir John's verses are compared "wth the best," not with those of Callimachus. In line 28 "Lute" translates for his sixteenth-century audience the "querulas . . . chordas" of Ovid. Lines 30-31 carry us to the Elizabethan court without the innuendo of

Illa placet gestu numerosaque bracchia ducit
Et tenerum molli torquet ab arte latus.

The deftness of Sir John's version is the more appreciated after reading Christopher Marlowe's labored English for the same Latin lines. For Marlowe's work see *Marlowe's Poems*, ed. L. C. Martin, New York, Dial Press, 1931, pp. 187-89, and pp. 14-17 of the Introduction (vol. iv of *Works*, ed. R. H. Case).

[223] *Loving in trewth, and fayn my love in verse to show*

Hand: Sir John Harington's, with the important heading in the same hand. The rest of the page is blank, as is the greater part of the verso, indicating that Harington intended to add others of Sidney's sonnets. The few lines of No. 224 on the verso, which are in another hand, were probably written in later.

This first sonnet in the *Astrophel and Stella* sequence was printed in Thomas Newman's two 1591 editions: (*A*) *Syr P. S. His Astrophel and Stella*, sig. B1^r (British Museum copy); (*B*) *Sir P. S. His Astrophel and Stella*, sig. A2^r (Huntington copy). It is also in the 1591 edition brought out by Matthew Lownes, where the text agrees with *A*. It was included in (*C*) *The Countesse of Pembrokes Arcadia*, 1598, p. 519 (Huntington copy). In *The Arcadian Rhetorike* [1588], sig. C8^r (Bodleian copy), Abraham Fraunce quotes the first four and one half lines of the sonnet to illustrate the figure *climax*. Fraunce's version of these lines agrees with *C* in line 1, but otherwise accords with *AH*. There are three other contemporary manuscript copies: (*D*) British Museum MS. Add. 15232, fol. 21^{r}. Mona Wilson in her edition of *Astrophel and Stella* (London, Nonesuch Press, 1931), p. xxxiv, briefly describes this manuscript, containing twenty-four sonnets and two songs from the sequence, as made "though not with perfect accuracy from a manuscript standing in very close relation with the Countess' copy." (*E*) Houghton MS., fol. 91^{r}. I am indebted to Professor William Ringler for the variants from this manuscript and to the present owner, Mr. Arthur H. Houghton, Jr., of New York City, for permission to use them in my collation. The Houghton MS., which contains an important body of Sidney poetry, will be fully described and evaluated by Professor Ringler in his edition of Sidney's poems. He tells me that he finds a close connection between it and manuscripts belonging to Sir John Harington. (*F*) Edinburgh University MS. De.5.96, fol. 4^{r}. This manuscript, presented to the University by William Drummond of Hawthornden, is also being carefully studied by Professor Ringler. I am indebted to him for the variants and to Mr. C. F. Finlayson, Keeper of Manuscripts, for information about the foliation.

1 my . . . verse] in verse my loue *C D*: my love *omitted* *F*
2 the] she *C*: thee *D*; deer shee] (dear thee) *D*; myght] must *D*
4 grace] great *D*
6 fyne] new *E*
7 thens] there *E*
8 showr] showers *C F*: flowers *D*; sunnburnd] Sunneburnt *A B E*
9 owt] forth *C D F*
10 stepdam] Stepdames *A B*
11 sute] feete *A-D F*
13 towng and] trewand *B-D F*

Although Harington's text of the first sonnet in *Astrophel and Stella* is very close to *A*, there is evidence that he had access to a manuscript source which had characteristics of both *A* and *C*, as well as some of its own. Evidence that Harington was acquainted with material by or relating to Sidney is indicated in several of his notes in his translation of the *Orlando Furioso*. In my Note on No. 71 I have pointed out that a statement made by Sir John in his notes following Book XI of the *Orlando* (ed. 1591, p. 87) makes it certain that he was familiar with a manuscript version of the original *Arcadia*. In the notes to Book XXXVII (pp. 314-15) he quotes from epitaphs on Sidney written by King James VI of Scotland and Alexander Nevile, who published in 1587 the volume in which both poems appeared, *Academiae Cantabrigiensis lachrymae tumulo D. Philippi Sidneii sacratae* (see M. W. Wallace, *The Life of Sir*

Philip Sidney, Cambridge University Press, 1915, pp. 106, 398). In the notes to Book XVI of the *Orlando* (ed. 1591, p. 126) Harington quotes Sidney's eighteenth sonnet, where the "sharp checks" of line 1 are in accord with the text of that sonnet as given in *C* (also in *D*), as opposed to the "strange checks" of *A B* (and the Lownes 1591 quarto). In lines 3 and 11, however, Sir John's text agrees with *A* against *B-D*. An independent reading in line 2, "reasons recknings," instead of "reasons audit," suggests an earlier writing of the line, perhaps revised by Sidney for better assonance.

Sir John's quotation of Sonnet XVIII is introduced thus:

> *and our English* Petrarke, Sir Philip Sidney, *or* (*as* Sir Walter Raulegh *in his Epitaph worthely calleth him*) *the* Scipio *and the* Petrarke *of our time, often comforteth him selfe in his sonets of* Stella, *though dispairing to attaine his desire, and* (*though that tyrant honor still refused*) *yet the nobilitie, the beautie, the worth, the graciousnesse, and those her other perfections, as made him both count her, and call her inestimably rich, makes him in the midst of those his mones, reioyce euen in his owne greatest losses, as in his eighteenth sonet which many I am sure haue read.*

In the light of Sir John's heading for No. 223 there can be no question of the pun on "Stella's" name in the significant use of the word *rich* in the above passage. His meaning would have been clear to the court circle in 1591. Many also would have been familiar with Ralegh's elegy on Sidney, not published until 1593, and then without attribution. Only by Sir John's heading to his copy of the elegy in *AH*, No. 225, do we have a positive attribution of Ralegh's authorship. In the same way his heading for No. 223 is the only clear contemporary statement that Sidney's sonnets were written to Lady Rich, as, indeed, is his statement that Henry Constable's sonnets were also addressed to the same lady (see No. 201).

Many scholars have taken part in the controversy concerning the identification of "Stella" with Penelope Devereux, who became the wife of Robert, Baron Rich, in October of 1581 (see the Note on No. 196). Sir John's statement above No. 223, which gives the key for interpretation of his more subtle reference in the notes to the *Orlando*, Book XVI, does invalidate the claims of those who have argued that there was no contemporary record of this identification. See, for example, James M. Purcell's note in "Comment and Criticism," *PMLA*, xlvi (1931), 945-46, and his book *Sidney's Stella*, New York, Oxford University Press, 1934; Theodore H. Banks' article "Sidney's *Astrophel and Stella* Reconsidered," *PMLA*, l (1935), 403-12; and Walter G. Friedrich's discussion "The Stella of Astrophel," *ELH*, iii (1936), 114-39. The autobiographical element in the sonnets is also discounted by such critics as

W. J. Courthope in *A History of English Poetry*, ii (2nd ed., London, Macmillan, 1904, reprint, 1935), 226-33, and Sir Sidney Lee in his Introduction to *An English Garner, Elizabethan Sonnets*, vol. i (New York, Dutton, 1904), p. xliii. In an admirable article, written as a rebuttal to Purcell's *Sidney's Stella*, Hoyt H. Hudson in "Penelope Devereux as Sidney's Stella," *The Huntington Library Bulletin*, No. 7 (1935), pp. 89-129, sets out and interprets a very complete and impressive body of circumstantial evidence leading to the identification of "Stella" as Lady Rich. This is the thesis also of Lisle C. John's discussion in *The Elizabethan Sonnet Cycles*, New York, Columbia University Press, 1938, pp. 179-88. Sir John's statement, as quoted in Hughey, p. 403, is there taken into account. This identification has indeed been accepted by the greater number of Sidney's critics and biographers, although the significance has been variously interpreted. See, for example, H. R. Fox Bourne, *A Memoir of Sir Philip Sidney*, 1862, pp. 283-91; A. B. Grosart, ed., *The Complete Poems of Sir Philip Sidney*, vol. i (1873), pp. xxv-xlviii; J. A. Symonds, *Sir Philip Sidney*, 1887, pp. 33, 106-44; A. W. Pollard, ed., *Sir Philip Sidney's Astrophel and Stella*, 1888, Introduction; Percy Addleshaw, *Sir Philip Sidney*, London, Methuen, 1910, pp. 321-35; M. W. Wallace (ref. above), pp. 169-70, 241-59; Emma M. Denkinger, *Immortal Sidney*, New York, Brentano, 1931, pp. 167-96; Mona Wilson, *Sir Philip Sidney*, New York, Oxford University Press, 1932, pp. 72, 167-206, and in her Introduction to her edition of the sequence, 1931. C. Henry Warren in *Sir Philip Sidney, A Study in Conflict*, London, Nelson, 1936, pp. 123-40, takes a somewhat uncertain position about the personal element in the *Astrophel and Stella* sonnets, and A. H. Bill in *Astrophel or The Life and Death of the Renowned Sir Philip Sidney*, New York, Farrar and Rhinehart, 1937, pp. 216-17, expresses the view that Penelope was chosen as the lady to be glorified according to the course recommended in *The Courtier*. All was to be understood in a Platonic sense.

I cannot enter here into a complete reconsideration of the identification of "Stella" as Lady Rich, as I am sure will be done by Professor Ringler in his edition of Sidney's poetry. This identity also plays an important part in a thesis written by one of my former students, Ephim G. Fogel, now at Cornell University. It is my own opinion that the circumstantial evidence set out by the late Professor Hudson, reinforced by Sir John's statement, and the vibrant quality of the sonnets themselves, leads inevitably to the conclusion that Penelope, Lady Rich, was certainly Sidney's "Stella," and that not merely in a literary sense.

[224] *Thow art pretty bvt vnconstant*

Hand: a slender contemporary italic not occurring elsewhere in the manuscript. The lines are written in the upper left-hand corner of the page, a part of the space left for Sir Philip Sidney's sonnets. See the Note on No. 223.

These delightful verses form the first stanza of a poem found in British Museum MS. Add. 10309, fol. 106^{v}, which reads:

Vpon his mistresses inconstancy

Thou art prettie, but inconstant
    Too too louely to be true
Thine affections in ane instant,
    Strugle which shall first be new.
This and that, and heere, and there
    Onely in thy thoughts appeare.
Thou art weary, thou art wauering
    Coy and in a while as kinde
All thy passions in a turning
    Shift as often as the winde.
Too and frow, and vp and downe
Change doth all thy actions crowne.
But to me thou ne're art chang'd
    In thy wonted crueltie
Still from me y^{u} keepes estrang'd
    There's thy only Constancie.
Oh then let thy next change be
ffrom neglect to Loue of me
If in that mind I could find yee
    I would hold the fast enou
This should be my tricke to bind yee
    Change I would as oft as you
Then by my example taught
    Thou should see y^{t} change is naught.

From the Add. MS., then "in Mr. Lloyd's Collection," George Ellis printed the poem in *Specimens of the Early English Poets*, iii (1803), 344-45.

[225] *To prayse thy lyfe and wayle thy worthy death*

Hand: Sir John Harington's, with the important superscription in the same hand.

Sir Walter Ralegh's elegy on Sidney was first printed anonymously in (*A*) *The Phoenix Nest*, 1593, sigs. B4^{v}-C1^{r,v} (ed. H. E. Rollins, 1931, pp. 16-18), where it is entitled, "An Epitaph vpon the right Honorable sir Philip Sidney knight: Lord *gouernor of Flushing*." From *A* it was carefully reprinted, again without ascription, in (*B*) Edmund Spenser's *Colin Clouts Come home againe*, 1595, sigs. K2^{r,v}-K3^{r}, among the several elegies on Sidney included in that volume. Catchwords are not included in the collation following:

1 and] or *A B*
2 pure hygh] high, pure *A B*
6 whose] And *A B*
8 that] Thy *A B*
15 princes] creatures *A B*
16 lyving] linage *A B*
18 which] That *A B*; thowght] found *A B*
19 meare] neere *A B*
29 When] Whence *A B*
33 Whear thou didst conquer] There didst thou vanquish *A B*
38 longe⟨r⟩] long *A B*
46 vallew] valure *A B*
50 long yeares] yeeres long *A B*
51 built] made *A B*
55 sythes] sighes *A B* *three times*
61 Heavens] heauen *B*

The reading "lyving" in line 16 of *AH* gives the sense: his virtue and princely living are no less than his princely birth. This meaning better accords with the intention of the stanza than does the "linage" of *A* and *B*. In line 19 of *AH* "meare," i.e., pure, unmixed, is preferable in the sense of the stanza to the "neere" of *A* and *B*. Agnes M. C. Latham in her revised edition of *The Poems of Sir Walter Ralegh*, 1951, p. 98, comments on Sir John's version, which she had examined in *N*, fol. 96^{r,v}, noting that it preserves Ralegh's spelling of "sythes" for "sighs."

The most important feature of the copy in *AH* is Sir John's positive statement of Ralegh's authorship. This attribution has long been deduced from a reference made by Sir John in the notes to Book XVI of his *Orlando Furioso* (1591, p. 126): "*our English* Petrarke, Sir Philip Sidney, *or* (*as* Sir Walter Raulegh *in his Epitaph worthely calleth him*) *the* Scipio *and the* Petrarke *of our time*." Similarly William Drummond of Hawthornden is reported to have remarked to Ben Jonson, "S. W. R. in an Epitaph on Sidney, calleth him our English Petrarch" (*Notes of Ben Jonson's Conversations with William Drummond of Hawthornden. January, M.DC.XIX*, ed. David Laing, Shakespeare Society, 1842, p. 49). In this connection see *Poems by Sir Henry Wotton, Sir Walter Raleigh and Others*, ed. John Hannah, 1845, pp. xxxvii-xxxviii; *The Poems of Sir Walter Raleigh . . . with Those of Sir Henry Wotton . . .*, ed. Hannah, 1875 (reprint, 1910), pp. 214-15; Rollins' notes in *The Phoenix Nest*, pp. 125-26; Miss Latham's notes in her 1929 edition of Ralegh's poems, p. 137, and also in her recent revised edition, pp. 97-98. These editors have further noted that lines of an inscription on Sidney formerly in old St. Paul's Cathedral are similar to lines 45-48 of Ralegh's elegy. Hannah's reference to the inscription as "(copied from the French)" is borne out by William Camden in his *Remaines*, 1605, sig. g 3^{r,v}:

> Sir *Philip Sidney* . . . hath this most happily imitated out of the French of *Mons. Boniuet*, made by *Ioach. du Bellay*, as it was noted by Sir *George Buc* in his *Poetica*.
>
> *England, Netherland, the heauens, and the arts,*
> *The souldiers, and the world hath made six parts*
> *Of noble Sidney; for who will suppose,*
> *That a small heape of stones, can* Sidney *enclose?*
>
> *England had his body for she it fed,*
> *Netherland his bloud in her defence shed*
> *The heavens haue his soule, the arts haue his fame,*
> *The souldiers the griefe, the world his good name.*

Rollins, p. 129, also quotes for comparison the last line of Surrey's epitaph on Wyatt, "The earth his bones, the heauens possesse his gost" (*TM*, I, 28). It might indeed be said that the tone of Ralegh's elegy as a whole shows that he owed much to Surrey's elegiac manner as exhibited in the three poems on Wyatt and in the epitaph on Thomas Clere (*The Poems of Henry Howard Earl of Surrey*, ed. F. M. Padelford, 2nd ed., 1928, pp. 97-99). Ralegh's lines 5-12 remind us of Surrey's lines on Wyatt in the sonnet beginning, "Dyvers thy death doo dyverslye bemone." The reference to the past envy of the living toward the dead poets is reiterated in Ralegh's lines 56-57, and in lines 21-24 there is a haunting echo of Surrey's tribute to Clere, beginning, "Norfolk sprang thee, Lambeth holds thee dead." As Ralegh compared Sidney the poet to Petrarch, so Surrey praised Wyatt as one "That reft Chaucer the glory of his wit."

[226] *Thease Thirtye things that Hellens fame did rayse*

Hand: the verses are in Sir John Harington's secretary. The heading, in faded brown ink, is in another secretary hand.

No. 227 is Sir John's copy of the Latin verses by Barthélemy de Chasseneux from which he made this translation.

No. 226 was included in Sir John's collection of epigrams, but it is now missing in the earlier autograph manuscript, British Museum Add. 12049. According to the index, it was written on p. 11, but that folio is now supplied by a modern blank leaf. See Hughey, p. 432. A version is in the fair copy made for Prince Henry in 1605, (*A*) Folger MS. 4455, p. 15, headed, "Of a fayr woman translated out of Casmeus,

Catalogus gloriae mundi." Not included in the 1615 edition of the *Epigrams*, it was first printed in (*B*) the 1618 edition, Book I, No. 15, headed as in *A*, with the author's name printed "*Casaneus*," and it was reprinted in the editions of 1625 and 1633-34. See my Note on No. 91. As there stated, for the *B* texts I have used N. E. McClure's edition of *The Letters and Epigrams of Sir John Harington* (1930), where this poem appears on p. 154. In Miller's folio edition of the *Epigrams*, appended to the 1634 edition of Sir John's *Orlando Furioso*, the text of No. 226 is printed on sig. Oo 6^{v}. It agrees with *B* except in line 8, as noted below.

2 must] should *A B*
5 Hear] and *B*
6 part] parts *A B*
8 showe good] haue ful *B*: have faire *1634*
9 ffeet] foot *A B*
10 Breast] brests *B*; Būme] hips *A B*
11 straight waste] small . . . *A B*; pryvye member] ( ) *B*
12 hears] hayr *A B*
13 Būme] necke *A B*; must . . . fatt] should be full smooth *A B*
14 may] can *A B*
16 be] are *B*

In his *Second Frutes*, 1591, fol. 131^{r}, John Florio introduced another Englishing of the same Latin verses:

L. Which are the partes that a woman ought to haue, to be accounted most faire?
G. In choyse of faire, are thirtie things required.
For which (they saie) faire Hellen was admired,
Three white, three black, three red, three short, three tall,
Three thick, three thin, three streight, three wide, three small,
White teeth, white hands, and neck as yuorie white,
Black eyes, black browes, black heares that hide delight:
Red lippes, red cheekes, and tops of nipples red
Long leggs, long fingers, long locks of her head,
Short feete, short eares, and teeth in measure short,
Broad front, broade brest, broad hipps in seemely sort,
Streight leggs, streight nose and streight her pleasure place,
Full thighes, full buttocks, full her bellies space,
Thin lipps, thin eylids, and heare thin and fine,
Smale mouth, smale waste, smale pupils of her eyne,
Of these who wants, so much of fairest wants,
And who hath all, her beautie perfect vauntes.

[227] *Trigenta hec habeat quae vult formosa viderj*

Hand: the first ten lines are certainly in Sir John Harington's secretary and the last eight may be his at a different writing.

These Latin verses, Englished by Sir John in No. 226, were printed in the collection of Barthélemy de Chasseneux (1480-1541), *Catalogus gloriae mundi, laudes, honores, excellentias ac prẹeminentias omniū fere statuū plurimarumque rerū illius continēs.* . . . So far as I am aware, the work in twelve parts was first published at Lyons in 1529. Another edition, from which the above title is quoted, was printed at Lyons in 1546. Other continental editions appeared in 1571, 1603, 1612, 1617, and 1649, but none seems to have been published in England. In the British Museum copy of the 1546 edition the verses are printed, fol. 53^r, col. b, as follows:

Trigenta haec habeat quae vult formosa vocari
foemina, sic Helenam fama fuisse refert.
Alba tria & totidem nigra, & tria rubra puella,
Tres habeat longas res, totidemque breues.
Tres crassas, totidemque graciles, tria stricta, tot ampla.
Sint ibidem huic formae sint quoque parua tria.
Alba cutis, niuei dentes, albique capilli.
Nigri oculi, cunnus, nigra supercilia.
Labra genẹ atque vngues rubri, sit corpora longa.
Et longi crines, sit quoque longa manus.
Sintque breues dentes, auris, pes, pectora lata,
Et clunes, distent ipsa supercilia.
Cunnus & os strictum, stringūt vbi cingula, stricta:
Sint coxae & cullus vuluaque turgidula.
Subtiles digiti, crines & labra puellis.
Paruus sit nasus, parua mamillia, caput.
Cum Nullae aut rarae sint haec, formosa vocari
Nulla puella potes, rara puella potest.

A study of Chasseneux has been made by J. H. Pignot, *Un Juris consulte au seizième siècle, Barthélemy de Chasseneuz . . . sa vie et ses oeuvres*, 1880, but I have not seen it.

[228] *Lady to yow, whose reverend bewty rare*

Hand: same as the last eight lines of No. 227, very probably that of Sir John Harington.

I have been unable to discover another copy of this dedicatory poem, which seems clearly to have been written for Mary Herbert, Countess of Pembroke, before the death of her "Noble Brother" in 1586. Line 14 indicates that it was an introduction to a work which had been assigned by the lady addressed.

[229] *Vnto the Caitife wretche, whome long affliction holdeth*

Hand: probably Sir John Harington's.

Like No. 191 this is another poem by Sir Philip Sidney which is found in *The Countesse of Pembrokes Arcadia*. Collation is given with the following manuscripts of the Old Arcadia (for further comment on these manuscripts, see the Note on No. 191):

(*A*) Huntington Library MS. HM 162, fols. 161^{v}-162^{v}

(*B*) British Museum MS. Add. 38892, fols. 166^{v}-168^{r}, wanting line 43 and sometimes showing confusion in sense

(*C*) British Museum MS. Add. 41204, fols. 159^{r}-160^{r}, wanting lines 19-20

(*D*) British Museum MS. Add. 41498, fol. 35^{r,v}

(*E*) Queen's College, Oxford, MS. R.38/301, fols. [112^{r,v}], [119^{r}]

(*F*) Bodleian MS. è Mus. 37, fol. 189^{v}-190^{r,v} (Professor W. R. Parker, to whom I am indebted for the variants from *E* and *F*, wrote me of the latter, "He doesn't seem to have understood in all instances what he was copying," and of *E*, "The Queen's copyist has even less understanding of what he's copying.")

(*G*) St. John's College, Cambridge, MS. I.7, fols. 190^{r,v}-191^{r}

(*H*) Folger Library MS. 400903, fols. 173^{v}-174^{v}, wanting lines 38-39. (This manuscript was used by Albert Feuillerat in his edition of the Old Arcadia in *The Complete Works*, vol. iv [1926], where this poem is printed on pp. 318-20.)

Professor William Ringler tells me that a long fragment of the poem, beginning with line 30 in *AH*, is contained in Jesus College, Oxford, MS. 150, fol. 241 ff. This is another manuscript of the Old Arcadia, deriving, according to Professor Ringler, from the same original as *E* above. I have not been able to include this in my collation.

The poem is in the three late sixteenth-century editions of the *Arcadia*:

(*I*) ed. 1590, fols. 246^{v}-247^{r,v} (British Museum copy)

(*J*) ed. 1593, fols. 122^{r,v}-123^{r} (Huntington copy)

(*K*) ed. 1598, pp. 237-39 (Huntington copy)

1 the] ⟨the⟩ a *G*: a *I-K*; whome] w^{ch} *D*; affliction] affection *E*

2 helpe] hoope *D*

3 yet] it *C*; to the last] to tast *B*: last *omitted* *C*; Monument] a moment *B*: mom^{t} *E*; his] this *F*

7 thy] the *C*; the . . . of] *omitted* *C*

9 th⟨è⟩ allure] the Allure *A-H*; home] ⟨w⟩hom *C*

10 thy] the *C*; those] these *B*

11 regard] rega [*sic*] *E*

12 thing] thinges *F*; cannot I] can I not *E*; giv⟨è⟩n] given *A-H*; my] an *E*: myne *F*

13 clause] cawse *E*; to a] to bee a *B*
14 thing] thinges *F*; knowes] knowe *E*; thy] y^{e} *C*
15 lyke] lyf *H*
16 those] these *C E*
18 kynde] kinde of a *C*; a] *omitted* *C*: an *F*
19 ne] no *E*; nor] ne *A-D F-K*: *omitted* *E*
Lines 19-20 are omitted in C.
20 that . . . not] that I do not *H*: that, that I do I not *I J K* though that] though *F*; me leefe weare] me sure *B*: me life were *F*: my blisse were *I-K*
21 yeares] *omitted* *E*
22 that, that] that *C H*; I doe not] doe I not *A B D-G J*; I do I not *J K*; Heav'ne] heaven *A-K*
23 to atcheeve] t'atchieue *I-K*; heavnly] heavenly *A-K*
24 But but] But nowe *D*: But *E*; alas] *omitted* *B*
25 Disastre] sorrowes *B*
26 th'approche] ye approach *B D*; inly] onely *E*; ougly *I*
27 an adewe to the world] to the Worlde an adewe *D*: a clyve . . . *E*
28 Right] *omitted* *B*; so] to *F*; inflam'de] enflame *B*: enflamed *C-E G H*; a faire eye] fire of a fare eye *A C-K*: a fyer of a faire eye *B*
29 signes] singes *B E*; hugie] huge *H*
31 thence] hence *H I*; where] when *C*; I] he *E I-K*; lived] lou'd *I*
32 the] *omitted* *A*: thy *C I-K*: to the *F*
33 suche] such a *A-D G I*
34 only the] the only *C*; angrye] angre *A*
that
36 shall] or *C*; that] the (*the scribe wrote in* that *above the line*) *H*
37 faith, and] mortall *E*
38 disdayne] disdaines *B*; vnendly] the deadly *C*
39 on] of *E*
Lines 38-39 are wanting in H.
42 the offence was] though sence weare *C*: though offence was *E*: thoffence was *F G I*: the offence ys *H*
43 All] Of *B*; then] thow *E*; I] *omitted* *B E*
44 doth] do *A-E G-K*: *omitted* *F*
Line 43 is wanting in B.
45 that] *omitted* *C*
46 never had me] had me neuer *D*: had neuↄ *E*; saw] have *F*; loved] lou'd *I-K*

47 that] *omitted* *E*; love] lou'd *I-K*
48 bodye it] body't *I-K*
49 Yf] you *F*; that] the *A C-H*; hate yow did] you hate *B*: you did hate *I-K*
50 those] these *A*
52 vailes] vaile *A*; then doe] do then *B*; prevaile] availe *B*
53 Lockes (those lockes] Lockes whose Lockes *B*: lookes, those lookes *C*; lock] lockes *B D*: lookt *C*
54 torne] Turne *E*
56 even] eu'n *I J*; I should] should I *C E*
57 with] what *B*; a] *omitted* *C G I-K*; hand] handes *E*; this] *omitted* *A C D H*
58 have] hyde *B*; evill] so ill *B*: ill *E I-K*
59 did] do *G I-K*; faire] fere *E*
60 to much] *omitted* *F*; sight] sighe *E*; cause] causes *F*; so true] such *B*
61 Cimmerian] Simeran *E*; only] onel' *J*: onl' *K*
62 myne] my *A*; pull'd] piled *E*
63 that] *omitted* *H*; doe] be *B*; such] so *J K*; excessive] an excessyve *B*; a] *omitted* *D E*
64 heav'nly] heavēly *A-K*; Iewell] revill *F*: evell *H*
65 not] no *I*; love] *omitted* *E*; affoorded] offered *C*
66 temprаunce] temperaunce *B-H*; a rages] rages *B D*: outragius *H*; event] eventes *C E-K*
67 simplicitye] Simphatie *E*; whence] whome *B C*
69 shall] should *D H*; pedantee] picture *B*: pendantes *E*: peclante *F*: pendaunte *D H*; found] framed *B*
70 I was] *omitted* *D*
71 to a] vnto a *B*
72 whats] what *D*; this] is *E*; be] is *D I*; abolish⟨è⟩d] abolished *A C-F H*: abolisht *B I-K*
73 inviolate] in violat *B*
76 not] *omitted* *C*; you, you] you me *B*: you haue *C*: you now *E*
77 whome] who *E*
78 thoughts] thought *E*; then] *omitted* *E*; my gaine] me giue *A-H*: me giu'n *I-K*
79 thinck what] I thinke what *G*; world] word *B*; who] what *D*; hart] haire *E*
80 of] *omitted* *B I-K*; such] soe much *D*; now] *omitted* *E*; so much] to much *B*: of such *D*: such *I-K*
81 fledd] fett *E*; remote] removed *B*

82 rosie] rosed *A-K*
83 well shuld] will . . . *A*: should well *J*
84 With] What *A*
86 banished] Banisht *A*; will] do all *G*: wee *H*; seeke] see *A*; a] *omitted* *C*; recou'rye] recovery *A-D F-H*
88 evill] ill *B I-K*

It is readily seen that the *AH* copy is a good one, closer to *G*, the final draft, than to *E*, a copy of an earlier draft (see William Ringler, "Master Drant's Rules," *PQ*, xxix [1950], 71, 74). For evidence that Sir John Harington had access to a copy of the earlier *Arcadia*, see the Note on No. 71.

Introduced as elegiacs in both versions, the lines are examples of Sidney's experiments with "measured" verse. (For the scansion pattern see Feuillerat, iv, 118). In this connection Abraham Fraunce first printed two lines from the poem in *The Arcadian Rhetorike* [1588], sig. C3^{v}. He quotes line 71 to illustrate "*Elegum*, or the Elegiacall verse of a *Dactylus* or *Spondæus* in the first place, and in the third place of a *Spondæus* with two *Anapæsti*." On the same page Fraunce quotes lines 70 and 71 to illustrate "*Hexameters* ioyned with *Pentameters*." Both lines agree with the reading in *AH*. Professor Ringler has recently made available Sidney's "rules obserued in thies English measurde verses" (ref. above, p. 74, quoted from Sidney's "Nota" in St. John's College, Cambridge, MS. I.7, fol. 40^{v}). Helpful also is the study by G. L. Hendrikson, "Elizabethan Quantitative Hexameters" (*PQ*, xxviii [1949], 237-60).

In the older *Arcadia* these "*Elegiackes*" are introduced seriously as written by Philisides for "that sweete and incomparable *Mira*." In the revised version the lines are mockingly introduced as the laboriously written testimony of mourning affection which Musidorus leaves in the "standish" of the wavering Pamela. Surely no better criticism of the verses can be made than was written by Sidney himself as he describes Musidorus

> . . . chusing the *Elegiac* as fittest for mourning. But pen did never more quakingly performe his office; never was paper more double moistned with inke & teares; never words more slowly maried together, & never the *Muses* more tired, then now with changes & rechanges of his devises: fearing howe to ende, before he had resolved how to begin, mistrusting ech word, condemning eche sentence. This word was not significant, that word was too plain: this would not be cõceived; the other would be il conceived. Here Sorow was not inough expressed; there he seemed too much for his owne sake to be sory. This sentence rather shewed art, then passion; that sentence rather

foolishly passionate, then forcibly moving. At last, marring with mending, and putting out better, then he left, he made an end of it; & being ended, & diverse times ready to teare it: till his reason assuring him, the more he studied, the worse it grew, he folded it up, devoutly invoking good acceptation unto it . . . [quoted from *Complete Works*, ed. A. Feuillerat, i (1912, reprint, 1939), 356].

[230] *A stearles shipp in stormy waves*

Hand: Sir John Harington's. In line 2 the *s* in "fors't" is written in another ink over *c*. As I have indicated, the poem is closely written in double columns.

Although this poem is copied in the hand of Sir John, the style is similar to that of the earlier or mid-Tudor period. The second stanza, however, suggests that the verses were perhaps inspired by the Spanish menace and the troubles connected with Mary Stuart, Queen of Scots. If this is a correct supposition, the poem was probably written between 1569 and 1586, possibly about 1572, when the Duke of Norfolk was executed for his machinations with Mary Stuart.

[231] *In this one Wight, three mighty Princes strave*

Hand: Sir John Harington's.

Although we are told that three princes strive for first place in this lady, we are actually informed of the strife of two only: Nature and Fortune. Nature gives beauty and wit; Fortune, wealth. Since the poem has no "finis," it may be unfinished.

[232] *Of Auncyent Howse, and gentle bloud descended*

Hand: Sir John Harington's.

This personal tribute is written in the manner of the elder Harington as exemplified in his verses on Admiral Seymour, Nos. 2 and 3, and in his epitaph "Of the death of master Deuerox the lord Ferres sonne" (*TM*, No. 169). Similar also are lines in the tribute to Henry Stanley, Earl of Derby, No. 146, which may have been written by Harington. The probable pun on the name *Markham* in line 9 of No. 232 and the tenor of the poem as a whole suggest that John Harington addressed this tribute to Sir John Markham of Cotham, whose daughter Isabella became the beloved second wife of John Harington (see the Introduction, pp. 64, 66).

That Sir John Markham was of ancient house and gentle blood is attested in several records. A manuscript history of the family prepared in 1601 by Sir John Markham's great-grandson Francis Markham was a major source for the following accounts: (1) Joseph Hunter's "Familiae Minorum," 1831, in British Museum MS. Add. 24458, pp. 412-14 (for the printed version see *Familiae Minorum Gentium*, ed. John W. Clay, vol. iii, Harl. Soc., xxxix [1895], 964-71); (2) David F. Markham, *A History of the Markham Family*, 1854; (3) Clements R. Markham, *Markham Memorials*, 1872; (4) accounts of several earlier members of the family in the *D. N. B.*, including Sir John Markham, Judge of the Common Pleas, an adviser to Henry of Lancaster in 1399, whose achievements are recorded by Edward Foss in *Judges of England*, iv (1851), 172. A pedigree of the family is also given in *The Visitation of the County of Nottingham in the Years 1569 and 1614*, ed. George W. Marshall, Harl. Soc., iv (1871), 23-26. Sir John Markham's grandfather Sir Robert was a Knight of the Bath. His father, another Sir John, fought with Henry VII at Stoke in 1488, and later, by chance, entertained the king's mother, Margaret, Countess of Richmond and Derby. As a result, she arranged a marriage for the son John (the Sir John of our present concern) with her kinswoman Anne Neville. Sir John Markham was married three times, and his "Chilldren broght vpp well" were many: by his first wife he had one, possibly two, sons; by his second wife, Margery Langford, he had fifteen children; by his third wife, Anne Strelley, he had four, of whom one was Isabella. The compliment to the wife given in line 12 would obviously refer to Isabella's mother.

As a young man John Markham fought with King Henry VIII in 1513 at the siege of Tournay, where he was knighted for his services (*Letters and Papers, Foreign and Domestic, of the Reign of Henry VIII*, vol. i, part 2, ed. J. S. Brewer, rev. R. H. Brodie, 1920, pp. 1027-28). In 1537 Cranmer in a letter to Thomas Cromwell highly commended Sir John Markham as "an old soldier and as a favourer of God's word" (*Narratives of the Days of the Reformation Chiefly from the Manuscripts of John Foxe the Martyrologist*, ed. John G. Nichols, Camden Soc., lxxvii [1859], 173, note e). Sir John Markham served Notts and Derby as High Sheriff and Notts as Knight of the Shire (*Letters and Papers*, vol. xx, part 2, ed. James Gairdner and R. H. Brodie [1907], p. 450; vol. xxi, part 2, same editors [1910], p. 222). Sometime after December 19, 1547, and before November 1, 1549, Protector Somerset appointed Sir John Markham Lieutenant of the Tower (*Acts of the Privy Council of England*, New Series, ed. John R. Dasent, ii [1890], 154, 353), and was in charge when John Harington was a prisoner in 1549 (same ref., p. 371). After Somerset fell, Markham was removed from office (*Literary Remains of King Edward the Sixth*, ed. John G. Nichols, Roxburghe Club, ii [1857], 358, under date October 31, 1551).

According to Add. MS. 24458, p. 412, Sir John Markham died in 1558, aged nearly one hundred. His will, however, was not made until April 1, 1559, and was proved the same year. It includes mention of a marriage dowry for his daughter Isabella Markham (50 Chaynay, *PCC Wills, 1558-83*, ed. S. A. Smith and L. L. Duncan, British Record Society, xviii [1898], 205).

We may suppose that John Harington addressed this tribute to the old gentleman not long before his death, and that years later Sir John Harington copied the lines into the *AH* MS.

[233] *If Love should rule w*th *even and vpright hand*

Hand: Sir John Harington's, written in double columns, as indicated.

This unknown poem was very probably written by one of the Haringtons, for there is a noticeable similarity between parts of it and Sir John's *Orlando Furioso*, 1591, Book XXXI, stanzas 1, 3, and 4, which are as follows:

What state of life more pleasing may we find,
Then theirs, that true & heartie loue do beare?
Whom that sweet yoke doth fast together bind
That mā in Paradice first learnd to weare:
Were not some so tormēted in their mind,
With that same vile suspect, that filthie feare,
That torture great, that foolish frenesie,
That raging madnesse, called ielousie.

[Stanza 2 on peace and war, omitted.]

Though eyes want sight, of that they would see faine,
The thought yet sees, & harts with patiēce take it,
Long absence grieues, yet when they meet againe
Absence delights, & doth more pleasant make it:
To serue and sue long time for litle gaine,
(So that all hope do not eu'n quite forsake it)
One may endure, for when the paine is past,
Reward, though long it stay, yet comes at last.

The sharpe repulses, and the deepe disdaines,
And all the torments that in loue are found,
At last with pleasure recompence the paines,
And make contentment far more to abound:
But if this hellish plague infect the braines,
Though afterward it seeme both whole and sound
The qualitie therof is so mischieuous,
The verie thought is to a louer grieuous.

The stanzas of No. 233 like those in the *Orlando* are written in *ottava rima*, and both are concerned with the madness of jealousy as it conflicts with the blessed state of contented love. The first three stanzas of No. 233 have something of the manner of the elder Harington, who certainly knew the *Orlando*. See No. 3 and Note; also, for comparison, see Nos. 21 and 23, and Notes. Since, however, Sir John translated the stanzas in the *Orlando*, there is no reason why he could not have written this poem.

[234] *To thee yet Deare, thoe most disloyall Lord*

Hand: Sir John Harington's secretary, with proper names in his italic hand. Corrections are in the same hand. As indicated in the text, the poem is written in double columns, and lines 65, 130, 195, and 260 are simply catch words for the following column. On the left side of fol. 160v, at the end of the poem, are some odd symbols and these words in secretary, "I my lord// According."

H. Sellers in "A Bibliography of the Works of Samuel Daniel, 1585-1623, with an Appendix of Daniel's Letters," *Oxford Bibliographical Society Proceedings and Papers*, ii (1930, for 1927-30), 29-54, describes six editions of works by Daniel which include this poem. The present collation includes readings from four of these editions, made from copies in the Huntington Library.

1 (*A*) *The Poeticall Essayes of Sam. Danyel. Newly corrected and augmented. . . . Printed by P. Short for Simon Waterson. 1599* (*S.T.C.* 6261). This poetical epistle appears with its own title-page, *A Letter From Octavia To Marcus Antonius. Samuel Daniel. . . . Printed by P. Short for Simon Waterson, 1599*, and separate signatures, [A]^2, B-C^4, D^2, the third set of separate signatures in the quarto volume. The two leaves of sig. [A] were evidently set up by the printer as the latter half of the D gathering. *A Letter* includes the dedicatory sonnet, "To the right Honourable and most vert*uous Ladie, the Ladie Margaret Countesse of Cumberland* (sig. [A]2r); "The Argument" (sig. B1r,v), the text, separately entitled, "A Letter sent from *Octauia* to her husband *Marcus Antonius* into Egypt" (sigs. B2r-D2v).

The epistle was entered on the Stationers' Register, January 9, 1598/99, to Waterson, under the title last quoted (*Transcript*, ed. Arber, iii [1876], 134). It appears that the sheets were separately printed and that they were bound separately and also in *The Poeticall Essayes*. Thomas Corser infers that he was aware of a separate volume (*Collectanea Anglo-Poetica*, Part V, Chetham Society, xci [1873], 33), and a copy was in the White collection (*Catalogue of Early English Books, Chiefly of the Elizabethan Period. Collected by William Augustus White and catalogued by Henrietta C. Bartlett*, New York: Privately printed, 1926, p. 30). Neither Sellers nor the *S.T.C.*, however, mention such a volume, and I have not seen it. I do not know whether the binding was contemporary.

2 (*B*) *The Works of Samuel Daniel Newly augmented*, 1601

(*S.T.C.* 6236), where *A Letter* is reprinted at sigs. D1r-E4r, with the text of the epistle at sigs. D4r-E4r. This is the second set of signatures.

3 *Certaine Small Poems Lately Printed: with the Tragedie of Philotas*, 1605 (*S.T.C.* 6239). Not included in this collation. As described by Sellers (p. 38), *A Letter* appears at sigs. A1r-B3v, with the text at sigs. A4r-B3v, the first set of signatures.

4 (*C*) *Certaine Small Workes Heretofore Divulged by Samuel Daniel . . . & now againe by him corrected and augmented*, 1607 (*S.T.C.* 6240). *A Letter* is given on sigs. F2r-G2v.

5 *Certaine Small Workes*, 1611 (*S.T.C.* 6242). Not included in this collation. As described by Sellers (p. 42), *A Letter* is printed on sigs. D5r-E1v, with the text on D8r-E1v.

6 (*D*) *The Whole Workes of Samuel Daniel Esquire in Poetrie*, 1623 (*S.T.C.* 6238). *A Letter* appears on sigs. A1r-B2r, with the text of the epistle on A4r-B2r, the second set of signatures.

Preceding the epistle itself in these printed editions are a dedication and an argument, not found in *AH*. The dedication, as given in *A*, sig. [A]2r, reads:

To the right Honourable and most vertu-
ous Ladie, the Ladie Margaret Countesse
of Cumberland.

Although the meaner sort (whose thoughts are plac'd
As in another region, far below
The Sphere of greatnesse) cannot rightly taste
What touch it hath, nor right her passions know:
Yet haue I here aduentur'd to bestow
Words vpon griefe, as my griefes comprehend,
And made this great afflicted Ladie show
Out of my feelings, what she might haue pend.
And here the same, I bring forth, to attend
Vpon thy reuerent name, to liue with thee
Most vertuous Ladie, that vouchsaf'st to lend
Eare to my notes, and comfort vnto me,
That one day may thine owne faire vertues spread
Be'ing secretarie now, but to the dead.

The hope expressed in the last two lines was fulfilled a few years later when Daniel published his fine poetical epistle to the Countess of Cumberland (*A Panegyrike Congratulatorie To The Kings Maiestie. Also certaine Epistles* [1603?], sigs. E1r-E3r, as described by Sellers, p. 36). Martha Hale Shackford in "Samual Daniel's Poetical *Epistles*, Especially That to the Countess of Cumberland" (*SP*, xlv [1948], 180-95), comments on the significance of the dedication of *A Letter from Octavia* to the Lady Margaret, whose marriage, contracted in 1577 by arrangement of her father, Francis Russell, second Earl of Bedford, to George Clifford, third Earl of Cumberland, was as unhappy as Octavia's. As a naval commander George Clifford was frequently away from home, and, furthermore, he engaged in an intrigue with a lady of the court, which led to a separation from his wife (see the *D.N.B.*). Lines in the epistle to the Countess of Cumberland (see especially 60-99), depict her as a woman of lofty ideals and strong character, similar to the Octavia portrayed by the poet. In this connection we may recall that in 1596 Spenser dedicated his *Fowre Hymnes* to the Lady Margaret and her sister, Lady Anne, Countess of Warwick. About 1599 or 1600 Daniel entered the household of the Countess of Cumberland as tutor to her daughter, Lady Anne Clifford (see *The Complete Works in Verse and Prose of Samuel Daniel*, ed. A. B. Grosart, i [1885], xx; *D.N.B.*), and it is probable, as Miss Shackford suggests, that Daniel's dedication for Octavia's epistle was written when he was expecting to assume this position.

The dedicatory epistle is followed in the printed texts by an argument, which I quote from *A*, sig. B1^{r,v}, reversing the use of the italic and roman type.

THE ARGUMENT.

Vpon the second agreement (the first being broken through iealousie of a disproportion of eminencie) betweene the *Triumuiri Octauius Cæsar, Marcus Antonius*, and *Lepidus: Octauia* the sister of *Octauius Cæsar*, was married to *Antonius*, as a linke to combine that which neuer yet, the greatest strength of nature, or anie power of nearest respect could long holde togither, who made but the instrument of others ends, and deliuered vp as an Ostage to serue the oportunitie of aduantages, met not with that integritie she brought: but as highlie preferred to affliction encountered with all the greeuances that beate vppon the miserie of greatnes, exposed to stand betwixt the diuers tending humours of vnquiet parties. For *Antonie* hauing yet vpon him the fetters of Ægypt, layde on by the power of a most incomparable beautie, could admit no new lawes into the state of his affection, or dispose of himselfe being not himselfe, but as hauing his heart turned Eastwarde whither the point of his desires were directed, touchte with the strongest allurements that ambition, and a licencious soueraintie could draw a man vnto: could not trulie descend to the priuate loue of a ciuill nurtred Matrone, whose entertainment bounded with modestie, and the nature of her education, knew not to cloth her affections in any other colours then the plaine habit of truth: wherein she euer suted al her actions, and vsed all her best ornaments of honestie, to win the good liking of him that helde her but as a Curtaine drawne betweene him and *Octauius* to shadow his other purposes withall; which the

> sharpe sight of an equallie iealous ambition could soone pierce into, and as easily looke thorow and ouer bloud and nature as he to abuse it: And therefore to preuent his aspiring, he armes his forces either to reduce *Antonie* to the ranke of his estate, or else to disranke him out of state and al. When *Octauia* by the imploiment of *Antonie* (as being not yet ready to put his fortune to her triall) throwes her selfe, great with child, and as big with sorrowe, into the trauaile of a most laboursome reconciliation: taking her iourney from the farthest part of *Greece* to find *Octauius*, with whom her care and teares were so good agents that they effected their Commission beyond all expectation: and for that time quite disarmed their wrath, which yet long could not hold so. For *Antonius* falling into the relaps of his former disease, watching his oportunity got ouer againe into *Egypt*, where he so forgot himselfe, that he quite put off his own nature, and wholly became a pray to his pleasures, as if hee had wound himselfe out of the respect of Country, bloud and alliance, which gaue to *Octauia* the cause of much affliction, and to me the Argument of this letter.

The basis of the Argument, as of the poem itself, including the conception of the nobility of Octavia's character, is found in the account of "Antonius" as presented in Sir Thomas North's translation of Plutarch's *Lives*, 1579 (see the Shakespeare Head Press edition, vi [1928], 333-67). The "second agreement," to which Daniel refers, was made by Octavius Caesar and Mark Antony by the treaty of Brundisium in 40 B.C. Although Antony was already deeply infatuated with Cleopatra, whom he had met in Syria the preceding year, he agreed to a marriage, arranged by Caesar, with the latter's half-sister Octavia, a young widow. Antony's wife Fulvia had recently died. After bearing Antony a daughter, Octavia accompanied him to Athens. Reverting to a feeling of enmity toward Caesar, Antony set sail for Italy to make war on his brother-in-law. Octavia, described in North's *Plutarch* (p. 338) as at that time "great with child," effected a reconciliation between the two at Tarentum. There were feasts and exchanges of military forces; then they parted. In North's words:

> *Antonius* also leaving his wife *Octavia* and litle children begotten of her, with *Cæsar*, and his other children which he had by *Fulvia*: he went directlie into ASIA. Then beganne this pestilent plague and mischiefe of *Cleopatræs* love (which had slept a long tyme, and seemed to have bene utterlie forgotten, and that *Antonius* had geven place to better counsell) againe to kindle, and to be in force, so soone as *Antonius* came neere unto SYRIA [p. 339].

The account relates further that "*Antonius dronke with the love of Cleopatra*" failed thereby to make good use of his "great and puisant army" in his war against the Parthians. Eventually Octavia, then in

Rome, obtained permission from Caesar to go to Antony, but in Athens she received letters from him telling her to await his coming. In reply she offered to send the gifts and military equipment which she had for him. Cleopatra, hearing about Octavia through Antony's friend Niger, then used her "*flickering enticements*" all the more to hold Antony. When Octavia returned to Rome, Caesar commanded her to leave Antony's house, but this she refused to do (p. 362). Daniel's epistle is conceived as written after this time (see lines 74-81) and before she was forced to leave the house by Antony's order (p. 367).

The collation bears out A. B. Grosart's statement about the printed texts of the letter from Octavia, "Exceptionally, a collation of the successive editions reveals practically no variations" (*Works*, i, 116, in a note preceding Grosart's text of *A Letter*, pp. 117-38). Grosart, of course, did not use the *AH* version, which does show marked differences from those of the printed editions. Close study of the texts reveals conclusively, I think, that Sir John Harington's copy of the poem represents an earlier version, which was considerably revised for the first printing of the epistle in 1599. Thus, Daniel's practice of revision is evident in this composition, as in others, even though he effected little change after it was published. For the collation, in which I have been assisted by one of my former students, Mr. Karl E. Schmutzler, a film of copies *A*, *B*, *C*, and *D* in the Huntington Library has been used. Catch words are not included.

1 Lord] Lotd *C* *misprint*
4 at] by *A-D*
5 Great] Grant *A*
7 dost] doest *C*
12 it] them *A-D*
13 while] Whilst *A-D*
16 being] staying *A-D*
17 yt comes indeed] indeed it comes *A-D*
21 this] the *A-D*
25 And] an *C*
28 that] As *A-D*
29 once let in] let in once *A-D*
30 confirme] confirmed *A C*: confirmd *B D*; ⟨ffa⟩] *omitted A-D*
34 true] trne *B* *turned letter*
36 w^{ch}] wihch *C*
38 vnto . . . made] I made my selfe, vnto *A-D*
39 thy] my *D*
40 y^{t} still] which yet *A-D*; kept] keepes *C*
47 Yet . . . be] But ô how soone are they *A-D*

48 shame theirs] their shame *A-D*
49 doth . . . lay] hath open layd *A-D*
50 revollt] relaps *A-D*; relapse] revolt *A-D*
52 lefte] made *A-D*
55 are] comes *A-D*
Lines 57-64 and 66-73, i.e., stanzas 8 and 9, are reversed in order in A-D.
57 th'eye] the eie *A-D*
61 vndeserved] vndeseruing *A-D*
63 selldome] neuer *A-D*
66 must I] I may *A-D*
68 w^{ch}] that *A-D*
69 rob'd me to] lost me too *A-D*
70 But] Yet *A B D*; that beare] bearing *A-D*
72 is not] be not *A-D*
74 labored] counsell//d *C*
79 th'obiects] the obiects *A-D*
80 That] What *A-D*
84 the] thee *A-D*
85 and] Ile *A-D*
90 want . . . thy] absence, and this *A-D*
93 having] That haue *A-D*
94 seeing] Since that *A-D*
98 ô] yet *A-D*; his] this *A-D*
100 contemne] coutemne *C* *turned letter*
102 add] giue *A-D*
103 doth] must *A-D*
106 else peculyer ought] ought peculiar else *A-D*
110 And] For *A-D*; all but] but all *A-D*
112 yf] though *A-D*
117 owr] ours *D*
119 be] are *A-D*
120 say] shewes *A-D*
121 sith] since *A-D*; sayth] saies *A-D*

A-D here insert three stanzas, i.e., 24 lines. In A they are:

Vnequall partage to b'allow'd no share
Of power to do of lifes best benefite;
But stand as if we interdicted were
Of vertue, action, libertie and might:
Must you haue all, and not vouchsafe to spare
Our weaknes any intrest of delight?
Is there no portion left for vs at all,
But sufferance, sorrow, ignorance and thrall?

Thrice happie you in whom it is no fault,
To know, to speake, to do, and to be wise:
Whose words haue credit, and whose deeds though naught
Must yet be made to seeme far otherwise:
You can be onely heard whilst we are taught
To hold our peace, and not to exercise
The powers of our best parts, because your parts
Haue with our fredome robb'd vs of our hearts:

We in this prison of our selues confin'd
Must here shut vp with our own passions liue
Turn'd in vpon vs, and denied to find
The vent of outward means that might relieue:
That they alone must take vp all our mind;
And no roome left vs, but to thinke and grieue,
Yet oft our narrowed thoughts look more direct
Than your loose wisdoms borne with wild neglect.

122 But . . . wee] For should we to *A B D*: For whould we do *C*
124 interest] int'rest *A-D*
125 owr . . . repay] Our wronged patience paie *A-D*
127 followe] Succeed *A-D*
128 to] in *A-D*
129 eternall] immortall *A-D*
132 firme, and] sure, though *A-D*
133 have you priviledge] are you priuilidg'd *A-D*
136 truth] loue *A-D*
137 While] Whilst *A-D*; loos'de] stretch'd *A-D*; vnto] vpon *D*
140 lett] make *A-D*; owt] to doubt *A-D*
142 manhood] valour *A-D*
143 vpp] in *A-D*
144 vs] them *A-D*
146 would] will *A-D*
147 takes never] doth take no *A-D*
149 setts] drawes *A-D*
150 while] Whilst *A-D*; of] in *C*; y^{t}] what *A-D*
152 that, that] that what *A-D*
154 th'occasion] the occasion *A-D*
156 or Loving] For louing *A-D*; lyves] loues *A-D*
157 whiles] Whilst *A-D*
158 ffalsehood is] And falshood *A-D*
159 they . . . in] she fares in whom is *A-D*; lesser] lesse *D*
160 belov'de, y^{t} be] is lou'd that is *A-D*

161 w^{ch} . . . you] Which (pardon me) shewes no great strength of mind *A-D*
162 To . . . vntrew] To be most theirs, that vse you most vnkind *A-D*

A-D here insert a stanza, quoted from A:

Yet wel it fits for that sinne euer must
Be tortur'd with the racke of his own frame,
For he that holds no faith shall find no trust,
But sowing wrong is sure to reape the same:
How can he looke to haue his measure iust
That fils deceipt, and reckons not of shame,
And being not pleas'd with what he hath in lot
Shall euer pine for that which he hath not?

163 didst] couldst *A-D*
165 by] of *A-D*
166 they ofts doe] That oft they *A-D*
167 ffor why] Because *A-D*
169 yet] it's *A-D*
170 inwardly] secretly *A-D*
171 is] to *A-D*
172 quite] left *A-D*
173 succors] comforts *A-D*
175 Anthony] Antony *A-D*
176 I must be] must be made *A-D*
177 owr] her *D*
179 had] haue *A-D*
180 thee to] So great *A-D*
181 did] doth *A-D*
182 to . . . that, that] For to dislike what *A-D*; should] doth *A B*
183 or else] Because *A-D*; the] his *C*; willing to] gladlie would *A-D*
185 be] are *A-D*
186 Doe] Will *A-D*; would] will *A-D*
188 only] wholy *A-D*
189 cause] side *A-D*; and] their *A*
190 might seeme] would shew *A-D*
191 That] For *A-D*
192 vpbraides] obraides *A-D*; sinne is] fault, were *ABD*: fault where *C*
193 their error thrusts] doth follie thrust *A-D*
199 doe] doth *A-D*
203 wast] were *A-D*

204 do] doth *A-D*
206 doth . . . th'inward] more doth touch that tender *A-D*
208 Anthony] Antony *A-D*; thy] thine *A-D*
209 ye hart] th'hart *A-D*; still yet] yet still *A-D*
210 Yf ever any] To iudge if euer *A-D*
211 wofull] wretched *A-D*
214 labor] sorrow *A-D*
216 travell] trauaile *A*
218 stepp] moue *A-D*; to] for *A-D*
220 what . . . first] first what great ado had I *A-D*
221 m'offended] My' offended *A*
222 ply'de] praid *A-D*; prayd] cride *A-D*; turne ye ill] staie the sinne *A-D*
224 what a case] in what case *A-D*; woefull] wretched *A-D*
225 plaste betweene] Set betwixt *A-C*: Set twixt *D*; of] with *A-D*
226 (quoth I)] said I *A-D*
227 wins] win *A-D*
228 And] For *A B D*
230 should . . . should] shall . . . shall *A B D*
231 th'enkyndled] Th'inkindeled *C*; fyres] fire *A-D*
234 and] an *A-D*
235 Th'agent] The Agent *A-D*
236 With . . . infortunate] With praiers, vowes and tears, with vrging hard *A-D*
238 such] the *A-D*; provisions] provision *C*; as I gate] I prepard *A-D*
239 fo^{r}⟨ode⟩ . . . haste] For thy (intended *Parthian* war) made haste *A-D*
240 not . . . estate] Weighing not how my poore weake body far'd *A-D*
242 I came] And came *A-D*
243 tell] shew *A-D*
246 I sent] sent I *A-D*
247 wth horse] With th' horse *A-D*
248 Which . . . ells] Whereat perhaps when some *A-D*
249 hart] soule *A-D*
250 But . . . grownd] Th'Inchantres straight steps twixt thy hart & thee *A-D, except D*: stept
251 Of . . . vnsownd] And intercepts all thoughts that came of mee *A-D*
252 Now] She *A-D*; th'ingines] the ingins *A-D*
253 falshood] batterie *A-D*
254 dryve] bring *A-D*

255 strength] powre *A-D*
256 wann] faint *A-D*; languisheth] languishes *A-D*; straight] striaght *A misprint*
257 to remove] more to moue *A-D*
258 While] Whilst *A-D*; followers] fellowes *D*
259 tales] passions *A-D*
263 lying] Lie thus *A-D*
265 whiles] Whilst *A-D*
267 Lifte vpp] Aduance *A-D*; thee] it *A-D*; thy grace] his right *A-D*
268 chase] quit *A-D*
273 the meane] yet the *A-D*
274 that] Who *A-D*; dost] doest *C*
276 betweene] betwixt *A-D*
278 travells] trauails *A C*
279 linck] locke *A-D*
283 his] thy *A-C D*: thine *B*; did] caus'd *A-D*
285 wear] haue *A-D*; so] beene *A-D*
286 still feare] feare still *C*
287 ye Love] that ful *A-D*
290 the . . . that] those . . . which *A-D*
291 is left behynd] must still be left *A-D*
293 Vnhappy . . . how] Wretched mankinde, wherefore *A-D*
295 pleasures] pleasure *A-D*
296 and more t'inflame] t'ad greater flame *A-D*
297 wear but] but as *A-D*; invade] lade *A-D*
298 owr . . . and] Our heart with passions *A-D*
299 Yf . . . foule] Which though it be, yet ad not worse to ill *A-D*
300 wth . . . soule] Do, as the best men do, bound thine owne will *A-D*
301 Vnyte] Redeeme *A-D*
302 passions tyr'de] hart opprest *A-D*
303 Cease from] Breake vp *A-D*
304 thoughts . . . now] passions to thy passions *A-D*
305 seeke only] only seeke *A-D*
309 truth] loue *A-D*
314 that] Who *A-D*; to be] to haue beene *A B D*: t'haue beene *C*

Lines 317-24, i.e., stanza 40 in AH, are not included in A-D.

328 to vex] t'offend *A B D*: to offend *C*
329 whiles] Whilst *A-D*; labor] labour'd *A C*
331 And] To *A-D*; against] to hurt *A-D*
332 make] moue *A-D*
336 inrowled] inrolled *C*

338 in . . . wast] for a thought to thinke I was disgrac'st *A-D*
341 Come . . . happly] And therefore come deer Lord, least *A-D*
345 thoughts] thought *A-D*; do] doth *A-D*
346 doe] doth *A-D*
347 sorrowes] horror *A-D*
348 Th'event] The'euent *D*; except] vnlesse *A-D*
A-D have here 24 lines, i.e., 3 stanzas not in AH. Quoted from A, these lines are:

With what strange formes and shadowes ominous
Did my last sleepe, my grieu'd soule intertaine?
I dreamt, yet ô, dreames are but friuolous,
And yet Ile tell it, and God grant it vaine.
Me thought a mighty *Hippopotamus*
From *Nilus* floting, thrusts into the maine,
Vpon whose backe a wanton Mermaide sate,
As if she ruld his course and steerd his fate.

In the right margin by line 5 is the explanation, "A sea Horse."

With whom t'incounter, forth another makes,
Alike in kind, of strength and powre as good:
At whose ingrappling *Neptunes* mantle takes
A purple colour dyde with streames of bloud,
Whereat, this looker on, amaz'd forsakes
Her Champion there, who yet the better stood;
But se'ing her gone straight after her he hies
As if his hart and strength laie in her eyes.

On followes wrath vpon disgrace and feare,
Whereof th'euent forsooke me with the night,
But my wak'd cares, gaue me, these shadowes were
Drawne but from darknes to instruct the light,
These secret figures, natures message beare
Of com̄ing woes, were they desciphered right;
But if as clouds of sleepe thou shalt them take,
Yet credit wrath and spight that are awake.

349 ⟨aryse⟩ begin] begin *A-D*
353 thyne . . . thyne] thy . . . thy *A-D*
354 dost] doest *C*
357 Warr] wrong *A-D*
359 those] these *A-D*; *blank*] thy *A-D*
360 dangers] torment *A-D*; feares] griefe *A-D*
361 whether . . . sorrowes] whither am I caried *A-D*
362 their] my *A-D*

363 My wordes] Words still *A-D*; greife do] sorrowes *A-D*
364 to have] t'haue *A-D*; and] but *A-D*
366 is] that's *A-D*

A study of the variants shows that the revisions consisted not only in changes of diction, which sometimes affect the tone of a stanza, and the substitution of entire lines and couplets in the *ottava rima* stanza, but also the reversal in order of two stanzas, the omission of one stanza, and the addition of seven stanzas. It is not possible here to consider all changes, but some may be noted for illustration.

90 *A-D* eliminates both the antithetical balance of structure as it is given in *AH* and the idea that Octavia's power consists in Antony's wrong. The *AH* version is closer to North's *Plutarch* (p. 363).

125 Through the introduction of "wronged," *A-D* changes the emphasis of the lines.

129 The "eternall" of *AH* is surely a more suitable word in the context than is "immortall."

136 The meaning is shifted when the "loue" of *A-D* replaces "truth."

156 The either-or sense of *AH* is changed to a causal one in *A-D*.

161-62 The couplet in *AH* places the emphasis on Antony's wrong toward Cleopatra, but that in *A-D* upon his weakness in being held by an unkind mistress.

236 The line in *A-D* shows a gain in climactic power over that in *AH*. The change in the rhyme word necessitates revisions in lines 238 and 240.

250-51 The couplet in *AH* gives an incomplete construction, and therefore runs on to the next stanza for its verb in line 252. In *A-D* the couplet is closed.

267 The plea in *AH* is directed to Antony's spirit; in *A-D* to his mind.

293, 299-300 These lines of the same stanza are more personal and more appealing in *AH* than in *A-D*.

301 The "Vnyte" of *AH* relates more closely to the sense of the next line than does the "Redeeme" of *A-D*.

338 The reading in *A-D* places the emphasis upon Octavia's disgrace; the *AH* line upon her appeal to Antony, with the promise to remember only what he once was.

341 The *AH* line is more intimate than that in *A-D*.

347 The "sorrowes" of *AH* is more in keeping with Octavia's mood than the "horror" of *A-D*.

There are numerous changes in tense. *AH* tends to present the older forms, such as, "quoth" and "sayth" rather than "saies" and "said"; "sith" instead of "since"; "ffor why" rather than "because."

It is evident that variants such as these discussed above are not casual but show studied intention. The same conclusion is reached on examining the other divergences in the texts. The order of lines 57-64 and 66-73 is more logical in *AH*, though presumably Daniel himself approved the reversed order of the printed texts. The three stanzas inserted in *A-D* between lines 121 and 124 of *AH* develop further the theme begun in the preceding stanza (lines 114-21). The added lines on womankind's enslavement by custom to masculine power and the contrasting freedom of men are a perceptive amplification on the particular situation, but the sense in *AH* is continuous without them. Similarly the three stanzas inserted in *A-D* between lines 348 and 349 of *A-H* relate Octavia's dream and form an entity. The sense is clear and continuous without these added lines. The stanza inserted in *A-D* between lines 162 and 163 of *AH* actually tends to interrupt the sense, which moves logically in *AH*. Just why the one stanza found only in *AH*, lines 317-24, should have been omitted from the printed copies is not clear, for it is closely related to the preceding stanza.

In general one may say that the poem as it stands in *AH* is more personal, more intimate, with the emphasis placed upon the sorrowing but essentially forgiving Octavia, appealing to a basically noble spirit in Antony. The poem in *A-D* is more formal, less personal, tending to include wronged womankind more than does the other version. Greater stress is placed upon the disgrace of Octavia and upon hatred for the designing Cleopatra. The appeal is rather to Antony's sense of justice and, consequently, is less emotional in effect. Perhaps the poem was given its revised form after Daniel became associated with the Countess of Cumberland, but Octavia's story had certainly been in his mind, if not written, for several years.

A Letter from Octavia is linked in theme and in tone with Daniel's play *The Tragedie of Cleopatra*, printed for the fourth time in *The Poeticall Essayes* of 1599, in which, as noted, the epistle was first published. *Cleopatra* had previously appeared in 1594, 1595, and 1598 (see Sellers, pp. 33-35, and his "Supplementary Note to a Bibliography of the Works of Samuel Daniel," same volume, p. 341). The play's dedication to Mary Herbert, Countess of Pembroke, introduces the work as imposed by her, required as company for her "well grac'd *Anthony*." In 1592 the Countess had published her *Antonius* (*Antonie*, ed. 1595), which was translated from the French *Marc Antoine* (1578, 1585) of Robert Garnier (see *The Countess of Pembroke's Antonie*, ed. Alice Luce, *Litterarhistorische Forschungen*, vol. iii [1897]). The important influence of Garnier's refined, intellectual Senecan tragedies upon the Countess of Pembroke and her coterie, of whom Daniel was one, is fully set out and critically evaluated in Alexander M. Witherspoon's study *The Influence of Robert Garnier on Elizabethan Drama* (Yale Studies in English, vol. lxv [1924]). Witherspoon points out that Garnier's plays reveal an interest "in states of mind, and tragic and pathetic situations" (p. 12); that they introduce characters which tend to show a "Christian spirit of submission" rather than a "pagan attitude of unyielding hostility and hatred" (p. 43); and that they are largely concerned with women, who "are quite modern in many respects" (pp. 53, 71). It is easy to see the bearing of Garnier's influence not only upon *Cleopatra*, as Witherspoon demonstrates (pp. 99-111), but also upon *A Letter from Octavia*, with the second characteristic especially marked in the *AH* version. But it was the Countess of Pembroke, a woman who was herself "modern in many respects," who led Daniel to his interest in the type of writing represented by Garnier. In his dedication to the 1594 edition of *Cleopatra*, Daniel praises her as the one

> Who only doth predominate my Muse:
> The starre of wonder, which my labours chose
> To guide their way in all the course I vse.
> She, whose cleare brightnes doth alone infuse
> Strength to my thoughts, and makes mee what I am.
> (quoted from Daniel's *The Tragedie of Cleopatra nach dem Drucke von 1611*, ed. M. Lederer. *Materialien zur Kunde des alteren Englischen Dramas*, begruendet und herausgegeben von W. Bang. Vol. xxxi [Louvain, Uystpruyst, 1911], p. 73)

Even more significant for the present purposes are lines in Daniel's dedication to the revised *Cleopatra*, where the Countess of Pembroke is addressed as the one

> . . . who didst at first disclose
> Vnto our times, what noble powers there are
> in womens harts, and sent example farre
> To call vp others to like studious thoughts.

Influences at Wilton, he further says:

> Made me attempt t'attire her miserie
> In th'habit I conceiued became her care
> Which if to her it be not fitted right
> Yet in the sute of nature sure it is
> And is the language that affliction might
> Perhaps deliuer when it spake distresse
> And as it was I did the same addresse
> To thy cleere vnderstanding . . .
> (the same volume, pp. 3-4).

Daniel thus attributes to the primary guidance of the Countess of Pembroke not only his concern with the Antony-Cleopatra story, but also his interest in the psychology of superior women and in the language of affliction. This influence led, as we have noted, to the acquaintance with Garnier's writings, which, in turn, contributed to Daniel's portrayal of feminine character in distress. We may then raise the question as to whether *A Letter from Octavia* might not well have been written in an earlier version, similar to that in *AH*, about the time of, or shortly after, the composition of *Cleopatra*, especially since the Octavia of the *AH* version is closer to the Garnier ideal. Miss Shackford (ref. above) in her discussion of the influences upon Daniel's poetical epistles includes the possibility of the various *Elogia* by Paulus Jovus, whose *Imprese* Daniel published as early as 1585. Moreover, as Miss Shackford also notes, Daniel's epistles in their formal, objective manner have some similarity to Ovid's *Epistolae Heroidum*, which, like *A Letter from Octavia*, are dramatic complaints of classical heroines addressed to unfaithful lovers. Although Daniel undoubtedly knew the Latin, he also would have seen George Turbervile's verse translation, which went through five editions between 1567 and 1600 (see *The Heroycall Epistles of the Learned Poet Publius Ovidius Naso. Translated into English Verse by George Turbervile*, ed. Frederick Boas, London: Cresset Press, 1928). The model of the epistle form, therefore, was readily available to Daniel. It is, nevertheless, admittedly strange that *A Letter from Octavia*, if then written, was not added to the editions of *Cleopatra* which were printed in 1595 and 1598, especially since in the latter year Michael Drayton's *Englands Heroical Epistles* was published in a new and enlarged edition, the first having appeared in 1597. Use of the epistle form may, of course, have been suggested to Daniel by Drayton's publications.

It is difficult to determine whether the work of the all but unknown Samuel Brandon had any influence upon Daniel's first poetical epistle. Brandon's play *The Tragicomoedi of the vertuous Octavia* was entered on the Stationers' Register on October 5, 1598 (*Transcript*, ed. Arber, iii, 127). The title-page of the one early edition states that it was "Done by Samuel Brandon. 1598," but Ponsonby's imprint is not dated. Even if, as Dr. R. B. McKerrow says in his brief introduction to the Malone Society's reprint of the play (1909), it was most likely published in 1598, it was not necessarily in print before Daniel's *Letter* was entered upon the Register in January 1598/99. The point is of peculiar interest not only because the Octavia of Brandon's drama has some similarity to the Octavia of Daniel's *Letter*, but because Brandon's book contains two epistles: "Octauia to Antonius" and "Antonius to Octauia." These epistles, however, are very different from Daniel's *Letter*, both in tone and in form. Written in fourteeners, Brandon's epistles never rise above the level of mediocrity, and Octavia's consists mainly in lamentation and recriminations against Antony, whom she pities for the revenge which Justice will bring him. These epistles seem to have been written in imitation of several in Turbervile's translation of Ovid, where the fourteener is frequently used. *The vertuous Octauia*, which is of higher literary merit than the epistles, belongs to the Garnier school and is closely modeled on Daniel's *Cleopatra* (see McKerrow, p. v, and Witherspoon, pp. 112-13). Although *The vertuous Octauia*, based primarily on the account in North's *Plutarch*, presents a heroine who is somewhat too conscious of her merit to gain our sympathy as much as does Daniel's Octavia, there is enough similarity in the conception and in occasional passages to suggest a possible connection. Comparison of the following will illustrate:

D.	B.	
25-40	614-73	Octavia maintains that the report of Antony is false.
49-56	1042-49	Octavia admits the truth.
57-58	1274-77	The vulgar people make Octavia's actions a pattern for their deeds.
106-13	1194-1211	Noble minds should be careful of the right and not imitate the multitude.
122-29	1298-1309	Women are not faithless and unconstant, but ever strive for the perfect good; women are inflamed with the "true zeale of vertues loue."

Witherspoon conjectures that Brandon was a member of the Pembroke circle and that he and Daniel were friends. In such a circumstance we might suppose that Brandon's play was inspired not only by *Cleopatra* but by a manuscript version of Daniel's *Letter from Octavia.* Since Daniel's epistle was entered on the Stationers' Register only three months after *The vertuous Octauia*, it seems unlikely that Daniel was led to write his epistle after reading Brandon's work in book form. It is to be hoped that some one will discover more about Samuel Brandon.

In evaluating the *AH* version of Daniel's *Letter from Octavia*, we should keep in mind that both he and Sir John Harington were Somersetshire men, and that Harington addressed an epigram "*To my good friend Master* Samuel Daniel" (McClure, No. 126). Sir John's copy was probably taken directly from Daniel's manuscript.

A thorough study of *A Letter from Octavia* has been made by my former student Miss Ann L. Hentz in her Ph.D. dissertation, an edition of Daniel's epistles.

[235] *ffarewell fallse love the oracle of lyes*

Hand: the first seven lines are in Sir John Harington's secretary hand, but the remaining lines are in the hand of No. 180.

A version of No. 235, now regarded as written by Sir Walter Ralegh, was printed without ascription in (*A*) William Byrd's *Psalmes, Sonets, & songs of sadnes and pietie*, 1588, No. XXV, sig. E4^{r}, "BASSVS" (copy in the British Museum). Three contemporary manuscript copies add an additional stanza: (*B*) Bodleian MS. Rawl. Poet. 85, fol. 48^{r,v}, anonymous; (*C*) Folger MS. 1.112, fols. 9^{v}-10^{r}, anonymous; (*D*) British Museum MS. Harl. 7392, fol. 37^{r}, ascribed, "Ra." A three-stanza version headed "Mr. Rawleigh" and subscribed "R" (*E*) was printed by Bertram Dobell in 1901 from a contemporary manuscript in his possession, now lost ("Poems by Sir Thomas Heneage and Sir Walter Raleigh," *Athenaeum*, No. 3855 [1901], p. 349).

1 the] thou *B-E*
2 a mortall foe] *omitted* *A*; an] & *A B E*; vntoe rest] to rest, to rest *A*: to rest *B-E*
3 whome] whence *D*
4 vyled] vile *A E*: borne *B-D*
5 of] for *B*; temple . . . treason] *repeated* *A*
6 contrary] a Contrarye *B*; vnto] to *B*
9 sobbes] sorows *A C D*: Sorrowe *B E*
10 lendes] lend *A*
11 Schole] porte *C*: poole *D*; nette] breast *B*: neast *C*
12 golden] guilded *A C-E*; w^{ch}] that *A-C E*
13 foild] soyld (?) *B*; w^{ch}] whom *B C E*
14 Syrens] Syren *A C*; to] of *A-E*
15 affeccõns find] affection finds *A-E*
16 raging] cunnynge *B*: ranginge *C D*; runnes] flees *B*: roves *D*
18 runne] tunne *A*
Lines 19-24 are wanting in *E*.
20 a] ⟨fire⟩ a *C*; ⟨of⟩ and] and *A-D*
21 of] to *B*
22 leynes on] sleepes in *A-D*
24 a] And *D*; doubtfull] doubtless *B*

The stanza added in *B-D* is quoted from *C* with variants from *B* and *D* given below:

Sithe then thy traynes my yonger yeares betrayed
and for my faythe ingratitude I fynde
and sithe repentance hathe thy wronges bewrayed
whose course I see repugnant vnto kinde
false love desire and bewtye frayle adewe
dead is the roote from whence such fancy grewe

1 Sithe] Since *D*; then] thou *D*; betrayd] betray *D*
3 hathe] *omitted* *D*; thy] my *B*; bewrayed] bewray *D*
4 course] cause *D*; I . . . vnto] was euer contrarye to *B*
6 from whence] whence all *B*; such fancy] these fancyes *B*: such fancies *D*

Pierre Lefranc ("A Miscellany of Ralegh Material," *N & Q*, ccii [1957], 24-26) has called attention to a contemporary copy in Dr. Williams Library, MS. Jones B60 PRO MS. SP 46/126, fol. 123ᵛ, which, he says, agrees with the Byrd version except for "raginge" instead of "ranging" in line 16. As noted, the Bassus text has "raging"; however, Agnes M. C. Latham's text, taken, she states, from Byrd, Contra Tenor (with the final stanza from *C*) has "ranging" (*The Poems of Sir Walter Ralegh*, 1928, p. 28; rev. ed., London, Routledge and Kegan Paul, 1951, pp. 7-8, 98-100).

Dobell (ref. above) notes that the *E* version answers line by line one of six accompanying poems by Sir Thomas Heneage, who, Dobell suggests, is responsible for the Ralegh attribution. As printed by Dobell, Heneage's pertinent verses run:

Sr. Thomas Heneage

Most welcome love, thou mortall foe to lies,
thou roote of life and ruiner of debate,
an impe of heaven that troth to vertue ties,
a stone of choise that bastard lustes doth hate
a waye to fasten fancy most to reason
in all effects, and enemy most to treason.

A flowre of faith that will not vade for smart,
mother of trust and murderer of oure woes
in sorowes seas, a cordiall to the hart
that medcyne gives to every grief that growes;
a schoole of witt, a nest of sweet conceit,
a percynge eye that findes a gilt disceit.

A fortress sure which reason must defend,
a hopefull toyle, a most delyghtinge band,
affection mazed that leades to happy ende
to ranginge thoughtes a gentle ranginge hande,
a substance sure as will not be undone,
a price of joye for which the wysest ronne.

finis.

For Sir John Harington's unsuccessful attempt to obtain a copy of Heneage's poem, see No. 236 and Note.

Although the style and tone of No. 235 support the *E* attribution of authorship to Ralegh, it was not considered to be his by earlier editors. See, for example, *Poems by Sir Henry Wotton Sir Walter Raleigh and Others*, ed. John Hannah, 1845, and his later collections of 1870 and 1875. Attributions of the poem to Thomas Deloney and to John Lyly need not be seriously considered. For Deloney see *The Garland of Good Will*, 1631, Part III, No. 6; F. O. Mann, *The Works of Thomas Deloney* (Oxford, Clarendon Press, 1912), pp. 378, 584; Miss Latham's two editions of Ralegh, 1929, pp. 132-34, and, 1951, pp. 98-99. On Lyly, see R. W. Bond, *The Complete Works*, iii (1902), 440, 471-72; and my Note on No. 194. See also Hoyt H. Hudson, "Notes on the Ralegh Canon," *MLN*, xlvi (1931), 286-89.

[235a] *A man that hath a good wife love her love her*

Hand: seventeenth-century italic, with some additional scribbling in the same hand. The sentence may have been written as a kind of comment on the bitter lines of No. 235.

[236] *Wellcome true love, the lanterne of my lyghte*

Hand: Sir John Harington's. The rest of the folio is blank, as if Sir John intended to complete his copy of the poem, which, undoubtedly, is represented in the verses quoted from Sir Thomas Heneage in the Note on No. 235. The *AH* heading reverses the relation of attack and reply as suggested by Dobell. On Heneage see No. 175 and Note.

[237] *As truthe, before tyme, ought placed to be*

Hand: resembles Hand A, and is clearly of the same period, but is less carefully formed, is smaller, and shows perhaps more character. In the left margin hands are drawn with the front forefinger pointing to the last lines of stanzas 1, 3, and 4.

I have found no other copy of this labored account of the conflict between truth and time. Lines 29-36 indicate that it was written late in Queen Mary's reign.

[238] *The dread of future foes exyle my present Ioy*

Hand: written in two late secretary hands, the first extending through line 4, as I have explained in the Introduction (p. 33). The neat second hand is similar to Sir John Harington's fair secretary. The ascription is in contemporary italic.

The poem is quoted by George Puttenham in (*A*) *The Arte of English Poesie*, 1589 (ed. G. Willcock and A. Walker, 1936, p. 248), where it is also attributed to Queen Elizabeth. A contemporary copy, written in late secretary, occurs in (*B*) Bodleian MS. Rawl. Poet. 108, fol. 44ᵛ, where it is headed, "Verses made by the Quenes M[atie]." In (*C*) British Museum MS. Harl. 6933, a collection of the late seventeenth or early eighteenth centuries, the poem is written on fol. 8^r, headed, "The following Ditty on the Factions raised by the Q of Scots while Prisoner in England, was composed by Q Elizabeth and was printed not long after, if not before the beheading of the said Scots Queen." This collation was made for me by Kathleen Tillotson. Willcock and Walker in their edition of Puttenham (p. 326) refer to a copy in Harl. MS. 7392, fol. 27^v, but I did not discover this in time to see the original, and I do not find the poem among the Harvard photostats from that manuscript (Ph M51 F*). No. 238 was included by Henry Harington in (*D*) the 1769 edition of *NA*, pp. 58-59, where it is again attributed to Queen Elizabeth. Curiously it is omitted in later editions of *NA*.

1 dread] doubt *A-C*; exyle] exiles *A-D*
3 subiects] subiect *A C*;
4 shold] would *A C*; wove] weu'd *A-C*
5 Ioyes] tois *A*; doth] do *A-C*
6 turne] turnes *B*; rage] raigne *A*: rain *C*; report] repent *A-C*; chaunged . . . minds] course of changed windes *A C* . . . windes *B*: course of changed kindes *D*
7 topps] toppe *A-C*; suppose] supposed *A*: supp[r]st *B*; of Rue] of ruth *A C*: vpreard *B*; shalbee] wil be *A C*
8 of] all *A-C*; graffed] grafted *B D*; guile] guiles *A*; yow] ye *A*: all *D*
9 The] Then *A*; with great] which great *A C*: And great *D*; blynde] blinds *A C*
11 discord ay] eke discord *A C*; doth] do ye *B*
12 still . . . know] hath taught stil peace to growe *A C*: . . . flowe *D*
14 brooks no] it brooks no *A C*: brokes not *B*; seditious sects] strangers force *A C*
15 My] Our *A C*; through] with *A C*
16 the] their *A-C*; seekes] seeke *A C D*; or] and *A C*; gapes] gape *A-D*; further] *omitted* *A*: future *B*: lawless *C*: such like *D*

The copy in *D* is another of the *NA* poems which indicates that Henry Harington had other manuscripts than *AH* available for his poetry selections (see the Introduction, p. 18). In *D* the poem is introduced in the fragment of a letter:

Good Madame,

Herewith I commit a precious jewel, not for your ear, but your eye; and doubt not but you will rejoyce to wear it even in your heart: It is of her Highness own enditing, and doth witness, how much her wisdom and great learning doth outweigh even the perils of state, and how little all worldly dangers do work any change in her mynde. My Lady Wiloughby did covertly get it on her Majesties tablet, and had much hazard in so doing; for the Queen did find out the thief, and chid for spreading evil bruit of her writing such toyes, when other matters did so occupy her employment at this time; and was fearful of being thought too lightly of for so doing. But marvel not, good Madam, her Highness doth frame herself to all occasions, to all times, and all things, both in business, and pastime, as may witness this her sonnet.

Following the poem, the letter continues:

> Now tell me, if this be not worthie your commendation, and then pray for the Poet. I will do myself the honour of your Lord's company to Cambridge as he doth so kindlie proffer, and there send what other matters are working. . . .

The style suggests that the letter was written by Sir John. In his note Henry Harington explains that the rest of the letter was not legible and had no date.

Puttenham, who quotes the poem to illustrate the figure of "*Exargasia* or The Gorgious," says that he finds "none example in English meetre, so well maintayning this figure as that dittie of her Maiesties owne making passing sweete and harmonicall" (p. 247). He explains that the queen wrote the poem to declare her awareness of the secret factions in league with Mary Stuart, who was then in England. Thus the poem was composed before the execution of Mary in 1587.

In Ewald Flügel's article "Die Gedichte Der Königin Elisabeth" (*Anglia*, xiv [1892], pp. 346-61), which may be described as a preliminary edition of Queen Elizabeth's poetic compositions, No. 238 is printed from *B* with reference to *A* and *D*. It has also been printed in a number of anthologies, e.g., John Hannah, *The Poems of Sir Walter Raleigh . . . and Other Courtly Poets*, 1892, p. 136; *Sir George* Ellis, *Specimens of the Early English Poets*, ii (1803), 162-63.

[239] *In youthfull yeares, when first my yonge desyres beganne*

Hand: same as No. 237. At the end G. F. Nott wrote, "By M. Edwards. See Paradise of Dainty Devices."

Attributed to "M. Edwardes," a version was printed in (*A*) *The Paradyse of daynty deuises*, 1576, sigs. A1ᵛ-A2ʳ (ed. Rollins, 1927, No. 7), where it is entitled, "Faire woordes make fooles faine." An anonymous copy written in secretary script is in (*B*) British Museum MS. Add. 15253, fols. 38ᵛ-39ʳ.

5 wayes] way *A B*
6 a] thy *A B*; poore] pare *B*; t'advaunce] to aduaunce *A*
7 but] Yet *A*: But ⟨yet⟩ *B*
9 appear'd] appeares *A B*
10 eye] eyes *A B*
talkes
11 tales] ⟨tales⟩ *B*: rales *A*
14 warmed] is warmd *A B*; flamyng] fleinge *B*
16 olde] true *A B*
17 wordes alwaies] speache alway *A B*; do] doeth *A*: dooth *B*; where] whearas *B*
18 doth alway ill] alway dooth euil *A B*
19 happ] hopes *A B*
20 stryke] strike it *A B*
21 they] them *A B*
22 often] ⟨often⟩ *B*
must
23 must . . . tell] must I tell *A*: ⟨must⟩ I ‸ tell *B*; few] *omitted* *A B*
24 by . . . fynde] proues true in them *A B*
prove
25 proves] turne *A*: ⟨turne⟩ *B*
turnde
26 turn'd] growē *A*: ⟨growne⟩ *B*
29 no faire] not faire *B*
31 that] which *A B*; no] me *A B*
32 myne] my *A B*; thee] you *A B*; ffor] and *A B*; faire] let *A B*

The relation between *A* and *B* is strikingly close, but in lines 7, 25, and 26, the corrections in *B* agree with the readings in *AH* as opposed to those of the printed copy. Rollins in his note on the poem (pp. 185-88) points out that the *B* version was printed by J. O. Halliwell in his edition of John Redford's *Moral Play of Wit and Science* (Shakespeare Society, 1848, pp. 74-75).

Rollins has very full notes on the proverbs of the poem, and I shall not repeat his references, but the proverb of the title and the refrain was so old and so popular that it appeared in many works. Rollins has not called attention to line 4446 in *The Romaunt of the Rose*, "Hir faire biheest disceyveth fele" (Chaucer, *Works*, ed. Skeat). Sir David Lyndsay in *Ane Satyre of the thrie Estaits* gives a Scottish version, "Quhen fuillis ar fow, then ar thay faine" (*Works*, ed. F. Hall, Part iv, E.E.T.S., xxxvii [1869], p. 534, line 4274). No. 239, built as it is upon proverbial lore, conceived as the advice of a father to a son who is setting out in the world, belongs to a tradition which includes the famous speech of Polonius to Laertes (*Hamlet*, I, iii, 58-81); but I think Edwards has no hint of humor in his verses. For some comparison with the work of Thomas Churchyard, see the Note on No. 171.

[240] *The Subtile slylye slyghtes, that worldlye wittes do worck*

Hand: same as that of No. 239. Beneath the poem G. F. Nott wrote, "M. Edwards: See Paradise of Dainty Devices."

With the ascription as given by Nott, the poem was printed in (*A*) *The Paradyse*, 1576, sigs. H2^{v}-H3^{r} (ed. Rollins, 1927, No. 66). In the second edition of 1578 the title "Euill to hym that euill thinketh" was added. A contemporary copy is given also in (*B*) Brit. Mus. MS. Add. 26737, fol. 107^{r}, without attribution.

1 wittes] men *A*
3 yearly] yernfull *A*: earnefull *B*
4 seekes] seeke *B*
5 brought] caught *A B*
6 the] Eche *A B*
7 nature] nature's *B*
8 seekes] seeke *B*
10 subtillie] subtelly *A B*; he . . . hymself . . . he] shee . . . herselfe . . . shee *B*
11 I see] And yet *A*: And eke *B*; his ffosters] her fostred *B*; his learing] her lyinge *B*
12 seekes] seeke *B*
13 ffawning] fainyng *A*; on] one *A*; that do] for to *B*
14 ffrendly] faithlesse *B*; hartes] harte *A B*
16 seekes] seeke *B*

It is interesting to find that the wily serpent is feminine in *B*. The version changes entirely the meaning of line 11: And also her nourished poison her lying looks betray, or reveal. As Rollins has pointed out in his note in *A*, the line, referring to a fable of Aesop, means that the serpent's leering looks reveal that he will harm his protector. This is also the sense in *AH*.

[241] *Deeme all my deedes by dew desertes, wch shew foorth everie ffrute*

Hand A.

Other copies are in: (*A*) *Churchyardes Charge*, 1580, sigs. D2^{v}-D3^{r}, with the heading, "Written to a vertuous gentlewoman, whose name is in the verses," printed in black letter except for the first letters of lines

1-8, which are in roman type, thereby indicating the acrostic of the lady's name as *Dampport*; (*B*) Folger MS. 1.112, fol. 15^{v}, written in a secretary script which resembles that of Hand A. For collation with *A* the British Museum copy has been used.

1 Deeme . . . dew desertes] . . . true desarts *A*: By due desertes deme all my deedes *B*; w^{ch}] that *A*; w^{ch}] that *A*; shew foorth] sheweth *A B*
3 truthe] troth *A*; my retyre] me retire *A B*
4 luck] hap *A*
5 Passe] Prease *A*; saith] quothe *B*
6 harmes] harme *B*; do rise] dothe fall *B*
8 Wherfore] Therefore *A*; wisdome] reason *A B*; thie] the *A*; raigne] rage *B*; reason] wisdome *A B*; guyd] master *A*; thie] *omitted* *A*
9 my] myne *A*; is] rose *B*; betwixt] betwene *A*; hope and dread] ⟨hope a⟩ dread & hope *B*
10 my] by *B*; ffancyes] fancie *A*; to procead] thus I feed *A*: to ꝓvocke *B*
11 good] & *B*
12 all this] this great *A*; appeas'd] a peace *A*

B has two additional lines as follows:

Yet welcome hope but lucklesse happ I now will quite forsake
& onelye cleave to good desertes y^{t} yow at lengthe may pytye take

A has ten more lines than AH:

The tossed shipp maie hauen it, that anker holde hath none,
As rainie dropps by length of tyme, maie pearce the Marble stone:
What fort or holde is halfe so strong, that euer man could make,
But poulders force and Cannon blast, can make it doune to shake.
The pelletts all that I must bryng, vnfained faithe must be,
The ladder for to scale the walls, is trothe when tried is he:
This aunswere maie the captaine make, to whom my siege I laie,
Whose fort is wonne by sutche a sault, or by none other waie.
With Ensigne spred, and battrie set, I hope to make a breache,
And trust to winne by suite at length, that now is past my reache.

The collation shows that neither *AH* nor *B* keep perfectly the acrostic of the lady's name. In *AH* it is *Dampporwt*, including line 9; and in *B* it is *Bampporwt*, with line 9. Presumably, since the *Charge* was supervised by Churchyard, the printed version is correct, although it probably represents a later stage of the poem. For some account of Churchyard and the *Charge*, see the Note on No. 171. It is interesting to find Churchyard the soldier using specific battle imagery in the added lines of *A*.

[242] *Now Leave and lett me rest*

Hand: same as the preceding.

I have found no other copy of this repentant farewell to "Dame Pleasure," a theme which occurs frequently among the poems of *The Paradise of Dainty Devices.*

An earlier form of the proverb in line 14 is given by Langland, *Piers* C, xiii, 223 (ed. W. W. Skeat, E.E.T.S., liv [1873], 228): "And that that rathest rypeth roteth most saunest." It is included in *Iohn Heywoodes woorkes*, 1562, Pt. I, ch. x (Spenser Society, i [1867], 22), "But soone rype soone rotten, yong seynt olde deuill." Other examples are cited by Bartlett J. Whiting in *Proverbs in the Earlier English Drama*, Cambridge: Harvard University Press, 1938, pp. 121, 290. Compare similar expressions in No. 254.

[243] *Attend ye, goe play ye, my Love I am busye*

Hand: same as the preceding. In line 30 the changed reading is given in another hand.

A longer version, with many variants, was printed in (*A*) Clement Robinson's miscellany, *A Handful of Pleasant Delights*, 1584, sigs. A6^{v}-A7^{r,v} (ed. Rollins, 1924, pp. 12-14), with the following heading:

The scoffe of a Ladie, as pretie as may be,
to a yong man that went a wooing:
He wēt stil about her, & yet he wēt without her,
because he was so long a dooing.

Even more different is the version included in (*B*) Folger MS. 2071.7, fol. 120^{r,v}, entitled, "The louer scoffed." This appears to be an early seventeenth-century copy. In both *A* and *B* the line arrangement differs from that in *AH*, but I have, of course, followed the latter for the collation.

1 ye . . . ye] thee . . . thee *A B*; my] Sweet *A B*; Love] youth *B*
2 silke and] silken *B*; yet vnsponne] not yet spun *A B*
3 she do send for] that she send for *A*: she name *B*
4 my] all my *B*; work] worke to be *A*
5 then] *omitted* *B*; how will] How shall *A*: will *B*; it] I *A*: she *B*
6 shall . . . Love] To say loue *A*: To say you *B*
7 no . . . fitly] Fie no, it will not fit me *A*: ffie noe it must not be *B*
8 *omitted* *A B*
9 were retayned] were attained *A*: once were gained *B*; Ioyes] ioye *B*; reclaymed] vnfained *A B*

10 silk and seame] seame and silke *A B*; wold] wil *A*: *omitted* *B*
11 prov'd] proofe *A*: *omitted* *B*
12 wanton] *omitted* *B*
13 say, nowe goe] say go *A B*; pyke] pack *A B*
15 Seeke out dame] Go seeke . . . *A*: Go seeke the *B*
16 most . . . brydle] More fit for thy bridle *repeated* *A*: Then thou maist bridle *B*
The rest of B differs so radically that the verses are quoted complete following the collation.
17 worth] worthie *A*; yor] thy *A*; detracting] detaining *A*
18 is in vayne] vayne it is *A*; you have] thou hast *A*
19 for you] now to *A*; and] Go *A*; yor] thy *A*
20 goe] and *A*; yor] thy *A*; you have] thou hast *A*
21 goe say] Say this *A*; now] Then *A*; than as] *omitted* *A*; youe] thee *A*
22 yor] the *A*
Between lines 23 and 24 A inserts:
And needeth no threatning
24 *Repeated in A*
25 Now . . . wandring] The boy is gone lurking *A*; the Ladies] Good Ladies *A*
26 you] we *A*
27 oft] All *A*
28 *Omitted* *A*
29 and . . . all] The frost bites *A*
30 Lett . . . owers] Lets work at due howres *A*
Hartes ease
31 ⟨Haste vs⟩] Haste, haste *A*
32 *Repeated in A*

Following line 32 A adds:

Now Ladies be merie,
Because you are werie:
leaue worke I say, and get you home,
Your businesse is slacking,
Your louer is packing:
your answer hath cut off his comb.

How then?
The fault was in him sir,
He wooed it so trim sir,
Alas poore seelie fellow,

Make much of thy pillow.
Make much of thy pillow,

The poem in B after line 16 reads:

Cupid is lurking
I heede my working
Go way now that I haue don
Tide will not tarie
I will not marie
Out of the light of the sunne
Stay not

Seene at all houres
I am in haste
No time to waste

Now ladies be merie
I am but wearie
Leaue worke and gett you home
My louer is packing
ffor all his craking
And I haue cut of his combe
Now then
The fault was in him for
He wooed to trim her
Poore selie fellow
Make much of thy willow.

The *B* version is, of course, closer to that of *A* than to the one in *AH*.

A poem in *A gorgious Gallery, of gallant Inuentions*, 1578 (ed. Rollins, 1926, pp. 38-39), seems to be an answer to this delightful song. The *Gallery* poem is entitled, "The Louer exhorteth his Lady to bee constant. To the Tune of Attend thee go play thee." In his note, p. 162, Rollins calls attention to a song by Wantonness in the *Marriage of Wit and Wisdom*, 1579 (ed. J. O. Halliwell, Shakespeare Soc. [1846], p. 20), which was sung "to the tune of 'Attend the goe playe the.'" Consequently, there is no question that before 1578 No. 243 was well known as a song. In his note in *A Handful*, p. 86, Rollins surmises that it had appeared in Robinson's collection of 1566, *Plesant Sonnets*. It is probable that the copy in *AH* represents this earlier version. The later *B* version was evidently sung to a different tune, for the variants change the rhythm noticeably.

[244] *Longer to prove ye, what may it availe me*

Hand: same as the preceding. The correction in line 8 is in the same hand. The "true" in line 26 looks like "trut," but surely "true" is intended.

From the refrain one may suppose that this was a song, very probably sung in answer to No. 243.

[245] *ffalce may he be and by the powres above*

Hand A. In the margin there is a penciled note by Bishop Percy, "Printed in Surrey's Poems. fo. 83."

Printed among the Uncertain Authors in *TM*, sigs. Aa3^{v}-Aa4^{v} (ed. Rollins, also No. 245), No. 245 is there entitled, "Against him that had slaundered a gentlewoman with him selfe." In his note Rollins gives variants from the *AH* transcript, *N* fols. 108^{v}-109^{v}, which differs in a few instances from the original.

3 and] or
4 lyer] .R.
10 nor . . . or] no nor neuer
12 over chardge] charge so large
16 deede] dedes
20 Colatyne] Collatiue *misprint*
21 Traytours] trayterous
22 vndid] fordid
23 Rodapeiane mayde] R. so depe can auoyde
25 Crok'st] crokest; agayne] agaynst
26 Cadge] brag
27 foyse] voyce
32 shuld'st] shouldest
37 delightes] delight
41 leade] treade
42 advowe] here auowe
43 sett] settest
48 the] in; to] eke
58 trothe] trouth
59 stode] stande; thie] the
60 wonne] one
62 may . . . thee] on thee may light

The *TM* variant in line 23 makes no sense, but the compositor's mistake was corrected in succeeding editions, in which the line agrees with *AH*. In his note Rollins identifies the maid as Phyllis, daughter of King Sithon, who hung herself when her lover Demophoön failed to come. Rollins quotes from the first line of her epistle in Ovid's *Heroides* (II.I), beginning, "Hospita, Demophoön, tua te Rhodopeia Phyllis."

Perhaps a *TM* editor is responsible for the toning down of line 26 by the substitution of "brag" for "cadge." According to the *N.E.D.* early meanings of "cadge" as a verb are obscure, but in the fourteenth through the sixteenth centuries it seems to have meant: to bind, fasten, or knot. The significance of the word here is evidently related to the subsequent meaning, cited for 1695 to 1854, "to load or stuff the belly," and to the later adjectival meaning as wanton or lustful (eighteenth century, Scottish and northern dialectical).

It is interesting to find personal invective as early as this written in decasyllabic couplets.

[246] *Honour is highe, and hard for to attayne*

Hand A. The following heading is written in modern script, possibly G. F. Nott's, "On Henry Stanley, Lord Strange. H: S.," deduced no doubt from the fact that the poem is an acrostic, "Henri Stanlei Lorde Strange H S." No. 247 is a companion piece, as line 39 in that poem makes it clear that it was addressed to his wife, Lady Margaret Stanley. So far as I know, neither poem has been printed, and I have found no other manuscript copies.

Henry Stanley (1531-1593) was eldest son of Edward Stanley, third Earl of Derby, by his first wife, Katherine, daughter of Thomas Howard, second Duke of Norfolk. Henry was styled Lord Strange. He succeeded his father as fourth Earl of Derby on the latter's death in 1572. He was knighted at the coronation of King Edward VI, February 20, 1546/47, and also then became a member of the Privy Chamber. At the conclusion of a peace in March, 1550, Strange was sent as a hostage to France. A project, not carried out, was under way to marry him to Margaret Seymour, daughter of Edward, Duke of Somerset and Lord Protector. It appears that Somerset was attempting to use the young Lord Strange to further other designs. Edward VI recorded in his journal for October 26, 1551 (*Literary Remains of King Edward the Sixth*, ed. John Gough Nichols, ii, Roxburghe Club [1857], 361):

> The lord Straung confessid how the duke willed him to sturre me to mary his third daughter the lady Jane, and willed him to be his spie in al mattieres of my doynges and saynges, and to knowe when some of my counsel spake secretly with me. This he confessed of himself.

At the trial of Somerset in December, 1551, Lord Strange reiterated on oath the truth of the charge against Somerset, although the latter denied it.

Probably because of the Catholic tendencies of his father, Lord Strange in July, 1554, became a Gentleman of the Privy Chamber to King Philip.

On February 7, 1554/55, Lord Strange married Lady Margaret Clifford, only daughter of Henry de Clifford, second Earl of Cumberland, by his wife, Eleanor Brandon. Lady Eleanor was second daughter of Henry VIII's younger sister Mary and Charles Brandon, Duke of Suffolk. The eldest daughter of this match, Lady Frances, who married Henry Grey, Marquis of Dorset and Duke of Suffolk, was mother of the ill-fated Lady Jane Grey. According to the will drawn up by Edward VI on the succession to the Crown, Lady Margaret Clifford was declared next in line after Lady Jane Grey (*Chronicle of the Grey Friars of London*, ed. J. G. Nichols, Camden Society, liii [1852], 79).

During the reign of Queen Elizabeth, Henry Lord Strange frequently served as a member of ecclesiastical commissions and was a member of the Council of the North. He is said not to have shared his father's Catholic sympathies and to have been an enemy to the recusants in Lancashire. He was made Knight of the Garter, April 24, 1574, and was appointed ambassador extraordinary to confer the insignia of the order of the Garter on King Henry III of France, January 20, 1580. He was a commissioner for the trial of Mary Queen of Scots in 1586, and was appointed Lord High Steward in 1589. His name is best known in literature for his patronage of a company of actors who became more famous under his son Ferdinando (1559-1594), who succeeded his father as fifth Earl of Derby on the latter's death in 1593. Apparently it is the son Ferdinando whom Sir John Harington praises in his notes to Book XXXII of his translation of the *Orlando Furioso* (ed. 1591, p. 266). After speaking of Charles Brandon, Duke of Suffolk, Sir John continues:

> *of whose ofspring there remaine yet some most worthie branches, but the likest to him for armes and cauallarie (as we terme it) is my noble good Lord, the Lord* Straunge, *whose value and vertue, need not this my barren and briefe testimonie.*

(In addition to the references cited above, the account of Henry Stanley, Lord Strange and Earl of Derby, is taken from the *D.N.B.*, G. E. Cokayne, *Complete Peerage of England, Scotland, Ireland, Great Britain, and the United Kingdom*, iii [1890], 71, and notes given by Nichols in his edition of *Literary Remains.*)

It is, I think, very probable that the elder Harington wrote the tributes to Ferdinando Stanley's parents. No. 247 was certainly written after Lady Margaret's marriage to Lord Strange in 1555, and presumably both poems would have been written before 1572, when Henry Stanley succeeded as Earl of Derby. For similarities in style, or in kind, both poems should be compared with Nos. 2, 21 (and its companion poem in the Notes), 23, 177, 232, 262, and with the first two poems in the Appendix. Related also is the elegy on "master Deurox" in *TM* (ed. Rollins, No. 169), which was written by John Harington. In this connection the word "degrace" in line 11 of No. 246 is of special interest. It is not given in the *N.E.D.*, but it does occur again in a Harington poem, No. 262, line 47. Characteristic of Harington's experimental rhyming tendencies (e.g., Nos. 2 and 3), is the irregularity of the third quatrain, which instead of introducing two new rhymes as do the others, carries over the *d* rhyme of the second quatrain.

It should be noticed that both Nos. 246 and 247 show an indebtedness to Surrey's elegy on Wyatt (*Poems*, ed. Padelford, 1928, No. 46). Like the latter, No. 246 employs the binding closing couplet following alternately rhyming quatrains—an extension of the English sonnet form.

Whether Harington or not, the writer reveals a nice sense of decorum in line 5 of No. 246 with his use of the archaic "Awntrus," i.e., adventurous, to describe the acts of "Awcetours olde," i.e., ancestors.

[247] *The Daughters deare of mightie Iove the great*

Hand A. In the same modern script used in the title of No. 246, a companion piece, this poem is headed, "On the Lady Margaret Strange." In confirmation of this, note the play on the name in line 41. A "margaret Stone" is, of course, a marguerite, i.e., a pearl.

A further example of a play on Lady Strange's name occurs in a letter written by Richard Bertie in 1568 to Sir William Cecil:

> Having to send to Lady Strange, it would seem strange, if I did not thank you for courtesies received. Peradventure, you will think it strange, to hear from me out of the south [quoted from Lady Cecilie Goff, *A Woman of the Tudor Age*, London, J. Murray, 1930, p. 285].

Something about Lady Strange has been said in the Note on No. 246, which was addressed to her husband, Henry Stanley, Lord Strange and Earl of Derby. I have also indicated that the poems were probably written by John Harington.

Some further details about Lady Strange may be of interest. According to the *D.N.B.*, she was born in 1540, but Charlotte C. Stopes, *Shakespeare's Environment* (London, G. Bell, 1914), p. 257, points out that in February, 1562, Lady Margaret testified that she was twenty-four. This would place the date of her birth in 1538, a year after the marriage of her parents, Lady Eleanor Brandon and the Earl of Cumberland. Despite the fact that Lady Margaret was designated by Edward VI as next in succession to the crown after her cousin Lady Jane Grey, she got on well with Queen Mary, and was one of the Ladies of the Bedchamber. She is said, however, to have boasted of her right to the throne over her cousins Katherine and Mary Grey (Richard Davey, *The Sisters of Lady Jane Grey*, New York, Dutton, 1911, pp. 293-99). Reasons for Lady Margaret's favor with Queen Mary are not hard to find. The Earl of Cumberland showed himself an astute politician. In 1553, before the death of Edward VI, a marriage was arranged by John Dudley, Duke of Northumberland, between his brother Sir Andrew Dudley and Lady Margaret Clifford. Sir Andrew accordingly sent jewels, plate, and robes to Cumberland, who, on the death of Edward VI, took possession of the gifts in the name of Queen Mary. Some of the Dudley gifts were turned over to Mary; others remained with the Cliffords. This circumstance led to a suit with the Dudley family, 1559-62. On Mary's accession in 1553 the Dudleys were imprisoned, and Queen Mary warned Cumberland that the marriage of his daughter Margaret must meet with her approval. That favor was granted in the match with Henry Stanley, Lord Strange. The ceremony took place at Westminster. The Queen gave a feast and presented Lady Margaret with some of the Dudley jewels, linen, and robes (Stopes, pp. 249-57). Lady Margaret was not happy with her husband, and in 1560 wrote to Sir William Cecil about dissension between them (*C.S.P.D.*, *1547-80*, ed. Robert Lemon [1856], p. 167, nos. 33, 34).

In 1568 Lady Strange was one of Queen Elizabeth's Ladies of the Privy Chamber (Goff, p. 285, note), and in 1570 Queen Elizabeth wrote the Earl of Derby that she desired his daughter-in-law Lady Strange to continue in attendance on her (*C.S.P.D.*, same vol., p. 363, no. 39). As another of the Ladies of the Privy Chamber, Isabella Harington would have been closely associated with Lady Strange (see the Note on No. 177). About 1578 Lady Margaret, then Countess of Derby, fell from court favor and was accused of conspiring by magic arts against Queen Elizabeth and of entertaining Jesuits (Stopes, p. 257; Davey, p. 301). The remaining years of Lady Margaret's life, spent under supervision on the Queen's order, were unhappy and at times morbid. She communed with soothsayers, who promised that her son Ferdinando should be king. William Camden in *The History or Annals of England During the Reign of Elizabeth* (*A Complete History of England* [Kennett White], ii [1706], 596) refers to her in an account of important men who died in 1596:

> Amidst these Gentlemen, I must take the Liberty to mention one of the other Sex, *viz. Margaret Clifford* Countess of *Derby*, the only Daughter of *Henry Clifford*, Earl of *Cumberland*, by *Eleanor Brandon*, Niece to King *Henry* VIII. 'Tis remarkable of this Lady, that through an idle mixture of Curiosity and Ambition, supported by sanguine Hopes and a credulous Fancy, she much used the Conversations of Necromancers and Figure-Flingers; upon which account she lost a great share in the Queen's Inclinations a little before her death.

There can be no denying that the facts about the latter part of Lady Margaret's life refute the encomium of her expressed in this poem. In view of these later events, it is ironic to read that she was "A constant Corps," "not fearing secreat foes," and "not thristing [i.e., pressing] rule." No. 247 is, however, clearly addressed to a young woman. In the

Note on No. 246 I have suggested that these two poems were written by John Harington. No. 247 is very close in style to No. 262, which was written before Elizabeth became queen in 1558. Nos. 246 and 247 were probably composed about the same time, possibly on the occasion of, or shortly after the marriage between Lord Strange and Lady Margaret in 1555.

The use of "state," or "staight," should be noticed. In lines 38 and 47 it clearly means "prince," or "person of high rank." The sense in line 35 is not clear, but from the context it seems to be: such a lady a lesser noble is not like to be. Or do we have: such a lady, in rank last, likes not to be? But this is contrary to the sense of the stanza. The *N.E.D.* notes no use of "furnyture" (line 39) as "ornament" earlier than 1548.

[248] *The mightie Macedon king, tooke in good part*

Hand A.

The story to which this couplet seems to refer was told not of Alexander, the "mightie Macedon king," but of Artaxerxes II, king of the Persians. Plutarch in his *Moralia*, 172.B (trans. F. C. Babbitt, Loeb Library, iii [1931], 8-9) says:

> Artaxerxes, the king of the Persians, O Trajan, Emperor Most High and Monarch Supreme, used to think that, as compared with giving large gifts, it was no less the mark of a king and a lover of his fellow-men to accept small gifts graciously and with a ready goodwill; and so, on a time when he was riding by, and a simple labourer, possessed of nothing else, took up water from the river in his two hands and offered it to the king, he accepted it pleasantly and with a cheerful smile, measuring the favour by the ready goodwill of the giver and not by the service rendered by the gift.

Plutarch tells the same story in the account of Artaxerxes in his *Lives*.

[249] *Oh, god the Heathen people vyle*

Hand A. The "Spal" is a scribal error.

Since this Psalm is numbered lxxix in accord with the practice adopted by the Reformers, and since the elect are referred to in line 36, we may conclude that the metrical version has a Calvinistic origin. It may be a translation of a continental version. Lines 31-32 are not in the Vulgate, and lines 37-48 are fairly free. Use of an introductory argument is in the manner of Wyatt's Psalms (Nos. 154-67).

[250] *Scarse can I me refrayne/ from teares when I thinck on*

Hand A.

This story of Paris, the golden apple, and the three goddesses, written in popular poulter's measure, might very well have been included among the poems of Uncertain Authors in *TM*. So far as I know, however, it has not been published, nor have I come across another manuscript copy.

[251] *Not she for whome prowde Troye did fall and burne*

Hand A.

This sonnet was printed in *A gorgious Gallery, of gallant Inuentions*, 1578, sig. F4v (ed. Rollins, 1926, p. 56), where it is entitled, "The Louer in the prayse of his beloued and conparison of her beauty."

4 a] an; to] did
6 was sprẽnt] *omitted*
8 The] Th'
11 .N. N.] the; and] and the
13 heaven] Ioue
14 happie he] happy is hee

The words omitted in line 8 of the *Gallery* version are needed for the iambic measure. It is interesting to find that "N. N.," evidently the initials of the lady for whom the sonnet was written, is not designated in the published copy. The last two lines imitate the closing couplet of Surrey's sonnet on Lady Elizabeth Fitzgerald (*Poems*, ed. Padelford, 1928, No. 29; quoted in full in the Note on No. 72). Surrey's lines are:

Bewty of kind, her vertues from above
Happy ys he that may obtaine her love.

[252] *Syns thought hath leave to thinck at least*

Hand A.

A contemporary copy is in (*A*) Bodleian MS. Ashmole. 840, p. 610, written in the hand of Robert Cook, principal herald and king of arms. This is evident from a statement on the same page signed by him and dated May 24, 1568. Another contemporary copy is in (*B*) Bodleian MS. Rawl. Poet. 85, fol. 114v.

2 and tyde] vntryed *A*: vntrewe *B*
3 so is it] for that is *A*: for so is *B*
4 so] their *B*

[253] *You halting howres that passen all to slowe*

Hand A.

These anonymous verses, of which I have found no other copy, are written in the manner of the mid-sixteenth century.

[254] *Sone highe, sone Lowe, sone Ryche, sone poore*

Hand A.

The sententious observations of this quatrain are similar to the proverb given in No. 242, line 14, for which a few parallels are cited in the Note. In *Iohn Heywoodes woorkes*, 1562, Pt. II, chap. vi (Spenser Society, i [1867], 62), a variation of the third line of No. 254 appears as, "Soone gotten, soone spent, yll gotten yll spent."

[255] *My lyfe, is stryfe my ease, disease*

Hand A.

No doubt this was intended to be written as six lines of rhymed dimeter couplets.

[256] *Who so that lyst to note well this*

Hand A.

This sonnet on the weakness of divided strength may have been developed from two verses in Ovid's *Remediorum Amoris*, lines 445-46:

> Grandia per multos tenuantur flumina rivos,
> Saevaque diducto stipite flamma perit.

The sonnet follows the English rhyme pattern but is written in tetrameter instead of the customary pentameter. Its experimental form and its sententious subject matter suggest that it was written no later than the third quarter of the sixteenth century.

[257] *In ioye thow arte, for whome I Sorowe sore*

Hand A. Above the poem is a note by G. F. Nott, "On Jone Aleine. T. L." This is clearly deduced from considering the poem an acrostic, built on the name of the diseased lady with the author's initials given in the closing couplet. Since the name "Allen" was frequently spelled "Aleyn," or "Aleine," there is no reason why this could not be an epitaph on one Joan Allen, and there were several whose names appear in genealogies of the period. Harl. MS. 1463 (a record of the visitation of 1568, augmented), fol. 3ᵛ, lists the family of Sir William Allen, Mayor of London in 1572, whose wife was Joane Daborne. Their daughter, Joanne, married Thomas Starkey of London. The same manuscript, fol. 30ʳ, gives the pedigree of Richard Allen of London, whose son married Joane Woodgate. These same pedigrees are given in Harl. MS. 1096, fols. 38ʳ and 61ʳ. However, the poem seems to have been written by the lady's husband or lover, the latter certainly if we accept the "T L" of the last two lines as the initials of the writer. Hence, the epitaph was probably written on another Joan Allen. The undistinguished style is that of the third quarter of the sixteenth century.

[258] *Remember well from whome ye have*

Hand A.

Like No. 256 this poem is an example of a sonnet in iambic tetrameter which otherwise follows the English type. This is true in the organic sense. Each alternately rhyming quatrain is separated in form and in thought, yet parallel, with a somewhat more distinctive break before the third quatrain, and the closing couplet expresses the point. As in Surrey's poetry, roughness is avoided by careful use of monosyllables and dissyllables and strong line endings. The familiar reference to nature's mold and an expression like "fordge and fyle" suggest the poetry of *TM*, but use of the sonnet for moral admonition to a fellow poet (or to himself) and as expression of simple piety reflects rather the temper of some of the verses in *The Paradise of Dainty Devices.*

[259] *When Cancer creapt was out of sight*

Hand A. No other copy known.

This is the first of a series of three poems, Nos. 259-61, which belong essentially to the pastoral tradition. The first two have a Chaucerian note in their opening lines and occasionally in diction. The narrator, a franklin, cares for his sheep, cultivates his land (No. 260, lines 11, 44), and dwells in a "homlye Cribb," or cottage, with his "best beloved dame" (No. 259, lines 39-40). In No. 259 the franklin's vivid description of a royal hunt is the means for a panegyrike on the virgin queen, who holds all pursuers at bay. In Nos. 260 and 261 the franklin's account of a meeting, while he was searching for his one lost sheep, with an aged man who in vain had spent his time at court, gives the opportunity for the expression of themes common in Tudor poetry: criticism on the evils of the court, praise of the simple life, moralizing on Time and misspent youth, chastisement of the "vyle goddesse" Fortune, who is to be blamed when "thow in furye fall."

Although No. 259 is written in the common fourteener, the author effectively conveys by the rhythm in several lines the hurry and excitement of the hunt, and the diction often adds to the sense of reality (see especially lines 7-8, 21-22). As I read the poem, I am reminded of lines in Surrey's elegy on the Duke of Richmond (*Poems*, ed. Padelford, No. 31), not only in the stanza of that poem on the hunting of the hart, but in the mingling of the playful love element with outdoor activity. Perhaps the "Iolye woes" of line 25 was suggested by Surrey's use of the expression in his sonnet "When Windesor walles sustained my wearied arme" (ed. Padelford, No. 30).

In several lines the diction, which occasionally has a studied effect of the archaic, is worthy of comment:

6. "ffrithe," a wood or a deer park, possibly the latter as more rarely used and then mainly in Middle English.

9. "pight," seated, or placed, old past participial form of "pitch." "prick," probably an error for "prickt," in the sense, rode on horseback.

11. "glymsing," glimpsing, glimmering. "glitt'raunt," not in the

N.E.D., but clearly derived from "glitter," signifying sparkling, or gleaming.

12. "molde," earth.

13. "startling," capering, prancing.

14. "amayne," literally, at main, at full force, or speed; according to the *N.E.D.* first used about 1540.

21. "mote," note of a horn or bugle; not used in this sense after 1575 (*N.E.D.*), except in Scottish speech. "take the say," i.e., open the inner parts of the stag or buck to see how fat he is; earliest example noted in the *N.E.D.* is dated 1611.

22. "Cabadge," a variant spelling of "cabache," to cut off the head of a deer close behind the horns. "baye," literally, in close quarters, referring in hunting to the relative position of the hunted animal and the hounds. This line presumably means: the keeper can cut off the head of the deer close behind the horns, thereby proving that the hunted animal has been brought completely to bay.

38. "thrust," a crowd, or press, often used with "throng" between 1565 and 1620 (*N.E.D.*).

[260] *This royall hunting ended thus*

Hand A. No other copy known.

For some introductory comments on this poem, see the preceding Note. As in No. 259 the diction is occasionally of interest.

8. "yshent," put to shame, old past participial form of "shend." Compare Chaucer, *The Freres Tale*, line 14, "And smale tytheres weren foule y-shent" (quoted from ed. Skeat). Spenser in *The Shepheardes Calender*, "*August*," line 139, uses "yshend."

9. "by said Chadd said I." The passage should read, I think, "by saint Chadd said I." The first "said" could easily have resulted from a copyist's error. Saint Chadd, or Ceadda (d. 672), was brother of Saint Cedd, whom he succeeded as abbot of Lastingham. Eventually he became Bishop of Mercia. In the account of Ceadda given by Bede in *The Ecclesiastical History of the English People*, Book IV, chap. III, he is said to have built a monastery "in the place which is called *Aet Bearwe*, that is By the Wood," in Lincolnshire, and to have preferred walking afoot to do the work of the gospel (see the 1565 translation by Thomas Stapleton, ed. Philip Hereford, London: Burns, Oates and Washbourne, 1935, p. 191). It is consequently quite appropriate that the franklin call upon Saint Chadd as he starts forth on foot to the wood. This reference to Saint Chadd suggests that the author of Nos. 259-61 may have come from Lincolnshire, or from the Midlands, where this saint's name would more probably have been used than in some other parts of England.

24. "to pitche and pay," to pay ready money, in other words, cash.

32. "at poynt to sterve," just about to starve. This expression seems to have been first used in the early sixteenth century.

[261] *When I had heard his tale to end*

Hand A. No other copy known.

For introductory comments see the Note on No. 259.

6. "frayned," asked. Compare Chaucer, *The Prioresses Tale*, line 148, "she frayneth and she preyeth pitously" (ed. Skeat). The *N.E.D.* records no example after 1536.

8. "playne plat Contrey tearmes," plain, blunt speech. Compare Chaucer, *The Tale of the Man of Lawe*, lines 787-88:

> This messenger tormented was til he
> Moste biknowe and tellen, plat and plein.

13. "as hownd hunting at gaze," i.e., as the hound hunting by sight, after he has spotted his quarry, runs quickly toward it, no longer needing to sniff his way. The only example quoted in the *N.E.D.* of the phrase "at gaze" used in hunting is dated 1865, but its appearance in the text of this poem is proof that it was in use some three hundred years earlier. The meaning in lines 13-14 seems to be: instead of rashly running away, you should behave as a hound hunting by sight, confront your quarry by blaming each person for want of stay, and then you might cause some consternation.

19. "with busye Cure," relating to the diligent application of oneself. The *N.E.D.* has no example of the phrase after 1556.

[262] *The great Dyana, chaste*

Hand A. In line 25 the *s* in "Markhams" is written in another ink, though in the same hand, over the comma; in line 45 the *c* in "mace" is written over an *s*.

A slightly different version of the poem is in the *NA*, 1769, pp. 88-90 (ed. 1779, iii, 261-64; ed. 1804, ii, 390-92), entitled, "*The Prayse of Six Gentle Women attending of the Ladye* ELIZABETH *her Grace, at* Hatfield *House*." According to an appended note by Henry Harington, this version was printed from a copy in the handwriting of John Harington. As explained in the Introduction (p. 18), the *NA* copy may have been printed directly from John Harington's manuscript, which was then destroyed. The variants in lines 28 and 34 are evidently a result of failure to read the manuscript properly. The poorest variant in the *NA* occurs in the "Pyramus" of line 16, which makes no sense in the context. We may wonder whether Henry Harington or the printer made the alteration because "Alsyon" was not understood.

3 me commaunded] did commande
7 How she meanes] Thus meaning

16 Alsyon] Pyramus
20 heale and hurt] wounde and heal
22 Shall] And
28 Grysylde] Gryfelde
32 that . . . enbrace] Such beautie to embrace
34 eares is] cares we eares is *1779, 1804*
36 the] That
38 thinges] thing
46 mightie Hercules] Hercules stout
47 degrace] disgrace
58 worthie] gracious
61 sacred] favour'd *1779, 1804 only*

The Princess Elizabeth was officially granted the manor of Hatfield on June 22, 1550 (*Acts of the Privy Council*, ed. J. R. Dasent, iii [1890], p. 52), but she had set up an establishment there and at Cheshunt sometime after June of 1548, when she was removed from the household of her step-mother, Catherine Parr, then wife of Sir Thomas Seymour (Sir John MacLean, *A Life of Sir Thomas Seymour*, 1869, p. 55). After Mary came to the throne in July of 1553, Elizabeth's position became precarious, and from March until October of 1554 she was confined as a prisoner, first in the Tower and then at Woodstock. On her release, October 16, she took up residence again at Hatfield, where she lived the greater part of the time until her accession to the throne in 1558 (*D.N.B.*). On the basis of available information it is not possible to determine definitely whether this poem was written during the earlier or the later period at Hatfield. Official dated lists would, of course, answer the question, but the earliest records I have seen of Elizabeth's attendants are dated 1558 and refer to her Chamber after she became queen. These are set out in British Museum MS. Lansdowne 3, Nos. 88 and 89, fols. 191^{r}-200^{v}. As is noted below, five of the names mentioned in the poem occur on these lists, with "Grey" only omitted.

Inference of John Harington's authorship of the poem rests not merely on the statement about the copy in his handwriting, but more significantly on the poem itself, especially lines 25-32, which pay the superlative compliment to Isabella Markham, who later became Harington's second wife (see Nos. 21, 22, 177, and Notes). His poem beginning, "Whence comes my love," is headed, "*A* SONNET *made on* ISABELLA MARKHAME, *when I firste thought her fayer as she stood at the Princess's Windowe in goodlye Attyre, and talkede to dyvers in the Courte-Yard*" (*NA*, 1769, p. 129). This indicates that Harington fell in love with her after she entered the service of the princess. This seems to have been in 1548 or 1549, as two other poems, said to have been written by Harington for Isabella, are dated 1549 (*NA*, ed. 1775, pp. 256-58). No. 262 may also belong to this period. As a member of Seymour's household, Harington had become closely associated with the Princess Elizabeth while she was living with Catherine Parr, and without doubt he often visited Hatfield both before and after his imprisonment in the Tower in 1549 (see the Introduction, p. 64, and Nos. 2, 3, 291, and Notes). In 1554 Harington was again in the Tower (see No. 20 and Note), and it has been said that he was then married to Isabella Markham (David F. Markham, *A History of the Markham Family*, 1854, p. 23; *D.N.B.*), but this is clearly an error. His first wife, Ethelreda, or Audrey, a natural daughter of King Henry VIII, to whom he was married about 1546, was still living in 1555 (John Collinson, *The History and Antiquities of the County of Somerset*, i [1791], 128; Francis J. Poynton on the Haringtons of Kelston, *Miscellanea, Genealogica, et Heraldica*, New Series, iv [1884], 191, 207; *Calendar of the Patent Rolls . . . Philip and Mary*, iii [1938], 95-96 [m. 15]). Further, in the will of Isabella's father, Sir John Markham of Cotham, which was made in 1558, is the significant statement, "I give and bequethe to Isabella Markham my daughter and her assignes three hundreth pounds for her preferment to her marriage" (taken from D. F. Markham, p. 115, who prints the complete will in Appendix E, pp. 114-16). Thus as late as 1558 Isabella might be referred to as "Markham." On the accession of Elizabeth, Isabella was appointed one of the Ladies of the Privy Chamber, an honor she held for twenty years (see the Note on No. 177). In the list for the Privy Chamber of 1558, the name appears as "Elizabeth Markham" (Lansd. MS. 3, No. 88, fol. 191^{v}), but "Isabella" and "Elizabeth" seem to have been regarded as variants. An example of this is given in an account of the Stanley family (Francis Blomefield and Charles Parkin, *An Essay towards a Topographical History of the County of Norfolk*, ii [1805], 442).

As I interpret them, the lines addressed to Markham in No. 262 not only reveal the poet's love for her, but in the comparison of her with "Gryselde" imply that she had needed patience in his long, complicated courtship of her. This then suggests the period between 1554 and 1558 as the time of composition. A few details in the information I have come across about the other five ladies tend to support this conclusion. As a guide to their identity, I have used a list of the Princess Elizabeth's Maids of Honor given by C. R. Markham in his introduction to Sir John Harington's *A Tract on the Succession to the Crown (A.D. 1602)* (Roxburghe Club, 1880, p. ii). Unfortunately, he does not state his source, and I have not found it.

The "Grey" of lines 9-16 is identified by C. R. Markham as Honora, only daughter of Sir William Grey, thirteenth Baron Grey of Wilton. Although he was arrested at the time of the Northumberland uprising in 1553, he was pardoned a few days later and claimed "to be master of the queen's hawkes the day of the coronacion" (G. E. Cokayne, *The Complete Peerage*, ed. H. A. Doubleday, Duncan Warrand, and Lord Howard De Walden, vi [London, St. Catherine Press, 1926], 184, as quoted from the *Chronicle of Queen Jane*, p. 13). This may have a bearing on line 10 in the poem. Sometime before 1562 Honora became the wife of Henry Denny, son of Sir Anthony, of Cheshunt, as her father died at her home there on December 14 or 15 of that year (same ref., p. 185). Lines 11-16 suggest that the betrothal had taken place when this poem was written. Their eldest son, Arthur, was born in 1563 and their fourth son, Edward, in 1569. Honora must have died shortly after, as Henry Denny was married a second time before his death in March, 1573/4, aged thirty-three (same ref., vol. ix [1936], pp. 767-69; J. E. Cussans, *History of Hertfordshire*, vol. iii [1879-81], "Hundred of Cashio," p. 75). The son Edward was created first Earl of Norwich in 1626. Since the Princess Elizabeth was removed to Cheshunt in 1548 and continued to spend time there until 1558, it is easy to account for the attachment between one of her Maids and Henry Denny. It is, however, tempting to think that these lines might refer to Lady Catherine Grey, younger sister of Lady Jane, who is famous for her devotion to her second husband, Edward Seymour, second Earl of Hertford. Her first marriage to Henry Herbert, second Earl of Pembroke, was dissolved in 1554, and the romance of Lady Catherine and Seymour sprang up during Mary's reign. After a secret marriage in 1560, they were imprisoned. Although Elizabeth is said to have given Lady Catherine a place at court after her accession, I find no indication that she belonged to the Privy Chamber, or that she had earlier served Elizabeth, who, of course, feared Lady Catherine and her sister, Lady Mary, because of their claim to the throne (*D.N.B.*).

The "willobe" of lines 17-24 is identified by C. R. Markham as Margaret Willoughby, daughter of Sir Henry Willoughby of Wollaton, Nottinghamshire. On Queen Elizabeth's accession, "Margaret Willoby" was appointed one of the "Gentlewomen of our Privie chamber" (Lansd. MS. 3, fol. 191^{v}; on fol. 193^{r}, she is listed as "M^{ters} Willoughby"). The comparison of her to an "Egle" in line 18 was evidently suggested by the Willoughby arms, which displayed three eaglets in the fourth quarter (*The Visitations of the County of Nottingham in the Years 1569 and 1614*, ed. G. W. Marshall, Harl. Soc., iv [1871], 145, and pp. 148-49 for the immediate pedigree). In 1559 or early in 1560 she was married to Sir Matthew Arundell of Wardour Castle, Wiltshire, a collateral descendant of Queen Catherine Howard (for accounts of the Arundells of Wardour, see J. P. Yeatman, *The Early Genealogical History of the House of Arundel*, 1882, pp. 268-74; J. J. Howard, *Roman Catholic Families of England*, Part III [1887], pp. 151-52).

Their son Thomas (1560-1639), who was at Eton with Sir John Harington and whose signature appears on the last page of the *AH* MS., was created first Baron Arundell of Wardour in 1605 (see the Introduction, pp. 34-36). Many years later than the time of this poem Sir John Harington referred with wry affection to his father's old friend Sir Matthew Arundell (see the Note on No. 20), who had Catholic sympathies. A sonnet beginning, "Marvaylous be thie matcheles gyftes of mynde," is headed "JOHN HARINGTON to sweete ISABEL MARKHAM" in the *NA* (1769, p. 198), but it is written in the form of an acrostic, "Margaret Wilobe," and must have been intended for this lady, whether composed by Harington or someone else.

The "Norwyche" of lines 33-40 is said by C. R. Markham to have been Elinor Norwich. He then continues, "More than this we have not been able to discover. The widow of Robert Baron Norwich, who died in 1535, survived until 1556. Conceivably it is she; but she would have been much older than her companions. We have found no record of a daughter." It is not necessary, however, to consider the widow of Robert Norwich, Justice of the Common Pleas (*D.N.B.*), as Elinor, or Ellen, Norwich was the daughter of Simon Norwich (d. 1588) of Brampton, Northamptonshire (Harl. MS. 1188, pp. 89-90). She was married first to Humphrey Mariott and then to one Middleton (Harl. MS. 1553, fol. 103^r). In 1558 "M^{ters} Norwiche" was appointed to the "quenes Chamber" (Lansd. MS. 3, fol. 193^r). In another entry "Elizabeth Norwiche" is listed as one of three "Gentelwomen of oure bedde chamber" (Lansd. MS. 3, fol. 191^v). This first name may be an error for Ellen.

The "Seintloe" of lines 41-48 is said by C. R. Markham to have been Mary St. Loe, daughter of Sir William St. Loe of Tormarton, Gloucestershire, a Captain of the Guard to Queen Elizabeth, by his first wife. I have found no verification of this statement. Sir William St. Loe's second wife was the notorious "Bess of Hardwick," who later became the wife of George Talbot, sixth Earl of Shrewsbury. In 1558 "Elizabeth Saintelowe" was appointed one of the Ladies of the Privy Chamber (Lansd. MS. 3, fol. 191^v; also, fol. 193^r, as "M^{ters} Sentlowe"). This would seem to refer to "Bess of Hardwick" herself, who was married to Sir William St. Loe in 1558, and who was one of Queen Elizabeth's Ladies (*D.N.B.*, Violet Wilson, *Queen Elizabeth's Maids of Honour*, London, John Lane, 1922, p. 27). Mary St. Loe may earlier have been at Hatfield with the Princess Elizabeth. Maud Stepney Rawson, in her book on *Bess of Hardwick and Her Circle* (London, Hutchinson, 1910), does not mention Bess's step-daughter.

The "Skypwith" of lines 49-56 was Bridget, daughter of Sir William Skypwith of Lincolnshire and his wife, Elizabeth Tyrwit. C. R. Markham includes the name in his list, and Thomas Wotton describes her as "one of the maids of honour, and bedfellow to Queen Elizabeth, who afterwards married—Cave, of Leicestershire, Esq." (*The English Baronetage*, iii [1741], 532, in an account of the Skipwith family). The records show that she was appointed one of the Ladies of the Privy Chamber in 1558 (Lansd. MS. 3, fol. 191^{v}; also, fol. 193^{r}, as "M^{ters} Skipwith").

Harington's charming *jeu d'esprit* on the Princess Elizabeth's Maids of Honor has more poetic grace than a similar composition by Richard Edwards. Beginning, "My fance fanned onne me somwhat of ye to see," it is addressed to eight ladies, "Hawarde," "Dacars," "Baynam," "Arundell," "Dormor," "Mancell," "Coke," and "Briges," who "nowe serves one noble Quene" (*The Life and Poems of Richard Edwards* by Leicester Bradner, Yale Studies in English, lxxiv [1927], p. 102). Printed by Thomas Park in his edition of the *NA* (ed. 1804, ii, 392), it is headed, "The prayse of eight Ladyes of Queen Elizabeth's Court," but Leicester Bradner in his study of Edwards argues convincingly that these ladies served Mary Tudor (pp. 94-96). The only one of particular interest here is "Arundell." Park identifies her as one of the daughters of Thomas Arundell, and hence, a sister of Sir Matthew Arundell, but Bradner points out that Thomas Arundell's daughters were married before 1558. Bradner surmises that "Arundell" refers to Mary, daughter of Henry Fitzalan, Earl of Arundel. In view of the identity of the other ladies, this must be correct. However, after her marriage in 1559 or 1560 Margaret Willoughby would have been designated as "Arundell," and it is at least interesting to see that the lines would be appropriate:

> Arundell is aunciante in thes her tender yeares
> in harte in voce in talke in deade a matrons wit appere[s].

[263] *The Sowles that lacked grace*

Hand A.

No. 263 was first printed among the poems by Uncertain Authors in the second edition of *TM*, sig. Y4^{v}-Z1^{r} (ed. Rollins, No. 272), where it is entitled, "The louer declareth his paines to excede far the paines of hell."

6 boylde] boile; sckalding lead] leade againe
8 from . . . head] with deadly paine
11 theise] their
19 are] be; put] kept
20 Angells be] are aungels
26 thowsandt] thousand
35 syth . . . not] So that I know
41 Beholding . . . this] And as I am thy

The poem is ordinary, and the variants of no great importance, but the *AH* readings in lines 6, 8, 26, and 41 are preferable. Line 20 in *TM* probably represents a change made for metrical reasons.

[264] *Soyled in Syñnes o lord/ a wretchid synfull ghoost*

Hand A.

Attributed to "Ro. Burdet Esquyer," and dated, "Anno. 1565. Aprilis. 14.," No. 264 was printed as a broadside by Richard Jones, with the title, "The Refuge of a Sinner/ Wherein are briefely declared the chiefest Poinctes of true Saluation." It was reprinted by Herbert L. Collmann in his *Ballads & Broadsides chiefly of the Elizabethan Period* (Roxburghe Club, 1912, No. 15). The collation following is made from a photostat of the unique copy of the broadside in the Huntington Library (*S.T.C.* 4104).

2 crye] call; mercyes] mercie
4 mend] mends; know'st] knowest
6 sence] Sith
7 powre eke] power
8 hand] handes
11 dost] doest
13 is offred] thou offeredst
14 mans synne] his wrath; favour toke] father put
16 for] of
17 ffor] Nowe
18 he] who; seekes] seeketh
In the printed copy the order jumps here to lines 21-24, followed by six lines omitted in AH; then picks up lines 19-20 of AH, followed by lines 25ff.
20 devysed by] deisde in
21 to . . . Lord] (O Lorde) on thee
24 cleane] here
The six lines added in the printed copy are:

There is no mummynge Masse, can make amendes for me:
Nor of the Sainctes departed hence, I trust in none but thee.
No pardon can me purge, but thy pardon alone,
  Nor yet no pillynge Pilgreimage, made vnto Stocke or Stone.
No Psalter nor yet Psalmes, saide to thy Creatures:
  No ryng of Belles, no Organe Pypes, nor Song that my soule cures.

25 seist] seest; both] *omitted*
27 better] bett
30 my] me
31 shew] sounde
35 I my selfe do] of my selfe I
36 walke] walckte; rest] suckte
38 helpp] grace; in] for
39 wherefore . . . lord] Shall I than ceace to call

40 it] to; do] that
41 and of] than and
42 lengthe] ende; blisse] Ioyes

Below the author's name in the printed copy is the following motto, "*Bonum quo communius eo melius.*"

It is clear enough in both versions that Robert Burdet was a believer in the "New," or Reformed religion with a Calvinistic bias, but the strong anti-Catholic, Puritanical point of view appears, unusually, in the published version rather than in that of the manuscript. It is possible that the six lines peculiar to the broadside, where these views are so vehemently expressed, were added to the poem by some one other than Robert Burdet. This supposition is the more reasonable if the author was the Robert Burdet of Bramcote in Warwickshire who died January 11, 1548/9 (William Dugdale, *The Antiquities of Warwickshire*, ii [1730], 847-49). Presumably this is the Robert Burdet whose name appears (as was noted by Collmann) in an acrostic written by Robert Vaughan in his address to the reader which introduces *A Dyalogue defensyue for women*, printed by Robert Wyer in 1542 and usually attributed to Vaughan (*S.T.C.* 24601). Beatrice White, however, in "Three Rare Books About Women" (*Huntington Library Bulletin*, No. 2 [1931], pp. 165-72) argues that *A Dyalogue* may have been written by Burdet. In this connection see also Francis L. Utley, *The Crooked Rib*, 1944, pp. 255-56, 272-76.

[265] *In dumppes but late wheare as I laye*

Hand A.

A shorter version of No. 265 was printed in (*A*) *TM*, sig. R2^{r,v} (ed. Rollins, No. 180), where it is entitled, "Of the mutabilitie of the world." In 1565-66 it was entered upon the Stationers' Register to Alexander Lacey for publication as a ballad entitled, "*the fantises of a Trubbled mans hed*" (*Transcript*, ed. Arber, i, 313). Under that title and with attribution to "I.C.," the shorter version was published as (*B*) a broadside, now preserved in the Huth collection in the British Museum (Huth 50). It was printed with three other ballads in double columns on one side of a sheet. Two of these three are attributed to "B.G." and "Ber. Gar.," no doubt the same person; the third (also in *TM*, No. 177) is ascribed to "I. Canand," who must be the "I.C." of No. 265. Reprints of the ballad form of the poem are in Huth's *Ancient Ballads and Broadsides*, Philobiblon Society, 1867, pp. 217-19, and in Joseph Lilly's *A Collection of Seventy-nine Black-Letter Ballads and Broadsides*, 1867, pp. 147-49. In 1597 the shorter version was included by Nicholas Breton in (*C*) *The Arbor of amorous Deuises*, sig. B3^{r,v} (facsimile edition of the copy in the Huntington Library, with introduction by H. E. Rollins, 1936). There it is entitled, "Fantasma."

1 In . . . laye] By fortune as I lay in bed *A B*: In fortune as I lay *C*
2 had] hath *B*
3 full] all *B*
4 than] that *B*
5 even theare] *omitted* *A-C*; of Sorrowes] of wofull sorrowes *A B*
6 waves] wayes *A B*; bredd] brought *C*; my] mine *A B*: me *C*
7 the] this *A-C*
8 how sone] And that *A-C*; ofte graunted] ygraunted *A-B*: graunted *C*
9 how envie yet] . . . it *A C*: eke how Envie *B*
11 saw also] also saw *C*; that] fowle *B*; moche] my *A-C*
12 some] me *A-C*; the] my *A-C*
Lines 13-14 and 15-16 are transposed in order in A-C.
13 saw also] also saw *C*; a . . . straunge] most straunge of all *A B*: most strange *C*
14 the wombe] her womb *A-C*
15 saw also] also saw *C*; desyre] deceit *C*
16 an] in *A B*
17 retaỹne] remaine *C*; she] her *C*
20 a . . . trulye] A fleyng birde, but seldom seen *A B*: A bird, but truely seldome seene *C*
In A-C lines 27-28 of AH follow here.
21 our] my *A-C*
22 tyme and] tide to *C*
A-C insert two lines (quoted from A):
I saw the yeares, that I had spent, and losse of all my gayn [payne *B*]
And how the sport of youthfull [youthly *B*] playes my foly dyd retayn
23 Antt] Ants *B*; did] dothe *A-C*
24 her] their *B*
25 wheare . . . sytt] eke vertue, how she sat *A-C*
26 worke] thing *C*; doth] doeth *C*
27 tymes] Time *C*; flowers] flowers doe *A B*
28 lyeth] falleth *A B*
Lines 29-36 are omitted in A-C.
37 with . . . perfectlye] I thus beheld with many mo pardy *A B*: I saw, with many moe perdie *C*
38 my] me *A B*; thought] thoughts *C*
Lines 39-42 are represented by two different lines in A-C (quoted from A):

And then I said vnto my self: a lesson this shalbe
For other: that shall after come, for to beware by me.

Just why lines 29-36, written in praise of the mean estate and in condemnation of wrong in the land, should have been omitted from the printed copies is not clear. Other more biting criticisms were published. See, for example, No. 321. It is interesting to find the *AH* version independent of the three printed copies, which differ only in details.

[266] *When Phebus gan hym self assend*

Hand A. A cross above "farleys" in line 24 directs the reader to a marginal penciled note in Bishop Percy's handwriting, "Farleys i e Wonders."

From Percy's gloss it is evident that the noun "farley," or "ferly," was all but unknown in eighteenth-century English. Described in the *N.E.D.* as now Scottish and dialectic, it seems to have been chiefly that in the sixteenth century. The one example quoted for the period is from a Scottish source, dated 1535. However, a quotation from Sternhold illustrates its use as an adjective in the English of 1549.

Even more rare is the "myskyns" of line 13. The word appears twice in the works of Michael Drayton, and, as Kathleen Tillotson has noted, no other use of the word is recorded except in No. 266 (*The Works of Michael Drayton*, vol. v, ed. Kathleen Tillotson and B. H. Newdigate, 1941, p. 6). In "The Second Eglog" of Drayton's *The Shepheards Garland*, 1593, is the line, "Now would I tune my miskins on this Greene." In the revised eclogue, published in 1619 (*Pastorals Contayning Eglogues*, "Second Eglogue"), Drayton uses the same line, and fortunately glosses it, "*A little Bagpipe*" (*Works*, vols. i and ii, ed. J. W. Hebel, 1931 and 1932, pp. 50 and 522, respectively).

Like Nos. 259-61, this poem is another addition to sixteenth-century pastoral poetry; and if my analysis of the manuscript is correct, all four are pre-Spenserian. This poem is particularly delightful in the first six stanzas, becoming more conventional with the introduction of the allegory presented by the dream framework.

[267] *The Sheening season heare to so͞me*

Hand A. At the top of fol. 182v is the comment in pencil by Bishop Percy, "Very good"; and in the right margin, "only the first Stanza printed in Surrey's Poems fo. 74."

The first stanza, entitled, "A happy end excedeth all pleasures and riches of the worlde," is in *TM*, sig. Y1r (ed. Rollins, No. 216), with the following variants:

4 great . . . right] in the worldes sight
6 glytt'ring] glitteryng

7 aye seemyng] that semes so
9 theare to] wherto

It is probable that the "some" of line 3 in both *AH* and *TM* should be "sonne," which would better fit the sense and the rhyme. Rollins in his note in *TM* has printed the poem from the *AH* transcript, *N*, fols. 120^{v}-121^{r,v}. He has also called attention to an imitation of the manuscript poem by D. S. in *The Paradise*, sigs. C1^{r,v} (ed. Rollins, 1927, No. 22).

The moral of the poem is, of course, to the effect that the happy end can best be obtained by leading the simple life, as so many of these poems advise.

[268] *Muse ye no whytt at all*

Hand A.

This unknown poem clearly belongs to the period of *TM*.

[269] *To this my songe if you geve eare*

Hand A.

Addressed to some one who is about to be married, this unknown poem offers advice on the ways by which marriage can be made an "earthlye paradyce" or can become a "Purgatorye." The points rest not on any consideration of physical beauty, nor on the problems of chastity versus infidelity, as we might expect, but on "amytie" as opposed to "discorde." The biblical injunction that a man and his wife shall become one flesh (Genesis 2:24; St. Matthew, 19:5) is expanded to include one "will and mynde." And this "knott," which "to vndoe no man hath might" (St. Matthew, 19:6), becomes not a "band but Lybertie" when there is "amytie," which, pleasantly enough, includes "merry meales and quyet rest."

Thus the poem reflects the ideals on marriage which were given impetus by the early humanists. One of the first of these treatises was the *Encomium Matrimonii* (1518) of Erasmus, translated into English about 1530 by Richard Tavernour as "A ryght frutefull epystle in laude and prayse of matrymony" (*S.T.C.* 10492), and later incorporated by Thomas Wilson into *The Arte of Rhetorique.* The following excerpts, quoted from Wilson (ed. 1560, ed. G. H. Mair, 1909, pp. 53-58), might almost lead us to believe that our unknown poet had a copy of Erasmus' epistle beside him as he wrote:

> For what can be more pleasant then to liue with her, with whom not onely you shall be ioyned in fellowship of faithfulnesse, and most heartie good will, but also you shall be coupled together most assuredly, with the company of both your bodies: If we count that great pleasure, which we receiue of the good will of our friends and acquaintance, how pleasant a thing is it aboue all other to haue one, with whom

you may breake the bottome of your heart, with whom you may talke as freely as with your self, into whose trust you may safely commit your self, such a one as thinketh all your goodes to bee her charge. Now what an heauenly blisse (trowe you) is the companie of man and wife together, seeing that in all the world there can nothing bee found, either of greater weight & worthines, or els of more strength and assurance. For with friends we ioyne onely with them in good wil, and faithfulnesse of mind, but with a wife we are matched together, both in heart and mind, in body and soule, sealed together with the bond & league of an holy sacrament, and parting all the goods we haue indifferently betwixt vs. Againe, when other are matched together in friendship, doe we not see what dissembling they vse, what falshod they practise, & what deceiptful parts they play? .... Now last of all, when you are thus lincked in Loue, the same shall bee so fastned and bounde together, as though it were with an Adamant stone, that Death it selfe can neuer bee able to vndoe it. . . . Thus I see you remember all such men, as by Mariage haue been vndone. Well, goe to it, tell as many as you can, and spare not: you shall finde all these were the faults of the persons, and not the faultes of Marriage. For beleeue me, none haue euill wiues, but such as are euill men. And as for you sir, you may chuse a good wife if you list. . . . And as for Ielousie, you shall not neede to feare that fault at all. For none bee troubled with such a disease but those only that are foolish Louers. Chast, godlie, and lawfull loue, neuer knewe what Ielousie ment. . . . For if libertie bee delightfull, I would thinke you should get a mate vnto you, with whom you should part stakes, and make her priuie of all your ioyes. Neither can I see any thing more free, then is the seruitude of these two, where the one is so much beholding and bound to the other, that neither of them both would be lose though they might. You are bound vnto him, whom you receiue into your friendship: but in Marriage neither partie findeth fault, that their libertie is taken away from them. . . . But if you consider things within the compasse of mankinde, there is nothing either more safe, more quiet, more pleasaunt, more to be desired, or more happie then is the married mans life.

Laudation of marriage was carried forward by the Reformers in various treatises and sermons, of which one of the most influential was that by Heinrich Bullinger, translated into English by Miles Coverdale as *The Christen State of Matrimonye*, 1541. Francis Lee Utley in *The Crooked Rib*, 1944, pp. 72-73, note 37, lists a number of these tracts on marriage. They are discussed by Chilton L. Powell in *English Domestic Relations, 1487-1653*, New York, Columbia, 1917, *passim*. Likewise, some of them are considered by Louis B. Wright, *Middle-Class Culture in Elizabethan England*, Chapel Hill: University of North Carolina Press, 1935, pp. 201-27; also by William and Malleville Haller in "The Puritan Art of Love," *HLQ*, v (1941-42), 235-72.

[270] *My frend the lyfe I lead at all*

Hand A. The letters "bell" in line 48 are written over an erasure. In the right margin is Bishop Percy's note in pencil, "Very good."

A copy, without ascription, written in a mid-sixteenth-century secretary hand is in Bodleian MS. Ashmole 48, fols. 25^{v}-26^{v}. H. E. Rollins has a brief account of this manuscript in *MLN*, xxxiv (1919), 342. The poem was printed from the Ashmole MS. in *Songs and Ballads With Other Short Poems Chiefly of the Reign of Philip and Mary*, ed. Thomas Wright, Roxburghe Club, 1860, pp. 38-39. My readings from that manuscript do not always accord with Wright's. Presumably the poem was printed as a broadside by Thomas Colwell, for in 1565-66 an entry to him was made on the Stationers' Register "for the prynting of a ballett intituled, *my frynde the lyfe I leade at all etc.*" (*Transcript*, ed. Arber, i, 306). So far as I know, however, no copy of the broadside is extant.

The variants following indicate that the *AH* copy is preferable.

2 lynes] wordes
4 do] cane
9 two, I] I do
10 eye] yeys
12 the] my
15 till] whylst
25 There] This; I] *omitted*
28 that] y^{e}
30 that] the; whiche] y^{t}
36 me knew] myght know
37 manour wyse] manner of wys
40 of] as
Lines 47-48 and 49-50 are reversed in order in the Ashmole MS.
47 lynnett] levythe
49 holle] creast
51 with red] w^{t} the rede
55 aye] ev^{r}

Although the main theme of the poem expresses the desire of the lover to be in the presence of his "dearest frynd," from whom he is barred, it nevertheless rises above the common level by the freshness of the lines describing the walk to the mountain in the early morning, and by the unifying device of wishing himself like one of the beasts or birds of the field so that he might more easily find admittance to his "frynd." Lines 5-29 particularly deserve Percy's dictum.

Lines 25-28: There may I see how the false fox beats the badger from the rocks, notwithstanding all the latter can do; through subtle trickery soon can the fox win that narrow passage from the badger.

[271] *My frend I see the pale and wan*

Hand A. In line 28 the words "kepe none thoe" are written over an erasure, and in line 52 the letters "ys."

This unknown poem, clearly of the *TM* period, is interesting for its anti-Petrarchan sentiments. The emphasis upon the lady's delight in her liberty and in her "hartie Laughters" over his woe echoes notes found frequently in the poetry of Wyatt, and later Spenser in the *Amoretti* (xviii, lxv) writes of his lady similarly, though in a different context.

[272] *When wynter with his Shivering blastes*

Hand A. This is clearly a fragment, as is indicated by the incomplete sense, the lack of a "finis," and the fact that fols. 189-91 are lacking.

In his *Surrey and Wyatt*, i (1815), 291, in a note on Surrey's poem "When Summer took in hand the Winter to assail," G. F. Nott printed the first four lines of No. 272 from *AH*, correctly noting that it was imperfect, and describing it as an imitation of Surrey's poem, but "not of sufficient merit to be printed." Rollins printed the fifty-eight lines of No. 272 from the *AH* transcript, *N* fol. 126^{r,v}, in his note on Surrey's poem in *TM*, ii, 133. It may be pointed out that No. 272 is also indebted somewhat to Surrey's poem "In winters iust returne, when Boreas gan his raigne" (*TM*, No. 18). Lines 11-18 are perhaps worthy of more approval than Nott accorded them.

[273] *that serven Mars in Armour bright*

Hand A. This is the fragmentary ending of a longer poem which I have been unable to identify. Fols. 189-91 are wanting in *AH*.

[274] *My deare sith chaunce hath Chosen me*

Hand A. Commas are placed in a straight line in the right margin after lines 1, 8, 14, 15, and 22. They appear to have been added later. There is also a comma between the *l* and *o* of "love," line 24. The comma in line 13 may have been added with the others. The "prosperpyne" of line 17 is probably a copyist's error for "proserpyne."

The poem is apparently written in fourteeners, but the lines break up into ballad measure with lines of four and three feet, alternately rhyming *a b a b*. The longer lines may have been kept to give a greater show of dignity.

A parallel exists between the thought of the first six lines and lines 21-

22 in a poem of the Uncertain Authors of *TM* (sig. Q1^{r,v}, ed. Rollins, No. 168), which read:

> Then did I me submit with humble hart and minde
> To be her man for euermore: as by the Goddes assinde.

The *TM* poem, however, addressed to ladies in general, is but another lament in the Petrarchan manner of the lover's lack of success in his suit, and the Platonic note in the phrase "as by the Goddes assinde" is not developed. The similar expression in line 6 of No. 274, "with this the godes devyse," is a key phrase for a poem on marriage (line 9). In the Note on No. 269 I have commented on the impetus given the marriage theme by the humanists, as illustrated by the passage quoted from Erasmus. That poem emphasizes that the oneness of the twain must include will and mind, and is concerned with harmony in living. No. 274 interprets the knitting of "vs two in one" as attained through an eternal love which was divinely appointed "long tyme our births before," is recognized at a "fatall howre," and must be accepted "Happ good or yll." Here, then, are elements of Platonism, derived ultimately from the accounts of the androgynous nature of primitive man in the *Symposium* (189-93), and of the pre-existence of the soul, its subsequent fall and occasional recollection of its former state, with which it seeks to be re-united through love, as given in the *Phaedrus* (246-57). These doctrines were adopted into the Kabbalistic tradition in the Middle Ages (see S. L. Macgregor Mathers, *The Kabbalah Unveiled*, London, Kegan Paul, Trench, Trubner and Co., 1926, pp. 34-35, especially), as is partly illustrated by the following passage in *The Zohar* (trans. Harry Sperling and Maurice Simon, i [London and Bournemouth, The Soncino Press, 1949], 300-01):

> Said R. Abba: "Happy are the righteous whose souls are beatified before the Holy King before they come into this world. For we have learnt that when God sends souls into the world they are formed into pairs of male and female, and thus united are placed in the hands of an emissary who has charge of conception, and whose name is Night. After that they are separated, and subsequently taken down among mankind (not always both at the same time). When their time of marriage arrives, God, who knows each spirit and soul, joins them as at first, and proclaims their union. Thus when they are joined they become one body and one soul, right and left in unison, and in this way 'there is nothing new under the sun.' "

In the fifteenth and sixteenth centuries the Italian Neoplatonists gave expression to similar beliefs (see Nesca A. Robb, *Neoplatonism of the Italian Renaissance*, London, G. Allen and Unwin, 1935, pp. 122-23, especially). Pertinent to lines 7-13 in No. 274 are views expressed by

Pico della Mirandola in his Commentary on Girolamo Benivieni's *Canzone dello Amore* (*A Platonick Discourse upon Love*, ed. Edmund G. Gardner [from the translation of Thomas Stanley], The Humanist's Library, VII [Boston, The Merrymount Press, 1914]). In Bk. II, No. XVII, Pico says:

> Venus is said "to command Fate." The order and concatenation of causes and effects in this sensible World, called Fate, depends on the order of the Intelligible World, Providence. Hence Platonists place Providence (the ordering of Ideas) in the first Minde, depending upon God its ultimate end, to which it leads all other things. Thus Venus being the order of those Ideas whereon Fate, the World's order, depends, commands it.

Thus Venus, "the powre devyne," appointed "that fatall howre." In Book III, in the commentary on "Stanzas VI, VII, VIII" of Benivieni, Pico refers to the doctrine of the stars:

> Many imagine the Rational Soul descending from her Star, in her "Vehiculum Coeleste," of her self forms the Body, to which by that Medium she is united. Our Author upon these grounds supposeth, that into the "Vehiculum" of the Soul, by her endued with Power to form the Body, is infused from her Star a particular formative vertue, distinct according to that Star . . . our Author infers, that the figures of two Bodies being formed by vertue of the same Star, this Conformity begets Love.

And in this way love may have been appointed long before birth. The idea expressed in line 8 of No. 274, that they should "dwell/in love for evermore," derives perhaps from the doctrine of the stair of love, given first by Plato in the *Symposium*, and by Pico (pp. 43-44, 73-74), and, perhaps more familiarly, by Castiglione, in the words of Bembo, in Book IV of *The Courtier*. But the idea is perfectly expressed in a short passage in the *Phaedrus*:

> For those who have once begun the heavenward pilgrimage may not go down again to darkness and the journey beneath the earth, but they live in light always; happy companions in their pilgrimage, and when the time comes at which they receive their wings they have the same plumage because of their love [*The Works of Plato*, ed. Irwin Edman, Modern Library, 1928, p. 299].

No. 274, which clearly belongs in general to the *genre* of *TM*, is remarkable for its expression of these ideas. There is nothing quite like it in the other poetry of the period. It foreshadows the ideas later expressed so elaborately and so much more completely by Edmund Spenser. The distinctive charm of the first part of this poem is further enhanced by its note of personal sincerity. There is, of course, a decided falling off in the second half.

This poem may be another of those addressed to Isabella Markham by John Harington.

[275] *When I do call to memorye, what learned bookes do shoe*

Hand A.

This anonymous poem is a contribution to the catalogues of "good" women which were current in the later medieval period; e.g., Chaucer's *Legend of Good Women*, Gower's *Confessio Amantis*, and Boccaccio's *De Claris Mulieribus*. Popularity of both Chaucer's and Gower's poems in the sixteenth century is evident from the number of editions of both. A portion of Boccaccio's work was translated into middle English, and in the reign of King Henry VIII, Henry Parker, Lord Morley, turned forty-six of Boccaccio's lives into English. Both translations remained in manuscript until the present century (see *Die mittelenglische Umdichtung von Boccaccios De claris mulieribus*, ed. Gustav Schleich, *Palaestra*, vol. cxliv [1924]; *Forty-six Lives Translated from Boccaccios De Claris Mulieribus by Henry Parker, Lord Morley*, ed. Herbert G. Wright, E.E.T.S., vol. clxvii [1943]), but Boccaccio's work, both in Latin and in French translation, was available to sixteenth-century English readers through continental editions. It is probable that the author of No. 275 was acquainted with *De Claris Mulieribus*, or at least with some account based on parts of it not represented in either of the English versions mentioned. Another major source for references to women famous "for love" was, of course, Ovid's *Heroides*, translated by George Turbervile (see the Note on No. 234).

5-8. "Arthemysya," i.e., Artemisia II, Queen of Caria in Asia Minor. In B.C. 365 she married her brother Mausolus, and on his death erected a tomb called Mausoleum. Noted writers of the day were invited to attend the funeral and to engage in a literary contest in his memory. Among these was Aulus Gellius, who in his *Noctes Atticae* (X.18) relates the story referred to in the lines of this poem. The story is also told by Valerius Maximus (*Facta et Dicta*, IV.6). Boccaccio, Chap. LV, gives an account of Artemisia, including this story, but he combines her activities with those of Artemisia I. (Since the original Latin is not available to me, I have used *Boccaccio De Claris Mulieribus Deutsch Übersetzt Von Stainhöwel*, ed. Karl Drescher, *Bibliothek des Litterarischen Vereins in Stuttgart*, vol. ccv [1895]).

9-12. "Hipsicratea," Hipsicrathea. Boccaccio, Chap. LXXV, has an account of her service to Mithridates.

13-16. Julia, daughter of Julius Caesar and Cornelia. She was married to Cn. Pompeius Magnus in B.C. 59, and died in childbirth in B.C. 54, a year after she had suffered a miscarriage on seeing Pompey bespattered with blood (*The Oxford Classical Dictionary*, ed. M. Cary and Others, Oxford University Press, 1950). Boccaccio, Chap. LXXVIII, has an account of her.

17-20. Lucrecia. The well known story of Tarquin's rape of Lucrece is told both by Chaucer in the *Legend* and by Boccaccio, Chap. XLVII. Ovid has a full account in his *Fasti*, II. 685-852.

21-24. Penelope. References to the faithful wife of Ulysses are common in Tudor poetry. Her story is told by Boccaccio, Chap. XXXVIII, and her epistle to Ulysses is the first in Ovid's *Heroides*.

25-28. Clawdia. We should expect to find here an account of Claudia Quinta, a Roman matron of the third century B.C., whose continency was dramatically proved, as told by Ovid in his *Fasti*, IV. 305-30, and by Boccaccio, Chap. LXXIV. The author of No. 275 refers, however, to the wife of Publius Papinius Statius (ca. 40-96 A.D.), basing his lines on the beginning of Statius' "Ecloga ad Uxorem" (*Silvae*, III, v), which is misinterpreted. Statius is there pleading with Claudia to return from Rome to Naples, his birthplace, and, after assuring her of his entire trust, he says (with the Penelope story implied) that he knows that if he were away from his native land for twenty years she would continue to be faithful. Statius seems never to have been separated from his wife.

29-30. Porcia, or Portia, daughter of Cato Uticensis, and wife of Marcus Brutus; died in B.C. 42. Plutarch in his account of Brutus says that the story of Portia's death from swallowing fire was told by Valerius Maximus and Nicolaus the philosopher, but he discounts it, maintaining that she died in a swoon (*Plutarch's Lives. The Translation Called Dryden's*, rev. by A. H. Clough, v [no date], 240). Boccaccio, Chap. LXXIX, relates the story of her death from fire.

33-34. Ariadne. Plutarch in his account of Theseus gives several different versions of the affair with Ariadne, pointing out their inconsistencies (*Lives*, same ed. i, 15-18). Her story is told by Virgil in the *Aeneid*, VI, 20-30, and by Chaucer in the *Legend*. Ovid, *Heroides*, X, has an epistle from Ariadne to Theseus.

35-36. "Elyssa," i.e., Dido. Every Tudor school boy would have known the dramatic story of Dido, who took her life when she was abandoned by Aeneas (Virgil, *Aeneid*, IV, 663-65). Many would-be poets would have been familiar with her epistle to Aeneas in Ovid's *Heroides*, VII, which ends with a reference to herself as "Elissa Scychaei," and the inscription for her tomb. But the description of her as "that true wight" may have resulted from Chaucer's including her story in his *Legend*, or from the lengthy exoneration given her by Boccaccio, Chap. XL.

37. "Ero," i.e., Hero, priestess of Aphrodite in Sestos, beloved of Leander, who swam the Hellespont each night to visit her. According to the legend of Musaeus, when Leander failed to come one night, she

threw herself into the sea. Ovid, *Heroides*, XIX, has only the premonition of her death.

38. "phadra," i.e., Phaedra, wife of Theseus. She was "despysed" by her step-son Hippolytus, as is sufficiently clear from her epistle to him in the *Heroides*, IV.

39-40. Phillis, daughter of King Sithon of Thrace. Ovid, *Heroides*, II, represents her as writing despairingly to her lover Demophoön, who was in Attica, ending with the prediction of her death and the inscription for her tomb. Her story is told by Chaucer in the *Legend* and by Gower in the *Confessio Amantis*, IV, 731 ff.

41-42. "Saphon," i.e., Sappho of Lesbos, the poetess. The legend of her unhappy love for Phaon is most fully told in Ovid's *Heroides*, XV, where she threatens to leap from the Leucadian rocks. Statius, *Silvae*, V, iii, 155-56, speaks of her heroic leap from Mt. Leucas. Boccaccio, Chap. XLV, praises her as a poet but blames her for her excessive love of one who did not return it. Phaon is not named.

43-44. "thesbe," i.e., Thisbe, beloved of Pyramus. This familiar story is told by Ovid, *Metamorphoses*, IV, 55-166; by Chaucer in the *Legend*; by Gower in *Confessio Amantis*, III, 1331 ff.; and Boccaccio, Chap. XII.

[276] *The great conflyct and cruell overthroe*

Hand A. In line 16 the letters "yn" and "att" are written over erasures.

This unknown poem may well owe something to Petrarch's *Sonetto in Vita* 91, which was translated both by Wyatt and by Surrey (see *AH* No. 99 and Note). In that sonnet the poet's Lord, Love, actually Desire, boldly spreads his victorious banner in the poet's face, thus causing the lady to reprimand the poet for "lustes negligence" and to urge more virtuous behavior. Surrey's lines on Love's (i.e., Lust's) retreat are paradoxically pertinent to the description of Love in lines 12 and 19 of No. 276 and to the final defeat of Lust by Love when aided by Virtue.

> And cowarde Love, then, to the hart apace
> Taketh his flight, where he doth lurke and playne
> His purpose lost, and dare not shew his face.
>
> (ed. Padelford, No. 4)

[277] *It pleasid Iove that iudge devyne*

Hand A.

It is not often that we can read the author's account of his own death as in these mediocre verses.

2. "Sagittare," the ninth sign of the zodiac, which the sun enters about November 22, is represented by a centaur with bow. The writer

seems to have in mind not the good centaur Chiron, who is sometimes said to have been transformed into Sagittarius, but the other wild and savage centaurs. The sign is cruel also because it is, like Cupid, an archer.

8-9. "the furies" are evidently used for the Fates, who were responsible for the Line of Life.

13-20. "Theise eyes" of line 13 are the writer's; the "glearing eye," the "celestiall eyes," and "those starres" of lines 15, 17, and 19 are really the eyes of his lady, whom he suddenly recognizes as having the cruel gaze of the cockatrice, the fabulous serpent, akin to the basilisk, which was proverbially said to slay by sight. In using the form "Cokatrill," actually an old variant for *crocodile*, the writer is following a confusion which had taken place in Old French. The crocodile, unlike the "Cokatrill" of No. 277, was said to cloak evil designs with tears (see John Lyly, *Euphues: The Anatomy of Wit. Euphues & His England*, ed. M. W. Croll and Harry Clemons, London, Routledge, 1916, p. 60, note 2). Lines 13-16 may be compared with a passage in George Pettie's *Petite Pallace*, 1576 (as quoted by M. P. Tilley in *Elizabethan Proverb Lore in Lyly's "Euphues" and in Pettie's "Petite Pallace,"* University of Michigan Publications, Language and Literature, vol. ii [New York, Macmillan, 1926], pp. 358-59, taken from the edition of I. Gollancz, i, 17), which reads:

> so though her face and looks were fine and sweet, and brought delight to all the beholders else, yet to him they brought only torment and trouble of mind; and notwithstanding he perceived her beauty to breed his bane, and her looks to procure the loss of his liberty, and that as (7) *the cocatrice by sight only slayeth*, so she by courteous countenance only killed and wounded his heart, yet he could not refrain his eyes from beholding her, but according to the nature of (8) *the sickly patient, which chiefly desireth that which chiefly is forbidden him*, he so incessantly threw his amorous glances towards her, that his eyes were altogether bleared with her beauty.

Spenser in the *Amoretti*, XLIX, employs the conceit of the killing gaze of the cockatrice in describing the power of his lady's eyes.

21-40. Petrarch, Pygmalion, and Orpheus, whom the writer had hoped would aid him, all betray him, so dazzled are they by "those killing eyes," which at last perform their function and send the author to join "theise dead men." And thus the "Cokatrill" slays by sight.

[278] *Vppon the hill Olympiade*

Hand A. The following are written over erasures: lines 7, 24, the *r* in "syr" and the *T* in "Tyme"; line 33, "prest." In the upper right margin is a penciled note, "May be printed." The handwriting is the same as that of the marginal notes by Nos. 1 and 2.

This poem was first printed in the *NA*, 1769, pp. 99-102, with the heading, "*A Description of* TYME. *The Book in which this is found bears Date* 1564, *a Manuscript.*" The poem was reprinted in Henry Harington's two succeeding editions of the *NA*, ed. 1779, iii, 273-78; ed. 1792, ii, 273-78; and in Park's edition, 1804, ii, 396-99. Variant readings in the 1769 *NA* are:

11 hartes] harte
12 who fledd as] Well seeminge they
15 tyme how he] how his tyme
23 toyles and travailes] toyl and travaile
27 you shall rewarded] and your rewarde
41 Then . . . ronneth] Hym to receave, then comethe
43 plast] placed
47 sightes] syght
53 cryed fame] FAME cryed
54 that so consumes] Who so consume
55 sorte] race
60 a . . . them] 'Twas heaven suche
67 curious] envious
68 the] they
71 Orpheus sate] Sweet Orpheus, lo!; good] stood
74 to . . . prayses] JEHOVA'S prayse he
75 as] wyth
77 Oh] Of
78 everye] ev'ry
88 once] And

In the Introduction, pp. 18-26, I have discussed in detail the relation of the *NA* to the *AH* MS., and also the matter of the manuscript dated 1564. It is evident from the above variants that the *NA* copy of this poem was not printed directly from *AH*. In addition to the word variants given above, there are many spelling variants. The punctuation in the *NA* is clearly added, and the variants in lines 60 and 71 suggest that a little eighteenth-century editing may have gone into the *NA* version.

There is nothing either in *AH* or in *NA* to indicate the authorship of this ballad on Sir Time, which is actually a dramatic description real or imaginary, of scenes depicted in a painting (line 5). It is the method used so effectively by Spenser in the August eclogue of *The Shepheardes Calender*, when Willye is describing the mazer (lines 25-36), and by Shakespeare, less successfully, in *The Rape of Lucrece* (lines 1366-1568). And, indeed, it looks back to Chaucer in *The Romaunt of the Rose*, in which the word "depeynted" is used (line 478).

29. "pight," i.e., situated, as in Spenser, *The Faerie Queene*, III, v, 40:

In whose enclosed shadow there was pight
A faire Pauilion, scarcely to be seene. (Oxford edition)

See also No. 259, line 9.

38. "bolde rebatant blowes," i.e., bold blows which beat back or down. The word "rebatant" is not in the *N.E.D.*, but it clearly is made from "rebate" (6), in the sense of repulsing or driving back, for which examples are cited from 1590 to 1633 only.

61. "eache Scyence called seven," i.e., the trivium and quadrivium.

[279] *In autume when mynerves men*

Hand A. In line 19 "eye" was first written "iye." In line 21 "Th" is written over an erasure, and in line 45, "did I an." To the right of the title there is a penciled note in Bishop Percy's handwriting, "Might have been printed, if it had been perfect." Since fols. 197-204, immediately following, are now supplied by blank pages of nineteenth-century paper, the remaining lines of No. 279 are missing, and, unfortunately, I have found no other copy of the poem.

The fifty-four lines of this fragment on "The black Lady" indicate a poem based on the seasonal myth of Persephone, which is quite possibly linked with the analogous one of Adonis. Because of her role as promoter of agriculture, the Athenians called Athene (Minerva) their Persephone, and their statue of Athene Nike bore in one hand her helmet and in the other a pomegranate, the symbol by which Pluto holds Persephone from her mother, Demeter (Ceres), for a part of every year (K. Kerényi, *The Gods of the Greeks*, trans. from the German by Norman Cameron, London and New York, Thames and Hudson, 1951, p. 127). Thus after her men have gathered the harvest yielded by her mother earth (lines 1-4, 35), the goddess in her Persephone role dons black raiment in preparation for her annual return to Hades as Pluto's queen. In a "greene grove" (line 9), possibly of olive trees, which were sacred to Athene, the poet hears the story which she relates to her companions (lines 10-31). The device of the walk and the overheard story is common in medieval literature. The lady begins her account with the idyllic period before her abduction by Pluto, when Nature, her mother (i.e., Demeter) delighted in her (lines 33-36). Fittingly, though somewhat surprisingly, the poet introduces as companions for his Black Lady two ladies who were famous for a chastity that was assailed (lines 37-40). Without the complete poem it is impossible to do more than suggest an interpretation of the remaining lines, but I think it quite reasonable to suppose that the reference to the lover, at first indulgently allowed her by Aphrodite, and from whom she is separated by envy, connects with the legend of Adonis (Spring), whose mythical nature is similar to that of Persephone, and who was claimed finally both by Aphrodite and

Persephone. When Hermes, after the abduction of the maiden by Pluto, descended to Hades to demand her release, Spring accompanied him. Perhaps the rest of the poem would tell us that Aphrodite, smitten with love for Adonis, arranged for Pluto to take the Black Lady so that the beautiful youth might be left for the goddess of beauty. As it is, the ladies now share him.

It will no doubt occur to the reader, as to this editor, that the Black Lady might perhaps represent the mourning mother of Persephone, Demeter, whose mother was the earth goddess Rhea (lines 34-35), but it is difficult in such an interpretation to understand lines 36-54. (For helpful reference on these myths, see, in addition to the work cited above, *Funk and Wagnalls Standard Dictionary of Folklore Mythology and Legend*, ed. Maria Leach, 1949; *The Oxford Companion to Classical Literature*, ed. Sir Paul Harvey, rev., ed., 1946; *The Classic Myths in English Literature and in Art*, ed. Charles M. Gayley, rev. ed., Boston, New York: Ginn and Co., 1939).

[280] *immortall thanckes to geve*

Hand A.

This is the last line of a poem which I am unable to identify. The missing lines were evidently written on one or more of the folios now wanting between Nos. 279 and 280.

[281] *The rare and greattest guyfte of all*

Hand A. Just why No. 281 was left incomplete is not clear, for fol. 206, which is of the original paper, is blank on the recto. It appears that space was left for the remaining lines, which were never copied.

The three petitions of Solomon set out in these verses are in reality one: a request for the mean between riches and poverty, according to the Greek, not the Hebraic, tradition. Therefore biblical accounts offer no authority for these requests, as given in lines 18-62. Lines 11-15 are based on Solomon's first petition, which was granted by God. In the words of I Kings 3:9 Solomon asks, "Give therefore thy servant an understanding heart to judge thy people, that I may discern between good and bad: for who is able to judge this thy so great a people?" Pleased, the Lord granted this request and promised Solomon also riches, honor, and long life, if he kept the commandments of the Lord (verses 10-14). A slightly different version of this covenant is recorded in II Chronicles 1:7-12. In his second petition, made before his people in the temple which he had built for the glory of God, Solomon asked first that God remember the promise made to his father, David: that if the people continued to obey the commandments of God, there should not fail to be a man to sit upon the throne of Israel. In the second part of this petition Solomon asked God to dwell with his people and hear them in their need (I Kings 8:25-60; II Chronicles 6:14-42). Then God appeared to Solomon a second time and said that these requests should be fulfilled if the King and the people remained faithful to Him; but if they turned away to follow other gods, they should be plucked up by the roots and the temple should become a byword among nations (I Kings 9:1-9; II Chronicles 7:12-22).

[282] *What natures worke is this, in one wightes Corps to hyde*

Hand A. The copyist mistakenly considered No. 283 to be a continuation of No. 282 and therefore made no division between the two. Then a line was drawn to separate them, and a "ffinis" in Hand A written in the right margin. The "finis" in the left margin is in another hand. The ascription to Sir John Cheke in the right margin is written in a distinctive secretary hand, which resembles that of the elder John Harington (see the Introduction, p. 34). Nos. 284 and 285, also ascribed to Cheke by this same hand, were likewise copied as one poem by Hand A and are separated in the same way as Nos. 282 and 283. The ascription to Cheke of No. 283 is written, I am confident, by the same person, but the letters are italic in style.

Copies of these four poems, in the same order, and with little difference in text, but without ascriptions, are in another Harington MS., Brit. Mus. Add. 36529, fols. 80r-81r. In the instance of No. 282 there are spelling variants only. The relationship of this manuscript (*P*) to *AH* is discussed in the Introduction, pp. 40-44. That these poems are preserved in Harington MSS. is not surprising. I have pointed out in the Introduction, pp. 38-39, that many of Cheke's letters are contained in another Harington MS., Brit. Mus. Add. 46367, and in the *NA*. Included is a letter showing warm friendship, written by Cheke to Harington in 1554 (*NA*, 1769, pp. 171-72). Also of interest is a letter of June, 1578, from William Cecil, Lord Burghley, to the younger John Harington, who was then at Cambridge, urging the young student to "follow the trade of Sir John Cheeke (who was one of the sweetest flowers that hath coomen in my tyme ovt of the garden you growe in)" [*NA*, 1775, pp. 238-40].

So far as I have been able to discover Nos. 282-85 have not been printed, nor are they mentioned in accounts of Sir John Cheke (1514-57) and his work. In the year of Cheke's death John Bale had ready for the press the first volume of his *Scriptorum Illustriū maioris Brytannię*, commonly referred to as his *Centuria* (Basel, 1557-59, 2 vols. in one, but with separate title-pages; copy in the English Department Library of the Ohio State University), and in it was included a list, not always easy to interpret, of Cheke's writings (vol. i, pp. 698-700, No. XCVII). Among the items is "Epitaphiorum Lib. 1," but particular poems, which might include Nos. 284 and 285, are not specified. John Strype in *The*

*Life of the Learned Sir John Cheke, K^t^*., which remains the most complete study of this distinguished humanist, devotes a chapter to Cheke's writings, based primarily on Bale's list (rev. ed., 1821, pp. 165-72). In the section on the "Epitaphiorum" two of Cheke's Latin elegies are quoted, as well as one in Greek, and others are mentioned, but nothing is said of the one on William Grindal (No. 285), although Cheke's connections with Grindal are briefly related earlier in the book (p. 9). No reference is made to Nos. 282-84. Thompson Cooper in his valuable article on Cheke in the *D.N.B.* also includes the imposing list of the latter's writings, usually of a scholarly nature and written in Latin, of which many, Cooper notes, are now lost. Again there is no reference to these English poems.

Both Strype and Cooper were indebted to Roger Ascham (1515-68), who was closely associated with Cheke at St. John's College, Cambridge, between 1531 and 1544, when Cheke left his post as Regius Professor of Greek and Public Orator to become tutor to the young prince, later King Edward VI. Readers of *The Scholemaster* (1570) will recall among passages where Ascham defers to Cheke in terms of highest praise the one on Sallust, quoted almost entirely from Cheke, who is introduced as, "My dearest frend, and best master, that euer I had or heard in learning, Syr *I. Cheke*, soch a man, as if I should liue to see England breed the like againe, I fear, I should liue ouer long" (*English Works*, ed. William A. Wright, Cambridge University Press, 1904, p. 297). Ascham then quotes Cheke's opinion that Sallust's writing was "more Arte than nature, and more labor than Arte," and, further, that Caesar and Cicero excelled because they "gaue themselues to vse soch speach as the meanest should well vnderstand, and the wisest best allow" (p. 298). Views on the "rude beggerly ryming" of English poets and the desirability for a proper imitation of classical poetry were the subject for "pleasant talke" at Cambridge, Ascham says, with "*M. Cheke and M. Watson*" (pp. 289-91). Ascham praises Watson's *Absalon*, modeled on the classic drama (p. 284), but is apparently unaware of these poems by Cheke, which are written in unrhymed hexameters. They are, however, metrical, as was Surrey's paraphrase of Psalm LV, and as were his unrhymed pentameters in his translations from the *Aeneid*, which Ascham approved for lack of rhyme but termed "feete without ioyntes" (p. 291). There can be no doubt, however, that in using unrhymed hexameters in Nos. 282-85, Cheke was deliberately attempting an adaptation of the classical to the native measure, after the manner of Surrey. This is not to say that Cheke was necessarily imitating Surrey. The diction, which is plain but not eccentric, exemplifies Cheke's theory on language as noted above. His insistence upon English that was "pure, unmixt and unmangeled with borowing of other tunges" (from his prefatory letter to Sir Thomas Hoby's *The Courtier*, Everyman ed., 1937,

p. 7) did lead him to eccentricity in his biblical translation (*The Gospel according to Saint Matthew and Part of the First Chapter of the Gospel according to Saint Mark*, ed. James Goodwin, 1843), but these poems are written in what might be called the mean style.

On turning more particularly to No. 282, we find that it has to do with a poet, evidently a contemporary, "worthie Chawcers mate" in the excellence of poetic skill, but "Vncerten is the rest which shame will not discrye." Only two of Cheke's contemporaries could very well be compared with Chaucer: Wyatt and Surrey. I suggest that in No. 282 Cheke has reference to Surrey, who was arraigned for treason in 1546 and was executed January 17, 1546/47. At the time Cheke was still engaged as tutor to Prince Edward, whose uncles, Edward and Thomas Seymour, were Surrey's bitter enemies. The charge, made as early as 1543, when Surrey was confined in the Fleet prison, that the young nobleman had said he was "like to be King" (*Surrey*, ed. Padelford, p. 23) would not be regarded lightly by the man who became the loyal servant of the Crown, and who in 1549 published a prose treatise on *The hurt of sedicion.*

12-19. Apelles painted the Aphrodite Anadyomene, i.e., the goddess rising out of the sea, and so left unmade the body; but the head was "Porterid with shape of lif," i.e., fashioned. The *N.E.D.* cites but one instance of date 1535 of the verb "porture" used in this sense.

27-30. These elliptical lines seem to mean: how shall I express the rest, which is better understood than spoken, not denying just praise from envy, but restrained by a careful style so that your great lack may be forgotten. That I might have praised you entirely had you been without this fault remains to be wished.

[283] *I praye to god whoe weldithe aye, the starrye heavens*

Hand A. The ascription is in contemporary italic. The "I" in line 1 is unusually large, written in Hand A over a smaller "I." For comments on the copying of this poem, the measure in which it is written, and the author, see the preceding Note.

A copy in the *P* MS., fol. 80^{v}, has the following variants:

3 dothe knitt] do knit

day
8 at the howre] at the ⟨wie⟩ *correction in a different hand*
11 doth call] do call

These verses were evidently written as a compliment for two people who were about to be married. Lines 2-4, 9, and 21 indicate influence from the "New Religion," which Cheke adopted while he was at Cambridge, 1529-44. In the Note on No. 269 I have mentioned the emphasis placed by the Reformers on marriage.

5. "stailesse happ," i.e., a course which does not lose its freshness or

interest. This adjective is not in the *N.E.D.*, but it is clearly derived from the verb "stale" (3).

11. "vngreeved of disease," i.e., unaffected by illness. The *N.E.D.* lists the verb "ungrieve" as used only by Warner in *Albion's England*, 1589, and the past participle as first employed by Hobbes in 1676.

[284] *The fainted shade of life painted with natures hand*

Hand A. The ascription and the "finis" are in two different secretary hands. On the copying of this poem and its author, see the Note on No. 282. In line 1 a word was erased after "shade," and a mark made over the erasure. A copy in the *P* MS., fol. 80ᵛ, has no variants.

This little poem makes us wish that we had more from the pen of Sir John Cheke. With classic simplicity the poet comments on the transient quality of life by using the Platonic metaphor of the shadow, which in the morning of youth is long and streaked with glimmerings of light. But it is a "fainted shade," and as the sun abates and drops into the sea, the shadow subtly loses its touches of light, becomes "shroncken with withred fear," and finally, appalled, falls down, with dreary aspect to behold. There is no Christian note of hope.

[285] *Vncertaine certaine deathe free grindall hath thee caught*

Hand A. The ascription is in a different secretary hand. The initial "V" in line 1 is written over a smaller capital "V." A copy of the poem in the *P* MS., fol. 81ʳ, has no variants. For introductory comments on No. 285, see the Note on No. 282.

This elegy was probably written in 1548, for William Grindal, tutor to the Princess Elizabeth, died of the plague in the summer of that year (lines 1-2; *D.N.B.*). Grindal had been a favorite pupil of Roger Ascham's at St. John's College, Cambridge, in whose rooms he had lived and studied for seven years. Ascham's praise of his dear friend more than supports that of Cheke: "Mores, ingenium, memoriam, judicium tale habuit, quale vix cuiquam in Anglia contigit quem ego unquam vidi" (*The Whole Works of Roger Ascham*, ed. Rev. Dr. Giles, I, ii [1865], 272, letter No. CXVII). In 1544 Ascham seems to have tried to secure a post at St. John's for Grindal, who is described as so poor he had not enough to live upon, and failing in that, Ascham had appealed to Cheke, who had recently assumed his duties as tutor to Prince Edward. Ascham was delighted when Cheke was able to arrange for the young man to become tutor to the Princess Elizabeth (the same ref.; also, vol. I, pt. i, pp. 53-57, letter No. XXIII). Two letters from Ascham to Grindal after the latter had left Cambridge are preserved, and another to the Princess Elizabeth, praising her progress under her tutor (same ref., pp. 62-63, letter No. XXVI; pp. 73-76, letters No. XXX, XXXI).

[286] *So Luckye be your twisted holde of Coopled youthe*

Hand A. A copy in the *P* MS., fol. 81^{v}, has no variants. In that manuscript, as here, No. 286 follows Nos. 282-85.

Since this poem, like Nos. 282-85 by Sir John Cheke, is written in unrhymed hexameters, and, again, since it is similar to No. 283 in content, we may well question whether it also was written by Cheke. For introductory comments on those poems, see the Note on No. 282.

2. "I knitt," i.e., aye, forever, knit.
6. "fore thinck," i.e., anticipate.
20. That is, by practice of wisdom's teaching the skilled to pursue.

[287] *Attend good Ladies and geve heede/ my dolefull playnt to heare*

Hand A. In line 14 "vassall" was written "vessell," and the two *e's* have been made into *a's* in another ink.

It would be interesting to know whether these plaintive verses were actually written by a woman as they purport to be. The apparent fourteeners, it will be noticed, break up into the common ballad measure stanza: 4, 3, 4, 3, rhyming *a b a b*.

[288] *O god that rul'ste both Sea and Land/ even by thie Heavenlye powre*

Hand A. Several words are written over erasures: line 10, "Corps"; line 20, "Corps," "and put"; line 21, "hollye"; line 43, "vndoubtelye."

A copy of No. 288 in Brit. Mus. MS. Cotton Titus A. XXIV, fols. 85^{v}-87^{v}, written in secretary hand, is ascribed, "R.E.," i.e., Richard Edwards. This manuscript and its contents are described by Leicester Bradner in *The Life and Poems of Richard Edwards* (New Haven: Yale Studies in English, lxxiv [1927], 93-94), and the text of this poem is printed (pp. 105-08), but without reference to the copy in *AH*.

1 god] lorde; rul'ste] ruleste; Sea and Land] lande seae
2 the] thes
4 Seas] see; drowning shore] drenchinge showre
5 among'st] amyddes
6 whole] *omitted*
8 it chaunced] that chaunsethe
9 myne] my; doth] do; theise] this
10 dreve forthe] forthe drive; drowned] drenched
11 wight] man
12 in] withe; their] his
15 onlye] won lye; his] this
17 rufull] ruthefull

19 perfect] farvente
20 this] the; put it] winde hit
21 beare it] bringe hit; Kirke] churche
22 theare] so; to lodge] will put
23 in] as
24 That] and; t'attempt] to attempte
27 that man] the manne; whearwith] whereby
28 To see] and see
30 drowned] wretched
33 bequeathe] begyns; springe] pryme
37 and] even
38 fforgeve] for in
39 Sea and Land] lande and sea
40 hath pointed] appoynted
41 be in perfect] bene in tender
42 thinck] thinkes; thyne Ire] theire sinnes
43 nede] nedes
46 it] me
49 In . . . trust] In the in the I truste o lorde; thie bloode onlye] thi blodde thy blodde
50 my spryt] me sprite; thie] the
51 beholde] lo now
52 O . . . it] o christe o christe take thow my sprite that

The *AH* copyist did not understand the "on lye" in line 15 and so made one word of two. In line 33 the *AH* "springe" destroys the rhyme pattern. On the other hand, words are clearly omitted in lines 1 and 6 of the Cotton MS. version. A particularly interesting reading is the Scottish "Kirke" in line 21 of *AH*.

Bradner describes the poem as "rapid, vivid, and dramatic," expressing unusual "force and feeling," and thinks that it was probably written as the result of an actual experience belonging to the "lost years" of Edwards, just after leaving Oxford, that is, between about 1550 and 1555 (pp. 97-98).

[289] *Geve eare, to me my god/ and heare my mourning voyce*

Hand A. The ascription, "Io. Warwick," also in Hand A, was first written as "I.W." The *o* was clearly added between the *I* and the first period; the *a* is written over the second period. Several words are written over erasures: line 2, "swarminge"; line 5, "guyftes"; line 15, "and mynde"; line 18, "god and"; line 30, "mye giltles."

In 1547 John Dudley (1502?-1553), then Baron Lisle, was created Earl of Warwick, and in 1551, Duke of Northumberland. Thus for four years he was known as Warwick, and it is therefore possible that he is the "Io. Warwick" to whom the ascription refers. More probably, however, as I have suggested in my earlier study on the Arundel MS. (Hughey, p. 422), the author of No. 289 was Northumberland's eldest son, John (d. 1554), who after 1551 was called Earl of Warwick (William Camden, *Britannia*, 1610, p. 571; *D.N.B.*). To him, so designated, Thomas Wilson dedicated *The Arte of Rhetorique*, first published in 1552/3. Acknowledging that the inception of the book was due to Warwick, Wilson thus praises his patron:

> *And because that aswell by your Lordshippes most tender imbracing of all such as be learned, as also by your right studious exercise: you do euidently declare, not onely what estimation you haue, of all learning and excellent qualities in generall, but also what a speciall desire and affection, you beare to Eloquence: I therefore, commend to your Lordshippes tuition and patronage, this treatise of Rhetorique, to the ende that ye may get some furtheraunce of the same, & I also be discharged of my faithfull promise, this last yere made vnto you* [quoted from *Wilson's Arte of Rhetorique 1560*, ed. G. H. Mair, Oxford, Clarendon Press, 1909, "The Epistle," sig. A3r].

Wilson's prediction that Warwick's eloquence would be greatly increased by "*perfect experience of manifolde and weightie matters of the Commonweale*" is ironic, for within the year the power of the Dudleys fell. As a result of machinations to place his son Guilford's young wife, Lady Jane Grey, on the throne immediately after the death of Edward VI, July 6, 1553, the elder John Dudley, lately the Lord Protector of the realm, now attainted and disgraced, was executed for high treason August 22, 1553. His brother Sir Andrew and his sons, John, Ambrose, Guilford, Robert, and Henry, arrested for complicity in the plot, remained as prisoners in the Tower. Following the uprising in January, 1553/54, connected with Queen Mary's plans for marriage to Philip II of Spain, Lord Guilford and Lady Jane Dudley were executed February 12. (For a review of the historical role of Northumberland and pertinent events in Queen Mary's reign, see, for example, *The Cambridge Modern History*, ed. Sir A. W. Ward, Sir G. W. Prothero, and Sir Stanley Leathes, vol. ii, "The Reformation" [1907], pp. 474-530; A. F. Pollard, *The History of England from the Accession of Edward VI, to the Death of Elizabeth (1547-1603)*, New York, Henry Holt, 1910, pp. 42-111; Conyers Read, *The Tudors*, New York, Henry Holt, 1936, pp. 101-44.) Robert Dudley (1532?-1588), later Earl of Leicester, then took the place of Guilford as Warwick's cell-mate on the second floor of Beauchamp Tower, where they remained until their release in October, 1554. Warwick died at Penshurst on October 21, only a few days after regaining his freedom. According to the *D.N.B.* and John Bayley, *The History and Antiquities of the Tower of London*, 1830, p. 449, Warwick was released October 11; but Frederick Chamberlin, *Elizabeth and Leycester* (New York, Dodd, Mead & Co., 1939), p. 83, and Milton Waldman, *Elizabeth and Leicester* (Cambridge, Mass., Houghton Mifflin, 1945), p. 48, state that Warwick was released with his brothers on October 18.

During these months of confinement, the brothers occupied some of the tedious time in carving their names and coats of arms on the walls of the cell (see Chamberlin, p. 81, and the illustration facing p. 80; Waldman, p. 47), and, I conjecture, in writing Nos. 289 and 290, and probably other poems now lost.

No. 289, ascribed to Warwick, is a free paraphrase of Psalm 55 (Hebrew numbering; 54 in the Vulgate), adapted as a passionately personal plea to God for vengeance against enemies who once posed as friends. Warwick may have had in mind such men as the Earls of Arundel and Sussex, and there were others. No. 290, ascribed to Robert Dudley, is a similar paraphrase of Psalm 94 (Vulgate 93), where the emphasis on vengeance is even more pronounced. The two paraphrases seem clearly to be companion poems, inspired by the same unhappy circumstances. One of their fellow prisoners was the elder John Harington, who may have taken copies of the poems during the year (see Hughey, pp. 422-23, and the Introduction, p. 65. We may recall that only a few years earlier another young Tudor nobleman, Henry Howard, Earl of Surrey, also accused of treason by former friends, had written a metrical paraphrase of Psalm 55 (see No. 84), but Warwick's version shows no indebtedness to Surrey's. A comparison of No. 289 with the Latin of the Vulgate at once indicates the freedom of the paraphrase, which often intensifies the cry for vengeance against personal enemies. In some instances passages not in the Latin are inserted; in others clauses, or verses, in the Latin are omitted; in still others the sense is deliberately twisted. The main theme, however, expressed in lines 9-14, follows the Latin fairly closely (C, verses 13-16). For the reader's convenience I give below a copy of the Vulgate version.

LIV.

Intellectus David.

1. *In finem; in carminibus.*

A 2. Exaudi, Deus, orationem meam, et ne despexeris deprecationem meam;

3. intende mihi, et exaudi me.

Contristatus sum in exercitatione mea; et conturbatus sum

4. a voce inimici, et a tribulatione peccatoris.

Quoniam declinaverunt in me iniquitates, et in ira molesti erant mihi,

5. cor meum conturbatum est in me, et formido mortis cecidit super me.

6. Timor et tremor venerunt super me, et contexerunt me tenebrae;
B 7. et dixi; Quis dabit mihi pennas sicut columbae, et volabo, et requiescam?
8. Ecce, elongavi, fugiens et mansi in solitudine.
9. Exspectabam cum, qui salvum me fecit a pusillanimitate spiritus, et tempestate.
10. Praecipita, Domine; divide linguas corum, quoniam vidi iniquitatem, et contradictionem in civitate.
11. Die ac nocte circumdabit eam super muros ejus iniquitas, et labor in medio ejus,
12. et injustitia;
et non defecit de plateis ejus usura et dolus.
C 13. Quoniam, si inimicus meus maledixisset mihi, sustinuissem utique;
et si is, qui oderat me, super me magna locutus fuisset, abscondissem me forsitan ab eo?
14. Tu vero, homo unanimis, dux meus, et notus meus,
15. qui simul mecum dulces capiebas cibos; in domo Dei ambulavimus cum consensu.
16. Veniat mors super illos; et descendant in infernum viventes, quoniam nequitiae in habitaculis eorum, in medio eorum.
17. Ego autem ad Deum clamavi; et Dominus salvabit me.
18. Vespere, et mane, et meridie narrabo et annuntiabo; et exaudiet vocem meam.
19. Redimet in pace animam meam ab his, qui appropinquant mihi, quoniam inter multos erant mecum.
D 20. Exaudiet Deus; et humiliabit illos, qui est ante saecula.
Non enim est illis commutatio, et non timuerunt Deum;
21. extendit manum suam in retribuendo.
Contaminaverunt testamentum ejus;
22. divisi sunt ab ira vultus ejus, et appropinquavit cor illius.
Molliti sunt sermones ejus super oleum; et ipsi sunt jacula.
23. Jacta super Dominum curam tuam; et ipse te enutriet, non dabit in æternum fluctuationem justo.
24. Tu vero, Deus, deduces eos in puteum interitus.
Viri sanguinum, et dolosi non dimidiabunt dies suos; ego autem sperabo in Te, Domine.

[290] *O mightie Lorde to whome/ all vengeaunce doth belonge*

Hand A. The ascription is in the same hand.

For some account of the circumstances in which I conjecture No. 290 to have been written, see the Note on No. 289. The further comment may be added that Robert Dudley, to whom No. 290 is ascribed, was created Earl of Leicester in 1564, and after that date an ascription to him would give his title.

As I have said in the preceding Note, No. 290 is a paraphrase of Psalm 94. The text of the Vulgate (93) is more closely followed than is true of No. 289. For purposes of comparison the Vulgate text follows.

XCIII.

Psalmus, ipsi David.
Quarta sabbati.

A 1. Deus ultionum Dominus; Deus ultionum libere egit.
2. Exaltare, qui judicas terram; redde retributionem superbis.
3. Usquequo peccatores, Domine; usquequo peccatores gloriabuntur,
4. effabuntur, et loquentur iniquitatem; loquentur omnes, qui operan-
tur injustitiam?
5. Populum Tuum, Domine, humiliaverunt, et hæreditatem Tuam
vexaverunt.
6. Viduam, et advenam interfecerunt, et pupillos occiderunt.
B 7. Et dixerunt: Non videbit Dominus, nec intelliget Deus Jacob.
8. Intelligite, insipientes in populo; et stulti, aliquando sapite.
9. Qui plantavit aurem, non audiet? aut qui finxit oculum, non con-
siderat?
10. Qui corripit gentes, non arguet; qui docet hominem scientiam?
11. Dominus scit cogitationes hominum, quoniam vanae sunt.
12. Beatus homo, quem Tu erudieris, Domine, et de lege Tua docueris
eum.
C 13. Ut mitiges ei a diebus malis, donec fodiatur peccatori fovea,
14. quia non repellet Dominus plebem suam, et hæreditatem suam
non derelinquet.
15. Quoadusque justitia convertatur in judicium; et qui juxta illam
omnes qui recto sunt corde?
16. Quis consurget mihi adversus malignantes? aut quis stabit mecum
adversus operantes iniquitatem?
17. Nisi quia Dominus adjuvit me, paulominus habitasset in inferno
anima mea.
D 18. Si dicebam: Motus est pes meus, misericordia Tua, Domine,
adjuvabat me.
19. Secundum multitudinem dolorum meorum in corde meo, consola-
tiones Tuae lætificaverunt animam meam.
20. Numquid adhæret Tibi sedes iniquitatis; qui fingis laborem in
præcepto?
21. Captabunt in animam justi, et sanguinem innocentem condemna-
bunt.

22. Et factus est mihi Dominus in refugium, et Deus meus in adjutorium spei meae,
23. Et reddet illis iniquitatem ipsorum, et in malitia eorum disperdet eos; disperdet illos Dominus Deus noster.

[291] *ffor geatting god*

Hand A. In line 22 *N* is written over an erasure of a small *n*. In line 28 *I* is superimposed on "Hee." The ascription in contemporary italic was first written "T.S." The *e* is written over the second period. In the Introduction, pp. 36-37, I have discussed the similarity of the handwriting in the ascription to specimens in Seymour's autograph. In the lower right-hand margin a penciled note by Bishop Percy reads, "Lord Admiral Seymour written the week before he was beheaded."

Percy's note accords with the heading to the poem in (*A*) *NA*, 1769, p. 86, which reads, "*Verses found written by the Lord Admiral* SEYMOUR *the Week before he was beheaded*, 1549." Collation with *A* indicates that it was not set up from the *AH* MS. The text was slightly changed in (*B*) *NA*, 1779, iii, 259, which *NA*, 1804, ii, 328-29, follows.

13 Loves He] he loves *B*
14 and not correcte] muste be correcte *A*: he muste correcte *B*
20 Hym] God *A B*
21 Who] Lord *A B*
24 His] thys *A B*
27 as in His] That in thy *A B*
28 $\overset{I}{\langle\text{Hee}\rangle}$ may have] he maie find *A B*

The author of these verses, Sir Thomas Seymour, Baron Sudeley, and Lord High Admiral, was executed for treason March 20, 1548/49. In the Introduction, pp. 63-65, and in the Note on No. 2 some account is given of John Harington's close relations with Seymour. These verses were probably left with Harington, who had followed Seymour to the Tower.

[292] *Eache thinge must have his tyme/ and tyme tryes out mens trowthe*

Hand A. In the margin is Bishop Percy's note in pencil, "Surrey fo. 69."

The poem was printed in (*A*) *TM*, sig. $V4^v$ (ed. Rollins, No. 206), where it is entitled, "Time trieth truth." It is also in (*B*) *A gorgious Gallery, of gallant Inuentions*, 1578, sig. $F4^{r,v}$ (ed. Rollins, 1926, pp. 47-48), entitled, "Of a happy wished time." There is a copy in a late sixteenth-century commonplace book (*C*) Brit. Mus. MS. Add. 26737, fol. 107^r, with the marginal comment, "Tempus omnia probat ffestina lente."

1 must have his] I se hath *A C*: must haue a *B*; and] which *A C*; tryes out mens] must trye my *A C*: doth try mens *B*; trowthe] truth *A*: troth *B C*
2 and trothe] Which truth *A*: Which troth *C*; growth] groweth *A C*
3 never fayles] may not faile *A C*: is full fast *B*; when] where *A-C*
4 faithfulnesse is] faythfull thinges be *B*; are] be *A-C*
5 in] at *A C*
6 worthie] precious *A C*; lightlye not] seldome ner *A*: seld or ne'er *C*
7 this . . . bring] these thinges times tries *A*: those thinges time tryes *C*
8 trothe] truth *A-C*
9 And] For *A C*; a . . . fownde] I found a time *A*: I had a time *C*
10 do I] I do *A*; a] an *B*; happie] lucky *A*; at . . . shewe] for to declare *A*: for to enioy *C*
11 fortune answere] hap may answere *A C*; his] her *B*: its *C*

It is evident that the text of *C* is closer to that of *AH* than are the other two, which are clearly related.

Rollins in his notes on the poem in both *A* and *B* suggests that the idea may have been taken from Ecclesiastes, iii, 1-8. This may well be, but the theme of the poem was a proverb. John Heywood, *woorkes*, 1562, Pt. II, chap. v (Spenser Society, i [1867], 59), has the line, "Let tyme trie, Tyme tryeth trouth in euery doubt." Similar is a line in *Respublica*, 1553 (ed. L. A. Magnus, E.E.T.S., Extra Series, xciv [1905], 2, line 27), "yet tyme trieth all and tyme bringeth truth to lyght." Perhaps pertinent also is the sentence noted by Publius Syrus (*Sententiae*, ed. Jules Chenu, 1835, p. 112), "Quae fieri fas est, tempore haec fiunt suo."

[293] *Experience now doth shew/ what god vs taught before*

Hand A. An ascription in ink to "Edward Somerset" is written in modern italic beneath the poem. In the left upper margin is Bishop Percy's note in pencil, "Surrey fo. 68."

This poem was printed in *TM*, sig. V3^{r} (ed. Rollins, No. 200), with the title, "The pore estate to be holden for best." In the second edition of *TM*, sig. R3^{v}, the complete acrostic "EDWARDE SOMERSET" is indicated in the printing, the final *T* being the last letter of the poem. Other editions of *TM* do not capitalize this letter, and the acrostic therefore appears to be incomplete. The *TM* version has the following variants:

3 state] fate
9 they have] haue they
10 fynde] fele
11 the] they
12 their] the
13 lyv'ste] liues

The subject of the poem is without doubt Edward Seymour (1506?-1552), Duke of Somerset, who became Lord Protector on the accession of his nephew Edward VI in 1547, was removed from that high office in January of 1549/50, and was finally executed for treason, January 22, 1551/52. He was twice a prisoner in the Tower: October 14, 1549 to February 6, 1549/50, and October 16, 1551, until the day of his execution. During the first confinement the elder John Harington was a fellow prisoner. Possibly this poem, written by Somerset or by another in comment on his losing career, came into Harington's hands at that time. Rollins in his note on the poem argues against Somerset's authorship, and suggests it was written after his execution. It is well to keep in mind, however, that during his first imprisonment Somerset wrote a preface for *A Spyrytual and most precyous Pearle* (1550), translated from the German of Otto Wermueller by Miles Coverdale. A fellow prisoner Sir Thomas Smith was writing verses to pass the time (see the Note on No. 323), and another one, John Harington, was translating *De Amicitia* (see the Introduction, p. 64). We must again recognize that imprisonment gave opportunity for reflection and writing (see Nos. 289, 290, and 291). Consequently I do not find it difficult to suppose that Somerset could have written this sonnet either in 1549 or in 1551, but I do not press the point. The experimental rhyme pattern and the hexameters, as well as the common theme in praise of the quiet life, do not indicate that No. 293 was the work of a practiced poet. (For accounts of Somerset, see A. F. Pollard's article in the *D.N.B.* and his *England under Proctector Somerset. An Essay*, London, Paul, Trench, and Trubner, 1900; also *The Cambridge Modern History*, ii [1907], 495-505.)

[294] *A pierlesse Prynce, of worthie weldinge witt*

Hand A.

This anonymous sixain was in all probability written by an admirer of Edward VI after his death at the age of sixteen, July 6, 1553. The young king's precocious abilities and advanced learning are evident in the *Literary Remains of King Edward the Sixth*, ed. John G. Nichols, 2 vols., Roxburghe Club, 1857.

In line 1 "weldinge" is a variant of "wielding," used in the sense of governing, or ruling.

[295] *ffrom vyle estate, of base and low degree*

Hand A. The ascription is in the same hand. In line 8 "good" is inserted in another ink and hand.

The poem was printed from *AH* by G. F. Nott, *Surrey and Wyatt*, vol. i (1815), "Memoirs," p. xcvii, footnote, but appears to be otherwise unknown. Nott is mistaken in saying that the author, George Blage, came from a Kentish family, and in supposing that this bitter epitaph on Sir Thomas Wriothesley (1505-1550), first Baron Wriothesley of Titchfield, first Earl of Southampton, and Lord Chancellor (1545-1546/47), was inspired primarily from the Chancellor's active part in bringing about the execution of Henry Howard, Earl of Surrey, in January, 1546/47. As printed out in the Note on No. 82, Blage's attitude toward the Howards in 1546 was not friendly, and it is clear that he had other reasons for his condemnation of Wriothesley.

"G. Blage," that is, Sir George Blage, or Blagge, son of Robert, of Broke Montague, Somersetshire, baron of the exchequer, was born in 1512. He attended Cambridge University, and in 1530 was admitted to Gray's Inn (*D.N.B.*, under the father; John and J. A. Venn, *Alumni Cantabrigienses*, I, i [1922]; C. H. and T. Cooper, *Athenae Cantabrigienses*, ii [1858], 104; *The Register of Admissions to Gray's Inn, 1521-1889*, ed. Joseph Foster, 1889, col. 8). In 1539 he was king's agent for making payments to Sir Thomas Wyatt, then Ambassador to the Emperor Charles V (Brit. Mus. MS. Arundel 97, fol. 17^{v}). In 1544, described as "King's servant," he was named chief steward of the manor of Maidston in Kent (*Letters and Papers . . . of King Henry VIII*, XIX, i, ed. James Gairdner and R. H. Brodie [1903], p. 643, No. 1036 [37]). Not long after he was serving with the English forces in France under the leadership of the Earl of Surrey (see the Note on No. 82). Probably before that time he had become a member of the Privy Chamber of Henry VIII, "who was very fond of him, and, for what reason is unknown, used to call him his *Pig*" (Patrick F. Tytler, *England under the Reigns of Edward VI and Mary*, i [1839], 146). As it turned out, the king's favor saved Blage, who was a follower of the "New Religion," from being burned as a heretic. In 1546 Stephen Gardiner, Bishop of Winchester, and Lord Chancellor Wriothesley began investigations connected with allegiance to the Six Articles. Blage was confined in Newgate prison and condemned to be burned, but Henry VIII "rated the Chancellor for coming so near him, even to his Privy Chamber, and commanded him instantly to draw out a pardon. On his release Blagge flew to thank his master; who, seeing him, cried out, 'Ah! my *Pig*! are you here safe again?' 'Yes, sire,' said he, 'and, if your majesty had not been better than your bishops, your *Pig* had been roasted ere this time.' " (Tytler, same ref., taken from the preface to testimony given by Blage at the trial of Admiral Seymour, 1548/49.) The pardon, granted July 17, 1546, states that on May 9 of that year in St. Paul's Cathedral, Blage had said, "That the Sacrament of the Altar did no good, neither to quick nor dead; and, further said That the good Lord's body could not in any means be minished ne impaired, and if it were laid up there as a mouse might come to it the mouse would eat it every whit; saying further, That in his opinion it were well done that the mouse were taken and put in the pix" (*Letters and Papers*, XXI, i, ed. Gairdner and Brodie [1908], No. 1383 [72]). In 1546 these were dangerous words, and it is hardly surprising that Blage was put in Newgate. Although Wriothesley was forced to countersign the pardon, he no doubt disliked Blage more after the king's interference, and it is clear enough from No. 295 that Blage hated Wriothesley. Possibly because of his alignment with the Seymour faction rather than that of the Howards in the closing months of Henry VIII's reign, Blage was knighted in September, 1547 (William A. Shaw, *The Knights of England*, ii [1906], 62), after Edward Seymour, Duke of Somerset, had become Lord Protector. In the fatal rift between the Protector and his brother Sir Thomas in 1549, Blage's allegiance was with the Protector (Tytler, i, 148). Wriothesley, on the other hand, now first Earl of Southampton (1547), joined the forces led by John Dudley, Earl of Warwick, which were directed toward the fall not only of Sir Thomas but also of Protector Somerset (see the Note on No. 293). On Dudley's success in 1550, Wriothesley was abandoned and dropped from the Council. He died on July 30 of that year, possibly from self-administered poison (*D.N.B.*). And his old enemy George Blage then wrote these invective lines as an epitaph. Blage himself died in less than a year, June 17, 1551. At the time he was constable of Caernarvon Castle and was succeeded in this office by the elder John Harington (*Kalendars of Gwynedd*, ed. Edward Breese and W. W. Wynne, 1873, p. 127). Perhaps in some way this connection gave Harington an opportunity to take a copy of No. 295.

Although Wriothesley did not spring from one of the old families, he could scarcely be described as in line 1, for his grandfather Sir John Wriothesley, or Writh, was head of the College of Heralds on its incorporation in 1483. Sir Thomas' father, William, became York herald, and his uncle, Sir Thomas, was Garter king-of-arms. A cousin, Charles, Winchester herald, compiled *A Chronicle of England during the Reigns of the Tudors* (ed. William Douglas Hamilton, Camden Society, New Series, vols. xi, xx [1875, 1877]). The family gained its greatest fame, of course, through Henry Wriothesley (1573-1624), third Earl of Southampton, Shakespeare's patron, years after Blage was writing with such obvious loathing on Henry's grandfather. A glance at the career of the first Lord Wriothesley (as given in such a general account as that of the *D.N.B.*) is sufficient to indicate reasons why he could be described as advancing "by false disceyt, by craft and subtile waies." Patronized by Thomas Cromwell, leader of the Reforming party, Wriothesley nevertheless testified against Cromwell on his fall in 1540, and then became friendly with Cromwell's enemy Stephen Gardiner, Bishop of Winchester, leader of the Catholic faction (in this connection see James A. Muller, *Stephen Gardiner and the Tudor Reaction*, New York: Macmillan, 1926, pp. 11-368, *passim*). After he became Chancellor, Wriothesley attempted to bring about an alliance with Spain, which may have been in Blage's mind when he wrote line 6. Despite this alignment with the Catholic element, Wriothesley was active against the Howards: when Queen Catharine was tried in 1541 and when Surrey and his father were arrested in 1546. This collaboration with the Seymour faction did not last, however, for, as noted, Wriothesley joined the Dudley forces—only to be cast off.

For sheer personal invective, I do not know that No. 295 is excelled in the Tudor period, unless it be by Surrey's sonnet directed against King Henry VIII, "Th'Assyrans king—in peas, with fowle desyre," (ed. Padelford, No. 40). It would be interesting to know whether Sir George Blage wrote other verses.

[296] *When tender youthe and pleasaunt yeares are past*

Hand A, with the ascription in the same hand.

In 1584 John Astley (d. 1595) published a prose treatise on *The Art of Riding*, but I have not discovered any other poems by him. The style and content of this sixain suggests that it was written before 1584 and that it might well have been included in *TM*.

Astley is probably best known today as the friend to whom Roger Ascham addressed *A Report and Discourse . . . of the affaires and state of Germany and the Emperour Charles his court*, 1553. In a prefatory letter written to Ascham from Hatfield and dated October 19, 1552, Astley speaks nostalgically of their pleasant fellowship at Cheston and Hatfield, when both were attached to the household of the Princess Elizabeth. After mentioning their reading in Aristotle, Cicero, and Livy, Astley reminds him of "our trimme cōferences of that present world: and to true iudgementes of the troublesome tyme that followed" (*Roger Ascham. English Works*, ed. W. A. Wright, 1904, p. 123. Astley was one of the gentlemen present at the dinner in 1563 which led to the writing of *The Scholemaster*. See p. 175. J. E. B. Mayor in his edition of the latter, 1863, pp. 203-04, has a good note on Astley). He is undoubtedly referring to complications arising from the treasonable charges directed against Admiral Thomas Seymour in 1548-49, which involved Seymour's attentions to the Princess Elizabeth. Both Astley and his wife were arrested for their suspected complicity in this matter. Mistress Catherine was sent to the Tower January 21, 1548/49, and

Astley was put in the Fleet on the twenty-third (*Acts of the Privy Council of England, New Series*, ed. J. R. Dasent, ii [1890], 239-40). During Seymour's trial his "man," John Harington, also a prisoner in the Tower (same ref., p. 239), quoted statements made to him by Mistress Astley about the Admiral's attentions to the Princess Elizabeth (Cecil Papers 150, p. 74; printed in *A Collection of State Papers . . . Left by William Cecil Lord Burghley*, ed. Samuel Haynes, 1740, p. 93, where are given most of the confessions made at Seymour's trial in January and February of 1548/49). As is evident from No. 262, Harington was well acquainted with the Princess Elizabeth's household, and from such an association may have come his copy of No. 296.

On the accession of Mary Tudor in 1553, Astley became an exile in Frankfurt. He returned in 1558 to become Queen Elizabeth's Master of the Jewel House and to enjoy many other favors from her. (*D.N.B.*; Thomas Tanner, *Bibliotheca Britannico-Hibernica*, 1748, p. 54.)

[297] *The secreat flame that made all Troye so hot*

Hand A. The following are written over erasures: line 14, "did tend"; line 49, "rke." In the upper left-hand margin is Bishop Percy's note in pencil, "Surrey's Poems fo. 93."

The poem was first printed in the second edition of *TM*, sigs. Aa^{v}-Aa2^{v} (ed. Rollins, No. 279), with the heading, "Of the troubled comon welth restored to quiet by the mighty power of god." The variants are not significant:

6 did] *omitted*
30 As] As sad
36 Troyans stroyed] stroied Troians
41 eke] *omitted*
54 over turneth] oreturneth
59 his] this
65 health] welth
77 case] ease

As Rollins says in his note, the poem may have been written after the rebellion led by Sir Thomas Wyatt the younger early in 1553/4, when plans were being made for the marriage of Mary Tudor and Philip II of Spain; or, as I think more likely, after the uprising in July, 1553, connected with the attempt to place Lady Jane Grey on the throne (see the Note on No. 289). Note especially line 48.

[298] *Brittle bewtie that nature made so fraile*

Hand A. The ascription is in another secretary hand. In line 8 the corrected reading, "never," is in a different secretary hand. In line 11 the *r* in "frost" is written over an *e* or an *o*. In the upper right-hand margin is Bishop Percy's penciled note, "In Surrey fo. 5."

No. 298 was printed in *TM*, sig. B$1^{r,v}$ (ed. Rollins, No. 9), among the poems attributed to Surrey, entitled, "The frailtie and hurtfulnes of beautie." The *TM* version presents the poem as a complete sonnet.

2 shorter is] short
7 Slipperer] slipper; than] as
never
8 obtayne] attaine; ⟨and not⟩] not
9 Well] Iewel
Inserted between lines 9 and 10:
False and vntrue, enticed oft to treason
10 men] may I
Inserted between lines 10 and 11:
Ah bitter swete infecting as the poyson
11 the] *omitted*

The important contribution of the *AH* version is the ascription to "L vawse," that is, Thomas, second Baron Vaux of Harrowden (1510-1556), to whom the unknown poem No. 173 is attributed with the more common spelling "vaux," and No. 299 in the form given here. This second spelling, which occurs also in the ascription to a copy of "I lothe that I did love" in Bodley MS. Ashmole 48, fols. 23^{v}-24^{v}, very probably indicates sixteenth-century pronunciation. G. F. Nott prints the *TM* version of No. 298 in his *Surrey and Wyatt*, i (1815), 20-21. In his note on the poem, p. 288, he mentions the copy in *AH*, and continues:

> As both the language, and the style of thought bear no resemblance to Surrey's, we may readily believe the piece not to be his. The circumstances of the double rhymes strengthens this conclusion. Surrey studiously avoided them. His natural good taste made him perceive that double rhymes were calculated for light or ludicrous composition only. In serious poems they produce a bad effect, by taking from the gravity of the versification, and throwing over the idea expressed an air of lightness and familiarity. If this poem be Surrey's, it is the only piece of his in which double rhymes occur.

From this context it seems to me clear that by "double rhymes" Nott refers to "season," "reason," "peason," "geason," "taken," and "shaken," which are double in the sense that both final syllables rhyme. We now speak of these as weak, or feminine, endings, and Nott's critical observations on the effect is sound. It is quite true that Surry's practice in rhyme is use of the strong final syllable or word as the rhyme sound, as is illustrated in "so fraile," "to faile," "availe," "Eeles tayle," and "bewayle." Padelford, who also prints the poem from *TM* in his edition of Surrey (*Poems*, 1928, No. 7), misunderstands Nott's meaning and connects the expression "double rhymes" with the rhyme pattern, which, he notes, is the same as in Surrey's sonnet "Alas so all thinges nowe doe holde their peace" (*Poems*, No. 1). Padelford and Rollins, however, agree with Nott in thinking it doubtful that Surrey wrote the poem, a conclusion with which this editor is in agreement, and mainly on the basis of Nott's comments. The ascription in *AH* to Vaux is in all probability correct. A. B. Grosart, however, in his edition of the work of Vaux (*Miscellanies of the Fuller Worthies Library*, iv [1872], 364-93) does not include No. 298, but neither does he include Nos. 173 and 299.

Rollins in his note suggests that the poem was developed from lines 761-74 in Seneca's *Hippolytus*, and both he and Padelford compare the beginning lines with Petrarch's sonetto in morte 63, lines 1-2. George Puttenham's imitation of No. 298 in *The Arte of English Poesie*, 1589 (ed. Willcock and Walker, 1936, p. 123), is well known.

[299] *O temerous taunters delighting in toyes*

Hand A. The ascription is in the same hand as that of No. 298. In line 2 the remains of a long *s* can be seen under the *T* of "Tossinge." In the upper right-hand margin is Percy's penciled note," In Surrey fo. 74."

The poem was printed among the Uncertain Authors of *TM*, sig. Y1[r] (ed. Rollins, No. 217), headed, "Against an vnstedfast woman."

1 taunters delighting] tauntres that delights
2 Tossinge] tottryng
3 gesters depravers of all] iestres deprauerers of swete
4 wheare] whence
5 envenomyd] enuironned; spight] dispite
6 will] doest

The *TM* poem is addressed certainly to one woman, a tauntress, whereas the *AH* version need not be so interpreted. The latter reading in line 5 is correct. For some comment on the author, Thomas, Baron Vaux, see the Notes on Nos. 173 and 298.

[300] *Staye gentle ffrend that passeth bye*

Hand A. In line 2 the *t* in "that" is added in another ink and hand. In the upper left-hand margin is Percy's penciled note, "In Surrey fo 99."

This poem was printed among the Uncertain Authors in (*A*) the second edition of *TM*, sig. Bb3[v] (ed. Rollins, No. 289), where the heading, "An other of the same," indicates that it is a second answer to No. 287 in *TM*. Another contemporary copy is in (*B*) Brit. Mus. MS. Cotton Titus A. XXIV, fol. 79[v], ascribed, "norton."

1 passeth] passest *A B*
2 leadith] ledes the *B*
3 they] we *A*: the *B*; hye] gye *B*
4 to stand] and stand *A*
5 the] that *A B*
6 and] withe *B*
7 resist] withstand *A*
9 my] me *A B*
14 on] in *A B*
17 shall we meete] we shall use meate *B*
19 shall] will *A*; of] for *A*
20 Now] Thus *B*

Presumably "norton" refers to Thomas Norton (1532-1584), who also wrote No. 148.

[301] *Whoe is a Shrew and seemes a saincte*

Hand A.

This epigram appears to be otherwise unknown.

[302] *The more ye desyre her the soner ye mysse*

Hand A.

The epigrammatic quality of these unknown lines is obtained, effectively, through parallelism and contrast. The first three lines may be compared with *Tom Tyler and His Wife*, about 1550 (ed. G. C. Moore Smith and W. W. Greg, Malone Society, 1910, p. 3), lines 83-85:

> The more that I please her, the worse she doth like me,
> The more I forbear her, the more she doth strike me,
> The more that I get her the more she doth glike me.

[303] *A worlde of wittes wear far to faynt*

Hand A.

Although the sense and implications of this unknown poem are not entirely clear, it is probable that it was written after the agrarian uprisings of 1549, as typified by the one in Norfolk led by Robert Kett. Thus by action of the "Symple sorte" (described as aided by God and truth), Britain regained briefly her common farm plots, which had been enclosed for pasturage (line 14); yet now, says the writer, "turnde to losse is all our gaynes"; little can be claimed from that enterprise (lines 7, 16); and "Cheape," that is, plenty, is changed for scarcity (line 39). Northumberland and his followers used the uprisings as one means of bringing about the downfall of Protector Somerset, and after Northumberland became Protector in 1550, abuses against the peasantry were even greater. The debased coinage contributed to the poverty of the people. For references on this period, see the Note on No. 289. G. M. Trevelyan in his *History of England* (New York, Longmans, 1928), pp. 314-17, gives a brief but cogent account of the situation in 1549-50.

[304] *Whan Cressyde came from Troye*

Hand A.

This anonymous ballad was printed from the *AH* transcript, *N*, fol. 141^{r}, by Rollins in his edition of *TM*, ii, 294-95, in his note on the *TM* poem beginning, "I read how Troylus serued in Troy" (No. 237), which also compares the love of the poet with that of Troilus for Cressida. On this story see Rollins' article, "The Troilus-Cressida Story from Chaucer to Shakespeare," *PMLA*, xxxii (1917), 383-429.

Unusual is the use of the adjective "wath," a variant of "wothe," that is, dangerous (line 50). The *N. E. D.* records only one example of this adjective, taken from *Cursor Mundi*, 1300. The last example of the word as substantive is of date 1470.

[305] *The thoughtes of men do daylye chaūnge*

Hand A.

Contemporary copies also occur in: (*A*) *Churchyardes Chance*, 1580, sigs. $B4^{v}$-$C1^{r}$, entitled, "Of the fickle faithe of men" (Huntington copy); (*B*) Folger MS. 1232.3, fol. $10^{r,v}$, written in a mid-sixteenth-century secretary; (*C*) Brit. Mus. MS. Add. 15225, fol. 38^{r}, a version of four stanzas in a book of sixteenth-century poetry. In addition a copy of stanza 1 only, not collated, is in Harl. MS. 6910, fol. 168^{r}.

1 men] man *C*; do] do⟨th⟩ *B*
2 fancye] phansies *A B*; breedes] growes *C*; brestes] brest *B*
3 And] for *C*; nature is] natures are *A B*
4 that] ⟨but can⟩ a *C*; may] can *A-C*; restes] rest *B*
Lines 5-6 in C read:
the hautie hart soe plentie growes
that everie weede doth seeme a rose
7 that] w^{ch} *B*; professe] profeste *A B*
8 from them] from mē *B*: a way *C*; and] or *A B*
9 doth . . . possesse] hath a perfaite freende possest *A B*: hath soe sure a frend possest *C*
10 by] In *A*; is] was *A-C*
11 wheare . . . fownd] but where thou findst *C*
12 failes] faile *B C*

Stanzas 3 and 4 are reversed in order in A and C; the stanzaic order of B is 4, 5, 3.

13 ffor . . . trees will] The . . . tree doth *C*

14 well] faire *B*; those] these *A*: they *B*; that frewt] that good fruites *C*; shall] doo *B*: *omitted C*

15 whose bark] And boughes *C*; seemes] beene *C*; as] soe *C*; faire] feare *A*

16 tree] trees *B*; fielde] fieldes *B*

20 spring] well *C*

21 he] thei *A*: those *B*; is] are *A B*

22 dothe] Doe *A B*; hope] looke *C*; frute] fruites *B C*; on] of *C*

Lines 23 and 24 are omitted in C and are replaced by a version of lines 35 and 36, which end the version in C:

but there as wordes and deedes agree
accept that frend and credit mee

26 prove] trie *B*

27 so shall] Wherein *A B*; not be] is not *A B*

28 trye] spie *A*

30 me to] the blont *A*: the blinde *B*

32 thowe] you *A*; list] lists *A*

34 are] be *B*

35 as] that *A B*

A adds the following couplet:

For he that giu's, this councell here,
Hath bought his witte, and freendshipp dere.

As I have explained in the Note on No. 171, *A* was printed under the author's supervision. It is evident from the collation that *B* is closer to the printed copy than are the other manuscript versions. *C* is obviously a poor text. Since No. 305 is copied in Hand A in *AH* and is there placed with the older poetry, it is reasonable to believe that the *AH* version pre-dates that in the *Chance*, which contains many compositions which were written a number of years before 1580 (see the Note on No. 171).

No. 305 was sufficiently regarded in the late seventeenth century to be set to music in *Cantus, Songs and Fancies*, printed by John Forbes in Aberdeen in 1682. Given as "The VII. Song" on sigs. $C4^{v}$-$D1^{r}$, it has the stanzaic order of the *AH* version, but there are a number of independent readings. The author is not named.

The poem is conventional in the manner of the Uncertain Authors of *TM*, but was evidently more popular than Nos. 171 and 321, also by Churchyard. They are nevertheless more distinctive in style, not simply literary imitations. Churchyard may have learned to use this six-line stanza in tetrameter by studying poems by his master, Surrey (see *Poems*, ed. Padelford, 1928, Nos. 13, 18, 19).

[306] *Misshapp doth holde the Helme/ the Sease my shipp doth shake*

Hand A.

There is little poetic merit in these unprinted lines, written in the manner of the Uncertain Authors of *TM*.

Line 9, "fatche," or fetch, that is, a trick.

[307] *My care to kepe my worde by promesse dewe*

Hand A. The following are written over erasures: line 3, "all"; line 4, the *w* in "well"; line 21, "know." A "Finis" following the poem has been erased.

It appears that Nos. 307 and 308, ascribed to "Cordall," that is, Sir William Cordell (see No. 172 and Note), should be considered one poem. This conclusion is supported by an anonymous copy in (*A*) Huntington MS. HM 198, vol. ii, fols. 42^{v}-43^{r}, where the two poems, wanting some lines, are written as one; and by a similar copy in (*B*) Folger MS. 1.112, fols. 12^{v}-13^{r}, which is ascribed to "G M." In a volume of the Conway papers, however, (*C*) Brit. Mus. MS. Add. 23229, fol. 52^{r}, an incomplete version of No. 307 only appears. This anonymous copy, entitled, "A Precept," is written in a seventeenth-century italic hand.

It is evident from the collation following, given here for No. 307 only, that the copy in *AH* has a few faulty readings, as in lines 7, 8, and 11, but it gives on the whole the superior text, as well as the most complete one.

2 that . . . best] when I must seke *A*: where I must seeke *C*
4 I may well] most I may *A C*: I might best *B*
5 force] mooue *A-C*; wote] knowes *C*
6 that] w^{ch} *A C*
7 And] But *B*; thought] taught *A-C*
8 moste] might *A C*; false] fault *A C*: faultes *B*; this] my *A C*
10 faith in worde doth not abyde] wordes & workes doe not agree *A C*: . . . woordes . . . *B*
Lines 11 and 12 are omitted in B, and variants of lines 23 and 24 are there given as the closing couplet of stanza 2.
11 style] skill *A C*
12 with] in *A C*
Lines 13-18 are omitted in A-C; lines 19-22 are also omitted in B.
19 th'effecte] the effect *A*

22 full fitt the] most meete such *A C*; wight] wightes *A C*
23 Whearefore take heede] wherefore beware *A C*: take heede therfore *B*
24 Among] amongst *B*; no poyson] no poysoned *B*: som̃e poysoned *A C*
In C the first word of the next line, "althoug[h]" is written as a catchword at the bottom of fol. 52^{r}, but lines 25-30 are wanting.
25 And thoughe] Although *A*; in] in in *B*; spend] driue *A*
26 be that thinck] are wch thinck *A*: be wch saye *B*; geason] gasonne B
27 you] on *B*; pleasant] worthy *A*
28 whiche] that *A B*; guyle] cryme *B*
29 lyeth] sittes *A*: lyes *B*
30 weales] wailes *A B*

It is curious that a poem of which there are four contemporary manuscript copies has not been printed before the present time. G. F. Nott, *Surrey and Wyatt*, i (1815), 290, quotes lines 25-30 to illustrate use of "geason," in its sense of being a "thing of no worth." Compare No. 298, line 8, the particular poem Nott is considering. Nott's appraisal of these lines as "very pleasing" is justified by the closing couplet especially.

[308] *Be frend to few, but foe to none at all*

Hand A. In line 18 "matche alw" is written over an erasure. The ascription to "Cordall" is in the same hand. For some further account of Sir William Cordell, see the Note on No. 172.

As pointed out in the Note on No. 307, a shorter version in (*A*) Huntington Library MS. HM 198, vol. ii, fols. 42^{v}-43^{r}, is written as a continuation of No. 307. Another copy of the double shorter version is in (*B*) Folger MS. 1.112, fol. 13^{r}, where it is ascribed, "G M."

2 Curteis speeche] curtesy alike *A*: curtesye *B*
3 your] thy *A*
4 by . . . you] by virtue winne wth the in league *A*: in vertues leauge be bounde . . . *B*
5 all ways] often *B*; fynd great] breed much *A*
7 your] thy *A*; you have proved] thou hast tried *A*
8 you do] thou doe *A*: that yow *B*; now is rarely] rarely here is *A*
9 your] thy *A*: thyne *B*
10 it . . . never] me now his faith is neuer *A*: them not their fruites are nothinge *B*

11 them] thou *A*; thoughe] if *B*; you] thou *A*
12 but] yet *B*; they] he *A*
Lines 13-18 are wanting in A and B.

[309] *When ffortune gave good wynde vnto my saile*

Hand A. In line 2 the crossed-out revised reading "that tyme" is written in another ink and hand. In line 3 the same hand has added "but" in the left margin.

See No. 61 and Note. No. 61 is a copy of the same lines, and the revisions noted above appear to have been made from it.

[310] *The flamyng Sighes that boile within my brest*

Hand A. In the upper right-hand margin is Bishop Percy's penciled note, "In Surrey's Poems fo 37."

This double sonnet was printed among the poems of Sir Thomas Wyatt in *TM*, sig. I3^{r,v} (ed. Rollins, No. 101), entitled, "The louer describeth his restlesse state." Rollins is mistaken when he says in his note that the poem occurs also in the *E* MS. The *TM* version differs little from that in *AH*.

5 eyes] eyen
9 list] lust
21 tasting] trifling
24 the] my

G. F. Nott, *Surrey and Wyatt*, ii (1816), 15, note p. 543, printed the poem from *AH*, with modernized spelling. Kenneth Muir used the *AH* copy for his text in *Collected Poems*, 1949, No. 175. Although Miss Foxwell is not very clear about her source, a comparison shows that she has printed from the *TM* version, *Poems*, i (1913), 43. She makes no mention there of the *AH* text, but in *A Study of Sir Thomas Wyatt's Poems*, 1911, p. 9, she mentions this as one of the four poems found in the *AH* transcript and in *TM*, but in no other manuscripts.

As has been noted by others, this very personal poem was probably written when Wyatt was in prison in 1541. Lines 13-14 echo the close of his epigram addressed to Sir Francis Bryan from prison:

> Sure I am Brian, this wounde shall heale agayne
> But yet, alas, the scarre shall styll remayne.
> (Foxwell, i, 62)

Rollins has other references on this expression.

[311] *Stond who so list vpon the Slipper toppe*

Hand A. In the upper right-hand margin is Percy's penciled note, "In Surrey fo 44."

No. 311 was printed among the poems of Wyatt in *TM*, sigs. K4^{v}-L1^{r}

(ed. Rollins, No. 118), entitled, "Of the meane and sure estate." There seems to be no other contemporary copy. The *TM* variants in lines 2, 3, 5, 7, and 9 were probably introduced to effect a smoother iambic rhythm.

1 toppe] whele
2 courtes] hye; estates] astate
3 vse . . . stoppe] vse my life in quietnesse eche dele
4 vnknowe] Vnknowen; suche brackishe ioyes] the wanton toyes
5 so . . . forthe] my time shall slowly
6 that] And; done] past
7 I . . . aged] Let me dye olde
8 ffrom . . . croppe] For gripes of death doth he to hardly passe
9 is . . . other] knowen is to all; and of] but to
10 Doth dye] He dyeth

As has been noted, the poem is adapted from lines 391-403 in Seneca's *Thyestes* (*Seneca's Tragedies*, ed. and trans. by F. J. Miller, Loeb Library, vol. ii [London, Heinemann; New York, Putnam, rev. ed., 1929]). As may be seen, neither version gives an exact translation:

Stet quicumque volet potens
aulae culmine lubrico;
me dulcis saturet quies;
obscuro positus loco
leni perfruar otio,
nullis nota Quiritibus
aetas per tacitum fluat.
sic cum transierint mei
nullo cum strepitu dies,
plebeius moriar senex.
illi mors gravis incubat
qui, notus nimis omnibus,
ignotus moritur sibi.

Line 8 in *AH* is a vivid projection of "illi mors gravis incubat," but this result is not gained in the *TM* line. In line 4 the "brackishe ioyes" of *AH* is more forthright, and more like Wyatt, than the "wanton toyes" of *TM*; but neither is in the Latin.

Wyatt's editors have judiciously chosen to print the *AH* version: Nott, *Surrey and Wyatt*, ii (1816), 74; Muir, *Collected Poems*, 1949, No. 176; Foxwell, *Poems*, i (1913), 366, taken from the *AH* transcript, *N*, fol. 143^{v} (see her note, vol. ii, p. 177).

[312] *Hart oppressyd with desp'rat thought*

Hand A.

A copy of the poem, written in a very individual, scrawling, pre-Elizabethan secretary hand, occurs also in the *D* MS., fols. 47^{v}-48^{r}, where it is followed by several of Wyatt's poems. The spelling of the *D* MS. version differs remarkably, but otherwise the variants are relatively unimportant.

1 desp'rat] dessperott; thought] thoughtes
5 must] do
8 had had] had
10 and for all] butt yett ffor all
11 thearfore] Wherffor; must] do
13 well moght] mowt wyell
17 Whearby] Wherffor; must] do
18 Sence . . . use] & cruell wyll theroff acvys

Using the *D* text modernized, Nott, *Surrey and Wyatt*, ii (1816), 227, included this unsigned poem as Wyatt's, perhaps because it is grouped with Wyatt poems in the *D* MS. In his note, p. 583, he makes no mention of the copy in *AH*, which, it should be noticed, follows two of Wyatt's poems, and comments only, "It is a piece which boasts of no particular merit." Muir, *Poems*, 1949, No. 217, includes the poem under his section of "Doubtful Poems." He also prints from the *D* text, but my readings differ slightly from his (lines 1, 13, 17, 18).

In my earlier study of *AH* (Hughey, pp. 417-18, 430-31) and in the Introduction (pp. 27-29), I have called attention to the ordered arrangement of parts of the *AH* MS. Consequently, on that basis alone we might suppose that the Haringtons considered No. 312 one of Wyatt's poems (see Nos. 310, 311). As noted, the order in the *D* MS. may also be indicative of Wyatt's authorship. Neither Nott nor Muir have considered the poem itself, which seems to me to be written in Wyatt's manner. No one would suppose that it was written by Surrey, and I think of no minor poet who might have given us the first line, which is striking and effective. Furthermore, Josephine Miles in her analysis of Wyatt's poetry (*Major Adjectives in English Poetry*, Berkeley: University of California Press, 1946, pp. 316, 323-28) points out that *heart* is the most frequently used word and that *cruel* is a favorite adjective. She also contrasts Wyatt's use of language with that of Surrey.

[313] *What thing is that, that I both have and lack*

Hand A. In the upper right-hand margin is Percy's penciled note, "In Surrey's Poems fo. 62."

The poem was printed among the Uncertain Authors of (*A*) *TM*, sig. $T1^{r,v}$ (ed. Rollins, No. 187), entitled, "Of the louers vnquiet state." A copy of the first stanza is in (*B*) British Museum MS. Harl. 78, fol.

29^{r}, headed, "Ridle." This last collation was made by Kathleen Tillotson.

1 that, that] that which *A*
2 yet is] yet yt is *A B*
3 How . . . receav'd and] alwayes forwarde and yet full fare *B*
4 Alway] Ever more *B*
5 that] that which *A*: that y^{t} *B*
6 Thus . . . say I] Still thus to seke, and *A*: whearby I *B*
7 And] ffor *B*; that] y^{t} that *B*; new] newest *A*: now *B*
Lines 8-14 are wanting in B.
8 wilfull . . . found] riches finde I wilfull
9 and] *omitted*; I lyved] liue I
10 too] *omitted*; lacked] lacke my
Line 11 is wanting in A.
12 was] am
13 I shuld] that I shall
14 a] *omitted*; suffred] suffer

The copy in *B* is followed by an "Aunswer," which is printed by Rollins in his note on the poem.

Like No. 312, this may be another of Wyatt's poems. Muir, *Collected Poems*, 1949, No. 223, prints the poem from *AH*, among the "Doubtful Poems," apparently on the basis of its position in the *AH* MS. Though of poorer quality, No. 313 may be compared with No. 120, a riddle written by Wyatt; further, No. 313 exemplifies Wyatt's use of conflict in emotion, with his often repeated emphasis on pain and liberty. In this connection see the analysis by Josephine Miles, *Major Adjectives in English Poetry*, 1946, pp. 316, 323, 329.

[314] *Who so desyres, to know in what estate*

Hand A. In line 13 the "u" in "houer" is written over another letter. A wormhole now in the paper where line 27 should begin was evidently there when the poem was copied, as this one line is indented.

I have found no other copy of this poem, which clearly belongs to the *TM* period. It is not of sufficient poetic quality to be considered, like Nos. 312 and 313, as possibly written by Wyatt, but it might well have been printed among the Uncertain Authors.

[315] *Moste happie is that wight, whiche borne is so to en'd*

Hand A. The "finis" may be in a different hand. The reason for the apostrophe in line 1 is not clear.

I have found no other copy of these lines.

[316] *Be sure the slipper tyme, so slyde not slighlye his way*

Hand A. The "finis" is in a different hand.

From the form and content I should judge that the same person wrote Nos. 315 and 316, both of which are otherwise unknown.

[317] *What wight in wealth doth walke, and weald at will*

Hand A. The "finis," as in Nos. 315 and 316, is in another hand.

These unknown verses, which offer good examples of the vice of excessive alliteration, are similar to some of those among the Uncertain Authors of *TM.* In the transcript of *AH, N,* fol. 145ʳ, the copyist has mistakenly written "slearing" in line 2. The "flearing" face is one which smiles obsequiously. In line 5 the occurrence of "blyvelye" is interesting. The *N.E.D.* quotes only one example, dated 1400, of this expressive adverb, *belively*, which means "quickly."

[318] *No storme nor bitter breathe, of Boreas blustring blast*

Hand A. As in the preceding, the "finis" is in a different hand. These unknown verses are similar to those of Nos. 315-17.

[319] *In all extreames as trobles move*

Hand B. See the Introduction, pp. 33-34.

These observations on the follies and troubles of youth seem familiar, but these particular verses appear to be otherwise unknown. They might have been published in *TM* or in *The Paradise of Dainty Devices.*

In line 53 the copyist of the transcript, *N,* fol. 146ʳ, has incorrectly written, "it breedes—a corfye so extreame," thus destroying the sense. The proper word, "corsye," i.e., corsie, in the sense of grievance was current between 1548 and 1601 (*N.E.D.*).

[320] *Amazed to see, nought vnder heavens cope*

Hand B. The ascription "E.R.," placed as indicated in the text, is written in a different ink, in large capital letters of printed character. There can be no question that they signify "Elizabetha Regina," to whom No. 238 is ascribed. The contraction beneath the initials is in small secretary, not that of Hand B, and appears to be "scr̄," i.e., "scripsit." Conceivably, however, it should be read "sec̄," i.e., "secundus," which would refer to the second year of Elizabeth's reign, thereby indicating exactly the time of composition. G. F. Nott interpreted the contraction as referring to the regnal year, but from a reading which I do not accept. In the transcript, *N,* fol. 147ᵛ, he has the penciled note:

'Et(2r̂
2 Elizabeth.'

The use of Hand B in *AH* shows, at any rate, that the composition was copied into the manuscript at a comparatively early period in Elizabeth's reign, whether or not the precise year 1560 is designated for the work itself, which could have been done before Elizabeth became queen. Since a finis is omitted and the last line of the selection is marked by a colon, and, furthermore, since the greater part of fol. 220^{v} and the following six pages, all of the original paper, are blank, we may suppose that the *AH* compiler hoped to add to his copy of this incomplete translation, "Triumphe Petrarcke."

So far as I can discover, no other copies of this translation by Elizabeth are extant, and it seems to be unknown to scholars. Nott, of course, knew it, but he did not call attention to it. No mention is made of it by Ewald Flügel in his article "Die Gedichte Der Königin Elisabeth" (*Anglia*, xiv [1892], 346-61), nor by Caroline Pemberton in her edition of *Queen Elizabeth's Englishings of Boethius, "De Consolatione Philosophiae," A.D. 1593, Plutarch, "De Curiositate," A.D. 1598, Horace, "De Arte Poetica" (part), A.D. 1598* (E.E.T.S., cxiii [1899]). Mary A. Scott in *Elizabethan Translations from the Italian* (Boston, Houghton Mifflin, 1916) refers only to Henry Parker Lord Morley's translation of the *Trionfi*, published about 1565 (pp. 112-13).

The eighty-eight lines of No. 320 present an economical translation of the first ninety lines of the "Trionfo Dell'Eternita" (*Francesco Petrarca, Le Rime Sparse E I Trionfi*, a cura Ezio Chiòrboli, Bari, Gius, Laterza & Figli, 1930, pp. 363-65). Elizabeth's intention was evidently to make a close, line-by-line translation, and she almost succeeded—to the detriment of the poetry. Although she does not always follow constructions, her frequently awkward syntax indicates the extent to which the original bound her. She has changed the rhyme scheme, for, as usual, the English language would not permit so few rhymes as the Italian. There is no evidence of any influence from Morley's more diffuse translation, which uses 124 lines for this same passage (*The Triumphes of Petrarch, Translated by Henry Parker Lord Morley 1554*, reprinted by Stafford Henry, Earl of Iddesleigh, Roxburghe Club, 1887, pp. 93-97). Miss Scott comments that Morley's translation is "in irregular and uncouth verse, and is not very faithful to the original." For purposes of comparison I give below lines 43-90 in the original (according with lines 43-88 in No. 320), and the corresponding translation in Morley.

Beat' i spirti che nel sommo coro
si troveranno, o trovano, in tal grado
che sia in memoria eterna il nome loro!
O felice colui che trova il guado
di questo alpestro e rapido torrente
c'ha nome vita, e a molti è si a grado!

Misera la volgare e cieca gente,
che pon qui sue speranze in cose tali
che'l tempo le ne porta si repente!
O veramente sordi, ignudi e frali,
poveri d'argomenti e di consiglio,
egri del tutto e miseri mortali!
Quei che'l mondo governa pur coi ciglio,
che conturba et acqueta gli elementi,
al cui saver non pur io non m'appiglio,
ma li angeli ne son lieti e contenti
di veder de le mille parti l'una,
et in ciò stanno desiosi e'ntenti!
O mente vaga, al fin sempre digiuna,
a che tanti penseri? Un'ora sgombra
quanto in molt'anni a pena si raguna:
quel che l'anima nostra preme e 'ngombra,
dianzi, *adesso*, *ier*, *deman*, *matino* e *sera*,
tutti in un punto passeran com'ombra;
non avrá loco *fu*, *sará*, ned *era*,
ma è solo, *in presente*, et *ora*, et *oggi*,
et sola *eternitá* raccolta e 'ntera.
Quasi spianati dietro e nanzi i poggi,
ch'oscupavan la vista, non fia in cui
vostro sperare e rimembrar s'appoggi;
la qual varietá fa spesso altrui
vaneggiar si, che'l viver par un gioco,
pensando pur—che sarò io? che fui?—
Non sará piú diviso a poco a poco,
ma tutto inseme, e non piú state o verno,
ma morto il tempo, e variato il loco;
e non avranno in man li anni il governo
de le fame mortali; anzi chi fia
chiaro una volta, fia chiaro in eterno.
O felici queele anime che'n via
sono o seranno di venire al fine
di ch'io ragiono, quandunque e' si sia!
e tra l'altre leggiadre e pellegrine,
beatissima lei che Morte occise
assai di qua dal natural confine!
Parranno allor l'angeliche divise,
e l'oneste parole, e i penser casti,
che nel cor giovenil natura mise.

Morley's translation of this passage reads:

But happye and blessed be those spirites certenly
That be found in that holy state eternally
Sure and very certayne in honor to encrease
Without terme or tyme neuer to sease
O howe happye is he that fyndeth that way
To passe this Rabidus and dul passage I say
That is called in this vnstable world a lyfe
And is so troublouse and so ful of stryfe
Blynd and wretched I say are the mortal
That hoopeth in thynges that sone doth fall
Which tyme taketh away with a thought
And turneth al our fancis and foly to nought
Surely they are both vnwise deffe and frayle
Poore of iudgment and of Counsayle
Yea & worse then sike in dead & wretched therto
That doth not as our deutie is regard hym so
That with his becke may trouble and appease
The elementes al as it doth hym please
Whome to honour we are not bound onlye
But the Aungels that sit in the heauen hye
Are contented of the thousand partes as one
With y[e] sight of his godhed in his gloriouse trone
And so stand stedfast with a feruent Intention
Are not our myndes then worthy of reprehenciō
To loke on that which in the very ende
Commeth to no profite therevnto to pretende
For that which we so fast gather together
With much paine in mani years hether & thether
With great and troubles cumbrance of mynd
To day and to morowe at the last we fynde
As the shadowe doth passe away and glyde
Euen at the poynt so shall all our pryde
Then remember ye well I truly counsell this
That after goddes great dreadfull iudgement is
Was and shalbe shall haue no more time and place
But one eternitie together in one selfe space
Nor further there shalbe none obiecte at all
To hurte by our sight our weake memoriall
Which is the occacion and the very cause
Many an vnprudent person in vanitie to pause
That the lyfe present semeth but a playe
Thinking they are to morowe as to day

But then all otherwyse shalbe no diuision at all
But litle and litle the hole vniuersall
Shalbe together and wynter and somer paste
And tyme quiete gone and no lenger laste
Nor these yeares y^t^ we do nowe presently name
Shall haue no more the domynion of fame
But ones theyr famouse that shall neuer disseuer
But in eternitie to endure famouse foreuer
O happie are those soules that are in that way
Of which so much I nowe speake of and say
In ioy glory and rest styll to Endure
That are and shalbe perpetually, so sure
And amonge the other that so gracious be
Most blessed of all other playnly is she
That cruell death kylled or she came to age
There shalbe seene in that angelyke vysage
The honest wordes the thought cleane and chast
That nature had set in her in olde tymes past

Both translations fall far below the original, but in such lines as 60-65 and 85-88, the queen's verses attain real poetic quality.

Selections of Elizabeth's translations from Cicero and Seneca were also among the Harington papers, from which they were printed in the *NA* (1769, pp. 135-38; 1775, pp. 235-37).

[321] *As witt is seldome good, till it be dearely bought*

Hand B.

Entitled *Churchyardes farewell*, No. 321 was printed as a broadsheet, presumably in 1565 or 1566. A "ballett" by that name was entered to Edward Russell between July 22, 1565 and the same day of 1566 (*Stationers' Register*, ed. E. Arber, i [1875], 308). The lines of poulter's measure are printed as four lines instead of two, with three columns on the sheet. The unique copy in the Huntington Library (*S.T.C.* 5221) is cut away at the bottom, partially obliterating the ascription, "qd. Churchyarde." Printed from the broadsheet, the poem is included as No. 30 in *Ballads and Broadsides chiefly of the Elizabethan Period*, ed. Herbert L. Collmann, Roxburghe Club, 1912. The collation with the Huntington copy shows no striking variants.

1 seldome] neuer
4 worthi'ste] worthiest
5 them] him
10 The] And; lies] lye
12 no] not
14 forthe] out; for] there

15 dothe] Doo
17 gothe] goeth
20 Youe] Ye; yor . . . fynde] to finde your freendes
21 youe] Ye
24 with . . . thynne] through thick & thinne for loue with you
28 swarves] swayes; wold] *omitted*
31 hastie happe] heapinge hope
34 wav'ring] wauereth
35 with the] with their
37 beare] stare
38 Wheare, for] Where lo, for
41 preace] preest
46 stand] runne
47 chamber] chambers
53 your sleeve] their . . .
56 you] ye
57 you] ye; throwklye] throughly; play'd] plaies
60 might] shoulde; flatt'rers] flatterers
61 Seat] state
62 doth] doo
64 the] *omitted*; in . . . pleasure] or . . . pleasures
65 charme] chaunce
67 Whil'ste] Whilest; eche . . . humo^{r}] euell honour
69 sicklye] sickle
71 twitling] twittell; Larom̃]larm
72 shrillie] shortly
73 aye] sure
74 flatt'rers] flatterers; fittest] finest
76 Or Aley] An alie
The lines scratched out, 77-78, are, of course, not so given in the printed copy.
80 and past] ye wot; Lordens] Lordinges
84 Latter] later; Lammasse] Lammas
85 departure] departinge
88 bowgetts] budgets
89 cow'ldest] canst
90 hand] handes; a] the
91 they have . . . do] he hath . . . doth
93 whoe] That; gaine] game
94 to be] *omitted*
97 Caryon] carraine; seing] steyng
98 foole] fell; fast] too
99 luck] hap
100 Court] Courts

103 in] my
106 Thus] As; and so] so now
108 among'st] amonge
110 blessid] blesse

For an introductory account of Churchyard and his work, see the Note on No. 171.

No. 321 is one of several "farewells" which Churchyard addressed to the Court. Also published as a broadsheet and entered on the *Stationers' Register* the same year was "A Farewell cauld, Churcheyeards, rounde. From the Courte to the Cuntry grownd" (ed. Arber, i [1875], 308). "A Farewell when I went to studie, written to the worlde," printed in his *Chippes*, 1575 (sigs. B5^{r}-C2^{r}), is another assertion of preference for the country as opposed to the Court. "Churchyardes farewell from the Courte, the seconde yere of the Queenes Maiesties raigne," in the *Charge*, 1580 (sigs. B3^{r}-C3^{v}), reveals the author as guilty of some of the tricks he is condemning in No. 321:

> And blushe to make an honest shrifte,
> I sent eche Lorde a Newe yeres gifte:
> Suche treasure as I had that tyme,
> Some thinke this is a crauyng guise,
> Tushe holde your peace, world waxeth wise.
> A dulled horse that will not sturre,
> Must be remembred with a spurre. (sig. C2^{r})

There are a number of other satires on the Court or on false friends who hang about the Court. The *Chance* of 1580 has among others: "Of a Flatterer and a Backbiter," "A warnyng from Courte," "Of a Courtiers life, and how the worst sorte findes beste Fortune" (sigs. C1^{r,v}, C2^{v}, C3^{r}). The *Challenge* of 1593 includes "A discourse of Gentlemen lying in London that were better keepe house in their Countrey" (sigs. P3^{v}-Q3^{r}).

As Wyatt's satire "A spending hand" (No. 141) exceeds "Myne owne I. P." (No. 140) in the biting quality of the satire, so No. 321 exceeds No. 171. No. 321 offers no solace from the mean estate but seethes with personal rancor and harsh invective against the "Buzzing Bees" who "creape in place wheare Churcheyardes creditt was"; against the "flearing fawners"; the "Caryon Crowes" of Cheapside; and finally against the fool who stays at Court "To linger out in yeares/ for Moone shyne in the well." So he will take his leave to go where fortune shall assign. The virulence of the satire is attained by graphic colloquial diction.

21. "fleezing fists," i.e., fleecing, or grabbing, fists. The *N.E.D.* does

not note the form *fleeze*, but gives *fleese* and *fliese*. Compare the German *flüsz*.

26. To give (a person) the fig was to make a contemptuous gesture to him, expressed also as "The Fig of Spain," as in Shakespeare, *Henry V*, III, vi, 62. Pertinent are lines in *England's Helicon*, 1600, "The Sheepheards Slumber" (ed. Rollins, I, 181, lines 36-39):

> And where you see these women nice,
> and looking to be sought:
> With scowling browes their follies check,
> and so giue them the Fig.

In No. 321 it is the hangers-on who give the Court the fig by their swarming in like trash to get what they can from those who trust too much. In line 45 the verb "figg" describes the restless moving about of these same seekers. They also indulge in "twitling twatling tales" (line 71), not in plain talk, as does the writer.

55. As a servant to Henry Howard, Earl of Surrey, Churchyard first learned about the "crooked crafts" of some at Court. See the Note on No. 171.

81. The meaning of "haunce" is not certain. If "haunce" is understood as an old form of *hance* (Old French *hauce*, *hausse*), signifying rise or elevation, then the sense in lines 81-82 would be that the poet, who has been nothing but the lowly Vice, or fool, since he came to Court, is thankful that he is free of any exalted place. If, however, "haunce" is understood as a variant of *haunch* (which it was), there are two possible interpretations, both arising from West Country and Scottish usage: (1) a bite like a dog's, hence (lines 79-82), my plain speaking is only that of the Vice, and free of all ill-natured biting remarks; (2) a throw under the leg, which by extension could mean a dirty trick, with a meaning obvious in the context. This last usage of the word, however, seems not to have been known earlier than the nineteenth century. See the *N.E.D.* and *The English Dialect Dictionary*, ed. Joseph Wright, English Dialect Society, vol. iii (1905).

84. The reckless ladies are, like the simple woodcock, so easily caught in the nets that they are seldom thriving by Latter Lammas, that is, never.

89. "Sr Dawe," or Sir Jackdaw, simpleton.

101-102. For "Curtall" in the sense of a person with his ears cut off, compare Robert Greene in *A Quippe for an Vpstart Courtier*, 1592 (*Life and Complete Works*, ed. A. B. Grosart, xi [1882], 259): "I haue plaied many mad pranckes, for which cause, you may apparently see I am made a curtal, for the Pillory (in the sight of a great many good and sufficient witnesses) hath eaten off both mine eares."

[322] *Shonne the bywaies, of wightes whiche walke a wrie*

Hand B. The "finis" is in a different hand.

The form of this unknown little poem is interesting, for it is composed of an iambic pentameter quatrain plus a stanza of rhyme royal. The introductory trochees are effectively used to convey the imperative sense.

[323] *Theise are the Hollie Commaund'mentes tenñe*

Hand: similar to Hand B, but not, I think, the same. The ascription is in the same hand. Wormholes in the paper have necessitated supplying letters in the title. In Hughey, p. 423, note 5, the first word of the poem is erroneously given as "Choise."

The "Tho. Smithe" who wrote these lines on the ten commandments was without doubt Sir Thomas Smith, 1512-1577, a devout Protestant humanist, who served as secretary of state under Edward VI and Elizabeth. When Protector Somerset was sent to the Tower, October 14, 1549 (see the Note on No. 293), Smith as a loyal adherent was also imprisoned. He was released March 10, 1549/50 (*D.N.B.*). During these tedious months he had ample opportunity for writing, as Royal MS. 17 A.XVII testifies. Written as fair copy in a contemporary hand, this little volume is entitled, "Certaigne Psalmes or Songues of David translated into Englishe meter by Sir Thomas Smith, Knight, then prisoner in the Tower of London, with other prayers and songues by him made to pas the tyme there, 1549." Included are paraphrases of eleven Psalms (102, 141, 142, 119, 85, 30, 40, 70, 54, 144, 145, Vulgate numbering) eight prayers, and three other poems. No. 323 is not included, but I conjecture that it was written at this time, and possibly given to his fellow prisoner, John Harington (see the Introduction, p. 64). A copy of Smith's oration on Queen Elizabeth's marriage is also in the Harington papers (Introduction, p. 38). In addition to the article in the *D.N.B.*, the best account of Smith seems still to be that of John Strype, *The Life of the Learned Sir Thomas Smith, Kt. D.C.L.*, rev. ed., 1820.

[324] *With Heavie hart I call to the*

Hand: same as the preceding. Lines 13-17 are indented to avoid a long wormhole. The extraneous matter written beneath this poem is described in the Introduction, pp. 34-36.

With this unknown metrical prayer, the *AH* MS. poetry collection is concluded.

Comments on Poems In Appendix I

I

In all respectes that nature may commend

This poem is an acrostic on *Iane Fleming*. A comparison with other poems in *AH* which were probably written by the elder John Harington suggests that this is another of his compositions. See Nos. 2, 21, 23, 177, 232, 246, 262. Several years ago Professor William R. Parker called my attention to the use of acrostics in poems presumably written by the elder Harington.

II

Of hew right faire, a face both good and sweete

This sixain, an acrostic on *Osborn*, was perhaps addressed by John Harington to Mistress Anne Osborne, the wife of his friend Peter Osborne (1521-92), a strong supporter of the Reformation and Keeper of the Privy Purse to King Edward VI. He married Anne Blythe, niece of Sir John Cheke, who died at their home in 1557 (*D.N.B.*). John Harington collected some of Osborne's letters. The compliment is turned in a manner similar to the preceding.

III

Now to the myndes of twelve it is - - referd

Implications here of the snares placed about the person to whom the poem is addressed would accord with John Harington's attitude about the fall of Thomas Seymour, Baron Sudeley. See the Introduction (pp. 63-64) and Notes on Nos. 2 and 3. The last two lines suggest that the poem was written three days after the death of the person, with the clearly implied meaning that vengeance for an innocent death would be given later by the Lord. It is obvious that there is a parallel in the poem to the trial and death of Christ.

IV

The Sonne hath twyse brought forthe - - -

See the Note on No. 74.

Glossary

Glossary

Words are arranged according to the spelling of the manuscript. Cross references are given for spellings which may present difficulty in finding. Interchangeable uses of *i* and *y* and *u* and *w* and the initial double *f* are not so indicated. Reference is to number and line of poem. The *N.E.D.* has been used as a guide in usage and definition throughout.

abid, pa. pple. — *undergone*, 184.2.
abhorr, v. — *make* (*one*) *shudder*, 229.84.
able, v. — *enable, empower*, 22.36; *strengthen*, 168.81.
abode, v. pa.t. — *endured*, 85.36.
abroach, adv. — in the phr., "to set abroach," *to pierce and leave running*, 182.151.
accombred, ppl. adj. — *overwhelmed*, 139.51.
accompte, sb. — *account*, 165.16.
acited, pa. pple. — *summoned*, 144.2.
adrad, ppl. adj. — *dreaded, greatly feared*, 154.64.
adresse, v. — *direct*, 161.60.
advowe, v. — see "avow."
advyse, v. — *look at*, 279.25.
advysing, pres. pple. — *observing*, 113.1.
afeard, ppl. adj. — *afraid*, 156.10.
affecte, sb. — *desire, feeling*, 95.14; *feeling towards or in favor of*, 158.25.
affrayes, v. — *alarms or disturbs*, 160.26.
affryght, v. — *frighten, terrify*, 234.346.
afore, affore, adv. — *before* (time), 100.6; 140.68; 161.50; 186.81.
afore, affore, prep. — *before, in front of, into the presence of*, 144.2; 154.34, 68; 186.52; 286.27.
afore, affore, conj. — *before* (*the time that*), 157.10; 167.27.
againe, agayne, prep. — *against, in resistance to*, 109.2; 114.11; 160.28; 245.25; 282.7.
agaste, pa. pple. — *afraid*, 161.21.
agree, v. — *to be suitable, appropriate*, 87.4.
aley (addle), adj. — in the phr., "aley head," — *empty, muddled*, 321.77.
algate, adv. — *always*, 163.63.
all be it, conj. — *although*, 73.37.
all to, adv. phr. — *wholly*, 128.8; in the phr., "all to breake," *break into pieces*, 129.8.
alonely, adv. — *only*, 67.9.
amanza, pres. pple. used as sb. (?) — *loving one, lover*, 23.1 (apparently coined from the pres. pple. of the Latin v. *amo.*, and here used as a term of endearment).
amayne, adv. — *at full speed*, 259.14.
amaze, v. — *infatuate*, 259.18; *confuse*, 261.14.
amazed, amazd, ppl. adj. — *bewildered, confused*, 5.2; *lost in wonder*, 67.7; 69.20; 260.12; 278.85; *terror-stricken*, 154.40; 270.22; *astonished*, 320.1.
anon, anone, adv. — *presently, soon*, 121.7; 155.53; 168.97; *at once, instantly*, 142.37, 73; 154.3.

annoy, anoy, anoye, annoye, sb. — *trouble, vexation,* 19.33; 105.14; 149.24; 184.20; 189.8; 214.6; 230.47; 238.2.

apace, apase, adv. — *swiftly, with speed,* 66.32; 78.12; 85.21; 112.7; 167.28; 259.19; 276.41.

appaire, appayre, v. — *become weaker,* 73.11; 81.16; *to injure, weaken, damage,* 83.7.

assaulted, ppl. adj. — *attacked, assailed,* 5.1.

assay, assaye, sb. — *trial,* 14.1, 16; *tribulations,* 22.29; *attempt,* 139.59; 260.38; in the phr. "at all assayes," *at all events, on every occasion, always,* 278.44.

assay, assaie, v. — *endeavor, attempt,* 2.6; 155.110; 160.28; 168.36; 182.154; 219.5; *set oneself,* 279.7 (pa.t.).

assayde, pa. pple. — *put to the proof,* 166.23.

assemble, sb. — *assembly, congregation,* 156.22.

asslake, v. — *mitigate,* 90.34.

assoyle, v. — *clear up, resolve,* 170.3.

asswage, v. — *pass away,* 76.20; *allay, calm, appease,* 78.25; 288.42; *mitigate, alleviate,* 85.40.

astart, v. — *to start up,* 270.54.

attire, v. — *adorn, array,* 194.9.

atweene, prep. — *between,* 164.19.

aulture, sb. — *height,* 84.29.

availe, avayle, sb. — *help, aid,* 82.8; 87.61; 89.22; 298.5; *profit, beneficial effect,* 260.4.

availe, avayle, v. — *afford help, assist,* 133.2, 6, 10, 14, 18, 22, 26; 192.16; 303.27.

avawnt, v. — *be off, be gone,* 66.66.

avow, avowe, advowe, v. — *to take a vow* (to do something), 130.3; *say, declare,* 182.187; 245.42.

avoyde, v. — *depart,* 155.96.

awcetours (authors) sb. — *ancestors, progenitors,* 246.5.

awe, sb. — *fear, dread,* 5.34.

awntrus (M.E. auntrous), adj. — *adventurous, hazardous,* 246.5.

ay, aye, I, interj. — *even so, even, yea,* 163.19; 179.19, 20; 272.34; 284.5; in the expression, "ay me," *alas,* 234.319.

aye, ay, ey, adv. — *ever, always,* 11.10; 13.9; 19.4; 23.29; 59.6; 89.55; 98.10; 106.6; 108.10; 161.12; 163.68; 167.49; 168.24, 96; 171.8; 175.28; 186.4; 238.11; 246.24; 247.21; 249.23; 250.24, 38; 260.24; 261.37; 262.14; 264.13; 266.50, 61, 84; 267.7, 12, 47; 270.55; 271.6; 272.53; 274.25; 276.26, 44; 278.66; 281.28, 43; 283.1; 289.19; 290.22; 295.7; 303.18; 320.45, 60; 321.73; 323.19; 324.20.

baale, sb. — see "bale."

bable, sb. — *bauble, the baton carried by the Court Fool or jester as a mock emblem,* 321.104.

bake meat, sb. — *pastry, a pie,* 142.27.

bale, baale, sb. — *woe, harm,* 264.19; 281.6; 319.4.

banckrowtes, sb. — *bankrupts*, 180.36.
bane, baine, bayne, sb. — *woe, harm, hapless fate*, 66.59; 90.44; 172.12; 240.11; *death*, 160.13; 275.30, 44; 288.3; 289.3.
bankerout, adj. — *bereft, destitute*, 182.60.
barb'd, ppl. adj. — *relating to a horse, caparisoned with a barb, i.e., a covering for the breast and flanks of a war horse*, 143.7.
bare (bore), v., pa.t. — "bare in hande," *abused with false pretences*, 149.55.
bashe, v. (imperative) — *be abashed or ashamed*, 245.52.
bate, v. — *abate, decrease*, 139.42.
bawson, sb. — *badger*, 270.26.
baye, sb. — in the hunting phr., "to make the baye," or, "to bring to the bay," *to put or bring into close quarters* (referring to the relative position of the hunted animal and the hounds), 181.18; 259.22.
bayne, sb. — see "bane."
bayne, v. — *bathe*, 81.16 (pa.t.), 89.4.
be, pa. pple. — *been*, 72.20.
beadell, sb. — *herald*, 304.47.
beadseman, sb. — "*humble servant*," 199.18.
bearing, vbl. sb. — in the phr., "bearing in hand," *pretending, deluding*, 107.13 (see "bare").
beck, sb. — *bow*, 78.13; *nod*, 261.29.
behest, beheste, sb. — *command*, 75.21; *vows, promise*, 90.14; 167.3; 307.8.
behight, sb. — *promise*, 83.60.
behight, v. — *promise*, 21.25.
beknow, v. — *confess*, 161.16.
beknowen, ppl. adj. — *known, familiar*, 186.18.
bell, sb. — in the phr., "bear the bell away," *carry off the prize, take first place*, 66.48; 180.117; 182.120.
bene, v., pres. subj. pl. — *be*, 246.2.
beredd, pa. pple. — *planned, advised*, 196.18.
beshrewe, beshrow, v. — *devil take! hang!*, 181.12; 182.107.
besyttes, v. — *suits, becomes*, 247.38.
bet, adv. — *better*, 90.15.
betane, pa. pple. — *betaken*, 163.22.
betyde, v. — *befall*, 123.6 (pa.t.); *become (of)*, 147.42; 148.42; *happen*, 317.7.
betyme, adv. — *early, in good time*, 87.54; 271.16; 283.16.
betymes, adv. — *before it is too late*, 66.99; 167.31.
bewray, bewraye, v. — *reveal, expose*, 139.50; 240.11; *betray trust*, 247.16.
bide, byde, v. — *await*, 14.22; 186.20; 241.3; *continue in a certain state or condition*, 16.12; 180.85; 186.65, 82; *dwell*, 23.22; *suffer, endure*, 73.34; 193.3; *remain, stay*, 86.18; 155.96.
blaze, v. — *celebrate, make known*, 182.34.
blazed, blased, p. pple. — *published, made known*, 67.5; *celebrated*, 81.27.
blazer, sb. — *defamer, decrier*, 245.52 (no example in the *N.E.D.*, but evidently from the v. "blaze," i.e., to defame or decry).
blynde, adj. — *secret*, 154.31.

blyvelye, adv. — *quickly*, 317.5 (the only example in the *N.E.D.* is of date 1400, "belively").
bode, sb. — *biding, tarrying, delay*, 186.20.
bode, v. — *presage*, 78.64.
bodkins, sb. — *daggers*, 267.36.
boisteous, boyst'ous, adj. — *violent*, 95.21; 117.9.
bolded, ppl. adj. — *emboldened*, 121.12.
bolt (pl., boltts), sb. — *arrow*, 180.45, 50.
bonne, sb. — name given sportively to the squirrel, 270.24.
boord (board), v. — *make up* (*with* or *to*), *make advances*, 182.6.
boote, sb. — *profit, use, advantage*, 90.50; *booty, plunder*, 230.46; *shoe* (pl.), as a sexual pun, 182.72.
boote, v. — *help*, 78.76; *remedy*, 264.19.
borrow, sb. — *deliverer, surety*, 165.4.
botts (possibly an error for "botte"), sb. — probably used as a pun in several senses: "bott," *a large pimple*; "botts," *small worms in the intestines of horses*; "bott," as a variant of *boot*; "bott" as a variant of *butt* (signifying both the verb and the noun "buttock"), 180.72.
bowgetts (budgets), sb. — *wallets, pouches*, 321.88.
bowle, sb. — *ball*, 129.2.
bownd, sb. — *bond*, 6.2.
brace, v. — *encircle, encompass*, 161.3.
brall, v. — *to raise a clamor*, 319.13.
bray, v. — *utter a harsh cry*, 84.3.
breaches, sb. — *gaps in a fortification made by a battery*, 230.39.
breake, v. — in the phr. "breake thye mynd," *to reveal what is in one's mind*, 245.40.
breathd, ppl. adj. — *having emitted an odor*, 182.193.
brent, v., pa.t. — *burned*, 128.1; 271.44.
brentt, pa. pple. — *burned*, 267.39.
breviat, v. — *shorten*, 272.34.
brewte, sb. — see "brute."
brickell, adj. — *easily broken, fragile, brittle*, 244.8.
brittle, brittel, adj. — *fragile*, 106.12; 115.12; *perishable*, 298.1.
broach, brotche, v. — *pierce*, 180.60; 182.105.
bronds, sb. — *swords*, 168.41.
broyle, sb. — *tumult, turmoil*, 16.3.
brute, brewte, sb. — *report, tidings*, 81.8; 87.53; 146.6; *reputation, fame*, 86.23; 87.81.
brydelith, v. — *restrains*, 113.8.
brydelid, ppl. adj. — *checked, restrained*, 111.1.
brym (breme), adj. — *raging, fierce*, 171.2.
buckeled, ppl. adj. — *united*, 84.4.
buntinge, sb. — *bobolink*, 181.18.
byddinge, vbl. sb. — *waiting*, 96.42.

cabadge (cabache), v. — *to cut off the head of a deer close behind the horns*, 259.22.

cace, sb. — see "case."

cadge (cage), v. — *be wanton*, or *lustful* (deriving from *bind, fasten* and related to the Scottish adjective *cadgy*, meaning *wanton*, or *amorous*), 245.26.

caitife, sb. — *wretch*, 155.52.

caitife, adj. — *miserable*, 229.1.

can, v. — *know*, 169.4; *know*, passing into the meaning, *be able*, 305.18; in the phr., "can be roate," *know by heart*, 77.25.

cantt, sb. — *share, portion*, 141.45.

cappe, v. — *take off the cap in respect*, 321.51.

carde (cared), v., pa.t. — *regarded*, 18.40.

care, sb. — *sorrow, grief, trouble*, 12.46, 48; 18.35, 36; 21.23; 23.7, 16, 17; 81.35, 42; 83.49; 84.5, 16, 24; 87.66; 88.23; 90.63; 122.7; 139.7; 142.79, 91; 144.56; 149.38; 168.14; 184.21; 240.6; 260.12; 262.52; 269.57; 276.47; 279.49; 286.8; 291.7; 293.4, 9; 310.10; 321.98; 324.5; elsewhere in current uses.

carefull, carfull, adj. — *mournful, sorrowful*, 15.50; 74.1; 134.4; 260.18; *attended with trouble or sorrow*, 68.5; 88.41; 130.16; *troubled, full of care*, 81.35; 147.30; 265.2; 276.7; 290.35; *heedful, solicitous*, 289.21.

carelesse, adj. — *untended, uncared for*, 294.6.

carpett knight, sb. — contemptuous term for a knight whose achievements belong to the lady's boudoir, 180.42.

case, cace, sb. — *deed*, 180.6; elsewhere in current uses.

castinge, vbl. sb. — *something given to a hawk to purge the gorge*, 180.66.

castrells (kestrel's), sb., poss. — *hawk's*, 181.15.

certes, adv. — *certainly*, 274.7.

chapmen, sb., pl. — *traders*, 180.111 (here a play on the surname *Chapman*).

chapps, sb. — *the jaws*, 76.17.

chardge (charge), sb. — *care, custody, responsibility*, 15.10; 72.8, 12; 104.9; 157.59; 168.13; 181.43; 276.20; *accusation*, 72.22; 142.28; *burden, load*, 139.22; 157.12; *order*, 182.11.

chardge, v. — *entrust, commission*, 5.8; *order*, 72.32 (pa.t.); *load to capacity*, 139.59.

charged, chardged, pa. pple. or ppl. adj. — *burdened*, 64.6; 83.40; 87.66; 90.2; 144.5; *laden to capacity*, 5.4; 112.1.

chaste, adj. — *disciplined, subdued*, 243.23.

chaw, v. — *chew*, 141.19.

cheape, sb. — *plenty, abundance*, 303.39.

Cheappe, pr. n. — *Cheapside*, 321.97.

cheare, cheere, chere, sb. — *expression of the face, aspect*, 23.13; 66.37; 78.15; 139.77; 250.39, 55; 259.18; 261.18; 266.77; 271.10; 284.7; *face*, 154.43, 69; 155.84; 279.41; *mirth, gaiety*, 77.19; 134.15; 321.67; *frame of mind, showing by outward action*, 78.2; 154.34; 159.55; 289.12; *kindly welcome, entertainment*, 104.89; 124.9; 279.20; *fare, provisions*, 142.49; 171.17.

check, checke, sb. — *exposed position, as of the King in chess*, 181.7; *reprimand, rebuke*, 275.41.
cheered, v., pa.t. — *entertained with feasting and "good cheer,"* 142.49.
chevin, sb. — *chevron, a device on the escutcheon*, 182.267.
chone, pron. — *one*, 289.13.
chopp and chaunge, vbl. phr. — *to chop and change, exchange*, 76.12.
clad, v. — *clothe*, 154.52.
clap, sb. — probably in the double sense of *a stroke of misfortune* and *gonorrhea*, 182.46.
clappe, v. — *imprison at once*, 321.98; as pa.t., *went suddenly and decisively*, 306.30.
Clarentieux, sb. — *King-of-arms at the College of Heralds*, 182.243.
clatter, v. — *babble*, 182.221.
clatt'ring, ppl. adj. — *chattering, prating*, 144.76.
cleape, clepe, v. — *call*, 79.50; *name*, 250.40.
clippers, sb. — *those who mutilate coins by fraudulently cutting the edges*, 182.61.
clippes, clypes, sb. — *eclipse*, 180.55; 303.8.
clip'st, ppl. adj. — *eclipsed*, 234.73.
clogg, clogge, sb. — *impediment, hindrance*, 68.5; *block of wood*, 104.81.
cloke (cloak), v. — *disguise, conceal*, 104.18, 56; 154.37; 238.5; 250.62.
cloked, ppl. adj. — *disguised, secret*, 268.43; 290.12; 301.4.
close, v. — *enclose, confine*, 95.1.
closures, sb. — *bounds, limits*, 75.47.
clowts, sb. — in the phr., "swadling clowts," *swaddling clothes*, 65.12.
clyppes (clips), v. (3rd per. sing.) — *embraces*, 69.30.
cockbote, sb. — *very light boat*, 299.2.
cockhorse, sb. — in the phr., "on cockhorse," *mounted, astride*, signifying exalted position, 182.74.
cockes combe, coxecome, sb. — *fool's cap on which was a strip of red cloth notched like the comb of a cock*, 180.155 (pl.); *a fool*, 321.105.
cockolds, sb., poss. — *cuckold's*, 180.267.
cogg, v. — *cheat*, 182.223.
cogging, vbl. sb. and ppl. adj. — *underhand dealing*, 180.207; *cheating*, 180.149.
cokatrice, sb. — *a serpent identified with the Basilisk, fabulously said to kill by its mere glance, and to be hatched from a cock's egg*, 265.10.
cokatrill, sb. — *cokatrice*, 277.14.
coltes, sb. — *wantons*, 180.43.
compasse, compace, sb. — *skilful devising*, 66.9; *area*, 79.4.
compasse, v. — *attain*, 16.1; 87.10, 34 (pa.t.), 60; *surround*, 155.106; 157.48.
compassed, pa. pple. — *attained, accomplished*, 234.214.
complishe, v. — *accomplish, fulfill*, 167.2.
compte, sb. — *computation, reckoning*, 87.31.
conceytes, sb. — *fanciful notions*, 69.18.
condytes (conduits), sb. — *channels*, 87.15.
coneies, sb. — *rabbits*, 142.88.

coniured, ppl. adj. — *conspired, resulting from a conspiracy*, 84.13.
coniures, sb. — *conspiracies*, 89.41.
conning, conninge (cunning), sb. — *skill*, 143.2, 6; *dexterity*, 275.47; *ability*, 282.24.
conning, connyng, adj. — *showing skill or expertness*, 95.1; 258.2; 282.16.
conster, v. — *construe, explain*, 97.7.
constrayne, v. — *bring about*, 265.43.
consume, v. — *waste away*, 19.17; 77.29; 81.6; 83.50; 157.27; 249.36; *make away with*, 87.47; 264.22; 289.13; *occupy wastefully*, 90.51; 278.54; *perish*, 276.6; *cause to disappear*, 278.83; *burn up*, 281.59; *devour, destroy*, 289.13; 290.35.
consumed, consumde, pa. pple. — *wasted away*, 161.50; 321.95; *caused to vanish by evaporation*, 168.60; *burned up*, 203.6.
consuming, consumynge, pres. pple. — *devouring, destroying*, 249.24; 260.25; 289.29.
convayers, sb. — *nimble thieves*, 182.61.
convert, converte, convart, v. — *turn, direct (one's) attention to*, 75.7; *change to another state of mind*, 77.17; 174.17; *direct*, 85.39; 269.20; *turn about*, 154.3; *restore, turn back*, 164.28; 166.19; 272.54.
copesmates, sb. — *accomplices in cheating*, 180.149.
corps, corce, sb. — *person*, 247.29; *live body*, 245.22; 260.14; 276.7; 282.1; 300.14; 315.2; *dead body*, 288.5, 10, 20, 30, 44; 295.10.
corsye (corsie), sb. — *grievance*, 319.53.
coullours, sb. — *pretexts*, 104.54.
counterpayse (counterpoise), v. — *balance*, 154.70.
courser, cowrser, sb. — *swift, or large and powerful, horse*, 143.7; 278.39.
cownter, sb. — *debtor's prison*, 321.98.
cownterchaunged, ppl. adj. — *Heraldry, of a charge (on a field of two tinctures): having the tinctures of the field reversed*, 182.268.
coxecomes, sb. — see "cockes comb."
coyners, sb. — *makers of counterfeit coin*, 182.61.
crackes, v. — *boasts, brags*, 267.24.
craft, crafte, sb. — *skill, art, dexterity*, 87.41; 95.5, 9; 143.16; 158.16; 282.17; *fraud, guile*, 6.20; 66.107; 72.4; 75.54; 78.46; 84.17; 104.28; 180.127; 234.357; 240.2, 6; 287.7; 295.2.
craftye, craftie, adj. — *cunning, artful, wily*, 64.16; 72.15; 140.60; 155.109; 180.254; 321.22.
crashe, sb. — *a short spell*, 182.8.
cresset light, sb. — *the light of a cresset, i.e., of a vessel made to hold oil which is to be burned for light, used in a punning sense*, 180.102.
crewse (cruse), sb. — *pot, jar*, 171.27.
cribb, sb. — *cabin*, 259.39.
crisped, ppl. adj. — *stiffly curled*, 139.69; 140.4.
cromes, sb. — *crumbs*, 281.23.
crooper (crupper), sb. — *buttocks*, 180.72.
crucifige, sb. —*cry of the Jews to Pilate, therefore a popular clamor for the death of a victim*, 66.96.

cullions, sb., poss. — *rascal's*, 180.148.
cure, sb. — *heed, concern*, 87.11; 161.55; 168.14, 86; "with busye cure," *to apply oneself diligently*, 261.19.
curelesse, adj. — *incurable*, 5.5.
curtall, sb. — *a horse with its tail cut short, or ears cropped, hence, derisively applied to persons*, 181.30; 321.102; used adjectivally, 182.13.
cyphringe (ciphering), ppl. adj. — *secret (?), as drawn from the meaning of the v., to express by cryptogram*, 148.21.

dale (Scottish or North. form of *dole*), sb. — *dealing, having to do with (it)*, 264.20.
darckling, adv. — *in the dark*, 180.245.
darked, ppl. adj. — *obscure*, 139.40.
date, sb. — *end*, 19.2; *period*, 101.3.
daunger, v. — *imperil, expose to danger*, 148.21.
dawe, sb. — *simpleton, fool*, 321.89.
decay, decaye, sb. — *downfall, destruction*, 83.53; 155.107; 163.49; 180.36; 240.4, 8, 12, 16; *decline from a thriving condition*, 139.2; 320.51; *decline of the vital faculties*, 86.7; 189.22; 271.4.
decay, decaye, dekaye, v. — *fall off, lose strength or quality*, 66.4; 161.42; 268.63; 292.6; 305.6; *cause to fall off*, 163.79.
declynde, ppl. adj. — *debased*, 234.43.
deemd, deemde, deem'de, v., pa.t. and pa. pple. — *considered, held*, 181.71; 45.1; 234.167, 230.
deeme, v. — *discern*, 3.1; *judge, hold, consider*, 15.2; 35.1; 40.1; 47.2; 234.58; 241.1; 247.40; 290.12; *rule as a judge*, 59.6; *think in a specified way*, 307.14.
deface, sb. — *cause of being put out of countenance*, 18.28.
deface, v. — *discredit*, 155.109; 181.26; 324.23; *outshine by contrast*, 93.11; 168.17; 277.20.
defaced, pa. pple. — *destroyed*, 150.2; *cast in the shade*, 229.57.
default, sb. — *imperfection, blemish*, 86.33; *mistake, error*, 107.11; 164.29.
defawlte, v. — *fail, be wanting*, 162.20.
defenst, ppl. adj. — *protected, fortified*, 94.13.
degrace, v. — *disgrace, cast shame upon intentionally*, 246.11; 262.47 (not in the *N.E.D.*).
dekaye, — see "decay."
deleaved, pa. pple. — *defoliated*, 184.4 (given as nonce word, 1591, in *N.E.D.*).
demying (deeming), vbl. sb. — *estimating*, 169.4.
deniee (demi), adj. — "deniee lowt," *half-grown bumpkin*, 182.204.
depaynted, ppl. adj. — *depicted, delineated*, 105.5; 278.5.
depe, v. — *immerse deeply*, 142.102.
deprave, v. — *to decry, disparage*, 250.37.
depraver, sb. — *one who corrupts, perverts*, 299.3.
descyphred (deciphered) pa. pple. — *discovered*, 84.14.
desert, adj. — *deserted, abandoned*, 121.2.

device, devise, devyce, devyse, sb. — *purpose, intention*, 86.20, 44; 102.1; 132.1; *piece of work*, 88.12; *inventive faculty, ingenuity*, 88.36; 239.11; 282.4; *design*, 269.53; 282.20.

devynce, sb. — *diviners, seers*, 181.79 (not in the *N.E.D.*, but apparently from "divine," sb[2]).

devyse, v. — *scheme*, 104.54; *contrive*, 118.5; 270.38; *conceive, conjecture, imagine*, 140.25; 161.73; 250.27; *consider*, 143.5, 9; 265.43; *arrange*, 274.6.

devysed, ppl. adj. — *constructed, fashioned*, 143.21; *plotted, schemed*, 264.20.

devysing, pres. pple. — *meditating, considering*, 259.25.

dewd, ppl. adj. — *pregnant with dew*, 284.4.

did, v., pa.t. — *made, caused*, 139.5.

dight, pa. pple. — *fit out, furnished*, 142.10.

dischardge (discharge), v. — *unburden*, 85.28; 89.46; *unload*, 86.16; *disburden*, 289.28.

dischardged, dischargde, pa. pple. — *unburdened*, 226.6 (ppl. adj.), 290.36; *removed*, 282.7.

discipher (decipher), v. — *find out, discover*, 145.10.

discover, v. — *reveal*, 5.42; *find out*, 71.2; *manifest*, 139.51.

discryde (descried), ppl. adj. — *disclosed, revealed*, 140.23.

discrye, discrie, discry (descry), v. — *find out, detect*, 22.2; *spy out*, 216.2; *betray, reveal*, 181.77; 282.5.

discryve (descrive), v. — *describe, set forth in words*, 247.5; 250.53; 269.74; 272.27; 279.24; *perceive, see*, 272.22 (in a sense of *descry*).

discust, ppl. adj. — *declared, made known*, 168.15; 275.7.

disdaine, disdayne, sb. — *indignation, anger*, 64.10; 112.9; 144.12; 163.34; *loathing, aversion*, 89.12; 196.3; pl., "disdaynes," *fits of anger*, 139.84; elsewhere as *scorn, contempt*.

disease, sb. — *discomfort, disquiet, trouble*, 142.80; 154.68; 156.16; 163.28; *cause of distress, grievance*, 255.1.

dispartledlye, adv. — apparently an error for "disparkledlye," from the v. "disparkle," hence, *scattered abroad*, 289.8.

dispatche, v. — *hasten, be quick*, 243.26.

dispight (despite), sb. — *contempt, anger*, 78.28, 73; *open defiance*, 79.7.

displayse, v. — "displayse the not," *be (not) displeased*, 107.8.

dispoiled, dispoyled (despoiled), ppl. adj. — *stripped*, 90.47; 320.32.

disporte, sb. — *amusement*, 15.28.

disprayse, v. — *censure, blame*, 91.1.

disquiet, adj. — *disturbed*, 193.11.

distayne, v. — *sully, dishonor*, 83.30; *to cause to look pale*, 124.3.

distemperate, adj. — *diseased*, 94.3.

distills, distilles, v. — *exudes*, 154.59; *lets fall*, 158.12.

divers, dyvers, dyverse, adj. — *perverse, evil, unfavorable*, 77.4; 113.12; 320.34; *various, sundry*, 79.10; 144.43; 266.14; *varied*, 102.7; *differing from itself in certain circumstances*, 140.63; *many*, 157.65 (absolute use); *impelling in different directions*, 320.27.

dizard, sb. — *foolish fellow, blockhead*, 182.176.

do, pa. pple. — *done*, 79.38.

do waye, vbl. phr. — *go away, leave off*, 78.21; *put away, abandon*, 123.3; 161.9, 52; 166.10; 168.25.
doe, v. — *cause, make*, 127.7; 167.34.
dolour, dollor, sb. — *grief, sorrow*, 157.13; 229.28 (pl., *sorrows*).
dome, doome, sb. — *a judgment or decision*, 23.45; 66.136; 75.55; 83.36; 90.43; 92.2; 142.105; 169.5; 251.7; 261.33; *a great or last judgment*, 66.89; 265.39; *trial*, 88.47; 166.11; *final fate, destruction*, 262.40.
donge, sb. — *dung, manure*, 141.19.
donne (dun), adj. — *of a dull brown color*, 259.6.
doome — see "dome."
doubted, v., pa.t. — *dreaded*, 64.7.
doubtfull, adj. — *of uncertain issue*, 77.50; 171.30.
doubtlesse, doubtles, adj. — *undoubting, free from doubt*, 22.31; *not to be doubted, indubitable*, 64.16.
draff, draffe, sb. — *refuse, dregs*, 180.19; 182.264.
draught, sb. — *a privy*, 197.1.
dread, v. — *stand in awe of, reverence*, 155.13; *to fear greatly, be apprehensive*, 155.11; 159.53.
drenche, v. — *to be drowned*, 83.54.
drenchid, ppl. adj. — *drowned, immersed*, 284.5.
dresse, v. — *direct, guide*, 277.7.
driftes, dryftes, sb. — *schemes*, 20.11; 289.6.
droile, sb. — *drudge*, 180.19.
drownyge, pres. ppl. adj. — copyist's error for "drownynge," i.e., *drenching*, 288.31.
dryvling (drivelling), pres. ppl. adj. — probably *dribbling at the mouth*, although the second meaning *idiotic* would also fit, 180.19.
dumppes, sb. — *fits of musing, reveries*, 265.1; 272.19.
durance, sb. — *forced confinement*, 81.15.
dure, v. — *continue in existence*, 19.19; 162.21; 163.74; 225.43; *persist, continue in a certain state*, 249.22; *hold out in action*, 274.18.
durynge, pres. ppl. adj. — *lasting*, 66.144.
dyke, sb. — *ditch* (fig.), 180.2.
dynted (dented), ppl. adj. — *hollow, sunken*, 76.16.
dyvers, dyverse — see "divers."
dyverslye, adv. — *perversely, wickedly*, 90.21.
dyversnes, sb. — *diversity, variability*, 102.8, 9.

eake, adv. — see "eke."
earnest, sb. — *ardor, passion*, 184.18.
earst, earste (erst), adv. — *before a specified time or event*, 87.25; 139.74; 162.11; 320.6, 11, 26; *in the recent past*, 88.7; 89.40; 121.11; 128.8; 156.18; 158.26; 230.34, 40; *formerly*, 163.86; 266.23.
earst, adj. — in the phr. "after earst" (absolute use), *after the first in time*, 320.33.
easye, adj. — *gentle*, 77.7.
effectes, sb. — *appearances*, 235.6.

egall, adj. — *equal*, 140.10.
either . . . other, adj. — *each of the two, both*, 88.55.
eke, eake, adv. — *also, moreover*, used frequently in the text.
embrue, v. — *defile*, 289.30.
enbrace (embrace), v. — *have, possess*, 18.4; 85.11; *clasp in arms*, 88.19 (fig.), 262.31; 266.46; *accept*, 139.32; *adopt (doctrine)*, 172.13; *gain, compass*, 261.23.
enbraced, enbraste (embraced), pa. pple. — *eagerly accepted*, 5.20; *cultivated*, 17.7; *encircled*, 88.29.
endite, v. — see "indite."
endure, v. — *live*, 261.25; *remain, continue*, 268.52; 269.14.
endured, ppl. adj. — *hardened*, 75.50; 81.25; 142.5.
endyte, v. — see "indite."
engynes, ingines, sb. — *snares*, 155.98; *wiles*, 234.252.
enowe, adv. — *enough*, 234.364.
enrowlde (enrolled), ppl. adj. — *engrossed, given legal form on parchment*, 5.32.
ensue, v. — *result from*, 239.17; *follow as a result*, 239.29.
entent, sb. — see "intent."
entermeete, v. — *put (oneself) between*, 139.38 (this is the only example in the *N.E.D.*).
enterpryse, v. — *to undertake*, 86.43.
erring, erringe, ppl. adj. — *wandering*, 118.10; 140.31.
eschew, eschewe, eschue, v. — *avoid*, 21.22; 168.25; 246.14; 293.14; 302.4.
estate, sb. — *condition, or state, general or particular*, 19.4; 73.38; 88.27; 89.35; 147.21; 149.36; 171.35; 185.1; 222.7; 234.240, 311, 353; 261.34; 287.3; 314.1; *status, standing*, 148.21; 163.61; 281.45; 295.1; 311.2; 321.16; *account*, 270.59; *person of high standing*, 281.35; *worldly prosperity*, 293.8.
etearne (eterne), adj. — *eternal*, 165.22.
etearne, adv. — *eternally, forever*, 163.79 (the *N.E.D.* quotes only one example of date 1590 of this adverbial use).
execute, pa. pple. — *executed*, 157.14.
extreame, adv. — *to an extreme degree*, 85.30.
extreamlye, adv. — *with the uttermost severity*, 275.32.
ey, adv. — see "ay."

fact, sb. — *guilt*, 180.258.
faine, fayne (feign), v. — *pretend*, 14.7; *believe erroneously*, 66.101; 263.4; *put a false appearance upon*, 104.68; *invent* (fig.), 107.11.
faine, fayne (fain), adj. — *willing, eager*, 83.15; 89.46; 223.1; 230.26; *glad, well pleased*, 142.16; 186.16; 239.8, 16, 24, 32; *obliged*, 182.78.
faine, fayne (fain), adv. — *gladly, willingly*, 12.13, 31 (superl.), 69.26; 78.42; 110.10; 228.16; 234.184; 242.26; 305.15.
fained, fayned (feigned), ppl. adj. — *pretended, insincere*, 3.3; 122.4; 148.14; 149.71; 234.259; 240.14; *sham, counterfeit*, 90.17.

fainted, ppl. adj. — *that which has faded, lost color or brightness*, 284.1.
false, v. — *falsify, corrupt*, 230.10.
falsed, falst, pa. pple. — *corrupted*, 135.22 (ppl.adj.); *broken, violated*, 289.24.
fancye, fansye, phansie (fancy), sb., often in pl. — *love, amorous inclinations*, 130.1, 3, 5, 9, 14, 25; 143.23, 28; 149.17; 174.19; 196.4; 222.9; 228.4; 243.22; 305.2; 319.13, 20, 43, 63; *imagination, or products of the imagination*, 79.12; 143.10, 12; 174.3; 233.49; 292.9; *whims, caprice*, 88.13; 148.34; 150.10; 196.23; 242.37; 288.28; 317.3; *individual taste*, 222.44.
fantasye, sb. — *desire, inclination*, 130.18.
farleys, sb. — *wonders*, 266.24.
farrforth, adv. — "so farrforth as I can," *to the extent that I can*, 274.2.
fast, adv. — *very near*, 181.65; 270.11.
fatche, sb. — see "fetche."
faulttes, v. — *commits a wrong*, 45.2.
faute, sb. — *fault*, 156.18.
favell, sb. — *a personification of cunning or duplicity*, 104.62.
fawltye, adj. — *guilty of wrongdoing*, 73.4.
fayes, sb. — *religious beliefs*, 181.53.
fayninge (feigning), pres. ppl. adj. — *inventing* (relating to story), 149.69; *pretending, false*, 180.206.
feasted, v., pa.t. — *entertained sumptuously*, 140.1; 142.46.
feature, sb. — *form, fashion, proportion*, 69.21.
featurde, ppl. adj. — *beautiful, comely*, 143.23.
feavers, sb. — *states of intense agitation or excitement*, 10.33.
fee, sb. — *allotted portion*, 270.56.
feele, sb. — *perception, sense*, 95.7.
feere, feare (fere), sb. — *mate, spouse*, 78.1, 22; 84.23; 89.29; 279.43; *comrade*, 149.68; 273.5.
fell, ffell, adj. — *cruel or dire*, 95.18; 180.225; *angry, enraged*, 266.82.
feltred, ppl. adj. — *matted together*, 182.175.
fend, v. — *make a shift* (*for yourself*), 66.66.
fest (fast), ppl. adj. — *bound*, 15.56.
fetche, fatche, sb. — *trick, stratagem*, 20.39; 306.9.
fett, v. — *draw forth*, 135.2.
fflyeing, ppl. adj. — *fleeing*, 154.62.
fforgers, sb. — *deceivers*, 245.51, 65.
ffrancklyn, sb. — *freeholder, ranking below the gentry*, 259.1; 260.1, 43; 261.1.
ffrithe, sb. — *wood*, 259.6.
fieldishe, adj. — *inhabiting the fields*, 142.2.
fierlye, adv. — *ardently, furiously*, 141.10.
figg, sb. — "gives . . . a figg," *makes a contemptuous gesture*, 321.26.
figg, v. — *move about restlessly*, 321.44.
fine, fyne, sb. — in the phr. "in fine," *in the end, in short*, 15.6; 176.8; 222.47; 260.26; 261.35; 279.32; *a person of superior quality*, 180.115 (adj. used as sb.).

flearing, flyringe (fleering), pres. pple. — *smiling obsequiously*, 289.25; 317.2; 321.10; *laughing mockingly*, 318.5 (super.).

fleete, flete, v. — *slip away*, 19.14; 115.9; 139.15; *move swiftly*, *fly*, 152.2; 242.45.

fleezing (fleecing), pres. ppl. adj. — *robbing, stripping of wealth*, 321.21.

fletcher, sb. — *one who makes arrows*, 180.45; *an archer*, 180.49 (used in a punning sense).

fletinge, pres. ppl. adj. — *flowing*, 186.2.

flit, flytte, v. — *depart, be gone*, 72.13; 168.28; 244.7 (pa.t.); *change from one state to another*, 269.30.

flye, v. — *flee*, 84.9; 108.3; 174.25; 175.20; 288.8, 14, 26.

flyeste, v. (3rd sing.) — *frightens*, 94.13.

flyinge, vbl. sb. — *departing this life*, 66.164 (the only example in the *N.E.D.* is from *Cursor Mundi*, ca. 1300).

flyringe — see "flearing."

flytting, ppl. adj.— *describing that which is changing from one state to another*, 130.6.

fond, v. — *plays the fool*, 168.45.

force, sb. — "of force," *necessarily*, 129.8; 131.3.

foredone, pa. pple. — *done away with, put away*, 167.46.

for feobled, ppl. adj. — *prematurely enfeebled*, 5.7.

fordge, v. — see "forge."

forepointed, pa. pple. — *determined beforehand*, 283.9.

forespeake, v. — *proclaim*, 83.66.

foresterved, ppl. adj. — *completely starved*, 150.9.

forethinck, v. — *anticipate*, 286.6.

forge, fordge, v. — *fashion, frame*, 191.6; 227.6 (pa.t.); "forge and file," *bring into shape, fashion completely*, 258.4; *devise evil*, 265.11.

forged, forgid, ppl. adj. — *fabricated, "made up,"* 234.259; "forgid and fylde," *brought into shape, completely fashioned*, 164.6.

forpassed, ppl. adj. — *that has previously been passed*, 73.26.

forsoothe, adv. — *in truth, truly*, 91.23; 182.5, 121, 255, 277.

foster, sb. — *offspring*, 198.27; *forester*, 240.11 (poss.).

fowler, sb. — *one who hunts wild birds*, 172.2; 219.1.

foyled, pa. pple. — *tread upon, trampled*, 167.15.

foyne, v. — *lunge, make a thrust at*, 181.36.

foyse, sb. — *nourishment*, 245.27 (from "foison," Scottish and dial.).

fraight, pa. pple. — see "freight."

frailefull, adj. — *extremely frail or feeble*, 159.16.

frame, sb. — *order, regularity*, 137.10; 186.13; *mood, mental or emotional state*, 292.9.

frame, v. — *direct or shape thoughts or actions to a certain purpose*, 66.162; 93.4; 98.4; 108.4; 149.31; 234.98; 250.9, 36; 259.16; 266.99; *invent, fabricate, plot*, 72.36 (pa.t.); 147.6; 148.6; 166.17; *bring to pass*, 83.17; *make progress*, 104.51; *fashion, shape*, 143.13, 32; 237.20 (pa.t.); 258.9 (pa.t.); 288.27 (pa.t.); *conceive, imagine*, 166.17; 233.49; *conform*, 321.58.

framed, framd, fram'de, pa. pple. and ppl. adj. — *devised*, 83.53; *fashioned, shaped*, 2.2; 290.20; *directed*, 322.9; *made ready for use*, 194.12.
franck, adj. — *free*, 260.38.
fransy, franzye, phrenesie (frenzy), sb. — *folly, enthusiasm*, 196.5, 23; *disorder likened to madness*, 271.14; 233.55.
fraught, ffraught, pa. pple. — *laden*, 205.1; 262.13 (ppl. adj.).
fraughted, ffraughted, frawghted, pa. pple. — *laden*, 72.26 (ppl. adj.); 81.5; 139.60.
fraughteth, v. (3rd sing.) — *loads*, 88.24.
fraughtfull, adj. — *laden to capacity*, 289.28 (not in the *N.E.D.*).
frawdfull, adj. — *treacherous*, 289.26.
frayned, v., (pa.t.) — *asked*, 261.6.
freight, fraight, pa. pple. — *laden*, 260.14 (ppl. adj.); 303.40.
frenzy, sb. — see "fransy."
friowr, sb. — *friar*, 84.42.
fro, froe, prep. — *from*, 110.1; 139.24; 244.7; 274.15; 304.8.
fromward, adv. — *in a direction which leads away from an object*, 84.1 (this line is given in the *N.E.D.* as the earliest example).
froward, adj. — *counter to what is reasonable*, 77.4; *perverse, ill-humored*, 78.11; 88.9; *difficult to deal with*, 137.10; *hard to please*, 144.1; *evilly disposed*, 144.45; 272.49; 290.13; *adverse*, 277.6; 290.13.
frowardlye, adv. — *perversely*, 268.13.
frowardnes, sb. — *perversity*, 111.6.
fryse (frieze), sb. — *a kind of coarse woollen cloth with a nap*, 171.15.
fume, sb. — *smoke*, 77.30.
furnyture, sb. — *decoration, embellishment*, 247.39.
fygure, sb. — *part enacted*, 75.21.
fyldye, adj. — *pertaining to life in the fields*, 175.9.
fyle, sb. — *metal instrument* (fig. sig.), 93.3; 98.2; 108.1, 2; *thread, tenor (of a story)*, 277.6.
fyle, v. — *polish, bring to a certain condition*, 98.2; 108.2; 258.4; 282.23.
fyled, fylde, ppl. adj. — *polished*, 108.1; 143.4; 164.6; *smooth*, 250.41; 260.34; *elaborated*, 297.14.
fyr'de, ppl. adj. — *set on fire, kindled*, 297.9.
fytt, sb. — *sudden and transitory state*, 10.25, 35.

game, sb. — *jest*, 113.11; 184.18; *amorous play*, 78.75.
gan, v. — *began*, 78.12, 18, 26; 259.35; 277.7; 278.67; 279.9, 31; 281.17; 297.60.
gapes, v. (3rd sing.) — *longs for*, 90.35.
gayne, adv. — *at once, straight*, 261.7.
gaze, sb. — in the expression, "hownd hunting at gaze," *the hound has spotted his quarry and runs quickly toward it, no longer needing to sniff his way; hence, hunting by sight*, 261.13 (the only ex. quoted in the *N.E.D.* is of date 1865).
geason, adj. — *rare*, 298.8; 307.26.
Gecke, sb. used as pr. n. — *derider, scorner*, 180.269 (see Note).
gheste (guest), sb. — *friend*, 3.6.

ghost, goste, gooste, sb. — *spirit as opposed to body*, 73.23; 89.54; 102.12; 161.78; *person*, 264.1.
girninge, vbl. sb. — *snarling*, 168.37.
glad, v. — *make glad, cause to rejoice*, 142.30; 198.2; 244.9.
gleede, sb. — *fire*, 109.14.
gleeke, sb. — "gave the gleeke," *played a trick*, 180.39.
glister, sb. — *brilliance, luster*, 158.21.
glistringes, sb. — *sparklings, glitter*, 188.3.
glitt'raunt, adj. — *gleaming, sparkling*, 259.11 (not in the *N.E.D.*, but evidently comes from v. "glitter").
glose, sb. — *pretence, false show*, 161.72.
glose, v. — *to explain away, extenuate*, 148.33.
glymsing (glimpsing), pres. ppl. adj. — *shining intermittently*, 259.11.
glyntt (glent), sb. — *glance*, 77.46.
goodgyn (gudgeon), sb. — *small fresh-water fish*, 180.9 (here a play on the surname *Googe*).
gooste, goste, sb. — see "ghost."
graffe, sb. — *branch, plant*, 299.4.
graffed, grafte, grafted, pa. pple. — *implanted*, 18.43 (ppl. adj.); 86.30; 88.5 (ppl. adj.); 272.53 (ppl. adj.); *firmly fixed*, 269.32.
grafte, v., pa.t. — *implanted*, 87.14; 186.56.
grate (greet), v. — *pray for*, 73.4.
gredern, sb. — *gridiron* (fig.), 181.31.
gree, v. — *agree*, 60.6.
gresly, greeslye, adj. — see "grizzly."
griphin, sb. — *a representation in Heraldry of the figure of a fabulous animal having the head and wings of an eagle and the body and hindquarters of a lion*, 182.234, 246.
grizzly, gresly, greeslye, adj. — *horrible, terrible*, 66.105; 84.6; 88.39; 274.15.
groines, v. — *grunts*, 141.18.
grotes (groats), sb. — *hulled grain used as barter*, 181.22.
grudge, v. — "grudge at," *complain against*, 83.5.
grudging, vbl. sb. — *grumbling*, 159.27.
guird (gird), sb. — *gibe, "dig,"* 321.10.
guyse, sb. — *manner, custom, habit, practice*, 88.11; 142.57; 266.6; 270.6; 303.14; *course of life*, 102.4; 132.3; *behaviour, conduct*, 118.8; 274.5; *disguise, mask*, 113.5; *method*, 167.7.
gyn, v. — *begin*, 164.16; 278.39.
gynne (gin), sb. — *the female title for a jack of all trades*, 180.142 (here in a derogatory sense).
gyrtt, ppl. adj. — *clothed with a garment confined with a girdle*, 72.1.
gyves, sb. — *fetters, shackles*, 89.40.

hallde, v., pa.t. — *hauled*, 66.125.
halyd (haled), ppl. adj. — *struck or pulled down*, 159.20.

hap, happ, happe, sb. — *chance, fortune, lot,* 2.3; 8.1; 8a.1; 16.9; 78.67; 84.20; 95.15; 96.5; 147.9; 182.45; 184.29; 241.11; 250.5; 275.42; 281.31; 283.5, 19; 286.2; 308.18; 320.46; 321.23, 26, 110; *good fortune, success,* 70.29; 89.39; 114.1; 134.25; 193.4; 259.30; 285.7; 294.5; in pl., *events, happenings,* 193.14; 283.18; 286.6.

haplesse, adj. — *unfortunate, unlucky,* 283.17; 312.15.

happ, v. — *happen, come to pass, occur,* 186.67; 239.19; 261.37; 274.11; 310.13; 320.82.

happe, v. — *trust, have confidence in,* 321.31 (from v. "hope," Sc. "hape").

happid, pa. pple. — *happened,* 134.26.

harbor, harbour, v. — *lodge, take shelter,* 7.6; 7a.6.

harme, sb. — *hurt, damage,* 17.8; 84.19; 90.18; 141.62; 157.23; 179.13; 180.23; 193.15; 241.6; 310.12; *grief, pain, affliction,* 77.19; 131.19; 133.3; 135.7; 155.18; 157.45; 159.30; 173.6; 184.17; 297.42; *mischief, evil,* 84.42; 172.10; 297.38, 41.

harrold, — see "herrald."

hasted, v., pa.t. and pa. pple. — *driven, urged,* 144.43; *made haste,* 320.31.

hatcht, v., pa.t. — *fanned, brought forth,* 233.47.

haunce, sb. — meaning uncertain but perhaps old form of "hance," *rise, elevation,* or related to Scottish "haunch," *a jerked underhand throw,* or to West Country and Scottish "haunch," *a bite or snap as from a dog,* 321.77, 81 (see discussion in Note).

hawlberd, sb. — *weapon, a kind of combination spear and battle ax,* 142.78.

hawltie, adj. — *haughty, arrogant,* 290.6.

haye, sb. — *trap,* 142.88.

health, healthe, helth, sb. — *well-being, welfare,* 15.33; 77.50; 138.19; 155.110; 167.33; 297.45, 65; 308.18; 310.26; *joy,* 18.27; *cure,* 69.3; *spiritual or mental soundness,* 77.32; 161.47; 168.106, 109; 324.20; *safety,* 85.10; 310.26.

heap, heape, sb. — *large quantity,* usually in pl., 76.2; 77.45; 81.35; 84.17; 87.19; 89.20; 148.15; 209.10.

heastes, sb. — *commands,* 322.4.

heavye, adj. — *grievous,* 185.19; *most despondent,* 304.12.

heavynes, sb. — *sadness, grief,* 313.9.

heithe, sb. — i.e., *height,* in the phr. "in heithe," *in the highest degree,* 286.16; "from . . . heithe," *from (their) eminence,* 293.10.

helth, sb. — see "health."

hent, v. — *reach,* 268.21; 279.13.

herdman, sb. — *a man who herds cattle or sheep,* 17.17.

herrald, harrold, sb. — *officer who regulates armorial bearings,* 182.238, 256, 260.

hie, hye, v. — *hasten,* 186.85; 230.14; 300.3.

hight, v. — *is called,* 250.2, 4; 259.15; 279.22; as pa. pple., *promised,* 300.9.

hobby, sb. — *a small species of falcon,* 181.13.

hold, sb. — *stronghold,* 20.20.

Holland, sb. — *a linen fabric, originally called "Holland cloth,"* 180.43 (here used in a punning sense).

horishe, adj. — *somewhat hoary*, i.e., *white*, 76.19.
horn, horne, sb. — *referring to the fanciful saying that cuckolds wear horns on the brow*, 180.95, 156, 241, 264; 181.42; 182.40, 112, 116, 272.
horned, ppl. adj. or simply adj. — *describing a man who has been made cuckold*, 180.202.
hoy, sb. — literally, *a small vessel usually rigged as a sloop, and employed in carrying passengers and goods*, here used in a derogatory figurative sense, 181.75, 80.
hugie, adj. — *numerous*, 229.29.
hyed, pa. pple. — *made haste (to do something)*, 272.35.
hyre, hyer, sb. — *reward*, 86.30; 234.125; 292.11; 314.19; 324.14.

I, interj. — see "ay."
iade (jade), sb. — *a term of reprobation applied to a woman*, 180.21; *a contemptuous name for a horse, and, hence, for a man*, 182.13.
ianglinge (jangling), ppl. adj. — *describing noisy babbling or discordant speaking*, 299.3.
iape (jape), sb. — *joke, jest*, 142.31.
iarr, iarre (jar), sb. — *discord, quarrelling*, 8a.5; 233.10; "at iarr," *in a state of dissension*, 276.5; 320.54.
Iennet (jennet), sb. — *a small Spanish horse*, 182.14.
Iewry, sb. — *jury*, 66.54, 91.
igraved, ppl. adj. — *graven, carved*, 281.14.
ilke, adj. — *same, identical*, 273.3.
importune, adj. — *irksome through persistency of request, persistent*, 90.6; 162.31.
impp, ympe, ympp, sb. — *child*, 145.3; *fellow*, 180.184; *follower (maiden?)*, 262.60.
indiff'rently, adv. — *impartially*, 250.7.
indite, endite, endyte, v. — *inspire*, 65.5; 186.64; *compose*, 282.24.
infecte, ppl. adj. — *tainted with disease*, 159.29.
infortunate, adj. — *presaging ill luck, inauspicious*, 234.236.
ingines, sb. — see "engines."
inly, adj. — *heartfelt*, 229.26.
intent, intente, entent, sb. — *aim, purpose*, 98.2; 108.2; 148.31; 151.3; 159.66; *meaning, purport*, 104.12; *attention, heed*, 163.6; *mind, understanding*, 164.14.
intersower, v. — *intermix sourness with (delights)*, 234.288 (this line given as the only ex. in the *N.E.D.*).
inward, adv. — *within, internally*, 104.13; 142.112.
iolye (jolly), adj. — *delightful*, 266.5; "iolye woes," *amorous sorrows*, 259.25.
ioye (joy), v. — *rejoice, be glad*, 18.37 (pa.t.); 186.17; 304.3, 4; 320.57.

Kelkes, sb. — *perhaps a dialectical variant of kex, i.e., stem, used as a derogatory pun on a proper name*, 180.171.
kinde, kynd, kynde, sb. — *character or quality derived from birth, nature of beings*, 9.31; 44.47, 51; 78.2; 88.50, 54; 90.59; 163.21; 180.8;

234.272; 245.39; 247.41; *manner, way*, 10.5; 229.41; 265.16; *natural quality or property*, 77.44; 137.2; 140.27; 171.1; 244.14; *Nature*, 95.5, 9; 304.62; 320.88; *heritage, native right of birth*, 147.22; 148.22; 247.7; *sex*, 149.47; *race of man*, 163.41; 245.57, 60; *natural state*, 237.4; *offspring, progeny*, 245.63; elsewhere as *sort, variety, class.*

knowledging, vbl. sb. — *confessing, acknowledging*, 157.17.

lade, v. — *lay a burden upon*, 160.29.

Lammasse, sb. — phr. "at Latter Lammasse," *a day that will never come, humorously for "never,"* 321.84.

largesse, sb. — *liberality*, 5.27; 88.62.

larom, sb. — *alarm*, 321.71.

lasshe, sb. — phr., "lye at lasshe," *be left in the lurch*, 180.33.

lawd, lawde, sb. — *praise*, 161.67; 163.68; 167.42.

lawnes, sb. — *glades, pastures*, 230.15.

leache, sb. — *physician*, 155.23.

learne, v. — *teach*, 17.23; 99.5; 321.72.

leefe, lyefe, adj. — *glad*, 15.20; *dear, agreeable*, 186.4; 229.20.

leeke, sb. — *herb, taken as a type of something of little value*, 180.103.

leere (lear), sb. — *instruction, learning*, 145.9.

leese, v. — *lose*, 16.5; 17.6; 25.3; 77.42; 135.20; 139.35; 141.46; 260.8; 313.6.

lemans, sb. — *sweethearts*, 87.23.

let, lett, sb. — *hindrance, prevention*, 9.2; 186.30; 247.3; 268.32, 57; 311.3.

let that passe, vbl. phr. — *"allow that to go by,"* 182.51, 108.

let, lett, lette, v. — *prevent, hinder*, 72.37 (pa.t.); 77.13; 95.9 (pa. pple.); 104.89; 139.45 (ppl. adj.); 243.6 (pa. pple.); 319.21; *set free*, 111.6; elsewhere as *permit, allow.*

lever, adj. (comp. of "lief") — *dearer, more precious*, 106.8.

libell, sb. — *false and defamatory statements which tend to bring ill repute on a person or persons or institution*, 181, Title; 182, Title (the *N.E.D.* gives no example earlier than 1618 for this use of "libel," but these examples are about 1564).

lightsome, adj.— *radiant with light*, 87.43.

like, lyke, v. — *please, suit*, 259.16; 270.30; "it liked me," *I am pleased*, 75.11; 78.5; 189.10.

list, sb. — *inclination, desire*, 182.165.

list, liste, lyst, lyste, v. — *please, choose, like, care*, 15.54; 79.34; 104.15, 97; 141.26, 64; 142.29, 100; 148.42; 174.12; 271.63; 303.25; 305.32; 306.15; 310.9, 25; *harken*, 66.66; *to desire, like, wish (to do something)*, 72.3; 95.25; 100.1, 9; 104.19; 123.7; 175.2; 181.24; 230.4; 250.47, 50; 256.1; 267.35; 270.50; 311.1.

livlie, lyvely, lyvelye, adj. — *vital, life-giving*, 81.25; 185.17; *living, animate*, 81.29; 90.41; *sparkling, brisk*, 87.15; 139.70; *fresh, vivid*, 87.23; *bright, brilliant*, 118.1; *sprightly, vivacious*, 250.40; *intense*, 281.34.

livlie, lyvelye, lyvelye, adv. — *vivid life, "to the life,"* 76.3; 85.25; 143.18; 282.14; *nimbly, actively*, 247.14.
lodstarr, sb. — *a star that shows the way*, 68.13.
long, longe, v. — *belong*, 83.64; 234.96; 263.36.
loode mans, sb. poss. — *leader's, guide's*, 250.68.
lore, sb. — *teaching, doctrine*, 106.3; 172.13; 300.2; *counsel, instruction*, 161.41; 225.5; 285.10; 286.20.
lott, sb. — "to lott," *to (your) turn*, or, *take your turn*, 266.40 (the rhyme here demands "lett," but the word is certainly "lott").
lovely, adj. — *amorous*, 105.2; 111.12; 139.84.
lowe, sb. — "to sett a lowe," *to set on fire*, 104.6.
lust, sb. — *pleasure, delight*, 77.17; 123.2; 130.9; 134.3; 142.82; 222.1, 40; 242.18; *desire, inclination*, 72.37; 90.14, 59; 99.6; 104.6, 50; 142.81; 148.32; 250.10; 290.38; *vigor*, 300.10; elsewhere as *carnal desire*.
lust, v. — *choose, wish*, 168.11; 181.36; 265.17; 290.8; used impersonally, e.g., "me lustithe," etc., *I have a desire*, 106.14; 168.67; 244.22; *of sexual desire*, 323.27.
lustie, adj. — *pleasant, delightful*, 104.79; 168.96; 270.7; 272.3; *jocund, merry*, 182.146; *healthy*, 182.214; *valiant*, 278.37; *vigorous*, 300.5.
lustinesse, lustynes, sb. — *vigor, robustness*, 157.32; 167.15.
lusting, ppl. adj. — *taking on life-like quality*, 282.12 (drawn from "lust," sb., meaning *vigor, fertility*).
lycorishe (lickerish), adj. — *lecherous, lustful*, 180.82.
lyefe, adj. — see "leefe."
lyfesome, adj. — *delightful*, 85.21; *"in the very flesh,"* 268.26.
lyke, sb. — *good pleasure*, 266.99.
lyke after, quasi-prep. — *according to*, 102.3.
lykerows (lickerous), adj. — *having a keen relish or desire for something pleasant*, 71.22.
lyme, sb. — *sticky substance used for catching small birds*, 172.6.
lyned, v., pa.t — *covered* (with a play on the word as related to copulation), 180.52.
lystes, sb.— *scenes of combat*, 278.37.

mace, sb. — *spice of the nutmeg husk*, 91.19; *staff of office*, 142.78; *club*, 261.27; 262.45.
make, sb. — *mate*, 78.7; 154.22; 268.6.
manured, v., pa.t. — *tilled*, 184.3.
mar, marr, v. — *ruin, damage seriously*, 66.51; 180.137; *harm, injure*, 176.8; 185.12; 228.10.
mard, marde, ppl. adj. — *ruined*, 91.23; 180.125.
margaret (margarite), sb. — *pearl*, 247.41.
market steede, sb. — *market place*, 84.16.
mashe, v. — *enmesh*, 77.44.
mashed, ppl. adj. — *enmeshed*, 128.8.
masked, v., pa.t. — *hid (my) real character by outward pretense*, 15.26.

mate, sb. — *as in chess, when the king cannot make a move,* 174.18; 181.7 (see "check").

mattocke, sb. — in the phr. "mouthed like a mattocke when he drinks," *with a mouth like a mattock (the agricultural tool?)*, intended as an invidious comparison, 182.192.

mawgre, prep. — *in spite of,* 300.18; "mawgre his head," *notwithstanding all he can do,* 270.27.

maze, sb. — *a state of bewilderment,* 15.43; *a network of winding paths,* 105.4; *figurative network,* 235.15.

mead, sb. — *meadow,* 265.27.

mean, meane, sb. — *the middle, that which is equally removed,* 104.55; *the moderate or middle course of life,* 186.48; 265.32; 267.11; "without a meane," *without due proportion,* 282.2.

meane, adj. — *about average,* 93.50; *moderate in amount,* 88.61; 281.54; *describing the middle condition in fortune,* 171.35; *base, inferior,* 245.38.

meare (mere), adj. — *pure, unmixed,* 225.19.

measlid, ppl. adj. — *spotted,* 145.4.

meatt (mete), pa. pple. — *measured,* 303.44.

meete, adj. — *fit, suitable,* 70.29 (super.); 72.22; 78.22 (comp.); 102.5; 143.26; 149.42; *mild, gentle,* 139.85; 304.50.

meetred, pa. pple. — *composed in verse,* 66.100.

mewe, sb. — *cage,* 122.6; "in mewe," *in hiding,* 180.66.

mewe, v. — *put into a cage,* 174.6.

mickell (mickle), absol. adj. used as sb. — in the expression "made me your mickell," *made me your devoted (one),* 244.5.

mischeef, sb. — *misfortune, trouble, distress,* 133.13.

mishap, myshapp, myshappe, sb. — *misfortune, bad luck,* 135.8; 147.34; 148.9, 10, 34, 40; 235.20; 306.1.

mislyking, vbl. n. — *dislike, aversion,* 174.20.

mo, moe, sb. — *others,* 21.19; 244.3; 265.37.

mo, moe, adj. — *more,* 2.11; 17.18, 19; 9.31; absolute use as sb., 9.31; 19.16; 141.57; 186.15.

mo, moe, adv. — *again,* 88.13.

molde, sb. — *earth,* 259.12.

mome, sb. — *blockhead, dolt,* 181.50.

most, v. — *must,* 12.18.

mote, sb. —*note of a horn or bugle used in hunting,* 259.21.

motley, adj. — "motley cote," *parti-colored dress,* 171.14; *esp. of a jester or fool,* 321.86.

mowlde, pa. pple. — *created,* 295.3.

moyle, sb. — *mule,* 5.13; 141.65; 157.61.

moyst, moyste, v. — *to moisten, wet,* 113.2; 304.35.

mylded, ppl. adj. — *made mild or gentle,* 186.93.

myshappyness, sb. — *unhappiness,* 144.20 (this line is quoted as the first of two examples in the *N.E.D.*).

myskyns, sb. — *a little bagpipe,* 266.13 (the earliest example in the *N.E.D.* is from Drayton, 1593, who gives the above definition in his margin).

myslike, myslyke, v. — *dislike,* 141.87; 142.91; *displease,* 180.10.

mystryes, sb. — *personal secrets,* 67.10.

nappie, adj. — *heady, strong*, 141.16.
ne, adv. and conj. — adverbial meaning, *not*; conjunctival meaning, *nor*; used frequently in the text.
niggishe, adj. — *niggardly*, 90.58.
nilt (nill), v. — *refuse, reject*, 155.65.
no, adv. — *not*, 246.4.
nocking, vbl. sb. — *the fitting of the arrow to the bowstring, readying for shooting*, 180.46 (fig.).
nonce, nones, sb. — *for the particular purpose, on purpose*, 155.54; 182.29; 183.6; *used as a rhyme tag with no particular meaning*, 141.16; 154.8.
nor . . . nor, conj. — *neither . . . nor*, 1.4; 225.22.
not, v. — *know not*, 118.11; 121.14; 160.32.
note, v. — *to affix to (one) the stigma or accusation of some fault*, 274.23.
nother . . . nor, adv. (conj.) — *neither . . . nor*, 104.80; 144.50.
noye, v. — *vex, harass*, 20.40.
noyse, v. — *spread abroad*, 297.42.
noysome, adj. — *disagreeable, unpleasant*, 247.31.
noysomnes, sb. — *unwholesomeness, offensiveness, unpleasantness*, 23.24.

obiect, ppl. adj. — "obiect againste," *over against, opposite*, 140.19.
oft, adj. — *frequent*, 186.57.
onsse, adv. — *once, once more* (?), 180.70.
or, adv. — *now*, 321.76 (the *N.E.D.* records nothing after the fifteenth century).
or, conj. — *ere, or that*, 10.23; 12.40; 15.47; 284.4.
or, prep. — *ere*, 89.37.
ordyne (ordinee), adj. — *ordained, holy*, 186.80.
ought, owght, sb. — *aught, anything*, 71.5; 155.72; 157.20; 182.180; 245.13; 249.28; 264.33; *duty, obligation*, 234.106 (the earliest ex. of the word in this sense in the *N.E.D.* is of date 1678).
ought, v., pa.t. — *owned*, 17.20; *was beholden for*, 268.45.
outstarte, v. — *spring forth suddenly*, 110.13 (examples in the *N.E.D.* are from Middle English and Browning).
overchardge, v. — *lay an excessive burden upon, press hard*, 245.12.
overcharged, ppl. adj. — *over-burdened*, 5.13.
overfraught, ppl. adj. — *too heavily laden*, 184.21.
overthwarte, sb. — *contradiction*, 132.4.
overthwarte, adv. — *amiss, adversely*, 161.37.
owght, sb. — see "ought."
owtragious, adj., used absol. — *the excessively bold (one)*, 168.1.

packstaff, sb. — *staff on which a peddler supports his pack when standing to rest*, in the phr., "playne as packstaff," *very clear*, 171.8.
palfrey, sb. — *a saddle horse for ordinary riding*, 259.9.
panne, sb. — *piece of cloth, of which several were joined together to make one garment*, 180.193.
parcell gilt (parcel-gilt), sb. — *partly gilded substance*, 180.241.
parfyte, adj. — *perfect*, 143.13.

partie, adj. — *divided, separated,* 211.8, "partie p pawnch," *a parody on heraldic terminology,* i.e., *"party per pale," which signifies division of the shield by a vertical line through the middle*; "pawnch" is the stomach, 182.264.

passionatnes, sb. — *quality of being easily moved,* 23.21 (the first example in the *N.E.D.* is of date 1648).

payne, v. — *take pains, endeavor,* 18.6.

paynt, v. — *fawn, talk speciously,* 104.28; *describe,* 182.36; 214.6; 260.34; 282.4.

paynted, ppl. adj. — *disguised, colored* (fig.), 77.20; 171.24; 175.18; 239.11; 305.33.

payseth (peiseth), v., 3rd. sing. — *ponders, considers,* 162.10 (see "poise").

pcell gilt, adj. — see "parcell gilt."

peason, sb. — *peas, type of something of little value,* 298.6.

peaxe, sb. — *peace,* 5.30.

pedantee, sb. — *teacher, tutor,* 229.69.

pedder, sb. — *peddler,* 180.27, and in adjacent marginal note, used as a pun on a proper name.

percell (parcel), sb. — *small amount,* 74.2.

perfytnesse, sb. — *perfection,* 143.16.

perilous, adj. — *capable of inflicting or doing serious harm,* 148.19.

perrie, sb. — see "pirrye."

perrish, v. — *destroy,* 182.92.

phansie, sb. — see "fancye."

phillip, sb. — *a name formerly given to a sparrow, hence, "phillip sparrow,"* 270.41.

phrenesie, sb. — see "fransy."

pight, ppl. adj. — *placed, seated,* 259.9; *situated,* 278.29.

pirrye, perrie, sb. — *squall, small gale,* 61.3; 309.3.

pitche, v. — "pitche and pay," *pay ready money,* 260.24.

pitifull, pittyefull, adj. — *merciful, tender,* 58.12; 247.36.

plage, Scottish variant of "pledge," sb. — *a hostage,* 323.12.

plaged, ppl. adj. — *afflicted,* 295.12.

plague, plage, sb. — *calamity, affliction,* 18.50; 19.3; 233.35; 289.29; 297.57; *visitation of divine wrath,* 75.26; 249.22; *annoyance,* 104.94; *pestilence,* 196.3; *wound,* 285.2.

plague, v. — *harass,* 290.44.

plaint, plainte, playnte, playnt, sb. — *audible expression of sorrow, lamentation, grieving,* 5.8; 6.8; 65.6, 34; 68.17; 83.44; 84.11; 96.11; 117.14; 135.4, 5; 137.8; 139.54, 57, 62; 144.63; 149.9, 38, 67; 154.58; 155.75; 159.35; 160.24; 165.11; 234.201; 279.15, 31; 287.1; 303.33; 304.30; 324.1; *prayer,* 90.23; *a statement or representation of wrong, injury, or injustice suffered, a complaint,* 125.2; 127.3; 134.4; 303.3.

plat, adj. — *blunt,* 261.8.

platt (plait), sb. — *secret supporter,* 295.5.

playnd (plained), pa. pple. — *mourned, lamented,* 98.13; 108.13.

playne (plain), v. — *make complaint*, 20.28; 115.7; 127.2; 133.1; *lament, mourn*, 23.28; 81.10; 88.9; 124.2; 133.7, 8; 158.16.
playntfull, adj. — *mournfull*, 163.16.
pleasure, v. — *delight*, 242.34.
pleasuringe, vbl. sb. — *delighting*, 58.10.
plentuous, plentuouse, adj. — *abundant*, 83.1; 165.30; *abundantly provided*, 90.45.
plixt, adj. — see "prolixt."
pluckes, v. — "pluckes in plagues," *brings in troubles*, 297.57.
plyeth, v. — *yields, submits*, 302.4.
pocks, poxe, sb. — *general name applied to diseases characterized by skin eruptions*, 181.68; 295.12 (in these instances signifying venereal disease).
pockye, pockie, adj. — *marked with pocks, or infected with the pox*, 180.141, and marginal note by lines 25-30 (see "pocks").
poise, v. — *to consider, ponder*, 241.2 (see "payseth").
poltcat, sb. — *polecat*, 182.193 (this spelling clearly derived from "poult" plus "cat").
ponderith, v., 3rd. sing. — *weighs on a scale*, 77.8.
porte, sb. — *bearing, manner*, 78.4.
porterid (portured), ppl. adj. — *formed, fashioned*, 282.13.
posseede (possede), v. — *possess*, 168.29.
poxe, sb. — see "pocks."
poynt, poynct, sb. — *the lace or cord that holds the hose to the doublet*, 180.156; 182.78; "no poynct," *not a bit*, 260.9; "at poynt," *ready, just about to*, 260.32.
poyntes, v. — *hints, suggests*, 162.12.
preace, prease, sb. — see "presse."
precisions (precisians), sb. — *those who are precise in religious observance, Puritans*, 180.140, and marginal note by lines 139-44.
prelooked on, v. — *looked ahead hostilely* (?), 84.33 (see note).
presence, sb. — *company*, 23.28.
presentes, v. — *offers*, 18.2.
presse, preace, prease, sb. — *the action of crowding or thronging*, 104.3; *crowd, throng*, 175.43; 180.74; 321.41; "in presse," literally, *in the thick of the fight*, here relating to *tribulation*, 157.30.
presse, preace, v. — *push or strain forward*, 22.32; 246.33 (pa.t.); *push (its way)*, 99.3; *repress*, 104.58; *strive*, 175.53; 222.48; 290.30; 314.25; *weigh down, burden*, 186.24; 320.64; *harass*, 286.13.
prest, pa. pple. — *burdened*, 118.3.
prest, adj. — *at hand*, 3.3; *eager*, 19.40; 58.10; *in proper order*, 144.19; *ready for action*, 276.29; 278.33.
pretence, sb. — *expressed aim, proposed end*, 166.32.
pretend, v. — *claim, profess to have*, 231.3.
prick, pryck, v. — *incite, impel*, 106.6; 241.10; 245.51 (pa.t.); 260.13 (pa.t.); *stab*, 125.8 (pa.t.); *ride on horseback*, 259.9.
pricked, pa. pple. — *pierced* (fig.), 125.5.
pricking, pres. ppl. adj. — *inciting, impelling*, 157.31; *painful in the sense of irritation as from the stick of a pin*, 167.12.

prickinge, vbl. sb. — *stabbing*, 127.8.
procure, v. — *induce, persuade*, 244.19.
profe, prov, sb. — *issue, result*, 186.73; *knowledge gained by experience*, 285.5.
prolixt, adj. — *protracted, lengthy*, 259.28.
proper, adj. — *belonging to oneself*, 163.21; *admirable, commendable*, 180.191; 182.36.
prov, sb. — see "profe."
prove, v. — *come to be, become*, 239.25.
purchase, purchace, v. — *provide*, 87.7; *obtain*, 178.12; 321.66; *win, gain*, 259.30; 266.44.
purveyor, sb. — *one who supplies necessaries for others*, 182.69, 80.
pye, sb. — *magpie* (fig.), *a chattering person*, 260.37; 271.32.
pyke, v. — variant of "pike," *make off with (thee)*, 243.13; variant of "pick," *preen*, 260.34.

quarantos (courantes), sb. pl. — *dances with quick running steps*, 222.30.
quayle, v. — *fail*, 12.50; *put an end to*, 272.2.
quaynt, adj. — *pretty*, 260.33.
quente, pa. pple. — *quenched*, 128.3.
quite, v. — *requite, repay*, 147.5; 148.5.
quod, v., pa.t. — *said*, 140.5; 142.18, 42, 43, 45; 157.38; 179.11; 239.8; 261.11; 272.39; 279.33; 306.23.
quyck, adj. — *alive*, 84.26.

race, v. — *raze, tear down*, 88.11; *erase*, 277.24 (pa.t.), 310.14.
rack, racke, sb. — *mass of cloud driven before the wind*, 150.4; *torture instrument*, 253.4.
rakt, ppl. adj. — *strained, tortured*, 17.1.
rapp, v. — *take by snatching*, 234.99.
rashlye, adv. — *quickly*, 261.13.
rate, sb. — "after one rate," *in the same manner*, 102.10.
rathe, adv. — *early*, 269.62.
raught, v., pa.t. — *snatched*, 91.11.
reade, rede, reed, reede, v. — (1) signifying "rede": *agree*, 21.21; *advise*, 59.4; 90.11; 319.23; (2) signifying "read": *discover significance of*, 157.55; *interpret, discern meaning*, 234.7; 267.46; 272.29; *suppose*, 303.22 (pa.t., "readd").
reave, v. — *tears away, cuts in two*, 320.50, 61.
rebatant, adj. — *which beat back or down (?)*, 278.38 (not in the *N.E.D.* but would seem to come from the v. "rebate," in the sense of beating back or down).
rebates, v. — *diminishes, abates*, 154.50.
rechelesse, retcheles, retchelesse (reckless), adj. — *reckless, heedless*, 80.1; 242.21, 44; 321.83.
recure, sb. — "without recure," and "sans recure," *without hope of recovering*, 155.25; 261.24.

recure, v. — *retrieve*, 194.3; *remedy, redress*, 259.25.
rede, v. — see "reade."
redresse, sb. — *remedy*, 12.22; 131.12; 136.13; 139.54, 77, 89; *one who affords remedy*, 14.4; *correction, amendment*, 90.26.
reed, reede, v. — see "reade."
reede, sb. — *cane* (fig.), 133.23.
refrayne, v. — *restrain, check*, 6.15; 78.25; 124.7; 302.5; *abstain, forbear*, 78.74; 107.8; 180.260; 250.1.
refuse, sb. — *refusal*, 78.64.
reiecte, ppl. adj. — *rejected, cast away*, 166.30.
remembered, v., pa.t. — *put (her) in mind of*, 125.2.
remove, v. — *depart, go away*, 77.48.
repayre, v. — *return*, 88.42.
repugnant, adj. — *diverse, different*, 140.8; *divergent*, 140.32; *incompatible*, 161.4.
requearing (requiring), ppl. adj. — *begging*, 261.9.
requyre, requeare, v. — *beg, entreat*, 12.42; 89.54; 155.8; 167.6; 168.63; 216.1; 274.5; 302.2; *need, want*, 14.2; 85.6; 131.2; 139.25, 92; *claim, demand*, 72.36; 163.10; 237.25; 303.26; *request, desire*, 277.19.
resorte, v. — *spring*, 104.13.
rest, sb. — *support*, 237.40.
rest, reste, v. — *remain, continue without change*, 3.1; 57.2; 69.84; 170.1; 171.36; 233.4; 246.15; 305.4; 307.10; *have place*, 146.5; *stay*, 149.7; *lie*, 264.3.
resum'de, pa. pple. — *taken back*, 225.19.
retayne, v. — *continue, remain*, 265.17 (the only example given by the *N.E.D.* is from Donne, 1631).
retcheles, retchelesse, adj. — see "rechelesse."
retyre, sb. — *retreat, withdrawing*, 241.3.
revaile (reveil), v. — *to reveal, disclose*, 145.15.
revert, v. — *be changed, turn the other way*, 135.15.
rewe, v. — see "rue."
rid, ridd, ryd, v. — *clear away, dispose of*, 18.35; 167.36; 175.22, 41; *destroy, remove by violence*, 275.3; 304.31, 54.
rife, ryfe, adj. — *prevalent*, 5.30; 75.6; 245.34; *widespread*, 167.16; *abundant*, 193.12; *plentiful*, 233.12.
right way, sb. — *esophagus*, here used in the phr., "the gates of my right way," i.e., *the jaws*, 76.17 (not in the *N.E.D.*).
rod, sb. — in a double sense, *path* and *means of punishment*, 291.3.
roist, v. — *to play the part of a riotous fellow*, 260.46.
roo, rooe, sb. — see "row."
roote, v. — *uproot*, 281.60.
rore (roar), sb. — *tumult, confusion*, 124.8; 297.7.
roste (roast), v. — *ridicule, banter*, 293.9.
rote, roate, sb. — "knows by rote," *knows by heart*, 141.49; "can be roate." same meaning, 77.25.

route, rowte, sb. — *throng*, 89.45; 175.43; *violent movement*, 297.59.
row, rowe, rooe, roo, sb. — *set of people of a certain kind*, 186.91; "on roo," *one after another*, 19.23; "a rowe," *in order*, 253.17; 262.5.
royle, sb. — *clumsy female*, 180.58.
rudelesse, adj. — *without rudeness*, App. I [II].5 (not in the *N.E.D.*).
rue, sb. — *regret*, 238.7.
rue, rew, rewe, v. — *regret, think of with sorrow*, 66.94; 87.24; 94.2; 122.3; 168.27; 293.3; *be penitent*, 78.63; *feel sorrow, lament*, 149.4; 179.16; *regard with compassion*, 163.42; *have pity or compassion* (*on or upon*), 74.5; 135.14; 136.5, 10, 15; 153.43.
rufull, adj. — *lamentable, pitiable*, 149.70; 288.17.
ruthe, sb. — *pity*, 78.38; 163.49; 179.17; 303.33.
rutt, sb. — *the annually recurring sexual excitement of the male deer; by extension, copulation in general*, 180.1.
ruyne, ppl. adj. (?) — possibly to be interpreted not as "ruin," but as coined from the verb "rue" (see above), hence, *sorrowful*, or, *that which produces sorrow*, 163.23 (not in the *N.E.D.*).
ryding rime — *properly rhyming couplets of iambic pentameter, not tetrameter as here*, 182.34.
rygor, rygour, sb. — *harshness*, 68.4; 89.6; 272.2.
ryve, v. — *split by violent impact*, 230.3; *pull, drag*, 315.4.
ryvelyd (rivelled), pple. adj. — *wrinkled*, 266.85.

saluith, v., 3rd sing. — *salutes*, 85.25.
sans, prep. — *without*, 261.24.
save, v. — *remain safe, secure*, 14.5.
savour, v. — *taste*, 163.29.
sawe, sb. — *a saying*, 23.40.
say, sb. — "take the say," *open the inner parts of the stag or buck to see how fat he is*, 259.21 (the earliest example in the *N.E.D.* is of date 1611).
scan, v. — *discern*, 271.3; *interpret, assign a meaning to*, 281.14; *interpret rhythmically*, 278.72 (pa.t., "sckand").
scant, scantt, skant, adv. — *hardly, scarcely*, 83.14; 124.14; 139.16; 140.33; 168.97; 182.97.
scape, skape, v. — *escape*, 9.36 (pa.t.); 76.6; 84.12; 104.34; 106.8; 157.49; 181.68; 182.52, 87; 230.23; 289.6.
scarse, adv. — *hardly, scarcely*, 250.1.
scathe, sb. — *harm*, 84.4.
scited (cited), v., pa.t. — *summoned officially*, 64.1.
sckand, skand, ppl. adj. — *examined, considered*, 182.233; 319.61; see also "scan."
scortche, v. — *burn* (fig.), 180.1.
scowring, vbl. sb. — *scoring, in the sense of punishment*, 182.52.
scryppe, sb. — *small bag carried by a beggar*, 281.25.
scuse, skewse, sb. — *excuse*, 243.7, 8; 306.6.
seeche (seek), v. — *try to find*, 168.40.
seelye, adj. — see "silly."
seeme, adj. — *seemly, proper*, 186.50.
selde, seild, adv. — *seldom*, 225.11; 282.26.

selly, adj. — see "silly."
serven, sb. — *servant*, 273.1.
severall, adj. — *distinct, separate*, 140.66.
shalme (shawm), sb. — *a medieval musical instrument of the oboe class, having a double reed enclosed in a globular mouthpiece*, 164.5.
shape, v. — *take a course*, 75.33; *plan*, 142.33.
sharpe, sharppe, v. — *to sharpen*, 69.45; 87.59; 155.51.
shaw, v. — *show, make known, point out*, 72.8.
sheath, sheathe, sb. — "pointed sheath," *showy exterior*, 171.24; 180.197.
sheene, shene, sb. — *brightness, radiance*, 279.27; 282.13.
sheene, v. — *shine*, 79.5, 13; 87.43, 76; 168.95; 250.34; 261.16; 314.27.
sheening, pres. ppl. adj. — *shining*, 267.3.
shent, ppl. adj. — *disgraced, ruined*, 234.16.
shifte, sb. — *available means of effecting an end*, 142.60.
shilder (shielder), sb. — *protector*, 175.25.
shite, v. — *void excrement*, 182.165.
short, v. — *shorten*, 19.6 ("shortyth"); 283.18.
shright, sb. — *shrieking*, 279.31.
shright, v. — *to shriek*, 110.12; 297.11 (pa.t.).
shrowde, v. — *to protect oneself*, 155.73; *to conceal in a secret place or manner*, 240.10; *to hide from view as by a veil, darkness, cloud*, 253.6; 260.6.
shrowdid, ppl. adj. — *concealed*, 279.17.
sicklesse, adj. — *free from sickness*, 77.29 (first example in the *N.E.D.*).
sight, v., pa.t. — *sighed*, 76.4, 25.
silly, sillie, syllye, selly, seelye, adj. — *deserving of pity or compassion, helpless, defenceless*, 104.25; 219.2; 230.28; 288.18, 48; *innocent, harmless*, 66.53; *poor, miserable*, 142.64; *foolish, simple*, 150.5; 271.18.
singuler, adj. — *remarkable, rare*, 158.14.
sith, sithe, sythe, syth, conj. — *since the time that, from, seeing that*, 68.17; 149.57; 181.59; 182.153, 231, 288; 202.2, 10; 204.5; 205.2; 206.10; 216.13, 11; 217.12; 219.11; 226.15; 234.121; 237.2; 239.15; 261.29; 263.35; 270.4; 274.1; 275.18; 277.17; 303.48; 304.51; 319.63; 324.17.
sithens, conj. — *since, seeing that*, 100.8.
sithes, sythes, sb. — *sighs*, 189.8; 225.54.
sittes, syttes, v. — *to suit, be suitable, fitting*, 87.20; 139.58; 307.2.
skabbe (scab), sb. — probably to be taken in the double sense: *disease* (*of the skin, with venereal implications*) and *rascal*, 181.40.
skand, ppl. adj. — see "sckand."
skant, adv. — see "scant."
skantly, adv. — *barely*, 181.40.
skape, v. — see "scape."
skewse, sb. — see "scuse."
skills, v. — *matters, concerns*, 85.4.
skinks, v., 3rd sing. — *pours out* (*his odor*), 182.193 (from "skink," not "stink").
slaightlye, adv. — see "sleightlie."

slake, v. — *to reduce, diminish*, 78.52, 72; 124.5; 134.5 (pa.t.); *to put off, delay*, 144.54; *to diminish the intensity of one's efforts*, 274.28.

slapmond, sb. — not in the *N.E.D.*, *slopman* (?), 180.236.

sleightlie, slaightlye, adv. —*subtly*, 284.2; *adroitly*, 317.5.

slighlye (slyly), adv. — *stealthily, secretly*, 186.38; 316.1.

slight, sleight, sleyghte, slyght, slyghte, sb. — *trick, artful design*, 66.53; 180.205; 239.11; 240.1; 270.27; 321.18, 40; *skill, dexterity*, 93.7; 269.50; *strategy, trickery*, 147.24; 148.21.

slipper, slypper, adj. — *unstable*, 77.49; 88.2; *slippery, difficult to stand on*, 83.4; *liable to slip*, 269.28; *readily slipping from grasp*, 298.7 (comp.), 316.1; *unreliable*, 317.8.

sloggardie, sb. — *indolence*, 123.3.

slylye, adj. — *artful, cunning*, 240.1 (not given in the *N.E.D.*).

smacking, vbl. sb. — *foul kissing*, 180.118.

smocking, vbl. sb. — a play on the word in three senses: *denoting a woman, a woman's undergarment, loose conduct*, 180.44.

smokes, sb. — *vapors* (fig.), 193.8.

smokes, v. — *rises like smoke*, 90.13.

smokie, smokye, adj. — *describing vapor, etc. as having the appearance of smoke*, 64.14; 160.20; 168.60.

softe, v. — *to mollify, appease*, 184.23.

soile, soyle, sb. — *sexual intercourse*, 180.1, 56.

soile, v. — *roll in mud or water*, 230.14.

soothe, sb. — *truth*, 317.8.

sore, adj. — *difficult to bear or support*, 318.2; *grievous*, 113.13; 154.39.

sore, adv. — *laboriously*, 19.20; 87.67; 88.16; *painfully, grievously*, 23.41; 68.5; 76.9; 81.11; 88.43; 100.3; 101.4; 106.6; 141.54; 142.6, 60; 179.8; 181.53; 266.63; 271.43; 288.3; 290.31; 297.44; 312.3; *closely*, 129.2; 168.55; *greatly*, 182.200; 237.36; 293.3; *eagerly*, 77.31; 182.127; 297.72.

sored, ppl. adj. — *troubled*, 139.7 (this line given as only example in *N.E.D.*).

sort, v. — *consort (with)*, 225.20.

sorte, sb. — *manner*, 245.40.

sothefull, adj. — *truthful, true*, 303.12.

sower, adj. — *harsh*, 160.9.

sowne, sownd (swoon), sb. — "in a sownd," or "in sowne," *in a swoon or faint*, 234.257; 272.35.

soyled, ppl. adj. — *polluted*, 264.1.

sparkeling, pres. ppl. adj. — *animated*, 105.6.

sparkle, v. — *scatter*, 135.21.

sparkled, ppl. adj. — *scattered*, 90.46; *kindled*, 154.8.

spedd, ppl. adj. — *furthered*, 7.4; 7a.4.

spence, sb. — *pantry, buttery*, 87.76; 90.61.

spill, v. — *to waste by squandering or misusing*, 42.3; *bring to ruin or misery*, 277.13; 312.16; *damage*, 317.6.

spilt, pa. pple. — *shed*, 2.14; *wasted by squandering*, 77.14.

splendaunte, adj. — *brightly shining*, 188.4.

spoil, spoyle, v. — *deprive*, 64.28 (pa.t.); *pillage*, 249.2.

spoild, pa. pple. — *ravaged*, 230.12.

spoile, spoyl, spoyle, sb. — *spoliation, rapine*, 24.4; 78.66; *death*, 66.15.

sprite, spryte, sprighte, sb. — *spirit in various senses*, 65.4; 83.58; 89.51; 90.62; *passim*.

square, sb. — "out of square," *out of right order*, 182.20.

square, v. — *diverge*, 180.50.

stablish, v. — *strengthen*, 19.4; 168.51; *place firmly*, 168.7.

stablishte, ppl. adj. — *firmly placed*, 163.91.

staid, stayed, pa. pple. and ppl. adj. — *detained*, 21.20; *sustained*, 139.6 (pa. pple.); 167.33; *checked, restrained*, 282.30; *dignified, serious*, 247.17.

staight, sb. — see "state."

stailesse, adj. — *that which does not lose its freshness or interest*, 283.5 (not in the *N.E.D.*, but evidently derived from the adj. "stale").

stale, sb. — *decoy-bird*, 78.60.

stand, stond, pa. pple. — *stood*, 8.2; 8a.2; 123.12.

starting, pres. pple. — *capering, jumping*, 266.41.

startling, pres. pple. — *capering, prancing*, 259.13; 278.35.

startt, v., pa.t. — *moved swiftly*, 78.17; *issued forth violently*, 297.35.

starttes, sb., pl. — *sudden journeys*, 297.15.

state, staight, sb. — *person of high rank*, 247.47; *order or body of persons*, 247.35; 265.7.

stay, staye, stey, sb. — *delay*, 1.5; 234.341; *support*, 85.23; 96.2; 165.24; 186.7; 223.9; 261.14; 286.18; 295.4; *restraint, check*, 5.26; 146.10; 233.21; *suspension of action*, 320.17.

stay, staye, v. — *cease*, 17.28; 320.26 (pa.t.); *check, restrain*, 234.345; 314.24; *sustain, support*, 83.54; 139.1; 141.53; 168.69; 286.29; 290.34 (pa.t.); *pause, stop*, 143.13 (pa.t.); 233.49; *lean, rest upon*, 194.10; 320.49; *wait*, 92.3, 4; *remain*, 204.6; *remain without changing nature*, 303.27; *detain, hold back*, 21.13; 225.22.

stayed, pa. pple. — see "staid."

steed, steede, sb. — *high-mettled horse*, 266.41; 278.35.

stey, sb. — see "stay."

still, v. — *allay, assuage*, 22.9.

still, styll, adv. — *even yet*, 12.24; 20.4; 83.31; *now as formerly*, 10.18; 77.12; *from now on*, 72.38; *ever, always, continuously*, frequent examples in the text.

stilling, pres. ppl. adj. — *distilling*, 137.6.

stint, stintt, stynte, v. — *cause to cease, check*, 158.1; 182.266; 285.2 (pa.t.); *cease, leave off*, 270.15, 48; 274.28.

stintles, adj. — *without cessation*, 289.14.

stond, pa. pple. — see "stand."

stounde, sb. — *short time*, 320.87.

stoute, stowt, stowte, adj. — *valiant*, 5.28; 230.10; 234.142; *proud*, 232.6.

stoutlye, stowtlye, adv. — *resolutely*, 237.15; *bravely*, 246.6.

straight, strayght, streight, adv. — *immediately*, 69.42; 81.37; 87.33; 88.14; 142.83; 154.42, 46; 168.69; 222.12; 234.256; 250.52; 269.49; 275.16; 290.34.

straitlye, straightlye, adv. — *tightly*, 321.88; *strictly*, 323.2.
strave, v., pa.t. — *strove*, 87.12.
strayne, v. — *force, constrain*, 157.70; 160.18; *use the voice in song*, 160.31; *press beyond the normal degree*, 259.13.
strayned, ppl. adj. — *describing the voice as used in song*, 156.32.
streight, adv. — see "straight."
strengthe, v. — *strengthen*, 161.79; 168.107.
stroyed, pa. pple. — *destroyed*, 142.14; 297.36 (ppl. adj.).
sturdie, adj. — *obstinate, intractable*, 274.5.
styckes, v. — *hesitates*, 72.6.
sue, v. — *follow as a result*, 17.8; *follow (steps, tracks)*, 64.25; 245.6; 286.20; 322.7; *plead, appeal*, 161.61; 166.22; 222.8; 234.197; 264.2.
sured, ppl. adj. — *assured*, 166.31 (this line is quoted in the *N.E.D.* as earliest example).
suretye, suretie, sb. — *security, safety*, 86.28; 88.31; 142.68; 168.93; 242.48; 297.34.
surprys'de, ppl. adj. — *seized (with an emotion)*, 158.24.
suspect, sb. — *apprehensive expectation*, 16.2.
swadd, sb. — *country bumpkin*, 180.195.
swadge, v. — *relieve, mitigate*, 68.4.
syche, pro. — *such*, 18.30.

talents, sb. — *talons*, 182.247.
tane, pa. pple. — *taken*, 63.5; 72.18; 141.82; 155.48.
targe, sb. — *light shield*, 66.14.
taunters, sb. — *tauntress* (?), 299.1.
taynte, v. — *affect*, 211.9.
thacking, vbl. sb. — *thatching, putting the thatch on cottages, a symbol of a lowly occupation or loose conduct*, 180.116.
thackyd, pa. ppl. adj. — *thatched*, 267.32.
than, adv. — *then*, 3.3; 5.29, 30, 31; 12.6; 14.12, 17; 15.43; 19.20; 20.21, 41, 45; 22.9; 72.35; 73.13; 83.58; 88.31; 130.11; 141.61; 143.15, 30; 169.6; 181.52; 182.201; 241.5; 243.21; 245.50; 250.25; 261.18; 265.4; 266.59; 268.71; 277.29; 287.20; 297.20.
then, conj. — *than*, 2.12; 12.16; 17.20; 20.36; 23.3; 52.2; 64.10, 58; 66.36, 146; 69.77; 95.7; 104.11; 105.9; 118.4; 139.76; 141.23; 143.15; 144.10, 39; 148.20; 152.5; 161.8; 171.30, 32; 175.32; 180.32; 181.25; 182.136; 184.26; 186.15; 209.8; 215.10; 217.14; 225.14, 26; 229.21, 84; 233.36; 234.211; 246.8; 259.28; 262.47; 264.27; 265.17; 268.39; 272.22; 285.12; 287.14; 293.10.
tho, thoe, adv. — *then*, 142.61; 260.9, 11; 271.28; 277.3, 8, 17, 22.
thone, pro. — *the one*, 122.10; 126.8; 140.25.
thorough, adv. — *along*, 182.43.
thother, pro. — *the other*, 72.31 (poss.); 102.10; 126.8; 140.21, 24, 25, 48; 142.38; 144.72; 260.40.
thoughtfull, adj. — *sorrowful, melancholy*, 5.1; 139.51; 193.8.

thraldom, thraldome, thralldome, sb. — *servitude, bondage,* 10.39; 19.8; 91.10.

thrall, sb. — *captive,* 22.16; 23.24; 68.7; 90.57; 104.4; 136.6; 167.8; 172.1; 229.56; 234.136; 247.34; 266.51; 267.9, 25, 41; 287.14; 303.29.

thrall, v. — *hold captive,* 287.12.

thralled, thrallde, thralld, thrall'd, ppl. adj. — *held captive, imprisoned,* 66.34; 144.60; 148.30; 222.40; 233.34, 39.

threateth, v. — *threateneth,* 155.30.

threpe, v. — *press upon,* 84.3.

thristing, ppl. adj. — *crushing,* 247.24.

throwklye, adv. — *thoroughly, completely, fully,* 321.57 (not in the *N.E.D.*, but clearly related to the Scottish "throuch," i.e., "through").

throws, throwse, sb. — *throes, anguish, agony of mind,* 5.1; 139.51; 223.12; 287.19; *throws, twists, turns,* 285.7.

thrust, sb. — *crowd,* 259.38.

thweene, prep. — *between,* 112.3.

tickle, tickell, adj. — *inconstant,* 239.15; 244.6; 298.4.

tofore, adv. — *before, earlier,* 149.29; 164.6.

tone, pro. — *the one (of two),* 140.19.

tonne, sb. — *tun, barrel, large cask for beer,* 171.31; 182.151, 157.

tonne, v. — *put into a cask,* 180.139 (used in a punning sense).

toppe, v. — *fight,* 175.51 (the last example in the *N.E.D.* is of date 1440).

tord, torde, sb. — *turd,* 182.284, 285, 290, 291, 292, 293.

tother, pro. — *the other (of two),* 77.6 (poss.); 89.32; 140.19, 77; 144.70; *the second (of two or more),* 140.57; pl., *the rest,* 168.55.

tother, adj. — *the other,* 144.50; 158.28.

toye, sb., usually pl. — *jest, joke,* 15.19; 66.102; 299.1; *foolish behavior,* 242.19; *whim, caprice,* 306.16; *amorous sport,* 180.214 (used as a pun on the surname), 276.45.

trace, sb. — *way of doing something,* 311.7.

trackt (tract), sb. — "trackt of tyme," *course of time,* 239.10.

tract, v. — *discuss,* 247.3.

trade, sb. — *manner of life,* 15.4; *way, path,* 78.45; *practice or habit of doing something,* 87.67; 286.20.

traile, v. — *draw along wearily or with difficulty,* 175.7.

train, trayne, sb. — *following, retinue,* 5.20; 89.49; 239.7; *trap, decoy,* 22.10; 77.47; *trick, scheme,* 64.24; *treachery,* 154.31.

trappes, sb. — *snares,* 155.82 (the first example in the *N.E.D.* of this figurative use is of date 1681).

traunced, v., pa.t. — *was in extreme dread,* 154.12.

travaile, travell, trayvaill (often pl.), sb. — *labor, exertion, often mental or spiritual, implying suffering,* 42.3; 78.20, 56; 83.9; 86.6; 87.26, 61, 68; 89.12, 16; 100.3; 114.14; 142.28, 91, 102; 144.47; 145.5; 173.3; 234.216, 278; 275.10; 277.35; *task,* 86.31; *result of labor, outcome,* 278.28.

travail, traveil, v. — *harass, afflict,* 84.5; *labor,* 88.16 (pa.t.); 89.22; 90.36; 278.23.

traynd, pa. pple. — *allured, enticed,* 78.54; 139.14; 234.44.
traynes, v. — *allures, entices,* 242.22.
treate, v. — *entreat, beseech,* 139.61.
trentalls, sb. — *sets of thirty requiem masses,* 196.13.
trice, sb. — "in a trice," *instantly, forthwith,* 320.50.
tripps, sb. — *mistakes, blunders,* 289.26.
tro, troe, v. — see "trow."
trompp, sb. — see "trumpe."
trothe, trouthe, sb. — *loyalty, good faith,* 5.30; 130.12; 134.19, 20; 135.39; 144.73; 147.33; 148.33; 149.47; 167.4; 168.15; 169.1; 244.13; 245.58; 292.1, 2, 8; 303.11; 305.24; *promise, pledge,* 182.182; "of trouthe," *truly, verily,* 157.41.
trott, sb. — *an old woman, hag,* 146.11; 180.20.
trow, trowe, tro, troe, v. — *suppose, think,* 78.8, 16; 116.5; 142.87; 171.7; 182.106; 253.3, 15; 321.105.
trudge, v. — *go on foot,* 259.19; 276.40; 321.46; *go wearily,* 234.234.
trumpe, trompp, trumppe, sb. — *trumpet,* 66.5; 81.30; 250.73; 262.63; 276.13.
trusse, v. — *fasten, bind,* 76.26.
trye, sb. — *trial, test,* 186.73.
trymme, adv. — *smartly, finely,* 321.49.
twatling, vbl. sb. — *chattering, babbling,* 321.71.
twitling, vbl. sb. — *chattering, babbling,* 321.71.

vade (wade), v. — *escape from,* 88.13.
vaer, sb. — *vair, squirrel with gray and white fur,* 179.4.
vaile, v. — "vaile their Bonettes," *take off their caps in respect,* 321.51.
vapourd, vapour'de, ppl. adj. — *filled with moisture,* 156.25; 277.22.
varied, v., pa.t. — *hesitated,* 143.11 (the only example in the *N.E.D.* is of date 1477).
vaunt, vauntt, v. — *away! be off!* 94.13; *boast,* 83.16; 180.89; 243.19.
vaunting, ppl. adj. — *boasting,* 86.35.
vayleth, v. — *availeth, profiteth,* 118.2.
verye, vearye, adj. — *used to emphasize the trueness or certainty of the thing itself,* 135.40; 140.6.
vice, sb. — *fool, jester,* 321.79, 82.
vizard, sb. — *a mask,* 182.177.
vncowthe, adj. — *unknown, uncertain,* 160.21.
vndeathfull, adj. — *not subject to death,* 283.14, 15 (not in *N.E.D.*).
vndertake, v. — *cure* (fig.), 130.22 (the *N.E.D.* notes but two instances of the word as *cure* in the physical sense, late fifteenth century).
vndid, v., pa.t. — *destroyed, did away with,* 245.22.
vnegall, adj. — *unequal,* 77.8.
vnendly, adj. — *unending,* 229.38 (this line quoted in the *N.E.D.* as the only example).
vnfained, vnfayned, ppl. adj. — *without pretence, sincere,* 105.1; 124.9.
vngreeved, ppl. adj. — *unharmed, unaffected* (*by disease*), 283.11 (rare,

only example of the verb "ungrieve" in the *N.E.D.* is of date 1589; first example of the ppl. adj. is from Hobbes, 1676).

vnhappe, sb. — *misfortune, mishap,* 96.5.

vnhoped, ppl. adj. — *unexpected,* 89.39.

vnknowe, ppl. adj. — *unknown,* 311.4 (the last example in the *N.E.D.* is of date 1513).

vnlace, v. — *deprive,* 5.41.

vnmeete, adj. — *unsuitable,* 78.14; 141.40; 274.23.

vnneth, adv. — *hardly, with difficulty,* 85.31.

vnplaste, pa. pple. — *displaced,* 17.5.

vnreste, sb. — *turmoil, trouble,* 161.55; 213.6; 245.44; 250.24; 276.4; 310.3.

vnright, sb. — *wrong-doing, iniquity,* 75.16, 46; 157.37; "to do vnright," *to do wrong,* 234.149.

vnsaciate, adj. — *unsatisfied,* 107.9.

vnsav'reth, v., 3rd. sing. — *has no savor or agreeableness,* 89.58.

vnskill, sb. — *folly,* 22.35.

vnspot, v. — *remove the spot or blemish* (fig.), 245.46 (not in *N.E.D.*).

vnspotted, ppl. adj. — *unblemished,* 245.54.

vnstayd, vnstaide, ppl. adj. — *unstable,* 222.7; 286.31.

vnsypher, v. — *decipher,* 64.19.

vntwynde, v. — *untwine, become undone,* 168.104.

vnware, adj. — *unaware, ignorant,* 88.41; 94.14; *unforeseen,* 173.6; 296.2.

void, voyd, voyde, adj. — *free from, devoid of,* 20.5; 94.9; 161.54; 178.10; 229.66; 233.31; 234.19; 307.28; *worthless,* 90.24; *wanting something desirable,* 149.8; 320.52.

vppon, adv. — *on or upon that (in time),* 75.55.

vpraze, v. — *uproot, tear out,* 175.45 (not in the *N.E.D.*).

vpspringe, v. — *to arise, come into being,* 161.49.

vpsupped, pa. pple. — *swallowed up,* 160.25.

vre, sb. — *use, practice,* 86.43; 250.65.

vse, v. — *pursue or follow a custom,* 29.1; 116.3.

vyled (vild), adj. — *low, base,* 235.4.

waile, v. — *bewail, lament,* 5.16.

wailfull, waylefull, waylfull, adj. — *lamentable,* 83.18; 87.50; 89.10.

waker, adj. — *watchful,* 90.41; 124.1; 163.24.

wakye, adj. — *wakeful,* 144.58 (this line is quoted in the *N.E.D.* as the first of two examples).

walde, v. — *use, have to do with,* 68.12.

wan, wanne, v., pa.t. — *won, gained,* 175.19; 237.12; 251.7; 272.56.

wand, sb. — *stick,* 37.2.

wand'rid, pa. pple. — *confused,* 88.43.

wanishe, adj. — *lustreless,* 79.13.

wanne, v. — see "wan."

wantons, sb. — *young persons of playful conduct,* 171.6.

warde, sb. — *custody,* 157.49; *a guard,* 181.33; *a guarded place,* 181.37 (the last two used in a punning sense).

warde, v. — *keep guard*, 84.15; *keep off*, 181.40 (pun).
ware, adj. — *wary, cautious*, 58.8; *informed, aware*, 241.7.
ware, v. — old pa.t. of "wear," hence, *wore*, 89.40; 279.26; *beware of, take care*, 141.73; 180.134, 247.
watche, sb. — *wakefulness*, 265.4.
wath, adj. — *dangerous*, 304.50 (the *N.E.D.* gives but one example, from *Cursor Mundi*, 1300, of "wothe," or "wath," as an adj. and no example of the word as sb. after 1470).
waxe, sb. — *beeswax as used for writing tablets*, 244.17.
waxe, wexe, v. — *become, grow*, 157.27; 272.13 (pa.t.); 320.12.
waynes, sb. — *wagons*, 175.10.
weald, v. — see "welde."
weale, sb. — *happiness*, 4a.1; 104.80; 139.6; 271.13; 274.11; *well-being*, 75.52; *welfare*, 104.37; *prosperity*, 269.40.
wealth, wealthe, welth, sb. — *happiness, well-being*, 18.11, 25; 76.14; 77.49; 85.9; 88.24, 32; 90.25; 106.4; 113.11; 123.11; 124.8; 139.42, 58; 159.30; 168.35; 172.8; 225.43; 297.43; 300.6; 303.34; *abundance, plenty* (*non-material*), 144.77; 285.7; *prosperity, riches*, frequent use, as at present.
wealthie, adj. — *happy*, 286.14.
weate (wet), adj. — *bringing rain*, 272.17.
weede, sb. — *garment*, 245.29; 287.2; 308.17.
weene, wene, v. — *judge*, 53.1; *expect*, 101.13; *hope*, 109.6; *surmise, suspect*, 281.48.
weete, v. — *know* (*a fact or answer*), 72.29; 78.21; 250.42; 271.19; *make wet*, 304.35.
welbe, sb. — not in the *N.E.D.*, but perhaps a shortened form of *well-being*, for which early seventeenth-century examples are given; or perhaps an error for "welle," i.e., *well*, sb., *well-being*, 186.50.
welde, weald, wylde (wield), v. — *use, control, direct*, 168.34; 265.34; 317.1; *rule, reign over*, 168.79.
weldinge, ppl. adj. — *capable of ruling*, 294.1.
wem, sb. — *injury, defect*, 36.2.
wemlesse, adj. — *without stain of sin*, App. I[II].5 (the last example in the *N.E.D.* is of date 1420).
wends, v. — *thinks, supposes*, 172.8.
wene, v. — see "weene."
wexe, v. — see "waxe."
wheare, sb. — *place, locality*, 5.19; 85.32; 323.26.
whillome, adj. — *former*, 148.25.
whirly gigges, sb. — *derisively applied to court seekers because they are forever "whirling" from one nobleman to another*, 321.45.
whote, adj. — *hot*, 84.30.
whyllom, whylome, adv. — *sometime before*, 128.6; 259.34; 279.34.
wight, sb. — *a human being, man or woman, often implying contempt or commiseration*, 5.17; 23.10; 75.42; 85.42, *passim.*
willd, pa. pple. — *prayed*, 156.13.
willed, wild, v., pa.t. — *ordered*, 9.33; *entreated, requested*, 250.6; 266.89.

wis, v. — "I wis," *I know*, 126.3; 271.54.
wist, v. — *know*, 78.53, 70; 94.5; 141.28; 268.41; 320.9.
withstand, pa. pple. — *withstood, resisted*, 158.8.
wittoll, sb. — *a fool*, 180.84 (the context does not permit use of the meaning, "a man who is aware of and contented about the infidelity of his wife").
wold, wolde, v., pa.t. — *would*, used frequently.
wonderlye, adv. — *to a wonderful degree or extent*, 134.12.
wonne, v. — *live, dwell*, 260.22.
wont, v. — *be accustomed*, 139.39, 78, 85 (pa.t.); 182.42.
wont, wontt, woont, woonte, pa. pple. — *accustomed to, in the habit of*, 84.24; 85.11; 139.30; 185.13, 14, 15; 320.27, 30.
wonte, sb. — *custom, habit*, 161.12.
wonted, ppl. adj. — *accustomed*, 10.5; 76.25; 134.30; 150.7; 155.45; 266.6; 267.9; 272.5, 8; 318.3.
woodcock, sb. — *fool, simpleton, deriving from the ease with which the woodcock is taken in a net*, 321.84.
woode, adj. — *angry*, 266.53.
woomd, pa. pple. (of "womb," v.) — *enclosed, contained*, 176.3.
woonte, pa. pple. — see "wont."
worthe, sb. — "to take in worthe," or "taking in worthe," *to take (something) at its proper value*, 72.26; 88.61; 163.84.
wote, wot, wott, v.— *know*, 93.3; 120.3; 131.3; 135.9; 175.56; 180.91; 182.53, 141; 186.67; 245.12; 307.5.
wrack, wracke, wrak, sb. — *ruin, misfortune*, 149.10; 175.54; 193.3; 269.8.
wract, pa. pple. — *wrecked*, 230.6.
wrastling, pres. ppl. adj. — *contending*, 234.274.
wreake, sb. — *harm, injury*, 110.4.
wreak, wreake, v. — *avenge*, 9.39; *hurt*, 135.32; *give expression to (anger)*, 146.1.
wreakfull, adj. — *vengeful*, 203.3.
wrest, v. — *deflect the law from its proper course, pervert*, 20.27; 104.29; 290.37; *move*, 75.48 (pa.t.).
wylde, v. — see "welde."
wyse, sb. — *manner*, 12.14; 78.14; 141.43; 144.59; 161.75; 167.9; 171.35; 201.2; *reason, cause*, 251.7.
wyvelye, adj. — *wifely*, 287.19.

ycarried, pa. pple. — *carried*, 279.6.
ydrawne, pa. pple. — *drawn*, 278.11.
yeede, v. — *go, proceed*, 13.9; 159.48.
yfeared, ppl. adj. — *apprehensive*, 272.32.
yfixed, pa. pple. — *fixed*, 101.6.
yfraughted, ppl. adj. — *burdened*, 154.68.
ygoe, ppl. adj. — *gone*, 260.10.
ygrave, pa. pple. — *graven*, 272.29.
yolden, ppl. adj. — *submissive*, 77.43.
yonckers (younker's), sb. (poss.) — *gentleman's*, 180.185.

yore, adv. — *long time ago*, 119.1.
yseene, pa. pple. — *seen*, 142.56.
yshent, ppl. adj. — *put to shame*, 260.8.
ystalld, pa. pple. — *installed, inducted into a seat or position of dignity*, 259.34.
ystreeken, ppl. adj. — *stricken, struck*, 118.9.
ytasted, pa. pple. — *tasted*, 144.23.
ytryde, pa. pple. — *tried*, 260.28.

INDEX

ITEMS in the Index are in modernized spelling unless such form might lead to misunderstanding. Manuscripts are entered under that general heading, according to repository. As is indicated by cross reference, the most frequently used manuscripts are separately listed under their common designations: Arundel Harington MS., Devonshire MS., Egerton MS. *2711*, Nott's transcript of the Arundel Harington MS., Park MS. Texts in the Arundel Harington MS. are referred to by poem number in bold face. Other references are to volume and page, thus, 1. 2, or 1. 2n. The *n* added to the page number indicates reference to a footnote only. The following abbreviations are used: *AH*, for Arundel Harington MS.; *NA*, for *Nugae Antiquae*; *TM*, for *Tottel's Miscellany*.